Five Checks

to

Antinomianism

Five Checks to Antinomianism

By

John Fletcher

Compiled and edited by
Jeffrey L. Wallace

Foreword by
Britt Williams

ISBN-10: 0615533418
ISBN-13: 978-0615533414

Published by:

Apprehending Truth Publishers
Brookfield, Missouri
2011

Apprehending Truth Publishers is a division of Apprehending Truth Ministry.

Buy the Truth and sell it not. ~Proverbs xxiii, 23

http://www.ApprehendingTruth.net

Other Titles published by Apprehending Truth:

Defining Biblical Holiness

The Life of John Fletcher (forthcoming)

The Works of John Fletcher:
Volume One: Five Checks To Antinomianism
Volume Two: Creeds and Scripture Scales (forthcoming)
--Additional Volumes to follow--

Deceptions of Rome (forthcoming)

-----

www.publishers.apprehendingtruth.net

Jean Guillaume de la Flechere

The Works

of

John Fletcher

Volume One

Five Checks to Antinomianism

Apprehending Truth Publishers

Brookfield, Missouri

2011

CONTENTS

FOREWORD

In the church of the big, the plenty, the carefree, and the over-confident, all is business as usual. Of course, by their own admission, everyone is sinning, and sinning a lot. They sin every day and in numerous and varied ways. But, hey, according to their *"cracker-jack-box"* theology, that's the best a Christian can expect from the blood of *Jesus*, right? Ironically, many are tattooed, others are pierced, but few are blushing *(Phil. 3:19)*. All that really matters is *"we're forgiven and we're on our way to heaven"*, so why all the fuss over a little law-breaking? No need to worry: the numbers are up, the crowds are still coming, the coffers are full, life is grand, and surely, God couldn't be more pleased. Why put a damper on all the positive, upbeat ambiance with a fun-spoiling, offering-killing message of doom-and-gloom? Above all, don't wax critical and, God forbid, eschew judgment at any cost. The trick is to stay cool, hip, and optimistic. You may rap, rock, and roll, but avoid repentance, it's too negative. Make sure to put on your best smile, but clothes are not necessary. No need to worry about sin, God understands, that's why He sent Jesus, so be jolly.

Sadly, so it is in the average church of today. Many erroneously believe that the "covenant of grace" either de-emphasizes or cancels the Christian's obligation to fulfill the moral law. Few truly search the Scriptures and form their theological ideas from holy writ, but rather, glean *"here and there"* from the latest spiritual best-seller or the most popular TV evangelist. In the pulpit the situation isn't much better. Tragically, sound Biblical doctrine (that exposes sin and exalts *Jesus*) is unpopular. On the contrary, positive, up-beat, motivational, feel-good speaking is in unprecedented demand. Sadly, multitudes of professing Christians today violently reject any standard of morality as teachings of "law". With such thinking so prevalent and vehemently defended as orthodox, we are forced to ask ourselves these questions:

1. Are we, as Christians, to obey the commandments of God?

2. And if so, is it legalistic to teach Christians to obey God?

An honest examination of the current spiritual trends in today's professing church reveals that in an attempt to avoid *legalism* we have now succumbed to *Antinomianism*. We have so recoiled from a *"salvation by works"* that we have produced a *salvation lacking obedience*. Not surprisingly, the *false* and *blasphemous* doctrine of *"once saved always saved"* is the most popular doctrinal error of our times. Confusion abounds regarding the covenants of *law* and *grace* and to be zealous for the church to submit to Christ as Lord is equated with undermining Biblical grace. This spiritual malady in doctrine is referred to as *Antinomianism*.

Antinomianism, according to *Webster's 1828 Dictionary*, is a sect who maintains, that, under the gospel dispensation, the law is of no use or obligation; or who hold doctrines which supersede the necessity of good works and a virtuous life.

We would be wise to consider the warning of Christ regarding the spiritual atmosphere of the last days...

> *"…and because iniquity shall abound, the love of many shall wax cold."*
> —Matthew 24:12

The Greek word here translated *"iniquity"* means *"lawlessness"*. *Jesus* is clearly pointing out that the last day spiritual error will be one marked by a hatred for restraint, rather than a bent toward legalism. However, the church has sired a generation who fear legalism more than they hate sin. They ramble on and on about avoiding *"the bondage of law"* while they participate in unspeakable vice and compromise. They piously talk of *"defending the faith"* yet live cold, dry, uninspired lives void of passion for *Jesus*. When talking to such people it appears that nearly every basic Biblical term has been redefined; the plain meanings of *repentance*, *hate*, and yes, even *love* have been skewed to a humanistic understanding. Is there any wonder they have exchanged *spiritual bondage* for *spiritual liberty* and vice versa? Evidently, according to the modern gospel and the new cross, *Jesus* died to allow them to *"do as they please"*. As *Jeremiah the Prophet* scolded backslidden *Israel* of old…

> *"Behold, ye trust in lying words, that cannot profit. Will ye steal, murder, and commit adultery, and swear falsely, and burn incense unto Baal, and walk after other gods whom ye know not; And come and stand before me in this house, which is called by my name, and say, We are delivered to do all these abominations?"*
>
> *—Jeremiah 7:10*

…the professing church has fallen headlong into the demonic lie that twists and perverts grace into license, just as the N.T. writers prophesied *(Jude 1:4)*. It is a sad testimony and largely confirms the low ebb of spiritual life in the modern church when professing Christians are more grieved with the confrontation and exposure of sin than sin itself. Few today appreciate the light, but many worship a false God who abides in the shadowy twilight that is just dim enough to obscure and cloak compromise.

Interestingly, in many Christian circles the mentioning of the *law of God* is treated with greater disdain than gossip, cursing, and false doctrine. Is this Biblically sound? Ironically, neither *Jesus*, nor any of the Apostles ever spoke of the law of God in a derogatory manner. Many would be shocked to simply realize this one Biblical fact: *the Holy Ghost will never inspire anyone to speak negatively about the law of God*. True, the law cannot save, nor can it make anyone holy, however, it has its place even under the gospel dispensation (1 Tim. 1:8-10). Nevertheless, Christians today forget that it is the ceremonial law, not the moral law that is *"done away with in Christ."* Under the covenant of grace, the moral law is expressed and established in the love commandments of Christ *(Matthew 22:40)* and nowhere in the New Testament are we freed from our obligation to fulfill this moral law. The Bible teaches that *"Christ's righteousness"* was imputed to us[*], not

---

[*] In the context of Christ and His atoning ministry, the author makes a distinction here between His righteousness and obedience, though they are intrinsically linked; namely, Christ's righteousness is the outcome of His obedience, notwithstanding the eternal nature of His righteousness. This author postulates that "righteousness" is the moral virtue in character due to conformity to the moral law, while "obedience" is the actual conformity to the law. Christ's righteousness could be perceived as the divine answer for our sins past, coupled, of course, with divine pardon.

   Webster's 1828 dictionary says of righteousness as it concerns Christ; "The active and passive obedience of Christ, by which the law of God is fulfilled."

The Works of John Fletcher

His obedience - this we must offer ourselves through the power of the Holy Ghost (John 15:4-5). At justification, we are rendered *"righteous"* by virtue of the finished work of Christ as we are forgiven for all *"sins past"* *(Romans 3:25)*. However, as Christians, we are obligated to fulfill the law of God by daily *"walking in the Spirit"* *(Romans 8:4, Gal. 5:14-16)*. Furthermore, we are given "grace" that we might "walk in newness of life" and *"present our bodies a living sacrifice, holy, and acceptable unto God which is our reasonable service"*.

Nonetheless, the professing church's ear has been captivated by those who distort the Biblical view of grace. Yet, *Antinomianism* is not a new concept, but a lie as old as the *Father of lies* himself. Often, the key to unlocking the future is to search through the past. What is needed to challenge the sin-excusing lies of today is not something *new*, but something *old (Jer 6:16)*. Something tried, tested, and used in generations past to utterly expose and slay the blasphemous and uncircumcised giant of *Antinomianism* in our midst.

In the republishing of *Mr. John Fletcher's, "Works: Checks to Antinomianism"*, one of the greatest and most extensive theological critiques of false grace ever penned, a bright and shining theological light is preserved for the edification and instruction of future generations of Christians. Mr. *Fletcher's* work has, with sound doctrine, calculating logic, and riveting application, forcefully and systematically exposed the satanic lies of easy-believism and counterfeit grace. May the Spirit of God anoint afresh this new publication of Mr. Fletcher's work so as to instruct us in the way we should go and equip us to utterly hate every false work *(Ps 119:104)*.

Britt Williams
Woodville, Mississippi
August 2011

The aim of this statement is to communicate that God expects and requires us to render obedience. True, obedience ultimately must be attributed to the grace of God secured via faith in the finished work of Christ; however, this is something different than imputation. Christian obedience is something real, literal, experiential, and acceptable to God. On the other hand, imputation is something attributed to us merely judicially. Antinomians pervert the doctrine of imputation, claiming Christ's obedience to the law becomes our obedience to the law, unconditionally realized and irrespective of our actual behavior or choices.

PREFACE TO THE
APPREHENDING TRUTH 2011 EDITION

The Works of John Fletcher have long been difficult to locate in print, and when found prove themselves to be very expensive. Such a body of works, as important as they, should be available for every Christian in a format readily and reasonably accessible. This edition seeks to put an end to this difficulty.

While complete editions have been available in the past, the corpus of works was last published in 1974 by Schmul Publishers (this editor is unaware of the timing of the last printing of that edition), they are now out of print and as previously stated, very difficult to locate.

Because of the vast importance and purity of the doctrine therein contained, Apprehending Truth Publishers has desired for some time to republish the works. Much thought and prayer has gone in to the format and means whereby the volumes would be produced. The publishers have elected to print the volumes in an affordable paperbound edition initially in the desire that they may then find a wider distribution than would otherwise be the case with the more expensive hardbound alternative. Apprehending Truth Publishers has considered the option of a special hardbound edition once all volumes are complete.

With the current trend of antinomianism becoming exponentially worse as the years, yea even the days, go by, the republication of these works could not have come at a more important juncture. A vast number of people are being swept away in the current flood spewed forth from the dragon's mouth, the flood despicably ensconced in Reform Theology. Reform Theology has so vastly affected Christendom that it has become the leaven mixed in the flour. From "thou shalt not surely die" to "hath God said", the lie of the Calvinist's "Diana", as Fletcher puts it, has swept away many in its deceptive flood, yea deceiving even the very elect, promoting sin while decrying holiness as a wicked and evil doctrine. Of course, such a plain assertion would be denied by the proponents of the "Doctrines of ~~Grace~~ Lasciviousness"*, but there is no escaping the logical arrangement of the theology and the resultant ideology.

It is evident that even many who intellectually recognize the necessity of holiness refuse to practically apprehend it or have redefined it to fit with their own chosen mode of subdued worldliness. Very rarely are issues defined according to Scripture but rather by autonomy and experience in order to justify a very flawed theology.

Without holiness no man shall see the Lord. (Hebrews 12:14) Thus it would be incumbent upon any lover of Truth to first determine what holiness is according to Scripture and then to apprehend it with all expediency, and having apprehended, to retain it at the cost of all else. The doctrines of John Calvin are indeed a singular affront to holiness, though some may deny it. The denial comes, I believe in most cases, not in intended prevarication but rather in the fact that practical holiness is redefined in the corridors of Reformed Theology. In fact in Reformed Theology, holiness is not "practical" at all, but rather "theoretical".† This is nowhere more evident than in the camp of the Calvinist Theonomist.

> In reflecting the moral perfection of God the law exposes our sinfulness by sharp contrast. We have no reason to hope that God, who is immutably righteous, will lower His ethical norms in order to accommodate our unrighteousness. However, <u>God does credit the perfect obedience of Christ to our account</u>, thereby being just and the justifier of His people (cf. Rom. 3:26). Herein the law takes on a two-fold significance for Christians; *first*, obedience to the law by the Messiah plays an integral part in the accomplishment of salvation, and *second*,

---

* To refer to Calvinism as the Doctrines of "Grace" is to truly turn that glorious attribute into lasciviousness.
† Sadly this can be seen to be flooding into the most conservative of Churches. Some walk so very close to the precise which falls headlong into the world while supposedly disdaining that world. The principles of separation are utterly foreign to most of the Church.

followers of Christ thus have set before them the example and goal of lawful living by their Lord.[*]

But the goal is never apprehended, nor truthfully or honestly pursued, because Christ's obedience has already been imputed to the believer's account.

> Christ's perfect obedience to the law of God secures our release from the necessity of personally keeping the law as a condition of justification...Our righteousness before God must be that which is imputed to us, the righteousness of Christ who was sinless before the law...Although faith does not nullify the law, it does release us from the law's condemnation.[†]

A law with no code of jurisprudence or statutory enforcement is no law at all, but rather an insincere suggestion with no teeth to sentence. And thus the theonomist provision is made for sin even while advocating obedience to the law.[‡] Cornelius Van Til has stated, "There is no alternative but that of theonomy and autonomy.[§]", but is this simply rhetoric? The practical application of holiness in day to day life is at best a mediocre façade and association with the world is platonic and blasé. And why not, considering that every action of man is preconceived as ordained and orchestrated by God Himself. There exists no greater man centered theology than to teach that every autonomous act of man is ordained and orchestrated by God Himself.

From a theoretical position the theonomist stands on solid ground. But when practical application of his theory is suggested the dunes begin to shift and his theonomic castle of sand sifts back into the shifting wasteland of antinomianism.[**]

Of course we are speaking to the theoretical position itself and not to individual experience.

How can even the theonomist hold such a theoretical dictum to obedience? Because regardless of the cries and claims of the Calvinist, Reform

[*] Greg Bahnsen, Theonomy in Christian Ethics. Covenant Media Press, 2000. p. 149.
[†] Ibid, p. 130-131
[‡] We contrast here the practicle application of holiness and the theoretical view of Calvinistic theonomy.
[§] Greg Bahnsen, Van Til's Apologetic, P&R Publishing, 1998, p. 21n.
[**] See "Antinomianism in the Theonomic Principle", www.blog.apprehendingtruth.net

Theology points its fanatical finger toward antinomianism all the while screaming, "grace, grace" when there is no grace.

It is not the obedience of faith which is effectual to soteriological perseverance, as Hebrews 12:14 suggests; it is the unalterable, irresistible will of God which has decreed who will see Him and who will suffer eternal damnation because of his reprobation irresistibly thrust upon him by his loving Creator. This is not a divine being which can be found in Scripture, but is more readily located in the demonic prose of the Quran. This form of "sovereignty" has in essence dethroned Calvin's "god" in one fell swoop of his "institutions" biased idiomatic dogma. The doctrines of necessity and determinism invariably shackle God Himself with the chains of His own decrees. If God, before eternity, determined every event, not even He can now be said to be a free moral agent, and is therefore not sovereign. The dilemma is obvious, to those who would see.

This volume in Apprehending Truth's presentation of the Works of John Fletcher, Five Checks to Antinomianism, is a corpus in letters rebutting and refuting the errors which belie a theology so foreign to the dictates of Scripture. With the care of a surgeon's scalpel Fletcher removes the pestilent infection from the body of theological elucidation and this antinomian malady called Calvinism is systematically diagnosed and exposed for the fraud that it is. His presentation is masterful, and timeless. Fletcher, in a defense and vindication of John Wesley and his teachings conflicting with Calvinism, has slain the proverbial dragon, but the problem, in his day as well as in ours, is that the dragon does not know he is dead.

Jeffrey L. Wallace
Woodville, Mississippi
July 2011

FIRST CHECK TO ANTINOMIANISM;

OR,

A VINDICATION

OF THE

REV. MR. WESLEY'S MINUTES

OF A

PUBLIC CONFERENCE, HELD IN LONDON, AUGUST 7, 1770;

OCCASIONED BY

A CIRCULAR LETTER

INVITING

PRINCIPAL PERSONS, BOTH CLERGY AND LAITY,

AS WELL OF THE DISSENTERS AS OF THE ESTABLISHED CHURCH,
WHO DISAPPROVED OF THOSE MINUTES,

TO OPPOSE THEM IN A BODY, AS A DREADFUL HERESY;

AND DESIGNED TO REMOVE PREJUDICE, CHECK RASHNESS, PROMOTE
FORBEARANCE, DEFEND THE CHARACTER OF AN EMINENT MINISTER OF CHRIST,
AND PREVENT SOME IMPORTANT SCRIPTURAL TRUTHS FROM
BEING HASTILY BRANDED AS HERETICAL.

IN FIVE LETTERS,

TO THE HON. AND REV. AUTHOR OF THE CIRCULAR LETTER.

BY A LOVER OF QUIETNESS AND LIBERTY OF CONSCIENCE.

The Works of John Fletcher

PREFACE.

A COPY OF THE CIRCULAR LETTER,

WHICH

GAVE OCCASION TO THIS VINDICATION,

TO WHICH IS ANNEXED

A COPY OF THE REV. MR. WESLEY'S MINUTES.

———

"SIR, — Whereas Mr. Wesley's conference is to be held at Bristol, on Tuesday, the 6th of August next, it is proposed by Lady Huntingdon, and many other Christian friends, (real Protestants,) to have a meeting at Bristol, at the same time, of such principal persons, both clergy and laity, who disapprove of the under written Minutes: and as the same are thought injurious to the very fundamental principles of Christianity, it is farther proposed that they go in a body to the said conference, and insist upon a formal recantation of the said Minutes; and in case of a refusal, that they sign and publish their protest against them. Your presence, sir, on this occasion, is particularly requested. But if it should not suit your convenience to be there, it is desired that you will transmit your sentiments on the subject to such persons as you think proper to produce them. It is submitted to you, whether it would not be right, in the opposition to be made to such a dreadful heresy, to recommend it to as many of your Christian friends, as well of the dissenters as of the established Church, as you can prevail on, to be there, the cause being of so public a nature.

"I am, sir, your obedient servant,

"WALTER SHIRLEY."

"P. S. Your answer is desired, directed to the countess of Huntingdon, or the Rev. Mr. Shirley, or John Lloyd, Esq. in Bath; or Mr. James Ireland, merchant, Bristol; or to Thomas Powis, Esq. at Berwick, near Shrewsbury; or to Richard Hill, Esq. at Hawkstone, near Whitchurch, Shropshire. *Lodgings will be provided. Inquire at Mr. Ireland's Bristol.*"

EXTRACTS FROM THE MINUTES

OF SOME LATE CONVERSATIONS

BETWEEN THE REV. MR. WESLEY AND OTHERS,

AT A PUBLIC CONFERENCE, HELD IN LONDON, AUGUST 7, 1770,

AND PRINTED BY W. FINE, IN BRISTOL

"Take heed to your doctrine."

"WE said in 1744, 'We have leaned too much toward Calvinism.' Wherein?

"1. With regard to *man's faithfulness.* Our Lord himself taught us to use the expression. And we ought never to be ashamed of it. We ought steadily to assert, on his authority, that if a man is not 'faithful in the unrighteous mammon,' God will not 'give him the true riches.'

"2. With regard to *working for life.* This also our Lord has expressly commanded us. '*Labour,*' Εργαζεσθε, literally, '*work* for the meat that endureth to everlasting life.' And in fact every believer, till he comes to glory, works *for,* as well as *from* life.

"3. We have received it as a maxim, that 'a man is to do nothing *in order to* justification.' Nothing can be more false. Whoever desires to find favour with God, — should 'cease from evil, and learn to do well.' Whoever repents, should do 'works meet for repentance.' And if this is not *in order to* find favour what does he do them for?

"Review the whole affair.

"1. Who of us is *now* accepted of God?

"He that now believes in Christ, with a loving, obedient heart.

"2. But who among those who never heard of Christ?

"He that feareth God, and worketh righteousness according to the light he has.

"3. Is this the same with 'he that is sincere?'

"Nearly, if not quite.

"4. Is not this 'salvation by works?'

"Not by the m*erit* of works, but by works as a condition.

"5. What have we then been disputing about for these thirty years?

"I am afraid, *about words.*

"6. As to *merit* itself of which we have been so dreadfully afraid: we are rewarded, *according to our works,* yea, *because of our works.* How does this differ from, *for the sake of our works?* And how differs this from *secundum merita operum,* 'as our works deserve?' Can you split this hair? I doubt, I cannot.

"7. The grand objection to one of the preceding propositions is drawn from matter of fact. God does in fact justify those who by their own confession, 'neither feared God nor wrought righteousness.' Is this an exception to the general rule?

"It is a doubt whether God makes any exception at all. But how are we sure that the person in question never did 'fear God and work righteousness?' His own saying so is not proof: for we know how all that are convinced of sin undervalue themselves in every respect.

"8. Does not talking of a justified or sanctified *state* tend to mislead men? almost naturally leading them to trust in what was done in one moment? Whereas we are every hour and every moment pleasing or displeasing to God, *according to our works:* according to the whole of our inward tempers and our outward behaviour."

FIRST CHECK TO ANTINOMIANISM.

LETTER I.

HONOURED AND REVEREND SIR, — Before a judge passes sentence upon a person accused of theft, he hears what his neighbours have to say for his character. Mr. Wesley, I grant, is accused of what is worse than theft, *dreadful heresy*; and I know that whosoever maintains a dreadful heresy is *a dreadful heretic;* and that the Church of Rome shows no mercy to such. But may not "real Protestants" indulge, with the privilege of a felon, one whom they so lately respected as a brother? And may not I, an old friend and acquaintance of his, be permitted to speak a word in his favour, before he is branded in the forehead, as he has already been on the back?

This step, I fear, will cost me my reputation, (if I have any,) and involve me in the same condemnation with him whose cause, together with that of truth, I design to plead. But when humanity prompts, when gratitude calls, when friendship excites, when reason invites, when justice demands, when truth requires, and conscience summons, he does not deserve the name of a *Christian friend*, who, for any consideration, hesitates to vindicate what he esteems truth, and to stand by an aggrieved friend, brother, and father. Were I not, sir, on such an occasion as this to step out of my beloved obscurity, you might deservedly reproach me as a *dastardly wretch:* nay, you have already done it in general terms, in your excellent sermon on the fear of man. "How often," say you, "do men sneakingly forsake their friends, instead of gloriously supporting them against a powerful adversary, even when their cause is just, for reasons hastily prudential, for fear of giving umbrage to a superior party or interest?"

These generous words of yours, Rev. sir, together with the leave you give both Churchmen and Dissenters to direct to *you* their answers to your circular letter, are my excuse for intruding upon you by this epistle, and my apology for begging your candid attention, while I attempt to convince you that my friend's principles and Minutes are not heretical. In order to this, I shall lay before you, and the principal persons, both clergy and laity, whom you have, from all parts of England and Wales, convened at Bristol, by printed letters, —

I. A general view of the Rev. Mr. Wesley's doctrine.

II. An account of the commendable design of his Minutes.

The Works of John Fletcher

III. A vindication of the propositions which they contain, by arguments taken from Scripture, reason, and experience; and by quotations from eminent Calvinist divines, who have said the same things in different words.

And suppose you yourself, sir, in particular, should appear to be a strong assertor of the doctrines which you call a *dreadful heresy* in Mr. Wesley, I hope you will not refuse me leave to conclude, by expostulating with you upon your conduct in this affair, and recommending to you, and our other Christian friends, the forbearance which you recommend to others, in one of your sermons: "Why doth the narrow heart of man pursue with malice or rashness those who presume to differ from him?" Yea, and what is more extraordinary, those who agree with him in all essential points?

I. When, in an intricate case, a prudent judge is afraid to pass an unjust sentence, he inquires, as I observed, into the general conduct of the person accused, and by that means frequently finds out the truth which he investigates. As that method may be of service in the present case, permit me, sir, to lay before you a general view of Mr. Wesley's doctrine.

1. For above these sixteen years I have heard him frequently in his chapels, and sometimes in my church: I have familiarly conversed and corresponded with him, and have often perused his numerous works in verse and prose: and I can truly say that, during all that time, I have heard him, upon every proper occasion, steadily maintain *the total fall of man in Adam*, and his utter inability to recover himself, or take any one step toward his recovery, "without the grace of God preventing him, that he may have a good will, and working with him when he has that good will."

The deepest expressions that ever struck my ears on the melancholy subject of our natural depravity and helplessness, are those which dropped from his lips: and I have ever observed that he constantly ascribes to Divine grace, not only the good works and holy tempers of believers, but all the good thoughts of upright heathens, and the good desires of those professors whom he sees "begin in the Spirit and end in the flesh:" when, to my great surprise, some of those who accuse him of "robbing God of the glory of his grace, and ascribing too much to man's power," directly or indirectly maintain that Demas and his fellow apostates never had any grace; and that if once they went on far in the ways of God, it was merely by the force of fallen nature; a sentiment which Mr. Wesley looks upon as diametrically opposite to the humbling assertion of our Lord, "Without me ye can do nothing;" and which he can no more admit than the rankest Pelagianism.

2. I must likewise testify, that he faithfully points out *Christ as the only way of salvation;* and strongly recommends faith as the only mean of receiving him, and all the benefits of his righteous life and meritorious death: and truth obliges me to declare, that he frequently expresses his detestation of the errors of modern Pharisees, who laugh at original sin, set up the powers of fallen man, cry down the operation of God's Spirit, deny the absolute necessity of the blood and righteousness of Christ, and refuse him the glory of all the good that may be found in Jew or Gentile. And you will not without difficulty, sir, find in England, and perhaps in all the world, a minister who hath borne more frequent testimonies, either from the pulpit or the press, against those dangerous errors. All his works confirm my assertion, especially his sermons on Original Sin, and

Salvation by Faith, and his masterly Refutation of Dr. Taylor, the wisest Pelagian and Socinian of our age. Nor am I afraid to have this testimony confronted with his Minutes, being fully persuaded that, when they are candidly explained, they rather confirm than overthrow it.

His manner of preaching the fall and the recovery of man is attended with a peculiar advantage: it is close and experimental. He not only points out the truth of those doctrines, but presses his hearers to cry to God that they may feel their weight upon their hearts. Some open those great truths very clearly, but let their congregations rest, like the stony ground hearers, in the first emotions of sorrow and joy which the word frequently excites. Not so Mr. Wesley: he will have true penitents "feel the plague of their own hearts, travail, be heavy laden," and receive "the sentence of death in themselves," according to the glorious "ministration of condemnation:" and according to "the ministration of righteousness and of the Spirit which exceeds in glory," he insists upon true believers knowing for themselves, that Jesus "hath power on earth to forgive sins;" and asserts, that they "taste the good word of God, and the powers of the world to come," and that they "are made partakers of the Holy Ghost and the Divine nature; the Spirit itself bearing witness with their spirits that they are the children of God."

3. The next fundamental doctrine in Christianity is that of *holiness of heart and life;* and no one can here accuse Mr. Wesley of leaning to the Antinomian delusion, which "makes void the law, through" a speculative and barren "faith:" on the contrary, he appears to be peculiarly set for the defence of practical religion: for, instead of representing Christ "as the minister of sin," with Ranters, to the great grief and offence of many, he sets him forth as a complete *Saviour from sin.* Not satisfied to preach holiness begun, he preaches finished holiness, and calls believers to such a degree of heart-purifying faith, as may enable them to triumph in Christ, as "being made to them of God, sanctification as well as righteousness."

It is, I grant, his misfortune (if indeed it be one) to preach a fuller salvation than most professors expect to enjoy here; for he asserts that Jesus can "make clean" *the inside* as well as the *outside* of his vessels unto honour; that he hath power on earth "to save his people from their sins;" and that his blood "cleanses from all sin," from the guilt and defilement both of original and actual corruption. He is bold enough to declare, with St. John, that "if we say we have no sin, *either by nature or practice,* we deceive ourselves, and the truth is not in us: but if we confess our sins, God is faithful and just to forgive us our sins, and to cleanse us from all unrighteousness." He is legal enough not to be ashamed of these words of Moses: "The Lord thy God will circumcise thine heart, and the heart of thy seed, to love the Lord thy God with all thine heart, and with all thy soul, that thou mayest live." And he dares to believe that the Lord can perform the words which he spoke by Ezekiel: "I will sprinkle clean water upon you and you shall be clean: from ALL your filthiness and from ALL your idols will I cleanse you. A new heart also will I give you: I will take away the stony heart out of your flesh, and I will give you a heart of flesh; and I will put my Spirit within you, and cause you to walk in my statutes; and ye shall keep my judgments, and do them. I will also save you from *all* your uncleannesses." Hence it is that he constantly exhorts his hearers "to grow in grace, and in the knowledge of our Saviour;" till by a strong and lively faith they can continually "reckon themselves to be dead indeed unto sin, but alive unto God through Jesus Christ our Lord." He tells them, that "he who committeth sin, is the servant of sin;" — that "our old man is crucified with Christ that the body of sin might be destroyed, that henceforth we should not serve sin;" — that "if the Son shall make us free, we shall be free indeed;" — and that although "*the* law of the Spirit of life in Christ Jesus" will not deliver us from the innocent infirmities incident to flesh and blood, it will nevertheless make us "free from the law of sin and death," and enable us to say with holy triumph, "How shall we, that are dead to sin, live any longer therein?" In a word, he thinks that God can so "shed abroad his love in our hearts, by the Holy Ghost given unto us," as to "sanctify us wholly, soul, body, and spirit;" and enable us to "rejoice evermore, pray without ceasing, and in every thing give thanks." And he is persuaded, that He who "can do far exceeding abundantly above all that we can ask or think," is able to fill us with the "perfect love which casts out fear; that we, being delivered out of the hands of our enemies," may have "the mind which was in Christ;" be righteous as the *man* Jesus was righteous; "walk as he also walked," and be in our measure, "as he was in the world:" he as the stock of the tree of righteousness, and we as the branches, "having our fruit from him "unto holiness," and "serving God without fear in true holiness and righteousness all the days of our life."

This he sometimes calls *full sanctification,* the state of "fathers in Christ," or, the "glorious liberty of the children of God;" sometimes "a being strengthened, stablished, and settled;" or "being rooted and grounded in love;" but most commonly he calls it *Christian perfection:* a word which, though used by the apostles in the same sense, cannot be used by him without raising the pity or indignation of one half of the religious world; some making it the subject of their pious sneers and godly lampoons; While others tell you roundly "they abhor it above every thing in the creation."

Tantæne animia coelestibus iræ!

On account of this doctrine it is that he is traduced as a Pharisee, a papist, an antichrist; some of his opposers taking it for granted that he makes void the priestly office of Christ, by affirming that his blood can so completely wash us here from our sins, that at death we shall "be found of him in peace, without spot, wrinkle, or any such thing;" while others, to colour their opposition to the many scriptures which he brings to support this unfashionable doctrine, give it out, that he only wants the old man to be so refined in all his tempers, and regulated in all his outward behaviour, as to appear perfect in the flesh; or, in other terms, that he sets up Pharisaic SELF, instead of a "Christ *completely* formed in us as *the full* hope of glory." But I must (for one) do him the justice to say he is misapprehended, and that what he calls perfection is nothing but the rich cluster of all the spiritual blessings promised to believers in the Gospel; and, among the rest, a continual sense of the virtue of Christ's atoning and purifying blood, preventing both old guilt from returning and new guilt from fastening upon the conscience; together with the deepest consciousness of our helplessness and nothingness in our best estate, the most endearing discoveries of the Redeemer's love, and the most humbling and yet ravishing views of his glorious fulness. Witness one of his favourite hymns on that subject: —

> Confound, o'erpower me with thy grace;
> I would be by myself abhorr'd:
> (All might, all majesty, all praise,
> All glory be to Christ my Lord!)
> Now let me gain perfection's height,
> Now let me into nothing fall;
> Be less than nothing in my sight,
> And feel that *Christ is all in all.*

4. But this is not all: he holds also *general redemption,* and its necessary consequences, which some account *dreadful heresies.* He asserts with St. Paul, that "Christ, by the grace of God, tasted death for every man;" and this grace he calls *free,* as extending itself *freely* to all. Nor can he help expressing his surprise at those pious ministers who maintain that the Saviour keeps his grace, as they suppose he kept his blood, from the greatest part of mankind, and yet engross to themselves the title of *preachers of* FREE *grace!*

He frequently observes, with the same apostle, that "Christ is the Saviour of *all* men, but especially of them that believe;" and that "God will have all men to be saved," consistently with their moral agency, and the tenor of his Gospel.

With St. John he maintains that "God is love," and that "Christ is the propitiation not only for our sins, but also — for the sins of the *whole world.*" With David he affirms that "God's mercy is over *all* his works:" and with St. Peter, that "the Lord is not willing that any should perish, but that *all* should come to repentance;" yea, that God, without hypocrisy, "commandeth *all* men, *every where,* to repent." Accordingly he says with the Son of God, "Whosoever will, let him come and take of the water of life freely;" and after his blessed example, as well as by his gracious command, he "preaches the Gospel TO *every creature;*" which he apprehends would be inconsistent with common honesty, if there were not a Gospel FOR *every creature.* Nor can he doubt of it in the least, when he considers that Christ is a king as well as a priest; that we are under a law to him; that those men who "will not have him to reign over them, shall be brought and slain before him;" yea, that he will "judge the secrets of men," according to St. Paul's Gospel, and take vengeance on all them that obey not his *own* Gospel, *and* be the author of eternal salvation to *none but* them that obey him. With this principle, as with a key given us by God himself, he opens, those things which are "hard to be understood." in the Epistles of St. Paul, and "which they that are unlearned and unstable wrest, as they do some other scriptures, *if not* to their own destruction, *at least to* the overthrowing of the faith of some" weak Christians, and the hardening of many, very many infidels.

As a true son of the Church of England, he believes that "Christ redeemed him and all mankind;" that "for us men," and not merely for the *elect,* "he came down from heaven, and made upon the cross a full, perfect, and sufficient sacrifice, oblation, and satisfaction, for the sins of the *whole* world."

Like an honest man, and yet a man of sense, he so subscribed the seventeenth article as not to reject the thirty-first, which he thinks of equal force, and much more explicit; and, therefore, as the seventeenth article authorizes him, he "receives God's promises in suchwise as they are generally set forth in holy Scripture;" rejecting, after the example of our governors in Church and state, the Lambeth articles, in which the doctrine of *absolute unconditional* election and reprobation was maintained, and which some Calvinistic divines, in the days of Queen Elizabeth, vainly attempted to impose upon these kingdoms, by adding them to the thirtynine articles. Far, therefore, from thinking he does not act a fair part in rejecting the doctrine of particular redemption, he cannot conceive by what salvo the consciences of those ministers, who embrace it, can permit them to say to each of their communicants," The blood of Christ was shed for *thee*;" and to baptize promiscuously *all* children within their respective parishes, "in the name of the Father, and of the Son, and of the Holy Ghost," when all that are unredeemed have no more right to the *blood, name,* and Sp*irit* of Christ, than Lucifer himself.

Thus far Mr. Wesley agrees with Arminius, because he thinks that illustrious divine agreed thus far with the Scriptures, and all the early fathers of the Church. But if Arminius, (as the author of *Pietas Oxoniensis* affirms, in his letter to Dr. Adams,) "denied, that man's nature is totally corrupt; and asserted, that he hath still* a freedom of will to turn to God, but not without the assistance of grace," Mr. Wesley is no Arminian; for he strongly asserts the *total* fall of man, and constantly maintains that by nature man's will is only free to evil, and that Divine grace must first prevent, and then continually farther him, to make him willing and able to turn to God.

I must, however, confess, that he does not, as some *real Protestants,* continually harp upon the words FREE grace, and FREE will; but he gives reasons of considerable weight for this. (1.) Christ and his apostles never did so. (2.) He knows the word *grace* necessarily implies the *freeness* of a favour; and the word *will,* the *freedom* of our choice: and he has too much sense to delight in perpetual tautology. (3.) He finds, by blessed experience, that when the will is touched by Divine grace, and yields to the touch, it is as free to good, as it was before to evil. He dares not, therefore, make the maintaining *free will,* any more than *free breath,* the criterion of an unconverted man. On the contrary, he believes none are converted but those who have a *free will* to follow Jesus; and, far from being ashamed to be called a "free-willer," he affirms it as essential to all men to be "free-willing creatures," as to be "rational animals;" and he supposes he can as soon find a diamond or a flint without gravity, as a good or bad man without free will.

Nor will I conceal that I never heard him use that favourite expression of some good men, *Why me? Why me?* though he is not at all against their using it, if they can do it to edification. But as he does not see that any of the saints, either of the Old or New Testament ever used it, he is afraid to be humble and "wise

* This is worded in so ambiguous a manner, as to give readers room to think that Arminius held man hath a will to turn to God before grace prevents him, and only wants some Divine assistance to finish what nature has power to begin. In this sense of the words it is I deny Mr. Wesley is an Arminian.

above what is written," lest "voluntary humility" should introduce refined pride before he is aware. Doubting, therefore, whether he could say, *Why me? Why me?* without the self-pleasing idea of his being preferred to thousands, or without a touch of the secret self applause that tickles the Pharisee's heart, when he "thanks God he is not as other men," he leaves the fashionable exclamation to others, with all the refinements of modern divinity; and chooses to keep to St. Paul's expression, "He loved me," which implies no exclusion of his poor fellow sinners; or to that of the royal psalmist, "Lord, what is *man,* that thou art mindful of him; and the *son of man,* that thou visitest him."

5. As a consequence of the doctrine of general redemption, Mr. Wesley lays down two axioms, of which he never loses sight in his preaching. *The first* is, that ALL OUR SALVATION IS OF GOD IN CHRIST, and therefore OF GRACE; — all opportunities, invitations, inclination, and power to believe being bestowed upon us of mere grace; — grace most absolutely free: and so far, I hope, that all who are called Gospel ministers agree with him. But he proceeds farther; for, *secondly,* he asserts with equal confidence, that according to the Gospel dispensation, ALL OUR DAMNATION IS OF OURSELVES, by our obstinate unbelief and avoidable unfaithfulness; as we may "neglect so great salvation," desire to "be excused" from coming to the feast of the Lamb, "make light of" God's gracious offers, refuse to "occupy," bury our talent, and act the part of the "slothful servant;" or, in other words, "resist, grieve, do despite to," and "quench the Spirit of grace," *by our moral agency.*

The first of these evangelical axioms he builds upon such scriptures as these: — "In me is thy help. Look unto me and be saved. No man cometh unto me except the Father draw him. What hast thou that thou hast not received?. We are not sufficient to think aright of ourselves, all our sufficiency is of God. Christ is exalted to give repentance. Faith is the gift of God. Without me ye can do nothing," &c, &c.

And *the second* he founds upon such passages as these: "This is the condemnation, that light is come into the world, and men loved darkness rather than light. Ye always resist the Holy Ghost. They rejected the counsel of God toward themselves. Grieve not the Spirit. Quench not the Spirit. My Spirit shall not always strive with man. Turn, why will ye die? Kiss the Son, lest ye perish. I gave Jezebel time to repent, and she repented not. The goodness of God leads [not *drags,*] thee to repentance, who after thy hardness and impenitent heart treasurest up wrath unto thyself. Their eyes have they closed, lest they should see, and be converted, and I should heal them. See that ye refuse not him that speaketh from heaven. I set before you life and death, choose life! Ye will not come unto me that ye might have life. I *would* have gathered you, and ye *would not,*" &c, &c.

As to the *moral agency* of man, Mr. Wesley thinks it cannot be denied upon the principles of common sense and civil government; much less upon those of natural and revealed religion; as nothing would be more absurd than to bind us by laws of a civil or spiritual nature; nothing more foolish than to propose to us punishments and rewards; and nothing more capricious than to inflict the one or bestow the other upon us; if we were not *moral agents.*

He is therefore persuaded, the most complete system of divinity is that in which neither of those two axioms is superseded: He thinks it is bold and unscriptural to set up the one at the expense of the other, convinced that the prophets, the apostles, and Jesus Christ left us no such precedent; and that, to avoid what is termed *legality,* we must not run into refinements which they knew nothing of, and make them perpetually contradict themselves: nor can we, he believes, without an open violation of the laws of candour and criticism, lay a greater stress upon a few obscure and controverted passages, than upon a hundred plain and irrefragable Scripture proofs. He therefore supposes that those persons are under a capital mistake who maintain only the first Gospel axiom, and under pretence of securing to God *all* the glory of the salvation of *one* elect, give to perhaps *twenty* reprobates full room to lay *all* the blame of their damnation either upon their first parents, or their Creator. This way of making twenty *real* holes, in order to stop a *supposed* one, he cannot see consistent either with wisdom or Scripture.

Thinking it therefore safest not to "put asunder" the truths which "God has joined together," he makes all extremes meet in one blessed Scriptural medium. With the Antinomian he preaches, "God worketh in you both to will and to do of his good pleasure;" and with the Legalist he cries, "Work out, therefore, your own salvation with fear and trembling;" and thus he has all St. Paul's doctrine. With the Ranter he says, "God has chosen you, you are elect;" but, as it is "through sanctification of the Spirit and belief of the truth," with the disciples of Moses he infers, "make your calling and election sure, for if ye do these things ye shall never fall." Thus he presents his hearers with all St. Peter's system of truth, which the others had rent to pieces.

Again, according to the *first* axiom, he says with the perfect Preacher, "All things are now ready;" but with him he adds also, according to the *second,* "Come, lest you never taste the Gospel feast." Thinking it extremely dangerous not to divide the word of God aright, he endeavours to give to every one the portion of it that suits him, cutting, according to times, persons, and circumstances, either with the smooth or the rough edge of his two-edged sword. Therefore, when he addresses those that are steady, and "partakers of the Gospel grace from the first day until now," as the Philippians, he makes use of the *first* principle, and testifies his confidence, "that he who hath begun a good work in them, will perform it until the day of Christ." But when he expostulates with persons, "that ran well, and do not now obey the truth," according to his *second* axiom, he says to them, as St. Paul did to the Galatians, "I stand in doubt of you; ye are fallen from grace."

In short, he would think that he mangled the Gospel, and forgot part of his awful commission, if, when he has declared that "he who believeth shall be saved," he did not also add, that he "who believeth not shall be damned;" or, which is the same, that none perish merely for Adam's sin, but for their own unbelief, and wilful rejection of the Saviour's grace. Thus he advances God's glory every way, entirely ascribing to his mercy and grace all the salvation of the elect, and completely freeing him from the blame of directly or indirectly hanging the millstone of damnation about the neck of the reprobate. And this he effectually does, by showing that the former owe all they are, and all they have, to creating, preserving, and redeeming love, whose innumerable bounties they freely and continually receive; and that the rejection of the latter has absolutely no cause but their obstinate rejecting of that astonishing mercy which wept over Jerusalem; and prayed, and bled even for those that shed the atoning blood — the blood that expiated all sin but that of final unbelief.

I have now finished my sketch of Mr. Wesley's doctrine, so far as it has fallen under my observation during above sixteen years' particular acquaintance with him and his works. It is not my design, sir, to inquire into the truth of his sentiments, much less shall I attempt to prove them orthodox, according to the ideas that some *real Protestants* entertain of orthodoxy. This only I beg leave to observe: Suppose he is mistaken in all the scriptures on which he founds his doctrine of Christian perfection and general redemption, yet his mistakes seem rather to arise from a regard for Christ's glory, than from enmity to his offices; and all together do not amount to any heresy at all; the fundamental doctrines of Christianity, namely, *the fall of man, justification by the merits of Christ, sanctification by the agency of the Holy Spirit*, and *the worship of the one true God in the mysterious distinction of Father, Son, and Holy Spirit*, as it is maintained in the three creeds, not being at all affected by any of his peculiar sentiments.

But you possibly imagine, sir, that he has lately changed his doctrine, and adopted a new system. If you do, you are under a very great mistake; and to convince you of it, permit me to conclude this letter by a paragraph of one which I received from him last spring: —

"I always did (for between these thirty and forty years) clearly assert the total fall of man, and his utter inability to do any good of himself: the absolute necessity of the grace and Spirit of God to raise even a good thought or desire in our hearts: the Lord's rewarding no works, and accepting of none, but so far as they proceed from his preventing, convincing, and converting grace, through the Beloved; the blood and righteousness of Christ being the sole meritorious cause of our salvation. And who is there in England that has asserted these things more strongly and steadily than I have done?"

Leaving you to answer this question, I remain, with due respect, Hon. and Rev. sir, your obedient servant, in the bond of a peaceful Gospel,

J. FLETCHER.

MADELEY, *July* 29, 1771.

LETTER II.

HONOURED AND REVEREND SIR, — Having proved that Mr. Wesley's doctrine is not heretical, permit me to consider the propositions which close the Minutes of his last conference, on which, it seems, your charge of *dreadful heresy* is founded.

The Works of John Fletcher

They wear, I confess, a new aspect; and such is the force of prejudice and attachment to particular modes of expression, that at first they appear to be very unguarded, if not altogether *erroneous*. But when the din of the severe epithets bestowed upon them by some warm friends was out of my ears; when I had prayed to the Father of lights for meekness of wisdom, and given place to calm reflection, I saw them in quite a different light. Our Lord commands us "not to judge according to the appearance, but to judge righteous judgment;" appearances, therefore, did not seem to me sufficient to condemn any man, much less an elder, and such an elder as Mr. Wesley. I consider, beside, that the circumstances in which a minister sometimes finds himself with respect to his hearers, and particular errors spreading among them, may oblige him to do or say things, which, though very right according to the time, place, persons, and juncture, may yet appear very wrong to those who do not stand just where he does. I saw, for example, that if St. Paul had been in St. James's circumstances, he would have preached justification in as guarded a manner as St. James; and that if St. James had been in St. Paul's place, he would have preached it as freely as St. Paul; and I recollected that in some places St. Paul himself seems even more legal than St. James. See Romans ii, 7, 10, 14; Galatians vi, 7, &c, and 1 Timothy vi, 19.

These reflections made me not only suspend my judgment concerning Mr. Wesley's propositions, but consider what we may candidly suppose was his design in writing them for, and recommending them to the preachers in connection with him. And I could not help seeing that it was only to guard them and their hearers against Antinomian principles and practices, which spread like wild fire in some of his societies; where persons who spoke in the most glorious manner of Christ, and their interest in his complete salvation, have been found living in the greatest immoralities, or indulging the most unchristian tempers. Nor need I go far for a proof of this sad assertion. In one of his societies, not many miles from my parish, a married man, who professed being *in a state of justification and sanctification,* growing wise above what is written, despised, his brethren as legalists, and his teachers as persons not clear in the Gospel. He instilled his principles into a serious young woman; and what was the consequence? Why they talked about "finished salvation in Christ," and "the absurdity of perfection in the flesh," till a perfect child was conceived and born; and, to save appearances, the mother swore it to a travelling man that cannot be heard of. Thus, to avoid legality, they plunged into hypocrisy, fornication, adultery, perjury, and the depth of Ranterism. Is it not hard, that a minister should be traduced as guilty of *dreadful heresy,* for trying to put a stop to such dreadful practices? And is it not high time that he should cry to all that regard his warn-rags, *"Take* heed to your doctrine?" As if he had said,

"Avoid all extremes. While on the one hand you keep clear of the Pharisaic delusion that slights Christ, and makes the pretended merit of an imperfect obedience the procuring cause of eternal life; see that on the other hand you do not lean to the Antinomian error, which, under pretence of exalting Christ, speaks contemptuously of obedience, and "makes void the law through a faith that *does not* work by love." As there is but a step between high Arminianism and self-righteousness, so there is but one between high Calvinism and Antinomianism. I charge you to shun both, especially the latter.

"You know, by sad experience, that at this time we stand particularly in danger of splitting upon the Antinomian rock. Many smatterers in Christian experience talk *of finished salvation in Christ,* or boast of being in a state of justification and sanctification, while they know little of themselves and less of Christ. Their whole behaviour testifies, that their hearts are void of humble love, and full of carnal confidence. They cry, *Lord! Lord!* with as much assurance and as little right as the foolish virgins. They pass for sweet Christians, dear children of God, and good believers; but their secret reserves evidence them to be only such believers as Simon Magus, Ananias, and Sapphira.

"Some, with Diotrephes, 'love to have the pre-eminence, and prate malicious words,' and not content therewith, 'they do not themselves receive the brethren, and forbid them that would,' and even cast them out of the Church as heretics. Some have 'forsaken the right way, and are gone astray, following the way of Balaam, who loved the wages of unrighteousness; they are wells without water, clouds without rain, and trees without fruit:' with Judas they try to 'load themselves with thick clay,' endeavour to 'lay up treasures on earth, and make provision for the flesh to fulfil the lusts thereof.' Some, with the incestuous Corinthian, are led captive by fleshly lusts, and fall into the greatest enormities. Others, with the language of the awakened publican in their mouths, are fast asleep in their spirits; you hear them speak of the corruptions of their hearts, in as unaffected and airy a manner, as if they talked of freckles upon their faces. It seems they run down their sinful nature only to apologize for their sinful practices; or to appear great proficients in self-knowledge, and court the praise due to genuine humility.

"Others, quietly settled on the lees of the Laodicean state, by the whole tenor of their life say, 'they are rich and increased in goods, and have need of nothing;' utter strangers to 'hunger and thirst after righteousness,' they never importunately beg, never wrestle hard for the hidden manna. On the contrary, they sing a *requiem* to their poor dead souls, and say, 'Soul, take thine ease, thou hast goods laid up (in Christ) for many years, yea, for ever and ever;' and thus, like Demas, they go on talking of Christ and heaven, but loving their ease, and enjoying this present world.

"Yet many of these, like Herod, hear and entertain us gladly; but, like him also, they keep their beloved sin, pleading for it as a right eye, and saving it as a right hand. To this day their bosom corruption is not only alive, but indulged; their treacherous Delilah is hugged; and their spiritual 'Agag walks delicately,' and boasts that 'the bitterness of death is past,' and he shall never be 'hewed in pieces before the Lord:' nay, to dare so much as to talk of his *dying* before the body, becomes almost an unpardonable crime.

"Forms and fair shows of godliness deceive us: many, whom our Lord might well compare to 'whited sepulchres,' look like angels of light when they are abroad, and prove tormenting fiends at home. We see them weep under sermons; we hear them pray and sing with the tongues of men and angels; they even profess the faith that removes mountains; and yet, by and by, we discover they stumble at every mole hill; every trifling temptation throws them into peevishness, fretfulness, impatience, ill humour, discontent, anger, and sometimes into loud passion.

"Relative duties are by many grossly neglected: husbands slight their wives, or wives neglect and plague their husbands: children are spoiled, parents disregarded, and masters disobeyed: yea, so many are the complaints against servants professing godliness, on account of their unfaithfulness, indolence, pert answering again, forgetfulness of their menial condition, or insolent expectations, that some serious persons prefer those who have no knowledge of the truth, to those who make a high profession of it.

"Knowledge is certainly *increased;* 'many run to and fro' after it, but it is seldom experimental; the power of God is frequently talked of, but rarely felt, and too often cried down under the despicable name of *frames* and *feelings.* Numbers *seek,* by hearing a variety of Gospel ministers, reading all the religious books that are published, learning the best tunes to our hymns, disputing on controverted points of doctrine, telling or hearing Church news, and listening to, or retailing, spiritual scandal. But, alas! few *strive* in pangs of heartfelt convictions; few ' deny themselves and take up their cross daily;' few ' take the kingdom of heaven by *the holy* violence' of wrestling faith, and agonizing, pray; few *see,* and fewer live in 'the kingdom of God, which is righteousness, peace, and joy in the Holy Ghost.' In a word, many say, 'Lo! Christ is here; and lo! he is there;' but few can consistently witness that '*the* kingdom of heaven is within them.'

"Many assert that 'the clothing of the king's daughter is of wrought gold;' but few, very few experience that she is 'all glorious within;' and it is well if many are not bold enough to maintain that she is *all full of corruptions.* With more truth than ever we may say,

> *Ye different sects, who all declare,*
> *Lo! here is Christ, or Christ is there;*
> *Your stronger proofs divinely give,*
> *And show us where* the Christians *live:*
> *Your claim, alas! ye cannot prove,*
> *Ye want the genuine mark of* love.

"The consequences of this high, and yet lifeless profession, are as evident as they are deplorable. Selfish views, sinister designs, inveterate prejudice, pitiful bigotry, party spirit, self-sufficiency, contempt of others, envy, jealousy, *making men offenders for a word,* — possibly a Scriptural word too, taking advantage of each other's infirmities, magnifying innocent mistakes, putting the worst construction upon each other's words and actions, false accusations, backbiting, malice, revenge, persecutions, and a hundred such evils, prevail among religious people, to the great astonishment of the children of the world, and the unspeakable grief of the true Israelites that yet remain among us.

"But this is not all. Some of our hearers do not even keep to the great outlines of heathen morality' not satisfied practically to reject Christ's declaration, that 'it is more blessed to give than to receive,' they proceed to that pitch of covetousness and daring injustice, as not to pay their just debts; yea, and to cheat, and to extort, whenever they have a fair opportunity. How few of our societies are there where this, or some other evil, has not broken out, and given such shakes to the ark of the Gospel, that had not the Lord wonderfully interposed; it must long ago have been overset! And you know how to this day the name and truth of God are openly blasphemed among the baptized heathens, through the Antinomian lives of many, who 'say they are Jews when they are not, but *by their works declare* they are of the synagogue of Satan.' At your peril, therefore, my brethren, countenance them not: I know you would not do it designedly, but you may do it unawares; therefore 'take heed,' — more than ever 'take heed to your doctrine.' Let it be Scripturally evangelical: give not the children's bread unto dogs: comfort not people that do not mourn. When you should give emetics do not administer cordials, and by that means strengthen the hands of the slothful and unprofitable servant. I repeat it once more, warp not to Antinomianism, and in order to this, *take heed, O! take heed to your doctrine."*

Surely, sir, there is no harm in this word of exhortation; it is Scriptural, and Mr. Wesley's pen cannot make it heretical. Take we then heed to the design of the directions which follow: —

It is evident, that, in order to keep his fellow labourers clear from Antinomianism, he directs them, FIRST, Not to *lean too much toward Calvinism;* and, SECONDLY, Not to *talk of a justified and sanctified state* so unguardedly as some, even Arminians do; which *tends to mislead men,* and relax their watchful attention to their internal and external works, that is, to *the whole of their inward tempers and outward behaviour.* See No. 8.

He produces three particulars, wherein he thinks that both he and his assistants in the Lord's vineyard have leaned too much toward Calvinism, each of which has a natural and strong tendency to countenance the Antinomian delusion. The FIRST: — Being afraid or ashamed to maintain that every man is *faithfully* to employ his every talent; though our Lord himself goes so far in maintaining this doctrine, as to declare that ' if a man be not FAITHFUL in the unrighteous mammon, God will not give him the true riches.' The SECOND:- Being afraid to use the expression, *working for life;* although our Lord, who must be allowed perfectly to understand his own Gospel, uses it himself. And the THIRD: — Granting, without proper distinction, that a man *is to do nothing in order to justification,* "than which," says he, "nothing can be more false;" as common sense dictates, that a rebel must lay down his arms before he can receive a pardon from his prince.

This being premised, Mr. Wesley invites his fellow labourers *to review the whole affair;* and while he does it, he saps the foundations of the Babels built by those who call Christ "Lord! Lord!" without departing from iniquity. *Who* among Christians, says he, *is now accepted of God?* Not he, that, like Hymeneus, *formerly* believed, and "concerning faith hath now made shipwreck," nor he, that, like Simon Magus, actually believes with a speculative, Antinomian faith; but 'he that now believes in Christ with a loving and obedient heart," or, as our Lord and St. Paul express it, he whose "faith works by love, and whose love keeps God's commandments." This must at once overthrow the pretensions of those whose reigned faith, instead of producing a change in their hearts, only adds positiveness to their self-conceit, bitterness to their bad tempers, and perhaps licentiousness to their worldly lives.

Still carrying on his point, he observes next, to the shame of loose Christians, that none *are accepted of God* even among the heathens, but those *that* *fear him and work righteousness.* Nor is this observation improper, (you, sir, being judge,) for you tell us in your fifth sermon, page 84,* that "Cornelius was a man of singular probity, humanity, and morality; and that a view of his character may perhaps convince some, who consider themselves as Christians, how far short they are even of his imperfect righteousness."

This leads him, No. 4, to touch upon an important objection, that will naturally occur to the mind of a Protestant; and he answers it by standing *for the necessity of works,* as firmly as he does *against their merit* in point of *salvation;* thus cutting down, with one truly evangelical stroke, the arrogancy of self-righteous Papists, and the delusion of licentious Protestants. And lest Antinomians should, from the Protestant doctrine "that good works have absolutely no merit in point of salvation," take occasion to slight them that live in sin, he very properly observes, No. 6, that believers shall be *rewarded* in heaven, and are even often rewarded on earth, *because of their works,* and *according to their works,* which, he apprehends, does not so widely differ from *secundum merita operum,* as Protestants in the heat of their contentions with the Papists have been apt to conclude. No. 7, he starts another objection, which Antinomians will naturally make to St. Peter's declaration, that God accepts those "who fear him and work righteousness."

And now, Hon. sir, reserving for another place the consideration of his answer, let me appeal to your candour. From the general tenor of these propositions, is it not evident that Mr. Wesley, (who is now among Gospel ministers, what St. James formerly was among the disciples, and Mr. Baxter among the Puritan divines, that is, the person peculiarly commissioned by the Bishop of souls to defend the Gospel against the encroachments of Antinomians,) aims at stemming the torrent of their delusions, and not at all at "injuring the fundamental principles of Christianity," or bringing "a dreadful heresy into the Church."

You may reply, that you do not so much consider what he *aims* at doing, as what he *has actually* done. Nay, sir, the intention is what a candid judge (much more a loving brother) should particularly consider. If aiming to kill a wild beast that attacks my friend, I unfortunately stab him, it is a "melancholy accident;" but he wrongs me much, who represents it as a "dreadful barbarity." In like manner, if Mr. Wesley has unhappily wounded the truth, in attempting to give the wolf in sheep's clothing a killing stroke, his mistake should rather be called "well-meant legality" than dreadful heresy.

You possibly reply, "Let any one look at these Minutes, and say, whether all the unawakened clergy in the land would not approve and receive them." And what if they did? Would the propositions be the worse barely for this? Is nothing Gospel but what directly shocks common sense? And is the apostles' creed dreadfully heretical, because all the carnal clergy of the Church of England, yea, and of the Church of Rome, receive it? At this strange rate we must give up the Bible itself, for all the Socinians receive it. Ashamed of taking farther notice of an argument by which every Papist might attack the reasonable

---

* London, printed for J. Johnson, 1762.

simplicity of our communion service, and defend the gross absurdity of transubstantiation, I come to an objection of greater weight: —

"Mr. Wesley contradicts himself. He has hitherto preached salvation by faith, and now he talks of *salvation by works, as a condition:* he has a thousand times offered a *free pardon* to the worst of sinners, and now he has the assurance to declare that a *man is to do something in order to justification."* Where will you "find such inconsistencies?" Where! In the Old and New Testament, and especially in the epistles of the great preacher of free justification, and salvation by faith. There you will see many such *seeming* inconsistencies as these: — *Eternal life is the gift of God through our Lord Jesus Christ.* "Charge the rich to lay up in store for themselves a good foundation, that they may lay hold on eternal life: we are temperate, to obtain an incorruptible crown." *By grace ye are saved through faith.* "In so doing thou shalt save thyself. Work out your own salvation." *We are not sufficient of ourselves to think any thing as of ourselves.* "The Gentiles do by nature the things contained in the law." *God justifieth the ungodly and him that worketh not.* "He shall render to every man according to his works, even eternal life to them who by patient continuance in well doing, seek for glory." *God forbid that I should glory in any thing, save in the cross of Christ.* "As the truth of God is in me, no man shall stop me of this glorying," that I have kept myself from being burdensome. *I am the chief of sinners.* "I have lived in all good conscience before God until this day." *We rejoice in Christ Jesus, and have no confidence in the flesh:* "Our rejoicing is this, the testimony of our conscience, that in simplicity and godly sincerity we have had our conversation in the world." *Not by works of righteousness that we have done, but according to his mercy he saved us: not of works, lest any man should boast; for if it be of works, then it is no more grace, otherwise work is no more work.* "I keep under my body, lest I myself should be a cast-away: be not deceived; whatsoever a man soweth that shall he also reap: he that soweth little shall reap little; he that soweth to the Spirit, shall of the Spirit reap life everlasting." *I am persuaded that neither death, nor life, neither things present nor things to come, &c, shall be able to separate us from the love of God which is in Christ Jesus.* Those that fall away "crucify to themselves the Son of God afresh, and put him to an open shame: for the earth which beareth thorns and briers is rejected, and is nigh unto cursing, whose end is to be burned. Some of the branches were broken off by unbelief, thou standest by faith; be not high minded, but fear; continue in God's goodness, otherwise thou also shalt be cut off."

Now, sir, permit me to beg you would lay your hand upon your heart, and say, whether malicious infidels have not a fairer show of reason to raise wicked men against St. Paul, than you have to raise good men against Mr. Wesley? And whether a grain of the candour with which you would reconcile the *seeming** contradictions of the great apostle would not be more than sufficient to reconcile the *seeming* inconsistencies of the great minister whom you have so warmly attacked?

Some persons indeed complain aloud that "Mr. Wesley, in his new scheme of salvation by works as a condition, fairly renounces Christ's blood and righteousness." I grant that the words "blood and righteousness" are not found

---

* Most of these seeming inconsistencies of St. Paul, and those which are charged upon Mr. Wesley, will be reconciled with the greatest ease by considering the two axioms mentioned in my first letter.

in the Minutes, but "acceptance by believing in Christ" is found there; and he must be a caviller indeed, who asserts that he means a Christ without blood, or a Christ without righteousness. Beside, when he cuts off *the merit of works* from having any share in our salvation, far from forgetting the meritorious life and death of the Redeemer, he effectually guards them, and the Protestant ark, sprinkled with the atoning blood, from the rash touches of all merit mongers.* Add to this, that Mr. Wesley has sufficiently declared his faith in the atonement, in thousands of sermons and hymns, some of which are continually sung both by him and the *real Protestants,* so that "out of their own mouth" their groundless charge may be refuted.

Again, the doctrine of the atonement had been fully discussed in former conferences and Minutes, and Mr. Wesley is too methodical to bring the same thing over and over again; nor is it reasonable to expect it should be peculiarly insisted upon in a charge against Antinomians, who rather abuse than deny it. Once more: Mr. Wesley's extract of the Minutes is a memorandum of what was said in the latter part of a conference, or conversation; and no unprejudiced person will maintain, that those who do not expressly mention the atonement in every conversation do actually renounce it.

To conclude: if the author of the Minutes had advanced the following propositions which you have dropped in your second sermon, you might have had some reason to suspect his not doing the atonement justice, (page 36.) "Christ only did that to the human nature which Adam (had he stood upright) would have done." What! sir, would Adam have died for his posterity, or did not Christ die for them? You add, "See the true reason of his death; that he might subdue the earthly life in every sense." And page 45, "He certainly died for no other end but that we might receive the Spirit of holiness." Mr. Wesley is of a very different sentiment, sir; for, poor heretic! he believes with the Papists that "Christ died to make an atonement for us;" and with St. John, that "he is the propitiation for our sins, and for the sins of the whole world." Nevertheless, he will not cry out, *Dreadful heresy!* though he will probably think, that you were once a little too deeply in Mr. Law's sentiments. Leaving you to think with how much justice I might descant here upon this line of the satiric poet,

Dat veniam corvis, vexat censura columbas:

I remain, Rev. and dear sir, yours, &c,

J. FLETCHER.

---

* In the former part of the imaginary contradictions those servants of God make use of the first Gospel axiom; in the latter part they employ the second, and thus declare the whole counsel of God.

LETTER III.

HONOURED AND REVEREND SIR, — We have seen how exceedingly commendable was Mr. Wesley's design in writing what you have extracted from his last Minutes; and how far from being unanswerable are the *general* objections Which some have moved against them. Let us now proceed to a candid inquiry into the true meaning of the propositions. They are thus prefaced: —

"We said in 1744, *We have leaned too much toward Calvinism*. Wherein?"

This single sentence is enough, I grant, to make some persons account Mr. Wesley a heretic. He is not a Calvinist! And what is still more dreadful, he has the assurance to say that he has *leaned too much toward Calvinism!* This will sound like a double heresy in their ears; but not in *yours*, sir, who seem to carry your anti-Calvinistical notions farther than Mr. Wesley himself. He never spoke more clearly to the point of free grace than you do, page 85, of your sermons: — "God," say you, "never left himself without witness, not only from the visible things of the creation, but likewise from the inward witness, a spiritual seed of light sown in the soul of every son of man, Jew, Turk, or Pagan, as well as Christians, whose kindly suscitations whoever follows, will gladly perceive increasing gleams still leading farther on to nearer and far brighter advances, till at length a full and perfect day bursts forth upon his ravished eyes." In this single sentence, sir, you bear the noblest testimony to all the doctrines in which Mr. Wesley dissents from the Calvinists. You begin with GENERAL REDEMPTION, and end with PERFECTION: or, to use your own expression, you follow him "from the spiritual seed of light in a Turk," quite to the "full and perfect day, bursting forth upon the ravished eyes of the Pagan who follows the kindly suscitations" of Divine grace.

And far from making man a mere machine, you tell us, page 140, "it is true that faith is the gift of God, but the exertion of that faith, when once given, lieth in *ourselves*." Mr. Wesley grants it, sir; but permit me to tell you that the word *ourselves* being printed in italics, seems to convey rather more anti-Calvinism than he holds: for he is persuaded that we cannot exert faith without a continual influence of the same Divine power that produced it; it being evident, upon the Gospel plan, that "without Christ we can do nothing." From these and the like passages in your sermons, I conclude, sir, that your charge of *dreadful heresy* does not rest upon these words, "We have leaned too much toward Calvinism." Pass we then to the next, in which Mr. Wesley begins to show wherein he has consented too much to the Calvinists.

"I. With regard to *man's faithfulness* Our Lord himself taught us to use the expression. And we ought never to be ashamed of it. We ought steadily to assert, on his authority, that if a man 'is not faithful in the unrighteous mammon, God will not give him the true riches.'"

Now, where does the heresy lie here? Is it in the word *man's faithfulness?* Is there so much *faithfulness* to God and man among professors, that he must be *opposed* by all good men who dares to use the bare word?. Do *real Protestants* account "man's faithfulness" a grace of supererogation, and quoting Scripture a heresy? Or do they slight what our Lord recommends in the plainest terms, and will one day reward in the most glorious manner? If not, why are they going to enter a protest against Mr. Wesley because he is "not ashamed of Christ and his words before an evil and adulterous generation," and will not "keep back" from his immense flock any part of "the counsel of God," much less a part that so many professors overlook, while some are daring enough to lampoon it, and others wicked enough to trample it under foot?

O, sir, if Mr. Wesley is to be cast out of your synagogue unless he *formally recant* the passage he has quoted, and which he says "we are not to be ashamed of;" what will you do to the Son of God who spoke it? What to St. Luke who wrote it? And what to good Mr. Henry do not make a right use of who thus comments upon it? "If we do not make a right use of the gifts of God's providence, how can we expect from him those present and future comforts which are the gifts of his spiritual grace? Our Saviour here compares these; and shows that though our faithful use of the things of this world cannot be thought to merit any favour at the hand of God, yet our unfaithfulness in the use of them may be justly reckoned a *forfeiture* of that grace which is necessary to bring us to glory. And that is it which our Saviour shows, Luke xvi, 10-12, He that is unjust, *unfaithful*, in the least, is unjust, unfaithful also in *much*. The riches of this world are the *less;* grace and glory are the *greater*. Now, if we be unfaithful in the less, if we use the things of this world to other purposes than those to which they were given us, it may justly be feared we shall be so in the gifts of God's grace, that we will receive them also in vain, and therefore they will be denied us. He that is faithful in that which is least, is faithful also in much. He that serves God and does good with his money, will serve God and do good with the more noble and valuable talents of wisdom and grace, and spiritual gifts, and the earnests of heaven: but he that buries the one talent of this world's wealth, will never improve the five talents of spiritual riches."

Thus speaks the honest commentator: and whoever charges him with legality or heresy therein, I must express my approbation by a shout of applause. Hail Henry! Hail Wesley! Ye faithful servants of the most high God. Stand it out against an Antinomian world! Hail ye followers of the despised Galilean! You "confess him and his words before a perverse generation, he will confess you before his Father and his angels." Let not the scoffs, let not the accusations even of good people, led by the tempter appearing as an angel of light, make you give up one jot or tittle of your Lord's Gospel. Though thousands should combine to brand you as legalists, Papists, heretics, and anti-christs stand it out: Scripture, conscience, and Jesus are on your side. "Be not afraid of their terror, but sanctify the Lord God in your hearts." And when you shall have *occupied* a little longer, and been a little more abused by your mistaken companions, your master will come and find you employed in serving his family, and not in "beating your fellow servants." And while the unprofitable, unfaithful, quarrelsome servant is cast out, he will address you with a "well done good and faithful servants! Ye have been faithful over a few things; I will make you rulers over many things. Enter into the joy of your Lord."

Five Checks To Antinomianism

Excuse the length of this address: it dropped from me before I was aware, and is the fruit of the joy I feel to see "the John Goodwin of the age," and the oracle of the Calvinists so fully agree to maintain the Christian *heresy* against the Antinomian orthodoxy. Nay, and you yourself are of the very same way of thinking. For you tell us (page 89) "that God so far approved of the advances Cornelius had made toward him," (by praying, and giving, as you had observed before, much alms to the people,) "under the slender light offered him; of his earnest desire of a still nearer and more intimate acquaintance with him; and of the improvements he had made of the small talent he had committed to him; that he was now about to entrust him with greater and far better treasures."

In the mouth of two such witnesses as Mr. Henry and yourself, Mr. Wesley's doctrine might be established; but as I fear that some of our friends will soon look upon you both as tainted with his heresy, I shall produce some plain Scripture instances to prove, by the strongest of all arguments, *matter of fact,* that man's "unfaithfulness in the mammon of unrighteousness" is attended with the worst of consequences.

You know, sir, what destruction this sin brought upon Achan, and by his means upon Israel: and you remember how Saul's avarice, and his "flying upon the spoil of the Amalekites" cost him his kingdom, together with the Divine blessing. You will, perhaps, object that "they forfeited only temporal mercies." True, if they repented; but if their sin sealed up the hardness of their heart, then they lost all.

I can, however, mention two who indisputably forfeited both spiritual and eternal blessings: the one is the moral young man whose fatal attachment to wealth is mentioned in the Gospel. "Go," said our Lord to him, "sell all thou hast, give to the poor; come, follow me, and thou shalt have treasure in heaven." He was unfaithful in the "mammon of unrighteousness;" he would not comply with the proposal, and though "Jesus loved him," yet he stood firm to his word, he did not "give him the true riches." The unhappy wretch chose to have his good things in this world, and so lost them in the next.

The other instance is Judas. "He left all," at first, "to follow Jesus;" but when the devil placed him upon the high mountain of temptation, and showed him the horrors of poverty and the alluring wealth of this world, covetousness, his besetting sin, prevailed again: and as he carried the bag he turned thief, and made a private purse. You know, sir, that "the love of money" proved to him "the root of all evil;" and that on account of his "unfaithfulness in the mammon of unrighteousness" our Lord not only did "not give him the true riches," but took his every talent from him, his apostleship on earth, and one of the twelve thrones which he had promised him in common with the other disciples.

Some, I know, will excuse Judas by lathering his crime and damnation upon the decrees of God. But we who are not numbered among *real Protestants* think that sinners are reprobated as they are elected, that is, says St. Peter, "according to the foreknowledge of God." We are persuaded that because God's knowledge is *infinite* he foreknows future contingencies; and we think we should insult both his holiness and his omniscience if we did not believe that he could both foresee and foretell that Judas would be unfaithful, without necessitating him to be so, that the Scriptures might be fulfilled. We assert, then, that as Jesus loved the poor covetous young man, so he loved his poor covetous disciple. For had he hated him, he must have acted the base part of a dissembler, by showing him for years as much love as he did the other apostles; an idea too horrid for a Christian to entertain, I shall not say of "God made flesh," but even of a man that has any sincerity or truth! Judas's damnation, therefore, and the ruin of the young man, according to the second axiom in the Gospel, were merely of themselves, by their unbelief and "unfaithfulness in the mammon of unrighteousness:" for "how could they believe," seeing they reposed their "trust in uncertain riches!"

Thus, sir, both the express declaration of our Lord, and the plain histories of the Scripture agree to confirm this fundamental principle in Christianity, that when God works upon man he expects faithfulness from man; and that when man, as a moral agent, grieves and quenches the Spirit that strives to make him faithful, temporal and eternal ruin are the inevitable consequence.

Thus far, then, the Minutes contain a great, evangelical truth, and not a shadow of heresy; Let us see whether the dreadful snake lurks under the second proposition.

"II. We have leaned too much toward Calvinism; (2.) With regard to *working for life*. This also our Lord has expressly commanded us. *Labour* (Εργαζεσθε, literally, *work*) *for the meat that endureth to everlasting life.* And in fact every believer, till he comes to glory, works *for* as well as *from* life."

Here Mr. Wesley strikes at a fatal mistake of all Antinomians, many honest Calvinists, and not a few who are Arminians in sentiment, and Calvinists in practice. All these, when they see that man is by nature dead in trespasses and sins, lie easy in the mire of iniquity, idly waiting till, by an irresistible act of omnipotence, God pulls them out without any striving on their part. Multitudes uncomfortably stick here, and will probably continue to do so till they receive and heartily embrace that part of the Gospel which is now, alas! called *heresy*. Then shall these poor prisoners in giant Despair's castle find the key of their dungeon about them, and perceive that "the word is nigh them, yea, in their mouth and in their heart; stirring up the gift of God within them, and in hope believing against hope," they will happily "lay hold on eternal life, and apprehend," by the confidence of faith, "him that has apprehended them" by convictions of sin.

But now, instead of imitating Lazarus, who, when the Lord had called him and restored life to his putrefying body, "came forth" out of his grave, though he was "bound hand and foot;" these mistaken men indolently wait till the Lord drags them out, not considering that it is more than he has promised to do. On the contrary, he reproves by his prophet, those that "do not stir themselves up to lay hold on him;" and deciding the point himself, says, "Turn ye at my reproof: behold, I will pour out my Spirit upon you; because I called and ye refused, I stretched out my hands unto you, and no man regarded, I will mock when your fear cometh."

Should you object, "that the case is not similar, because the Lord gave life to the dead body of Lazarus, whereas our souls are *dead in sin by nature.*" True, sir, *by nature;* but does not "*grace* reign" to control nature? And "as by the offence of one, judgment came upon all men to condemnation; even so, by the righteousness of one, is not the free gift come upon all men to justification of life?" According to the promise made to our first parents, and of course to all men then contained in their loins, is not "the seed of the woman *always* nigh," both to reveal and "bruise the serpent's head?" Is not Christ "the light of men, — the light of the world, — come into the world? Shineth he not in the darkness of our nature, even when the darkness comprehends him not? And is not this "light the life," the spiritual "life of men?" Can this be denied, if the "light is Christ," and if "Christ is the resurrection and the life," who came that "we might have life, and that we might have it more abundantly?"

In this Scriptural view of free grace, what room is there for the ridiculous cavil that "Mr. Wesley wants the dead to work for life?" God, of his infinite mercy in Jesus Christ, gives to *poor* sinners, naturally dead in sin, *a talent* of free, preventing, quickening grace, which "reproves them of sin;" and when it is followed, of "righteousness and judgment." This, which some Calvinists call *common grace,* is granted to all without any respect of persons; so that even the poor Jew, Herod, if he had not preferred the smiles of his Herodias to the convincing light of Christ which shone in his conscience, would have been saved as well as John the Baptist; and that poor heathen, Felix, if he had not hardened his heart in the day of his visitation, would have sweetly experienced that Christ had as much tasted death for him as he did for St. Paul. The living light visited them; but they, not "working while it was day," or refusing to "cut off the right hand," which the Lord called for, fell at last into that "night wherein no man can work; their candlestick was removed, their lamp went out." They quenched their "smoking flax," or, in other words, *their talent* unimproved was justly "taken from them." Thus, though once through grace they could work, they died while they lived; and so were, as says St. Jude, "twice dead," *dead* in Adam by that sentence, "In the day that thou eatest thereof thou shalt surely die;" and *dead* in themselves, by personally renouncing Christ the life, or rejecting the light of his convincing Spirit.

This being premised, I ask, Where is the *heresy* in this paragraph of the Minutes? Does it consist in quoting a plain passage out of one of our Lord's sermons? Or in daring to produce in the original, under the horrible form of the decagrammaton, Εργαζεσθε, that dreadful tetragrammaton, *work?* Surely, sir, you have too much piety to maintain the former, and too much good sense to assert the latter. Does it consist in saying that *"believers* work from *life?"* (for of such only Mr. Wesley here speaks.) Do not all grant that *he who believeth hath life,* yea, *everlasting life,* and therefore can work? And have I not proved from Scripture that the very heathens are not without some light and grace to work suitably to their dispensation?

"The heresy," say you, "does not consist in asserting that the believer works *from,* but *for* life!" Does it indeed? Then the Lord Jesus is the *heretic;* for Mr. Wesley only repeats what he spoke about seventeen hundred years ago: "Labour," says he, Εργαζεσθε, "work for the meat that endureth to everlasting life." Enter therefore "your protest against" St. John's Gospel, if Christ will not "formally recant it;" and not against the Minutes of his servant who dares not "take away from his Lord's words," for fear "God should take away his part out of the book of life!"

But if the Son of God be a heretic for putting the unbelieving Jews upon *working by* that dreadful word, Εργαζεσθε, St. Paul is undoubtedly an arch-heretic for corroborating it by a strong preposition: Κατεργαζεσθε says he to the Philippians, *work out* — and what is most astonishing, "work out your own salvation." *Your own salvation!* Why, Paul, this is even worse than *working for life;* for *salvation* implies a deliverance from all guilt, sin, and misery; together with obtaining the life of grace here, and the life of glory hereafter. Ah! poor legal apostle, What a pity is it thou didst not live in our evangelical age! Some, by explaining to thee the mystery of "finished salvation," or by "protesting in a body against thy dreadful heresy," might have saved "the fundamental doctrines of Christianity;" and the Richard Baxter of our age would not have had thee to bear him out in his Pharisaical and Papistical delusions!

Here you reply, that "St. Paul gives God all the glory, by maintaining that ' it is he who works in us both to will and to do of his good pleasure.'" And does not Mr. Wesley do the same? Has he not for near forty years steadily asserted that all power to think a good thought, much more to will or do a good work, is from God, by mere grace, through the merits of Jesus Christ and the agency of the Holy Spirit? If any dare to deny it, myriads of witnesses who have heard him preach, and thousands of printed sermons, hymns, and tracts dispersed through the three kingdoms will prove it.

But let us come closer to the point. Is not Christ "the bread that came down from heaven to give life to the world?" Is he not "the meat that endureth to everlasting life?" "the meat which" he directs even the poor Capernaites "to work for?" Must we not *come to* him for that meat? Is not "coming" to Christ a "work" of the heart? Yea, "the work of God?" The work that God peculiarly calls for! John vi, 28, 29. Does not our Lord complain of those who will not work for life, that is, "come unto him that they might have life, or that they might have it more abundantly?" And must not every believer "do this work" — come to Christ for life, yea, and live upon him every day and every hour?

Again, sir, consider these scriptures, "He that believeth hath everlasting life: he that hath the Son hath life." Compare them with the following complaint' "None stirreth up himself to lay hold on God;" and with the charge of St. Paul to Timothy, "Lay hold on eternal life." And let us know whether "stirring up one's self to lay hold on the God of our life," and actually "laying hold on eternal life," are not "works," and works *for,* as well as *from* life! And whether believers are dispensed from these works till they come to glory!

Once more: please to tell us if praying, using ordinances, "running a race, taking up the cross, keeping under the body, wrestling, fighting a good fight," are not works; and if all believers are not to do them till death brings them a discharge? If you say that "they do them *from* life and not *for* life," you still point blank oppose our Lord's express declaration.

A similar instance will make you sensible of it. Lot flies out of Sodom. How many works does he do at once! He hearkens to God's messengers, obeys their voice, sacrifices his property, forsakes all, prays, runs, and "escapes *for* his life." "No," says one, "wiser than seven men who can render a reason," "you should not say that he escapes *for* life, but *from* life. Do not hint that he runs *to preserve his life;* you should say that he does it *because he is alive.* "What an admirable distinction is this!

Again: my friend is consumptive. I send for a physician who prescribes, "he must ride out every day *for* his life." Some other physicians see the prescription, and, by printed letters, raise all the gentlemen of the faculty to insist in a body on a formal recantation of this dreadful prescription; declaring the health of thousands is at stake, if we say that consumptive people are to ride *for* life as well as *from* life. *Risum teneatis, amici?*

But they who protest against Mr. Wesley for maintaining that we ought to work *for,* as well as *from* life, must protest also against a body of Puritan divines, who, in the last century, being shocked at Dr. Crisp's doctrine, thus bore their testimony against it: "To say, *Salvation is not the end of any good work we do,* or *we are to act* FROM *life, and not* FOR *life,* were to abandon the human nature; it were to teach us to violate the great precepts of the Gospel; it supposes one bound to do more for the salvation of others than our own; it were to make all the threatenings of eternal death, and promises of eternal life in the Gospel, useless, as motives to shun the one, or obtain the other: and it makes the Scripture characters and commendation of the most eminent saints, a fault:" for they all escaped out of Sodom or Babylon for their lives; they all wrestled for, and "laid hold on eternal life." (*Preface to Mr. Flavel's Book against Antinomianism.*)

Thus, sir, the very Calvinists were ashamed a hundred years ago of the grand Crispian tenet, "that we ought not to work *for* life."

And I am glad to find you are as far from this error as they were; for you tell us in your sermons, page 69, that "the gracious end of Christ's coming into the world was to give eternal *life* to those who were *dead* in sins; and that eternal life does consist in knowing the true God, and Jesus Christ whom he hath sent." You assure us next, that this life begins by "an exploring desire;" and that God, by giving it, "only means to be earnestly sought, that he may be more successfully and more happily found."

Perhaps some suppose the expression of working *for* life implies the working in order to *merit* or *purchase* life. But, as our Lord's words convey no such idea, so Mr. Wesley takes care positively to exclude it, by those words, "not by the merit of works:" for he knows that "eternal life is the gift of God;" and yet with St. Paul he says, "Labour to enter into rest, lest ye fall after the example of Israel's unbelief:" and with the great anti- Crispian divine, Jesus Christ, he cries aloud, "Strive *to walk* in the narrow way; agonize to enter in at the strait gate that leads to life."

I pass to the third instance which he produces of his having leaned too much toward Calvinism: —

"III. We have received it as a maxim, *that a man is to do nothing in order to justification.* Nothing can be more false. Whoever desires to find favour with God, should 'cease from evil, and learn to do well.' Whoever repents, should 'do works meet for repentance.' And if this be not *in order* to find favour, what does he do them for!"

To do Mr. Wesley justice, it is necessary to consider what he means by "justification." And, First, He does not mean that general benevolence of our merciful God toward sinful mankind, whereby, through the Lamb slain from the foundation of the world, he casts a propitious look upon them, and freely makes them partakers of "the light that enlightens every man that cometh into the world." This general loving kindness is certainly previous to any thing we can do to find it; for it always prevents us, saying to us in our very infancy, *Live;* and when we turn from the paths of life, still crying, "Why will ye die?" In consequence of this general mercy, our Lord says, "Let little children come unto me: for of such is the kingdom of heaven." Much less does Mr. Wesley understand what Dr. Crisp calls "eternal justification," which, because I do not see it in the Scripture, I shall say nothing of.

But the "justification" he speaks of, as something that we must "find," and "in order to which something must be done," is either *that public and final* JUSTIFICATION *which the Lord mentions in the Gospel,* "By thy words thou shalt be justified, and by thy words thou shalt be condemned." And in this sense no man in his wits will find fault with Mr. Wesley's assertion; as it is evident that we must absolutely "do something," that is, speak good words, in order to be "justified by our words." Or he means FORGIVENESS, *and the* WITNESS *of it;* that wonderful transaction of the Spirit of God, in a returning prodigal's conscience, by which the forgiveness of his sin is proclaimed to him through the blood of sprinkling. This is what Mr. Wesley and St. Paul generally mean. It is thus that "being justified by faith we have peace with God through our Lord Jesus Christ."

And now, do not Scripture, common sense, and experience, show that "something must be done in order to attain or find," though not to *merit* and *purchase* this justification?

Please to answer the following questions founded upon the express declarations of God's word: — "To him that ordereth his conversation aright will I show the salvation of God." Is "ordering our conversation aright," doing nothing? "Repent ye, and be converted, that your sins may be blotted out." Are "repentance and conversion" nothing? "Come unto me, all ye that are heavy laden, and I will give you rest," I will justify you. Is "coming" doing nothing? "Cease to do evil, learn to do well. Come now, let us reason together, and though your sins be red as crimson they shall be white as snow," you shall be justified. Is "ceasing to do evil and learning to do well," doing nothing? "Seek the Lord while he may be found, call upon him while he is near. Let the wicked forsake his way, and the unrighteous man his thoughts; and let him return unto the Lord, and he will have mercy upon him, and to our God, for he will abundantly pardon." Is "seeking, calling, forsaking one's way, and returning to the Lord," a mere nothing? "Ask, and you shall receive; seek, and you shall find; knock, and it shall be opened unto you." Be "violent, take even the kingdom of heaven by force." Is "seeking, asking, knocking, and taking by force," doing absolutely nothing? Please to answer these questions; and when you have done, I will throw one or two hundred more of the like kind in your way.

Let us now see whether reason is not for Mr. Wesley as well as Scripture. Do you not maintain that *believing* is necessary in order to our justification? If you do, you subscribe Mr. Wesley's *heresy;* for "believing" is not only "doing something," but necessarily supposes "a variety of things." "Faith cometh by hearing," and sometimes by *reading,* which implies "attending the ministry of the word, and searching the Scriptures," as the Bereans did. It likewise presupposes at least "the attention of the mind, and consent of the heart to a revealed truth;" or "the consideration, approbation, and receiving of an object proposed to us." Nay, it implies "renouncing worldly, and seeking Divine honour." For, says our Lord, "How can you believe who receive honour one of another, and seek not the honour that cometh of God only?" And if none can believe in Christ unto salvation but those who give up seeking worldly honours, by a parity of reason they must give up following fleshly lusts, and putting their trust in uncertain riches. In a word, they must own themselves sick, and renounce their physicians of no value, before they can make one true application to the invaluable Physician. What a variety of things is, therefore, implied in "believing," which we cannot but acknowledge to be previous to justification! Who can then, consistently with reason, blame Mr. Wesley for saying "*something* must be done in order to justification?"

Again, if nothing be required of us in order to justification, who can find fault with those that die in a state of condemnation? They were "born in sin, and children of wrath," and nothing was required of them in order to find favour. It remains, therefore, that they are — damned, through an absolute decree, made thousands of years before they had any existence! If some can swallow this camel with the greatest ease, I doubt, sir, it will not go down with *you,* without bearing very hard upon the knowledge you have of the God of love, and the Gospel of Jesus.

Once more Mr. Wesley concludes his proposition with a very pertinent question: "When a man that is not justified, 'does works meet for repentance,' *what does he do them for?*" Permit me to answer it according to Scripture and common sense. If he do them in order to *purchase* the Divine favour, he is under a self-righteous delusion; but if he do them as Mr. Wesley says, "in order to *find:*" what Christ has purchased for him, he acts the part of a wise Protestant.

Should you say that "such a penitent does works meet for repentance from a sense of gratitude for redeeming love:" I answer, this is impossible; for that "love must be shed abroad in his heart by the Holy Ghost given unto him," in consequence of his justification, before he can act from the sense of that love and the gratitude which it excites. I hope it is no heresy to maintain that the cause must go before the effect. I conclude, then, that those who have not yet found the pardoning love of God, do works meet for repentance "in order to *find* it." They abstain from those outward evils which once they pursued; they do the outward good which the convincing Spirit prompts them to: they use the means of grace, confess their sins, and ask pardon for them; in short, they "seek" the Lord, encouraged by that promise, "they that seek me early shall find me." And Mr. Wesley supposes they "*seek* in order to *find.*" In the name of candour, where is the harm of that supposition?

When the poor woman has lost her "piece of silver, she lights a candle," says our Lord, "she sweeps the house, and searches diligently till she find it." Mr. Wesley asks, "If she do not do ALL this *in order to find it,* what does she do it for?" At this the alarm is taken; and the post carries, through various provinces, printed letters against old Mordecai; and a synod is called together to *protest* against the dreadful error!

This reminds me of a little anecdote. Some centuries ago, one Virgilius, I think, a German bishop, was bold enough to look over the walls of ignorance and superstition which then enclosed all Europe; and he saw, that if the earth was round there must be *antipodes*. Some minutes of his observations were sent to the pope. His holiness, who understood geography as much as divinity, took fright, fancying the unheard — of assertion was injurious to the very fundamental principles of: Christianity. He directly called together the cardinals, as wise as himself; and by their advice, issued out a bull condemning the heretical doctrine, and the poor bishop was obliged to make a formal recantation of it, under pain of excommunication. Which are we to admire most? The zeal of the conclave, or that of the *real Protestants?* In the meantime let me observe, that as all the Roman Catholics do now acknowledge that there are *antipodes,* so all real Protestants will one day acknowledge that penitents seek the favour of God *in order to find it;* unless some rare genius should be able to demonstrate that it is in order to lose it.

Having defended Mr. Wesley's third proposition from Scripture and common sense, permit me to do it also from experience. And here I might appeal to the most established persons in Mr. Wesley's societies: but as their testimony may have little weight with you, I waive it, and appeal to all the accounts of *sound* conversions that have been published since Calvin's days. Show me one, sir, wherein it appears that a mourner in Sion found the above described justification, without *doing* some previous "works meet for repentance." If you cannot produce one such instance, Mr. Wesley's doctrine is supported by the *printed experiences* of all the converted Calvinists, as well as of all the believers in his own societies. Nor am I afraid to appeal even to the experience of your own friends. If any one of these can say, with a good conscience, that he found the above described justification without first stopping in the career of outward sin, without praying, seeking, and confessing his guilt and misery, I promise to give up the Minutes. But if none can make such a declaration, you must grant, sir, that experience is on Mr. Wesley's side, as much as reason, revelation, the best Calvinists, and yourself. I say *yourself:*

Give me leave to produce but one instance: page 76 of your sermons, you address those "who see themselves destitute of that knowledge of God which is eternal life," the very same thing that Mr. Wesley calls justification; and which you define, "a home-felt knowledge of God, by the experience of his *love* being *shed abroad in our hearts by the Holy Ghost given unto us: the Spirit of God bearing witness with our spirits that we are the children of God;"* and you recommend to them "to *seek* and *press* after *it.*" Now, sir, "seeking and pressing after it" is certainly "doing something in order to find it."

I must not conclude my vindication of the third proposition without answering a specious objection. "If we must do something *in order to justification,* farewell *free* justification! It is no more of grace, but of works, and consequently of debt. The middle wall of partition between the Church of Rome and the Church of England is pulled down, and the two sticks in the hands of that heretical juggler, John Wesley, are become one."

I reply, (1.) That some, who think they are *real* pillars in the Protestant Church, may be nearer the Church of Rome than they are aware of: for Rome is far more remarkable for lording it over God's heritage, and calling the most faithful servants of God *heretics,* than even for her Pharisaic exalting of good works. (2.) If the Church of Rome had not insisted upon the necessity of *unrequired, unprofitable, and foolish works;* and if she had not arrogantly ascribed *saving merit* to works, yea, to merely external performances, and by that means clouded the merits of Christ; no reasonable Protestant would have separated from her on account of her regard for works. (3.) Nothing can be more absurd than to affirm, that when "something is required to be done in order to receive a favour, the favour loses the name of *a free gift,* and directly becomes *a debt."* Long, too long, persons who have more honesty than wisdom, have been frightened from the plain path of duty, by a phantom of their own making. O may the snare break at last! And why should it not break now? Have not sophisms been wire-drawn, till they break of themselves in the sight of every attentive spectator?

I say to two beggars, "Hold out your hand; here is an alms for you." The one complies, and the other refuses. Who in the world will dare to say that my charity is no more *a free gift,* because I bestow it only upon the man that held out his hand? Will nothing make it *free* but my wrenching his hand open, or forcing my bounty down his throat? Again: the king says to four rebels, "Throw down your arms; surrender, and you shall have a place both in my favour and at court." One of them obeys, and becomes a great man; the others, upon refusal, are caught and hanged. What sophister will face me down that the pardon and place of the former are not *freely* bestowed upon him, because he did something in order to obtain them? Once more:

The God of providence says, "If you plough, sow, harrow, fence, and weed your fields, I will give the increase, and you shall have a crop." Farmers obey: and are they to believe that because they do so many things toward their harvest, it is *not the free gift* of Heaven? Do not all those who fear God know that their ground, seed, cattle, strength, yea, and their very life, are the gifts of God? Does not this prevent their claiming a crop as a *debt;* and make them confess, that though it was suspended on their ploughing, &c, it is the unmerited bounty of Heaven?

Apply this, sir, to the present case; and you will see that our *doing something in order to justification* does not in the least hinder it from being a *free gift;* because whatever we do in order to it, we do it "by the grace of God" preventing us, that we may have a good will, and working with us when we have that good will; all being of free, most absolutely free grace through the merits of Christ. And, nevertheless, so sure as a farmer, in the appointed ways of Providence, shall have no harvest if he does nothing toward it; a professor in the appointed ways of grace, (let him *talk* of "finished salvation" all the year round,) shall go without justification and salvation, unless he do something toward them. (My comparison is Scriptural:) "He that now goeth on his way weeping," says the psalmist, "and beareth forth good seed, shall doubtless come again with joy, and bring his sheaves with him." "Be not deceived," says the apostle, "whatsoever a man soweth, that shall he also reap; and he *only* that soweth to the Spirit shall of the Spirit reap life everlasting." David, therefore, and St. Paul must be proved enemies to free grace before Mr. Wesley can be represented as such: for they both did something in order to justification; they both "sowed in tears," before they "reaped in joy;" their doctrine and experience went hand in hand together.

Having now vindicated the three first propositions of the Minutes, leveled at three dangerous tenets of Dr. Crisp; and shown, that not only yourself, sir, but moderate Calvinists are, so far, entirely of Mr. Wesley's sentiment; I remain, honoured and reverend sir, your obedient servant in the bonds of a free and peaceful Gospel,

J. FLETCHER.

LETTER IV.

HONOURED AND REVEREND SIR, — If the three first propositions of the Minutes are Scriptural, Mr. Wesley may well begin the remaining part, by desiring the preachers in his connection to emerge, along with him, from under the noisy billows of prejudice, and to struggle quite out of the muddy streams of Antinomian delusions which have so long gone over our heads, and carried so many souls down the channels of vice, into the lake that burneth with fire and brimstone. Well may he entreat them to "review the whole affair."

And why should this modest request alarm any one? Though error dreads a revisal, truth, you know, cannot but gain by it.

Mr. Wesley says in this REVIEW,

"I. Who is now accepted of God? He that now 'believes in Christ with a loving, obedient heart.'"

Excellent answer! Worthy of St. Paul and St. James; for it sums up in one line the epistles of both. In the FIRST part of it, ("he that now believes in Christ,") you see St. Paul's Gospel calculated for lost sinners, who now fly from the Babel of self righteousness and sin, and find "all things" in Christ "ready" for their reception. And in the SECOND part, ("with a loving and obedient heart,") you see the strong bulwark raised by St. James to guard the truth of the Gospel against the attacks of Antinomian and Laodicean professors. Had he said, "He that shall believe the next hour is *now* accepted," he would have bestowed upon present unbelief the blessing that is promised to present faith. Had he said, *"He that believed a year ago is now* accepted of God," he would have opened the kingdom of heaven to apostates, contrary to St. Paul's declarations to the Hebrews. He therefore very properly says, "He that *now* believes:" for it is written, "He that believeth," (not he that *shall* believe, or he that *did* believe,) "hath everlasting life."

What fault can you then find with Mr. Wesley here? Surely you cannot blame him for proposing Christ as the object of the Christian's faith, or for saying that the *believer* hath a loving and obedient heart; for he speaks of the *accepted man,* and not of him who *comes for acceptance.* Multitudes, alas! rest satisfied with an *unloving, disobedient* faith; a faith that engages only the head, but has nothing to do with the heart; a faith that works by malice instead of "working by love;" a faith that pleads for sin in the heart, instead of purifying the heart from sin; a faith that St. Paul explodes, 1 Corinthians xiii, 2, and that St. James compares to a carcass, James ii, 28. There is no need that Mr. Wesley should countenance such a faith by his Minutes. Too many, alas! do it by their lives; and, God grant none may do it by their sermons! Whoever does, sir, it is not you: for you tell us in yours, page 150, that "Christ is to be found only by living faith; even a faith that worketh by love; even a faith that layeth hold of Christ by the feet, and worshippeth him;" the very faith of Mary Magdalene, who certainly had a loving and obedient heart, for our Lord testified that "she loved much," and ardent love cannot but be zealously *obedient*. There is not then the least shadow of heresy, but the very marrow of the Gospel in this article. Let us see whether the second is equally defensible.

"II. But who among those that never heard of Christ? He that feareth God and worketh righteousness, according to the light he has."

And where is the error here? Did not St. Peter begin his evangelical sermon to Cornelius by these very words, prefaced by some others that make them remarkably emphatical? "Of a truth I perceive that God is no respecter of persons; but in every nation he that feareth God and worketh righteousness is accepted of him." Surely, sir, you will never insist upon a formal recantation of a plain scripture.

FIRST OBJECTION. But perhaps you object to those words which Mr. Wesley has added to St. Peter's declaration, "according to the light he hath."

ANSWER. What, should it be "according to the light he has *not*?" Are not there people enough among us who follow the wicked servant that intimated his Lord "was a hard and austere man, reaping where he had not sown, and gathering where he had not strewed?" Must Mr. Wesley increase the number? Or would you have him insinuate that God is more cruel than Pharaoh, who granted the poor Israelites *daylight*, *if* he allowed them *no straw* to make bricks; that he requires a heathen to work without any degree of *light*, without a *day* of visitation, in the Egyptian darkness of a merely natural state. And that he will then damn and torment him everlastingly, either for not doing, or for marring his work? O sir, like yourself, Mr. Wesley is too evangelical to entertain such notions of the God of love.

"At this rate," say some, "a heathen may be saved without a Saviour. His *fearing God and working righteousness* will not go for the blood and righteousness of Christ." Mr. Wesley has no such thought. Whenever a heathen is accepted, it is merely through the merits of Christ; although it is in consequence of his *fearing God and working righteousness*. "But how comes he to see that God is to be feared, and that righteousness is his delight?" Because a beam of our Sun of righteousness shines in his darkness. All is therefore of grace; the light, the works of righteousness done by that light, and acceptance in consequence of them. How much more evangelical is this doctrine of St. Peter than that of some divines, who consign all the heathens by millions to hell torments because they cannot explicitly believe in a Saviour whose name they never heard? Nay, and in whom it would be the greatest arrogancy to believe, if he never died for them? Is it not possible that heathens should, by grace, reap some blessings through the second

Adam, though they know nothing of his name and obedience unto death; when they, by nature, reap so many curses through Adam the first; to whose name and disobedience they are equally strangers? If this is a heresy it is such a one as does honour to Jesus and humanity.

SECOND OBJECTION. "Mr. Wesley, by allowing the possibility of a righteous heathen's salvation, goes point blank against the eighteenth article of our Church, which he has solemnly subscribed."

ANSWER. This assertion is groundless. Mr. Wesley, far from presuming to say that a heathen "can be saved by the law or sect that he professes, if he frames his life according to the light of nature," cordially believes that all the heathens who are saved, attain salvation through the name, that is, through the merits and Spirit of Christ; by framing their life, not according to I know not what light naturally received from fallen Adam, but according to the supernatural light which Christ graciously affords them in the dispensations they are under.

THIRD OBJECTION. "However, if he does not impugn the eighteenth article, he does the thirteenth, which says, that 'works done before justification, or before the grace of Christ and the inspiration of his Spirit, forasmuch as they proceed not from faith in Christ, are not pleasant to God, yea, have the nature of sin.'"

Nay, this article does not affect Mr. Wesley's doctrine; for he constantly maintains that if the works of a Melchisedec, a Job, a Plato, a Cornelius, are accepted, it is only because they follow the general justification above mentioned, (which is possibly what St. Paul calls the "free gift that comes upon all men to justification of life," Romans v, 18,) and because they proceed FROM "the grace of Christ, and the inspiration of his Spirit," they are not therefore done BEFORE that grace and inspiration, as are the works which the article condemns.

FOURTH OBJECTION. "But 'all that is not of faith is sin, and without faith it is impossible to please God.'"

ANSWER. True: therefore, "he that cometh to God must believe that he is, and that he is a rewarder of them that diligently seek him." Cornelius had undoubtedly this faith, and a degree of it is found in all sincere heathens. For Christ, the Light of men, visits all, though in a variety of degrees and dispensations. He said to the carnal Jews that believed not on him, "Yet a little while the light is with you; walk while ye have the light, lest darkness come upon you. While ye have the light, believe in the light, that ye may be the children of the light." All the heathens that are saved are then saved by a lively faith in Jesus, "the Light of the world;" or to use our Lord's own words, by "believing in the light" of their dispensation, before the day of their visitation is past, before total "darkness comes upon them," even the night when "no man can work."

FIFTH OBJECTION. "But if heathens can be saved without the Gospel, what need is there of the Christian dispensation?"

ANSWER. (1.) None of them were ever saved without a beam of the internal light of the Gospel, which is preached "in εν every creature under heaven," Colossians i, 23. (2.) The argument may be retorted. If sinners could be saved under the patriarchal dispensation, what need was there of the Mosaic? If under the Mosaic, what need of John's baptism? If under the baptism of John, what need of Christianity? Or to answer by a comparison: If we see our way by starlight, what need is there of moonshine? If by moonshine, what need of the dawn of day? If by the dawn of day, what need of the rising sun?

The brightness of Divine dispensations, like the light of the righteous, "shines more and more unto the perfect day." And though a heathen may be saved in his low dispensation, and attain unto a low degree of glory, which the apostle compares to the shining of a star, ("for in my Father's house," says Christ, "there are *many mansions*,") yet it is an unspeakable advantage to be saved from the darkness attending his uncomfortable dispensation, into the full enjoyment of the "life and immortality brought to light by the *explicit* Gospel." Well might then the angel say to Cornelius, who was already accepted according to his dispensation, that Peter should "tell him words whereby he should be saved;" saved from the weakness, darkness, bondage, and tormenting fears attending his present state, into that blessed state of light, comfort, liberty, power, and glorious joy, where "he that is feeble is as David, and the house of David as God, or as the angel of the Lord."

Having thus briefly answered the objections that are advanced against St. Peter's and Mr. Wesley's doctrine, proceed we to the third query, in the review of the whole affair.

"III. Is this the same with, *he that is sincere?* Nearly, if not quite."

In the name of charity where is the error of this answer? Where the shadow of heresy? Do you suppose by — *he that is sincere,* Mr. Wesley means "a carnal, unawakened wretch who boasts of his imaginary sincerity?" No, sir, he means "one who, in God's account, and not barely in his own, sincerely and uprightly follows the light of his dispensation." Now, if you expose Mr. Wesley as guilty of heresy, for using this word once, what protests will you enter against St. Paul for using it over and over? How will you blame him for desiring the Ephesians, (according to the beautiful reading of our margin,) to "be sincere in love!" αληθευονες εν αγαπη. Or, for wishing nothing greater to his dear Philippians, than that they might be "sincere in the day of Christ!" O, sir, to fear, and much more, to love the Lord "in sincerity," is a great and rare thing! Ephesians vi, 24. We find every where too much of the "old leaven of malice," and too little of "the unleavened bread of sincerity and truth," 1 Corinthians v, 8. Think not therefore that Mr. Wesley betrays the cause of God, because he thinks that "to be sincere," and to "fear God and work righteousness," are expressions nearly, if not quite synonymous.

But you do not perhaps find fault with Mr. Wesley for setting accepted heathens too low, but too high, by giving them the character of being sincere. For you know that our translators render the Hebrew word תמים sometimes "sincere," at other times "upright, undefiled," and most commonly" perfect." As in these sentences, "Noah was a *perfect* man, Job was a *perfect* man," &c. May not then Mr. Wesley secretly bring in his abominable doctrine of PERFECTION, under the less frightful expression of *sincerity?* Of this more by and by.

In the meantime, I shall close my vindication of the second and third query by the sentiments of two unquestionable Protestants on the present subject. The one is Mr. Henry, in his comment on St. Peter's words' "God," says he, "never did, nor ever will reject an honest Gentile who fears God, and worships him. and works righteousness: that is, is just and charitable toward all men, who lives up to the light he has, in a sincere devotion and regular conversation. Wherever God finds an *upright* man, he will be found an up*right* God, Psalm xviii, 25. And those that have not the knowledge of Christ, and therefore cannot have an explicit regard to him, may yet receive grace for his sake, 'to fear God and work righteousness;' and wherever God gives grace to do so, as he did to Cornelius, he will, through Christ, accept the work of his own hands." Here, sir, you have the very doctrine of Mr. Wesley quite down to the heretical word *sincere.*

The other divine, sir, is yourself. You tell us in your sermon on the same text, that "we cannot but admire and adore God's universal tenderness and pity for every people and nation under heaven, in that 'he willeth not the death of any single sinner,' but accepteth every one into Gospel covenant with him, 'who feareth him and worketh righteousness,' according to the light imparted to him."

Now, sir, where is the difference between your *orthodoxy* and Mr. Wesley's *heresy?* He asserts, God accepts "him that *fears God and works righteousness according* to the light he has" Mr. Henry says, "him that lives up to the light he has "" and you, sir, "him *who feareth God and worketh righteousness* according to the light imparted to him." If Mr. Wesley must share the fate of Shadrach for his heresy, I doubt Mr. Henry will have that of Meshech, and you, of Abednego; for you are all three in the same honourable condemnation.

But Mr. Wesley, foreseeing that some will be offended at St. Peter's evangelical declaration concerning the acceptance of sincere heathens who work righteousness, proposes and answers the following objection: —

"IV. Is not this *salvation by works?* Not by the *merit* of works, but by works as a *condition."*

In the former part of this answer Mr. Wesley freely grants all you can require to guard the Gospel against the Popish doctrine of making satisfaction for sin, and meriting salvation by works: for he maintains, that, though God accepts the heathen who work righteousness, yet it is not through the merit of his works, but solely through that of Christ. Is not this the very doctrine of our Church, in her eleventh article, which treats of justification? "We are accounted righteous before God only for the *merit of our Lord Jesus Christ* by faith, and not for our own works, or *deservings."* Does not the opposition of the two sentences, and the explanatory word *deservings,* evidently show that "works meet for repentance" are not excluded from being in the sinner that comes to be justified, but from having any *merit* or worth to *purchase* his justification?

Our Church expresses herself more fully on this head in the homily on salvation, to which the article refers. "St. Paul," says she, "declares nothing [necessary] on the behalf of man concerning his justification, but only a true and lively faith; and yet [*observe*] that faith does not shut out repentance, hope, love, [of *desire* when we are coming, love of *delight* when we are come,] dread, and the fear of God to be joined with it in every man that is justified; but it shutteth them out from the office of justifying: so that though they be all present together in him that is justified, yet they justify not altogether." This is agreeable to St. Peter's doctrine, maintained by Mr. Wesley. Only *"faith in Christ"* for CHRISTIANS, and *"faith in the light* of their dispensation" for HEATHENS, is necessary in order to acceptance. But though FAITH ONLY justifies, yet it is never alone; for "repentance, hope, love of desire, and the fear of God," necessarily accompany this faith if it is true and living. Our Church, therefore, is not at all against works proceeding from, or accompanying faith in all its stages. She grants, that whether FAITH *seeks* or *finds* its object, whether it *longs for,* or *embraces* it, it is still a lively, active, and working grace. She is only against the vain conceit that WORKS have any hand in *meriting* justification or *purchasing* salvation, which is what Mr. Wesley likewise opposes.

If you say, that "his heresy does not consist in exploding the merit of works in point of salvation, but in using that legal expression, *salvation by works as a condition*;" I answer, that as I would not contend for the word *trinity,* because it is not in the Bible; no, nor yet for the word *perfection,* though it is there; neither would I contend for the expression, *salvation by works, as a condition:* but the thing Mr. Wesley means by it is there in a hundred different turns and modes of expression. Therefore it is highly worth contending for: and so much the more, as it is, next to the doctrine of the atonement, the most important part of "the faith once delivered unto the saints."

Any candid person acquainted with Mr. Wesley's principles, (and for such only the Minutes were written,) cannot but see that he meant absolutely nothing but what our Saviour means in these and like scriptures; namely, that salvation is suspended on a variety of things which divines call by various names, and which Mr. Wesley, with a majority of them, chooses to call *conditions*. "Except ye repent, ye shall all perish. Except ye be converted, and become as little children, ye shall not enter into the kingdom of heaven." Here *repentance* and *conversion* are conditions of eternal salvation. "If ye believe not, ye shall die in your sins; for this is the work of God, [the work that God requires and approves,] that ye believe on him whom he hath sent." Here the *work of faith* is the condition. "I am Alpha and Omega, the first and the last. Blessed are they that do his commandments, that they may have right to the tree of life," and "may enter in through the gates of the city." And here it is *doing God's commandments.*

St. Paul, the evangelical Paul, says the same thing in a variety of expressions: "If any man love not the Lord Jesus, let him be anathema." If *love,* the noblest work of the heart, does not take place, the fearful curse will: — "If ye live after the flesh, ye shall die;" but "if ye through the Spirit do mortify the deeds of the body, ye shall live." *Spiritual mortification* is here the condition. "Without holiness no man shall see the Lord." Here *holiness* is the condition. "Be not deceived, neither fornicators, nor covetous, nor drunkards, nor thieves, nor revilers, shall inherit the kingdom of God." Here ceasing from *fornication, drunkenness, &c,* is the same condition.

St. John is in the same condemnation as Mr. Wesley, for he declares, "There shall in no wise enter into the New Jerusalem any thing that defileth, neither whatsoever worketh abomination, or maketh a lie." Here the condition is, *not working abomination, &.c.* "Whosoever hateth his brother is a murderer," and "ye know that no murderer hath eternal life." Here the condition is, *ceasing from hatred,* the murder of the heart. St. Peter is equally deep in the heresy. In a variety of expressions he describes the misery and fatal latter end of those "who escape the pollution of the world, through the knowledge of the Lord Jesus, and are again entangled therein," through the non-performance of this condition, "*If ye do these things, ye shall never fall.*"

As for St. James, I need not quote him. You know that, when Luther was in his heat, he could have found it in his heart to tear this precious epistle from among the sacred books, and burn it as *an epistle of straw.* He thought the author of it was an enemy to *free grace,* an abettor of Popish tenets, an antichrist. It is true, the scales of prejudice fell at last from his eyes; but, alas! it was not till he had seen the Antinomian boar lay waste the Lord's flourishing vineyard all over Protestant Germany. Then was he glad to draw against him St. James's despised sword; and I shall be happily mistaken, sir, if you are not obliged one day to make use of the *heretical Minutes,* as he did of the epistle of straw.

If any still urge, "I do not love the word *condition;*" I reply, it is no wonder; since thousands so hate the thing that they even choose to go to hell rather than perform it. But let an old worthy divine, approved by all but Dr. Crisp's disciples, tell you what we mean by *condition.* "An antecedent condition," says Mr. Flavel, in his *Discourse of Errors,* "signifies no more than an act of ours; which, though it be neither perfect in any degree, nor in the least meritorious of the benefit conferred, nor performed in our own natural strength; is yet, according to the constitution of the covenant required of us, in order to the blessings consequent thereupon, by virtue of the promise: and consequently, benefits and mercies granted in this order are, and must be, suspended by the donor, till it be performed" *Such a condition* we affirm *faith* to be, with all that faith necessarily implies.

When Dr. Crisp, in the last century, represented all the sober Puritan divines as *legal,* they answered, "The covenant, though *conditional,* is a dispensation of grace. There is grace in giving ability to perform the condition, as well as in bestowing the benefits. God's enjoining the one in order to the other makes not the benefit to be less of grace; but it is a display of God's wisdom, in conferring the benefit suitable to the nature and condition of men in this life, who are here in a state of trial; yea, the *conditions* are but a meetness to receive the blessings."

"The reason," added they, "why we use the word *condition,* is, because it best suits with man's relation to God, in his present dealings with us as his subjects on trial for eternity. Christ, as a priest, has merited all: but, as a priestly king, he dispenseth all; he enjoins the conditions in order to the benefits, and makes the benefits motives to our compliance with the conditions. He treats with men as his subjects, whom he will now *rule,* and hereafter *judge.* Now, what word is so proper to express the duties as *enjoined means* of benefit, as the word *conditions?* The word *conditions* is of the same nature as *terms* of the Gospel. There are few authors of note, even of any persuasion, that scruple using this word in our sense; as Ames, Twisse, Rutherford, Hooker, Norton, Preston, Owen, synod of New England, the assembly of divines, &c. And none have reason to scruple it, except such as think *we are justified before we are born."* — See *"Gospel Truth Vindicated,"* by Williams, against Dr. Crisp.

If all the Protestant divines who have directly or indirectly represented REPENTANCE and FAITH as *conditions of present salvation;* and HOLINESS OF HEART AND LIFE as *conditions of eternal glory,* as things *sine quibus non,* without which salvation and glory neither can nor will follow. If all those divines, I say, are guilty of heresy, ninety-nine out of a hundred are heretics, and none of them deeper in the heresy than yourself.

In your Sermons, page 39, clearing yourself of the slander that "you do not preach up, recommend, and insist on *the necessity of good works;*" you add, "I not only preach this or that part of the moral law, but I preach the whole moral law; and I tell you plainly, that *if you do not perform the whole will of God, you cannot be finally saved.*" Then you add, "Surely, they who contend for the doctrine of *good works* will be satisfied with this, or they are very unreasonable," Indeed, sir, Mr. Wesley is quite satisfied with it; I only wonder what in the world can make you so dissatisfied with his Minutes; for he never gave Antinomianism a more legal thrust.

And as you make *works* so absolutely necessary to eternal salvation, so do you make a *law work* a universal prerequisite of the present salvation. Speaking of the fear and dread that seize a sinner under convictions of sin, you say, page 111, "This inward shock of perturbation must pass upon the soul of every *returning* sinner more or less, before he can possibly be rendered a proper object of Divine grace and mercy." Hold, sir, you go one step beyond Mr. Wesley; for he steadily maintains, that if the sinner was not *a proper object of Divine grace* BEFORE he feels the inward shock you speak of, he would never *be shocked and return.*

Do not all unprejudiced persons see, that what Mr. Wesley calls *condition,* others call *way, means,* or *terms,* &c? And that you have as little reason to pick a quarrel with him as to raise a *body* of men against a quiet traveler for calling a certain sum *a guinea,* whereas you think it more proper to call it *one pound one,* — *twenty-one shillings,* — *forty-two sixpences,* — or *sixty-three groats.* O, sir, what reason have we to be ashamed of our chicaneries; and to beseech the Lord that they may not stumble the weak, and harden infidels!

How justly does Mr. Wesley ask next: —

"V. What have we then been disputing about for these thirty years? I am afraid, about words."

Pardon me sir, if here also I cannot, with you, cry *heresy!* Far from doing it, I admire the candour of an aged servant of God, who, instead of stiffly holding, and obstinately maintaining an old mistake, comes down as a little child, and freely acknowledges it before a respectable body of preachers, whose esteem it is his interest to secure. O how many are there that look upon Mr. Wesley as a rotten threshold, and themselves as pillars in the temple of God, who would not own themselves mistaken for the world!

He says, "I am afraid we have disputed about words:" perhaps he might have said, "I am very sure of it." How many disputes have been raised these thirty years among religious people, about those works of the heart which St. Paul calls "repentance toward God, and faith in our Lord Jesus Christ!" Some have called them *the only way* or *method* of receiving salvation, others *the means* of salvation, others *the terms* of it. Some have named them *duties* or *graces* necessary to salvation, others *conditions* of salvation, others *parts* of salvation, or *privileges* annexed to it; while others have gone far round about, and used I know not what far-fetched expressions and ambiguous phrases to convey the same idea. I say *the same idea;* for if all maintain that although *repentance* and *works meet for it,* and *faith working by love*, are not meritorious, they are nevertheless absolutely necessary; that they are a thing *sine qua non*, all are agreed; and that if they *dispute*, it must be, as Mr. Wesley justly intimates, *about words*.

A comparison will at once make you sensible of it. A physician tells me that the *way*, the *only way* or *method* in which we live, is by abstaining from poison, and taking proper food. "No," says another, "you should say, that *abstaining from poison* and *taking proper food* are the MEANS by which our life is preserved." "You are quite mistaken," says a third, "rejecting *poison* and *eating* are the TERMS God hath fixed upon for our preservation." "No,!' says a fourth, "they are *duties* without the performance, or *blessings*, without *the receiving* of which we must absolutely die." "I believe, for my part," says another, "that Providence hath engaged to preserve our life, on *condition* that we should forbear taking poison, and eat proper food." "You are all in the wrong, you know nothing at all of the matter," says another, who applauds himself much for his wonderful discovery, "turning from poison and receiving nourishment are the *exercises* of a living man; therefore they must absolutely be called *parts* of his life, or *privileges* annexed to it. You quite take away people's appetite, and clog their stomach, by calling them *duties, terms, conditions*. Only call them PRIVILEGES, and you will see nobody will touch poison, and all will eat most heartily." While they are all neglecting their food, and taking the poison of this contention, he that hath mentioned the word *condition*, starts up and says, "Review the whole affair; take heed of your assertions; I am afraid we dispute about words." Upon this all rise against him, all accuse him of robbing the Preserver of men of his glory, or holding a tenet injurious to the very fundamental principles of our constitution.

Let us leave them to the uneasy workings of their unaccountable panic, to consider the next article of the Minutes.

"VI. As to *merit itself*, of which we have been so dreadfully afraid: We are rewarded *according to our works*, yea, *because of our works*. How does this differ from, *for the sake of our works?* And how differs this from *secundum merita operum?* 'as our works *deserve?'* Can you split this hair? I doubt, I cannot."

If Mr. Wesley meant that we are saved by the *merit of works*, and not by the alone merits of Christ, you might exclaim against his proposition as erroneous; and I would echo back your exclamation. But as he flatly denies it, No. 4, in those words, "not by the merit of works," and has constantly asserted the contrary for above thirty years, we cannot, without monstrous injustice, fix that sense upon the word *merit* in this paragraph.

Divesting himself of bigotry and party spirit, he generously acknowledges truth, even when it is held forth by his adversaries: an instance of candour worthy of our imitation! He sees that God offers and gives his children, here on earth, particular rewards for particular instances of obedience. He knows that when a man is saved meritoriously by Christ, and *conditionally by* (or if you please, *upon the terms of) the work of faith, the patience of hope*, and *the labour of love*, he shall particularly be rewarded in heaven *for this work*. And he observes, that the Scriptures steadily maintain, "we are recompensed *according to* our works, yea, *because* of our works."

The former of these assertions is plain from the parable of the talents, and from these words of our Lord, Matthew xvi, 27, "The Son of man shall come in the glory of his Father, and reward every man *according to his work.*" UNBELIEVERS according to the various degrees of demerit belonging to their vile works, (for some of them shall comparatively be "beaten with few stripes;") and BELIEVERS according to the various degrees of excellence found in their good works; for as "one star differeth from another star in glory, so also is the resurrection of the righteous dead."

The latter assertion is not less evident from the repeated declarations of God: "BECAUSE thou hast kept the word of my patience, I also will keep thee from the hour of temptation, which shall come upon all the world," Revelation iii, 10. "BECAUSE Phinehas was zealous for his God," in killing Zimri and Cosbi, "behold! give unto him my covenant of peace, and he shall have it, and his seed after him, even the covenant of an everlasting priesthood." And again: "BECAUSE thou hast done this, and hast not withheld thy son, by myself have I sworn that in blessing I will bless thee, *because* thou hast obeyed my voice." Now, says Mr. Wesley, "How differs this from, 'I will bless thee, for the sake of thy obedience to my voice?' And how differs this from *secundum merita obedientioe*? 'as thy obedience deserves?'" And by comparing the difference of these expressions to the splitting of a hair, or to a metaphysical subtilty, he very justly insinuates that we have been too dreadfully afraid of the word *merit*. Surely, sir, you will not divest yourself of the candour that belongs to a Christian, to put on the bitter zeal of a bigot. You will not run, for fear of Popery, into the very spirit of it, by crying, *Heresy! heresy!* before you have maturely considered the question' or, if you have done so once, you will do it no more. And if Mr. Wesley should ever propose again "the splitting of a hair," I hope you will remember that equity (to say nothing of brotherly love) requires you to split the hair *first* yourself, before you can with decency stir up people far and near against him, for modestly doubting whether he can do it or no.

But suppose some are determined to cry *heresy!* whenever they see the word *merit;* I hope others will candidly weigh what follows in the balance of unprejudiced reason.

If we detach from the word *merit* the idea of "obligation on God's part to bestow any thing upon creatures who have a thousand times forfeited their comforts and existence;" if we take it in the sense we fix to it in a hundred cases: for instance, this, "A master may reward his scholars according to the *merit* of their exercises, or he may not; for the *merit* of the best exercise can never bind him to bestow a premium for it, unless he has promised it of his own accord." If we take, I say, the word *merit* in this simple sense, it may be joined to the word *good works,* and bear an evangelical meaning.

To be convinced of it, candid reader, consider, with Mr. Wesley, that "God accepts and rewards no work but so far as it proceeds from his own grace through the Beloved." Forget not that Christ's Spirit is the savour of each believer's salt, and that he puts excellence into the good works of his people, or else they could not be *good.* Remember, he is as much concerned in the good tempers, words, and actions of his living members, as a tree is concerned in the sap, leaves, and fruit of the branches it bears, John xv, 5. Consider, I say, all this; and tell us whether it can reflect dishonour upon Christ and his grace, to affirm that "as his personal merit, — the merit of his holy life and painful death, —

'opens the kingdom of heaven to all believers,' so the merit of those works which he enables his members to do, will determine the peculiar degrees of glory graciously allotted to each of them."

I own, I believe there is such a dignity in every thing in which the Son of God has a hand, that the Father, who is always well pleased with him and his works, cannot but look upon it with peculiar complacency. Even a "cup of water given in his *dear* name," that is, by the efficacy of his loving Spirit, hath that in it which "shall in no wise lose its reward;" for it has something of the love of the God-man, Jesus Christ, which merits all the approbation and smiles of the Father.

In our well-meant zeal against Popery we have been driven to an extreme, and have not done *good works* justice. "I am the Vine," says Jesus, "and ye are the branches: he that abideth in me bringeth forth much fruit. Herein is my Father glorified, that ye bear much fruit." What! is the Father glorified in the fruit of believers? And shall this fruit be represented to us always grub-eaten, and rotten at the core? Do we honour either the Vine or the husbandman, while one hour we speak wonders of the Vine and its fruit, and the next represent the branches and their fruit as full of deadly poison? O God of mercy and patience, forgive us, for we know not what we do! We even think we do thee service. O give us *genuine,* and save us from *voluntary* humility!

Believer, let not the virtue of thy Saviour's righteousness, the only good thing that is in thee, be evil spoken of. "Thou art grafted upon the good olive tree; be not high minded, but fear;" fear to be *cut off* like the branch that "beareth not fruit." But be not afraid to suck the balmy sap, till the peaceful olive ripens in thy soul, and drops the oil of joy that makes a cheerful countenance. Thou art "married to Christ, that henceforth thou shouldest bring forth fruit unto God." O let not thy mistaken brethren discourage thee from doing all the good that thy heart and hand find to do, and that "with all thy might!"

I write these allusions as they occur to my mind, to raise thy thoughts above spiritual sloth and barrenness of heart, by showing thee, through a Scriptural glass, something of thy Husband's glory, and of the excellence of the "labour of love," wherein thou hast the honour of being "a worker together with him." Let not what I say puff thee up, but encourage thee to "be steadfast, unmovable, always abounding in the work of the Lord, forasmuch as thou knowest thy labour shall not be in vain in the Lord." Remember thou hast nothing to boast of, but much reason to be humbled. If thy works are compared to a rose, the colour, odour, and sweetness are Christ's; the aptness to fade, and the thorns are thine. If to a burning taper, the snuff and smoke come from thee; the bright and cheering light from thy Bridegroom. The excellence and merit of the performance flow from him; the flaws and imperfections from thee. Nevertheless, the whole work is as truly thine, as grapes are truly the fruit of the branch that bore them. And yet, "as the branch cannot bear fruit of itself, except it abide in the vine, no more canst thou, except thou abide in Christ; for without him thou canst do nothing."

Having thus cautioned thee against the Popish abuse of Mr. Wesley's doctrine of the excellence of works, and shown thee the evangelical use that a *real Protestant* should make of it; I return to the word "merit, of which we have been so dreadfully afraid." Let a comparison help thee to understand how a believer may use it in a very harmless sense.

The king promises rewards for good pictures, to miserable foundlings, whom he has charitably brought up, and graciously admitted into his royal academy of painting. Far from being masters of their art, they can of themselves do nothing but spoil canvass, and waste colours by making monstrous figures. But the king's son, a perfect painter, by his father's leave, guides their hands; and, by that mean, good pictures are produced, though not so excellent as they would have been had not he made them by their stiff and clumsy hands. The king, however, approves of them, and fixes the reward of each picture according to its peculiar *merit*. If thou say, "that the poor foundlings, owing all to his majesty, and the prince having freely guided their hands, themselves *merit* nothing; because, after all they have done, they are miserable daubers still, and nothing is properly theirs but the imperfections of the pictures, and therefore the king's reward, though it may be of promise, can never be of debt;" I grant, I assert it. But if thou sayest, "The good pictures have no *merit*," I beg leave to dissent from thee, and tell thee thou speakest as unadvisedly for the king, as Job's friends did for God. For if the pictures have absolutely no *merit*, dost not thou greatly reflect upon the king's taste and wisdom in saying that he *rewards*, them? In the name of common sense, what is it he rewards? The *merit* or *demerit* of the work?

But this is not all: if the pictures have no *merit*, what hath the king's son been doing? Hath he lost all his trouble in helping the novices to sketch and finish them? Shall we deny the excellence of *his* performance because *they* were concerned in it? Shall we be guilty of this glaring partiality any longer? No: some Protestants will dare to judge righteous judgment, and acknowledging there is *merit* where Christ *puts* it, and where God *rewards* it, they will give "honour to whom honour is due," even to him "that worketh all *the good* in all" his creatures.

For my part, I entirely agree with the author of the Minutes, and thank him for daring to break the ice of prejudice and bigotry among us, by restoring *works of righteousness* to their deserved glory, without detracting from the glory of "the Lord our righteousness." I am as much persuaded that the grace of Christ *merits* in the works of his members, though they themselves merit nothing but hell, as I am persuaded that gold in the ore hath its intrinsic worth, though it is mixed with dust and dross, which are good for nothing. As there is but one Mediator, one prevailing Intercessor "between God and us," even "the man Christ Jesus;" and, nevertheless, his Spirit in us "maketh intercession for us, with groanings which cannot be uttered:" so there is but one man whose works are truly meritorious; but when he works in us by his Spirit, our works cannot, (so far as he is concerned in them,) but be in a sense meritorious; because they are his works. Real Protestant, if thou deniest this, thou maintainest an antichristian proposition, namely, that Christ has lost his power of *meriting*. Herein I must dissent from thee, nor will the cry, "Heresy! Popery!" make me give up this fundamental truth of Christianity, that "Jesus is the same," the very same *deserving* Lord, "yesterday, to-day, and for ever."

In this evangelical view of things, the Redeemer is much exalted by the doctrine of the "merit" of good works; and believers are still left in their native dust to cry out," Not unto us, not unto us, but to thy name give we the praise!"

In the light of this precious truth we see and admire the endearing contest that is always carried on between God's loving kindness and the humble gratitude of believers. God says, "Well done, good and faithful servants! reap what ye have sown:" and they answer, "Lord, THY pound hath gained all; thou hast wrought all our works in us." God says, "They shall walk with me in white, for they are worthy:" and they reply, "Worthy is the Lamb that was slain, and hath washed us from our sins in his own blood." Christ crowns faith by this gracious declaration, "Thy faith hath saved thee." And believers, in their turn, crown Christ by this true confession, "Not by works of righteousness that we have done, but according to thy mercy thou hast saved us; for thou hast quickened us by thy Spirit, when we were dead in sin; yea, thou didst redeem us unto God by thy blood," hundreds of years before we had done any one good work. In a word, they justly give God all the glory of their salvation, agreeable to the first axiom in the Gospel plan; and God graciously gives them all the reward, according to the second.

And now, is it not a pity, that any good men should be so far biassed by the prejudice of their education, or influenced by the spirit of their party, as to account this delightful, harmonizing view of evangelical truths, "a dreadful heresy?" Is it not pity, that, by so doing, they should expose their prepossession, strengthen the hands of Antinomians, harden the hearts of Papists, deprive their Saviour of part of the honour due to him, leave *seeming* contradictions in the Scriptures unexplained, and trample under foot, as unworthy of their Protestant orthodoxy, a powerful motive to obedience, by which neither Moses nor Jesus was above being influenced? For the one "looked to the recompense of reward;" and the other, "for the joy that was set before him, both despised the shame, and endured the cross."

It may not be amiss to illustrate what has been advanced upon the merit or rewardableness of works, by Scriptural instances of old and modern saints who have pleaded it before God. David speaks thus in the eighteenth psalm: — "The Lord rewarded me according to my righteousness, according to the cleanness of my hands hath he recompensed me: I was upright before him, therefore hath he recompensed me according to my righteousness," &c. And in the one hundred and nineteenth psalm, having mentioned his spiritual comforts, he says, "This I had, because I kept thy precepts." Another instance, no less remarkable, is that of Hezekiah, who prayed thus in his sickness, "Remember now, O Lord, I beseech thee, how I have walked before thee in truth, and with a perfect heart, and have done that which is good in thy sight!"

We see instances of this boldness in the New Testament also: "We have left all to follow thee," said once the disciples of our Lord, and "what shall we have" for this sacrifice? Jesus, instead of blaming their question, simply told them they should have "a hundred fold" for all they had left, and made it a standing rule of distribution for all the Church. St. John, legal St. John, is not ashamed to say, that "if our heart condemn us not, then have we confidence toward God, and whatsoever we ask we receive of him, because we keep his commandments, and do those things that are pleasing in his sight." He even exhorts the elect lady to "look to herself that she might not lose the things that she had wrought, but receive a full reward." And the evangelical Apostle Paul desires the Hebrews "not to cast away their confidence, which," says he, "hath great recompense of reward;" and charges the Colossians to see "that none beguiled them of their reward, in a voluntary humility."

From these and the like scriptures, I conclude, that those who have a clear witness they have done what God commanded, may, without "heresy," humbly demand the promised reward: which they can never do without this idea, that, according to the tenor of the Gospel covenant, they are fit subjects for it.

I know some will take the alarm; and, to save the ark, which they think totters by this doctrine, will affirm, that "in the above mentioned passages, David personates Christ; and Hezekiah the Pharisee." But this is contradicting the whole context, to say nothing of all sober commentators. Mr. Henry tells us, that David, in these verses, "reflects with comfort upon his own integrity, and rejoiceth, like St. Paul, 'in the testimony of his own conscience, that he had had his conversation in godly sincerity.'" And he informs us, that the psalmist lays down in this psalm "the rules of God's government, that we may know, not only what God expects from us, but what we may expect from him." With regard to Hezekiah, it is plain his prayer was heard; a strong proof that it was inspired by the Spirit of Jesus, and not that of the Pharisee.

But if you reject, sir, the testimony of David and Hezekiah because they were Jews, receive, at least, that of "real Protestants;" for which we need only go as far as Bath or Talgarth parish; there we shall find chapels, where the Protestants have agreed together to ask *rewards* as solemnly as ever David and Hezekiah did. In the Hymns you have revised for another edition, and by that means made your own with respect to the doctrine, one is calculated to "welcome a messenger of Jesus's grace." and all the congregation sings,

> Give *reward* of grace and glory
> To thy faithful labourer there.

What, sir, do you allow the labours of a minister to be of such dignity, and his faithfulness to have such uncommon merit, that a thousand people can boldly ask God a reward for him, and that not only of gifts and temporal blessings, but of grace; and not of grace only, but of glory too? You have in those two lines the very quintessence of the three grand heresies of the Minutes, "faithfulness, works, and merit." Permit me to add one passage more, from page 312, of *Baxter's Methodus Theologiæ Christianæ.*

"The word *merit*, rightly explained, is not amiss. All the fathers of the primitive Church have made use of it without opposition, to the best of my remembrance. It may be used by believers who do not make it a cloak for error; by wise men who will not be offended at it, and by those who want to defend the truth, and convey clearer ideas in the explanation of things intricate. There is no word that fully conveys the same idea; that which comes nearest to it is *dignity*, and suspicious persons will not like it much better. We have three words in the New Testament that come very near it, αξιος, μισθος, and διχαιος, and they occur pretty frequently there. We render them *worthy, reward,* and *just;* and the abuse which Papists make of them ought not to make us reject their use. The English word *worthy* conveys no other idea than that of the Latin word *meritum,* taken actively; nor has the word *reward* any other signification than the word *meritum*, taken passively; therefore, they who can put a candid sense upon the words *worthy*, and *reward*, should do the same with regard to the word *merit.* "

Having explained and vindicated the sixth article of the Minutes, I proceed to the

"VII. The grand objection to one of the preceding propositions is drawn from matter of fact. God does, in fact, justify those who, by their own confession, neither 'feared God, nor wrought righteousness.' Is this an exception to the rule? It is a doubt, if God make any exception at all. But how are we sure that the person in question never did 'fear God and work righteousness?' His own saying so is not proof: for we know how all that are convinced of sin undervalue themselves in every respect."

Do you think, sir, the "heresy" of this proposition consists in intimating that God does, in fact, justify those who fear him, and not those who make absolutely no stop in the downward road of open sin and flagrant iniquity? If it does, I am sure the sacred writers are heretics to a man. See the account we have of conversions in the Scripture; please to remember what Mr. Wesley means by justification, and then answer the following questions: —

Did not the prodigal son "come to himself," repent, and return to his father, before he received the kiss of peace? Did not the woman that was a sinner forsake her wicked course of life before our Lord said to her, *"Go* in peace, thy sins are forgiven thee?"

Again: was not the woman of Samaria convinced of sin, yea, of "all that ever she did," before our Lord revealed himself to her, to enable her to believe unto justification? Did not Zaccheus evidence his *fear of God,* yea, and "work righteousness," by hearty offers of restitution, before Christ testified that he was "a son of Abraham?" Did not St. Paul express his fear of God, and readiness to work righteousness, when he cried out, "Lord, what wouldst thou have me to do?" Yea, did he not produce "fruit meet for repentance," by praying three days and three nights, before Ananias was sent to direct him "how to wash away his sins?" Did not the eunuch and Cornelius fear God? Did not David himself, whom the apostle mentions as a grand instance of justification without the merit of works, fear God from his youth? And when he had wrought folly in Israel, was he not humbled for his sin, before he was washed from it? Did he not confess his crime, and say, "I have sinned," before Nathan said by Divine commission, "The Lord hath put away thy sin?"

Does not St. Paul himself carry Mr. Wesley's "heresy" so far as to say, "Whosoever among you feareth God, to you is the word of this salvation sent?" Acts xiii, 26. Must we so understand Romans iv, 5, as to make him contradict, point blank, his own declarations, his own experience, and the account of all the above mentioned conversions? Certainly not. Those words, "God justifies the ungodly, and him that worketh not, but believeth in Jesus," when candidly explained, agree perfectly with Mr. Wesley's doctrine. (1.) By "the ungodly," the apostle does not mean "the wicked that does not forsake his way;" but the man who, before he believed to justification, was ungodly, and still remains ungodly in the eye of the law of works, needing daily forgiveness by grace, even after he is made godly in a Gospel sense. (2.) By "him that worketh not" St. Paul does not mean a lazy, indolent wretch, who, without any reluctance, follows the stream of his corrupt nature; but "a penitent," who, whatever works he does, has no dependence upon them, esteems them as nothing, yea, "as dung and dross *in comparison of* the excellency of Christ;" and, in short, one who does not work to merit or purchase his justification, but comes to receive that invaluable blessing as a free gift. (3.) That this is the meaning of the apostle is evident from his adding, that he who "worketh not," yet "believeth." For if he took the word "worketh not," in an absolute sense, he could never make it agree with "believing," which is certainly a *work*, yea, a work of our noblest part; for "with the heart man believeth to righteousness." Add to this, sir, that justifying faith, as I observed before never comes without her fore-runner, conviction; nor conviction of sin without suitable tempers or inward works. "There is nothing," says Dr. Owen, "that I will more firmly adhere to in this whole doctrine, than the necessity of convictions previous to true believing; — as also displacency, sorrow, fear, a desire of deliverance, With other necessary effects of true convictions." St. Paul, therefore, is consistent with himself, and Mr. Wesley with St. Paul.

Again if God justify sinners merely as "ungodly," and people that "work not" why should he not justify *all* sinners; for they are all ungodly, and there is "none of them that does good, no, not one?" Why did not the Pharisee, for example, go to his house justified as well as the publican? You will probably answer, that "he was not convinced of sin." Why, sir, this is just what Mr. Wesley maintains. Express yourself in St. Peter's words, "He did *not fear God;*" or in those of John the Baptist, "He did not *bring forth fruits meet for repentance.*"

Should some ask, "*What works meet for repentance* did the woman caught in adultery do, before our Lord justified her?" I would ask, in my turn, how do they know that the Lord justified her? Do they conclude it from those words, "Neither do I condemn thee?" Does not the context show, that as the Pharisees had not condemned her to be stoned, according to the Mosaic law, neither would our Lord take upon himself to pass sentence upon her, according to his declaration on another occasion, "I am not sent to condemn the world, but that the world through me might be saved?" This by no means implies, that the world is justified in St. Paul's sense, Romans v, 1. But supposing she was justified, how do you know that our Lord's' words, writing, looks, and grace, had not brought her to godly shame and sorrow, that is, to "the fear of God," and "the working of *internal* righteousness," before he gave her the peace that passes all understanding?

After all, Mr. Wesley says, with modesty and wisdom, "It is a doubt whether God makes any exception at all:" and it lies upon you to show there is in these words any thing contrary to the humility of the true Christian, and orthodoxy of the sound divine. But please to remember, that if you judge of orthodoxy according to the works of Dr. Crisp, we will take the liberty to appeal to the word of God.

But you make, perhaps, Mr. Wesley's heresy in this proposition consist in his refusing to take the word of persons convinced of sin, when they say they never "feared God nor wrought righteousness." "For we know," says he, "how all that are convinced of sin, undervalue themselves in every respect."

Had Mr. Wesley imagined that some Christian friends (O my God, deliver me from such friendship!) would leave no stone unturned to procure a copy of his Minutes, in order to find some occasion against him, he would probably have worded this with more circumspection. But he wrote for real friends; and he knew such would at once enter into his meaning, which is, that "persons deeply convinced of sin are apt, very apt, to form a wrong judgment both of their state and performances, and to think the worst of themselves in every respect, that is, both with regard to what Divine grace does in them, and by them."

And this is so obvious a truth, that he must be a novice indeed in Christian experience who doubts of it for a moment; and a great lover of disputing, who will make a man an offender for so true an assertion. Do not we daily see some, in whom the arrows of conviction stick fast, who think they are as much past recovery as Satan himself? Do not we hear others complain, "they grow worse and worse," when they only discover more and more how bad they are by nature? And are there not some, who bind upon themselves heavy burdens of their own making, and when they cannot bear them, are tormented in their consciences with imaginary guilt; while others are ready to go distracted through groundless fears of having committed the sin against the Holy Ghost? In a word, do we not see hundreds, who, when they have reason to hope well of their state, think there is no hope for them? In all these respects do they not act like Jonah in the whale's belly, and complain, "I am cast out of thy sight?" And have not they need to encourage themselves in their God, and say, "Why art thou cast down, O my soul?"

But let your conscience speak, sir, on this matter. When some deep mourners have complained to you of their misery, danger, and desperate state, did you never drop a word of comfort to this effect — "You undervalue yourselves; you write too bitter things against yourselves; your case is not so bad as your unbelieving fears represent it: God's thoughts are not as your thoughts. Many, like the foolish virgins, think themselves sure of heaven, when they stand on the brink of hell; and many think they are just dropping into it, who are not far from the kingdom of God."

Yea, and as it is with real seekers, so it is with real believers. Did not they undervalue, yea, degrade themselves, by the remains of their unbelief; or, which is the same, did they live up to their dignity, and every where consider themselves as "members of Christ, children of God, and inheritors of the kingdom of heaven," "what manner of persons," yea, what angels "would they be in all holy conversation!"

Sometimes their light shines with peculiar lustre, like Moses' face, and they "know it not." Thousands "see their good works, and glorify their Father who is in heaven;" but the matter is hid from them: they complain, perhaps, that they are the most unprofitable of all his children. Let me instance in one particular: St. Paul, Mr. Whitefield, and thousands of the brightest stars of the Church, have called themselves both "the chief of sinners," and "the least of all saints." Now, as in a chain there is but one link that can be called *the first*, or *the last;* so in the very nature of things, there can be but one man in the immense file of Christ's soldiers, that is actually "the chief of sinners," and "the least of all saints." If a thousand believers, therefore, say, those two appellations belong to themselves, it is evident that at least nine hundred and ninety-nine undervalue themselves. For my part, I cannot but think they suit me ten thousand times better than they did St. Paul. I must therefore insolently think myself a less sinner and a greater saint than him; or of necessity believe that he, and "all that are partakers of the same convincing grace," undervalue themselves in every respect.

One more. article remains, and if it does not contain "the dreadful heresy," which hitherto we have looked for in vain, the Minutes are, from first to last, Scripturally orthodox, and you have given Churchmen and dissenters a false alarm.

"VIII. Does not talking of a justified and sanctified state tend to mislead men? Almost naturally leading them to trust in what was done in one moment? whereas we are every hour, and every moment, pleasing or displeasing to God, according to our works — according to the whole of our inward tempers and outward behaviour."

To do this proposition justice, and prevent misunderstandings, I must premise some observations.

1. Mr. Wesley is not against persons talking of justification and sanctification in a Scriptural sense: for when he "knows the tree by the fruits," he says himself to his flocks, as St. Paul did to the Corinthians, "Some of you are sanctified and justified." Nor does he deny that God justifies a penitent sinner in a moment, and that in a moment "he can manifest himself" unto his believing people "as he does not to the world, and give them an inheritance among them that are sanctified, through faith in Jesus." His objection respects only the idea entertained by some, and countenanced by others, that when God forgives us our sins, he introduces us into a state where we are unalterably fixed in his blessed favour, and for ever stamped with his holy image; so that it matters no longer whether the tree is barren or not, whether it produces good or bad fruit; it was set at such a time, and therefore it must be a "tree of righteousness" still. A conclusion directly contrary to the words of our Lord and his beloved disciple: "By their fruits ye shall know them. He that sinneth is of the devil. Every branch in me that beareth not fruit, [much more that beareth evil fruit,] my Father taketh away."

2. Permit me, sir, to observe also, that Mr. Wesley has many persons in his societies, (and would to God there were none in ours:) who profess they were justified or sanctified in a moment; but instead of trusting in the living God, so trust to what was done in that moment, as to give over "taking up their cross daily, and watching unto prayer with all perseverance." The consequences are deplorable; they slide back into the spirit of the world; and their tempers are no more regulated by the meek, gentle, humble love of Jesus. Some inquire with the heathens, "What shall we eat, and what shall we drink," to please ourselves? Others evidently "love the world, lay up treasures on earth," or ask, "wherewith shall we *be fashionably* clothed?" Therefore "the love of the Father is not in them." And not a few are "led captive by the devil at his will;" influenced by his unhappy suggestions, they harbour bitterness, malice, and revenge; none is in the right but themselves, and "wisdom shall die with them."

Now, sir, Mr. Wesley cannot but fear it is not well with persons who are in any of these cases. Though every body should join to extol them as "dear children of God," he is persuaded that "Satan has beguiled them as he did Eve;" and he addresses them as our Lord did the angel of the Church of Sardis, "I know thy works, that thou hast a name that thou livest, and art dead, [or dying:] repent, therefore, and strengthen the things which remain, that are ready to die; for I have not found thy works perfect before God." Mr. Wesley hath the word of prophecy, which he thinks more sure than the opinion of a world of professors; and, according to that word, he sees that "they who are led by the Spirit of God are the sons of God," and that God's Spirit does not lead into the vanities of the world, or indulgences of fleshly lusts, any more than into the pride or malice of Satan. Nor does he think that those are not "under the law" who can merrily laugh at the law, and pass jests upon Moses, the venerable servant of God. But with St. Paul he asserts, that when people are "under grace, and not under the law, sin hath not dominion over them." With our Lord he declares, "He who committeth sin, is the servant of sin;" and with his prophet, that "God is of purer eyes than to behold iniquity" with the least degree of approbation. In short, he believes that God, being unchangeable in his holiness, cannot but always "love righteousness and hate iniquity;" and that, as the heart is continually working either iniquity or righteousness, and as God cannot but be pleased at the one, and displeased at the other, he is continually pleased or displeased with us, according to the workings of our hearts, and the fruits which they outwardly produce.

Perhaps you object to the word "every moment." But why should you, sir? If it be not *every moment,* it is *never.* If God do not approve holiness, and disapprove sin every moment, he never does it, for he changes not. If he do it only now and then, he is such a one as ourselves; for even wicked men will approve righteousness and condemn unrighteousness by fits and starts. I may every moment harbour malice in my heart, and so commit internal murder. If God winks at this one instant, why not two? And so on to days, months, and years? Does the *duration* of moral evil constitute sin? May not I be guilty of the greatest enormity in the twinkling of an eye? And is it not the ordinary property of the most horrid crimes, such as robbery and adultery, that they are soon finished?

Do not say, sir, that this doctrine sets aside "salvation by faith." It is highly consistent with it. He that, in God's account, does the best works, has the most faith, most of the sap of eternal life that flows from the heavenly Vine. And he that has most faith has most of Christ's likeness, and is of course most pleasing to God, who cannot be pleased but with Christ and his living image. On the other hand he that in God's account does the worst works, and has the worst tempers, has most unbelief. He that has most unbelief, is most "like his father, the devil;" and must consequently be most displeasing to him that accepts us "in the Beloved," and not "in the wicked one."

Having premised these observations, I come closer to the point, and assert that if we are not every moment pleasing or displeasing to God, according to the works of our hearts and hands, you must set your seal to the following absurdities: —

(1.) "God is angry with the wicked all the day," and yet there are moments in which he is not angry at them. (2.) Lot *pleased* God as much in those moments in which he got drunk and committed incest with his daughters, as in the day he exercised hospitality toward the disguised angels. (3.) David did not *displease* God more when he committed adultery with Bathsheba, and imbrued his hands in her husband's blood, than when he danced before the ark, or composed the 103d Psalm. (4.) Solomon was as acceptable to God in the moment when "his wives turned away his heart after other gods," as when he chose wisdom, and his speech pleased the Lord, when he went after the goddess Ashtaroth, and built a high place to bloody Moloch, as when he represented our Melchisedec, and dedicated the temple. (5.) Again: you must set your seal to these propositions of Dr. Crisp: "From the time thy transgressions were laid upon Christ, thou ceasest to be a transgressor to the last hour of thy life; so that now thou art not an idolater, thou art not a thief, &c; thou art not a sinful person, whatsoever sin thou committest." Again: "God does no longer stand offended nor displeased, though a believer, after he is a believer, do sin often; except he will be offended where there is no cause to be offended, which is blasphemy to speak." Yet again: "It is thought that elect persons are in a damnable, estate in the time they walk in excess of riot; let me speak freely to you that the Lord has no more to lay to the charge of an elect person, yet in the height of iniquity, and in the excess of riot, and committing all the abominations that can be committed." "There is no time but such a person is a child of God." (6.) In short, sir, you must be of the sentiment of the wildest Antinomian I ever knew, who, because he had once a bright manifestation of pardon, not only concludes that he is safe, though he lives in open sin, but asserts God would no more be *displeased* with him for whoring and stealing, than for praying and receiving the sacrament.

Again: It is an important truth, that we may please God for a time, and yet afterward displease him. St. Paul mentions those who, by putting away a good conscience, "concerning faith made shipwreck," and therefore pleased God no longer, "seeing that without faith it is impossible to please him."

Of this the Israelites are a remarkable instance. "They did all drink of that spiritual Rock that followed them, and that rock was Christ. Yet with many of them God was not well pleased." Then comes the proof of the Divine displeasure; for "they were overthrown in the wilderness. Now," adds the apostle, "these things happened unto them for examples, and they are written for our admonition, that we should not lust after evil things, and tempt Christ as they did. Therefore, let him that thinketh he standeth, take heed lest," after their example, "he fall" into wilful sin, the Divine displeasure, and utter destruction.

Our Lord teaches the same doctrine, both by parables and positive assertions. He gives us the history of a man to whom his lord and king compassionately "forgave a debt of ten thousand talents." This ungrateful wretch, by not forgiving his fellow servant who owed him a hundred pence, forfeited his own pardon, and drew upon himself the king's heaviest displeasure; "for he was wroth, and delivered him to. the tormentors till he should pay all that was due to him;" and to the eternal overthrow of Dr. Crisp's fashionable tenets, our Lord adds, "So likewise shall my Father do unto you, if ye from your hearts forgive not every one his brother their trespasses." Agreeably to this, he assured his disciples that his Father "pruneth every branch in him that beareth fruit, and taketh away every one that beareth not fruit;" and to show how far this displeasure may proceed, he observes that such a barren branch is "cast forth, is withered, gathered, cast into the fire, and burned."

Here, sir, I might add all those scriptures that testify the possibility of falling away from the Divine favour. I might bring the alarming instances of those apostates who once "tasted the good word of God, and the powers of the world to come," and afterward "fell from their steadfastness, lost their reward, became enemies to God by wicked works, hated the light" which they rejoiced in, because it reproved their evil deeds; "trod under foot the Son of God, forgot they were washed from their old sins, and counted the blood of Christ, wherewith they were sanctified, an unholy thing." But I refer you, sir, to the two John Goodwins of the age, the Rev. Mr. Wesley and the Rev. Mr. Sellon, who have so cut down and stripped the *Crispian orthodoxy,* that some people think it actually lies without either root, bark, or branches, exposed to the view of those who have courage enough to see and think for themselves.

Should all they have advanced to show that "we are every hour and every moment pleasing or displeasing to God, according to our internal and external works," have no weight with you, let me conclude by producing the testimony of two respectable divines, against whom you will not enter a protest.

The one is the rector of Loughrea. You tell us, sir, in your sermons, page 88, that the acceptance of Cornelius "was not absolutely final and decisive;" and you add, "So long as we continue in the flesh, we are doubtless in a probationary state. Even after Cornelius had been endued with the Holy Ghost, had he wilfully done despite to the Spirit of grace, he might have" [not only *displeased God,* which is all Mr. Wesley asserts in this proposition, but] "fallen as deep into perdition as ever Judas did."

I know one, sir, who was burned as "a dreadful heretic," that did not go farther in this heresy than you do. And that is good Bishop Latimer, my second witness. He not only affirmed that "Christ shed as much blood for Judas as he did for Peter," but roundly asserted, "We may one time be in the book, and another out; as it appeareth by David, who was written in the book of life; but when he sinned with a high hand, [which, by the by, we may do every moment,] he, at the same time, was out of the favour of God, until he had repented; out of Christ, who is the book in which all believers are written." (*Latimer's* Sermon on the Third Sunday after Epiphany.)

Thus, sir, have I looked out for "the heresy," the dreadful heresy, of Mr. Wesley's Minutes, by bringing all the propositions they contain to the touchstone of Scripture and common sense; but, instead of finding it, I have found the very marrow of the Gospel of Christ, so far as it is opposed to Dr. Crisp's Antinomian Gospel; which at this time would overflow our little Sion, if God did not sit above the water floods, and say to the proudest billows of error, "Hitherto shall ye come, and no farther." I have showed that the Minutes contain nothing but what is truly Scriptural, and nothing but what the best Calvinist divines have themselves directly or indirectly asserted; except perhaps the sixth proposition concerning *the merit of works;* and with respect to this, I hope I have demonstrated, upon rational and evangelical principles, that Mr. Wesley, far from "bringing in a damnable heresy," has done the Gospel justice, and Protestantism service, by candidly giving up an old prejudice, equally contrary to Scripture and good sense, a piece of bigotry which hath long hardened the Papists against the doctrine of "salvation by the merit of Christ," and hath added inconceivable strength to the Antinomian delusion among us. One difficulty remains, and that is, to account for your attacking Mr. Wesley, though you could not wound him without stabbing yourself. Reserving my reflections upon this amazing step for another letter, I remain your astonished servant, in the bonds of a peaceful Gospel,

J. FLETCHER.

LETTER V.

HONOURED AND REVEREND SIR, — Having vindicated both some important doctrines of the Gospel, and an eminent servant of Christ, from the charge of "dreadful heresy;" I will now take the liberty of a friend to expostulate a little with *you*.

When Brutus, among other senators, rushed upon Cesar, the venerable general, as he wrapped himself in his mantle, just said, "And art thou also among them? Even thou, my son?" May not Mr. Wesley address you, sir, in the same words, and add, "If a body of men must be raised to attack me, let some zealous follower of Dr. Crisp, some hot-headed vindicator of reprobation and eternal justification blow the trumpet, and put himself at their head: but let it not be *you*, who believe with me that we are moral agents; that God is love; that Jesus tasted death for every man; and that the Holy Spirit shall not always strive with sinners. If you do not regard my reputation, consider at least your own; and expose me not as a heretic for advancing propositions, the substance of which you have avowed before the sun."

But had those propositions at length appeared to you unsound, yea, and had you never maintained them yourself, should you not, as a Christian and a brother, have written to him, acquainted him with your objections, and desired him to solve them and explain himself, or you should be obliged publicly to expose him?

Was this condescension more than was due from you, sir, and our other friends, to a gray-headed minister of Christ; an old general in the armies of Emmanuel; a father who has children capable of instructing even masters in Israel; and one whom God made the first and principal instrument of the late revival of internal religion in our Church?

Instead of this friendly method, as if you was a Barak, "commanded by the Lord *God* of Israel, you call together the children of Naphtali and Zebulun:" you convene, from England and Wales, clergy and laity, Churchmen and Dissenters, to meet you at Bristol, where they are, it seems, to be entertained in good and free quarters. And for what grand expedition? Why, on a day appointed you are to march up "in a body," not to attack Sisera and his iron chariots, but an old Caleb, who, without meddling with you, quietly goes on to the conquest of Canaan; not to desire in a friendly manner, after a fair debate of every proposition that appears dangerous, and upon previous conviction that what is exceptionable may be given up, but to do what I think was never done by nominal, much less by "real Protestants" — O let it not be told in Rome, lest the sons of the inquisition rejoice! — This mixed, this formidable body, is to "insist upon" Mr. Wesley, and the preachers in his connection, "formally recanting" their Minutes, as appearing "injurious to the very fundamental principles of Christianity, and being dreadfully heretical." And this, (astonishing!) without the least inquiry made into their meaning and design — without a shadow of authority from our superiors in Church or state — without an appeal to "the law and to the testimony" — without form of process — without judge or jury — without so much as allowing the poor "heretics," (who are condemned six weeks before they can possibly be heard,) to answer for themselves!

As I was fortunate enough to stop, some months ago, such rash proceedings in Wales, permit me, sir, to bear my testimony against them in England, and to tell you they exceed the late transactions in Edmund Hall. The six students, against whom wrath was gone forth, were allowed to say what they could in their own defence before they were sentenced, as unfit members of a literary society. Likewise the vice-chancellor had the statutes of the university of Oxford, seeming to countenance his proceedings: but what statute of the university of Jesus can you produce, even to save appearances? Surely not that which the Papists made use of, "Compel them to come in;" for I am persuaded, that although clergy and laity, Churchmen and Dissenters, are convened to go in a body to Mr. Wesley's conference, you mean no external compulsion. Much less are you authorized to "insist" upon his owning himself "a heretic," by these words of the apostle, "As much as lieth in you, live peaceably with all men, and esteem ministers highly in love for their works' sake." Neither by his command, "A heretic, after the first and second admonition, reject," &c; for you have neither proved Mr. Wesley a *heretic,* nor *once admonished* him as such.

Surely our Lord will not smile upon your undertaking; for he has left his sentiments upon record; the reverse of your practice. He had said, "Whosoever shall receive," not provoke, "one of such children in my name, receiveth me. But John answered him, saying, Master, we saw one casting out devils in thy name, and we forbad him, because he followeth not with us. Forbid him not," said Jesus, "for there is no man who can do a miracle in my name, that can lightly speak evil of me." Festus himself, though a poor heathen, will disapprove of such a step: "It is not the manner of the Romans," says he, "to deliver any man to die," (or to insist on his publicly giving up his reputation, which in some cases is worse than death,) "before that he who is accused have the accusers face to face; and have license to answer for himself concerning the crime laid against him." The lordliness of your procedure even exceeds, in one respect, the severity of the Council of Constance, where poor Jerome of Prague had leave to plead his own cause before he was obliged to acknowledge himself a heretic; and make "a formal recantation" of the propositions he had advanced.

Beside, how could you suppose, sir, that Mr. Wesley, and the preachers who shall assemble with him, are such weak men as tamely to acknowledge themselves heretics upon your *ipse dixit?* Suppose Mr. Wesley took it in his head to convene all the divines that disapprove the extract of Zanchius, to go with him in a body to Mr. Toplady's chapel, and demand a formal recantation of that performance, as heretical; yea, to insist upon it, before they had "measured swords, or broken a pike together;" would not the translator of Zanchius, from the ramparts of common sense, deservedly laugh at him, and ask whether he thought to frighten him by his protests, and bully him into orthodoxy?

O sir, have we not fightings enough *without* to empty all our time and strength? Must we also declare war and promote fightings *within?* Must we catch at every opportunity to stab one another, because the livery of truth which we wear is not turned up in the same manner? What can be more cruel than this? What can be more cutting to an old minister of Christ, than to be traduced as "a dreadful heretic," in printed letters sent to the best men in the land, yea, through all England and Scotland, and signed by a person of your rank and piety; to have things that he knows not, that he never meant, laid to his charge, and dispersed far and near? While he is gone to a neighbouring kingdom to preach Jesus Christ, to have his friends prejudiced, his foes elevated, and the fruit of his extensive ministry at the point of being blasted! Put yourself in his place, sir, and you will see that the wound is deep, and reaches the very heart. I can apologize for the other "real Protestants." Some are utter strangers to polemic divinity; others are biassed by high Calvinism; and one, whose name is used, never saw your circular letter till it was in print. But what can I say for you, sir? Against hope I must believe in hope, that an unaccountable panic influenced your mind, and deprived you for a time of the calmness and candour which adorn your natural temper. If this is the case, may you act with less precipitancy for the future! And may the charity "that hopeth all things, believeth all things, does not provoke, and is not provoked," rule in our hearts and lives! So shall the heathen world drop their just objections against our unhappy divisions, and once more be forced to cry out, "See how these Christians love!" And so shall we give over trying to disturb, or pull down a part of the Church of Christ, because we dislike the colour of the stones with which it is built; or because our fellow builders cannot pronounce *Shibboleth* just as we do.

One word more about Mr. Wesley, and I have done. Of the two greatest and most useful ministers I ever knew, one is no more. The other, after amazing labours, flies still with unwearied diligence through the three kingdoms, calling sinners to repentance, and to the healing fountain of Jesus' blood. Though oppressed with the weight of near seventy years, and the care of near thirty thousand souls, he shames still, by his unabated zeal and immense labours, all the young ministers in England, perhaps in Christendom. He has generally blown the Gospel trump, and rode twenty miles, before most of the professors, who despise his labours, have left their downy pillow. As he begins the day, the week, the year, so he concludes them, still intent upon extensive services for the glory of the Redeemer, and the good of souls. And shall we lightly lift up our pens, our tongues, our hands against him? No, let them rather forget their cunning! If we *will* quarrel, can we find nobody to fall out with but the minister upon whom God puts the greatest honour?

Our Elijah has lately been translated to heaven. Gray-headed Elisha is yet awhile continued upon earth. And shall we make a hurry and noise, to bring in railing accusations against him with more success? While we pretend to a peculiar zeal for Christ's glory, shall the very same spirit be found in us, which made his persecutors say, "He hath spoken blasphemy," (or heresy,) "what need we any farther witnesses?" Shall the sons of the prophets, shall even children in grace and knowledge, openly traduce the venerable seer and his abundant labours? When they see him run upon his Lord's errands, shall they cry, not, "Go up, thou bald head," but, "Go up, thou heretic?" O Jesus of Nazareth, thou rejected of men, thou who wast once called "a deceiver of the people," suffer it not! lest the raging bear of persecution come suddenly out of the wood upon those sons of discord, and tear them in pieces.

And suppose a Noah, an old preacher of righteousness, should have really nodded under the influence of an honest mistake, shall we act a worse part than that of Canaan? Shall we make sport of the nakedness which, we say, he has disclosed, when we have boldly uncovered it ourselves? O God, do not thou permit it, lest a curse of pride, self sufficiency, bigotry, Antinomianism, and bitter zeal, come upon us; and lest the children, begotten by our unkind preaching and unloving example, walk in our steps and inherit our propagated punishment!

Rather may the blessing of *peace makers* be ours. May the meek, loving Spirit of Jesus fill our hearts! May streams, not of the bitter waters which cause the curse, but of the living water which gladdens the city of God, flow from our catholic breasts, and put out the fire of wild zeal and persecuting malice! May we know when Sion is really in danger; and when the accuser of the brethren gives a false alarm to disturb the peace of the Church, and turn the stream of undefiled, lovely, and loving religion, into the miry channel of obstinate prejudice, imperious bigotry, and noisy vain jangling. And may we at last unanimously worship together in the temple of peace, instead of striving for the mastery in the house of discord!

Should this public attempt to stop the war which has been publicly declared be in any degree successful, — should it check a little the forwardness that has lately appeared to stir up contention, under pretence of opposing heresy, — should it make warm men willing to let the light of their moderation shine before the world, and to "keep a conscience void of offence" toward their neighbours, instead of openly opposing their liberty of conscience, — should it cause the good that is in an eminent servant of Christ to be less evil spoken of, — and above all, should it convince any of the great impropriety of exposing precious truths as "dreadful heresies;" and of preferring the gospel of Dr. Crisp to "the truth as it is in Jesus," — I shall be less grieved at having been obliged to expostulate with you, sir, in this public manner.

In hopes this will be the case, and with a heart full of ardent wishes that all our unhappy divisions may end in a greater union, I remain, Hon. and Rev. sir, your obedient servant in the peaceable Gospel of Jesus Christ,

J. FLETCHER

July 29, 1771.

SECOND CHECK TO ANTINOMIANISM;

OCCASIONED BY A LATE NARRATIVE.

In Three Letters

TO THE HON. AND REV. MR. SHIRLEY.

BY THE

VIDICATOR OF THE REV. MR. WESLEY'S MINUTES.

Reprove, rebuke, exhort, with all long-suffering and (Scriptural) doctrine; for the time will come when they will not endure sound doctrine. 2 Timothy iv, 2, 3.

Wherefore rebuke them sharply, that they may be sound in the faith. But let brotherly love continue. Titus i, 18; Hebrews xiii, 50.

PREFACE.

THE publication of the "Vindication of Mr. Wesley's Minutes" having been represented by some persons as an act of injustice, the following letter is made public to throw some light upon that little event, and serve as a preface to the SECOND CHECK TO ANTINOMIANISM.

To the Rev. Mr. John Wesley.

"REV. AND DEAR SIR, — As I love open dealing, I send you the substance, and almost the very words, of a private letter I have just written to Mr. Shirley, in answer to one, in which he informs me he is going to publish his Narrative. He is exceedingly welcome to make use of any part of my letters to Mr. Ireland, concerning the publication of my Vindication, and you are equally welcome to make what use you please of this. Among friends all things are, or should be, common.

"I am, Rev. and dear sir, yours, &c,   J. FLETCHER.
"MADELEY, *Sept.* 11, 1771."

To the Hon. and Rev..Mr. Shirley.

"REV. AND DEAR SIR, — It is extremely proper, nay, it is highly necessary, that the public should be informed how much like a minister of the Prince of Peace, and a meek, humble, loving brother in the Gospel of Christ you behaved at the conference. Had I been there, I would gladly have taken upon me to proclaim these tidings of joy to the lovers of Zion's peace. Your conduct at that time of love is certainly the best excuse for the hasty step you had taken; as my desire of stopping my Vindication, upon hearing it, is the best apology I can make for my severity to you.

"I am not averse at all, sir, to your publishing the passages you mention, out of my letters to Mr. Ireland. They show my peculiar love and respect for you, which I shall at all times think an honour, and at this juncture shall feel a peculiar pleasure, to see proclaimed to the world. They apologize for my calling myself *a lover of quietness,* when I unfortunately prove *a son of contention:* and they demonstrate, that I am not altogether void of the fear that becomes an awkward, unexperienced surgeon, when he ventures to open a vein in the arm of a person for whom he has the highest regard. How natural is it for him to tremble, lest by missing the intended vein, and pricking an unseen artery, he should have done irreparable mischief, instead of a useful operation.

"But While you do me the kindness of publishing those passages, permit me, sir, to do Mr. Wesley the justice of informing him I had also written to Mr. Ireland, that 'whether my letters were suppressed or not, the Minutes *must* be vindicated, — that Mr. Wesley owed it to the Church, to the *real Protestants,* to all his societies, and to his own aspersed character; — and that, after all, the controversy did not seem to me to be so much, whether the Minutes should stand, as whether the Antinomian gospel of Dr. Crisp should prevail over the practical Gospel of Jesus Christ.'

"I must also, sir, beg leave to let my vindicated friend know, that in the very letter where I so earnestly entreated Mr. Ireland to stop the publication of my letters to you, and offered to take the whole expense of the impression upon myself, though I should be obliged to sell my last shirt to defray it, I added, that 'if they were published, I must look upon it as a *necessary evil* or *misfortune;*' which of the two words I used I do not justly recollect. A *misfortune* for you and me, who must appear inconsistent to the world: you, sir, with your Sermons, and I with my title page; and nevertheless *necessary* to vindicate misrepresented truth, defend an eminent minister of Christ, and stem the torrent of Antinomianism.

"It may not be improper also, to observe to you, sir, that when I presented Mr. Wesley with my Vindication, I begged he would correct it, and take away whatever might be unkind or too sharp; urging that, though I meant no unkindness, I was not a proper judge of what I had written under peculiarly delicate and trying circumstances, as well as in a great hurry; and did not therefore dare to trust either my pen, my head, or my heart. He was no sooner gone, than I sent a letter after him, to repeat and urge the same request; and he wrote me word he had 'expunged every tart expression.' *If he has,* (for I have not yet seen what alterations his friendly pen has made,) I am reconciled to their publication; and *that he has* I have reason to hope from the letters of two judicious London friends, who calmed my fears lest I should have treated you with unkindness.

"One of them says, 'I reverence Mr. Shirley for his candid acknowledgment of his hastiness in judging. I commend the Calvinists at the conference for their justice to Mr. Wesley, and their acquiescence in the declaration of the preachers in connection with him. But is that declaration, however dispersed, a remedy adequate to the evil done, not only to Mr. Wesley, but to the cause and work of God? Several Calvinists, in eagerness of malice, had dispersed their calumnies through the three kingdoms. A truly excellent person herself, in her mistaken zeal, had represented him as *a Papist unmasked, a heretic, an apostate.* A clergyman of the first reputation informs me *a Poem on his apostasy* is just coming out. Letters have been sent to every serious Churchman and Dissenter through the land, together with the Gospel Magazine. Great are the shoutings, *And now that he lieth, let him rise up no more!* This is all the cry. His dearest friends and children are staggered, and scarce know what to think. You, in your corner, cannot conceive the mischief that has been done, and is still doing. But your letters, in the hand of Providence, may answer the good ends you proposed by writing them. You have not been too severe to dear Mr. Shirley, moderate

Calvinists themselves being judges; but very kind and friendly to set a good mistaken man right, and probably to preserve him from the like rashness as long as he lives. Be not troubled, therefore, but cast your care upon the Lord.'

"My other friend says, 'Considering what harm the Circular Letter has done, and what a useless satisfaction Mr. Shirley has given by his vague acknowledgment, it is no more than just and equitable that your letters should be published.'

"Now, sir, as I never saw that *acknowledgment*, nor the *softening corrections* made by Mr. Wesley in my Vindication; as I was not informed of some of the above mentioned particulars when I was so eager to prevent the publication of my letters; and as I have reason to think, that through the desire of an immediate peace, the festering wound was rather skinned over than probed to the bottom; all I can say about this publication is, what I wrote to our common friend, namely, that 'I must look upon it as a necessary *evil.*'

"I am glad, sir, you do not direct your letter to Mr. Olivers, who was so busy in publishing my Vindication; for, by a letter I have just received from Bristol, I am informed he did not hear how desirous I was to call it in, till he had actually given out before a whole congregation it would be sold. Beside, he would have pleaded with smartness that he never approved of the patched-up peace, that he bore his testimony against it at the time it was made, and had a personal right to produce *my* arguments, since both parties refused to hear *his* at the conference.

"If your letter is friendly, sir, and you print it in the same size with my Vindication, I shall gladly buy ten pounds' worth of the copies, and order them to be stitched with my Vindication, and given gratis to the purchasers of it; as well to do you justice as to convince the world that we make a loving war; and also to demonstrate how much I regard your respectable character, and honour your dear person. Mr. Wesley's heart is, I am persuaded, too full of brotherly love to deny me the pleasure of thus showing you how sincerely I am, Rev. and dear sir, your obedient servant,

JOHN FLETCHER.

"MADELEY, *September* 11, 1771."

SECOND CHECK TO ANTINOMIANISM

LETTER I.

HONOURED AND REVEREND SIR, — I cordially thank you for the greatest part of your Narrative. It confirms me in my hopes that your projected opposition to Mr. Wesley's' Minutes proceeded in general from zeal for the Redeemer's glory. And as such a zeal, though amazingly mistaken, had certainly something very commendable in it, I sincerely desire your Narrative may evidence your *good meaning*, as some think my Vindication does your *mistake*.

In my last private letter I observed, Rev. sir, that if your Narrative was *kind*, I would buy a number of copies, and give them gratis to the purchasers of my book, that they might see all you can possibly produce in your own defence, and do you all the justice your proper behaviour at the conference deserves. But as it appears to me there are some important mistakes in that performance, I neither dare recommend it *absolutely* to my friends, nor wish it in the religious world the *full* success you desire.

I do not complain of its severity; on the contrary, considering the sharpness of my fifth letter, I gratefully acknowledge it is *kinder* than I had reason to expect. But permit me to tell you, sir, I look for *justice* to the Scriptural arguments I advance in defence of truth, before I look for *kindness* to my insignificant person; and could much sooner be satisfied with the former than with the latter alone. As I do not admire the fashionable method of advancing general charges without supporting them by particular proofs, I shall take the liberty of pointing out some mistakes in your Narrative, and by that means endeavour to do justice to Mr. Wesley's declarations, your own sermons, my Vindication, and, above all, to the cause of practical religion.

Waiving the repetition of what I said in my last, touching the publication of my Five Letters to you, I object first to your putting a wrong colour upon Mr. Wesley's declaration. You insinuate, or assert, that he, and fifty-three of the preachers in conference with him, give up the doctrine of "justification by works in the day of judgment." "It appears," say you, "from their subscribing the declaration," notwithstanding Mr. Olivers' remonstrances, "that they do not maintain a second justification by works."

Surely, sir, you wrong them. They might have objected to some of Mr. Olivers' expressions, or been displeased with his readiness to enter the lists of dispute; but certainly so many judicious and good men could never so betray the cause of practical religion, as tamely to renounce a truth of that importance. If they had, one step more would have carried them full into Dr. Crisp's eternal justification, which is the very centre of Antinomianism; and without waiting for the return of the next conference, I would bear my *legal* testimony against their *Antinomian* error. Mr. Wesley I reverence as the greatest minister I know, but would not follow him one step farther than he follows Christ. Were he really guilty of rejecting the evangelical doctrine of a second justification by works, with the plainness and honesty of a Suisse I would address him, as I beg you will permit me to address you.

1. Neither you, Rev. sir, nor any divine in the world, have, I presume, a right to blot out of the sacred records those words of Jesus Christ, St. James, and St. Paul: "Blessed are they that do his commandments, that they may have right to the tree of life. Not every one that says to me, *Lord! Lord!* shall enter into the kingdom of heaven, but he that does the will of my Father. Be ye therefore doers of the word, and not hearers only, deceiving your own selves. For we are under the law to Christ. Not the hearers of the law shall be just before God, but the doers of the law shall be justified. Every man's work shall be made manifest: for the day shall declare it, because it shall be revealed by fire, and the fire shall try every man's work of what sort it is." His very words shall undergo the severest scrutiny. "I say unto you, [O how many will insinuate the contrary!] that every idle word that men shall speak they shall give account thereof in the day of judgment, for by thy words shalt thou [then] be justified, and by thy words shalt thou [then] be condemned."

Can you say, sir, that the justification mentioned by our Lord in this passage is the same as that which St. Paul speaks of as the present privilege of all believers, and has no particular reference to "the day of judgment" mentioned in the preceding sentence? Or will you intimate our Lord does not declare we shall be justified in the last day by *works*, but by *words?* Would this evasion be judicious? Do not all professors know that *words* are *works* in a theological sense; as being both the signs of the "workings" of our hearts, and the positive "works" of our tongues? Will you expose your reputation as a divine, by trying to prove, that although we shall be justified by the *works* of our tongues, those of our hands and feet shall never appear for or against our justification? Or will you insinuate that our Lord "recanted" the legal sermons written Matthew v, and xii? If you do, his particular account of the day of judgment, chap. xxv, which strongly confirms and clearly explains the doctrine of our second justification by works, will prove you greatly mistaken, as will also his declaration to St. John, above forty years after, "Behold, I come quickly, and my reward is with me, to give to every man as his work [not faith] shall *be."*

O, if faith alone turn the scale of justifying evidence at the bar of God, how many bold Antinomians will claim relation to Christ, and boast they are interested in his imputed righteousness! How many will say, with the foolish virgins, "Lord! Lord! we are of faith, and Abraham's children. In thy name' we publicly opposed all legal professors, traduced their teachers as enemies to thy *free grace;* and, 'to do thee service,' made it our business to expose the righteousness, and cry down the good works of thy people; therefore 'Lord! Lord! open to us!'" But, alas! far from thanking them for their pains, without looking at their boasted faith, he will dismiss them with a "Depart from me, ye that work *iniquity!" As* if he said —

"Depart, ye that made the doctrine of my atonement a cloak for your sins, or 'sewed' it as a 'pillow under the arms of my people,' to make them sleep in carnal security, when they should have 'worked out their salvation with fear and trembling.' You profess to know me, but I disown you. My sheep I know: them that are mine I know. The seal of my holiness is upon them all: the motto of it, (Let *him that nameth the name of Christ depart from iniquity,*) is deeply engraven on their faithful breasts, — not on yours, ye 'carnal, ye sold under sin!'

"'And why called ye me, LORD! LORD! and did not the things which I said?' Why did you even use my righteousness as a breastplate, to stand it out against the word of my righteousness; and as an engine to break both tables of my law, and batter down my holiness? Your heart condemns you, ye 'sinners in Zion! Ye salt without savour!' Ye believers without charity! And am not I 'greater than your heart?' And 'know' I not 'your works?' Yes, 'I know that the love of God is not in you,' for you despised one of these my brethren. How could you think to deceive me, 'the Searcher of hearts and Trier of reins?' And how did you dare to call yourselves by my name? As if you were my people? my dear people? mine elect? Are not all my peculiar people 'partakers of my holiness,' and' zealous of good works? Have not I chosen to myself the man that is godly,' and protested that 'the ungodly shall not stand in judgment, nor sinners,' though in sheep's clothing, 'in the congregation of the righteous?' And say I not to the wicked, though he should have been one of my people, *Lo ammi, Thou art none of my people now.* 'What hast thou to do with taking my covenant in thy mouth?' You denied me in works, and did not wash your hearts from iniquity in my blood; therefore, according to my word, 'I deny you,' in my turn, 'before my Father and his holy angels.' Perish your hope, ye hypocrites: and utter darkness be your portion, 'ye double minded! Let fearfulness surprise you,' ye tinkling cymbals! Let the fall of your Babels crush you, ye towering professors of my humble faith! Fly, 'ye clouds without water; ye chaff,' fly before the blast of my righteous indignation! 'Ye workers of iniquity! Ye Satans transformed into angels of light! Ye cursed, depart!'"

II. Nor is our Lord singular in his doctrine of justification, or condemnation, by works in the day of judgment. If it is a heresy, the patriarchs, prophets, and apostles are as great heretics as their Master. Enoch, quoted by St. Jude, prophesied, that when the Lord shall "come to execute judgment upon all men," he will "convince the ungodly among them of all their ungodly deeds and hard speeches." This *conviction* will no doubt be in order to condemnation; and this condemnation will not turn upon unbelief, but its effects, "ungodly deeds and hard speeches." Solomon confirms the joint testimony of Enoch and St. Jude, where he says, "He that knoweth the heart, shall render to every man according to his works;" and again, "Know, O young man, that for all these things, for all thy ways, God shall bring thee into judgment."

St. Paul, the great champion for faith, is particularly express upon this anti-Crispian doctrine. "The Lord," says he, "in the day of wrath and revelation of the righteous judgment of God, will render to every man according to his *deeds;* to them that *continue in well doing*," (here is the true perseverance of the saints!) "eternal life! Indignation upon every soul of man that *does* evil, and glory to every man who *worketh* good; for there is no respect of persons with God. We shall all appear before the judgment seat of Christ, that every one may receive the things *done* in the body," not according to that he hath *believed,* whether it be true or false, but "according to that he hath *done,* whether it be good of bad." St. Peter asserts, that the Father, "without respect of persons, judgeth according to every man's *work.*" And St. John, who, next to our Lord, gives us the most particular description of the day of judgment, concludes it by these awful words: "And the dead were judged out of the things written in the books, according to their *works.*" It is not once said, "according to their *faith.*"

Permit me, sir, to sum up all these testimonies in the words of two kings and two apostles. "Let us hear the conclusion of the whole matter," says the king who chose wisdom, "Fear God, and keep his *commandments,* for this is the whole duty of man; for God shall bring every *work* into judgment, whether it be good or evil." "They that have *done* good," says the King who is wisdom itself, (and the Athanasian creed after him,) "shall go into everlasting life; and they that have *not done* good," or "that have done evil, to everlasting punishment." "You see then," and they are the words of St. James, "that a man is justified by his works, and not by faith only." By faith he is justified at his conversion, and when his backslidings are healed. But he is justified by works, (1.) In the hour of trial, as Abraham was when he had offered up Isaac: (2.) In a court of spiritual or civil judicature, as St. Paul at the bar of Festus: and, (3.) Before the judgment seat of Christ, as every one will be whose faith, when he goes hence, is found working by love; for there, says St. Paul, as well as in consistoral courts, "circumcision is nothing, and uncircumcision is nothing, but the keeping of the commandments of God," 1 Corinthians vii, 19.

III. This doctrine is so obvious in the Scriptures, so generally received in all the Churches of Christ, and so deeply engraven on the consciences of sincere professors, that the most eminent ministers of all denominations perpetually allude to it; yourself, sir, not excepted, as I could prove from your sermons if you had not recanted them. How often, for instance, has that great man of God, the truly reverend Mr. Whitefield, said to his immense congregations, "You are warned; I am clear of your blood; I shall rise as a swift witness against you, or you against me, in the terrible day of the Lord! O, remember to clear me then!" or words to that purpose. And is not this just as if he had said, "We shall all be 'justified or condemned in the day of judgment' by what we are now *doing:* I by my preaching, and you by your hearing?"

And say not, sir, that" such expressions were only *flights of oratory,* and prove nothing." If you do, you "touch the apple of God's eye." Mr. Whitefield was not a *flighty orator,* but spoke the words of soberness and truth, with Divine pathos, and floods of tears declarative of his sincerity.

Instead of swelling this letter into a volume, (as I easily might,) by producing quotations from all the sober Puritan divines, who have directly or indirectly asserted a second justification by works, I shall present you only with two passages from Mr. Henry. On Matthew xii, 37, he says, "Consider how strict the judgment will be on account of our words. 'By thy words thou shalt be justified or condemned,' — a common rule in men's judgment, and here applied to God's. Note the constant tenor of our discourse, according as it is gracious or not gracious, will be an evidence for us, or against us, at that day. Those that 'seemed to be religious, but bridled not their tongue,' will then be found to have put a cheat upon themselves with a vain religion. It concerns us to think much of the day of judgment, that it may be a check upon our tongues." And again:

Upon those words, Romans ii, 13, "Not the hearers of the law are just before God, but the doers of the law shall be justified;" the honest commentator says, "The Jewish [Antinomian] doctors bolstered up their followers with an opinion that all that were Jews, [the elect people of God,] how bad soever they lived, should have a glorious place in the world to come. This the apostle here opposes. It was a very great privilege that they had the law, but not a saving privilege, *unless they lived up to the law they had.* We may apply it to the Gospel: it is not hearing, but *doing that will save us,*" John xiii, 17; James i, 22. Who does not perceive that Mr. Henry saw the truth, and spoke it so far as he thought his Calvinistic readers could bear it? Surely, if that good man dared to say *so much,* we, who have "done leaning too much toward Calvinism," should be inexcusable if we did not say *all.*

IV. These testimonies will, I hope, make you weigh with an additional degree of candour the following arguments, which I shall produce as a logician, lest any should be tempted to call me *a bold metaphysician,* or *almost a magician:* —

The voice that St. John heard in heaven did not say, "Blessed are the dead that die in the Lord, for their FAITH follows them:" no, it is *their works.* Faith is the hidden root, hope the rising stalk, and love, together with good works, the nourishing corn: and as the king's agents, who fill a royal granary, do not take in the roots and stalks, but the pure wheat alone; so Christ takes neither faith nor hope into heaven, the former being gloriously absorbed in sight, and the latter in enjoyment.

If I may compare faith and hope to "the chariot of Israel and the courser thereof," they both bring believers to the everlasting doors of. glory, but do not enter in themselves. Not so *love* and *good works;* for love is both the nature and element of saints in glory; and good works necessarily follow them, both in the books of remembrance which shall then be opened, and in the objects and witnesses of those works, who shall then be all present; as it appears from the words of our Lord, "You have done it," or "You have not done it, to one of the least of these my brethren;" and those of St. Paul to his dear converts, "You shall be 'my joy and my crown' in that day." Thus it is evident, that although *faith* is the temporary measure according to which God deals out his mercy and grace in this world, as we may gather from that sweet saying of our Lord, "Be it done to thee according to thy FAITH;" yet *love* and *good works* are the eternal measures, according to which he distributes justification and glory in the world to come. On these observations, I argue,

We shall be justified in the last day by the grace and evidences which shall then remain.

Love and good works, the fruits of faith, shall then remain.

Therefore we shall then be justified by love and good works, that is, not by faith, but by its fruits.

V. This doctrine, so agreeable to Scripture, the sentiments of moderate Calvinists, and the dictates of reason, "recommends" itself likewise "to every man's conscience in the sight of God." Who, but Dr. Crisp, could (after a calm "review of the whole affair,") affirm, that in the day of judgment, if I am accused of being actually a hypocrite, Christ's sincerity will justify me, whether it be found in me or not?

Again: suppose I am charged with being a drunkard, a thief, a whoremonger, a covetous person; or a fretful, impatient, ill-natured man; or, if you please, a proud bigot, an implacable zealot, a malicious persecutor, who, notwithstanding fair appearances of godliness, would raise disturbances even in heaven if I were admitted there: will Christ's sobriety, honesty, chastity, generosity: or will his gentleness, patience, and meekness, justify me from such dreadful charges?. Must not I be found really sober, honest, chaste, and charitable?. Must I not be inherently gentle, meek, and loving? Can we deny this without flying in the face of common sense, breaking the strongest bars of Scriptural truth, and opening the flood gates to the foulest waves of Antinomianism? If we grant it, do we not grant a second justification by works? And does not St. Paul grant, or rather insist upon as much, when he declares, that "without holiness no man shall see the Lord?"

VI. You will probably ask, what advantage the Church will reap from this doctrine of a second justification by works? I answer, that, under God, it will rouse Antinomians out of their carnal security, stir up believers to follow hard after holiness, and reconcile fatal differences among Christians, and seeming contradictions in the Scripture.

1. It will *re-awaken Antinomians*,* who fancy "there is no condemnation to

---

* I beg I may not be understood to level the following paragraphs, or any part of these letters, at my pious *Calvinist* brethren. God knows how deeply I reverence many, who are immovably fixed in what some call "the doctrines of grace;" how gladly (as conscious of their genuine conversion and eminent usefulness) I would lie in the dust at their feet to honour our Lord in his dear members; and how often I have thought it a peculiar infelicity in any degree to dissent from such excellent men, with whom I wanted both to live and die, and with whom I hope soon to reign for ever!

As these *real* children of God lament the bad use Antinomians make of their principles, I hope they will not be offended if I bear my testimony against a growing evil, which they have frequently opposed themselves. While the *Calvinists* guard the foundation against *Pharisees,* for which I return them my sincere thanks, they will, I hope, allow the Remonstrants to guard the superstructure against *Antinomians.* If in doing those good offices to the Church, we find ourselves obliged to bear a little hard upon the peculiar sentiments of our opposite friends, let us do it in such a manner as not to break the bonds of peace and brotherly kindness; so shall our honest reproofs become matter of useful exercise to that "love which thinketh no evil, hopeth all things, rejoiceth even in the *galling* truth," and is "neither quenched by many waters," nor damped by any opposition.

I have long wished to see, on both sides the question about which we unhappily divide, moderate men step out of the unthinking noisy crowd of their party, to look each other lovingly in the face, and to convince the world that with impartial zeal they will guard both the foundation and the superstructure against all adversaries, those of their own party not excepted. Whoever does this *omne tulit punctum,* he is a real friend to both parties, and to the whole Gospel; for he cordially embraces all the people of God, and joins in one blessed medium the seemingly incompatible extremes of Scriptural truth. Ye men of clear heads, honest hearts, and humble loving spirits, nature and grace have formed you on them," whether they "walk after the Spirit" in love, or "after the flesh" in malice; whether they "forsake all" to follow Christ, or like Judas and Sapphira "keep back part" of what should be the Lord's without reserve. Thousands boldly profess justifying faith, and perhaps eternal justification, who reverence the commandments of God just as much as they regard the scriptures quoted in Mr. *Wesley's* Minutes.

Upon their doctrinal systems they raise a tower of presumption, whence they bid defiance both to the law and Gospel of Jesus. His law says, "Love God with all thy heart, and thy neighbour as thyself, that thou mayest live" in glory. "If thou wilt enter into the life" (of glory,) "keep the commandments." But this raises their pity, instead of commanding their respect, and exciting their diligence. "Moses is buried," say they: "we have nothing to do with the law! We are not under the law to Christ! Jesus is not a lawgiver to control, but a Redeemer to save us."

The Gospel cries to them, "Repent and believe!" and just as if God was to be the penitent, believing sinner, they carelessly reply, "The Lord must do all; repentance and faith are his works, and they will be done in the day of his power;" and so without resistance they decently follow the stream of worldly vanities and fleshly lusts. St. Paul cries, "If ye live after the flesh, ye shall die." "We know better," answer they; "there are neither *ifs* nor conditions in all the Gospel." He adds, "This one thing I do, leaving the things that are behind, I press toward the mark for the prize of my high calling in Christ Jesus — the crown of life. Be ye followers of me. Run also the race that is set before you." "What!" say they, "would you have us *run* and *work for life?* Will you always harp upon that legal string, *Do! do!* instead of telling us that we have nothing to do, but to believe that all is done?" St. James cries, "*Show your faith by your works; faith without works is dead* already, much more that which is accompanied by bad works." "What!" say they, "do you think the lamp of faith can be put out as a candle can be extinguished, by not being suffered to shine? We orthodox hold just the contrary: we maintain both that faith can never die, and that living faith is consistent not only with the omission of good works, but with the commission of the most horrid crimes." St. Peter bids them "give all diligence to make their election sure, by adding to their faith virtue," &c. "Legal stuff!" say they, "The covenant is well ordered in all things and sure: neither will our virtue save us, nor our sins damn us." St. John comes next, and declares, "He that sinneth is of the devil." "What!" say they, "do you think to make us converts to Arminianism, by thus insinuating that a man can be a child of God to-day, and a child of the devil to-morrow?" St. Jude advances last, and charges them to "keep themselves in the love of God;" and they supinely reply, "We can do nothing." Beside, "We are as easy and as safe without a frame as with one."

With the seven-fold shield of the Antinomian faith they would fight the twelve apostles round, and come off, in their own imagination, more than conquerors. Nay, were Christ himself to come to them *incognito*, as he did to the

purpose to do the Church this important service. Therefore, without regarding the bigots of your own party, in the name of the loving Jesus, and by his catholic Spirit, give professors public lessons of *moderation* and *consistence*, and permit me to learn those rare virtues with thousands at your feet.

disciples that went to Emmaus, and say, "Be ye perfect, as your Father who is in heaven is perfect:" it would be well if, while they measured him from head to foot with looks of pity or surprise, some were not bold enough to say with a sneer, "You are a perfectionist, it seems, a follower of poor John Wesley! are you? For our part, we are for Christ and free grace, but John Wesley and you are for perfection and free will."

Now, sir, if any doctrine, humanly speaking, can rescue these mistaken persons out of so dreadful a snare, it is that which I contend for. Antinomian dreams vanish before it, as the noxious damps of the night before the rising sun. St. Paul, if they would but hear him *out*, with this one saying, as with a thousand rams, would demolish all their Babels: "Circumcision is nothing, uncircumcision is nothing, but the keeping of the commandments of God:" or, to speak agreeable to our times, "Before the tribunal of Christ, forms of godliness, Calvinian and Arminian notions *are nothing*: confessions of faith and recantations of error, past manifestations and former experiences 'are nothing, but the keeping of the commandments of God;'" the very thing which Antinomians ridicule or neglect!

2. This doctrine is not less proper to *animate feeble believers in their pursuit of holiness*. O if it were clearly preached and steadily believed, — if we were fully persuaded, we shall soon "appear before the judgment seat of Christ," to answer for every thought, word, and work, for every business we enter upon, every sum of money we lay out, every meal we eat, every pleasure we take, every affliction we endure, every hour we spend, every idle word we speak, yea, and every temper we secretly indulge, — if we knew we shall certainly "give account" of all the chapters we read, of all the prayers we offer, all the sermons we hear or preach, all the sacraments we receive; of all the motions of Divine grace, all the beams of heavenly light, all the breathings of the Spirit, all the invitations of Christ, all the drawings of the Father, reproofs of our friends, and checks of our own consciences, — and if we were deeply conscious, that every neglect of duty will rob us of a degree of glory, and every wilful sin of a jewel in our crown, if not of our crown itself; what humble, watchful, holy, heavenly persons should we be! How serious and self denying! How diligent and faithful! In a word, how angelical and divine, "in all manner of conversation!"

Did the *woman,* the professing Church, cordially embrace this doctrine, she would no more stay "in the wilderness, *idly* talking of her beloved;" but actually "leaning upon him," she would "come out of it," in the sight of all her enemies. No more wrapped up in the showy cloud of ideal perfection or imaginary righteousness, and casting away her cold garments, her moonlike changes of merely doctrinal apparel, she would shine with the dazzling glory of her Lord; she would burn with the hallowing fires of his love: once more she would be "clothed with the sun, and have the moon under her feet!"

Ye lukewarm talkers of Jesus' ardent love, if you were deeply conscious that nothing but love shall enter heaven, instead of judging of your growth in grace by the warmth with which you espouse the tenets of Calvin or Arminius, would you not instantly try your state by the thirteenth chapter of the first Epistle to the Corinthians, and by our Lord's alarming messages to the falling or fallen Churches of Asia? Springing out of your Laodicean indifference, would you not

earnestly pray for the "faith of the Gospel, the faith that works by *burning* love?"
If the fire be kindled, would you not be afraid of putting it out by "quenching the
Spirit?" Would you not even dread "grieving" him, lest your love should grow
cold? Far from accounting the "shedding abroad of the love of God in your
hearts" an unnecessary frame, would you not be "straitened" till you were
baptized, every one of you, with "the Holy Ghost and with fire?"

Ye who hold the doctrine of perfection without "going on to
perfection," and ye who explode it as a pernicious delusion, and inconsistently
publish hymns of solemn prayer for it, how would you agree, from the bottom of
your reawakened hearts, to sing together, in days of peace and social worship, as
you have carelessly sung asunder,

> *O for a heart to praise our God!*
> *A heart from sin set free!*
> *A heart in every thought renew'd,*
> *And fill'd with love divine!*
> Perfect, *and right, and pure, and good,*
> *A copy, Lord, of thine. —*
> *Bigotry from us remove,*
> Perfect *all our souls in love, &c.*

O ye halcyon days! Ye days of brotherly love and genuine holiness! if
you appeared to pacify and gladden our distracted Jerusalem, how soon would
practical Christianity emerge from under the frothy billows of Antinomianism,
and the proud waves of Pharisaism, which continually break against each other,
and openly "foam out their own shame!" "What carefulness" would *godly sorrow*
work in us all! "What clearing of ourselves," by casting away our dearest idols!
"What indignation" against our former lukewarmness! "What fear" of offending
either God or man! "What vehement desire" after the full image of Christ! "What
zeal" for his glory! And "what revenge" of our sins! "In all things we should
approve ourselves," for the time to come, "to be clear" from the Antinomian
delusion. Then would we see, what has seldom been seen in our age, distinct (not
opposed) societies of meek professors of the *common faith* walking in humble love,
and supporting each other with cheerful readiness, like different battalions of the
same invincible army. And if ever we perceived any contention among them, it
would be only about the lowest place and the most dangerous post. Instead of
"striving for mastery," they would strive only who should stand truest to the
standard of the cross, and best answer the neglected motto of the primitive
Christians: *Non magna loquimur sed vivimus;* "Our religion does not consist in high
words, but in good works."

3. I observed that this doctrine will likewise *reconcile seeming contradictions in
the Scriptures, and fatal differences among Christians.* Take one instance of the former:
What can those who reject a second justification by works make of the solemn
words of our Lord, already quoted, "By thy words thou shalt be justified, *or* by
thy words thou shalt be condemned?" Matthew xii, 37. And by what art can they
possibly reconcile them with St. Paul's assertions, Romans iv, 5, "To him that
worketh not, but believeth on him that justifieth the ungodly, his faith is imputed

to him for righteousness?" and Romans v, 1, "Being justified by faith, we have peace with God through our Lord Jesus Christ." Accept an example of the latter. In the Antinomian days of Dr. Crisp arose the honest people we call Quakers. Shocked at the general abuse of the doctrine of *justification by faith*, they rashly inferred it never could be from God; and seeing none "shall be justified *in glory* but the doers of the law," they hastily concluded there is but one justification, namely, the being made inherently just, or the being sanctified, and then declared holy. Admit our doctrine, and you have both parts of the truth, — that which the Antinomians hold against the Quakers, and that which the Quakers maintain against the Antinomians. Each alone is dangerous; both together mutually defend each other, and make up the Scriptural doctrine of justification, which is invincibly guarded on the one hand by FAITH against Pharisees, and on the other by WORKS against Antinomians. Reader, may both be thy portion! So shalt thou be eternally reinstated both in the *favour* and *image* of God.

VI. But while I enumerate the benefits which the Church will reap from a *practical* knowledge of our second justification by works, an honest Protestant, who has more zeal for, than acquaintance with the truth, advances, with his heart full of holy indignation, and his mouth of objections, which he says are unanswerable. Let us consider them one by one.

FIRST OBJECTION. "Your Popish, antichristian doctrine I abhor, and could even burn at a stake as a witness against it. Away with your new-fangled Arminian tenets! I am for old Christianity; and with St. Paul, 'determined to know nothing *for justification* but Christ, and him crucified.'"

ANSWER. Do you, indeed? Then I am sure you will not deny both Jesus Christ and St. Paul in this old Christian doctrine; for Christ says, "By thy words shalt thou be justified;" and St. Paul declares, "Not the hearers, but the doers of the law (of Christ) shall be justified." Alas, how often are those who say they "will know" and have "nothing but Christ," the first to "set him at nought" as a prophet, by railing at his holy doctrine: or to reject him as a king, by trampling upon his royal proclamations! But "I wot that through ignorance they do it, as do their rulers."

SECOND OBJECTION. "This legal doctrine robs God's dear children of their comforts and Gospel liberty, binds Moses' intolerable burden upon their free shoulders, and 'entangles them again in the *galling* yoke of bondage.'"

ANSWER. If God's dear children have got into a false liberty of doing the devil's works, either by "not going into the vineyard" when they have said, "Lord, I go," or by "beating their fellow servants" there, instead of working with them; the sooner they are robbed of it the better: for if they continue thus free, they will ere long be "bound hand and foot, and cast into outer darkness." It is the very spirit of Antinomianism to represent God's "commandments as grievous," and the keeping of his law "as bondage." Not so the dutiful children of God: "Their hearts" are never so much "at liberty," as when they "run the way of his commandments, and so fulfil the law of Christ." Keep them from obedience, and you keep them "in the snare of the devil, promising liberty *to others*, while they themselves are the servants of corruption."

Again: you confound the heavy yoke of the circumcision and ceremonial bondage, with which the Galatians once entangled themselves, with the "easy yoke of Jesus Christ." The former was intolerable, the latter is so "light a burden," that the only way to "find rest unto our souls is to take it upon us." St. Paul calls a dear brother his "yoke fellow." You know the word BELIAL in the original signifies "without yoke." They are *sons of Belial* who shake off the Lord's yoke; and though they should boast of their *election* as much as the Jews did, Christ himself will say concerning them, "Those mine enemies that *refused my yoke,* and would not that I should reign over them, bring hither, and slay them before me!" So inexpressibly dreadful is the end of lawless liberty!

THIRD OBJECTION. "Your doctrine is the damnable error of the Galatians, who madly left Mount Sion for Mount Sinai, made Christ the *Alpha,* and not the *Omega,* and after ' having begun in the Spirit *would be* made perfect by the flesh.' This is *the other Gospel* which St. Paul thought so diametrically contrary to his own, that he wished the teachers of it, though they were 'angels of God,' might be even 'accursed and cut off.'"

ANSWER. You are under a capital mistake: St. Paul could never be so wild as to curse himself, anathematize St. James, and wish the Messiah to be again cut off: for he himself taught the Romans, that "the doers of the law shall be justified." St. James evidently maintains a justification by works; and our Lord expressly says, "By thy words thou shalt be justified." Again' the apostle, if he had foreseen how his Epistle to the Galatians would be abused to Antinomian purposes, gives us in it the most powerful antidotes against that poison. Take two or three instances. (1.) He exhorts his fallen converts to the fulfilling of all the law: "Love one another," says he, "for all the law is fulfilled in this one word, *Thou shalt love thy neighbour as thyself,*" because none can "love his neighbour as himself," but he that: "loves God with all his heart." How different is this doctrine from the bold Antinomian cry, "We have nothing to do with the law!" (2.) He enumerates the works of the flesh, "adultery, hatred, variance, wrath, strife, envyings, heresies, &c; of which," says he, "I tell you before, as I have told you in time past, that they who do such things" shall not be justified in the day of judgment, or, which is the same thing, "shall not inherit the kingdom of God." How different a Gospel is this from that which insinuates, "impenitent adulterers may be dear children of God, even while such, and in a very safe state, and quite sure of glory!" And (3.) As if this awful warning were not enough, he point blank cautions his readers against the Crispian error: "Be not deceived," says he, "whatever a MAN (not *whatever* CHRIST) soweth, that shall he also reap. He that soweth to the flesh shall reap corruption, and he that soweth to the Spirit shall reap life everlasting." How amazingly strong therefore must your prejudice be, which makes you produce this epistle to thrust love and good works out of the important place allotted them in all the word of God! And no where more than in this very epistle!

FOURTH OBJECTION. "Notwithstanding all you say, I am persuaded you are in the dreadful heresy of the Galatians; for they were, like you, for 'justification by the works of the law;' and St. Paul resolutely maintained against them the fundamental doctrine of *justification by faith.*"

ANSWER. If you once read over the Epistle to the Galatians without prejudice, and without comment, you will see, that (1.) They had returned "to the beggarly elements of this world," by superstitiously "observing days, months, times, and years." (2.) Imagining they "could not be saved except they were circumcised," they submitted even to that grievous and bloody injunction. (3.) Exact in their useless ceremonies, and fondly hoping to be justified by their partial observance of Moses' law, they well nigh forgot the merits of Christ, and openly trampled upon his law, and "walked after the flesh." Stirred up to contentious zeal by their new teachers, they despised the old apostle's ministry, hated his person, and "devoured one another." In short, they trusted partly in the merit of their superstitious performances, and partly in Christ's merits; and on this preposterous foundation they "built the hay" of Jewish ceremonies, and "the stubble" of fleshly lusts. With great propriety, therefore, the apostle called them back, with sharpness, to the only sure foundation, the merits of Jesus Christ; and wanted them to "build upon it gold and precious stones," all the works of piety and mercy that spring from "faith working by love."

Now which of these errors do we hold? Do we not preach present justification *by faith,* and justification at the bar of God *according to what a man soweth,* the very doctrine of this epistle? And do we not "secure the foundation," by insisting that both these justifications are equally through *the merits of Christ,* though the second, as our Church intimates in her twelfth article, is by the evidence of works?

Will you bear with me if I tell you my thoughts? We are all in general condemned by the Epistle to the Galatians, for we have too much dependence on our forms of piety, speculative knowledge, or past experience; and too little heart-felt confidence in the merits of Christ: "We sow *too little* to the Spirit, and *too much* to the flesh." But those, in the next place, are peculiarly reproved by it, who "return to the beggarly elements," the idle ways and vain fashions "of this world." Those who make as much ado about the beggarly element of water, about baptizing infants and dipping adults, as "the troublers" of the Church of Galatia did about circumcising their converts, "that they might glory in their flesh." Those who "zealously affect *others,* but not well:" those who now despise their spiritual fathers," whom they *once* received as angels of God:" those who "turn our enemies when we tell them the truth," who "heap to themselves" teachers, smoother than the evangelically legal apostle, and would call us blind if we said, as he does, "Let every man prove his own work, and then shall he have rejoicing in himself alone, and not in another," Galatians 6:4. Those who plead for spiritual bondage while they talk of Gospel liberty, and affirm "that the son of the bondwoman" shall always live "with the son of the free;" that sin can never be cast out of the heart of believers, and that Christ and corruption shall always dwell together in this world. And, lastly, those who say there is no "falling away from grace," when they are already fallen like the Galatians, and boast of their stability chiefly because they are ignorant of their fall!

FIFTH OBJECTION. "However, your Pharisaic doctrine flatly contradicts the Gospel summed up by our Lord, Mark 16:16, 'He that believeth shall be saved, and he that believeth not shall be damned.' Here is not one word about works. All turns upon faith."

ANSWER. Instead of throwing such hints, you might as well speak out at once, and say that Christ in these words flatly contradicts what he had said, Matthew xii, 37, "By thy words thou shalt be justified, or by thy words thou shalt be condemned." But drop your prejudices, and you will see that the contradiction is only in your own ideas. We steadily assert, as our Lord, that "he who believeth," or "endureth unto the end believing," (for the word implies both the reality and the continuance of the action,) "shall *infallibly* be saved;" because faith, which continues living, "works" to the last" by love" and good works, which will infallibly justify us in the day of judgment. For when faith is no more, love and good works will evidence, (1.) That we were grafted into Christ by true faith' (2.) That we did not "make shipwreck of the faith;" that we were not "taken away as branches in him which bear not fruit, *but* abode fruitful branches in the true Vine." And (3.) That we are still in him by HOLY LOVE, the precious and eternal fruit of true persevering faith. How bad is that cause which must support itself by charging an imaginary contradiction upon the Wisdom of God, Jesus Christ himself!*

SIXTH OBJECTION. "Your doctrine exalts man, and by giving him room to boast, robs Christ of the glory of his grace. 'The top stone' is no more ' brought forth with shouting, Grace! Grace!' but, Works! Works! ' unto it!' And

---

* This is frequently the stratagem of those who have no arguments to produce. I bore my testimony against it in the Vindication, and flattered myself that serious writers would be less forward to oppose the truth, and expose the ministers of Christ by that injudicious way of discussing controverted points. Notwithstanding this, I have before me a little pamphlet, in which the editor endeavours to *answer* Mr. Wesley's *Minutes,* by extracting from his writings passages supposed to stand in direct opposition to the Minutes. Hence, in a burlesque upon the *Declaration,* he tries to represent Mr. Wesley as a knave.

I would just observe upon that performance, (1.) That by this method of raising dust, and avoiding to reason the case fairly, every malicious infidel may blind injudicious readers, and make triumphing scoffers cry out, Jesus against Christ! Saul against St. Paul! or John the divine against John the evangelist! as well as Wesley against John! and John against Wesley. (2.) Mr. Wesley having acknowledged, in the beginning of the Minutes, he "had leaned too much toward Calvinism," we may naturally expect to meet in his voluminous writings with a few expressions that look a little toward Antinomianism: and with some paragraphs which (when detached from the context, and not considered as spoken to deep mourners in Zion, or to souls of undoubted sincerity,) seem directly to favour the delusion of the present times. (3.) This may be easily accounted for without flying to the charges of knavery or contradiction. When after working long without cheering light we discover the ravishing day of luminous faith, we are all apt, in the sincerity of our hearts, to speak almost as unguardedly of works as Luther did; but when the fire of Antinomian temptations has frequently burned us, and consumed thousands around us, we justly dread it at last; and ceasing to lean toward Crisp's divinity, we return to St. James, St. John, and St. Jude, and to the latter part of St. Paul's Epistles which we too often overlooked, and to which hardly two ministers did, upon the whole, ever do more justice than Mr. Baxter and Mr. Wesley. (4.) A man who gives to different people, or to the same people at different times, directly contrary directions, does not always contradict himself. I have a fever, and my physician, under God, restores me to health by cooling medicines; by and by I am afflicted with the cold rheumatism, and he prescribes fomentations and warming remedies, but my injudicious apothecary opposes him, under the pretence that he goes by no *certain rule,* and *grossly contradicts himself.* Let us apply this to Mr. Wesley and the Versifier, remembering there is less difference between a burning fever and a cold rheumatism, than between the case of the trifling Antinomian and that of the dejected penitent. (5.) Whoever considers without prejudice what our satiric poet produces as *contradictions,* will find some of them not so much as amount to an *opposition,* and that most of them do not *seem* so contradictory as numbers of propositions that might be extracted from the oracles of God. If the editor of the *Answer to the Minutes* will compare this note with the [28th] page of the Vindication, I hope he will find his performance answered, his direct attack upon the Minutes frustrated, and Mr. Wesley's honesty fully vindicated.

the burden of the song in heaven will be, — Salvation to our works! and no more; Salvation to the Lamb!"

ANSWER. I no less approve your godly jealousy, than I wonder at your groundless fears. To calm them, permit me once more to observe, (1.) That this doctrine is Christ's, who would not be so unwise as to side with our self-righteous pride, and teach us to rob him of his own glory. It is absurd to suppose Christ would be thus against Christ, for even Satan is too wise "to be against Satan." (2.) Upon our plan, as well as upon Crisp's scheme, free grace has absolutely *all the glory*. The love and good works by which we shall be justified in the day of judgment, are the fruits of faith, and "faith is the gift of God." Christ is the great object of faith, the Holy Ghost, called the Spirit of faith, the power of believing, the means, opportunities, and will to use that power, are all the rich presents of God's free grace. All our sins, together with the imperfections of our works, are mercifully forgiven through the blood and righteousness of Christ: our persons and services are graciously accepted merely for his sake, and through his merits: and if rewards are granted us according to the fruits of righteousness we bear, it is not because *we* are profitable to God, but because the meritorious sap of the Root of David produces those fruits, and the meritorious beams of the Sun of righteousness ripen them. Thus you see, that, which way soever you look at our justification, God has all the glory of it, but that of turning moral agents into mere machines, — a glory which, we apprehend, God does no more claim than you do that of turning your coach horses into hobby horses, and your servants into puppets.

If *faith* on earth gives Christ the glory of all our salvation, you need not fear that *love* (a superior grace) will rob him in heaven: for "love is not puffed up, seeketh not her own, and does not behave herself unseemly" toward a beggar on earth; much less will she do so toward the Lord of glory, when she has attained the zenith of heavenly perfection. Away then with all the imaginary lions you place in your way to truth! Notwithstanding Crisp's prohibitions, like the Bereans, receive Christ in his holy doctrine, and be persuaded that in the last day you will shout as loud as the honest doctor, *Grace! Grace! and Salvation to the Lamb!* Without suggesting, with him, to those on the left hand, the blasphemous shouts of *Partiality! Hypocrisy! Barbarity! and damnation to the Lamb!* Thus shall you have all *the free grace* he justly boasts of, without any of his horrid reprobating doctrine.

SEVENTH OBJECTION. "How will the converted thief, that did no good works, be justified by works?"

ANSWER. (1.) We mean by WORKS "the whole of our inward tempers and outward behaviour;" and how do you know *the outward behaviour* of the converted thief? Did not his reproofs, exhortations, prayers, patience, and resignation, evidence the liveliness of his faith, as there was time and opportunity? (2.) Can you suppose his *inward temper* was not love to God and man? Could he go into paradise without being born again? Or could he be born again and not love? Is it not said, "He that loveth is born of God;" consequently, he that is born of God loveth? Again does not he who "loveth, fulfil all the law," and do, as says Augustine, all good works in one? And is not "the fulfilling of the law of Christ" work enough to justify the converted thief by that law?

EIGHTH OBJECTION. "You say, that your doctrine 'will make us zealous of good works;' but I fully discharge it from that office: for 'the love of Christ constraineth us to abound in every good word and work.'"

ANSWER. (1.) St. Paul, who spoke those words with more feeling than you, thought the contrary; as well as his blessed Master, or they would never have taught this doctrine. You do not, I fear, evidence the temper of *a babe* when you are so exceedingly" wise above what" Christ preached, and "prudent above what" the apostle "wrote." (2.) If the love of Christ in professors is so *constraining* as you say, why, do good works and good tempers bear so little proportion to the great talk we hear of its irresistible efficacy? And why do those who have tasted it "return to sin as dogs to their vomit?" Why can they even curse, swear, and get drunk? Be guilty of idolatry, murder, and incest? (3.) If love alone is always sufficient, why did our Lord work upon his disciples' hearts, by the hope of "thrones and a kingdom," and by the fear of a "worm that dieth not, and a fire that is not quenched?" Why does the apostle stir up believers to "serve the Lord with godly fear," by the consideration that "he is a consuming fire?" Illustrating his assertion by this awful warning, "If they (Korah and his company) escaped not," but were consumed by fire from heaven, because they "refused him (Moses) that spake on earth; much more shall not we escape, if we turn away from him that speaketh from heaven!" Why did St. Paul himself, who, no doubt, understood the Gospel as well as Crisp and Saltmarsh, "run a race for an incorruptible crown, and keep his body under, LEST he himself should be a castaway?" O ye *orthodox* divines, and thou ludicrous versifier of an awful declaration! instead of attempting to set St. Paul against St. Paul, and to oppose Wesley to Wesley, answer these Scriptural questions; and if you cannot do it without betraying *heterodoxy,* for the Lord's sake, for the sake of thousands in Israel, keep no more from the feeble of the flock those necessary helps which the "very chief of the apostles," evangelical Paul, without any of your Crispian refinements, continually recommended to others, and daily used himself. And for your own souls' sake, never more prostitute these awful words, "The love of Christ constraineth us;" never more apply them to yourselves, while you refuse to treat the most venerable ambassador of Christ, I shall not say, *with respected love,* but *with common decency.*

NINTH OBJECTION. "All the formal and Pharisaical ministers, who are sworn enemies to Christ and the Gospel of his grace, preach your legal doctrine *of justification by works in the day of judgment.*"

ANSWER. And what do you infer from it? That the doctrine is false? If the inference be just, it will follow there is neither heaven nor hell; for they publicly maintain the existence of both. But suppose they now and then preach our doctrine without zeal, without living according to it, or without previously preaching the fall, and a present *justification by faith in Christ,* productive of peace and power, what can be expected from it? Would not the doctrine of the atonement itself be totally useless, if it were preached under such disadvantages? The truth is, such ministers are only for the roof, and you, it seems, only for the foundation. But a roof, unsupported by solid walls, crushes to death; and a foundation without a roof is not much better than the open air. Therefore, "wise master builders," like St. Paul, are for having both in their proper places. Like him, when the foundation is. well laid, "leaving the first principles of the doctrine of Christ, they go on to perfection;" nor will they forget, as they work out their salvation, to shout, Grace! Grace! to the last slate that covers in the building; or to "the top stone," the key that binds the solid arch.

TENTH OBJECTION. "Should I receive and avow such a doctrine, the generality of professors would rise against me; and while the warmest would call me a *Papist, an antichrist,* and what not; my dearest Christian friends would pity me as an unawakened Pharisee, and fear me as a blind legalist."

ANSWER. "Rejoice, and be exceeding glad when all men (the godly not excepted) shall say all manner of evil of you falsely for Christ's sake," — for preferring Christ's holy doctrine to the loose tenets of Dr. Crisp: and remember, that, in our Antinomian days, it is as great an honour to be called *legal* by fashionable professors, as to be branded with the name of *Methodist* by the sots who glory in their shame.

VII. As I would hope my objector is either satisfied or silenced, before I conclude, permit me a moment, Rev. sir, to consider the two important objections which you directly, or indirectly, make in your Narrative.

1. "I should tremble," say you, (page 21,) "lest some bold metaphysician should affirm, that a second justification by works is quite consistent with what is contained in Mr. Wesley's declaration; but that it is expressed in such *strong and absolute terms* as must *for ever* put the most exquisite refinements of metaphysical distinctions *at defiance."*

ANSWER. "For ever at *defiance!"* You surprise me, sir: I, who am as perfect a stranger to *"exquisite refinements"* as to Dr. Crisp's *eternal justification,* defy you (pardon a *bold* expression to a *bold metaphysician*) ever to produce out of Mr. Wesley's declaration, I shall not say (as you do) "strong and absolute terms," but one single word or tittle denying or excluding a second justification by works; and I appeal both to your second thoughts and to the unprejudiced world, whether these three propositions of the declaration, "We have no trust, or confidence, but in the alone merits of Christ *for* justification in the day of judgment. Works have no part in *meriting or purchasing* our justification from first to last, *either in whole or in part.* He is not a real Christian believer, (and consequently cannot be saved,) *who does not good works* where there is time and opportunity." I appeal to the unprejudiced world, whether these three propositions are not highly consistent with this assertion of our Lord, "By thy words thou shalt be justified," that is, "although from first to last the merits of my life and death purchase, or deserve, thy justification; yet in the day of judgment thou shalt be justified by thy works; that is, thy justification, which is purchased by my *merits,* will entirely turn upon the *evidence* of thy works, according to the time and opportunity thou hast to do them."

Who does not see, that, "to be justified by the *evidence* of works," and "to be justified by the *merit* of works," are no more phrases of the same import than *minutes* and *heresy* are words of the same signification? The latter proposition contains the error strongly guarded against, both in the declaration and the Minutes: the former contains an evangelical doctrine, as agreeable to the declaration and Minutes as to the Scriptures; a doctrine of which we were too sparing when we "leaned too much toward Calvinism," but to which, after the example of Mr. Wesley, we are now determined to do justice.

Whosoever is "ashamed of Christ's words," we will proclaim them to the world. Both from our pulpits and the press we will say, "By thy words thou shalt be condemned." Yea, "Whoever shall say to his brother, Thou fool! shall be in danger of hell fire; and whosoever maketh a lie shall have his part in the lake which burneth with fire and brimstone;" for as "with the heart man believeth unto righteousness," or disbelieveth to unrighteousness, so "with the mouth confession is made to salvation," or "hard speeches" are uttered to "damnation." Reserve, therefore, Rev. sir, our public praises for a more proper occasion than that which caused their breaking out in your Narrative. "Blessed be God!" say you, (page 16,)" Mr. Wesley and fifty-three of his preachers do not agree with Mr. Olivers in the material article of a *second justification by works*." Indeed, sir, you are greatly mistaken, for we *do* agree with him; and shall continue so to do, till you have proved he does not agree with Jesus Christ, or that our doctrine is not perfectly consistent both with the Scriptures and the declaration.

2. Your second objection is not so formal as the first; it must be made up of broad hints scattered through your Narrative, and they amount to this: "Your pretended difference between justification by the *merit* of works, by the *evidence* of works, and between a first and a second justification, is founded upon the *subtilties of metaphysical distinctions*. If what you say wears the aspect of truth, it is because *you give a new turn to error, by the almost magical power of metaphysical distinctions*," pages 16, 20, 21.

Give me leave, sir, to answer this objection by two appeals, one to the most ignorant collier in my parish, and the other to your own sensible child; and if they can at once understand my meaning, you will see that my "metaphysical distinctions," as you are pleased to call them, are nothing but *the dictates of common sense*. I begin with the collier.

Thomas, I stand here before the judge, accused of having robbed the Rev. Mr. Shirley, near Bath, last month, on such an evening; can you speak a word for me? Thomas turns to the judge, and says, "Please your honour, the accusation is false, for our parson was in Madeley Wood; and I can make oath of it, for he even reproved me for swearing at our pit's mouth that very evening." By his evidence, the judge acquits me. Now, sir, ask cursing Tom whether I am acquitted and *justified*, by his *merits*, or by the simple *evidence* he has given, and he will tell you, "Ay, to be sure by the *evidence;* though I am no scholar, I know very well that if our Methodist parson is not hanged, it is none of my deservings." Thus, sir, an ignorant collier, as great a stranger to *your metaphysics* as you are to *his mandrel*, discovers at once a material difference between justification by the *evidence*, and justification by the *merits* of a witness.

My second appeal is to your sensible child. By a plain comparison I hope to make him at once understand, both the difference there is between our first and second justification, and the propriety of that difference. The lovely boy is old enough, I suppose, to follow the gardener and me to yonder nursery. Having shown him the operation of *grafting*, and pointing at the crab tree newly grafted, "My dear child," would I say, "though hitherto this tree has produced nothing but crabs, yet by the skill of the gardener, who has just fixed in it that good little branch, it is now made an *apple tree:* I *justify* and warrant it such. (Here is an emblem of our *first* justification *by faith!*) In three or four years, if we live, we will come again and see it: if it thrives and 'bears fruit,' *well;* we shall then by that mark justify it a second time, we shall declare that it is a *good* apple tree indeed, and fit to be transplanted from this wild nursery into a delightful orchard. But if we find that the old crab stock, instead of nourishing the graft, spends all its sap in producing wild shoots and sour crabs; or if it is a ' tree whose fruit withereth, without fruit, twice dead, (dead in the graft and in the stock,) plucked up by the root,' or quite cankered, far from declaring 'it a good tree,' we shall pass sentence of condemnation upon it, and say, 'Cut it down; why cumbereth it the ground? For every tree that bringeth not forth good fruit is hewn down and cast into the fire.'" Here is an emblem of our *second* justification *by works,* or of the condemnation that will infallibly overtake those Laodicean professors and wretched apostates, whose faith is not shown by works, where there is time and opportunity.

Instead of offering an insult to your superior understanding, in attempting to explain by "metaphysical distinctions," what I suppose your sensible child has already understood by the help of a grafting knife, I shall leave you to consider whether Scripture, reason, and candour do not join their influence to make you acknowledge, at least, in the court of your own conscience, that you have put a wrong construction upon Mr. Wesley's declaration as upon his Minutes, and by that mean inadvertently given another *rash* touch to the ark of practical religion, and to the character of one of the greatest ministers in the world.

I am, with due respect, Hon. and Rev. sir, your obedient servant, in the bond of the practical Gospel of Christ,

THE VINDICATOR.

LETTER II.

HONOURED AND REVEREND SIR, — Having endeavoured in my last to do justice to the practical Gospel of Christ, and Mr. Wesley's awful declarations, I pass on to the other mistakes of your Narrative. That which strikes me next is "the public recantation of your *useful* sermons, in the face of the whole world." (Page 22.)

1. O! sir, what have you done! Do you not know that your sermons contain not only the legally evangelical doctrine of the Minutes, but likewise all the doctrine which moderate Calvinists esteem as the marrow of the Gospel! And shall all be treated alike? "Wilt thou also destroy the righteous with the wicked? That be far from thee to do after this manner!" Thus did a good man formerly plead the cause of a *wicked* city, and thus I plead that of your *good* sermons, those

twelve valuable, though unripe fruits of your ministerial labours. Upon this plea the infamous city would have been spared, had only "ten" good men been found in it. Now, sir, spare a valuable book for the sake of a "thousand" excellent things it contains. But if you are inflexible, and still wish it "burned," imitate, at least, the kind angels who sent Lot out of the fiery overthrow, and except all the evangelical pages of the unfortunate volume.

Were it not ridiculous to compare wars which cost us only a little ink, and our friends a few pence, to those which cost armies their blood, and kingdoms their treasures, I would be tempted to say to you, Imitate the Dutch in their last effort to balance the victory, and secure the field. When they are pressed by the French, rather than yield, they break their dykes, let in the sea upon themselves, and lay all their fine gardens and rich pastures under water: but before they have recourse to that strange expedient, they prudently save all the valuable goods they can. Why should you not follow them in their prudential care, as you seem to do in their bold stratagem? When you publicly lay your useful book under the bitter waters of an anathema, why do you save absolutely nothing? Why must Gospel truths, more precious than the wealth of Holland and the gold of Ophir, lie for ever under the severe scourge of your recantation? Suppose you had "recanted" your third sermon, *The way to eternal life*, in opposition to mysticism; and "burned" the fourth, *Salvation by Christ for Jews and Gentiles*, in honour of Calvinism, could you not have spared the rest?

If you say, you may do what you please with your own; I answer, Your book, publicly exposed to sale, and bought perhaps by thousands, is, in one sense, no more your own; it belongs to the purchasers, before whom you lay, I fear, a dangerous example: for when they shall hear that the author has "publicly recanted it in the face of the whole world," it will be a temptation to them to slight the Gospel it contains, and perhaps to ridicule it "in the face of the whole world."

You add, "It savours too strongly of mysticism." Some passages (are a little tainted with Mr. Law's capital error, and you might have pointed them out: but if you think mysticism is intrinsically bad, you are under a mistake. One of the greatest Mystics, next to Solomon, is Thomas a Kempis, and a few errors excepted, I would no more burn his" Imitation of Jesus Christ," than *the Song of Solomon*, and Mr. Romaine's edifying" Paraphrase of the 107th Psalm."

You urge also, your sermons "savour too much of *free will*." Alas! sir, can you recant "free will?" Was not your will as *free* when you recanted your sermons as when you composed them? Is there not as much free will expressed in this one line of the Gospel as in all your sermons, "I would have gathered you, and ye would not?" Do not "free-will offerings, with a holy worship," delight the Lord more than *forced*, and, if I may be allowed the expression, *bond-will* services? Is not the free will with which the martyrs went to the stake as worthy of our highest admiration, as the mysticism of the Canticles is of our deepest attention? If all that strongly "savours of free will" must be "burned," ye heavens! what Smithfield work will there be in your lucid plains! Wo to saints! Wo to angels! for they are all free-willing beings — all full of free will. Nor can you deny it, unless you suppose they are *bound* by irresistible decrees, as the heathens fancied their deities were *hampered* with the adamantine chains of an imaginary something they called "fate:" witness their *Fata vetant,* and *Fata jubent,* and *ineluctabile Fatum.*

Pardon, Rev. sir, the oddity of these exclamations. I am so grieved at the great advantage we give infidels against the Gospel, by making it ridiculous, that I could try even the method of Horace, to bring my friends back from the fashionable refinements of Crisp, to the plain truth as it is in Jesus.

Ridiculum acri
Fortius ac melius stultas plerumque secat res.

Nor is this the only bad tendency of your new doctrine: for by exploding the freedom of the will, you rob us of free agency. You afford the wicked, who determine to continue in sin, the best excuse in the world to do it without either shame or remorse; you make us mere machines, and indirectly reflect upon the wisdom of our Lord, for saying to a set of Jewish machines, "I would, and ye would not." But what is still more deplorable, you inadvertently represent it an unwise thing in God to judge the world in righteousness; and your *new* glass shows his vindictive justice in the same unfavourable light, in which England saw two years ago the behaviour of a great monarch, who was exposed in the public papers, for unmercifully cutting with a whip, and tearing with spurs, the horses worked in a tapestry of his royal apartment, because they did not prance and gallop at his nod.

If a commendable, but immoderate fear of Pelagius' doctrine drove you into that of Augustine, the oracle of all the Dominicans, Thomists, Jansenists, and all other Roman Catholic predestinarians, you need not go so far beyond him as to recant all your sermons, because you mention perhaps three or four times, the freedom of our will, in the whole volume. "Let no one," says judicious Melancthon, "be offended at the words free will, (*liberum arbitrium,*) for St. Augustine himself uses it in many volumes, and that almost in every page, even to the surfeit of the reader."

The most ingenious Calvinist that ever wrote against free will is, I think, Mr. Edwards, of New-England. And his fine system turns upon a comparison by which it may be overturned, and the freedom of the will demonstrated.

The will, says he, (if I remember right,) is like an even balance which can never turn without a weight, and must *necessarily* turn with one. But whence comes the weight that *necessarily* turns it? From the understanding, answers he; the last dictate of the understanding necessarily turns the will. And is the understanding also necessarily determined? Yes, by the effect which the objects around us necessarily have upon us, and by the circumstances in which we necessarily find ourselves; so that from first to last, our tempers, words, and actions, necessarily follow each other, and the circumstances that give them birth, as the second, third, and fourth links of a chain follow the first, when it is drawn along. Hence the eternal, infallible, irresistible, universal concatenation of events, both in the moral and material world. This is, if I mistake not, the scheme of that great, divine, and he spends no less than four hundred and fourteen large pages in trying to establish it.

I would just observe upon it, that it makes the First Cause or First Mover, the only *free Agent* in the world; all others being necessarily bound with the chain of his decrees, drawn along by the irresistible motion of his arm, or, which is the same, entangled in *forcible* circumstances unalterably fixed by his immutable counsel.

And yet, even upon this scheme, you needed not, sir, be so afraid of free will; for if the will be like an even balance, it is free in itself, though it is only with what I beg leave to call "a mechanical freedom;" for an even balance, you know, is *free* to turn either way.

But with respect to our ingenious author's assertion, that the will cannot turn without a weight, because an even balance cannot, I must consider it as a mere begging the question, if not as an absurdity. What is a balance but *lifeless matter?* And what is the will but *the living, active soul, springing up in its willing capacity, and self-exerting, self-determining power?* O how tottering is the mighty fabric raised, I shall not say upon such a fine spun metaphysical speculation, but upon so weak a foundation as a comparison, which supposes that two things, so widely different as spirit and matter, a *living soul* and a *lifeless balance,* are exactly alike with reference to self determination! Just as if a spirit, made after the image of the living, free, and powerful God, was no more capable of determining itself, than a horizontal beam supporting two equal copper bowls by six silken strings!

I am sorry, sir, to dissent from such a respectable divine as yourself; but, as I have no taste for new refinements, and cannot even conceive how far actions can be *morally* good or evil, any farther than our free will is concerned in them, I must follow the universal experience of mankind, and side with the author of the sermons against the author of the Narrative concerning the freedom of the will.

Nor is this freedom derogatory to free grace: for as it was free grace that gave an upright free will to Adam at his creation; so whenever his fallen children think or act aright, it is because their free will is mercifully prevented, touched, and so far rectified by free grace.

However, it must be granted, that many fashionable professors, and the large book of Mr. Edwards, are for you: but when you maintained *the freedom of the will,* Jesus Christ and the Gospel were on your side. To the end of the world this plain, peremptory assertion of our Lord, "I would and ye would not," will alone throw down the sophisms, and silence the objections of the most subtle philosophers against free will. When I consider what it implies, far from supposing that the will is a lifeless pair of scales, necessarily turned by the least weight, I see it is such a strong, selfdetermining power, that it can resist the effect of the most amazing weights; keep itself inflexible under all the warnings, threatenings, miracles, promises, entreaties, and tears of the Son of God; and remain obstinately unmoved under the strivings of his Holy Spirit. Yes: put in one scale the most stupendous weights, for instance, the hopes of heavenly joys, and the dread of hellish torments; and only the gaudy feather of honour, or the breaking bubble of worldly joy, in the other; if the will casts itself into the light scale, the feather or bubble will instantly preponderate. Nor is the power of the rectified will less wonderful; for though you should put all the kingdoms of the world and their glory in the one scale, and nothing but "the reproach of Christ" in the other; yet, if the will *freely* leap into the infamous scale, a crown of thorns easily outweighs a thousand golden crowns, and a devouring flame makes ten thousand thrones kick the beam.

Thus it appears the will can be persuaded, but never forced. You may bend it by moral suasions; but if you do this farther than it freely gives way, you *break,* you absolutely *destroy* it. A will forced, is no more a *will;* it is mere *compulsion;* freedom is not less essential to it than moral agency to man. Nor do I go, in these observations upon the freedom of the will, one step farther than honest John Bunyan, whom all the Calvinists so deservedly admire. In his "Holy War" he tells us, "There is but one *Lord Will-be-Will* in the town of Man's-soul:" whether he serves Diabolus or Shaddai, he is *Lord Will-be-Will* still, "a man of great strength, resolution, and courage, whom in his occasion no one can turn," if he does not freely turn, or yield to be turned.

I hope, sir, these hints upon the harmlessness of mysticism, and the important doctrine of our free agency, will convince you, and the purchasers of your sermons, that you have been too precipitate in "publicly recanting them in the face of the whole world," especially *the ninth.*

If you ask, why I particularly interest myself in behalf of that one discourse, I will let you into the mystery. At the first reading I liked and adopted it: I cut it out of the volume in which it was bound, put it in my sermon case, and preached it in my church. The title of it is, you know, "Justification by Faith;" and, among several striking things on the subject, you quote twice this excellent passage out of our homilies: "Justification by faith implies a sure trust and confidence which a man hath in God, that by the *merits* of Christ his sins are forgiven, and he is reconciled to the favour of God." O sir, why did you not except it in your recantation, both for the honour of our Church and your own?

Were I to print and disperse such an advertisement as this' "Eight years ago I preached in my church a sermon, entitled *Justification by Faith,* composed by the honourable and reverend Mr. Shirley, to convince Papists and Pharisees that we are accepted through the alone *merits* of Christ: but I see better now; *I wish this sermon had been burned, and I publicly recant it in the face of the whole world;*" how would the Popish priest of Madeley rejoice! And how will that of Loughrea triumph when he hears *you* have actually done it in your Narrative! What will your Protestant parishioners, to whom your book is dedicated, say, when the surprising news reaches Ireland? And what will the world think, when they see you warmly plead in August for *justification by faith,* as being *"the* foundation that must by all means be secured;" and publicly recant, in September, your own excellent sermon on "Justification by Faith?"

Indeed, sir, though I admire your candour in acknowledging there are some exceptionable passages in your discourses, and your humility in readily giving them up, I can no more approve of your readiness in making, than in insisting upon "formal recantations." We cannot be too careful in dealing in that kind of ware; and it is extremely dangerous to do it by wholesale; as by that mean we may give up, or *seem* to give up, "before the whole world," precious truths, delivered by Christ himself, and brought down to us in streams of the blood of martyrs.

Among some blunt expostulations that Mr. Wesley erased in my Fifth Letter, as being too severe, he kindly but unhappily struck out this: "Before you could with candour insist upon 'a recantation' of Mr. Wesley's Minutes, should you not have recanted yourself the passages of your own sermons where the same doctrines are maintained; and have sent your recantation through the land, together with your Circular Letter?" Had this been published, it might have convinced you of the unseasonableness of your "recantation." Thus, this *second hasty step* would have been prevented; and if I dwell so long upon it now, believe me, sir, it is chiefly to prevent a *third.*

And, now your sermons are recanted, is the Vindication of Mr. Wesley's Minutes invalidated? Not at all; for you have not yet recanted the Bath Hymnbook, nor can you ever get Mr. Henry, Mr. Williams, and a tribe of other anti-Crispian, though Calvinist divines, now in glory, to recant with you; much less the prophets, apostles, and Christ himself, on whose irrefragable testimony we chiefly rest our doctrine.

II. As I have pleaded out the cause of free will against bound will, or that of your sermons against your Narrative, and am insensibly come to the Vindication, give me leave, sir, to speak a word also for that performance and the author of it.

You say he has "*attempted* a vindication of the Minutes;" but do not some people think he has likewise *executed* it? And have you proved he has not?

You reply, "There would be a great impropriety in my giving a full and particular answer to those letters, because the author did all he could to revoke them, and has given me ample satisfaction in his letters of submission." Indeed, sir, you quite mistook the nature of that "submission:" it had absolutely no reference to the *arguments* of the Vindication; it only respected the *polemic dress* in which the vindicator had put them. You might have been convinced of it by this paragraph of his letter of submission: "I was going to preach when I had the news of your happy accommodation, and was no sooner out of church than I wrote to beg my Vindication might not appear in the *dress* in which I had put it. I did not then, nor do I yet, repent having written upon the Minutes; but, *as matters are now,* I am very sorry I did not write in a general manner, without taking notice of the Circular Letter, and mentioning your dear name." He begs, therefore, you will not consider his letter of submission as a reason for not giving "a full or particular answer" to his *arguments.* On the contrary, if you can prove they want solidity; *a letter of thanks* shall follow his "letter of submission:" if he is wrong, he sincerely desires to be set right.

You add, however, that he has "broken the Minutes into sentences and half sentences; and by refining upon each of the detached particles, has given a new turn to the whole." But he appeals to every impartial reader whether he has not, like a candid man, first considered them all together, and then every one asunder. He begs to be informed, whether an artist can better inquire into the goodness of a watch, than by making first his observations on the whole movement in general, and then by taking it to pieces, that he may examine every part with greater attention. And he desires you would show, whether what you are pleased to call "a new turn," is not preferable to the *heretical turn* some persons give them; and whether it is not equally, if not better adapted to the literal meaning of the words, as well as more agreeable to the Antinomian state of the

Church, the general tenor of the propositions, and the system of doctrine maintained by Mr. Wesley for near forty years?

The vindicator objects likewise to your asserting, (page 21,) that "when he first saw the Minutes, he expressed to Lady Huntingdon his *abhorrence* of them." Had you said SURPRISE, the expression would have been strictly just; but that of *abhorrence* is far too strong, Her ladyship, who testified her *detestation* of them in the strongest terms, might easily mistake his *abhorrence* of the sense fixed upon the Minutes, for an abhorrence of the Minutes themselves; but she may recollect, that, far from ever granting they had that sense, he said again and again, even in their first conversation upon them, "Certainly, my lady, Mr. Wesley can mean no such thing' he will explain himself."

But supposing he had a first been so far influenced by the jealous fears of Lady Huntingdon, as to express as great an *abhorrence* of the Minutes as the mistaken disciples did of the person of our Lord, when they took him for an apparition, and "cried out for fear;" would this have excused either him or you, sir, for resolutely continuing in a mistake, in the midst of a variety of means and calls to escape from it? And if the vindicator, before he had weighed the Minutes in the balance of the sanctuary, had even taken his pen, and condemned them as dangerously legal, what could you fairly have concluded from it, but that he was not partial to Mr. Wesley, and had also "leaned so much toward Calvinism," as not instantly to discover, and "rejoice in the truth?"

In your last page you take your friendly leave of the vindicator, by saying, you "desire in love to cast a veil over all apparent mistakes of his judgment on this occasion;" but as he is not conscious of "all these apparent mistakes," he begs you would in love take off "the veil" you have cast upon them, that he may see, and rectify at least those which are capital.

III. And that you may not hastily conclude he was "mistaken" in his Vindication of that article that touches upon *merit*, he embraces this opportunity of presenting you with another quotation from the JOHN WESLEY of the last century, he means Mr. BAXTER, the most judicious divine, as well as the greatest, most useful, and most laborious preacher of his age.

In his "Catholic Theology," answering the objections of an Antinomian, he says: "Merit is a word, I perceive, you are against; you may therefore choose any other of the same signification, and we will forbear this rather than offend you. But yet tell me, (1.) What, if the words Greek αξιος and αξια were translated *deserving* and *merit*, would it not be as true a translation as *worthy* and *worthiness*, when it is the same thing that is meant? (2.) Do not all the ancient teachers of the Churches, since the apostles, particularly apply the names αξια and *meritum* to believers? And if you persuade men that all these teachers were Papists, will you not persuade most that believe you to be Papists too? (3.) Are not *reward*, and *merit* or *desert*, relative words, as *punishment* and *guilt*, *master* and *servant*, *husband* and *wife*? And is there any reward which is not *meriti præmium*, "the reward of some merit?" Again:

"Is it not the second article of our faith, and next to 'believing there is a God,' that 'he is the rewarder of them that diligently seek him?' When you thus extirpate faith and godliness, on pretence of crying down *merit*, you see what *overdoing* tends to. And indeed by the same reason that men deny a *reward* to duty, (the faultiness being pardoned through Christ,) they would infer there is no *punishment* for sin; for if God will not do good to the righteous, neither will he do evil to the wicked; he becomes like the god of Epicurus, he does not trouble himself about us, nor about the merit or demerit of our actions. But David knew better: 'The Lord,' says he, 'plenteously rewardeth the proud doers; and verily there is a reward for the righteous, for there is a God that judgeth the earth;' that sees matter of praise or dispraise, rewardableness or worthiness of punishment, in all the actions of men." This is, sir, all Mr. Baxter and Mr. Wesley mean by *merit* or *demerit;* and if the vindicator be wrong in thinking they are both in the right, please to remove "the veil" that conceals his "mistake."

IV. As one of his correspondents desires him to explain himself a little more upon the article of the Minutes which respects *undervaluing ourselves*; and as you probably place the arguments he has advanced upon that head among his "apparent mistakes," he takes likewise this opportunity of making some additional observations on that delicate subject.

How we can "esteem every man better than ourselves," and ourselves "the chief of sinners," or "the least of saints," seems not so much a calculation for the understanding, as for the lowly, contrite, and loving heart. It puzzles the former, but the latter at once makes it out. Nevertheless, the seeming contradiction may, perhaps, be reconciled to reason by these reflections: —

1. If friendship brings the greatest monarch down from his throne, and makes him sit on the same couch with his favourites; may not brotherly love, much more powerful than natural friendship; may not humility, excited by the example of Christ washing his disciples' feet; may not a deep regard for that precept, "He that will be greatest among you, let him be the least of all," sink the true Christian to the dust, and make him lie in spirit at the feet of every one?

2. A well-bred person uncovers himself, bows, and declares, even to his inferiors, that he is their "most humble servant." This affected civility of the world is but an apish imitation of the genuine humility of the Church; and if those who customarily speak humble words without meaning, may yet be honest men, how much more the saints, who have "truth written in their inward parts," and "speak out of the abundance of their *humble* hearts!"

3. He who walks in the light of Divine love, sees something of God's spiritual, moral, or natural image in all men, the worst not excepted; and at the sight, that which is merely creaturely in him, (by a kind of spiritual instinct found in all who are "born of the Spirit,") directly bows to that which is of God in another. He imitates the captain of a first rate man of war, who, upon seeing the king or queen coming up in a small boat, forgetting the enormous size of his ship, or considering it is the king's own ship, immediately strikes his colours; and the greater vessel, consistently with wisdom and truth, pays respect to the less.

4. The most eminent saint, having known more of the workings of corruption in his own breast, than he can possibly know of them in that of any other man, may, with great truth, (according to his present views and former feelings of the internal evil he has overcome,) call himself "the chief of sinners."

5. Nor does he know, but if the feeblest believers had all his talents and graces, with all his opportunities of doing and receiving good, they would have made far superior advances in the Christian life; and in this view also, without

hypocritical humility, he prefers the least saint to himself. Thus, although, according to the humble light of *others*, all true believers certainly "undervalue," yet, according to *their own* humble light, they make a true estimate of "themselves."

V. The vindicator having thus solved a problem of godliness, which you have undoubtedly ranked among his "apparent mistakes," he takes the liberty of presenting you with a list of some of *your own* "apparent mistakes on this occasion."

1. In the very letter in which you recant your Circular Letter, you desire Mr. Wesley to "give up the fatal errors of the Minutes," though you have not yet *proved* they contain one; you still affirm, "They appear to you evidently subversive of the fundamentals of Christianity," that is, in plain English, still "dreadfully heretical;" and you produce a letter which asserts, also, without shadow of proof, that the "Minutes were given for the establishment of another foundation than that which is laid;" that they are "repugnant to Scripture, the whole plan of man's salvation under the new covenant of grace, and also to the clear meaning of our Established Church, as well as to all other Protestant Churches."

2. You declare in your Narrative that, "when you cast your eye over the Minutes, you are just where you was," and assure the public, that "nothing inferior to an *attack upon the foundation* of our hope, through the allsufficient sacrifice of Christ, could have been an object sufficient to engage you in its defence." Thus, by continuing to insinuate such an ATTACK was really made, you continue to wound Mr. Wesley in the tenderest part.

3. Although Mr. Wesley and fifty-three of his fellow labourers have let you quietly "secure the foundation," (which, by the by, had only been shaken in your own ideas, and was perfectly secured by these express words of the Minutes, "not by the merit of works," but by *"believing* in Christ,") yet, far from allowing them to *secure the superstructure* in their turn, which would be nothing but just, you begin already a contest with them about "our second justification by works in the day of judgment."

4. Instead of frankly acknowledging the rashness of your step, and the greatness of your mistake, with respect to the Minutes, you make a bad matter worse, by treating the Declaration as you have treated them; forcing upon it a dangerous sense, no less contrary to the Scriptures, than to Mr. Wesley's meaning, and the import of the words.

5. When you speak of the dreadful charges you have brought against the Minutes, you softly call them "misconstructions you *may seem to* have made of their meaning." (Page 22, line 4.) Nor is your "acknowledgment" much stronger than your "may seem;" at least it does not appear, to many, adequate to the hurt done by your Circular Letter to the practical Gospel of Christ, and the reputation of his eminent servant, thousands of whose friends you have grieved, offended, or stumbled; while you have confirmed thousands of his enemies in their hard thoughts of him, and in their unjust contempt of his ministry.

6. And, lastly, far from candidly inquiring into the merit of the arguments advanced in the Vindication, you represent them as mere "metaphysical distinctions;" or cast, as a veil over them, a friendly submissive *letter of condolence,* which was never intended for the use to which you have put it.

Therefore the vindicator, who does not admire a peace founded upon a "may seem" on your part, and on Mr. Wesley's part upon a "declaration," to which you have already fixed a wrong unscriptural sense of your own, takes this public method to inform you, he thinks his arguments in favour of Mr. Wesley's anti-Crispian propositions rational, Scriptural, and solid; and once more he begs you would remove the veil you have hitherto "cast over all the apparent mistakes of his judgment on this occasion," that he may see whether the *Antinomian* gospel of Dr. Crisp is preferable to the *practical* Gospel which Mr. Wesley endeavours to restore to its primitive and Scriptural lustre.

VI. Having thus finished my remarks upon the mistakes of your Narrative, I gladly take my leave of controversy for this time. Would to God it were for ever! I no more like it than I do applying a caustic to the back of my friends; it is disagreeable to me, and painful to them; and nevertheless, it must be done, when their health and mine is at stake.

I assure you, sir, I do not like the warlike dress of the vindicator, any more than David did the heavy armour of Saul. With gladness, therefore, I cast it aside, to throw myself at your feet, and protest to you, that, although I thought it my *duty* to write to you with the utmost *plainness, frankness,* and *honesty,* yet the design of doing it with *bitterness* never entered my heart. However, for every "bitter expression" that may have dropped from my sharp vindicating pen, I ask your pardon; but it must be *in general,* for neither friends nor foes have yet *particularly* pointed out to me *one* such expression.

You have accepted of "a *letter* of submission" from me; let, I beseech you, a concluding *paragraph* of submission meet also with your favourable acceptance. You condescend, Rev. sir, to call me your "learned friend." *Learning* is an accomplishment I never pretended to; but your *friendship* is an honour I shall always highly esteem, and do at this time value above my own brother's love. Appearances are a little against me: I feel I am a thorn in your flesh; but I am persuaded it is a *necessary* one, and this persuasion reconciles me to the thankless and disagreeable part I act.

If Ephraim must vex Judah, let Judah bear with Ephraim, till, happily tired of their contention, they feel the truth of Terence's words, *Amantium* (why not credentium?) *iræ amoris redintegratio est.** I can assure you, my dear sir, without metaphysical distinction, I love and honour you, as truly as I dislike the rashness of your well-meant zeal. The motto I thought myself obliged to follow was *E bello pax;†* but that which I delight in is, *In bello pax;‡* may we make them harmonize till we learn war and polemic divinity no more!

My Vindication cost me tears of fear, lest I should have wounded you too deeply. That fear, I find, was groundless; but should you feel a little for the great truths and the great minister I vindicate, these expostulations will wound me, and probably cost me tears again.

If, in the meantime, we offend our weak brethren, let us do something in order to lessen the offence till it is removed. Let us show them we make war

---

* The misunderstandings of lovers (why not of *believers*) end in a renewal and increase of love.
† We make war in order to get peace.
‡ We enjoy peace in the midst of war.

without so much as shyness. Should you ever come to the next county, as you did last summer, honour me with a line, and I shall gladly wait upon you, and show you, (if you permit me,) the way to my pulpit, where I shall think myself highly favoured to see you "secure the foundation," and hear you enforce the doctrine of *justification by faith*, which you fear we attack. And should I ever be within thirty miles of the city where you reside, I shall go to submit myself to you, and beg leave to assist you in reading prayers for you, or giving the cup with you. Thus shall we convince the world, that controversy may be conscientiously carried on without interruption of brotherly love; and I shall have the peculiar pleasure of testifying to you, in person, how sincerely I am, Hon. and dear sir, your Submissive and obedient servant, in the bond of a PRACTICAL Gospel,

J. FLETCHER.

LETTER III.

HONOURED AND REVEREND SIR, — If I mistake not the workings of my heart, a concern for St. James' "pure and undefiled religion" excites me to take the pen once more, and may account for the readiness with which I have met you in the dangerous field of controversy. You may possibly think mere partiality to Mr. Wesley has inspired me with that boldness; and others may be ready to say as Eliab, "We know the pride and haughtiness of thy heart. Thou art come down that thou mightest see the battle." But may I not answer with David, "Is there not a cause?"

Is it not highly necessary to make a stand against Antinomianism? Is not that gigantic "man of sin" a more dangerous enemy to King Jesus, than the champion of the Philistines was to King Saul? Has he not defied more than forty days the armies and arms, the people and truths of the living God? By audaciously daring the thousands in Israel, has he not made all the faint hearted among them ashamed to stand "in the whole armour of God," afraid to defend the important post of *duty?* And have not many left it already, openly running away, flying into the dens and caves of earthly mindedness, "putting their light under a bushel," and even burying themselves alive in the noisome grave of profaneness?

Multitudes indeed still keep the field, still make an open profession of godliness. But how few of these "endure hardship as good soldiers of Jesus Christ!" How many have already cast away "the shield of *Gospel* faith, the faith which works by love!" What numbers dread the *cross*, the heavenly standard they should steadily bear, or resolutely follow! While in pompous speeches they extol the cross of Jesus, how do they, upon the most frivolous pretence, refuse to "take up" their own! Did the massy staff of Goliah's spear seem more terrible to the frighted Israelites than *the daily cross* of those dastardly followers of the Crucified?

Five Checks To Antinomianism

What Boanerges can spirit them up, and lead them on "from conquering to conquer?" Who can even make them look the enemy in the face? Alas! "in their hearts they are *already*, gone back to Egypt. Their faces are *but half* Sion ward." They give way, — they "draw back;" O may it not be "to perdition*!*" May not the king of terrors overtake them in their retreat, and make them as great monuments of God's vengeance against cowardly soldiers, as Lot's wife was of his indignation against halting racers!

But setting allegory aside, permit me, sir, to pour my fears into your bosom, and tell you with the utmost plainness my distressing thoughts of the religious world.

For some years I have suspected there is more imaginary than "unfeigned faith" in most of those who pass for believers. With a mixture of indignation and grief have I seen them carelessly follow the stream of corrupt nature, against which they should have manfully wrestled. And by the most preposterous mistake, when they should have exclaimed against their *Antinomianism*,* I have heard them cry out against "the *legality*† of their wicked hearts; which" they said "still suggested they were to *do something* in order to salvation." Glad was I, therefore, when I had attentively considered Mr. Wesley's Minutes, to find they were levelled at the very errors which give rise to an evil I had long lamented in secret, but had wanted courage to resist and attack.

I. This evil is *Antinomianism;* that is, any kind of doctrinal or practical *opposition to God's law*, which is the perfect rule of right, and the moral picture of the God of love, drawn in miniature by our Lord in these two exquisite precepts, "Thou shalt love God with all thy heart, and thy neighbour as thyself."

As "the law is good, if a man use it lawfully," so *legality* is excellent, if it be evangelical. The external respect shown by Pharisees to the law is but feigned and hypocritical legality. Pharisees are no more truly legal, than Antinomians are truly evangelical. "Had ye believed Moses," says Jesus to people of that stamp, "ye would have believed me:" but in your hearts you hate his law as much as you do my Gospel.

We see no less Gospel in the preface of the ten commandments, "I am the Lord thy God," &c, than we do legality in the middle of our Lord's sermon on the mount, "I say, Whosoever looketh on a woman to lust after her, hath already committed adultery in his heart." Nevertheless, the latter "has in all things the pre-eminence" over the former. For if "the law," shortly prefaced by the Gospel, "came by Moses;" *grace*, the gracious, the full display of the Gospel, *and truth*, the true explanation and fulfilling of the law, "came by Jesus Christ."

This evangelical law should appear to us "sweeter than the honeycomb, and more precious than fine gold." We should continually spread the tables of our hearts before our heavenly Lawgiver, beseeching him to write it there with his

---

* The word Antinomianism is derived from two Greek words, *anti* and *nomos*, which signify "against the law," and the word "legal" from the Latin *legalis*, which means "agreeable to the law."

† The *legality* contended for in these letters is not a *stumbling at Christ*, and a *going about to establish our own righteousness* by faithless works: this sin, which the Scripture calls *unbelief*, I would no more countenance than murder. The evangelical legality I want to see all in love with, is a cleaving to Christ by faith which *works righteousness;* a "following him as he went about doing good;" and a showing by St. James' *works* that we have St. Paul's faith.

own finger, the powerful Spirit of life and love. But alas! God's commandments are disregarded; they are represented as the needless or impracticable sanctions of that superannuated legalist, Moses; and if we express our veneration for them, we are looked upon as people who are always strangers to the Gospel, or are fallen into the Galatian state.

Not so David. He was so great an admirer of God's law, that he declares the godly man "doth meditate therein day and night." He expresses his transcendent value for it, under the synonymous expressions of *law, words, statutes, testimonies, precepts,* and *commandments,* in almost every verse of the 119th Psalm. And he says of himself, "O how I love thy law! It is my meditation all the day!"

St. Paul was as evangelically legal as David; for he knew the law is as much contained in the Gospel, as the tables of stone, on which the moral law was written, were contained in the ark. He therefore assured the Corinthians, that "though he had all faith," even that which is most uncommon, and performed the greatest wonders, it would "profit him nothing," unless it was accompanied by "charity," unless it "worked by love," which is "the fulfilling of the law;" the excellency of faith arising from the excellent end it answers in producing and nourishing love.

Should it be objected, that St. Paul says to the Galatians, "I through the law am dead to the law, that I might live to God;" and to the Romans, "Ye are become dead to the law by the body of Christ:" I answer, in the apostle's days, that expression, *the law,* frequently meant "the whole Mosaic dispensation;" and in that sense every believer is dead to it, dead to all that Christ has not adopted. For, (1.) He is dead to the *Levitical law,* "Christ having abolished in himself the law of ordinances. Touch not, taste not, handle not." (2.) He is dead to the *ceremonial law,* which was only "a shadow of good things to come," a typical representation of Christ and the blessings flowing from his sacrifice. (3.) He is dead to the *curse* attending his past violations of the *moral law;* for "Christ hath delivered us from the curse of the law, being made a curse for us." And *lastly,* he is dead to the hopes of recommending himself to God by the *merit* of his obedience to the moral law; for in point of *merit,* he "is determined to know nothing but Christ and him crucified."

To make St. Paul mean more than this, is, (1.) To make him maintain that no believer can sin: for if "sin is the transgression of the law," and "the law is dead and buried," it is plain, no believer can sin, as nobody can transgress a law which is abolished: for "where no law is, there is no transgression." (2.) It is to make him contradict St. James, who exhorts us to "fulfil the royal law, according to the Scripture, Thou shalt love thy neighbour as thyself." And, (3.) It is to make him contradict himself: for he charges the Galatians "by love to serve one another; all the law being fulfilled in one word, even in this, Thou shalt love thy neighbour as thyself." And he assures the Hebrews, that under the new covenant, believers, far from being "without *God's* laws, have them written in their hearts; God *himself* placing them in their minds." We cannot, therefore, with any shadow of justice, put Dr. Crisp's coat upon the apostle, and press him into the service of Antinomians.

And did our Lord side with Antinomians? Just the reverse. Far from repealing the two above mentioned royal precepts, he asserts, that "on them hang all the law and the prophets;" and had the four Gospels been then written, he would no doubt have represented them as subservient to the establishing of the law, as he did the book of Isaiah, the evangelical prophet. Such high thoughts had he of the law, that when a lawyer expressed his veneration for it, by declaring that "the love of God, and our neighbour, was more than all whole burnt offerings and sacrifices, Jesus, seeing that he had answered discreetly, said unto him, Thou art not far from the kingdom of God."

The Gospel itself terminates in the fulfilling of the commandments. For as the curse of the law, like the scourge of a severe schoolmaster, drives, so the Gospel, like a loving guide, brings us to Christ, the great Law Fulfiller, in whom we find inexhaustible treasures of pardon and power; of pardon for past breaches of the law, and of power for present obedience to it. Nor are we sooner come to him than he magnifies the law, by his precepts, as he formerly did by his obedience unto death. "If ye love me," says he, "keep my commandments." "This is his commandment, that we should love one another; and he that loveth another hath fulfilled the law."

Again: the Gospel displays Jesus' dying love, that by "believing" it "we may" love him, that is, "have everlasting life," the life of *love* which *abideth* when the life of faith is no more. Hence St. John sums up Christianity in these words, "We love him because he first loved us!" And what is it to love Jesus, but to fulfil the whole law at once, to love God and man, the Creator and the creature, united in one divinely human person!

Did the Son of God "magnify the law," that we might vilify it? Did he "make it honourable," that we might make it contemptible? Did he "come to fulfil it," that we might be discharged from fulfilling it according to our capacity? That is, discharged from loving God and our neighbour? Discharged from the employment and joys of heaven? No: the "Word was *never* made flesh" for this dreadful end. None but Satan could have become incarnate to go upon such an infernal errand as this! Standing, therefore, upon the rock of evangelical truth, we ask, with St. Paul, "Do we then make void the law through faith? God forbid! Nay, we establish the law." We point sinners to that Saviour in and from whom they may Continually have the law-fulfilling power; "that the righteousness of the law may be fulfilled in us, who walk not after the flesh but after the Spirit."

Such are the glorious and delightful views which the Scriptures give us of the law, disarmed of its curse in Christ; the law of holy, humble love, so strongly enforced in the discourses, and sweetly exemplified in the life and death of the "Prophet like unto Moses!" So amiable, so precious is the book of the law, when delivered to us by Jesus, sprinkled with his atoning blood, and explained by his loving Spirit! And so true is St. Paul's assertion, "We are not without law to God, but under the law to Christ!"

Instead then of dressing up the law as a scarecrow, let us in our degree "magnify it, and make it honourable," as did our Lord. Instead of representing it as "an intolerable yoke of bondage," let us call it, with St. Paul, "the law of Christ;" and, with St. James, "the perfect law of liberty." And let every true believer say, with David, "I love thy commandments above gold and precious stones: I shall alway keep thy law, yea, for ever and ever; I will walk at LIBERTY, for I seek thy precepts."

But, alas! how few give us these evangelical views of the law, and practical views of the Gospel! How many intimate Christ has "fulfilled all righteousness," that we might be the children of God with hearts "full of unrighteousness!" If some insist upon our "fulfilling all righteousness" also, is it not chiefly when they want to draw us into their peculiarities, and *dip* us into their narrow denomination? And what numbers, under the fair pretence that they "have a living law *written in their hearts*," insinuate, "there is no need of preaching the law" to them, either to show them more of God's purity, endear the atoning blood, regulate their conduct, or convince them of the necessity of perfecting *holiness!*

But suppose these objectors love, as they say, "the law written in their inward parts," (which the actions and tempers of some make rather doubtful,) is the writing so "perfectly finished," that no one stroke need to be added to it? Is not the law an important part of "the word of righteousness?" And could not the Holy Ghost retouch the writing, or deepen the engraving, by the ministry of "the word of righteousness?" Again: if the internal teachings of the Holy Spirit supersede the letter of the *law*, must they not, by the same reason, supersede the letter of the *Gospel?* Is there any more need of preaching the Gospel than the law to believers? Or have they not the Gospel "written in their hearts," as well as the law?

At what amazing heights of unscriptural perfection must our objectors suppose themselves to have arrived! What palpable errors do they run into, that they may have the honour of passing for evangelical! And who will envy them the glory of countenancing the Antinomian delusion, by standing in direct opposition to Christ, who thus decides the controversy: "Think not that I am come to destroy the law and the prophets: I am not come to destroy but to fulfil. For verily I say unto you, till heaven and earth pass away, one jot or tittle shall in no wise pass from the law, till all be fulfilled," either in what it requires or, denounces: for the law is "fulfilled" not only when its precepts are obeyed, but when rewards are given to the observers, and punishments inflicted upon the violators of it. "Whosoever, therefore, shall DO my commandments, and TEACH them, shall be great in the kingdom of heaven."

Do not imagine, Rev. sir, I thus cry up God's law to drown the late cries of *heresy* and *apostasy*. I appeal to matter of fact and your own observations. Consider the religious world, and say, if ANTINOMIANISM is not in general a motto better adapted to the state of professing congregations, societies, families, and individuals, than HOLINESS UNTO THE LORD, the inscription that should be even upon our "horses' bells."

II. Begin with CONGREGATIONS, and cast first your eyes upon the hearers. In general" they have curious "itching ears, and will not endure sound doctrine." Many of them are armed with the "breastplate of a righteousness" which they have vainly* imputed to themselves: they have on the showy "helmet

---

* Our imputation of Christ's righteousness to ourselves is a trick of our Antinomian hearts, and is a dreadful delusion: but God's imputing of Christ's righteousness to true believers is a most blessed reality, for which we cannot too much contend. "He speaks the word and it is done;" his imputation is not an *idea*, but a *fiat*; wherever it takes place, "Jehovah our righteousness, or Christ the righteous,

of a *presumptuous* hope," and hold fast the impenetrable shield of strong prejudice. With these they "quench the fiery darts of" convincing truth, and stand undaunted under volleys of reproof.

They say, they "will have nothing, but Christ." And who could blame them, if they would have Christ in all his offices? Christ, with all his parables and sermons, cautions and precepts, reproofs and expostulations, exhortations and threatenings? Christ, preaching to the multitudes upon a mountain, as well as honourably teaching in the temple? Christ, fasting in the wilderness, or praying in Gethsemane; as well as Christ making the multitude sit down upon the grass to receive "loaves and fishes," or promising "thrones" to his disciples? Christ, "constraining them to get into a ship, and toil in rowing all night with a contrary wind;" as well as Christ "coming in the morning," and causing "the ship to be immediately at the land whither they went?" Christ upon Mount Calvary, as well as Christ upon Mount Tabor? In a word, who would find fault with them if they would have Christ with his poverty and self- denial, his reproach and cross, his Spirit and graces, his prophets and apostles, his plain apparel and mean followers?

But alas! it is not so. They will have *what* they please of Christ, and that too *as* they please. If he come accompanied by legal Moses and honest Elijah, who talk of the crucifixion of the body, and "decease" of the flesh, they can do very well without him. If he preach "free grace, free will, faithfulness, or heavenly mindedness," some turn to the right, some wheel about to the left, others go directly back, and all agree to say or think, "This is a hard saying, who can hear it?"

They admire him in one chapter, and know not what to make of him in another. Some of his words they extol to the sky, and others they seem to be ashamed of. If he assert his authority as a Lawgiver, they are ready to treat him with as little ceremony as they do Moses. If he say, "Keep my Commandments: I am a king;" like the Jews of old, they rise against the awful declaration; or they "crown him" as *a Surety*, the better to "set him at naught" as *a Monarch*. And if he add, to his ministers, "I am the prophet that was to come; go in my name, and teach all nations to observe all things whatsoever I have commanded you;" they complain, "This is *the law; give us the Gospel;* we can relish nothing but *the Gospel!*"

They have no idea of "eating the paschal lamb" whole, "his head with his legs, and the purtenance thereof;" nor do they take care of "not breaking his bones;" they do not like him roast with fire neither; but "raw or sodden with water" out of their own "broken cisterns." If you present him to them as the type of the "Lamb of God that taketh away the sin of the world, and maketh an end of it;" their hearts heave, they say, "Pray have me excused" from thus feeding upon him: and though it is said, "Ye shall let nothing of it remain until the

---

dwells in the heart by faith." I wish that with respect to *imputed righteousness* we paid more regard to the late Mr. Hart's sentiment. This experienced and *sound* Calvinist, in the account of his conversion, prefixed to his Hymns, says, with great truth: "As much as Lazarus coming out of the grave, and feeling himself restored to life, differed from those who only saw the miracle, or believed the fact told them; so great is the difference between a souls *real* coming to Christ out of himself and having the righteousness of Christ imputed to him by the precious faith of God's elect; and a man's bare believing the doctrine of imputed righteousness, because he sees it contained in the Scripture, or assenting to the truth of it when proposed to his understanding by others."

morning, you shall eat it in haste," they postpone, they beg leave to keep it till the article of death: and if, in the meantime, you talk to them of "bitter herbs," they marvel at your Jewish, legal taste, and complain that you spoil the Gospel feast.

They do not consider we must "give every one his portion of meat," or proper medicine, "in due season;" and that sweet things are not always wholesome. They forget we must "leave all" Antinomian refinements "to follow Christ," who sometimes says to decent Pharisees, "How can you escape the damnation of hell?" And to a beloved disciple that shuns the cross, "Satan, thou savourest not the things of God, but the things of men." They will have nothing but the atonement. Nor do they choose to remember, that St. Paul, who "did not shun to declare the whole counsel of God," preached Christ to Felix, by "reasoning of temperance, righteousness, and judgment to come."

Hence it is that some preachers must choose comfortable subjects to please their hearers; just as those who make an entertainment for nice persons are obliged to study what will suit their difficult taste. A multitude of important scriptures may be produced, on which no minister, who is unwilling to lose his reputation as "an evangelical preacher," must dare to speak in some pulpits, unless it be to explain away or enervate their meaning. Take some instances: —

The good old Calvinists, (Archbishop Leighton for one,) questioned whether a man was truly converted who did not sincerely "go on to perfection," and heartily endeavour to "perfect holiness in the fear of God." But now, if we only quote such passages with an emphasis, and enforce their meaning with some degree of earnestness, the truth of our conversion is suspected: we even pass for enemies to Christ's righteousness.

If we have courage to handle such scriptures as these, "To do good and to distribute forget not, for with such sacrifices God is well pleased. Show me thy faith by thy works. Was not Rahab justified by works? By works was Abraham's faith made perfect," &c, the bare giving out of our text prejudices our Antinomian hearers against us, and robs us of their candid attention, unless they expect a charity sermon; for on such an occasion they will yet allow us, at the close of our discourse, to speak honourably of good works: just as those who run to the opposite extreme, will yet, on some particular days, such as Christmas and Good Friday, permit us to make honourable mention of Jesus Christ.

The evil would be tolerable if we were only obliged to select smooth texts in order to gratify an Antinomian audience; but, alas! it is grown so desperate, that unless we "adulterate the sincere milk of the word," many reject it as poison. It is a doubt whether we could preach in some celebrated pulpits on "the good man, who is merciful and lendeth, who hath dispersed abroad and given to the poor, and whose righteousness remaineth for ever;" or on "breaking off our sins by righteousness, and our iniquities by showing mercy to the poor;" or on "the righteousness which exceeds that of the scribes and Pharisees;" or on "the robes washed and made white in the blood of the Lamb," without giving general disgust; unless, to keep in the good grace of our Nicolaitan hearers, we were to dissent from all sober commentators, and offer the greatest violence to the context, our own conscience, and common sense, by saying, that *the righteousness* and *robes,* mentioned in those passages, are Christ's *imputed,* and not our *performed* obedience.

Five Checks To Antinomianism

How few of our evangelical congregations would bear from the pulpit an honest explanation of what they allow us to read in the desk! We may open our service by saying, that "when the wicked man turneth away from his wickedness, and doth that which is lawful and right, he shall save his soul alive;" but wo to us, if we handle the Scripture in the pulpit, unless we wrest it by representing CHRIST as "the wicked man who DOES that which is lawful and right, to save our souls alive," without any of our *doings*.

Were we to preach upon these words of our Lord, "This DO and thou shalt live," Luke x, 25, the sense of which is fixed by the thirty-seventh verse, "Go and DO thou likewise;" or only to handle, without deceit, those common words of the Lord's prayer, confirmed by a plain parable, "Forgive us our trespasses, as we forgive them that trespass against us;" our reputation as Protestants would be in as much danger, from the bulk of some congregations, as our persons from the fire of a whole regiment in the day of battle. How would such a discourse, and the poor blind man that preached it, be privately exclaimed against; or publicly* exposed in a Magazine presented to the world under the sacred name of *Gospel!*

In short, whoever has courage enough to preach as St. Paul did at Athens, at Lystra, and before Felix, rebuking sin without respect of persons; whoever will imitate St. Peter, and exhort all his hearers to "save themselves from this perverse generation," assuring them that "the promise of the Holy Spirit is unto them, and their children;" must expect to be looked upon as unsound, if not as an enemy of free grace, and a setter forth of Pelagian or Popish doctrines. Moderate Calvinists themselves must run the gantlet, if they preach free grace as St. Peter did. A pious clergyman, noted for his strong attachment to what some call "the doctrines of grace," was, to my knowledge, highly blamed by one part of his auditory, for having preached to the other "repentance toward God," and exhorted them to call on him for mercy. And I remember he just saved his sinking reputation as a *sound* divine, by pleading, that two apostles exhorted even Simon Magus to "repent of his wickedness, and pray to God, if perhaps the thought of his heart might be forgiven him."

When such professors will not bear the plainest truth, from ministers whose sentiments agree with theirs; how will they rise against deeper truths advanced by those who are of a different opinion! Some will even lose all decency. Observing, in preaching last summer, one of them remarkably busy in disturbing all around him, when the service was over I went up to him, and inquired into the cause of the dissatisfaction he had so indecently expressed. "I am not afraid to tell it to your face," said he; "I do not like your doctrine. You are a free willer." "If I have spoken evil," replied I, "bear witness of the evil." He paused awhile, and then charged me with praying before the sermon, as if ALL might be saved. "That is false doctrine," added he, "and if Christ himself came down from heaven to preach it, I would not believe him."

I wondered at first at the positiveness of my rigid objector: but, upon second thoughts, I thought him modest, in comparison of numbers of professors, who see that Christ actually came down from heaven, and preached

---

* This was actually the case some months ago with respect to a sermon preached by Mr. Wesley.

the doctrine of perfection in his sermon upon the mount, and yet will face us down that it is an antichristian doctrine.

This Antinomian cavilling of hearers against preachers is deplorable; and the effects of it will be dreadful. If the Lord do not put a stop to this growing evil, we shall soon see every where, what we see in too many places, self-conceited, unhumbled men, rising against the truths and ministers of God; men who "are not *meek* doers of the law," but *insolent* judges, preposterously trying that law by which they shall soon be tried; — men who, instead of sitting as criminals before all the messengers of their Judge, with arrogancy invade the Judge's tribunal, and arraign even his most venerable ambassadors; — men, who should "fall on their faces before all, and give glory to God, by confessing that he is with his ministers," of every denomination, "of a truth;" but who, far from doing it, boldly condemn the word that condemns them, snatch the two-edged sword from the mouth of every faithful messenger, blunt the edge of it, and audaciously thrust at him in their turn; — men, who, when they see a servant of God in their pulpit, suppose he stands at their bar; try him with as much insolence as Korah, Dathan, and Abiram tried Moses; cast him with less kindness than Pilate did Jesus; force a fool's coat of their own making upon him; and then, from "the seat of the scornful," pronounce the decisive sentence: "He is legal, dark, blind, unconverted; an enemy to free grace. He is a rank Papist, a Jesuit, a false prophet, or a wolf in sheep's clothing."

III. But whence springs this almost general Antinomianism of our congregations? Shall I conceal the sore because it festers in my own breast? Shall I be partial? No, in the name of Him who is "no respecter of persons," I will confess my sin, and that of many of my brethren. Though I am the least, and (I write it with tears of shame) the most unworthy of them all, I will follow the dictates of my conscience, and use the authority of a minister of Christ. If Balaam, a *false* prophet, took in good part the reproof of his ass, I should wrong my honoured brethren and fathers, the *true* prophets of the Lord, if I feared their resenting some well-meant reproofs, which I first level at myself, and for which I heartily wish there was no occasion.

Is not the Antinomianism of hearers fomented by that of preachers? Does it not become us to take the greatest part of the blame upon ourselves, according to the old adage, "Like priest, like people?" Is it surprising that some of us should have an Antinomian audience? Do we not make or keep it so? When did we preach such a practical sermon as that of our Lord on the mount, or write such close letters as the epistles of St. John? Alas! I doubt it is but seldom. Not living so near to God ourselves as we should, we are afraid to come near to the consciences of our people. The Jews said to our Lord, "In so saying thou reproachest us;" but now the case is altered, and our auditors might say to many of us," In so saying you would reproach yourselves."

Some prefer popularity to plain dealing. We love to see a crowd of worldly-minded hearers, rather than "a little flock, a peculiar people zealous of good works." We dare not shake our congregations to purpose, lest our *five thousand* should, in three years' time, be reduced to *a hundred and twenty.*

Luther's advice to Melancthon, *Scandaliza fortiter,* "So preach that those who do not fall out with their sins may fall out with thee," is more and more unfashionable. Under pretence of drawing our hearers by love, some of us softly rock the cradle of carnal security in which they sleep. For "fear of grieving the dear children of God," we let "buyers and sellers, sheep and oxen," yea, goats and lions, fill "the temple" undisturbed. And because "the bread must not be kept from the hungry children," we let those who are wanton make shameful waste of it, and even allow "dogs," which we should "beware of," and noisy parrots that can speak *shibboleth,* to do the same. We forget that God's children "are led by his Spirit," who is "the Comforter" himself; that they are all afraid of being deceived, all "jealous for the Lord of hosts;" and therefore prefer a preacher who "searches Jerusalem with candles," and cannot suffer God's house to be made a "den of thieves," to a workman who "whitewashes *the noisome* sepulchres," he should open, and "daubs over with untempered mortar the *bulging* walls" he should demolish.

The old Puritans strongly insisted upon *personal holiness,* and the first Methodists upon the *new birth;* but these doctrines seem to grow out of date. The Gospel is cast into another mould. People, it seems, may now be "in Christ," without being "new creatures," and "new creatures" without casting "old things" away. They may be God's children without God's image; and "born of the Spirit" without "the fruits of the Spirit." If our unregenerate hearers get orthodox ideas about the way of salvation in their heads, evangelic phrases concerning Jesus' love in their mouths, and a warm zeal for our party and favourite forms in their hearts; without any more ado, we help them to rank themselves among the children of God. But, alas! this self adoption into the family of Christ will no more pass in heaven than self imputation of Christ's righteousness. The work of the Spirit will stand there, and that alone. Again:

Some of us often give our congregations particular accounts of *the covenant* between the persons of the blessed Trinity, and speak of it as confidently as if the King of kings had admitted us members of his privy council; but how seldom do we do justice to the Scriptures, where the covenant is mentioned in a *practical* manner! How rarely do the ministers., who are fond of preaching upon the covenant between God and David, dwell upon such scriptures as these! "Because they continued not in my covenant, I regarded them not; because they have transgressed the law, changed the ordinances, and broken the everlasting covenant, therefore hath the curse devoured the earth, and they that dwell therein are desolate: therefore the inhabitants of the earth are burned, and few men left. I say to the wicked, What hast thou to do to take my covenant in thy mouth? They kept not the covenant of God, and refused to walk in his law;" they would not be evangelically legal, "therefore a fire was kindled in Jacob, the wrath of God came upon them, he slew the fattest of them, and smote down the chosen, *the elect* of Israel!"

We frequently keep back from our hearers the very portions that honest Nathan or blunt John the Baptist would have particularly enforced. The taste of many is perverted; they "loathe the manna of the word," not because it is *light,* but *heavy* food. They must have "savoury meat, such as their soul loveth;" and we "hunt for venison," we minister to their spiritual luxury, and feast with them on our doctrinal refinements. Hence "many are weak and sickly among us." Some that might be "fat and well-liking, cry out, *My leanness! My leanness!*" And "many sleep" in a spiritual grave, the easy prey of corruption and sin.

How few Calebs, how few Joshuas are found among the many spies who bring a report of the good land! The cry is seldom, "Let us go up and possess it," unless the good land be the map of the Gospel drawn by Dr. Crisp. On the contrary, the difficulties attending the noble conquest are magnified to the highest degree. "The sons of Anak are tall and strong, and their cities are fenced up to heaven." "All our corruptions are gigantic. The castle where they dwell shall always remain a den of thieves. It is an impregnable citadel, strongly garrisoned by Apollyon's forces: we shall never love God here with all our souls: we shall always have desperately wicked hearts."

How few of our celebrated pulpits are there, where more has not been said *at times* for sin than against it! With what an air of positiveness and assurance has that Barabbas, that murderer of Christ and souls, been pleaded for! "It will humble us, make us watchful, stir up our diligence, quicken our graces, endear Christ," &c. That is, in plain English, pride will beget humility; sloth will spur us on to diligence; rust will brighten our armour; and unbelief, the very soul of every sinful temper, is to do the work of faith! Sin must not only be always lurking about the walls and gates of the town of Man's Soul, (if I may once more allude to Bunyan's *Holy War,)* but it shall dwell in it, in the King's palace, "in the inner chamber," the inmost recesses of the heart; there is no turning it out. Jesus, who cleansed the lepers with a word or a touch, cannot, with all the force of his Spirit and virtue of his blood, expel this leprosy. It is too inveterate. Death, that foul monster, the offspring of sin, shall have the important honour of killing his father. He, he alone is to give the great, the last, the decisive blow. This is confidently asserted by those who cry, *Nothing but Christ!* They allow him to lop off the branches; but death, the great savior death, is to destroy the root of sin. In the meantime "the temple of God shall have agreement with idols, and Christ concord with Belial: the Lamb" of God shall "lie down with the roaring lion" in our hearts.

Nor does the preaching of this internal slavery, this bondage of spiritual corruption, shock our hearers. No: this mixture of light and darkness passes for Gospel in our days. And what is more astonishing still, by making much ado about "finished salvation," we can even put it off as "the only pure, genuine, and comfortable Gospel:" while the smoothness of our doctrine will atone for our most glaring inconsistencies.

We have so whetted the Antinomian appetite of our hearers, that they swallow down almost any thing. We may tell them St. Paul was, at one and the same time, "carnal, sold under sin," crying, "Who shall deliver me from this body of death?" and triumphing that he did "not walk after the flesh, but after the Spirit, rejoicing in the testimony of a good conscience," and glorying that "the law of the Spirit of life in Christ Jesus had made him free from the law of sin and death!" This suits their experience; therefore they readily take our word, and it passes for "the word of God." It is a mercy that we have not yet attempted to prove, by the same argument, that lying and cursing are quite consistent with apostolic faith; for St. Paul speaks of his "lie," and St. James says, "With our tongues curse we men."

Five Checks To Antinomianism

We may make them believe, that though adultery and murder are damning sins in poor blind Turks and heathens, yet they are only the spots of God's children in enlightened Jews and favoured Christians: that God is the most partial of all judges; some being accursed to the pit of hell for breaking the law in the most trifling points; while others, who actually break it in the most flagrant instances, are richly "blessed with all heavenly benedictions:" and that, while God beholds "no iniquity in Jacob, no perverseness in Israel," he sees nothing but odious sins in Ishmael, and devilish wickedness in Esau; although the Lord assures us, "The wickedness of the wicked shall be upon him," and that "though hand join in hand the wicked shall not go unpunished," were he as great in Jacob as Korah, and as famous as Zimri in Israel.

We may tell our hearers, one hour, that "the love of Christ *sweetly* constrains" all believers to walk, yea, to "run the way of God's commandments," and that they cannot help obeying its forcible dictates: and we may persuade them, the next hour, that "how to perform what is good they find not; that they fall continually into sin; for that which they do they allow not, and what they would, that do they not; but what they hate, that do they." And that these inconsistencies may not shock their common sense, or alarm their consciences, we again touch the sweet-sounding string of "finished salvation:" we intimate we have the key of evangelical knowledge, reflect on those who expect deliverance from sin in this life, and "build up" our congregations in a most comfortable, I wish I could say, "most holy faith."

In short, we have so used our people to strange doctrines, and preposterous assertions, that, if we were to intimate, God himself sets us a pattern of Antinomianism, by disregarding his own most holy and lovely law, which inculcates perfect love, — if we were even to hint that he bears a secret grudge, or an immortal enmity to those very souls whom he commands us to "love as Christ has loved us;" that he feeds them only for the great day of slaughter, and has determined, (so inveterate is his hatred!) "before the foundation of the world" to "fit" them as "vessels of wrath," that he might eternally fill them with his fiery vengeance, merely to show what a great and sovereign God he is; I doubt whether some would not be highly pleased, and say we had "preached a sound and sweet discourse." This would probably be the ease, if we addressed them in such a manner as to make them believe they are *elect;* not, indeed, of those ancient, legal, and wrestling "elect, who cry to God day and night to be avenged of their spiritual adversary," but of those modern, indolent elect, who have found out a short way to heaven, and maintain, "We are absolutely to do nothing in order to salvation."

With joy I confess, however, that glorious and rousing truths are frequently delivered in the demonstration of the Spirit and of power. But, alas! The blow is seldom followed. You have seen fond mothers violently correcting their children one instant, and the next dandling them upon their knees; and, by foolishly kissing away their tears, spoiling the correction they had given. Just so it is with several of us: we preach a close discourse, and seem determined to drive the buyers and sellers out of the temple. Our Antinomian hearers begin to awake and look about them: some are even ready to cry out, "Men and brethren, what shall we do?" but, alas! We sound a retreat when we should shout for a second

The Works of John Fletcher

battle. By an unaccountable weakness, before we conclude, we soothe them up, and make a way for their escape; or, which is not much better, the next time we preach, by setting up Dr. Crisp's doctrine as much as ever, we industriously repair the breach we had made in the Antinomian Babel.

And suppose some of us preach against Antinomianism, is not our practice contrary to our preaching? We are under a dangerous mistake if we think ourselves clear from Antinomianism merely because we thunder against Antinomian principles' for as some, who zealously maintain such principles, by the happiest inconsistency in the world, pay nevertheless, in their practice, a proper regard to the law they revile; so not a few, who profess the deepest respect for it, are so unhappily inconsistent as to transgress it without ceremony. The God of holiness says, "Go and WORK in my vineyard;" the inconsistent Antinomian answers, "I will not be bound by any law; I scorn the ties of duty" but nevertheless "he repents and goes." The inconsistent legalist replies, "It is my bounden duty to obey; *I go, Lord:*" nevertheless "he does not go." Which of the two is the greater Antinomian? The latter, no doubt: his practical Antinomianism is much more odious to God and man than the speculative error of the former.

The Lord God help us to avoid both! Whether the hellish wolf comes barefaced, or "in sheep's clothing;" or, what is a still more dangerous disguise, in *Lamb's* clothing; in the clothes of the Shepherd, covered from head to foot with a righteousness which he has "imputed" to himself, and sings the siren song of "finished salvation."

IV. I shall close these reflections upon the Antinomianism of preachers, by presenting you with sketches of two very opposite ways of preaching. The first is an extract from Bishop Hopkins' twenty-fourth sermon, entitled, *Practical Christianity,* upon those words of St. Paul, "Work out your own salvation with fear and trembling," &c. This testimony will weigh so much the more with you: as he was a *sound Calvinist,* and a truly converted man.

"To work out our salvation, says the godly prelate, is to persevere in the ways of obedience until, through them, that salvation which is begun here on earth be perfected in heaven. This work implies three things: (1.) Pains and labour. Salvation is that which must be wrought out; it is that which will make the soul pant and breathe, yea, run down with sweat to obtain it. (2.) It implies constancy and diligence. A Christian that would 'work out his salvation' must be always employed about it. It is a web, into which we must weave the whole thread of our lives. That man who works at salvation only by some passionate fits, and then, within awhile, undoes it all again by foul apostasy and notorious sins, will never work salvation *out.* (3.) It promises success; though it be hard work, it shall not be long work; continue working, it shall be wrought out; what before was your work, shall be your reward; and this salvation, that was so painful in working, shall be most blessed in the enjoyment.

"Say not, 'We have no strength to work with.' What God commands us to do he will assist us in doing. We are impotent, but God is omnipotent. Work, therefore; for this omnipotent God 'works in you both to will and to do.'

"The proposition I shall lay down from the text is this: 'That it is the duty of every true Christian to work out his own salvation with fear and trembling:' or,' that every Christian, yea, every man, ought to work for his living, even for an eternal life.' To mention places for the proof of this, were to transcribe the Bible. We can no where open this blessed book but we find this truth proved to us, either directly or by consequence. And yet, it is strange in these days to see how dubiously some men, who would be thought admirers of free grace, speak of obedience and working, as if they were the badge of a legal spirit. O, it is a soft and easy doctrine to bid men sit still and believe, as if God would translate them to heaven upon their couches! Is it possible that these notions should be dispersed and entertained, but because it has always been the devil's policy to vent those doctrines that indulge the flesh under the patronage of free *grace and Gospel attainments?*

"Wherefore is it that we are commanded to 'strive that we may enter in at the strait gate? So to run that we may obtain?' So to *wrestle* that we may be 'able to stand?' So 'to fight, that we may lay hold on eternal life?' Can you strive and run, and wrestle and fight, and all this by doing nothing? If God would save you without working, why has he given you grace, an operative principle, that you might work? He might as well save you without grace as without works: for that is not grace that does not put forth itself in working. God, rather than we shall not work, will set us at work. He gives and promises assistance, only that we might work out our own salvation. 'We are not sufficient to think any thing.' What then? Must we therefore sit still? 'No,' says the apostle: for God, who finds us employment will also find us strength. '*Our sufficiency is of God.*'

"Wherefore is it that men are justly damned? Is it not because they will not do what they are able to do? And whence have they this ability? Is it not from the grace of God's Spirit? What is it that men expect? Must God drive them to heaven by force and violence, whether they will or not?

"If man will, he may work out his salvation. I speak not this to assert the power of man to work out salvation without the aid of special grace to incline his will. Where there is special grace given to make the will willing to convert, there is nothing more required to make him able, because conversion chiefly consists in the act of the will itself; only to make him willing is required special grace; which they, that favour the undue liberty of the will, deny. Our impotency lies in the stubbornness of our wills. The greatest sinner may work out his own salvation if he will. If he be but willing, he has that already that may make him able. God puts no new powers in the soul when he converts it.

"Are there any so desperately profane as not to have prayed unto God in their whole life? Why now, to what end have you prayed? Was it not for salvation? And did you work for salvation, and at the same time believe you could not work?. Thou art inexcusable, O man, whoever thou art, that wilt not work: it is in vain to plead thou wantest power! God will confute thee out of thy own mouth.

"Would a master, when he commands his servant to work, take this as a sufficient excuse for his sloth and idleness, that he has no power to work till God acts and moves him? Why, this is a truth, and it may as well be objected by' your servants to you, as by you unto God. Though it is impossible that men should stir without God's concurrence, yet this hinders not endeavour, no, nor is it any matter of discouragement to them. They put these things to the trial. Now, why should we not do so in spirituals as well as in temporals? Are they not of greater concernment? It is not inability, but wilful sloth, that destroys men. Sinners, wherefore will you perish? Why will you sleep away your souls into hell? Is it more painful for you to work than to be damned? Endeavour therefore to do what you can: labour and sweat at salvation's work, rather than fail of it for a wilful neglect. 'How shall you escape if you neglect so great salvation?'

"OBJECTION. Thus to press men to working is derogatory to Christ's merits, by which alone we are saved, and not by our works. Christ has done all for us, and wrought out our salvation by himself. Shall we piece out his work by our obedience, when all we have now to do is to believe on him?"

"ANSWER. There is the sweetest harmony between the merits of Christ and our 'working out of our salvation.' To make it evident, I shall show what Christ has done for us, and what he expects we should do for ourselves. He has merited grace, and purchased eternal happiness. And why did Christ merit grace?. Was it not that we might act it in obedience? If he merited grace that we might obey, is it sense to object, that our obedience is derogatory to his merit? If one end of his doing all that he did for us was to enable us to do for ourselves, will any man say, 'Now I am bound to do nothing, because Christ has done all?' How lost are such men both to reason and religion, who undertake so to argue! No: salvation was purchased and grace procured, that, by the acting and exercise of that grace, we might attain to that salvation. It is not by way of merit or purchase that we exhort men to work out their salvation. Those are guilty of practical blasphemy against the priestly office of Christ who think to merit it by their own works.

"As Christ has done two things for us, so he requires two things from us. (1.) That we should put forth all the strength of nature in laboring after grace: and (2.) That we should put forth the power of grace in labouring for the salvation purchased for us. (1.) Let every sinner know it is his work to repent and return, that he may live. You cannot sit down and say, 'What need is there of my working? Christ has already done all my work for me to my hands.' No: Christ has done his own work, the work of a *Saviour* and a *Surety;* but he never did the work of a *sinner.*

"If Christ, by m*eriting* grace, had bestowed it upon thee, and wrought it in thee, then indeed no more would be required of thee to become holy, but to cast back a lazy look at the purchase of Jesus Christ: then thy sloth would have some pretence not to labour. But this will not do. Our Saviour commands all men 'to seek first the kingdom of God:' and the apostle exhorts Simon Magus 'to pray.' Do not therefore cheat your own souls into perdition by lazy notions about Christ's merits. If you sit still, expecting till the meriting grace of Christ drop down into your souls, and change your hearts, truly, it may be, before that time you yourselves may drop down into hell, with your old unchanged hearts!

"(2.) Christ expects that those who have grace should put forth the utmost power thereof in labouring after the salvation he has purchased for them. He has merited salvation for them; but it is to be obtained by their own labour and industry. Is not what Christ has done sufficient? Must he *repent, believe,* and *obey* for them? This is not to make him a Saviour, but a drudge. He has done what was fit for a Mediator to do. He now requires of us what is meet for *sinners* to do; that is, to repent, &c. He now bids you 'wash and be clean.' Would you have the great Prophet come and strike off your leprosy, and you do nothing toward the cure? The way to heaven is made possible; but if you do not walk in the way that leads to it, you may still be as far from heaven as ever. Though Christ's bearing the punishment of the law by death does exempt us from suffering, yet his obeying of the law does not excuse our obedience to the law. Nor is our obedience derogatory to Christ's, because it proceeds from other grounds than Christ's did. He obeyed the law as a covenant of works, — we only as a rule of righteousness.

"To conclude upon this point: so work with that earnestness, constancy, and unweariedness in well doing, as if thy works alone were able to justify and save thee' and so absolutely depend and rely upon the merits of Christ for justification and salvation, as if thou never hadst performed one act of obedience in all thy life. This is the right Gospel frame of obedience, so to work, as if we were only to be saved by our own merits; and withal so to rest on the merits of Christ, as if we had never wrought any thing. It is a difficult thing to give to each of these its due in our practice. When we work, we are too apt to neglect Christ; and when we rely on Christ, we are too apt to neglect working. But that Christian has got the right art of obedience who can mingle these two together; who can with one hand 'work the works of God,' and yet, at the same time, lay fast hold on the merits of Jesus Christ. Let this Antinomian principle be for ever rooted out of the minds of men, that our working is derogatory to Christ's work. Never more think he has done all your work for you, but labour for that salvation which he has purchased and merited. Could ever such senseless objections prevail with men who have seriously read this scripture? 'He gave himself for us, that he might redeem us from all iniquity, and purify to himself a peculiar people zealous of good works.' But truly, when sloth and ignorance meet together, if you tell men what powers their natures, assisted by preventing grace, have to work, and how necessary obedience is to salvation, they, with the sluggard, fold their arms in their bosom, doing nothing; telling us these doctrines are *Arminianism* and flat *Popery*. But deceive not yourselves: whether this doctrine takes hold on your judgments now, I know not; but this I know assuredly, it shall take hold on your consciences either here or hereafter; and then it will not suffice you to say, either that you had no power to do any thing, or that Christ has already done all for you."

This excellent discourse should be in all the houses of professors. It would shame the careless remonstrants, and show them how orthodox some Calvinists are in point of works; and it would confound the slothful Calvinists, and make them see how they have left *practical Christianity* for *Antinomian Crispianity*. For east cannot be farther from west than the preceding extract of Bishop Hopkins' sermon is from the following propositions, extracted from Dr. Crisp's Works, which some make the standard of evangelical preaching. They are refuted also in "Gospel Truth Vindicated, by Mr. Williams," whose excellent refutation is recommended by fifty-three Calvinist divines of the last century. And Mr. Wesley's propositions, in the Minutes of the conference held in 1770, may be looked upon as the ground on which that refutation stands.

"Must not a believer, an elect, be reckoned to be a sinner while he does sin? No: though he does sin, yet he is not to be reckoned as a sinner; his sins are reckoned to be taken away from him. A man does sin against God; God reckons not his sin to be his; he reckons it Christ's, therefore he cannot reckon it to be his. There is no condition in the covenant of grace; man has no tie upon him to perform any thing whatsoever as a condition that must be observed on his part; and there is not one bond or obligation upon man to the fulfilling of his part of the covenant, or partaking of the benefits of it. There is no better way to know your portion in Christ, than, upon the general tender of the Gospel, to conclude absolutely he is yours: say, 'My part is as good as any man's:' set down thy rest here; question it not, but believe it. Christ belongs to sinners as sinners; and if there be no worse than sinfulness, rebellion, and enmity in thee, he belongs to thee, as well as to any in the world. Christ does justify a person before he believes; we do not believe that we may be justified, but because we are justified. The elect are justified from eternity, at Christ's death; and the latest time is before they are born. It is a received conceit among persons that our obedience is the way to heaven; and though it be not, say they, the cause of our reign, yet it is the way to the kingdom: but I must tell you, all this sanctification of life is not a jot the way of that justified person to heaven. To what purpose do we propose to ourselves the gaining of that by our labour and industry that is already become ours before we do one jot? Must they now labour to gain these things, as if it were referred to their well or evil walking, that as they shall walk so they shall speed? The Lord does nothing in his people upon conditions. The Lord intends not that by our obedience we shall gain something, which, in case of our failing, we shall miscarry of. While you labour to get by duties, you provoke God as much as in you lies. We must work from life, and not for life. There is nothing you can do from whence you ought to expect any gain to yourselves. Love to the brethren, universal obedience, and all other inherent qualifications, are no signs by which we should judge of our state. Every elect vessel, from the first instant of his being, is as pure in the eyes of God from the charge of sin as he shall be in glory. Though such persons do act rebellion, yet the loathsomeness and hatefulness of this rebellion is laid on the back of Christ; he bears the sin, as well as the blame and shame: and God can dwell with persons that act the thing, because all the filthiness of it is translated from them upon the back of Christ. It is the voice of a lying spirit in your hearts, that says, 'You that are believers (as David) have yet sin wasting your conscience.' David indeed says, *My sins are gone over my head,* but he speaks from himself, and all that he speaks from himself was not truth. There is as much ground to be confident of the pardon of sin to a believer, as soon as he committed it, as to believe it after he has performed all the humiliation in the world. A believer may be assured of pardon as soon as he commits any sin, even adultery and murder. There is not one fit of sadness in a believer, but he is out of the way of Christ. God does no longer stand displeased though a believer do sin often. There is no sin that ever believers commit that can possibly do them any hurt. Therefore, as their sins cannot hurt them, so there is no cause of fear in their sins committed. Sins are but scarecrows and bugbears to fright ignorant children, but men of understanding see they are counterfeit things. Sin is dead, and there is no more terror in it than in a dead lion. If we tell believers, except they walk thus and thus holily, and do these and those good works, God will be angry with them, we abuse the Scriptures, undo what Christ has done, injure believers, and tell God lies to his face. All our righteousness is filthy, full of men-struosity, the highest kind of filthiness: — even what is the Spirit's must be involved within that which is a man's own, under the general notion of *dung*. God has done every thing in Christ, and taken away all things that can disturb our peace; but man will be mincing the truth, and tell you, that if you keep close to God, and refrain from sin, God will love you. Christ does all his work for him as well as in him that believes. If persons are not united to Christ, and do not partake of justification before they do believe, there will be bringing to life again the covenant of works; you must of necessity press upon yourselves these terms, 'I must do, that I may have life in Christ; I must believe.' Now if there be believing first, then there is doing before living. To what purpose do we tell men of wrath and damnation? We had as good hold our tongues," &c, &c.

"I observe," Says my judicious Calvinist author, "the pretence for these opinions is, *that they exalt* CHRIST *and* FREE GRACE. Under this shadow Antinomianism set up in Germany. This was the great cry in England above fifty years since. The Synod of New-England expose this as one of the speeches of them whom they call Antinomians: 'Here is a great stir about grace and looking to hearts; but give me Christ! I seek not for graces, but for Christ: I seek not for promises, but for Christ: I seek not for sanctification, but for Christ: tell me not of meditation and duties, but tell me of Christ.' Dr. Crisp very often bears upon this point, as if all he said was to advance Christ and grace."

You will perhaps say that our Gospel ministers are far more guarded than the doctor. But I would ask whether all his scheme is not collected and made to centre in the one fashionable expression of *finished salvation?* which seems to be our *Shibboleth*.

If the *salvation* of the elect was *finished* upon the cross, then was their *justification* finished, their *sanctification* finished, their *glorification* finished. For justification, sanctification, and glorification *finished*, are but the various parts of our *finished salvation*. If our justification be *finished*, there is no need of believing in order to be justified. If our sanctification be *finished*, there is no need of mortifying one sin, praying for one grace, taking up one cross, parting with either right eye or right hand, in order to perfect holiness. Again:

Suppose our salvation be *finished*, it follows, Christ has done all, and we are to do nothing. Obedience and good works are no more necessary in order to it, than cutting and carrying stones are necessary to the completing of Westminster bridge. We are as perfect in Christ, as completely blameless and holy in the midst of all our sins, as ever we shall be in glory. In a word, if salvation be *finished*, well ordered in all things and sure, our sins cannot take any thing from it, nor our righteousness have any thing to do with it. The little flock of the elect shall be saved, nay, are fully saved now, do what they please; and the multitudes of the reprobates shall be damned, do what they can. Give me only the smooth ring of *finished salvation*, and without offering the least violence to common sense, I shall necessarily draw every link of Dr. Crisp's Antinomian chain.

I have often wondered how so many excellent men can be so fond of an expression which is the stalking horse of every wild ranter. Is it Scriptural? Which of the prophets or apostles ever used it on earth? Do even "the spirits of just men made perfect," ascribe *finished salvation* to the Lamb? If they did, would not their uncollected dust, and the souls "crying under the altar," prove their praises premature? Will salvation be *finished* till "the last enemy, death," is fully overcome by the general resurrection? Again:

Is the expression *of finished salvation* consistent with the analogy of faith? Does it not supersede our Lord's "intercession at the right hand of God?" Whether he intercede for the reprobate or the elect, acts he not a most unwise part? Is he not giving himself a needless trouble, whether he intercede for the justification of those whom he has himself *reprobated,* or for the salvation of those whose salvation is *finished?* Is it right to offer an insult to our High Priest upon his mediatorial throne, under pretence of honouring him on the cross? And may not I say, with judicious Baxter, "See what this overdoing tends to!" See what contempt it pours upon Him "who is the brightness of his Father's glory!"

If that favourite expression be neither Scriptural nor agreeable to the analogy of faith, is it at least *rational?* I doubt it is not. *Finished salvation* implies both a deliverance from bodily and spiritual evils, and a being made fully partakers of heavenly glory, in body and in soul. But waiving the consideration of glory and heaven, and taking the word *salvation* in its negative and lower sense, I ask, Can it be said, with any propriety, that bodily salvation is *finished,* while innumerable pains and diseases surround us, to drag us to the grave, and deliver us to putrefaction? And is spiritual 'salvation *finished?* "Is the *body* of sin destroyed?" Do not those very ministers, who preach finished salvation with one breath, tell us with the next," There is no deliverance, (that is, *no finished salvation,)* from sin in this life?"

And what end does that expression answer? I know of none but that of spreading Dr. Crisp's doctrine, and making thousands of deluded souls talk as if the "tower" of their salvation was finished, when they have not so much as "counted the cost;" or when they have just laid the foundation.

Therefore, with all due deference to my brethren and fathers who preach *finished salvation,* I ask, Would it not be better to drop that doctrine, with all the other dangerous refinements of Dr. Crisp,. and preach a *finished atonement, a present sovereign remedy, completely prepared* to heal all our spiritual infirmities, assuage all our miseries, and fit us for finished salvation in glory? Would not this be as well at least, as to help our patients to compose themselves to sleep upon the pillow of Antinomianism; by making them believe that the preparation of the remedy, and a complete cure, are all one; so that now they have absolutely nothing to do in order to saving health, and (as the apostles concluded about Lazarus,) "if they sleep they shall do well?" And should we not, even in speaking of *redemption,* imitate the judicious Calvinists of the last century, who carefully distinguished between redemption by the *price* of Jesus' blood, and redemption by the *power* of his Spirit? "The former," said they, "was finished upon the cross but the latter is not so much as begun in thousands; even in all that are unborn or unconverted."

V. To speak the melancholy truth, how few individuals are free from practical Antinomianism! Setting aside their attendance on the ministry of the word, where is the material difference between several of our genteel believers and other people? Do we not see the sumptuous furniture in their apartments, and fashionable elegance in their dress? What sums of money do they frequently lay out in costly superfluities to adorn their persons, houses, and gardens!

Wise heathens, by the help of a little philosophy, saw the impropriety of having any useless brittle vessels about them: they broke them on purpose that they might be consistent with the profession they made of *seeking wisdom*. But we, who profess to have "found CHRIST the Wisdom of God," purchase such vessels and toys at a high rate; and instead of hiding them for shame, as Rachel did her teraphim for fear, we "'write our *motto* over against the candlestick upon the plaster of the wall," and any man that fears the God of Daniel may, upon studying the Chinese characters, make out ANTINOMIANISM.

Our Lord, whose garment does not appear to have been cut in the height of the fashion, as it was made without seam, informs us that they who wear "soft clothing" and splendid apparel "are in kings' houses." But had he lived in our days, he might have found them in God's houses; in our fashionable churches or chapels. There you may find people professing to believe the Bible, who so conform to this present world, as to wear gold, pearls, and precious stones, when no distinction of office or state obliges them to it; in direct opposition to the words of two apostles: "Let not their adorning," says St. Peter, "be that outward adorning of plaiting the hair, and of wearing of gold, or of putting on of apparel." "Let them adorn themselves in modest apparel," adds St. Paul, "not with curled hair, or gold, or pearls, or costly array."

Multitudes of professors, far from being convinced of their sin in this respect, ridicule Mr. Wesley for bearing his testimony against it. The opposition he dares make to that growing branch of vanity, affords matter of pious mirth to a thousand Antinomians. Isaiah could openly reprove the "haughty daughters of Zion, who walked with stretched-forth necks, wanton eyes, and tinkling feet." He could expose "the bravery of their fashionable ornaments, their round tires like the moon, their chains, bracelets, headbands, rings, and earrings." But some of our humble Christian ladies will not bear a reproof from Mr. Wesley on the head of dress. They even laugh at him, as *a pitiful legalist:* and yet, O the inconsistency of the Antinomian spirit! they call Isaiah *the evangelical prophet!*

Finery is often attended with an expensive table, at least with such delicacies as our purse can reach. St. Paul "kept his body under, and was in fastings often;" and our Lord gives us directions about the proper manner of fasting. But the apostle did not *know* the easy way to heaven taught by Dr. Crisp; and our Lord did not *approve* of it, or he would have saved himself the trouble of his directions. In general, we look upon fasting, much as we do upon penitential flagellation. Both equally raise our pity. We leave them both to Popish devotees. Some of our good old Church people will yet fast on Good Friday; but our fashionable believers begin to cast away that last scrap of self denial. Their faith, which should produce, animate, and regulate works of mortification, goes a shorter way to work, — it explodes them all.

"But perhaps 'we wrestle not with flesh and blood,' because we are entirely taken up with 'wrestling against principalities, powers, and spiritual wickednesses in high places.'"

Alas! I fear this is not the case. Few of us know what it is "to cry out of the deep," to pray and believe, till in the name of Jesus we force our way beyond flesh and blood, come within the reach of the eternal world, conflict in an agony with the powers of darkness, vanquish Apollyon in all his attacks, and continue wrestling till the day of eternity break upon us, and the God of Jacob "bless us with all spiritual benedictions in heavenly places." John Bunyan's pilgrim, the old Puritans, and the first Quakers, had such engagements, and gained such victories; but they soon got over the hedge of internal activity, into the smooth easy path of Laodicean formality. Most of us, called Methodists, have already followed them; and when we are in that snare, Satan scorns to conflict with us; puny flesh and blood are more than a match for us. We fall asleep under their bewitching power, and begin to dream strange dreams. "Our salvation is finished, we have got above legality, we live without frames and feelings, we have attained Christian liberty, we are perfect in Christ, we have nothing to do, our covenant is sure," &c. True! But unhappily it is a covenant with the flesh. Satan, who is too wise to break it by rousing us in the spirit, leaves us to our delusions; and we think ourselves in the kingdom of God, when we are only in a fool's paradise.

"At midnight, I will rise and praise thee," said once a pious Jew; but we pious Christians, who enjoy both health and strength, are imprisoned within our bed curtains, long after the sun has "called the *diligent* to their labour." When "the fear of the Lord" was in us "the beginning of wisdom," we durst "not so confer with flesh and blood." We had then a little faith; and, so far as it went, it showed itself by our works. Then we could without hesitation and from our hearts pray, "Stir up, we beseech thee, O Lord, the wills of thy faithful people, that they, plenteously bringing forth the fruit of good works, may by thee be plenteously rewarded, through Jesus Christ our Lord." (*Collect for the last Sunday in Trinity.*) We believed there was some truth in these words of our Lord: "Except a man forsake all that he hath, deny himself, and take up his cross daily, he cannot be my disciple. He that wills save his life Shall lose it, and he that will lose his life for my sake shall find it. If thine eye offend thee, pluck it out: it is better for thee to enter into life with one eye, than having two eyes to be cast into hell fire. Strive to enter in at the strait gate; for I say unto you, that many shall seek to enter in, and shall not be able;" because they will seek to enter in at the *wide,* rather than the *strait gate;* the Antinomian or Pharisaic, rather than the evangelically legal gate of salvation. But now "we know better," say some of us, "we have got over our scruples and legality." We can "conform to this present world;" cleave to instead of "forsaking all we have," and even grasp what we have not. What a strange way this of "growing in grace, and in the knowledge of Christ crucified!"

Daniel informs us, that he "made his petition *three* times," and David, that he offered up his "praises *seven* times a day." Once also, like them, we had fixed hours for private prayer and self examination, for reading the Scriptures, and meditating upon them perhaps upon our knees; but we thought this was legality too; and under the specious pretence of going beyond forms, and learning "to pray always," we first threw away our forms, and, soon after, our endeavours to watch unto prayer. Now we scarcely ever, for any length of time, solemnly bend the knee before "our Father who sees in secret." And, instead of leaning on Christ's bosom in all the means of grace, we take our graceless rest on the bosom of that painted Jezebel, *formality.*

Five Checks To Antinomianism

If we are backward in performing that leading work of PIETY, *secret prayer*, is it a wonder if, in general, we are averse to every work of MERCY that costs us something, beside a little of our superfluous money? And would to God some did not even grudge this, when it is pressed out of their purses, by the importunate address of those who beg for the poor! However, we give yet at the door of a church, or at the communion; whether with indifference or joy, whether out of custom, shame, or love, we seldom examine. But that important branch of St. James' "pure and undefiled religion before God, even the Father," which consists "in visiting the fatherless and widows in their afflictions," is, with many, almost as much out of date as a pilgrimage to our Lady of Loretto.

O ye forsaken sons of poverty, and ancient daughters of sorrow, who pine away in your desolate garrets or cellars, without fire in winter, destitute of food, physic, or nurse in sickness! raise a moment your emaciated bodies, wrapped up in thread-bare blankets, if you are possessed of any such covering, and tell me, tell the world, how many of our gay professors of religion have sought and found you out in your deplorable circumstances! How many are come to visit, in you, and to worship, with you, "the Man of sorrows" who once lay on the cold ground in a bloody sweat! When did they "make your bed in your sickness?" When have they kindly inquired into all your wants, sympathized in all your temptations, supported your drooping heads in a fainting fit, revived your sinking spirits with suitable cordials, gently wiped your cold sweats, or mixed them with their tears of pity?

Alas! you sometimes find more compassion and assistance in your extremity from those who never "name the name of Christ," than from our easy, Antinomian, Laodicean *believers*. Their wants are richly supplied; that is enough: they do not inquire into yours, and *you* are ashamed or afraid to trouble them with the dismal story. Nor indeed would some of them understand you if you did. Their uninterrupted abundance makes them as incapable of feeling for you, as the warm inhabitants of Ethiopia are to feel for the frozen Icelanders.

While the table of some believers, (so called,) is alternately loaded with a variety of delicate meats and rich wines, what have *ye* to sustain sinking nature? Alas! one can soon see your all of food and physic. A pitcher of water stands by your bed side upon a stool, the only piece of furniture left in your wretched apartment. The Lord God bless the poor widow that brought it you, with her *two mites!* Heaven reward a thousand-fold the loving creature, that not only shares with you, but freely bestows upon you "all her living, even all that she has," when *they* forgot to inquire after you, and to send you something out of their luxurious abundance! "The Son of man, *once* forsaken by all the disciples, and comforted by an angel, make her bed in the time of sickness!" and a waiting band of celestial spirits "carry" her charitable soul "into Lazarus' bosom" in the awful hour of dissolution! I had rather be in her case, though she should not confidently profess the faith, than in *yours*, O ye caressed believers, who let your affluence overflow to those that have more need to learn frugality in the school of scarceness, than to receive bounties which feed their sensuality, and indulge their pride.

And ye women professing godliness, who enjoy the comforts of health and abundance, in whose "streets there is no complaining, no decay, whose daughters are as the polished corners of the temple!" when did *you* ever want visiters? Alas! ye have too many, for the good they do you, or that you do them. Does not your conversation, which begins with the love of Jesus, terminate in religious scandal; as naturally as your soul, which once "began in the spirit, ends now in the flesh?" O that your visiters were as ready to attend work houses, jails, infirmaries, and hospitals, as they are to wait upon you! O that at least, like the Dorcases, the Phebes, and Priscillas of old, you would teach them cheerfully to work for the poor, to be the free servants of the Church, and tender nurses of the sick! O that they saw in you all, now the holy women, "the widows who were widows indeed," formerly "entertained strangers, washed the saints' feet, instructed the younger women, and continued night and day in prayer!" But alas! "the love of many," once warm as the smoking flax, "is waxed cold," instead of taking fire, and flaming. They who once began "to seek the profit of many," now seek "their own" ease, or interest; their own honour, or indulgence.

Almost all, when they come to the foot of the hill Difficulty, take their leave of Jesus as a guide, because he leads on through spiritual death to the regeneration. Some, disliking that "door," like "thieves and robbers, climb up" an easier way. And others, leaving the highway of the *cross,* under the fair pretence that blind Papists walk therein, make for themselves and others broad and downward roads, to ascend the steep hill of Zion.

Those easy paths are innumerable, like the people that walk in them. O that "my eyes, like David's, did run down like water, because men," professing godliness, "keep not God's law," and are even offended at it! "Their mouth talketh of vanity; they dissemble with their double heart, and their right hand is a right hand of *sloth, or positive* iniquity." O that I had the tenderness of St. Paul, "to tell you, even weeping, of those who mind earthly things;" those "who have sinned and have not repented;" those who, while they boast they "are made free by the Son" of God, are "brought under the power of *many* things;" whom foolish desires, absurd fears, undue attachments, imported superfluities, and disagreeable habits, keep in the most ridiculous bondage!

"O that my head were waters, and my eyes fountains of tears," to deplore, with Jeremiah, "the slain of the daughter of God's people, who live in pleasure, and are dead while they live!" And to lament over spiritual Pharisees of every sort; those who say, "Stand by, I am holier than thou;" and those who fix the names of *poor creature! blind!* and *carnal!* Upon every publican they see in the temple; and boldly placing themselves among *the elect,* "thank God they are not as other men," and in particular as *the reprobates!*

Who can number "the adulterers and adulteresses, who know not that the friendship of the world is enmity against God?" The concealed idolaters, who have their "chambers of imagery within, and set up their idols in their hearts?" The envious Cains, who carry murder in their breasts? The profane Esaus, who give up their birthright for a sensual gratification; and covetous Judases, who "sell the truth" which they should *buy,* and part with Christ "for filthy lucre's sake?" The sons of God, who look at the fair daughters of men, and take to themselves wives of all whom they choose? The gay Dinahs, who "visit the daughters of the land," and come home polluted in body or in soul. The filthy Onans, "who defile the temple of God." "The prophets of Bethel," who deceive the "prophets of Judah," entice them out of the way of self denial, and bring the roaring lion and death upon them. The fickle Marcuses, who depart when they should "go to the work." The self-made prophets, who "run before they are sent," and scatter instead of "profiting the people." The spiritual Absaloms, who rise against their fathers in the Gospel, and in order to reign without them, raise a rebellion against them, The furious Zedekiahs, who "make themselves horns of iron to push" the true servants of the Lord, because they will not "prophesy smooth things and deceit," as they do?

Who can count the fretful Jonahs, who are "angry to death" when the worm of disappointment "smites the gourd" of their creature happiness? The weak Aarons, who dare not resist a multitude, and are carried by the stream into the greatest absurdities. The jealous Miriams, who rise against the ministers that God honours. The crafty Zibas, who calumniate and supplant their brethren. The treacherous Joabs, who *kiss* them, to get an opportunity of "stabbing them under the fifth rib." The busy sons of Zeruiah, who perpetually stir up resentment and wrath. The mischievous Doegs, who carry about poisonous scandal, and blow up the fire of discord. The hypocritical Gehazis, who look like saints before their masters and ministers, and yet can impudently lie, and impiously cheat. The Gibeonites, always busy in hewing wood and drawing water, in going through the drudgery of outward services, without ever aspiring at the adoption of sons. The halting Naamans, who serve the Lord anti bow to Rimmon. The backsliding Solomons, who once chose wisdom, but now pursue folly in her most extravagant and impious forms. The apostatizing Alexanders, who "tread under foot the Son of God, and count the blood of the covenant, wherewith they were sanctified, an unholy thing." And, to include multitudes in one class, the Samaritans, who, by a common mixture of truth and error, of heavenly and earthly mindedness, "worship the Lord, and serve their gods;" are one day for God, and the next for Mammon? Or the thousands in Israel, who "halt between two opinions," crying out when Elijah prevails, "The Lord, he is the God!" and when Jezebel triumphs, returning to the old song, "*O Baal, save us!* O trinity of the world, *money, pleasure,* and *honour,* make us happy!"

VI. Time would fail to describe the innumerable branches of Antinomianism, with all the fruits they bear. It may be compared to the astonishing tree which Nebuchadnezzar saw in his mysterious dream: "A strong tree set in the midst of the *church;* the height thereof reaches unto heaven, and the sight thereof unto the ends of the earth. Its leaves are fair, and its fruit much." Thousands sleep under its fatal shadow, and myriads feed upon its pernicious fruit. At a distance it looks like "the tree of life planted in the midst of paradise;" but it only proves "the tree of knowledge of good and evil." The woman, (the Antinomian Church,) is deceived by the appearance. "She sees that it is good for food, pleasant to the eye, and desirable to make one wise." She eats to the full, and flushed with fond hopes of heaven, nay, fancying herself as God, she presents of the poisonous fruit that intoxicates her, to the nobler part of the Church, the obedient members of the second Adam.

O ye sons of God, and daughters of Abraham, who, in compliance with the insinuation of this deceived Eve, have already stretched forth your hands to receive her fatal present, instantly draw them back, for eternal "death is in the *fruit!*" Flee from the tree on which she banquets to the tree of life, the despised cross of Jesus; and there feed on "him crucified," till you are "crucified with him;" till the "body of sin is destroyed," and you feel eternal life abundantly circulating through all your sanctified powers.

And ye uncorrupted, self-denying followers of Jesus, whom love and duty still compel to bear your cross after him, join to pray that "the Watcher and his holy ones may come down from heaven, and cry aloud, Hew down the tree of *Antinomianism;* cut off its branches, shake off its leaves, scatter its fruit, and let not even the stump of its roots be left in the earth! Your prayer is heard: —

> *He comes! he comes! the Judge severe!*
> *The seventh trumpet speaks him near.*

Behold, he appears in his glory, "with ten thousand of his saints, to execute judgment upon all. The thrones are cast down; the Ancient of days doth sit, whose garment is white as snow, and the hair of his head like pure wool; his throne is like the fiery flame, and his wheels as burning fire. A fiery stream issues, and comes forth from before him: thousand thousands minister unto him, and ten thousand times ten thousand stand before him. The trumpet sounds: the sea gives up the dead which are in it, death and hades deliver up the dead which are in them." The just are separated from the unjust; and while the "earth and the heaven flee away from the face of him that sits on the great *resplendent* throne, and there is found no place for them, the judgment is set, the books are opened, and the dead, small and great, are judged, every one according to their works."

Fear not, ye righteous. Ye are "in the hand of the Lord, and there shall no torment touch you. In the sight of the unwise ye seemed to die," they laughed at your dying daily: "but ye are in peace, and your joy is full of immortality." Having been a little chastised, you shall be greatly rewarded; for God proved you, and found you worthy for himself. And now that "the time of your visitation is come," judge the nations, and reign with your Lord for ever; for, "such as are faithful in love shall abide with him; grace and mercy are to his saints, and he careth for his elect: he sets his sheep on his right hand," and stretching it toward them with ravishing looks of benignity and love, he finally justifies *by works* those whom he freely justified *by faith*. How sublime and solemn is the sentence!

"'Come, ye blessed of my Father! inherit the kingdom prepared for you from the foundation of the world. For I was hungry, and ye gave me meat; I was thirsty, and ye gave me drink; I was a stranger, and ye took me in; naked, and ye clothed me; I was sick, and ye visited me; I was in prison, and ye came to me!' And do not ask, with astonishment, WHEN you gave me all these tokens of your love: for whatever you did out of regard to me, my law, and my people, you did it 'in my name;' and whatever you did 'in my name' to the least of my creatures, and in particular 'to the least of these my brethren, you did it unto me!'"

As if he said, "Think not that I am biassed by lawless partiality. No: I am the Author of eternal salvation to them that obeyed me,' and made a right use of my sanctifying blood. Such are 'the blessed of my Father;' and such are ye. 'Your faith unfeigned' produced unfeigned love: you 'loved not in word only, but in deed and in truth:' witness the works of mercy that adorned your lives, or the fruits of the Spirit that now replenish your souls. 'You, of all the families of the earth, have I known' with approbation. Ye have not 'denied me in works;' or, if ye have, bitter repentance, and purifying, renovating faith followed your denial; and by 'keeping that faith, ye continued in my covenant, and endured unto the end.'

"Thou seest it, righteous Father, for to thee the books are always open. Thou readest 'my laws in their minds,' and beholdest my loving precepts 'written in their hearts:' I therefore 'confess them before thee;' and before you, my angels, who have seen them agonize, and 'follow me through the regeneration.' I take the new heavens and the new earth to witness, that 'I am to them a God, and they are to me a people. They walked WORTHY of God, who called them to his kingdom and glory; *therefore* they are worthy of me.'

"I have confessed your PERSONS, O ye 'just men made perfect!' Ye precious jewels of my mediatorial crown; let me next reward your WORKS. In the days of my flesh I declared, that 'a cup of water given in my name,' (and my name ye know is Mercy, Goodness, and Love,) 'should in no wise lose its reward;' and that 'whosoever should forsake' earthly friends or property for righteousness' sake, should have 'a hundred fold, and everlasting life.' The pillars of heaven have given way; but my promise stands, firm as the basis of my throne. Triumph in my faithfulness, as you have in my forgiving love. I bestow, on all, crowns of blissful immortality; 'I appoint unto each a kingdom' which shall not be destroyed. Be 'kings and priests unto God for ever.' 'Prepare to follow me to the realms of glory, and there 'whatsoever is right (διχαιον) that shall ye receive;' in *just* proportion to the various degrees of perfection, with which you have obeyed my law, and improved your talents."

Thus are the persons of the righteous accepted, and their works "praised in the gate" of heaven, and "rewarded in the kingdom of their Father." Thus they receive crowns of life and glory; but it is only to cast them, to all eternity, with unutterable transports, grateful humble love, at the feet of Him who was crowned with piercing thorns, and hung bleeding upon the cross, to purchase their thrones.

While they shout, "Salvation to God and the Lamb!" the Judge turns to the left hand, where trembling myriads stand waiting for their fearful doom. O how does confusion cover their faces, and guilty horror rack their breasts, while he says, with the firmness of the eternal Lawgiver, and the majesty of the Lord of lords: — "Depart from me, ye cursed, into everlasting fire, prepared for the devil and his angels! For I was hungry, and ye gave me no meat; I was thirsty, and ye gave me no drink; I was a stranger, and ye took me not in; naked, and ye clothed me not; sick and in prison, and ye visited me not!"*

---

* Should some sincere followers of Christ read these lines, and be convinced they never visited Christ *in prison*, never entertained him as a *stranger, &c*, it is proper they should be humbled for having overlooked this important part of "pure religion;" and consider next how far it is in their power literally to practise it. Some live at a great distance from prisons, and are necessarily detained at home. Some (as women) could not, in many places, visit prisoners with decency. Others are altogether unable to do good to the souls or bodies of the sick and captives, being themselves sick, poor, and confined. If thou art in any of these cases, believer, canst not thou influence others to do what is out of thy power? Canst thou not send the relief thou art unable to carry, and show thy good will by cutting off thy superfluities, sparing some of thy conveniences, and at times a little of thy necessaries,

Some are not yet *speechless*; they only falter. With the trembling insolence of Adam, not yet driven out of paradise, they even dare to plead their desperate cause. While stubborn sons of Belial say, "Lord, thy Father is merciful: and if thou didst die for *all*, why not for *us*?" While the obstinate Pharisees plead the good they did in their own name to supersede the Redeemer's merit, methinks I hear a bold Antinomian address thus the Lord of glory: —

"'Lord, when saw we thee hungry, or athirst, or a stranger, or naked, or sick, or in prison, and did not minister to thee?' Had we seen thee, dear Lord, in any distress, how gladly would we have relieved thy wants! Numbers can witness how well we spoke of thee and thy righteousness: it was all our boast. Bring it out in this important hour. Hide not the Gospel of thy free grace. We always delighted in pure doctrine, in *salvation without any condition; especially without the condition* of WORKS. Stand, gracious Lord, stand by us, and the preachers of thy free grace, who *made us hope thou wouldest confirm their word.*

"While they taught us to call thee, *Lord! Lord!* they assured us that love would *constrain* us to do good works; but finding no inward constraint to entertain strangers, visit the sick, and relieve prisoners, we did it not; supposing we were not called thereto. They continually told us, '*human righteousness was mere filth before thee; and we could not appear, but to our everlasting shame, in any righteousness but thine in the day of judgment.*' As to works, we were afraid of doing them, lest we should have 'worked out' abomination instead of 'our salvation.'

"And indeed, Lord, what need was there of our 'working it out?' For they perpetually assured us, it was finished; saying, If we did any thing toward it, we worked for life, fell from grace like the bewitched Galatians, spoiled thy perfect work, and exposed ourselves to the destruction which awaits yonder trembling Pharisees.

"They likewise assured us, *that all depended on* THY *decrees; and if we could but firmly believe our election, it was a sure sign we were interested in thy salvation.* We did so; and now, Lord, for the sake of a few dung works we have omitted, let not our hope perish! Let not electing and everlasting love fail! Visit our offences with a rod, but take not thy loving kindness altogether from us; and break not David's covenant, 'ordered in all things and sure,' of which we have so often made our boast.

"May it please thee also to consider, that if we did not love and assist some of those whom thou callest *thy brethren*, it was because they appeared to us so exceeding legal; so strongly set against free grace, that we judged them to be obstinate Pharisees, and dangerous reprobates. We therefore thought, that, in

---

for thy sick, naked, hungry, or imprisoned Lord? If thou art so indigent and infirm, that thou canst absolutely do nothing for the bodies of thy fellow creatures, endeavour to do works of mercy for their souls; exhort, reprove, comfort, instruct, as thou canst, all, around thee in meekness of wisdom. If thou canst do works of mercy neither with thy tongue, hands, nor feet, then be the more diligent to do them with *thy heart.* In spirit, visit prisons and sick beds. If thou hast no house to take in strangers, open to them thy heart; earnestly recommend them to God, who can supply all their wants, and open to them the gate of heaven, when they lie under a hedge, as he once did to Jacob in the fields of Bethel. Give thy heart continually to the Lord, and thou givest more than a mountain of gold; and the moment thou canst "give a cup of water in his name," bestow it as freely as he did his blood; remembering, "God loves a cheerful giver, and that it is accepted according to what a man hath, and not according to what he hath not."

hating and opposing them, we did thee service, and walked in thy steps. For thou hast said, 'It is enough if the servant is as his Lord:' and supposing 'thou didst hate them,' as thou dost Satan; *we* thought we need not be more righteous than thou, by loving them more than thou didst.

"O suffer us to speak on, and tell thee, we were champions for thy free grace. Like true Protestants, we could have burned against the doctrine of a *second justification by works*. Let then 'grace' justify us 'freely without works.' Shut those books,* filled with the account of our deeds, open the arms of thy mercy, and receive us just as we are.

"If *free grace* cannot justify us alone, let *faith* do it, together with free grace. We do *believe* finished salvation, Lord; we can join in the most evangelical creeds, and are ready to confess the virtue of thy stoning blood. But if thou sayest, we have 'trampled it under foot, and made it a common thing,' grant us our last request, and it is enough.

"Cut out the immaculate garment of 'thy righteousness' into robes that may fit us all, and put them upon us by *imputation:* so shall our nakedness be gloriously covered. We confess we have not dealt our bread to the hungry; but impute to us thy feeding five thousand people with loaves and fishes. We have seldom given drink to the thirsty, and often 'put our bottle' to those who were not athirst; but impute to us thy turning water into wine, to refresh the guests at the marriage feast in Cana; and thy loud call, ' in the last day of the feast at Jerusalem: *If any man thirst, let him come to me and drink!* We never supposed it was our duty to 'be given to hospitality:' but impute to us thy loving invitations to strangers, thy kind assurances of receiving 'all that come to thee;' thy comfortable promises of 'casting out none,' and of feeding them even with thy 'flesh and blood.' We did not clothe the naked as we had opportunity and ability; but impute to us thy patient parting with thy seamless garment for the benefit of thy murderers. We did not visit sick beds and prisons, we were afraid of fevers, and especially of the jail distemper; but compassionately impute to us thy visiting Jairus' daughter, and Peter's wife's mother, who lay sick of a fever; and put to our account thy visiting putrefying Lazarus in the offensive prison of the grave.

"Thy imputed righteousness, Lord, can alone answer all the demands of thy law and Gospel. We did not dare to *fast;* we should have been called *legal* and *Papists* if we had; but thy forty days' fasting in the wilderness, and thy continual abstinence, imputed to us, will be self denial enough to justify us ten times over. We did not 'take up our cross;' but impute to us thy 'carrying THINE;' and even fainting under the oppressive load. We did not 'mortify the deeds of the flesh, that we might live:' this would have been evidently *working for life;* but impute to us the crucifixion of *thy* body, instead of our 'crucifying our flesh, with its affections and lusts.' We hated private prayer; but impute to us thy love of that duty, and the prayer thou didst offer upon a mountain all night. We have been rather hard to forgive; but that defect will be abundantly made up if thou impute to us thy forgiving of the dying thief: and, if that will not do, add, we beseech

---

* This plea is excellent when a man comes to Christ, his High Priest, as a sinner for pardon and holiness, or for his first justification on earth; but it will be absurd, when he "stands before the throne" of Christ as a rebellious subject, or "before his judgment seat" as a criminal in the last day.

thee, the merit of that good saying of thine, 'Forgive, and you shall be forgiven.' We have cheated the king of his customs; but no matter; only impute to us thy exact paying of the tribute money, together with thy good advice, 'Render unto Cesar the things which are Cesar's.'

"It is true, we have brought up our children in vanity, and thou never hadst any to bring up. May not thy mercy find out an expedient, and impute to us, instead of it, thy obedience to thy parents? And if we have received the sacrament unworthily, and thou canst not cover that sin with thy worthy *receiving,* indulge us with the imputation of thy worthy *institution* of it, and that will do yet better.

"In short, Lord, own us *freely* as thy children. Impute to us thy perfect righteousness. Cast it as a cloak upon us to cover our filthy souls and polluted bodies. *We will have no righteousness but thine.* Make no mention, we beseech thee, of *our* righteousness and personal holiness; they are but" filthy rags," which thy purity forbids thee to take into heaven; therefore accept us without, and we shall shout, *Free grace! Imputed righteousness! and finished salvation!* to eternity."

While the bold Antinomian offers, or prepares to offer, this most impious plea, the Lord, who "is of purer eyes than to behold iniquity," casts a flaming look upon all the obstinate violators of his law. It pierces their conscience, rouses all its drowsy powers, and restores their memory to its original perfection. Not one wish passed their heart, or thought their brain, but is instantly brought to their remembrance. "The books are opened" in their own breast, and every character has a voice which answers to the voice of "the Lion of the tribe of Judah."

"Shall I pervert judgment," says he, "and justify the wicked for a bribe? the bribe of your abominable praise? 'Think you,' by your base flatteries 'to escape the righteous judgment of God?' Is not my 'wrath revealed from heaven against all ungodliness, and unrighteousnes of men, who hold the truth in unrighteousness?' Much more against you, 'ye vessels of wrath;' who hold an impious absurdity in matchless insolence.

"Said I not to Cain himself at the beginning, 'If thou doest well shalt thou not be accepted?' Personal holiness, which ye scorned, is 'the wedding garment' I now look for. 'I swear in my wrath,' that without it, 'none shall taste of my *heavenly* supper. Ye have rejected my word' of commandment, 'and I reject you from being kings. Ye cried unto me and I delivered you. Yet have ye forsaken me and served other gods; therefore I will deliver you no more. Go and cry unto the gods whom ye have chosen. I wound the hairy scalp of such as have gone on still in their wickedness. Whosoever hath sinned against me *to the last,* him do I blot out of my book.' And this have you done, 'ye serpents, ye generation of vipers, awake to everlasting shame! Will ye set the briers and thorns against me in battle,' and make them pass 'for roses of Sharon and lilies of the valleys? I will go through them *with a look,* and consume them together. The day is come that burneth like an oven; all that have DONE wickedly are stubble, and *must* be burned up root and branch. Upon such I rain snares, fire and brimstone, storm and tempest: this is the portion of their cup. Drink the dregs of it. Ye hypocrites, DEPART! and wring them out in everlasting burnings.'

Five Checks To Antinomianism

"Said I not, 'He that does good is of God; but he that does evil is not of God? Be faithful unto death, and I will give you the crown of life; for he that overcometh, *and he only*, shall be clothed in white raiment, and I will not blot out his name out of the book of life?' And shall I keep *your* name in that book for having 'continued in doing evil?' Shall I give *you* the crown of life for having been *unfaithful* unto death, and clothe *you* with the bright robes of my glory, because you *defiled* your *garments* to the last? Delusive hope! Because 'your mind was not to do good,' be ye rather 'clothed with cursing, like as with a garment! Let it come into your bowels like water, and like oil into your bones!'"

VII. If "these shall go into eternal punishment;" if such will be the dreadful end of all the impenitent Nicolaitans; if our churches and chapels swarm with them; if they crowd our communion tables; if they are found in most of our houses, and too many of our pulpits; if the seeds of their fatal disorder are in all our breasts; if they produce Antinomianism around us in all its forms; if we see bold Antinomians in *principle*, barefaced Antinomians in *practice*, and sly *Pharisaical Antinomians*, who speak well of the law, to break it with greater advantage: should not every one "examine himself whether he be in the faith," and whether he have a *holy Christ* in his heart, as well as a *sweet Jesus* upon his tongue; lest he should one day swell the tribe of Antinomian reprobates? Does it not become every minister of Christ to drop his prejudices, and consider whether he ought not to imitate the old watchman, who, fifteen months ago, gave a "legal alarm" to all the watchmen that are in connection with him? And should we not do the Church excellent service, if, agreeing to lift up our voices together against the common enemy, we gave God no rest in prayer, and our hearers in preaching, till we all "did our first works," and "our latter end," like Job's, "exceeded our beginning?"

Near forty years ago, some of the ministers of Christ, in our Church, were called out of the extreme of self righteousness. Fleeing from it, we have run into the opposite with equal violence. Now that we have learned wisdom by what we have suffered, in going beyond the limits of truth both ways, let us return to a just Scriptural medium. Let us equally maintain the two evangelical axioms on which the Gospel is founded, (1.) "All our salvation is of God by free grace, through the alone merits of Christ." And (2.) "All our damnation is of ourselves, through our avoidable unfaithfulness."

This second truth, as important as one half of the Bible, on which it rests, has not only been set aside as useless by thousands, but generally exploded as unscriptural, dangerous, and subversive of true Protestantism. Thus has the Gospel balance been broken, and St. James' "pure religion" despised. What we owe to truth in a state of oppression, hath engaged me to cast two mites into the scale of truth, which Mr. Wesley has the courage to defend against multitudes of good men, who keep one another in countenance under their common mistake. I do not want *his* scale to preponderate to the disadvantage of free grace. If it did, far from rejoicing in it, I would instantly throw the insignificant weight of my pen into the other scale; being fully persuaded that Christ can never be so truly honoured, nor souls so well edified, when we overdo on either side of the question, as when we Scripturally maintain the *whole* "*truth* as it is in Jesus."

"But are we not in as much danger from overdoing in Pharisaic *works*, as in Antinomian *faith?*"

Not at present. The stream runs too rapidly on the side of lawless faith, to leave any just room to fear we shall be immediately carried into excessive working. There would be some ground for this objection, if we saw most professors of religion obstinately refusing to drink any thing but water, eat any thing but dry bread or cheap vegetables; fasting themselves into mere skeletons; wearing sackcloth instead of soft linen; lying on the bare ground, with a stone for their pillow; imitating Origen, by literally "making themselves eunuchs for the kingdom of heaven's sake;" turning hermits, spending whole nights in contemplation in churches and church yards; giving away all their goods, the necessaries of life not excepted; allowing themselves only three or four hours' sleep, and even breaking that short rest to pray or praise; overpowering their bodies the next day with hard labour, to keep them under; scourging their backs unto blood every day; or forgetting themselves in prayer for hours in the coldest weather, till they have almost lost the use of their limbs. But! ask any unprejudiced person, who knows what is now called "Gospel liberty," whether we are in danger of being thus "righteous overmuch," or legal to such an extreme?

I grant, however, we are not absolutely safe from any quarter: let us therefore continually stand on our guard. The right wing of Emmanuel's army, which defends living faith, is partly gone over to the enemy, and fights under the Nicolaitan banner. The left wing, which defends good works, is far from being out of the reach of those crafty adversaries. Therefore, as we are, or may be, attacked on every side, let us faithfully use "the word of truth, the power of God, and the armour of righteousness on the right hand and on the left." Let us gallantly fly where the attack is the hottest, which now, *in the religious world, is* evidently where gross CRISPIANITY (if I may use the word) is continually obtruded upon us as true *Christianity:* I say, *in the religious world:* for, in this controversy, "what have I to do to judge them also that are without? Do not ye judge them that are within," and represent them as opposers of free grace?

Should Pharisees, while we are engaged in repelling the Nicolaitans, try to rob us of present and free justification by faith, under pretence of maintaining justification by works, in the last day: or should they set us upon unnecessary and unscriptural works, we shall be glad of your assistance to repel them also.

If you grant it us, and do not despise ours, the world shall admire, in the *Shulamite,* (the Church at unity in herself,) "the company of two armies, ready mutually to support each other against the opposite attacks of the Pharisees and the Nicolaitans; *the Popish workers* who exclude the Gospel, and the modern Gnostics, *the Protestant Antinomians* who explode the law.

May the Lord God help us to sail safely through these opposite rocks, keeping at an equal distance from both, by taking Christ for our pilot, and the Scripture for our compass! So shall we enter full sail the double haven of present and eternal rest. Once we were in immediate danger of splitting upon "works without faith:" now we are threatened with destruction from faith "without works." May the merciful Keeper of Israel save us from both, by *a living faith,* legally productive of all good works, or by *good works,* evangelically springing from a living faith!

Should the Divine blessing upon these sheets, bring one single reader a step toward that good old way, or only confirm one single believer in it, I shall be "rewarded a hundred-fold" for this little "labour of love;" and I shall be even content to see it represented as the invidious labour of malice: for what is my reputation to the profit of one blood-bought soul!

Beseeching you, dear sir, for whom these letters are first intended, to set me right where I am wrong; and not to despise what may recommend itself in them to reason and conscience, on account of the blunt and Helvetic manner in which they are written, I remain with sincere respect, honoured and reverend sir, your affectionate and obedient servant in the practical Gospel of Christ,

J. FLETCHER.

POSTSCRIPT.

SINCE these Letters were sent to the press, I have seen a pamphlet, entitled, "A Conversation between Richard Hill, Esq., the Rev. Mr. Madan, and Father Walsh," a monk at Paris, who condemned Mr. Wesley's Minutes as "too near Pelagianism," and the author as "a Pelagian;" adding, that "*their* doctrine was a great deal nearer that of the Protestants." Hence the editor concludes, that "the principles in the extract of the Minutes are too rotten even for a Papist to rest upon; and supposes that Popery is about the midway between Protestantism and Mr. J. Wesley." I shall just make a few strictures upon that performance.

1. If an Arian came to me, and said, "You believe that 'Jesus Christ is God over all, blessed for ever!' *Pelagius, that heretic who was publicly excommunicated by the whole Catholic Church,* was of your sentiment, therefore you are a Pelagian; give up your heresy." Should I, upon such an assertion, give up the Godhead of our Saviour? Certainly not. And shall I, upon a similar argument, advanced by the help of a French monk, give up truths with which the practical Gospel of Jesus Christ must stand or fall? God forbid!

2. We desire to be confronted with all the pious Protestant divines, except those of Dr. Crisp's class, who are a party: but who would believe it? The suffrage of a Papist is brought against us! Astonishing! that our opposers should think it worth their while to raise one recruit against us in the immense city of Paris, where fifty thousand might be raised against the Bible itself!

3. So long as Christ, the prophets, and apostles are for us, together with the multitude of the Puritan divines of the last century, we shall smile at an army of Popish friars. The knotted whips that hang by their sides will no more frighten us from our Bibles than the *ipse dixit* of a Benedictine monk will make us explode, as heretical, propositions which are demonstrated to be Scriptural.

4. An argument, which has been frequently used of late against the anti-Calvinist divines, is, "This is downright Popery! This is worse than Popery itself!"

And honest Protestants have been driven by it to embrace doctrines, which were once no less contrary to the dictates of their consciences than they are still to the word of God. It is proper, therefore, such persons should be informed, that St. Augustin, the Calvin of the fourth century, is one of the saints whom the popes have in the highest veneration; and that a great number of friars in the Church of Rome are champions for Calvinism, and oppose St. Paul's doctrine, that "the grace of God bringing salvation has appeared unto all men," as strenuously as some "real Protestants" among us. Now, if good father Walsh be one of that stamp, what wonder is it that he should so well agree with the gentlemen who consulted him! If Calvinism and Protestantism are synonymous terms, as some divines would make us believe, many monks may well say, that "their doctrine is a great deal nearer that of the Protestants" than the Minutes; for they may even pass for "real Protestants."

5. But whether the good friar be a hot Jansenist, or only a warm Thomist, (so they call the Popish Calvinists in France,) we appeal from his bar to the tribunal of Jesus Christ, and from the published Conversation "to the law and the testimony." What is the decision of a Popish monk to the express declarations of the Scripture, the dictates of common sense, the experience of regenerate souls, and the writings of a cloud of Protestant divines? No more than a grain of loose sand to the solid rock on which the Church is founded.

I hope the gentlemen concerned in the Conversation lately published, will excuse the liberty of this postscript. I reverence their piety, rejoice in their labours, and honour their warm zeal for their Protestant cause. But that very zeal, if not accompanied with a close attention to every part of the Gospel truth, may betray them into mistakes which may spread as far as their respectable names: I think it therefore my duty to publish these strictures, lest any of my readers should pay more regard to the goodnatured friar, who has been pressed into the service of Dr. Crisp, than to St. John, St. Paul, St. James, and Jesus Christ, on whose plain declarations I have shown that the Minutes are founded.

THIRD CHECK TO ANTINOMIANISM;

IN A LETTER

TO THE

AUTHOR OF PIETAS OXONIENSIS.

BY THE VINDICATOR OF THE REV. MR. WESLEY'S MINUTES

Reprove, rebuke, exhort, with all long suffering and (*Scriptural*) doctrine; for the time will come when they will not endure sound doctrine, 2 Timothy iv, 2, 3.

Wherefore rebuke them sharply, that they may be sound in the faith. But let brotherly love continue, Titus i, 13; Hebrews xiii, 1.

THIRD CHECK TO ANTINOMIANISM.

HONOURED AND DEAR SIR, — Accept my sincere thanks for the Christian courtesy with which you treat me in your Five Letters. The title page informs me, that a concern for "mourning backsliders, and such as have been distressed by reading Mr. Wesley's Minutes, or the Vindication of them," has procured me the honour of being called to a public correspondence with you. Permit me, dear sir, to inform you, in my turn, that a fear lest Dr. Crisp's balm should be applied, instead of the *Balm of Gilead,* to Laodicean loiterers, who may haply have been brought to penitential *distress,* obliges me to answer you in the same public manner in which you have addressed me.

Some of our friends will undoubtedly blame us for not yet dropping the contested point. But others will candidly consider, that controversy, though not desirable in itself, yet, properly managed, has a hundred times rescued truth, groaning under the lash of triumphant error. We are indebted to our Lord's controversies with the Pharisees and scribes for a considerable part of the four Gospels. And, to the end of the world, the Church will bless God for the spirited manner in which St. Paul, in his Epistles to the Romans and Galatians, defended the controverted point of a believer's present justification by faith; as well as for the steadiness with which St. James, St. John, St. Peter, and St. Jude carried on their important controversy with the Nicolaitans, who abused St. Paul's doctrine to Antinomian purposes.

Had it not been for controversy, Romish priests would to this day have fed us with Latin masses and a wafer god. Some bold propositions, advanced by Luther against the doctrine of indulgences, unexpectedly brought on the reformation. They were so irrationally attacked by the infatuated Papists, and so Scripturally defended by the resolute Protestants, that these kingdoms opened their eyes, and saw thousands of images and errors fall before the ark of evangelical truth.

From what I have advanced in my *Second Check,* it appears, if I am not mistaken, that we stand now as much in need of a reformation from Antinomianism as our ancestors did of a reformation from Popery; and I am not without hope that the extraordinary attack which has lately been made on Mr. Wesley's anti-Crispian propositions, and the manner in which they are defended, will open the eyes of many, and check the rapid progress of so enchanting and pernicious an evil. This hope inspires me with fresh courage; and turning from the Hon. and Rev. Mr. Shirley, I presume to face (I trust in the spirit of love and meekness) my new respectable opponent.

I. I thank you, sir, for doing Mr. Wesley the justice in your *first letter* of acknowledging, that "man's *faithfulness* is an expression which may be used in a sober, Gospel sense of the words." It is just in such a sense we use it; nor have you advanced any proof to the contrary.

We never supposed that "the faithfulness of God, and the stability of the covenant of grace, are affected by the unfaithfulness of man." Our Lord, we are persuaded, keeps his covenant when he *spews a lukewarm,* unfaithful Laodicean *out of his mouth,* as well as when he says to the good and faithful servant, "Enter thou into the joy of thy Lord." For the same covenant of grace which says, "He that believeth shall be saved; — he that abideth in me bringeth forth much fruit," says also, "He that believeth not shall be damned; — every branch in me that beareth not fruit, is cast forth and burned."

Thanks be to Divine grace, we make our boast of *God's faithfulness* as well as you, though we take care not to charge him, even indirectly, with our own unfaithfulness. But from the words which you quote, "My covenant shall stand fast with his seed," &c, we see no more reason to conclude that the obstinately unfaithful seed of Christ, such as Hymeneus, Philetus, and those who to the last "tread under foot the blood of the covenant wherewith they were sanctified," shall not be cast off; than to assert that many individuals of David's royal family, such as Absalom and Amnon, were not cut off on account of their flagrant and obstinate wickedness.

We beseech you, therefore, for the sake of a thousand careless Antinomians, to remember that the apostle says to every believer, "Thou standest by faith; behold therefore the goodness of God *toward thee,* if thou continue in his goodness; otherwise thou also shalt be cut off." We entreat you to consider, that even those who admire the point of your epigram, "Whenever we say one thing, we mean quite another," will not be pleased if you apply it to St. Paul, as you have done to Mr. Wesley. And when we see God's covenant with David grossly abused by Antinomians, we beg leave to put them in mind of God's covenant with the house of Eli. "Thus saith the Lord God of Israel, I chose thy father out of all the tribes of Israel to be my priest; [but thou art unfaithful] thou honourest thy sons above me. I said indeed, *that thy house, and the house of thy father, should walk before me for ever:* but now be it far from me; for them that honour me, I will honour; and they that despise me, shall be lightly esteemed. Behold, the days come, that I will cut off thine arm, and the arm of thy house; and I will raise me up a faithful priest, that shall do according to that which is in my heart," 1 Samuel ii.

II. Your second Letter respects *working for life.* You make the best of a bad subject, and really some of your arguments are so plausible, that I do not wonder so many men should commence Calvinists, rather than be at the trouble of detecting their fallacy. I am sorry, dear sir, I cannot do it without dwelling upon *Calvinism.* My design was to oppose *Antinomianism alone:* but the vigorous stand which you make for it upon Calvinian ground, obliges me to encounter you there, or to give up the truth which I am called to defend. I have long dreaded the alternative of displeasing my friends or wounding my conscience; but I must yield to the injunctions of the latter, and appeal to the candour of the former. If impetuous rivers of Geneva Calvinism have so long been permitted to flow through England, and even deluge Scotland, have not I some reason to hope that a rivulet of Geneva anti-Calvinism will be suffered to glide through some of Great Britain's plains; especially if its little murmur harmonizes with the clearest dictates of reason, and loudest declarations of Scripture?

Before I weigh your arguments against *working for life,* permit me to point out the capital mistake upon which they turn. You suppose, that *free preventing grace* does not visit all men; and that all those in whom it has not prevailed, are as totally dead to the things of God, as a dead body is to the things of this life: and from this unscriptural supposition you very reasonably conclude, that we can no more turn to God than corpses can turn themselves in their graves; no more *work for life,* than putrid carcasses can help themselves to a resurrection.

This main pillar of your doctrine will appear to you built upon the sand, if you read the Scriptures in the light of that mercy which is over all God's works. There you will discover the various dispensations of the everlasting Gospel; your contracted views of Divine love will open into the most extensive prospects; and your exulting soul will range through the boundless fields of that grace which is both richly free *in* all, and abundantly free *for* all.

Let us rejoice with reverence while we read such scriptures as these: "The Son of man is come to save that which is lost, and to call sinners to repentance. This is a true saying, and worthy of all acceptation, — worthy of all men to be received, — that Christ Jesus came into the world to save sinners. To this end he both died and rose again, that he might be the Lord of the dead and living. He came not to condemn the world, but that the world through him might be saved, and that at the name of Jesus every knee should bow, and every tongue confess that he is Lord."

"Bound every heart, and every bosom burn," while we meditate on these ravishing declarations: "God so loved the world, that he gave his only begotten Son, that whosoever believeth on him should not perish, but have everlasting life. He was made under the law, to redeem them that were under the law," that is, all mankind; unless it can be proved that some men never came under the curse of the law. He is the Friend of *sinners,* the Physician of the sick, and the Saviour of the *world:* "He died, the just for the unjust; he is the propitiation, not for our sins only, but for the sins of the whole world. One died for all, because all were dead. As in Adam all die, even so in Christ," [during the day of their visitation,] all are blessed [with quickening grace, and therefore in the last day.] "all shall be made alive," to give an account of their blessing or talent. "He is the Saviour of all men, especially of them that believe:" and the news of his birth are "tidings of great joy to all people. As by the offence of one judgment came upon all men, even so by the righteousness of one, the free gift came upon all men; for Christ by the grace of God tasted death for every man; he is the Lamb of God who taketh away the sin of the world: therefore God commandeth all men every where to repent, — to look unto him and be saved."

Do we not take choice jewels from Christ's crown, when we explain away these bright testimonies given by his free grace? "It pleased the Father by him to reconcile all things to himself. The kindness and pity of God our Saviour toward man has appeared. I will draw all men unto me. God was in him reconciling the world unto himself." Hence he says to the most obstinate of his opposers, "These things have I spoken unto you, that ye might be saved. If I had not come and spoken unto them, they had not had sin, [in rejecting me,] but now they have no cloak for their sin," no excuse for their unbelief.

Once indeed, when the apostles were on the brink of the most dreadful trial, their compassionate Master said, "I pray for them, I pray not for the world." As if he had said, Their immediate danger makes me pray as if there were but these eleven men in the world, "Holy Father, keep them." But having given them this seasonable testimony of a just preference, he adds, "Neither pray I for these alone, but for them who shall believe, that they all may be one," may be united in brotherly love. And he adds, "that the world may believe, and may know that thou hast sent me."

If our Lord's not praying, for a moment, on a particular occasion, for the world, implies that the world is absolutely reprobated, we should be glad of an answer to the two following queries: — (1.) Why did he pray the next day for Pilate and Herod, Annas and Caiaphas, the priests and Pharisees, the Jewish mob, and Roman soldiers; in a word, for the countless multitude of his revilers and murderers? Were they all elect, or was this ejaculation no prayer, "Father, forgive them, for they know not what they do?" (2.) Why did he commission St. Paul to say, "I exhort, first of all, that supplications, prayers, and intercessions be made for all men; for this is acceptable in the sight of God our Saviour, who will have all men to be saved, and come to the knowledge of the truth. For there is one God, and one Mediator between God and men, the man Christ Jesus; who gave himself a ransom for all?"

Without losing time in proving that none but artful and designing men use the word *all* to mean the *less number!* and that *all*, in some of the abovementioned passages, must absolutely mean *all mankind*, as being directly opposed to *all* that are *condemned* and "die in Adam;" and without stopping to oppose the new Calvinian creation of "a whole world of elect;" upon the preceding scriptures I raise the following doctrine of free grace: — If *Christ tasted death for every man*, there is undoubtedly a Gospel for every man, even for those who perish by rejecting it.

St. Paul says, that "God shall judge the secrets of men, according to his Gospel." St. Peter asks, "What shall be the end of those who obey not the Gospel of God?" and the apostle answers, "Christ, revealed in flaming fire, will take vengeance on them who obey not the Gospel," that is, all the ungodly who "receive the grace of God in vain, or turn it into lasciviousness." They do not perish because the Gospel is a lie with respect to them, but "because they receive not the love of the truth, that they might be saved." God, to punish their rejecting the truth, permits that they should believe a lie; "that they all might be damned, who, *to the last hour of their day of grace*, believed not the truth, but had pleasure in unrighteousness."

The latitude of our Lord's commission to his ministers demonstrates the truth of this doctrine: "Go into all the world, and teach all nations, baptizing them in the name of the Father, and of the Son, and of the Holy Ghost." Hence those gracious and general invitations, "Ho, every one that thirsteth, [after happiness,] come ye to the waters; if any man thirst, [after pleasure,] let him come to me and drink. Come unto me, all ye that labour, [for want of rest,] and I will give it to you. Whosoever will, let him come and take the water of life freely. Ye adulterers, — draw nigh unto God, and he will draw nigh unto you, Behold, I stand at the door and knock; if any man open, I will come in and sup with him. Go out into the highways and hedges, preach the Gospel to every creature; and lo, I am with you to the end of the world."

If you compare all the preceding scriptures, I flatter myself, Hon. sir, you will perceive, that as the redemption of Christ is general, so there is a general Gospel, which is more or less clearly revealed to all, according to the clearer or more obscure dispensation which they are outwardly under.

This doctrine may appear strange to those who call nothing *Gospel* but the last dispensation of it. Such should remember that as a little seed, sown in the spring, is one with the large plant into which it expands in summer; so the Gospel, in its least appearance, is one with the Gospel grown up to full maturity. Our Lord, considering it both as sown in man's heart, and sown in the world, speaks of it under the name of "the kingdom of heaven," compares it to corn, and considers first the *seed,* then the *blade,* next the *ear,* and last of all *the full corn in the ear.*

1. The Gospel was sown in the world as a *little but general seed,* when God began to quicken mankind in Adam by the precious promise of a Saviour; and when he said to Noah, the second general parent of men, "With thee will I establish my covenant;" blessing him and his sons after the deluge.

2. The Gospel appeared as *corn in the blade,* when God renewed the promise of the Messiah to Abraham, with this addition, that though the Redeemer should be born of his elect family, Divine grace and mercy were too free to be confined within the narrow bounds of a peculiar election: therefore, "in his seed," that is, in Christ the Sun of righteousness, "all the families of the earth should be blessed;" as they are all cheered with the genial influence of the natural sun, whether he shines above or below their horizon, whether he particularly enlightens the one or the other hemisphere.

3. The Gospel word grew much in the days of Moses, Samuel, and Isaiah; "for the Gospel," says St. Paul, "was preached unto them as well as unto us," though not so explicitly. But when John the Baptist, a greater prophet than any of them, began to preach the Gospel of repentance, and point sinners to "the Lamb of God that taketh away the sins of the world," then *the ear* crowned *the blade,* which had long been at a stand, and even seemed to be blasted.

4. The great Luminary of the Church shining warm upon the earth, his direct beams caused a rapid growth. The Favonian breathings and sighs which attended his preaching and prayers, the genial dews which distilled on Gethsemane during his agony, the fruitful showers which descended on Calvary, while the blackest storm of Divine wrath rent the rocks around, and the transcendent radiance of our Sun, rising after this dreadful eclipse to his meridian glory; all concurred to minister fertile influences to the *Plant of Renown.* And on the day of pentecost, when power came from on high, when the fire of the Holy Ghost seconded the virtue of the Redeemer's blood, the *full corn* was seen *in the mystical ear;* the most perfect of the Gospel dispensations came to maturity; and

Christians began to bring "forth fruit unto" the "perfection" of their own economy.

As some good men overlook the gradual display of the manifold Gospel grace of God, so others, I fear, mistake the essence of the Gospel itself. Few say, with St. Paul, "The Gospel *of which* I am not ashamed, is the power of God unto salvation, to every one that believeth, — with the heart unto righteousness," according to the light of his dispensation. And many are afraid of his catholic doctrine, when he sums up the general everlasting Gospel in these words: "God *was* not the God of the Jews only, but of the Gentiles also; because that which may be known of God," under their dispensation, "is manifest in them, God having showed it unto them. For the grace of God, which bringeth salvation," or rather η χαρις η σωτηριος, *the grace* emphatically *saving*, "hath appeared unto all men; teaching us to deny all ungodliness and worldly lusts, and to live soberly, justly, and godly, in this present world."

"But how does this saving grace teach us?" By proposing to us the saving truths of our dispensation, and helping our unbelief, that we may cordially embrace them; for "without faith it is impossible to please God." Even the heathens who "come to God, must believe that he is, and that he is the rewarder of them that diligently seek him; for there is no difference between the Jew and the Greek, the same Lord over all being rich unto all them that call upon him."

Here the apostle starts the great Calvinian objection: "But how shall they believe, and call on him, of whom they have not heard?" &c. And having observed that the Jews had heard, though few had believed, he says, "So then faith cometh by hearing, and hearing by the word of God," which is nigh, even in the mouth and in the heart of all who receive the truth revealed under their dispensation. Then resuming his answer to the Calvinian objection, he cries out, "Have not they" (Jews and Greeks) all "heard" preachers, who invite them to believe that God is good and powerful, and consequently that he is the rewarder of those who diligently seek him? "Yes, verily," replies he, "their sound went into all the earth, and their words unto the end of the world."

If you ask, "Who are those general heralds of free grace, whose sound goes from pole to pole?" The Scripture answers with becoming dignity: "The heavens declare the glory of God, and the firmament showeth his handy work. Day unto day uttereth speech, and night unto night showeth knowledge. There is no speech or language [no country or kingdom] where their voice is not heard. Their [instructing] line went through the earth, [their vast parish,] and their words to the ends of the world," their immense diocese. For "the invisible things of God, [that is, his greatness and wisdom, his goodness and mercy,] his eternal power and Godhead, are clearly seen, being understood by the things that are made, [and preserved,] so that [the very heathens, who do not obey their striking speech,] are without excuse; because that when they knew God, they glorified him not as God, neither were thankful."

This is the Gospel alphabet, if I may be allowed the expression. The apostle, like a wise instructer, proceeded upon the plan of this free grace, when he addressed himself to the heathens: "We preach unto you," said he to the Lycaonians, "that ye should turn from these vanities to serve the living God, who made heaven and earth, and the sea, and all things therein; who, *even when he* suffered all nations to walk in their own ways, left not himself without witness;" that is, without preachers, according to that saying of our Lord to his disciples, *Ye shall be my witnesses, and teach all nations.* And these witnesses were *the good* which God did, "the rain he gave us from heaven, and fruitful seasons, and the food and gladness with which he filled our hearts."

St. Paul preached the same Gospel to the Athenians, wisely coming down to the level of their inferior dispensation: "The God that made the world, dwells not," like a statue, "in temples made with hands, nor hath he need of any thing; seeing he giveth to all life, and breath, and all things. He hath made of one blood all nations of men, to dwell on all the face of the earth," not that they might live like atheists, and perish like reprobates, but "that they might seek the Lord, if haply they might feel after him, and find him." Nor is this an impossibility, as "he is not far from every one of us; for in him we live, and move, and have our being, as certain of our own poets have taught," justly asserting that "we are the offspring of God." Hence he proceeds to declare that "God calls all men every where to repent," intimating that upon their turning to him, he will receive them as his dear children, and bless them as his beloved offspring.

These, and the like scriptures, forced Calvin himself into a happy inconsistency with Calvinism: "The Lord," said he, in an epistle prefixed to the French New Testament, "never left himself without a witness, even toward them unto whom he has not sent any knowledge of his word. Forasmuch as all creatures, from the firmament to the centre of the earth, might be witnesses and messengers of his glory unto all men, to draw them to seek him; and indeed there is no need to seek him very far, for every one might find him in his own self." And no doubt some have; for although "the world knew not God" by the wisdom that is "earthly, sensual, and devilish;" yet many have savingly known him by his general witness, that is, "the wonderful works that he doth for the children of men; for that which may be known of God," in the lowest economy of Gospel grace, "is manifest in them," as well as shown unto them.

"What! Is there something of God inwardly manifest in, as well as outwardly shown to, all men?" Undoubtedly: the grace of God is as the wind, "which bloweth where it listeth;" and it listeth to blow with more or less force successively all over the earth. You can as soon meet with a man that never felt the wind, or heard the sound thereof, as with one that never felt the Divine breathing, or heard the still small voice, which we call *the grace of God,* and which bids us turn from sin to righteousness. To suppose the Lord gives us a thousand tokens of "his eternal power and Godhead," without giving us a capacity to consider, and grace to improve them, is not less absurd than to imagine, that when he bestowed upon Adam all the trees of paradise for food, he gave him no eyes to see, no hands to gather, and no mouth to eat their delicious fruits.

We readily grant, that Adam, and we in him, lost all by the fall; but Christ, "the Lamb slain from the foundation of the world, Christ, the repairer of the breach," mightier to save than Adam to destroy, solemnly gave himself to Adam, and to us in him, by the free everlasting Gospel which he preached in paradise. And when he preached it, he undoubtedly gave Adam, and us in him, a capacity to receive it, that is, a power to believe and repent. If he had not, he might as well have preached to stocks and stones, to beasts and devils. It is offering an insult to "the only wise God," to suppose that he gave mankind the light, without giving them eyes to behold it; or, which is the same, to suppose that he gave them the Gospel, without giving them power to believe it.

As it is with Adam, so it is undoubtedly with all his posterity. By what argument or scripture will you prove, that God excluded part of Adam (or what is the same thing, part of his offspring, which was then part of his very person) from the promise and gift which he freely made him of "the seed of the woman, and the bruiser of the serpent's head?" Is it reasonable to deny the gift, because multitudes of infidels reject it, and thousands of Antinomians abuse it? May not a bounty be really given by a charitable person, though it is despised by a proud, or squandered away by a loose beggar?

Waiving the case of infants and idiots, was there ever a sinner under no obligation to repent and believe in a merciful God? O ye opposers of free grace, search the universe with Calvin's candle, and among your reprobated millions, find out the person that never had a merciful God: and show us the unfortunate creature whom a sovereign God bound over to absolute despair of his mercy from the womb. If there be no such person in the world — if all men are bound to repent and believe in a merciful God, there is an end of Calvinism. And unprejudiced men can require no stronger proof that all are redeemed from the curse of the Adamic law, which admitted of no repentance; and that the covenant of grace, which admits of, and makes provision for it, freely extends to all mankind.

"Out of Christ's fulness all have received grace, a little leaven" of saving power, an inward monitor, a Divine reprover, a ray of *true* heavenly *light,* which manifests, first moral, and then spiritual good and evil. St. John "bears witness of that light," and declares it was the spiritual "life of men, the true light which enlightens" not only every man that comes into the Church, but "every man that cometh into the world," without excepting those who are yet in darkness. For "the light shineth in darkness, *even when* the darkness comprehends it not." The Baptist bore also "witness of that light, that all men through *it,*" not through *him,* "might believe," φως, "light," being the last antecedent, and agreeing perfectly with Greek δι αυτου.*

Hence appears the sufficiency of that Divine light to make all men believe in Christ "the light of the world;" according to Christ's own words to the Jews, "While ye have the light, believe in the light, that ye may be the children of light. Walk while ye have the light, lest darkness come upon you," even that total night of nature, "when no man can work."

Those who resist this internal light, generally reject the external Gospel, or receive it only in the letter and history. And too many such there have been in all ages; for Christ "was in the world, *even when* the world knew him not:" therefore he was "manifest in the flesh." The same sun which had shined as the dawn, arose "with healing in his wings;" and came to deliver the truth which was held in unrighteousness, and to help the light which was not comprehended by the darkness. But alas! when "he came to his own," even then "his own received

---

* EDITOR'S NOTE: The Greek here in the original is difficult to read. The reference is to John 1:7 where the Greek reads "δι αυτου", thus we have opted for that reading here.

him not." Why? Because they were *reprobates?* No: but because they were *moral agents.*

"This is the condemnation," says he himself, "that light came into the world, but men" shut their eyes against it. "They loved darkness rather than light, because their works were evil." They would go on in the sins which the light reproved, and therefore they opposed it till it was quenched, that is, till it totally withdrew from their hearts. To the same purpose our Lord says, "The heart of this people is waxed gross, their ears are dull of hearing, and their eyes have they closed" against the light, "lest they should see with their eyes, and understand with their hearts, and should be converted, and I should heal them." The same unerring Teacher informs us, that "the devil cometh" to the way-side hearers, and "taketh away the word out of their hearts, lest they should believe and be saved." And "if our Gospel be hid," says St. Paul, "it is hid to them that believe not, and are lost, whose minds the god of this world hath blinded, lest the glorious Gospel of Christ should shine unto them."

From these scriptures it is evident that Calvin was mistaken, or that the devil is a fool. For if a man is now totally blind, why should the devil bestir himself *to blind him?* And why should he fear "lest the Gospel should shine to them that are lost," if there be absolutely no Gospel for them, or they have no eyes to see, no capacity to receive it?

Whether sinners know their Gospel day or not, they have one. Read the history of Cain, who is supposed to be the first reprobate; and see how graciously the Lord expostulated with him. Consider the old world: St. Peter, speaking of them, says, "The Gospel was preached to them also that are dead; for Christ went by the Spirit and preached even to those who were disobedient, when once the long suffering of God waited one hundred and twenty years in the days of Noah." Nor did the Lord wait with an intention of having them completely fattened for the day of slaughter; far be the unbecoming thought from those who worship the God of love! Instead of entertaining it, let us "account that the long suffering of our Lord is salvation," that is, a beginning of salvation; and a sure pledge of it, if we know and redeem the accepted time: for "the Lord is long suffering to us-ward, and not willing that any should perish, but that all should come to repentance."

Nor does God's long suffering extend to the elect only. It embraces also those "who treasure up unto themselves wrath against the day of wrath, by despising the riches of *Divine* goodness, and forbearance, and long suffering, not knowing that the goodness of God leads them to repentance." Of this the Jews are a remarkable instance: "What could God have done more to his *Jewish* vineyard? He gathered the stones out of it, and planted it with the choicest vine.; and yet when he looked that it should have brought forth grapes, it brought forth wild grapes; when he sent his servants to receive the fruits, they were abused and sent away empty." Hence it is evident that the Jews had a day in which they could have brought forth fruit, or the *wise God* could no more "have looked for it" than a wise man expects to see the pine apple grow upon the hawthorn.

Nay, the most obstinate, Pharisaic, and bloody of the Jews had a day, in which our Lord in person "would have gathered them" with as much tenderness "as a hen gathers her brood under her wings." And when he saw their free agency absolutely set against his loving kindness, he wept over them, and deplored their not having "known the things belonging unto their peace, before they were hid from their eyes."

Our gracious God freely gives one or more talents of grace to every man: nor was ever any man "cast into outer darkness, where shall be weeping and gnashing of teeth," but for the not using his talent aright, as our Lord sufficiently declares, Matthew xxv, 30. Alluding to that important parable, I would observe, that the Christian has *five talents*, the Jew *two*, and the heathen *one*. If he that has *two talents* lays them out to advantage, he shall "receive a reward," as well as he that has *five:* and the *one talent* is as capable of a proportionable improvement as the *two* or the *five.* The equality of God's ways does not consist in giving just the same number of gracious talents to all; but, FIRST, in not desiring *"to gather where he has not strewed,"* or, "to reap" above a proportion of his *seed;* and, SECONDLY, in graciously dispensing rewards according to the number of talents improved, and the degrees of that improvement; and in justly inflicting punishments according to the number of talents buried, and the aggravations attending men's unfaithfulness. "For unto whomsoever much is given, of him shall much be required; and to whom men have committed much, of him they will ask the more."

We frequently speak of God's secret decrees, the knowledge of which is as useless as it is uncertain, but seldom consider that solemn decree so often revealed in the Gospel: — "To him that has grace *to purpose,* more shall be given; and from him that has not," that has buried his talent, and therefore in one sense has it not, "shall be taken away even that which he hath" to no purpose: according to our Lord's awful command, "Take the talent from him" that hath buried it, "and give it to him that hath ten," for the good and faithful servant shall have abundance.* He who says, "Whatsoever a man soweth, that shall he also reap," is too just to look for an increase from those on whom he bestows no talent; and as he calls for repentance and faith, and for a daily increase of both, he has certainly bestowed upon us the seed of both, for he "gives seed to the sower," and does not desire "to reap where he hath not sown."

Methinks my honoured opponent cries out with amazement, "What! Have all men power to repent and believe?" And in the meantime a Benedictine monk comes up to vouch, that this doctrine is rank Pelagianism. But permit me to observe, that if Pelagius had acknowledged, as we do, the total fall of man, and ascribed, with us, to the free grace of God in Jesus Christ, all the power we have to repent and believe, none of the fathers would have been so injudicious and uncharitable as to rank him among heretics. We maintain, that although "without Christ we can do nothing," yet so long as the "day of salvation" lasts, all men, the chief of sinners not excepted, can, through his free preventing grace, "cease to do evil, and learn to do well," and use those means which will infallibly end in the repentance and faith peculiar to the dispensation they are under, whether it be that of the heathens, Jews, or Christians.

---

* I must do the Calvinists the justice to observe, that as our Lord says, "Ask and have;" so Elisha Coles says, "Use grace and have grace," which is all that we contend for, if the inseparable counterpart of the axiom be admitted, "Abuse grace and lose grace."

If the author of *Pietas Oxoniensis,* and father Walsh, deny this, they might as well charge Christ with the absurdity "of tasting death for every man" in order to keep most men from the very possibility of being benefited by his death. They might as well assert, that although "the free gift came upon all men," yet it never came upon a vast majority of them; and openly maintain, that Christ deserves to be called the *destroyer,* rather than the *Saviour* of the world. For if the greatest part of mankind may be considered as *the world,* if repentance and faith are absolutely impossible to them, and Jesus came to denounce destruction to all who do not repent and believe, let every thinking man say whether he might not be called with greater propriety the *destroyer* than the *Saviour* of the world; and whether preaching the Christian Gospel is not like reading the warrant of inevitable damnation to millions of wretched creatures. But upon the scheme of what you call the "Wesleyan orthodoxy," Christ is really "the Saviour of all men, but especially of those that believe:" for he indulges all with a day of salvation; and if none but believers make a proper use of it, the fault is not in his partiality, but in their own obstinacy.

In what a pitiful light does your scheme place our Lord! Why did he "marvel at the unbelief" of the Jews, as if they could no more believe than a stone can swim? And say not, "he marvelled *as a man;*" for the assertion absolutely unmans him. What man ever wondered that an *ass* does not bray with the nightingale's melodious voice? Nay, what child ever marveled that the ox does not fly above the clouds with the soaring eagle?

The same observation holds with regard to repentance. "Then he began," says St. Matthew, "to upbraid the cities wherein most of his mighty works were done, because they repented not." Merciful Saviour, forgive us! We have insulted thy meek wisdom, by representing thee as cruelly upbraiding the lame for not running, the blind for not seeing, and the dumb for not speaking!

But this is not all: if Capernaum could not have repented at our Lord's preaching, as well as Nineveh at the preaching of Jonas, how do we reflect upon his mild equity, and adorable goodness, when we represent him as pronouncing wo upon wo over the impenitent city, and threatening to sink it into a deeper hell than Sodom, "because it repented not!" and how ill does it become us to exclaim against Deists for robbing Christ of his *divinity,* when we ourselves divest him of common *humanity.*

Suppose a schoolmaster said to his English scholars," Except you instantly speak Greek you shall all be severely whipped," you would wonder at the injustice of the school tyrant. But would not the wretch be merciful in comparison of a Saviour, (so called,) who is supposed to say to myriads of men, that can no more repent than ice can burn, "Except ye repent, ye shall all perish?" I confess, then, when I see real Protestants calling this doctrine *the pure Gospel,* and extolling it as *free grace,* I no more wonder that real Papists should call their bloody inquisition *the house of mercy,* and their burning of those whom they call heretics an *auto de fe;* (an act of faith.)

OBJECTION. "At this rate our salvation or damnation turns upon the good or bad use which we make of the manifold grace of God: and we are in this world in a state of probation, and not merely upon our passage to the rewards, which everlasting love, or to the punishments, which everlasting hatred, has freely allotted us, from the foundation of the world."

ANSWER. Undoubtedly; for what man of sense, (I except those who through hurry and mistake have put on the veil of prejudice,) could show his face in a pulpit, to exhort a multitude of reprobates to avoid a damnation absolutely unavoidable; and invite a little flock of elect, to lose no time in making sure an election surer than the pillars of heaven?

Again: who but a tyrant will make the life of his subjects turn upon a thing that is not at all at their option? When Nero was determined to put people to death, had he not humanity and honesty enough not to tantalize them with insulting offers of life? To whom did he ever say, "If thou pluckest one star from heaven thou shalt not die; but if thou failest in the attempt, the most dreadful and lingering torments shall punish thy obstinacy?" And shall I, — shall my Christian brethren, represent the King of saints as guilty of (what my pen refuses to write) that which Nero himself was too merciful to contrive?

OBJECTION. "You do not state the case fairly. If *all have sinned in Adam,* and *the wages of sin is death,* God did the reprobates no wrong when he condemned them to eternal torments, before they knew their right hand from their left; yea, before the foundation of the world."

ANSWER. The plausibility of this objection, heightened by voluntary humility, has misled thousands of pious souls: God give them understanding to weigh the following reflections: —

1. If an unconditional, absolute decree of damnation passed upon the reprobates *before* the foundation of the world, it is absurd to account for the justice of such a decree, by appealing to a sin committed *after* the foundation of the world.

2. If Adam sinned necessarily according to the *secret will and purpose* of God, as you intimate in your fourth letter, many do not see how he, much more his posterity, could justly be condemned to eternal torments for doing an iniquity which "God's hand and counsel determined before to be done."

3. As we sinned only *seminally* in Adam, if God had not intended ourredemption, his goodness would have engaged him to destroy us *seminally,* by crushing the capital offender who contained us all: so there would have been a just proportion between the sin and punishment; for as we sinned in Adam without the least consciousness of guilt, so in him We should have been punished without the least consciousness of pain. This observation may be illustrated by an example: If I catch a mischievous animal, a viper for instance, I have undoubtedly a right to kill her, and destroy her dangerous brood, if she is big with young. But if, instead of despatching her as soon as I can, I feed her on purpose to get many broods from her, and torment to death millions of her offspring, I can hardly pass for the good man who regards the life of a beast. Leaving to you the application of this simile, I ask, Do we honour God when we break the equal beams of his perfections? when we blacken his *goodness* and *mercy,* in order to make his *justice* and *greatness* shine with exorbitant lustre? If "a God all mercy is a God unjust," may we not say, according to the rule of proportion, that "a God all justice is a God unkind," and can never be he whose "mercy is over all his works?"

4. But the moment we allow, that the blessing of the second Adam is as general as the curse of the first; that God "sets" again "life and death" before every individual; and that he mercifully restores to all a capacity of choosing life, yea, and of having it one day more abundantly than Adam himself had before the fall; we see his goodness and justice shine with equal radiance, when he spares guilty Adam to propagate the fallen race, that they may share the blessings of a better covenant. For, according to the Adamic law, "judgment was by one sin to condemnation; but the free gift of the Gospel is of many offences to justification. For if through the offence of one the many be dead, much more the grace of God, and the gift by grace, which is by one man, Jesus Christ, hath abounded unto the many."

5. Rational and Scriptural as the preceding observations are, we could spare them, and answer your objection thus: — You think God may justly decree that millions of his unborn creatures shall be "vessels of wrath" to all eternity, overflowing with the vengeance due to Adam's preordained sin; but you are not nearer the mark: for, granting that he could do it as a just, good, and merciful God; yet he cannot do it as the God of "faithfulness and truth." His word and oath are gone forth together; hear both: "What mean ye, that ye use this proverb, *The fathers have eaten sour grapes, and the children's teeth are set on edge?* as I live, says the Lord God, ye shall not have occasion any more to use this proverb. The soul that sinneth *personally* shall die *eternally*: every one shall die for his own *avoidable* iniquity. Every man that eateth sour grapes," when he might have eaten the sweet, "his teeth shall justly be set on edge." When God has thus made oath of his equity and impartiality before mankind, it is rather bold to charge him with contriving Calvin's election, and setting up the Protestant great image, before which a considerable part of the Church continually falls down and worships.

O ye honest Shadrachs, who gaze upon it with admiration, see how some Calvinian doctors deify it, *decreta Dei sunt ipse Deus,* "The decrees of God are God himself." See Elisha Coles advancing at the head of thousands of his admirers, and hear how he exhorts them to worship: "Let us make election our all; our *bread, water, munition of rocks,* and whatever else we can suppose ourselves to want," — that is, Let us make *the great image* our God. Ye candid Meshachs, ye considerate Abednegos, follow not this mistaken multitude. Before you cry with them, "Great is the Diana of the Calvinists!" walk once around the celebrated image, and, I am persuaded, that if you can make out FREE GRACE written in running hand upon her smiling face, you will see FREE WRATH written in black capitals upon her deformed back: and then, far from being angry at the liberty I take to expose her, you will wish speed to the "little stone" which I level at her "iron-clay feet."

Think not, honoured sir, that I say about free *wrath* what I cannot possibly prove: for you help me yourself to a striking demonstration. I suppose you are still upon your travels: you come to the borders of a great empire; and the first thing that strikes you is a man in an easy carriage, going with folded arms to take possession of an immense estate, freely given him by the king of the country. As he flies along, you just make out the motto of the royal chariot, in which he doses, FREE REWARD. Soon after you meet five of the king's carts, containing twenty wretches loaded with irons; and the motto of every cart is, FREE

Five Checks To Antinomianism

PUNISHMENT. You inquire into the meaning of this extraordinary procession, and the sheriff, attending the execution, answers: — "Know, curious stranger, that our monarch is *absolute;* and to show that *sovereignty* is the prerogative of his imperial crown, and that he is no *respecter of persons,* he distributes every day *free rewards* and *free punishments* to a certain number of his subjects." "What! without any regard to merit or demerit, by mere caprice!" "Not altogether so; for he *pitches upon the worst of men, and chief of sinners, and upon such to choose* for the subjects of his rewards. (Elisha Coles, page 62.) And that his punishments may do as much honour to *free* sovereign *wrath* as his bounty does to *free* sovereign *grace,* he pitches upon those that shall be executed before they are born." "What! have these poor creatures in chains done no harm?" "O yes!" says the sheriff, "the king contrived that their parents should let them fall and break their legs, before they had any knowledge: when they came to years of discretion he commanded them to run a race with broken legs; and, because they cannot do it, I am going to see them quartered. Some of them, beside this, have been obliged to fulfil the king's *secret will, and bring about his purposes;* and they shall be burned in yonder deep valley, called *Tophet,* for their trouble." You are shocked at the sheriff's account, and begin to expostulate with him about the *freeness* of the *wrath* which burns a man for doing the king's will; but all the answer you can get from him is, that which you give me in your fourth letter, (page 23,) where speaking of a poor reprobate, you say, "Such a one is indeed accomplishing" the king's, you say, "God's decree, but he carries a dreadful mark in his forehead, that such a decree is, that he shall be punished with everlasting destruction from the presence of the lord" of the country. You cry out, "God deliver me from the hands of a monarch who *punishes with everlasting destruction* such as accomplish his decree!" And while the magistrate intimates that your exclamation is *a dreadful mark,* if not *in your forehead,* at least upon your *tongue,* that you yourself shall be apprehended against the next execution, and made a public instance of the king's free wrath, your blood runs cold, you bid the postilion turn the horses; they gallop for your life, and the moment you get out of the dreary land you bless God for your narrow escape.

May reason and Scripture draw your soul with equal speed from the dismal fields of Coles' *sovereignty* to the smiling plains of primitive Christianity! Here you have God's *election,* without Calvin's *reprobation.* Here Christ chooses the Jews without rejecting the Gentiles; and elects Peter, James, and John, to the enjoyment of peculiar privileges, without reprobating Matthew, Thomas, and Simon. Here nobody is damned for not doing impossibilities, or for doing what he could not possibly help. Here all that are saved enjoy rewards, through the merits of Christ, according to the degrees of evangelical obedience which the Lord enables, not forces, them to perform. Here *free wrath* never appeared: all our damnation is of ourselves, when we "neglect such great salvation," by obstinately refusing to "work it out with fear and trembling." But this is not all: here *free grace* does not rejoice over *stocks,* but over *men,* who gladly confess that their salvation is all of God, who for Christ's sake rectifies their free agency, helps their infirmities, and "works in them both to will and to do of his good pleasure." And from the tenor of the Scripture, as well as from the consent of all nations, and the dictates of conscience, it appears, that part of God's "good pleasure" toward man is, that he shall remain invested with the awful power of choosing life or death, that his will shall never be forced, and, consequently, that overbearing, irresistible grace, shall be banished to the land of Coles' *sovereignty,* together with free, absolute, unavoidable wrath.

Now, honoured sir, permit me to ask, Why does this doctrine alarm good men? Why are those divines deemed *heretics,* who dare not divest God of his essential love, Emmanuel of his compassionate humanity, and man of his connatural free agency? What are Dominicus and Calvin when weighed in the balance against Moses and Jesus Christ? Hear the great prophet of the Jews: "I call heaven and earth to record this day against you, that I have set before you life and death, blessing and cursing, *heaven and hell;* therefore choose life that ye may live." And "he that hath ears," not yet absolutely stopped by prejudice, "let him hear" what the great Prophet of the Christians says upon the important question: "I am come that they might have life; all things are now ready, — but ye will not come unto me that ye might have life. I would have gathered you, and ye would not. Because I have called and ye refused, I will laugh when your destruction cometh. For that they did not choose the fear of the Lord, therefore shall they eat," not "the fruit" of my decree? or of Adam's sin, but "of their own *perverse* way: they shall be filled with their own doings."

If these words of Moses and Jesus Christ are overlooked, should not, at least, the experience of near six thousand years teach the world, that God does not force rational beings, and that, when he tries their loyalty, he does not obey for them, but gives them sufficient grace to obey for themselves? Had not all the angels sufficient grace to obey? If some "kept not their first estate," was it not through their own unfaithfulness? What evil has our Creator done us, or what service have devils rendered us, that we should fix the blot of Calvinian reprobation upon the former, to excuse the rebellion of the latter? Did not Adam and Eve stand some time, by means of God's sufficient grace; and might they not have stood for ever? Have not unconverted men sufficient grace to forsake or complain of some evil; to perform, or attempt some good? Had not David sufficient grace to avoid the crimes into which he plunged? Have not believers sufficient power to do more good than they do? And does not the Scripture address sinners, (Simon Magus not excepted,) as having sufficient grace to pray for more grace, if they have not yet sinned the sin unto death?

In opposition to the above-stated doctrine of *grace, free* FOR *all,* as well as *free* IN *all,* our Calvinian brethren assert, that God binds his free grace, and keeps it from visiting millions of sinners, whom they call *reprobates.* They teach that man is not in a state of probation, that his lot is absolutely cast; a certain little number of souls being immovably fixed in God's favour, in the midst of all their abominations; and a certain vast number under his eternal wrath, in the midst of the most sincere endeavours to secure his favour. And their teachers maintain, that the names of the former were "written in the book of life," without any respect to foreseen repentance, faith, and obedience; while the names of the latter were put in the book of death, (so I call *the decree of reprobation,)* merely for the sin of Adam, without any regard to personal impenitency, unbelief, and disobedience. And this *narrow grace* and *free wrath* they recommend to the world under the engaging name of FREE GRACE.

Five Checks To Antinomianism

This doctrine, dear sir, we are in conscience bound to oppose; not only because it is the reverse of the other, which is both Scriptural and rational; but because it is inseparably connected with doctrinal Antinomianism, as your fourth letter abundantly demonstrates: and, above all, because it appears to us that it fixes a blot upon all the Divine perfections. Please, honoured sir, to consider the following queries:-

What becomes of God's *goodness*, if the tokens of it, which he gives to millions, be only intended to enhance their ruin, or cast a deceitful veil over his everlasting wrath? What becomes of his *mercy*, which is "over all his works," if millions were for ever excluded from the least interest in it, by an absolute decree that constitutes them "vessels of wrath" from all eternity? What becomes of his *justice*, if he sentences myriads upon myriads to everlasting fire, *"because* they have not believed on the name of his only-begotten Son?" when, if they had believed that he was their Jesus, their Saviour, they would have believed a monstrous lie, and claimed what they have no more right to than I have to the crown of England. What becomes of his *veracity*, and the *oath he swears*, that "he willeth not the death of a sinner," if he never affords most sinners sufficient means of escaping eternal death? If he sends his ambassadors to every creature, declaring that "all things are now ready" for their salvation, when nothing but "Tophet is prepared of old" for the inevitable destruction of a vast majority of them? What becomes of his *holiness*, if, in order to condemn the reprobates with some show of justice, and secure the end of his decree of reprobation, which is, that *millions shall absolutely be damned*, he absolutely fixes *the means* of their damnation, that is, their sins and wickedness? What becomes of his *wisdom*, if he seriously expostulates with souls as dead as corpses, and gravely urges to repentance and faith persons that can no more repent and believe than fishes can speak and sing? What becomes of his *long suffering*, if he waits to have an opportunity of sending the reprobates into a deeper hell, and not to give them a longer time to "save themselves from this perverse generation?" What of his *equity*, if there was mercy for Adam and Eve, who, *personally* breaking the hedge of duty, wantonly rushed out of paradise into this howling wilderness? And yet there is no mercy for millions of their unfortunate children, who were born in a state of sin and misery, without any *personal* choice, and consequently without any *personal* sin. And what becomes of his *omniscience*, if he cannot foreknow future contingencies? If to foretell without a mistake that such a thing shall happen, he must do it himself? Was not Nero as wise in this respect? Could not he foretell that Phebe should not continue a virgin, when he was bent upon ravishing her; that Seneca should not die a natural death, when he had determined to have him murdered; and that Crispus should fall into a pit, if he obliged him to run a race at midnight in a place full of pits? And what old woman in the kingdom cannot precisely foretell that a silly tale shall be told at such an hour, if she is resolved to tell it herself, or at any rate to engage a child to do it for her?

Again: what becomes of God's *loving kindnesses*, "which have been ever of old" toward the children of men? And what of his *impartiality*, if most men, absolutely reprobated for the sin of Adam, are never placed in a state of personal trial and probation? Does not God use them far less kindly than devils, who were tried every one for himself, and remain in their diabolical state, because they brought it upon themselves by a *personal* choice? Astonishing! That the Son of God should have been flesh of the flesh, and bone of the bone of millions of men, whom, upon the Calvinian scheme, he never indulged so far as he did devils! What a hard-hearted relation to myriads of his fellow men does Calvin represent our Lord! Suppose Satan had become our *kinsman* by incarnation, and had by that means got "the right of redemption," would he not have acted like himself, if he had not only left the majority of them in the depth of the fall, but enhanced their misery by the sight of his partiality to the little flock of the elect?

Once more: what becomes of *fair dealing*, if God every where represent sin as the dreadful evil which causes damnation, and yet the most horrid sins "work for good" to some, and, as you intimate, *accomplish their salvation through Christ?* And what of *honesty*, if the God of truth himself promises, that "all the families of the earth shall be blessed in Christ?" when he has cursed a vast majority of them with a decree of absolute reprobation, which excludes them from obtaining an interest in them, even from the foundation of the world.

Nay, what becomes of his *sovereignty* itself, if it be torn from the mild and gracious attributes by which it is tempered? If it be held forth in such a light as renders it more terrible to millions, than the sovereignty of Nebuchadnezzar, in the plain of Dura, appeared to Daniel's companions, when "the form of his visage was changed against them," and he decreed that they should be" cast into the burning fiery furnace;" for they might have saved their bodily lives by bowing to the golden image, which was a thing in their power; but poor reprobates can escape at no rate. The horrible decree is gone forth; they must, in spite of their best endeavours, *dwell* body and soul *with everlasting burnings.*

And let none say, that we wrong the Calvinian decree of reprobation, when we call it *a horrible decree;* for Calvin himself is honest enough to call it so. *Unde factum est, tot gentes, una cum liberis eorum infantibus æternæ morti involveret lapsus Adæ absque remedio, nisi quia Deo ira visum est?* DECRETUM QUIDEM HORRIBILE, *fateor; inficiari tamen nemo poterit, quin præciverit Deus quem exitum habiturus esset homo, antequam ipsum conderet, et ideo præsciverit, quia decreto suo sic ordinaret.* That is, "How comes it to pass that so many nations, together with their infant children, are by the fall of Adam involved in eternal death without remedy, unless it is because God would have it so? A HORRIBLE DECREE, I confess! Nevertheless, nobody can deny that God foreknew what would be man's end before he created him, and that he foreknew it, because he had ordered it by his decree." *(Calvin's Institutes, book iii, chap. 23, sec. 7.)*

This is some of the contempt which Calvinism pours upon God's perfections. These are some of the blots which it fixes upon his word. But the moment man is considered as a candidate for heaven, a probationer for a blissful immortality; the moment you allow him what *free grace* bestows upon him, that is, "a day of salvation," with "a talent" of living light and rectified free agency, to enable him to *work for life* faithfully promised, as well as *from life* freely imparted; — the moment, I say, you allow this, all the Divine perfections shine with unsullied lustre. And, as reason and majesty returned to Nebuchadnezzar after his shameful degradation, so consistency and native dignity are restored to the abused oracles of God.

Five Checks To Antinomianism

Having thus shown the inconsistency of Calvinism, and the reasonableness of what you call the Wesleyan, and what we esteem the Christian orthodoxy, (so far at least as it respects the gracious power and opportunity that man, as redeemed and prevented by Christ, has to *work for life*, or to "work out his own salvation,") it is but just I should consider some of the most plausible objections which are urged against our doctrine.

FIRST OBJECTIONS. "Your Wesleyan scheme pours more contempt upon the Divine perfections than ours. What becomes of God's *wisdom*, if he gave his Son to die for all mankind, when he foreknew that most men would never be benefited by his death?"

ANSWER. (1.) God foreknew just the contrary. All men, even those who perish, are benefited by Christ's death: for all enjoy, through him, a "day of salvation," and a thousand blessings both spiritual and temporal. And, if all do not enjoy heaven for ever, they may still thank God for his gracious offer, and take the blame upon themselves for their obstinate refusal of it. (2.) God, by reinstating all mankind in a state of probation, for ever shuts the mouths of those who choose "death in the error of their ways," and clears himself of their blood before men and angels. If he cannot eternally benefit unbelievers, he eternally vindicates his own adorable perfections. He can say to the most obstinate of all the reprobates, "'O Israel, thou hast destroyed thyself. In me was thy help; but thou wouldst not come unto me that thou mightest have life.' Thy destruction is not from *my decree*, but *thine own determining*."

SECOND OBJECTION. "If God wills all men to be saved, and yet many are damned, is he not disappointed? And does not this disappointment argue that he wants either wisdom to contrive the means of some men's salvation, or power to execute his gracious designs?"

ANSWER. (1.) God's purpose is, that all men should have sufficient grace to believe according to their dispensation; that "he who believeth shall be saved, and he who believeth not shall be damned." God cannot, therefore, be disappointed, even when man's free agency throws in the weight of final unbelief, and turns the scale of probation for death. (2.) Although Christ is the author of "a day of salvation" to all, yet he "is the author of *eternal salvation*" to none but to such as "obey him, by working out their own salvation" while it is day. If you say, that "suppose God wills the salvation of *all*, and none can be saved but *the obedient*, he should make all obey." I reply, So he does, by a variety of gracious means, which persuade, but do not force them. For he says himself, "What could I have done more to my vineyard than I have done?" "O, but he should *force* all by the sovereign power of irresistible grace." You might as well say that he should renounce his wisdom, and defeat his own purpose. For if his wisdom places men in a state of probation; the moment he forces them, he takes them out of that state, and overturns his own counsel; he destroys the work of his hands; he unmans man, and saves him, not as a rational creature, but as a stock or a stone. Add to this, that *forced obedience* is a contradiction in terms; it is but another word for *disobedience*, at least in the account of Him who says, "My son, give me thy heart;" obey me with an unconstrained, free, and cheerful will. In a word, this many "are willingly ignorant of," that when God says, "he wills all men to be saved," he wills them to be saved as *men*, according to his own method of salvation laid down in the abovementioned scriptures, and not in their own way of wilful disobedience, or after Calvin's scheme of irresistible grace.

THIRD OBJECTION. "You may speak against *irresistible* grace, but we are persuaded that nothing short of it is sufficient to make us believe. For St. John informs us, that the Jews, toward whom it was not exerted, *could* not believe."

ANSWER. (1.) Joseph said to his mistress, "How can I do this great wickedness?" But this does not prove that he was not able to comply with her request, if he had been so minded. The truth was, that some of the Pharisees had "buried their talent," and therefore could not improve it; while others had so provoked God, that he had "taken it from them;" they had "sinned unto death." But most of them obstinately held that evil which was an insurmountable hinderance to faith; and to them our Lord said, "How can ye believe who receive honour one of another?" (2.) I wonder that modern Predestinarians should make so much of this scripture, when Augustine their father solves the seeming difficulty with the utmost readiness: "If you ask me," says he, "why the Jews *could* not believe? I quickly answer, Because they *would* not. For God foresaw their evil will, and foretold it by the prophet; and if he blinded their eyes, their own wills deserved this also." They obstinately said, "We *will* not see," and God justly said at last, "Ye *shall* not see."

FOURTH OBJECTION. "You frequently mention the parable of the *talents,* but take care to say nothing of the parable of the *dry bones,* which shows not only the absurdity of supposing that men can work for life, but the propriety of expostulating with souls as void of all spiritual life as the dry bones to which Ezekiel prophesied."

ANSWER. (1.) If you read that parable without comment, you will see that it is not descriptive of the spiritual state of souls, but of the political condition of the Jews during their captivity in Babylon. They were scattered throughout Chaldea, as dry bones in a valley; nor was there any human probability of their being collected to form again a political body. Therefore God, to cheer their desponding hearts, favoured Ezekiel with the vision of the resurrection of the dry bones. (2.) This vision proves just the reverse of what some imagine: for the dry bones are thus described by the Lord himself: "These bones are the whole house of Israel. Behold, they say," (this was the language of their despairing minds,) "our bones are dried, our hope is lost, we are cut off for our parts." Here these Israelites, (compared to dry bones,) even before Ezekiel prophesied, and the Spirit entered into them, knew their misery and complained of it, saying, "Our bones are dried up." How far then were they from being as insensible as corpses? (3.) The prophecy to the dry bones did not consist in threatenings and exhortations; it was only of the declarative kind. Nor was the promise of their resurrection fulfilled in the Calvinian way, that is, *irresistibly.* For although God had said, "I will open your graves," that is, your prisons, "and will bring you out of them into your own land," we find that multitudes, when their graves were opened, chose to continue in them. For when Nehemiah and Ezra breathed, under God, courage into the dry bones, the Jewish captives dispersed throughout Chaldea, many preferred the land of their captivity to their own land,

and refused to return' so that, after all, their political resurrection turned upon their own choice.

FIFTH OBJECTION. "We do not altogether go by the parable of the dry bones, when we affirm there is no absurdity in preaching to souls as dead as corpses. We have the example of our Lord as well as that of Ezekiel. Did he not say to Lazarus, when he was dead and buried, *Come forth?*"

ANSWER. If Christ had called Lazarus out of the grave without giving him power to come forth, his friends would have had some reason to suspect that he was "beside himself." How much more, if they had heard him call a thousand corpses out of their graves, denouncing to all, that if they did not rise they should be "cast into a lake of fire," and eaten up "by a worm that dieth not!" It is a matter of fact, that Christ never commanded but one dead man to come out of the grave; and the instant he gave him the command, he gave him also power to obey it. Hence we conclude, that as the Lord "commands all men every where to repent," he gives them all power so to do. But some Calvinists argue just the reverse. "Christ," say they, "called *one* corpse without using any entreaty, threatening, or promise; and he gave it power to obey: therefore when he calls *a hundred* dead souls, and enforces his call with the greatest variety of expostulations, threatenings, and promises, he gives power to obey only to *two* or *three.*" What an inference is this! How worthy of the cause which it supports!

In how contemptible a light does our Lord appear, if he says to souls as dead as Lazarus in the grave, "All the day long have I stretched out my hands unto you. Turn ye, why will ye die? Let the wicked forsake his way, and I will have mercy upon him: but if he will not turn, I will whet my sword, I have bent my bow and made it ready; I have also prepared for him the instruments of death."

I once saw a passionate man unmercifully beating and damning a blind horse, because he did not take to the way in which he would have him go; and I came up just when the poor animal fell a lamed victim to its driver's madness. How did I upbraid him with his cruelty, and charge him with unparalleled extravagance! But I now ask, if it is not more than paralleled by the conduct of the imaginary being, whom some recommend to the world as a wise and merciful God? For the besotted driver for some minutes expostulated, in his way, with a *living,* though blind horse; but the supposed maker of the Calvinian decrees expostulates "all the day long" with souls, not only as blind as beetles, but as dead as corpses. Again: the former had some hopes of prevailing with his living beast to turn; but what hopes can the latter have to prevail with dead corpses, or with souls as dead as they? What man in his senses ever attempted to make a corpse *turn,* by threatening it sword in hand, or by bending the bow and leveling an arrow at its cold and putrid heart?

But suppose the resurrection of Lazarus, and that of the dry bones, did not overthrow Calvinism, would it be reasonable to lay so much stress upon them? Is a dead soul in every respect like a dead body; and is *moral* death absolutely like *natural* death? Can a parabolical vision, wrested from its obvious meaning, supersede the plainest declarations of Christ, who personally addresses sinners as free agents? Should not metaphors, comparisons, and parables, be suffered to walk erect like reasonable men? Is it right to make them *go upon all four,* like the stupid ox? What, loads of heterodoxy have degraded parables brought into the Church? And how successfully has error carried on her trade, by dealing in *figurative expressions,* taken in a *literal sense!*

"This is my body," says Christ. "Therefore bread is flesh," says the Papist, "and transubstantiation is true." "These dry bones are the house of Israel," says the Lord. "Therefore Calvinism is true," says my objector, "and we can do no more toward our conversion, than dry bones toward their resurrection." "Lost sinners" are represented in the Gospel as a "lost piece of silver." "Therefore," says the author of *Pietas Oxoniensis,* "they can no more seek God, than the piece could seek the woman who had lost it." "Christ is the Son of God," says St. Peter. "Therefore," says Arius, "he is not co-eternal with the Father, for I am not so old as my parents." And I, who have a right to be as wise as any of them, hearing our Lord say, that "the seven Churches are seven candlesticks," prove by it that the seven Churches can no more repent than three pair and a half of candlesticks, or, if you please, seven pair of snuffers! And shall we pretend to overthrow the general tenor of the Scripture by such conclusions as these! Shall not, rather, unprejudiced persons of every denomination agree to turn such arguments out of the Christian Church, with as much indignation as Christ turned the oxen out of the Jewish temple?

Permit me, honoured sir, to give you two or three instances more of an undue stretching of some particular words for the support of some Calvinian errors. According to the oriental style, a follower of wisdom is called "a son of wisdom;" and one that deviates from her paths, "a son of folly." By the same mode of speech, a wicked man, considered as wicked, is called "Satan, a son of Belial, a child of the wicked one, and a child of the devil." On the other hand, a man who turns from the devil's works, and does the works of God, by believing in him, is called "a child or a son of God." Hence the passing from the ways of Satan to the ways of God, was naturally called *conversion* and *a new birth,* as implying a turning from sin, a passing into the family of God, and being numbered among the godly.

Hence some divines, who, like Nicodemus, carnalize the expressions of *new birth, child of God,* and *son of God,* assert, that if men who once walked in God's ways turn back, even into adultery, murder, and incest, they are still God's *dear people* and *pleasant children,* in the Gospel sense of the words. They ask, "Can a man be a child of God to-day, and a child of the devil to-morrow? Can he be born this week, and unborn the next?" And with these questions they as much think they have overthrown the doctrine of holiness, and one half of the Bible, as honest Nicodemus supposed he had demolished the doctrine of regeneration, and stopped our Lord's mouth, when he said, "Can a man enter a second time into his mother's womb and be born?"

The questions of our brethren would be easily answered, if, setting aside the oriental mode of speech, they simply asked, "May one who has 'ceased to do evil, and learned to do well *to-day,* cease to do well, and learn to do evil' *to-morrow?*" To this we could directly reply, If the dying thief, the Philippian jailer, and multitudes of Jews, in one day went over from the *sons of folly* to the *sons of wisdom,* where is the absurdity of saying, they could measure the same way back again in one day; and draw back into the horrid womb of sin as easily as Satan drew back into rebellion, Adam into disobedience, David into adultery, Solomon into idolatry, Judas into treason, and Ananias and Sapphira into covetousness? When Peter had shown himself a blessed son of heavenly wisdom, by confessing Jesus Christ, did he even stay till the next day to become a son of folly, by following the "wisdom which is earthly, sensual, and devilish?" Was not our Lord directly obliged to rebuke him with the utmost severity, by saying, "Get thee behind me, Satan?"

Multitudes, who live in open sin, build their hopes of heaven upon a similar mistake; I mean, upon the unscriptural idea which they fix to the Scriptural word *sheep*. "Once I heard the Shepherd's voice," says one of these Laodicean souls; "I *followed him*, and therefore I was one of his *sheep;* and now, though I follow the voice *of a stranger*, who leads me into all manner of sins, into adultery and murder, I am undoubtedly a sheep still: for it was never heard that a sheep became a goat." Such persons do not observe, that our Lord calls "sheep" *those who hear his voice*, and "goats" *those who follow that of the tempter*. Nor do they consider that if Saul, a grievous wolf, "breathing slaughter" against Christ's sheep, and "making havoc" of his little flock, could in a short time be changed both into a sheep and a shepherd; David, a harmless sheep, could, in as short a time, commence a goat with Bathsheba, and prove a wolf in sheep's clothing to her husband.

Pardon me, honoured sir, if, to make my mistaken brethren ashamed of their argument, I dedicate to them the following soliloquy, wherein I reason upon their own plan: —

"Those very Jews whom the Baptist and our Lord called 'a brood of vipers and serpents,' were soon after compared to 'chickens,' which Christ wanted 'to gather as a hen does her brood.' What a wonderful change was here! The *vipers* became *chickens!* Now, as it was never heard that chickens became vipers, I conclude that those Jews, even when they came about our Lord like 'fat bulls of Bashan,' like 'ramping and roaring lions,' were true chickens still. And indeed, why should not they have been as true chickens as David was a true sheep when he murdered Uriah? I abhor the doctrine which maintains that a man may be a chick or a sheep today, and a viper or a goat to-morrow.

"But I am a little embarrassed. If none go to hell but *goats,* and none to heaven but *sheep,* where shall the *chickens* go? Where 'the wolves in Sheep's clothing?' And in what *limbus* of heaven or hell shall we put that 'fox Herod,' the *dogs* who 'return to their vomit,' and the *swine,* before whom we must 'not cast our pearls?' Are they all species of goats, or some particular kind of sheep?

"My difficulties increase! The Church is called *a dove,* and Ephraim *a silly dove.* Shall the *silly dove* be admitted among the sheep? Her case seems rather doubtful. The hair of the spouse in the Canticles is likewise said to be like 'a flock of goats,' and Christ's shepherds are represented as 'feeding kids, or young goats, beside their tents.' I wonder if those *young goats* became young sheep, or if they were all doomed to continue reprobates! But what puzzles me most, is, that the Babylonians are in the same verse compared to 'lambs, rams, and goats.' Were they mongrel elect, or mongrel reprobates, or some of Elisha Coles' *spiritual monsters?'*

I make this ridiculous soliloquy, to show the absurdity and danger of resting weighty doctrines upon so sandy a foundation as the particular sense which some good men give to a few Scriptural expressions, stretched and abused on the rack of my countryman, Calvin; especially such expressions as these, "A child of God, a sheep, a goat," and, above all, "the dead in sin."

Upon this last expression you seem, honoured sir, chiefly to rest the merit of your cause, with respect to *working for life*. Witness the following words: — "That *we are to work for life* is an assertion most exceedingly self contradictory, if it be a truth that man is 'dead in trespasses and sins.'" Had you given yourself the trouble of reading, with any degree of attention, the thirty-eighth [forty-second in the original edition] * page of the Vindication,† you would have seen your difficulty proposed and solved: witness the following words, which conclude the solution: "In this Scriptural view of free grace, what room is there for the ridiculous cavil, that Mr. Wesley wants the *dead to work for life?*' Had I been in your place, I confess, honoured sir, I could not have produced that cavil again, without attempting at least to wipe off the ridicule put upon it. I should think truth has better weapons with which to defend herself than *a veil*. I grant that the reverend divine, whose second you are, has publicly *cast a veil* over all my arguments under the name of *mistakes:* but could you possibly think that his veil was thick enough to cover them from the eyes of unprejudiced readers, and palliate your answering, or seeming to answer me, without taking notice of my arguments? But if you cast a veil over them, I shall now endeavour to do yours justice, and clear the matter a little farther.

I. Availing yourself of St. Paul's words to the Ephesians and Colossians, "You hath He quickened, who were dead in trespasses and sins; and you, being dead in your sins, hath he quickened together with him;" you dwell upon the absurdity of "expecting living actions from a dead corpse," or living works from a dead soul.

1. I wonder at the partiality of some persons. If we assert, that "strong believers are *dead TO* sin," they tell us very properly that such are not so dead, but they may commit sin if they please, or if they are off their watch. But if we say, that "many who are *dead IN* sin, are not so dead, but in the strength imparted, together with the Light that enlightens every man, they may leave off some of their sins if they please," we are exclaimed against as using metaphysical distinctions. and *dead* must absolutely mean *impotent as a corpse*.

2. The word *dead,* &c, is frequently used in the Scriptures to denote a particular degree of helplessness and inactivity, very short of the total helplessness of a corpse We read of the *deadness* of Sarah's womb, and of Abraham's body being *dead;* and he must be a strong Calvinist indeed, who, from such expressions, peremptorily asserts, that Sarah's *dead* womb was as unfit for conception, and Abraham's *dead* body for generation, as if they both had been "dead corpses." Christ writes to the Church of Sardis, "I know thy works; thou

---

* The page numbers referenced by Fletcher to his own works have been edited to conform to this present series. The page numbers of the Schmul editions are reserved in brackets occasioning the desire of any to reference those works. –ed.
† Page 38 [30] of this volume.

hast a name to live, and art dead." But it is evident, that *dead* as they were, something remained alive in them, though like the smoking flax, it was "ready to die." Witness the words that follow: "Be watchful, and strengthen the things which remain, that are ready to die." Now, sir, if the dead Sardians could *work for life*, by "strengthening the things" belonging to the Christian "which remained" in them' is it modest to decide è *cathedra*, that the dead Ephesians and Colossians could not as well work for life, by "strengthening the things that remained and were ready to die," under *their own* dispensation? Is it not evident that a beam of "the Light of the world" still shone in their hearts, or that the Spirit still strove with them? If they had absolutely quenched him, would he have helped them to believe? And if they had not, was not there something of "the Light which enlightens every man" remaining in them; with which they both could, and did work for life, as well as the dead Sardians?

3. The absurdity of always measuring the meaning of the word *dead*, by the idea of *a dead corpse*, appears from several other scriptures St. Paul, speaking of one who grows wanton against Christ, says, "She that liveth in pleasure is dead while she liveth." Now, if this means that she is entirely devoid of every degree of spiritual life, what becomes of Calvinism? Suppose all that live in pleasure are as dead to God as corpses, what became of the everlasting life of Lot, when he lived in pleasure with his daughters? of David with Bathsheba, and Solomon with his idolatrous wives? When the same apostle observes to the Romans, that their "body was dead because of sin," did he really mean they were already *dead* corpses? And when he adds, "Sin revived and I died," did Calvinian death really pass upon him? Dead as he was, could not he complain like the dry bones, and ask, "Who shall deliver me from this body of death?" Again: when our Lord says to Martha, "He that believeth in me, though he were dead, yet shall he live," does he not intimate, that there is a work consistent with the degree of death of which he speaks? A believing *out of death* into life? A doing the work of God *for life*, yea, for eternal life?

4. From these and the like scriptures, it is evident, that there are different degrees of spiritual death, which you perpetually confound. (1.) Total death, or a full departure of the Holy Spirit. This passed upon Adam, and all mankind in him, when he lost God's moral image, fell into selfish nature, and was buried in sin, guilt, shame, and horror. (2.) Death freely visited with a seed of life in our fallen representative, and of course in all his posterity, during the day of their visitation. (3.) Death oppressing this living seed, and holding it "in unrighteousness," which was the death of the Ephesians and Colossians. (4.) Death prevailing again over the living seed, after it had been powerfully quickened, and burying it in sin and wickedness. This was the death of David during his apostasy, and is still that of all who once believed, but now live in Laodicean ease or Sardian pleasure. And, (5.) The death of confirmed apostates, who, by absolutely quenching "the Spirit of life in Christ Jesus," the second Adam, are fallen into the miserable state of nature and total helplessness, in which the first Adam was when God preached to him the Gospel of his quickening grace. These are said by St. Jude to be *twice dead;* dead by Adam's total apostasy from God, and dead by their own personal and final apostasy from "the Light of the world."

II. The foundation of the Crispian Babel is literally laid in confusion. When you have confounded all the degrees of spiritual death, we may naturally expect to see you confound all the degrees of spiritual life, which our Lord meant when he said, "I am come that they may have life, and that they may have it more abundantly." "All that are quickened," do you say, "are pardoned and justified!" As if a man could not be quickened to see his sins and reform, before he is quickened so to believe in Christ as to receive the pardon and justification mentioned Colossians ii, 13, and Romans v, 1.

If you read the Scriptures without prejudice, you will see that there are several degrees of spiritual life, or quickening power. (1.) The living "Light which shines in the darkness" of every man during the day of his visitation. (2.) The life of the returning sinner, whether he has always lived in open sin, as the publican, or once walked in the ways of God, as David. (3.) The life of the heathen, who, like Cornelius, "fears God and works righteousness" according to his light, and is accepted in his dispensation. (4.) The life of the pious Jew, who, like Samuel, fears God from his youth. This degree of life is far superior to the preceding, being cherished by the traditions of the patriarchs, the books of the Old Testament, the sacraments, priests, prophets, temples, Sabbaths, sacrifices, and other means of grace, belonging to the Jewish economy. (5.) The life of the feeble Christian, or disciple of John, who is "baptized with water unto repentance for the remission of sins," and believing in "the Lamb of God," immediately pointed out to him, enjoys the blessings of the primitive Christians before the day of pentecost. And, (6.) The still more abundant life, the life of the adult or perfect Christian, imparted to him when the love of God, or power from on high, is plentifully shed abroad in his believing soul, on the day that Christ "baptizes him with the Holy Ghost and with fire, to sanctify him wholly, and seal him unto the day of redemption."

III. When you have overlooked all the degrees of spiritual death and life, what wonder is it that you should confound all the degrees of acceptance and Divine favour, with which God blesses the children of men! Permit me, honoured sir, to bring also this article of the Christian faith out of the Calvinian tower of Babel, where it has too long been detained.

1. I have already proved, that in consequence of the love of benevolence and pity, with which "God loved the world," and through the "propitiation *which Christ made* for the sins of the whole world, the free gift of an accepted time, and a day of salvation, came upon all men." In this sense they are all *accepted*, and sent "to work in the vineyard of their respective dispensations. This degree of acceptance, with the seed of light, life, and power that accompanies it, is certainly previous to any work; and, in virtue of it, infants and complete idiots go to heaven, for "of such is the kingdom of God." As they are not capable of burying or improving their talent of inferior acceptance, they are admitted with it to an inferior degree of glory.

2. While many abandoned heathens, and those who follow their abominable ways, bury their talent to the last, and lose it, together with the degree of acceptance they once enjoyed in or through "the Beloved;" some, by improving it, are accepted in a higher manner, and, like Cornelius, receive tokens

of increasing favour. The love of pity and benevolence which God bore them, is now mixed with some love of complacence and delight.

3. Faithful Jews, or those who are, under their dispensation, improving a superior number of talents, are accepted in a superior manner, and as a token of it they are made "rulers over five cities," they partake of greater grace here, and greater glory hereafter.

4. John the Baptist and his disciples, — I mean Christians who have not yet been "baptized with the Holy Ghost and with fire," — are yet more highly accepted: for John, and the souls who live up to the height of his dispensation, are "great in the sight *and favour* of the Lord." They exceed all those who attain only to the perfection of inferior economists.

5. But those Christians who live in the kingdom of God, which was opened to believers on the day of pentecost, whose hearts burn with his love, and flame with his glory, are accepted in a still higher degree. For our Lord informs us, that great as John himself was, "the least in the kingdom of God is greater than he:" and as a token of superior acceptance, he shall be made "ruler over ten cities;" he shall enter more deeply "into the joy and glory of his Lord."

Although *concurrence with grace given* is necessary, in order to these four last degrees of acceptance, none enjoys them but *in* and *through* "the Beloved:" for as his blood is the meritorious spring of all our pardons, so his Spirit is the inexhaustible fountain of all our graces. Nor are we less indebted to him for power, to "be workers together with God" in the great business of our salvation, than for all the other wonders of his unmerited goodness and redeeming love.

Let nobody say, that the doctrine of these degrees of acceptance is founded upon metaphysical distinctions, and exceeds the capacity of simple Christians: for a child of ten years old understands that he may be accepted to run a race before he is accepted to receive the prize; and that a man may be accepted as a day labourer, and not as a servant; be as a steward, and not as a child; as a friend, and not as a spouse. All these degrees of acceptance are very distinct, and the confusion of them evidently belongs to the Calvinian Babel.

IV. As we have considered three of the walls of your tower, it will not be amiss to cast a look upon the fourth, which is the utterly confounding of the four degrees that make up a glorified saint's eternal justification: —

1. That which passes upon all infants universally, and is thus described by St. Paul: "As by the offence of one, judgment came upon all men to condemnation; even so, by the righteousness of one, the free gift came upon all men, unto *present* justification *from original sin, and future* justification *of life;*" upon their repenting and "believing in the light, *during* the day of their visitation." In consequence of this degree of justification, we may, without impeaching the veracity of God, say to every creature, "God so loved the world, that he gave his only begotten Son, to reconcile them unto himself, not imputing to them" original sin unto eternal death, and blotting out their personal transgressions in the moment "they believe with the heart unto righteousness."

2. The justification consequent upon such believing, is thus described by St. Paul: — This blessing of "faith imputed for righteousness" shall be ours, "if we believe on Him that was raised from the dead for our justification. We have believed in Jesus Christ, that we might be justified by the faith of Christ, and not

by the works of the law. Therefore, being justified by faith, we have peace with God through our Lord Jesus Christ," &c.

3. The justification consequent upon bringing forth the fruit of a lively faith in the truths that belong to our dispensation. This justification is thus mentioned by St. James: — "Rahab the harlot was justified by works. Abraham our father was justified by works. Ye see then how by works a man is justified, and not by faith only."

And, 4. Final justification, thus asserted by our Lord and St. Paul: In the day of judgment "by thy words shalt thou be justified, and by thy words shalt thou be condemned. Circumcision and uncircumcision avail nothing, but the keeping of the commandments; for the doers of the law shall be justified."*

All these degrees of justification are equally merited by Christ. We do nothing in order to the *first*, because it finds us in a state of total death. Toward the *second* we believe by the power freely given us in the first, and by the additional help of Christ's word and the Spirit's agency. We work by faith in order to the *third*. And we continue believing in Christ and working together with God, as we have opportunity, in order to the *fourth*.

The preaching distinctly these four degrees of a glorified saint's justification is attended with peculiar advantages. The *first* justification engages the sinner's attention, encourages his hope, and draws his heart by love. The *second* wounds the self-righteous Pharisee, who works without believing; while it binds up the heart of the returning publican, who has no plea but "God be merciful to me a sinner!" *The third* detects the hypocrisy and blasts the vain hopes of all Antinomians, who, instead of "showing their faith by their works, deny in *works* the Lord that bought them, and put him to an open shame." And while the *fourth* makes even a "Felix tremble," it causes believers to "pass the time of their sojourning here in *humble* fear" and cheerful watchfulness.

Though all these degrees of justification meet in glorified saints, we offer violence to Scripture if we think, with Dr. Crisp, that they are inseparable. For all the wicked who "quench the *convincing* Spirit," and are finally given up to a reprobate mind, fall from the FIRST, as well as Pharaoh. All who "receive the seed among thorns," all who "do not forgive their fellow servants," all who "begin in the Spirit and end in the flesh," and all "who draw back," and become sons or daughters of "perdition," by falling from the THIRD, lose the SECOND, as Hymeneus, Philetus, and Demas. And none partake of the FOURTH but those who "bear fruit unto perfection," according to one or another of the Divine dispensations; "some producing thirty-fold," like heathens, "some sixty-fold," like Jews, "and some a hundred-fold," like Christians.

---

* These four degrees of a glorified saint's justification are mentioned in the preceding Checks, though not so distinctly as they are here. If treating of our present justification by faith, and of justification by works in the day of judgment, I have called them "our first and second justification," it was not to exclude the other two, but to attack gradually reigning prejudice, and accommodate myself to the language of my honoured opponent, who called *justification in the day of judgment* "a second justification." I should have been more exact first; but I was so intent in demonstrating the *thing*, that I did not think then of contending for the most proper *name*. Nor did I see then of what importance it is to drag the monster *error* out of the den of *confusion*, in which he hides himself.

Five Checks To Antinomianism

From the whole it appears, that although we can absolutely do nothing toward our first justification, yet to say that neither faith nor works are required in order to the other three, is one of the boldest, most unscriptural, and most dangerous assertions in the world; which sets aside the best half of the Scriptures, and lets gross Antinomianism come in full tide upon the Church.

Having thus taken a view of the confusion in which Calvin and Crisp have laid the foundation of their schemes, I return to the arguments by which you support their mistakes.

I. "If you suppose," you say, "that there are any conditional works before justification, these works must either be the works of one who is in a state of nature, or in a state of grace, either condemned by the law or absolved by the Gospel."

A new sophism this! No works are previous to justification from original sin, and to the quickening "light which enlightens every man that comes into the world." And the works that a penitent does in order to the subsequent justifications, such as "ceasing to do evil, learning to do well," repenting, and persevering in obedient faith, are all done in a state of initial, progressive, or perfected grace; not under the Adamic law, which did not admit of repentance, but under the Gospel of Christ, which says, "Let the wicked forsake his way, and the unrighteous man his thoughts; and let him return unto the Lord, who will abundantly pardon his sins, cleanse him from all unrighteousness," and even "fill him with the fulness of God."

II. You proceed: "If a man in a state of nature do works in order to justification, they cannot please God, because he is in a state of utter enmity against him."

What, sir! do you think that a man *in a state of utter enmity against God* will do any thing in order to recover his favour? When Adam was in that state did he so much as once ask pardon? If he had, would he not have evidenced a desire of reconciliation, and consequently a degree of apostasy short of what you call *utter enmity?*

III. You quote Scripture: "He that does something in order to justification cannot please God, because he 'is alienated from the life of God, through the ignorance that is in him, because of the blindness of his heart.'"

An unhappy quotation this! For the apostle did not speak these words of those honest heathens, who, in obedience to "the Light of the world," did something in order to justification; but of those abandoned Pagans, who, as he observes in the next verse, "being past feeling, had given themselves over unto lasciviousness, to work all uncleanness with greediness." Thus, to prove that men have not a talent of power to "work the works of God," you produce men who have buried it, that they might "work all uncleanness" without control, yea, "with greediness."

You would have avoided this mistake if you had considered that the heathens mentioned there by St. Paul were of the stamp of those whom he describes, Romans i, and whom he represents as "given up" by God "to a reprobate mind, because when they knew God they glorified him not as God, and did not like to retain him in their knowledge." Here we may observe, (1.) That those reprobate heathens had once some knowledge of God, and, of course, some life: for "this is eternal life," to know God. (2.) That if they were given up, *because* they did not use that talent of Divine knowledge, it was not because they were eternally and unconditionally reprobated; whence I beg leave to conclude, that if eternal, unconditional reprobation is a mere chimera, so is likewise eternal, unconditional election.

You might have objected, with much more plausibility, that when the Ephesians were in the flesh they were "without hope, without Christ, and without God in the world:" and if you had, I would have replied, that these words cannot be taken in their full latitude, for the following reasons, which appear to me unanswerable: — (1.) The Ephesians, before their conversion, were not totally *without hope*, but without a *good* hope. They probably had as presumptuous a hope as David in Uriah's bed, or Agag when he thought the bitterness of death was past. (2.) They were *without Christ*, just as a man who has buried his talent is without it. But as he may dig it up and use it if he sees his folly in time, so could, and so did the Ephesians. (3.) If they were in every sense *without Christ*, what becomes of the doctrine maintained in your fourth letter, that they "were for ever and for ever complete in Christ?" (4.) They were not entirely *without God*: "for in him they lived, moved, and had their being." Nor were they without him as absolute reprobates; for they "knew the day of their visitation" before it was over. It remains, then, (5.) That they were *without God*, as the prodigal son was without his father when "he fed swine in a far country;" and that they could and did return to their heavenly Father as well as he.

IV. You go on: "He who does something in order to justification, not being grafted in Christ the true vine, cannot bring forth any good fruit; he can do nothing at all."

I beg, sir, you would produce one man who has not" sinned the sin unto death," that can absolutely do nothing, that cannot cease from one sin, and take up the practice of one duty. You will as soon find a saint in hell as such a man upon earth. Even those who in their voluntary humility say perpetually that *they can do nothing,* refute their own doctrine by their very confessions: for he who confesses his helplessness, undoubtedly does something, unless by some new rule in logic it can be demonstrated that confessing our impotence, and complaining of our misery, is *doing nothing.*

When our Lord says, "Without me ye can do nothing," does he say that *we are totally without him?* When he declares, that "no man cometh unto him unless the Father draw him," does he insinuate that the Father does *not draw all?* Or that he draws *irresistibly?* Or that those who are drawn at one time, may not *draw* back at any other? Is it right to press Scripture into the service of a system, by straining its meaning so far beyond the import of the words?

Again: though a man may not be "grafted in Christ," according to the Jewish or Christian dispensation, may he not partake of his quickening sap, according to the more general dispensation of that "saving grace which has appeared to all men?" May not the branches in which that "saving grace appears," have some connection with Christ, the heavenly vine, and bring forth fruit meet for repentance, as well as Job and his friends, Melchisedec, Plato, the wise men, Cornelius, some of his soldiers, and many more who brought forth fruits according to their dispensation? Does not the first general justification so graft all men in Him that if they bear not fruit during their "accepted time," they are justly "taken away, cast forth, and burned," as barren branches?

V. Your knowledge of the Scripture made you foresee this answer, and to obviate it, you say: "If you tell me *that I mistake, that although we must cease from evil, repent, &c, yet you are far from supposing we can perform these things in our own natural strength.* I ask then, In whose strength are they performed? You say, *In the strength of Christ, and by the power of the Holy Ghost, according to these scriptures: 'I can do all things through Christ strengthening me, being strengthened with might in the inner man.'"*

Permit me to tell you, honoured sir, that I do not admire your quoting Scripture for me. You take care to keep out of sight the passages I have quoted, and to produce those which are foreign to the question. To show that even a sinful heathen may work *for,* as well as *from* life, I could never be so destitute of common sense as to urge the experience of St. Paul, "a father in Christ;" and that of the Ephesians, who were Christians "sealed unto the day of redemption."

To do justice to free grace, instead of the above mentioned improper scriptures, you should have produced those which I have quoted in the Vindication: — Christ is "the Light of the world, which enlightens every man that cometh into the world. I am come that they might have life. Ye will not come unto me that ye might have life. The grace of God, which bringeth salvation, hath appeared unto all men. God's Spirit strives with man, *even with those who perish.* He commands all men every where to repent; nor does he desire to reap where he has not sown."

VI. Such scriptures as these would have been to the purpose. But I excuse your producing others: for if these had appeared, you would have raised more dust in six lines than you could have laid in sixty pages; and every attentive reader would have detected the fallacy of your grand argument: "As soon may we expect living actions from a dead corpse; light out of darkness; sight out of blindness; love out of enmity; wisdom out of ignorance; fruit out of barrenness, &c, &c, &c, as look for any one good work or thought from a soul who is not" (in some degree) "quickened by the Holy Ghost, and who has not yet found favour with God:" so far at least as to be blessed with "a day of salvation," and to be a partaker of" the free gift, which is come upon all men."

But, I pray, who is guilty of these absurdities? Who expects living actions from a dead corpse, &c, &c? You, or we? You, who believe that the greatest part of mankind are left as graceless as devils, as helpless as corpses; and yet gravely go and preach to them repentance and faith, threatening them with an aggravated damnation if they do not turn? or we, who believe that "Christ by the grace of God tasted death for every man;" and that his "saving, quickening grace hath appeared unto all men?" Who puts foolish speeches in the mouth of the "only wise God?" You, who make him expostulate with souls as dead as corpses, and say, "Ye will not come unto me that ye might have life?" or we, who assert, upon the testimony of the Holy Ghost, that God, by "working in us both to will and to do," puts us again in a capacity of "working out our salvation with fear and trembling?" Will not our impartial readers see that the absurdity, which you try to fix upon us, falls at your own door; and if your doctrine be true, at the door of the sanctuary itself?

VII. You pursue: "It is most clear that every soul who works in the strength of Christ, and by the power of the Holy Ghost, is already a pardoned and justified soul; he already has everlasting life."

Here is some truth and some error; let us endeavour to separate them. Every soul who works in the strength of Christ's preventing grace, and by his Spirit "convincing the world of sin," is undoubtedly interested in the first degree of justification' he is justified from the guilt of original sin, and, when he believes, from the guilt of his own actual sins; but it is absurd to suppose he is justified in the day of judgment, when that day is not yet come. He hath a seed of life, or else he could not work; but it is a doubt if this seed will take root; and in case it does, the heavenly plant of righteousness may be "choked by the cares of the world, the deceitfulness of riches, or the desire of other things, and *by that mean* become unfruitful."

As many barbarous mothers destroy the fruit of their womb, either before or after it comes to the birth, so many obstinate sinners obstruct the growth of the spiritual "seed *that* bruises the serpent's head;" and many flagrant apostates, in whose heart "Christ *was once* formed, crucify him afresh, and quench the Spirit" of his grace. Hence the many miscarriages and apostasies, for which Elisha Coles is obliged to account thus: There are "monsters in spirituals, in whom there is something begotten in their wills, by the common strivings and enlightenings of the Spirit, which attains to a kind of formality, but proves in the end a lump of dead flesh." Surely that great Calvinian divine was brought to a strait when he thus fathered *formality* and *dead flesh* upon the Holy Ghost!

VIII. I follow you: "Therefore all talk of *working for life, in order to find favour with God,* is not less absurd than if you were to suppose that a man could at the same moment be both condemned and absolved."

What, sir, may not a man be justly condemned, and yet graciously reprieved? Nay, may not the judge give him an opportunity to make the best of his reprieve, in order to get a full pardon and place at court? At Geneva, we think that the absurdity does not consist in asserting, but in denying it. "Awake and asleep!" What, sir, is it an absurdity to think that a man may be at the same moment *awake* in one respect, and *asleep* in another? Does not St. Paul say, "Let us awake out of sleep?" But this is not all; even in Geneva people can be drowsy, that is, half awake and half asleep. "Dead and alive!" I hope you will not fix the charge of absurdity upon Christ, for saying that a certain man was left "half dead," and of course *half alive;* and for exhorting the people of Sardis who were *dead,* to "strengthen the things which remained and were ready to die'" nor yet upon St. Paul, for saying that the "dead body" of Abraham begat Isaac, and for speaking of a woman who was "dead while she lived."

IX. You go on and say, that "it is as absurd to talk of *working for life,* as to assert that we can be at the same time loved and hated of God."

But you forget, sir, that there are a thousand degrees of love and hatred; and that, in Scripture language, *loving less* is called *hating:* "Jacob have I loved, and Esau have I hated. Except a man hate his father, &c, he cannot be my disciple." Yea, and we can without absurdity say, that we *love* the same person in one respect, and *hate* her in another. I may love a woman as a neighbour, and yet loathe her in the capacity of a wife. And what absurdity is there in asserting that while the day of grace lasts, God loves, and yet hates an impenitent sinner? He loves him as his redeemed creature, yet hates him as his rebellious creature: or, in other terms, he loves him with a love of benevolence, but has no more love of complacence for him than for the devil himself.

X. You proceed: "To talk of *working for life*, is not less absurd, than if you were to suppose that a man can be at the same moment one with Christ, by his Spirit dwelling in the heart, and yet not have redemption, peace, and reconciliation by the blood of his cross."

Here is, if I mistake not, the language of Babel.

(1.) You confound the various degrees of redemption. Are not thousands of souls redeemed by the blood of Christ's cross, who are not yet redeemed by the power of his Spirit? May not every rebellious sinner out of hell say, "God redeemeth my life from destruction?" Is it not a degree of redemption to be kept out of hell, enjoying the good things of this life, and called to secure the blessings of the next? Did not Cain, Esau, Pharaoh, Saul, and Judas, the five great reprobates, as some account them, enjoy this degree of redemption for many years? Have not believers a higher degree of "redemption, even the forgiveness of sins?" And do they not wait for the highest degree of it, even "the redemption of their body," when the trump of God will sound and awake the dead? Romans viii, 23.

(2.) As you confound all the degrees of redemption, so you do all the degrees of the "manifestation of the Spirit." He visits all, so as to strive with and reprove them, as he did mankind in the days of Noah; but this is no mark that their peace is made, and a firm reconciliation brought about: witness the deluge, which God sent upon those with whom his Spirit had striven particularly one hundred and twenty years, in the days of Noah. Again: some have "the spirit of bondage unto fear;" but this, far from being a sign that they have full reconciliation, is a Divine consciousness that they have it not. And others have had the Spirit of adoption, and after having begun in him, so grieve or quench him as to end in the flesh. But in the Calvinian Babel, these Scriptural, experimental distinctions are exploded as metaphysical, if not dreadfully heretical.

XI. You proceed: "You will not assert that a soul who is 'quickened together with Christ,' and in whom the Spirit of Jesus dwells by his gracious influences, can be in a state of enmity with God."

Still the same confounding of things which should be carefully distinguished! May not a sinner "be quickened" by the seed of life, and yet "hold it in unrighteousness?" May not a backslider "crucify Christ afresh," in *the gracious influences of his Spirit?* And are not such persons *in a state of enmity with God?* But if, by a soul "quickened together with Christ, and in whom the Spirit of Jesus dwells," you mean *a believer completely baptized with the Holy Ghost and with fire*, in whom he that once visited as a Monitor now fully resides as a Comforter, you are right; the enmity ceases, the carnal mind and body of sin are destroyed, and "God is all in all" to that just man "made perfect in love."

XII. You add: "If a man is not in a state of enmity, then he must be in a state of pardon and reconciliation."

What, sir! Is there no medium between these extremes? There is, as surely as the morning dawn intervenes between midnight and noonday. If the king say to some rebels, "Lay down your arms, surrender, kiss my son, and you shall be pardoned," the reconciliation on the king's part is undoubtedly begun. So far "was God in Christ reconciling the world unto himself." But can it be said that the reconciliation is begun on the part of the rebels, who have not yet laid down any of their arms? Does not the reconciliation gradually take place, as they gradually comply with the king's terms? If they are long in coming to kiss the king's son, is not their full reconciliation suspended till they have fulfilled the last of the king's terms? And though the king made the overtures of the reconciliation, is there the least absurdity in saying, that "they surrender, and kiss the son, in order to find reconciliation?" Nay, is it either sense or truth to assert, that "they are absolutely to do nothing toward it?"

XIII. What you say about the thirteenth article of our Church is answered beforehand. But what follows deserves some notice: "Whenever God puts forth quickening power upon a soul, it is in consequence of his having already taken that soul into covenant with himself, and having washed it white in the blood of the Lamb slain."

This is very true, if you speak of the covenant of grace, which God made with our first parent and representative after the fall; and of the washing of all mankind white in the blood of the Lamb from the guilt of original sin, so far as to remit the eternal punishment of it. But you are dreadfully mistaken, if you understand it of the three subsequent degrees of justification and salvation, which do not take place, but as we "work them out with fear and trembling, *as God works in us* both to will and to do of his good pleasure."

XIV. In the next page you ask some Scriptural questions, which I shall Scripturally answer: "What did the expiring thief do?" Some hours before he died he obeyed this precept, "To-day if ye will hear his voice harden not your heart;" he confessed his sin and believed in Jesus.

"What did Mary Magdalene do?" She forsook her lovers, and followed Jesus into Simon's house.

"What Lydia?" She "worshipped *God,* and resorted where prayer was wont to be made."

"What the Philippian jailer?" He ceased from attempting self murder, and "falling at the apostle's feet, *inquired* what he must do to be saved?"

"What the serpent-bitten Israelites?" They "looked at the brazen serpent."

"What Paul himself?" "For this cause I obtained mercy," says he, "because I did it ignorantly in unbelief," 1 Timothy 1:13. But this was not all; for he "continued praying three days and three nights;" and when Ananias came to him he tarried no longer, but "arose and washed away his sins, calling on the name of the Lord."

"What did the Corinthians do?" They "heard and believed," Acts viii, 8.

"And what the Ephesians?" They "trusted in Christ, after that they heard the word of truth," Ephesians i,13.

XV. In the next paragraph, (page 6, line 28,) you gravely propose the very objection which I have answered, without taking the least notice of my answer. And in the next page you advance one of Dr. Crisp's paradoxes: "Wherever God puts forth his power upon a soul, (and he does so whenever he

Five Checks To Antinomianism

visits it even with a touch of preventing grace,) pardon and reconciliation are already obtained by such a one. He shall never come into condemnation."

Young penitents, beware! If you admit this tenet, you will probably stay in the "far country,', vainly fancying you are in your "Father's house," because you have felt a desire to be there. Upon this scheme of doctrine, Lot's wife might have sat down at the gate of Sodom, concluding, that because the angels had taken her by the hand she was already in Zoar. A dangerous delusion this, against which our Lord himself cautions us by crying aloud, "Remember Lot's wife!"

I would take the liberty to expostulate with you, honoured sir, about this paradox, if I had not some hope, that it is rather owing to the printer's mistake than your own. If you wrote in your manuscript, "Pardon is already obtained *for*," not *by*, such a one, we are agreed; for "Christ made upon the cross a sufficient sacrifice and satisfaction for the sins of the whole world." But what he procured *for* us, is not obtained *by* us, till the Holy Ghost makes the application by faith. "If I had a mind," said the Rev. Mr. Whitefield, "to hinder the progress of the Gospel, and to establish the kingdom of darkness, I would go about telling the people, *they might have the Spirit of God, and yet not feel it;*" or, which is much the same, that the pardon which Christ procured *for* them, is already obtained *by* them, whether they enjoy a sense of it or not.

XVI. In the next paragraph, page 7, (who could believe it?) you come fully into Mr. Wesley's doctrine of' doing something in order to obtain justification." You was reminded *(First Check)* that "St. Paul and Mr. Wesley generally mean by *justification,* that wonderful transaction of the Spirit of God in a returning prodigal's conscience, by which the forgiveness of his sins is proclaimed to him through the blood of sprinkling." Nevertheless, speaking of the sense of pardon, and the testifying of it to a sinner's conscience, you grant that "this knowledge of our interest in Christ," (this experienced justification,) "is certainly to be sought in the use of all appointed means; we are to seek that we may find, to ask that we may have, to knock that it may be opened unto us. In this sense," (the very sense we generally fix to the word justification,) "all the texts you have brought to prove that man is to do something in order to obtain justification, and to find favour with God, admit of an *easy solution:*" that is, in plain English, easily demonstrate the truth of Mr. Wesley's proposition, which has been so loudly exclaimed against as *dreadfully heretical!*

O prejudice, thou mischievous cause of discord, why didst thou cast thy black veil in June, and the following months, over the *easy solution,* which has been found out in December? And what a pity is it, dear sir, you did not see this *solution* before you had attempted to expose our gray-headed Elisha, by the publication of that weak and trifling dialogue with the Popish friar at Paris!

XVII. Page 10. After showing that you confound the atonement with the application of it, the work of Christ with that of the Holy Ghost, you produce one of my arguments, (the first you have attempted to refute,) brought to prove, that we must do something in order to justification. I had asserted that we must *believe,* faith being previous to justification. You say, "*I deny the assertion!*" Do you, indeed, honoured sir? Upon what ground? "The Holy Ghost teaches," say you, "that all who believe *are* justified." And does this prove the point? The king says to a deserter, "Bow to my son, and thou shalt not be shot." "Bow to the prince," adds an officer; "all who bow to him *are* pardoned." Must the soldier conclude from the words, "*are* pardoned," that the *pardon* is previous to the *bow?* Again: you are sick, and your physician says, "Take this medicine; all who take it *are* cured." "Very well!" answers your nurse, "you need not then distress and perplex my master, by making him take your remedy. The taking of it cannot possibly be previous to his recovery; for you say, All who take it *are* cured." This is just such another argument as that of my honoured friend. O sir, how tottering is that system, which even such a writer as yourself cannot prop up, without putting so forced a construction upon the apostle's words, "All that believe *are* justified?"

Now we have seen upon what Scriptural ground you maintain, that believing cannot be previous to justification, permit me, honoured sir, to quote some of the many scriptures which induce us to believe just the reverse: "Believe in the Lord Jesus Christ, and thou shalt be saved;" that is, in the lowest sense of the word, thou shalt be justified: for God justifies the ungodly that believe in Jesus. "We have believed in Jesus Christ, that we might be justified by the faith of Christ — whom he hath set forth to be a propitiation through faith in his blood, for the remission of sins that are past. As Moses lifted up the serpent, even so must the Son of man be lifted up, that whosoever believeth in him should not perish;" should be pardoned, &c. "Faith shall be imputed to us for righteousness, if we believe on him who raised up Jesus. Being therefore justified by faith, we have peace with God. Without faith it is impossible to please God. He that believeth not," far from being justified, as is insinuated, "shall be damned; the wrath of God abideth on him; he is condemned already," John iii, 18. Light cannot be more opposite to darkness, than this doctrine of Christ to that which my honoured friend thinks it his duty to patronize.

XVIII. When you have ineffectually endeavoured to defend your sentiment from Scripture, you attempt to do it from reason. "Faith," say you, "can no more subsist without its object than there can be a marriage without a husband."

This is as proper an argument as you could advance, had you intended to disprove the doctrine you seem studious to defend; for it is evident that a woman must be married before she can have a husband, So sure then as marriage is previous to having a husband, faith is previous to receiving Christ: for we receive him by faith, John i, 12. However, from this extraordinary argument, you conclude that "the doctrine of believing before justification is not less contrary to reason than it is to Scripture;" but I flatter myself that my judicious readers will draw a conclusion diametrically opposite.

XIX. A quotation from St. Augustine appears next, and secures the ruin of your scheme. For if faith be compared to a *lantern,* and Christ to *the light in the lantern,* common sense tells us we must have the lantern before we can receive the candle which is to give us light. Or, in other words, we must have faith before we can receive Christ: for you very justly observe, that "faith receiveth Christ, who is the true Light."

XX. St. Augustine's lantern makes way for the witticism with which you conclude your second epistle. "No letters," says my honoured friend, "were sent through the various provinces against old Mordecai, for supposing that the woman, Luke xv, lights a candle, &c, in order to find her lost piece; but because he insists upon it, that the piece lights the candle, sweeps the house, and searches diligently in order to find the woman."

Permit me to ask, whether your wit here has not for a moment got the start of your judgment? I introduced *the woman seeking the piece she had lost,* merely to show that it is neither a heresy nor an absurdity to "seek something in order to find it;" and that instance proved my point, full as well as if I had fixed upon Saul seeking his father's asses, or Joseph seeking his brethren in Dothan.

If it be as great an absurdity to say, that sinners are "to seek the Lord," as it is to say, that "a piece seeks the woman that has lost it;" let me tell you, that Mr. Wesley has the good fortune to be countenanced in his folly, *First,* by yourself, who tell us, page 7, that the knowledge of Christ, and our interest in him, "is certainly to be sought in the use of all the appointed means." And, *Secondly,* by Isaiah, who says, "Seek ye the Lord while he may be found." By St. Paul, who tells the Athenians, that" all nations of men are to seek the Lord." And by Christ himself who says, "They that seek me early shall find me: — seek that you may find," &c.

I leave you to judge, whether it was worth your while to impeach Mr. Wesley's good sense, not only by reflecting upon your own, but by inevitably involving Isaiah, St. Paul, and our Lord himself, in the ridicule cast upon my vindicated friend! For the same sinner, who is represented by *the lost piece,* is, a few verses before, represented by *the lost son;* and, you know, Jesus Christ tells us that he came from far to seek his father's pardon and assistance.

REMARKS ON THE THIRD LETTER.

You begin this letter by saying, "How God may deal with the heathen world is not for us to pry into." But we may believe what God has revealed. If the Holy Ghost declares, that "in every nation he that feareth God and worketh righteousness, is accepted of him," we may credit what he says, without being "wise above what is written."

If you cannot set aside that apostolic part of the Minutes, you try however, to press it into the service of your doctrine. "There is," say you, "a material difference between saying, 'He that feareth God and worketh righteousness *is* accepted, and *shall be* accepted;'" and because "the verb is in the present tense," you conclude, there is no need of fearing God, or working righteousness in order to find acceptance. This is exactly such another argument as that which I just now refuted, "We need not believe in order to be justified, because it is said, 'all that believe *are* justified, and not *shall be* justified.'" You can no more prove by the one that Cornelius, provoking God and working unrighteousness, was accepted of him; than, by the other, that *unbelievers* ARE justified, because it is said that *believers* are so.

A similar instance may convince you of it: "All run," says St. Paul, "but one receiveth the prize." I, who am a stranger to refinements, immediately conclude from those words, that running is *previous* to the receiving of the prize, and *in order* to it. "No," says a friend, "there is a material difference between saying, 'one *receiveth* the prize,' and 'one *shall receive* the prize.' The verb is in the present tense, and therefore the plain sense of the passage is, (not that by running he does any thing to receive the prize, but) that he who runs *is* possessed of the prize, and proves himself to be so." Candid reader, if such an argument proselytes thee to Dr. Crisp's doctrine, I shall suspect there is no small difference between English and Suisse reason.

However, to make up the weight of your argument, you add, "Cornelius was a chosen vessel." True, for "God hath chosen to himself the man that is godly;" and such was Cornelius; "a devout man," says St. Luke, "and one that feared God with all his house." But if my honoured opponent speaks of an election which drags after it the horrors of absolute reprobation, and hangs the millstone of unavoidable damnation about the neck of millions of our fellow creatures, I must call for proof.

Till it comes, I follow you in your observations upon the merit or rewardableness of good works. Most of them are answered, First Check, p. 54*, &c, and Second Check, p. 98†. The rest I answer thus: —

1. If you do not believe Mr. Henry when he assures us David speaks *of himself*, "The Lord rewarded me according to my righteousness," &c, Psalm xviii, believe at least the sacred historian, who confirms my assertion, 2 Samuel xxii; and consider the very title of the psalm, "David spake unto the Lord the words of this song, in the day that the Lord delivered him from the hand of his enemies, and from the hand of Saul."

2. But "when David speaks in his own person, his language is very different." "Enter not into judgment with thy servant," says he, "for in thy sight shall no man living be justified." The psalmist does not here contradict what he says of the rewardableness of good works, Psalm xviii. He only appeals from the law of innocence to the law of grace, and only disclaims all merit in point of justification and salvation, a thing which Mr. Wesley takes care to do when he says, even in the Minutes, "Not by the merit of works," but by "believing in Christ."

3. My honoured correspondent asks next, — "Where is the man who has the witness of having done what God commanded?" I answer, Every one is who "walks in the light as God is in the light," and can say with St. John, "Beloved, if our heart condemn us not, then have we confidence toward God: and whatsoever we ask, we receive of him, *because* we keep his commandments, and do those things which are pleasing in his sight."

4. But Bishop Beveridge spoke just the reverse; for he said in his Private Thoughts, "I sin in my best duties," &c. That may be; for he was but a young convert when he wrote his Private Thoughts. I hope before he died he enjoyed more Gospel liberty. But whether he did or not, we appeal from his Private Thoughts to the above-mentioned public declaration and evangelical experience of St. John.

5. If many Roman Catholics do not ascribe merit to "mere external performances," I have done them "great injustice;" and, to repair that wrong, I declare my full approbation of that excellent passage upon merit which you quote

* [47]

† [95]

in French, from the works of the bishop of Meaux. I say, *in French*, because your English translation represents him as looking On *all* opinion of merit as *presumptuous*, whereas he blames only *l' opinion d' un merite presomptueux*, "the doctrine of a presumptuous merit," — of a merit which is not all derived from Christ, and does not terminate in the glory of his grace.

The dying challenge of Alexander Seton is answered in the Second Check, first letter. As to your quotation from Bishop Cooper, it does as little credit to his learning as to his charity; for St. Augustine, who had no more "the spirit of antichrist" than the bishop himself, uses perpetually the word *merit*, in speaking of man and his works.

Let us now see how you "split the hair," that is, fix the difference there is between being rewarded *according to our works?*[*] BECAUSE *of our works,* and *secundum merita operum,* "according to the *merit* or *rewardableness* which Christ gives to our works." "The difference," say you, "by no means depends upon the splitting of a hair; those expressions are as wide as east from west." Are they indeed? Then it must be the east and west of the map of the world, which meet in one common line upon the globe. This will appear, if we consider the manner in which you untie the Gordian knot.

"Good works," say you, "are rewarded, because God, of his own mere favour, rich grace, and undeserved bounty, has promised that he will freely give such rewards to those whom he has chosen in his dear Son." Now, sir, simplify this sentence, and you tell us just that "good works are rewarded because God freely promised to reward them."

And is this the east of my honoured opponent's orthodoxy? Surprising! It just meets the west of Popish heterodoxy. You know, sir, that Thomas Aquinas and Scotus are as great divines among the Romanists as Calvin and Luther among the Protestants; and in fleeing from Mr. Wesley, you are just gone over to Scotus and Baxter; for Scotus, and Clara, his disciple, maintain, that if God gives rewards to the godly, *non oritur obligatio ex natura actus, sed ex suppositione decreti et promissi,* "the obligation does not arise from the nature of the action rewarded, but from the decree and free promise of the rewarder." "Though so much be given in Scripture to good works," says the council of Trent, "yet far be it from a Christian to glory in himself, and not in the Lord, whose goodness is so great to all men, that he wills those things to be *their merits,* which are *his gifts.*" (*Can.* 16, de Justif.)

"Most Protestants," says Baxter, "will take *merit* to signify something which profiteth God, and which is our own, and not his *gift* and *grace;* but they are mistaken."

Some, however, are more candid: Bucer says, "If by m*eriting* the holy fathers and others mean nothing but to do *in faith, by the grace of God,* good works, which the Lord has *promised* to reward, in this sense," (which is that which Scotus, Baxter, and Mr. Wesley fix to *merit,)* "we shall in no wise condemn that word."

Hence it is that whole congregations of real Protestants have not scrupled at times to use the words *we merit,* in their humblest addresses to the

---

[*] See 1 John iii, 22, and First Cheek, pp. 47, 48. You have no right to throw out this middle term till you have proved that my quotations are false.

throne of grace. "Congregations of real Protestants!" says my honoured friend. "Popery is about midway between Protestantism and such worshippers. Who are they?" I answer, They are the orthodox opposers of the Minutes, the truly honourable the countess of Huntingdon, the Rev. Mr. Shirley, the Rev. Mr. Madan, and all the congregations that use their Hymns; for they all agree to sing,

> *Thou hast the righteousness supply'd,*
> *By which we* merit *heaven.*

See Lady Huntingdon's Hymns, British edition, page 399; and the Rev. Mr. Madan's Collection, which you frequently use, hymn xxv, page 27, last stanza. Come then, dear sir, while Mr. Madan shakes hands with his venerable father, Mr. Wesley, permit the vindicator of the Minutes to do the same with the author of *Pietas Oxoniensis,* and let us lovingly follow Scotus and Baxter, singing, "Christ hath the righteousness supplied, by which *we merit* heaven."

If you say, "True; but it is of God's own mere favour, rich grace, and undeserved bounty in his dear Son;" I answer, We are agreed, and before hand I subscribe a hundred such clauses, being fully persuaded of the truth of Mr. Wesley's proposition, when explained according to the analogy of faith, "There is no original *merit* but in the blood and obedience of Christ; and no derived *merit,* or, (if you dislike that word out of the Lock chapel,) no derived *rewardableness,* but that which we are supplied with through the Spirit of Christ, and the blood of his cross." If Mr. Wesley meant any more by the saying you have quoted, he will permit me to use his own words, and say that he "leaned too much toward Calvinism."

I cannot better close the subject of merit, and requite your quotation from Dr. Willet, than by transcribing a third passage from the pious and judicious Mr. Baxter: —

"We are agreed on the negative: (1.) That no man or angel can merit of God in proper commutative justice, giving him somewhat for his benefits that shall profit him, or to which he had no absolute right. (2.) No man can merit any thing of God upon the terms of the law of innocency, (but punishment.) (3.) Nor can he merit any thing of God by the law of grace, unless it be supposed first to be a free gift and merited by Christ.

"And affirmatively we are, I think, agreed: (1.) That God governs us *by a law of grace,* which hath a *promise,* and gives by way of *reward.* (2.) That God calls it *his justice* to reward men according to his law of grace, Hebrews 6:10; 2 Timothy 4:8. (3.) That this supposes that such works as God rewards have *a moral aptitude* for that reward, which chiefly consists in these things, that they spring from the Spirit of God, that their faultiness is pardoned through the blood and merits of Christ, that they are done in the love and to the glory of God, and that they are presented to God by Jesus Christ. (4.) That this *moral aptitude* is called in Scripture αξια, that is, *worthiness* or *merit;* so that thus far *worthiness* or *merit* is a Scripture phrase. And, (5.) That this worthiness or merit is only in point of *paternal governing justice,* according to the *law of grace,* ordering that which in itself is a *free gift merited by Christ.*

"All orthodox Christians hold the fore-described doctrine of merit in *sense*, though not in *words:* for they that deny *merit*, confess the *rewardableness* of our obedience, and acknowledge that the Scripture useth the term *worthy*, and that αξιος and αξια may be translated *meriting* and *merit*, *as* well as *worthy* and *worthiness*. This is the same thing, in other words, which the ancient Christians meant by *merit*. When godly persons earnestly extol holiness, saying that 'the righteous is more excellent than his neighbour,' and yet deny all *merit*, reviling all that assert it, they do but show that they understand not the word, and think others also misunderstand it: and so we are reproaching one another where we are agreed, and know it not; like the woman who turned away her servant upon the controversy, Whether the house should be swept with a *besom*, or with a *broom*.

"The partial teachers are the cause of this, while, instead of opening the doctrine, and showing in what sense we have or have not any *worthiness* or *merit*, they without distinction cry down *merit*, and reproach those that do otherwise. And if they do but say, 'Such a man speaks for merit and free will,' they think that they sufficiently render him odious to their followers; when yet all sober Christians in all ages have been for *merit* and *free will* in a sound sense. And is not this to be adversaries to truth, and love, and peace?

"I formerly thought, that though we agree in the *thing*, it is best to omit the *name*, because the Papists have abused it: and I think so still in such companies, where the use of it, not understood, will scandalize men, and do more harm than good. But in other cases I *now* think it better to keep the *word*, (1.) Lest we seem to the ignorant to be of another religion than* all the ancient Churches were. (2.) Lest we harden the Papists, Greeks, and others, by denying the sound doctrine in *terms*, which they will think we deny in *sense*. And, (3.) Because our penury of words is such, that for my part I remember no other word so fit to substitute instead of *merit, desert*, or *worthiness*. The word *rewardableness* is long and harsh. But it is nothing else that we mean." *(Baxter's End of Doctrinal Controversies,* page 294.)

REMARKS ON MR. HILL'S FOURTH LETTER.

I am glad that my honoured opponent, in the beginning of his fourth letter, does Mr. Wesley the justice to admit of the explanation I have given of that misunderstood assertion, "All who are convinced of sin undervalue themselves." Had you done otherwise, sir, you would have "shown judgment without mercy." Nevertheless, you still think that explanation *forced;* while many believe it not only natural and *agreeable* to Mr. Wesley's whole plan of doctrine, but *so solid* that no arguments can overthrow it. If you turn to the Second Check, (pp. 99, 100†) you will see more clearly that you do Mr. Wesley no favour in "dismissing this article of the Minutes."

---

* "It is a great advantage to the Papists," says our judicious author, "that many Protestants wholly disclaim the word *merit*, and simply deny the merit of Gospel obedience. For hereupon the teachers show their scholars that all the fathers speak for merit, and do tell them, that the Protestant doctrine is new and heretical, as being contrary to all the ancient doctors; and when their scholars see it with their eyes, no wonder if they believe it, to our dishonour."
† [95,96]

But you prepare to attack the next with the utmost vigour. *A part of the Minutes which you esteem most contrary to sound doctrine,* is, say you, that "we are every hour and every moment pleasing, or displeasing to God, according to the whole of our inward tempers and outward behaviour," &c. And it is, I own, diametrically opposite to the favourite sentiment which you thus express: "Though I believe that David's SIN displeased the Lord, must I therefore believe that David's PERSON was under the curse of the law?" (I suppose you mean *under God's displeasure,* for of this Mr. Wesley speaks; nor does he mention *the curse of the law* in all the Minutes.) You boldly answer, "Surely no. Like Ephraim, he was still a pleasant child, though he went on frowardly," in adultery and murder, "he did not lose the character of the man after God's own heart." You might as well have advanced at once that unguarded proposition of Dr. Crisp: "God does no longer stand displeased, though a believer do sin often. No sin can possibly do him any hurt." Is this what you call "sound doctrine?" And is that *the worst part of the Minutes,* which opposes such a dangerous tenet? Then how *excellent* must the *other* parts be! Indeed, sir, their vindicator could say nothing stronger to demonstrate their soundness, seasonableness, and importance. But let us consider your arguments; and that with such care as the importance of the subject requires.

I. "David's SIN displeased the Lord," but not "his PERSON." This is what you must mean, if you oppose Mr. Wesley's proposition. I like your shifting the terms; it is a sign that you are a little ashamed the world should see the good doctor's scheme without some covering. *Erubuisti, salva res est.* (1.) Your intimation, that the Lord was not displeased at David's *person,* bears hard upon the equity and veracity of God. David commits adultery and murder in Jerusalem, and Claudius in Rome. God sees them, and says, agreeably to your scheme, "They are both guilty of the same crimes, and both impenitent; but David is a Jew, an elect, a sheep, and therefore, though he sins against *ten* times more light than the other, I am not at all displeased at him. But Claudius is a heathen, a reprobate, a goat, and my anger smokes against him; he shall surely die." If this is God's method, how can he make the following appeal? "O house of Israel, are not my ways equal? Are not your ways unequal? The soul that sinneth it shall die: wherefore, turn ye, why will ye die, O house of Israel?" See Ezekiel xviii, and Second Check, pp. 112,113*.

(2.) Your distinction is overthrown by Scripture: for we read, Genesis xxxviii, 10, that "the thing which Onan did displeased the Lord." "True," might you say, upon your scheme, "this is the very thing I assert. This mode of speech shows that God was angry at Onan's *sin,* and not at his *person. "* But this would be a great mistake, honoured sir; for the sacred historian adds immediately, *Wherefore God slew him also.* He showed his heavy displeasure at his *person,* by punishing him with death, as well as his brother Er, who *was wicked in the sight of the Lord.*

(3.) But if you will not believe Mr. Wesley when he declares, that God is displeased at the *persons* of the righteous, the moment they do those *things* which displease him, believe at least the oracles of God. "God's anger was kindled against Moses," Exodus iv, 14. "The Lord was very angry against Aaron,"

---

* [109, 110]

Deuteronomy ix, 20; and with all Israel: witness those awful words, "Let me alone, that I may consume them in a moment!" Isaiah, whom you allow to be an elect, says, "Thou wast angry with me." God himself says, Isaiah xlvii, 6, "I was angry with my people:" and David, who frequently deprecates God's wrath in his penitential Psalms, observes, that "his anger smokes against the sheep of his pasture," when they go astray, Psalm lxxiv, 1.

(4.) The New Testament inculcates this doctrine as well as the Old. St. Paul having reminded the believers of Ephesus, that "no whoremonger, or covetous person, hath an inheritance in the kingdom of Christ and of God," subjoins this seasonable caution, "Let no man deceive you;" no, not those good men, Dr. Crisp and the author of *Pietas Oxoniensis:* "for because of these things the wrath of God cometh upon the children of disobedience." "Impossible!" say those orthodox Protestants; "you may be 'children of disobedience,' not only unto 'whoredom and covetousness,' but unto adultery and murder, without, fearing that 'the wrath of God will come upon you for these things.' No, no, you will be 'pleasant children still.'" See *Vindication*, pp. 66*.

II. You proceed: "Shall I believe, that, because David was ungrateful, God, whose *gifts and callings are without repentance,* was unfaithful?" And shall I believe that God is not as *faithful* when he accomplishes his threatenings, as when he fulfils his promises? You reply, "God's *gifts and callings are without repentance."* And does this prove that God's warnings are without meaning, and his threatenings without truth? St. Paul spoke those words of the election of the Jews; and, it is certain, God does not repent that he formerly *called* them, and *gave* them the land of Canaan; any more than he repents his having now *rejected* them, and *taken from them* the good land which he gave their fathers: for as he had once sufficient reasons to do the one, so he has now to do the other.

But if you will make this passage mean, that the Divine favour and blessings can never be forfeited through any fall into sin, I beg you will answer these queries. Had not God *given* all angels a place in his favour and glory? and did not many of them lose it by their fall? Was not innocent Adam interested in the Divine favour and image? and did he not lose both, together with paradise, when he fell into sin? Did not King Saul forfeit the crown which God had *given* him, and the throne to which he had *called* him? Were not Judas' *calling* and apostleship forfeited by his unfaithfulness, as well as one of the twelve *thrones* which Christ had promised him? What will you say of the unprofitable servant from whom his lord took the talent unimproved? Lost he not a blessing *given*, and *his calling to occupy* with it? And can you assert that the man who took his fellow servant by the throat did not lose *the forgiveness of a debt of ten thousand talents?* Or that those apostates, who "tread under foot the blood of the covenant wherewith they were sanctified," do not forfeit their sanctification by *doing despite to the Spirit of grace?* Is it right thus to set the author of the Epistle to the Romans against the author of the Epistle to the Hebrews?

III. Your bringing in "backsliding Ephraim, *the pleasant child,"* as a witness of the truth of your doctrine, is a most unhappy proof. "Rejoice not, O

---

* [59, 60]

Israel, as other people," says the Lord, Hosea ix, 1, "for thou hast gone a whoring from thy God." This whoring Israel is called Ephraim, verse 13. *Ephraim*, the pleasant child, *is planted as a pleasant plant*. Notwithstanding, "Ephraim shall bring forth his children for the murderer. All their wickedness is in Gilgal: for there *I hated* them. For the wickedness of their doings I will drive them out of mine house: *I will love them no more."* Hence the prophet observes immediately after, "Ephraim is smitten; my God will cast them away because they did not hearken unto him."

IV. However, my honoured friend still affirms, that "David, notwithstanding his horrible backslidings, did not lose the character of *the man after God's own heart."* But you will permit me to believe the contrary.

1. Upon the testimony of the Psalmist himself, who says, in your favourite Psalm, "Thou hast cast off and abhorred, thou hast been very wroth with thine anointed; thou hast made void the covenant of thy servant; thou hast profaned his crown by casting it to the ground," Psalm lxxxix, 38.

2. Where is David called *the man after God's own heart*, while he continued an impenitent adulterer? How much more guarded is the Scripture than your Letters? "David did that which was right in the eyes of the Lord, and turned not aside, SAVE only in the matter of Uriah," 1 Kings xv, 5. Here you see the immoral parenthesis of ten months spent in adultery and murder, expressly pointed at, and excepted by the Holy Ghost.

3. David himself, far from thinking that sin could never separate between God and *a just man* who *draws back* into wickedness, speaks thus in the last charge which he gave to Solomon: "And thou, Solomon, my son, know the God of thy father, and serve him with a perfect heart. If thou seek him, he will be found of thee; but if thou forsake him, he will cast thee off for ever," 1 Chronicles xxviii, 9. Hence it appears that the God of *Solomon's father is* very different from the picture which Dr. Crisp draws of *David's God!* The former can be so displeased at an impenitent backslider, as to cast him off for ever; while the latter accounts him *a pleasant child still.* But let us come to matter of fact.

4. Displeasure, anger, or wrath in God, is not that disturbing, boisterous passion so natural to fallen man; but an invariable disapprobation of sin, and a steady design to punish the sinner. Now God severely manifested his righteous displeasure at David's person, when he punished him by not restraining any longer the ambition of his rebellious son. How remarkably did his dreadful punishments answer his heinous crimes! He wanted the fruit of his adultery to live, but inflexible justice destroys it. "The crown of *righteousness* was fallen from his head," and his royal crown is "profaned and cast to the ground." He had not turned out "the way faring man," the hellish tempter; and he is turned out of his own palace and kingdom. He flees beyond Jordan for his life; and, as he flees, Shimei throws stones at him; volleys of curses accompany the *stones;* and the most cutting challenges follow the curses: — "Come out, thou bloody man," said he, "thou man of Belial! The Lord hath delivered thy kingdom into the hand of Absalom thy son; and behold, thou art taken in thy mischief, because thou art a bloody man." To which David could answer nothing, but "'*Let him curse; for the Lord,*' by not restraining his wickedness, *hath* permissively '*said unto him, Curse David.*' I see the impartial justice of a sin-avenging God, through the cruel abuse

of this raging man." This was not all. He had *secretly* committed adultery with Uriah's wife, and his son *publicly* commits incest with his wives. And, to complete the horror of his punishment, he leaves the most dreadful curse upon his posterity. "Thou hast slain Uriah with the sword of the children of Ammon," says the Lord, "now therefore the sword shall never depart from thy house," and thy own children shall murder one another. What a terrible punishment was this! And how strong must be the prejudice of those who maintain that God was not displeased at David's *person!*

V. Pass we now to an argument which you seem to consider as one of the main pillars of your doctrine: "If one believer sin by an unclean thought," say you, *"and* another by an unclean act, does the former continue in a state of grace, and the other forfeit his sonship? Take heed lest you should be forced to go to Rome for an answer to this query."

Without going even to the convent of the Benedictine monks in Paris, I answer, It is evident from Scripture that an adulterous thought, delighted in, is adultery. He that entertains such a thought is an adulterer, one who is absolutely unfit for the presence of a holy God. "Be not deceived," says St. Paul, "neither fornicators nor adulterers shall inherit the kingdom of God." Therefore adultery of heart certainly excludes an impenitent backslider out of heaven; though it will not sink him into so deep a hell, as if he had drawn another into the commission of his intended crime. You add:

"But if David had only had an angry thought, he had still been a murderer in the sight of God." Not so: for there is a righteous anger, which is a virtue and not a sin; or else how could Christ "have looked round about on the Pharisees with anger," and continued sinless? You mean, probably, that if David had only *hated* Uriah in his heart, he would have been a murderer. If so, your observation is very just, for, "he that hateth his brother," says St. John, "is a murderer; and you know," adds he, "that no murderer," though he were a royal psalmist, "hath eternal life abiding in him."

But what do you get by these arguments? Nothing at all. You only make it easier to prove that your doctrine is erroneous. For if David would have forfeited heaven by "looking on Uriah's wife, to lust after her in his heart," or by intending in his breast to murder her husband; how much more did he forfeit it when mental sin fully ripened into outward enormities! "Ye are of your father the devil, whose works ye do," said Christ to some of the chosen nation. And if adultery and murder are works of the devil, it follows from those words of our Lord, that while David continued impenitent, he was *not* "a man after God's own heart," as my honoured opponent too charitably supposes; but *a man after the own heart of him* "who abode not in the truth, and was a murderer from the beginning."

VI. But you add, "Sin did not reign in him as a king, it only for a time usurped as a tyrant." Nay, sir, sin is a tyrant wherever he reigns, and he reigns wherever he usurps. "Where will you draw the line" between the *reign* and *tyranny* of sin? Are not both included under the word *dominion?* "Sin," says St. Paul, "shall not have DOMINION over you that are under grace." Had I made such a distinction as this, some Protestants would deservedly have called it *metaphysical;* but as it comes from the orthodox author of *Pietas Oxoniensis,* it will probably pass for *evangelical.*

Very different, however, is St. Peter's orthodoxy. "Of whom a man is overcome," says he, "of the same is he brought into bondage. For if after they have escaped the pollution of the world through the knowledge of the Lord Jesus Christ, they are again entangled therein and overcome, the latter end is worse with them than the beginning." Nevertheless, even such apostates, so long as the day of their visitation lasteth, may again repent and believe; for, as you justly observe, they have still "an Advocate with the Father, Jesus Christ the righteous."

VII. You try to prove your point by Scripture. "There is," say you 'no condemnation to them who are in Christ." True: but it is while they "walk not after the flesh, but after the Spirit;" a clause which you prudently keep out of sight. And, surely, David walked after the flesh, when in the act of adultery and murder. You proceed: "Who shall lay any thing to the charge of God's elect?" Nobody, if God's elect are penitent believers, "who walk not after the flesh;" but if they are impenitent adulterers and hypocritical murderers, — Jews and Gentiles, law and Gospel, prophets and apostles, God and their own conscience, ALL will agree to lay their crimes to their charge. You urge, that "Christ, by one offering, hath for ever perfected them that are sanctified." True! But not those who are *unsanctified:* and, certainly, such are all adulterers and murderers. These ought rather to be ranked with those who "tread under foot the blood of the covenant wherewith they WERE sanctified."

It is said, however, "Ye," believing, loving, fruitful Colossians, see Colossians i, 4, 6, "are complete in him." It is so; but not, *ye impenitent backsliders, ye unclean defilers of another's bed*. Such are "complete" in *evil*, not in *good*, in Belial, not in Christ. Alas, for the prostitution of the sacred and pure word of God! Can it also be pressed into the service of profaneness and impurity? To rescue at least one sentence from such manifest abuse, I might observe, the original may with the greatest propriety be rendered, *filled with* (or *by*) *him*, instead of "complete in him;" and I think the context fixes this sense upon it. The apostle is cautioning the Colossians against vain philosophers, whose doctrine was empty and deceitful. Now, that he may do this the more effectually, he points out a more excellent Teacher, whose character and qualifications he describes when he says, *'In* him dwelleth the fulness, Greek ωληρωμα, of the Godhead." He immediately adds, ωεπληρωμενοι εν αυτω (a verb of the same etymology with the noun, and undoubtedly of a similar import,) "ye are filled *with* (or *by*) him." As if he had said, "Christ is filled with the Godhead of the Father, and ye with the Spirit of Christ, the Spirit of wisdom, righteousness, and strength. *Plenitudo Christi*, says the learned and pious Bengelius on the passage, *redundat in ecclesiam*, "The fulness of God dwelleth in the Mediator, and overflows upon his Church." The very sense our translators have given the very same two words in Ephesians iii, 19 Why they rendered them differently here is hard to say.

VIII. You go on: "No falls or backslidings in God's children can ever bring them again under condemnation, because *the law of the Spirit of life in Christ Jesus hath made them free from the law of sin and death." A* most dangerous proposition, exposed, (*First Check*, p. 66*) and contrary to the very Scripture by which you try

* [59]

to support it. (1.) To the context, where those to whom "there is no condemnation," are said to be persons "who walk not after the flesh," and are therefore very different from impenitent adulterers and murderers, who bring forth the most execrable fruits of the flesh. (2.) To the text itself: for if "the law, *or power* of the Spirit of life in Christ Jesus, hath made *the believer* free from the law *or power* of sin," how can he be represented as the same "servant of sin;" as "sold under sin;" sold under adultery and murder for ten months! But you are at a loss for an answer.

IX. "We are very apt," say you, "to set up mountainous distinctions concerning the various degrees of sin, especially of sins after conversion." This, together with your placing "an angry thought" upon a level with deliberate murder, seems to insinuate, that you make very little difference between an atrocious crime and a sin of surprise; so that, upon your scheme, a bloody murderer may plead that he is not more guilty than a man who has felt a motion of impatience; and the latter may be hurried out of his wits, as if he had committed murder. To remove this mistake, I need only observe, that if all are Papists who make a material difference between various sins, or between the same sins variously aggravated, my worthy opponent is as sound a Papist as myself: for when he acts as a magistrate, he does not promiscuously pass the same sentence upon every one. He commits one to prison, and dismisses another with a gentle reprimand. Our Lord himself sets you the example. Pharisees shall receive "the GREATER damnation," and it shall be "more tolerable for Sodom than for Chorazin in the day of judgment." Whence we may justly infer, that the sin of some is more "mountainous" than that of others.

But as you have made choice of David's case, permit me to argue from his experience. He was once, you know, violently angry with Nabal; but as he seasonably restrained his anger, and meekly confessed his sin, God forgave him without "breaking his bones." Not so when the unrestrained evil of his heart, in the matter of Uriah, produced the external fruits of treachery and murder. For *then* the Lord inflicted upon him all the dreadful punishments which we have already considered. "Hear the rod," therefore, and learn what *vast* difference the Lord makes between sins, whether committed after, or before conversion.

X. What follows is a sweet and smooth Antinomian pill, so much the more dangerous as it is gilt with gold taken from the sanctuary, from *the golden altar* itself. Hence it is that multitudes swallow it down as *rich grace*, without the least scruple or suspicion. Lord, dart a beam of thy wisdom into the mind of thy servant, that I may separate the precious from the vile, and expose the dangerous ingredient without depreciating the gold that covers it!

"What is all sin," do you say, "before the infinitely precious atoning blood of Jesus?" Nothing at all, when that blood is humbly apprehended by penitent believers, who depart from all iniquity. But when it is "accounted a common thing, and trodden under foot" by impenitent apostates; or wantonly pleaded in defence of sin, by loose Nicolaitans or lukewarm Laodiceans, it does not answer its gracious design. On the contrary, "How shall we escape," says St. Paul, "if we thus neglect such great salvation?" And "of how much sorer punishment *than others* shall they be thought worthy, who do such despite to the Spirit of grace?" See Hebrews ii, 5; x, 29. You go on: —

"If Christ has fulfilled the whole law and borne the curse, then all debts and claims against his people, be they more or be they less, be they small or be they great, be they before or be they after conversion, are for ever and for ever cancelled. All trespasses are forgiven them. They are justified from all things. They already have everlasting life." What! before they repent and believe? A bold assertion this! which sets Jesus against Christ, — our Priest against our Prophet. For Christ himself teaches us, that many for whom his "fatlings are killed, and all things are now ready," through an obstinate refusal of his *sincere* (I hope nobody will say *hypocritical*) invitation," shall never taste of his supper." And as if this were not enough to arm us against your doctrine, he commissioned an apostle to assure his Church, that some who have *tasted* of his Gospel supper, that is, who "have been enlightened, have tasted the heavenly gift, the good word of God, and the powers of the world to come, do crucify to themselves the Son of God afresh," and, by that means, so totally fall away, that "it is impossible to renew them again to repentance." A clear proof this that those who "once *truly* repented" and were even "made partakers of the Holy Ghost," may "quench the Spirit, and sin against the Holy Ghost;" may not only fall, but fall finally, Hebrews vi, 4.

2. Your doctrine sets also our High Priest against our heavenly King, who declares, that if he who was once his faithful servant, "begins to beat his fellow servants," much more to murder them, he will, as Judge of all, command him to be "bound hand and foot, and delivered to the tormentors." See Second Check, p. 75*.

3. Your doctrine drags after it all the absurdities of eternal, absolute justification. It sets aside the use of repentance and faith, in order to pardon and acceptance. It represents the sins of the elect as forgiven, not only before they are confessed, but even before they are committed; a notion which that strong Calvinist, Dr. Owen himself, could not but oppose. It supposes, that all the penitents who have believed that they were once "children of wrath," and that God was displeased at them when they lived in sin, have believed a lie. It makes the preaching of the Gospel one of the most absurd, wicked, and barbarous things in the world. For what can be more absurd than to say, "Repent ye, and believe the Gospel. He that believeth not shall be damned," if a certain number can never repent or believe, and a certain number can never be damned? And what can be more wicked than to distress elect sinners, by bidding them "flee from the wrath to come," if there is absolutely no *wrath*, neither past, present, nor *to come*, for them; if all their sins, "be they more or less, be they small or great, are for ever and for ever cancelled?" As for the reprobates, how *barbarous* is it to bid them flee, if adamantine chains, eternal decrees of past wrath perpetually bind them down, that they may never escape the repeated, eternal strokes of' the wrath to come!"

4. But what shocks me most in your scheme, is the reproach which it unavoidably fixes upon Christ. It says, The elect "are justified from all things," even before they believe. In all their sins "God views them 'without spot, wrinkle,

---

* [71]

or any such thing.' They stand always complete in the everlasting righteousness of the Redeemer." *"Black in themselves,* they are comely through his comeliness:" so that when they commit adultery and murder, He, "who is of purer eyes than to behold iniquity," can, nevertheless, address them with "Thou art ALL FAIR, my love, my undefiled, there is no spot in thee."

What a prostitution of the word of God is here! We blame a wild youth for dropping some bold innuendoes about Jupiter, in a play composed by a poor heathen. But I acquit thee of indecency, O Terence, if a vindicator of Christian piety has a right to represent our holy and righteous God as saying to a bloody adulterer, *in flagranti delicto,* "Thou art all FAIR, my love, my undefiled, there is no spot in thee." And are these the fat pastures and limpid waters where Gospel preachers "feed the sheep?" Where then! O where are the "barren pastures and muddled waters" in which barefaced Antinomians feed the goats? Is not this "taking the children's bread to cast it to the dogs?" I had almost asked, Is it not "the abomination of desolation standing in the holy place?" See ye not the Lord, O ye mistaken Christians, looking down from the habitation of his holiness? And do ye not hear him thunder this expostulation from heaven? *How long will ye blaspheme mine honour, and have such pleasure in deceit! Know ye not that I have chosen to myself the man that is godly; and that him who delighteth in iniquity doth my soul abhor?*

5. And plead not that you have quoted Scripture in defence of your point. If the Church says, in a mystical song, *"I am black* in the eyes of the world, *because* the *sun* of affliction and persecution *hath looked upon me,* while I *kept the vineyards;* but *I am comely* in the sight of God, whose Spirit enables me with unwearied patience *to bear the burden and heat of the day;"* you have absolutely no right, either from divinity or criticism, to make those words mean as they do upon your scheme, *"I am black* by the atrocious crimes which I actually commit, black by the horrors of adultery and murder: but no matter; *I am comely* by the purity and chastity of my Saviour. My sins, be they small or be they great, are for ever and for ever cancelled; I am justified from all things." Again: if God says to a soul actually "washed, walking with him as Enoch, and walking in white as the few names in Sardis, who had not defiled their garments," *Thou art all fair, my undefiled; is* it right to take those gracious words, and apply them to every lukewarm Laodicean we meet with; and to every apostate, who not only "defiles his garment, but wallows in the mire like the sow that was washed?"

6. Another great, and, if I am not mistaken, insurmountable difficulty attends your scheme. You tell us that "a believer's person stands absolved and always complete in the everlasting righteousness of the Redeemer." But I ask, Was he absolved *before* he was a believer? If you answer, "No, he was absolved the moment he began to believe," it follows, that he *does something,* that is, he *believes* toward his absolution. And thus your main pillars, "that faith is not previous to justification, that there is no wrath in God for the elect, and that all claims against his people before or after conversion are for ever cancelled," are not only broken, but ground to powder. Add to this, that if the believer be justified in consequence of his faith, it is evident that his justification, while he is on earth, can stand no longer than his faith, and that if he "make shipwreck of faith and a good conscience, as Hymeneus, he must again come into condemnation." But supposing, that to avoid these inconsistencies, you boldly

say, "He was justified from the time 'the Lamb was slain, that is, from the beginning of the world;'" you point blank contradict Christ, who says, that "he who believeth not is condemned already." Thus, either the veracity of our Lord, or the truth of your doctrine, must go to the bottom. A sad dilemma this, for those who confound *Crispianity* with CHRISTIANITY.

XI. You reply, "As soon shall Satan pluck Christ's crown from his head as his purchase from his hand." Here is a great truth, making way for a palpable error, and a dreadful insinuation.

Let us, FIRST, see the great truth. It is most certain, that nobody shall ever be able to pluck Christ's sheep, that is, penitent believers, who "hear his voice and follow him," John x, 27, out of his protecting, almighty hand. But if the minds of those penitent believers are "corrupted from the simplicity that is in Christ: if they wax wanton against him, turn after Satan, end in the flesh, and draw back to perdition;" if, "growing fat with kicking," like Jeshurun, they "neigh," like high-fed horses, "after their neighbours' wives," we demand proof that they belong to the fold of Christ, and are not rather *goats* and wolves in sheep's clothing, who cannot, without conversion, enter into the kingdom of heaven.

SECONDLY: The palpable error is, that none of those for whom Christ died can be cast away and destroyed; that no "virgin's lamp can go out;" no promising harvest be "choked with thorns;" no "branch in Christ cut off" for unfruitfulness; no pardon forfeited, and no "name blotted out of God's book:" that no "salt can lose its savour, nobody receive the grace of God in vain, bury his talent, neglect such great salvation, trifle away a day of visitation, look back after setting his hand to the plough, and grieve the Spirit" till he is "quenched, and strives no more." This error, so conducive to the Laodicean case, is expressly opposed by St. Peter, who informs us, that some "deny the Lord that bought them, and bring upon themselves swift destruction." Christ himself, far from desiring to keep his lukewarm purchase "in his hand," declares he will "spew it out of his mouth," Revelation iii, 16.

Pass we on, THIRDLY, to the "dreadful insinuation." While you perpetually try to comfort *a few elect* some of whom, for aught I know, comfort themselves already with their neighbours' wives, yea, and the wives of their fathers; please to tell us how we shall comfort *millions of reprobates,* who, for what you know, try "to save themselves from this adulterous generation?" Do ye not hear how Satan, upon a supposition of the truth of your doctrine, triumphs over those unhappy victims of what some call God's sovereignty? While that old murderer shakes his bloody hand over the myriads devoted to endless torments, methinks I hear him say to his fellow executioners of Divine vengeance, "As soon shall Christ's crown be plucked from his head as this his free gift from my hand. Let yonder little flock of the elect commit adultery and incest without any possibility of missing heaven. I object no more. See what crowds of reprobates may pray, and reform, and strive, without any possibility of escaping hell. Let those gay elect shout, *Everlasting love! Eternal justification!* and *Finished salvation!* I consent! See, ye fiends, see the immense prey that awaits us, and roar with me, beforehand, *Everlasting wrath! Eternal reprobation!* and *Finished damnation!*"

XII. "Our twelfth article maintains, that good works necessarily spring out of a lively faith, insomuch that by them a lively faith may be as evidently known as a tree discerned by its fruits." "This," you say, "I most firmly believe:" and nevertheless, to prove just the contrary — to show that when David committed adultery and murder, he had "a lively faith, and was in a state of justification and sanctification," you quote a verse of a hymn, composed by the Rev. C. Wesley, which only confirms what I say of *undervaluing, Vindication,* p. 61*. But you mistake him, if you suppose that, when "not one bud of grace appears to ourselves, many may not appear to others;" and if you apply to outward enormities greedily committed, what the poet means of inward motions of sin cordially lamented and steadily opposed. Nevertheless, as some expressions in this hymn are not properly guarded, the pious author will forgive me, if I transcribe part of a letter which I lately received from him: —

"I was once on the brink of Antinomianism by unwarily reading Crisp and Saltmarsh. Just then, warm in my first love, I was in the utmost danger, when Providence threw in my way BAXTER'S treatise, entitled, *A hundred Errors of Dr. Crisp demonstrated.* My brother was sooner apprehensive of the dangerous abuse which would be made of our unguarded hymns and expressions than I was. Now I also see and feel we must all sink, unless we call St. James to our assistance. Yet let us still insist as much, or more than ever, on St. Paul's justification. What God has joined together let no man put asunder. The great Chillingworth saw clearly the danger of separating St. James from St. Paul. He used to wish, that whenever a chapter of St. Paul's justification was read, another of St. James might be read at the same time."

XIII. When my honoured correspondent has endeavoured to prove, by the above-mentioned scriptures, arguments, and quotations, that an impenitent adulterer and murderer, instead of being under God's displeasure, is "a pleasant child still," to complete his work, he proceeds to show the good that falls into sin do to believers. Never did the pious author of *Pietas Oxoniensis* employ his pen in a work less conducive to piety!

"God," says he, "often brings about his purposes by those very means, which to the human eye would certainly defeat them. He has always the same thing in view, his own glory and the salvation of his elect by Jesus Christ. This Adam was accomplishing when he put the whole world under the curse." Hail, Adam, under the fatal tree! Pluck and eat abundantly, for "thou accomplishest the salvation of the elect!" O the inconsistency of your doctrine! If we insist upon "doing the will of God," in order to "enter his kingdom," we are boldly exclaimed against as proudly sharing the glory of our redemption with Christ. But here Adam is represented as his partner in the work of salvation, and a share of his glory positively assigned to the fall, that is, to his disobedience to the Divine will. St. Paul asserts, that "by one man [Adam] came death, and sin the sting of death; and so death [with his sting] passed upon all men." But you inform us, that Adam by his sin "accomplished the salvation of the elect." If this is not plucking

---

* [55]

---

a jewel from Christ's crown, to adorn the most improper head in the world, next to that of Satan, I am very much mistaken.

But if God "brought about his purpose" concerning "the salvation of the elect" by the fall of Adam; tell us, I pray, who brought about the purpose concerning *the damnation of the reprobates?* Had the Lord "always this thing in view" also? On the brink of what a dreadful abyss hath your doctrine brought me? Sir, my mind recoils; I fly from the God whose unprovoked wrath rose before the beginning of the world against millions of his unformed, and therefore guiltless creatures! He that "tasted death for every man" bids me fly! and he points me from Dr. Crisp to God, "whose mercy is over all his works," till they personally forfeit it by obstinately trampling upon his richest grace.

XIV. As if it was not enough to have represented our salvation in part "accomplished" by the transgression of our first parents, you bring in "Herod and Pontius Pilate," and observe, to the honour of the good which sin does to the elect, that those unrighteous judges did whatsoever God's hand and counsel determined before to be done! If you quote this passage to insinuate that God predetermined their sin, you reflect upon the Divine holiness, and apologize for the murderers of our Lord as you have for the murderer of Uriah.

I grant that when God saw, in the light of his infinite foreknowledge, that Pilate and Caiaphas would absolutely choose injustice and cruelty, he "determined" that they should have the awful opportunity of exercising them against his Anointed. As a skilful pilot, without predetermining, and raising a contrary wind, foresees it will rise, and predetermines so to manage the rudder and sails of his ship, as to make it answer a good purpose; so God overruled the foreseen wickedness of those men, and made it subservient to his merciful justice in offering up the true Paschal Lamb. But, as it would be very absurd to ascribe to the "contrary wind" the praise due to the "pilot's skill;" so it is very unevangelical to ascribe to the sin of Pilate, or of Joseph's brethren, the good which God drew from some of its extraordinary circumstances.

XV. "The Lord has promised to make 'all things work for good to those that love him;' and if all things, then their very sins and corruptions are included in the royal promise." A siren song this! which you unhappily try to support by Scripture. But, (1.) if "this is the love of God, that we keep his commandments," how will you prove that David *loved* God when he left his own wife for that of Uriah? Does not our Lord declare, that those who will not "forsake husband, wife, children, and all things for his sake, are not worthy of him," either as believers or lovers? And are those "worthy of him" who break his commandment, and take their neighbours' wives? Again: if St. John, speaking of one who does not relieve an indigent brother, asks with indignation, "How dwelleth the love of God in him?" May not I, with greater reason, say, "How dwelt the love of God in David?" who, far from assisting Uriah, murdered his soul by drunkenness, and his body with the sword! And if David did not love God, how can you believe that a promise made to "those who love God," respected him in his state of impenitency? (2.) When we extol free grace, and declare, that "God's mercy is over all his works," you directly answer, that the word ALL must be taken in a limited sense: but when you extol the profitableness of sin, *all*, ("in all things working for good,") must be taken universally, and include "sin and corruption," contrary to the context. (3.) I say, contrary to the context; for, just before the apostle declares, "If ye live after the flesh, ye shall die," ye shall evidence the truth of Ezekiel's doctrine, "When the righteous turneth away from his righteousness, in his sin that he hath sinned shall he die;" and at the end of the chapter, "the things that work for good" are enumerated, and they include "all tribulations and creatures," but not our own sin, unless you can prove it to be God's creature, and not the devil's production. (4.) It is nowhere promised, that sin shall do us good. On the contrary, God constantly represents it as the greatest evil in the world, the root of all other temporal and eternal evils: and as he makes it the object of his invariable disapprobation, so, till they repent, he levels his severest threatenings at sinners without respect of persons. But the author of *Pietas Oxoniensis* has made a new discovery. Through the glass of Dr. Crisp, he sees that one of the choicest promises in Scripture respects the commission of sin, of thefts and incest, adultery and murder! So grossly are threatenings and promises, punishments and rewards, confounded together by this fashionable divinity!

(5.) I grant that, in some cases, the *punishment* inflicted upon a sinner has been overruled for good: but what is this to the *sin itself*? Is it reasonable to ascribe to *sin* the good that may spring from the *rod* with which sin is punished? Some robbers have, perhaps, been brought to repentance by the gallows, and others deterred from committing robbery by the terror of their punishment; but by what rule in logic, or divinity, can we infer from thence, either that any robbers love God, or that all robberies shall work together for their good?

But "Onesimus robbed Philemon his master; and flying from justice, was brought under Paul's preaching and converted." Surely, sir, you do not insinuate that Onesimus' conversion depended upon robbing his master! Or that it would not have been better for him to have served his master faithfully, and stayed in Asia to hear the Gospel with Philemon, than to have rambled to Rome for it in consequence of his crime! The heathens said, "Let us eat and drink, for to-morrow we die." It will be well if some do not say, upon a fairer prospect than theirs, "Let us steal and rob, for tomorrow we shall be converted."

XVI. You add, that "The royal and holy seed was continued by the incest of Judah with Tamar, and the adultery of David with Bathsheba." And do you really think, sir, God made choice of that line to show how incest and adultery "work together for good?" For my part, I rather think that it was because, if he had chosen any other line, he would have met with *more* such blots. You know that God slew David's child conceived in adultery; and if he chose Solomon to succeed David, it was not because the adulterous Bathsheba was his mother, but because he was then the best of David's children: for I may say of God's choosing the son, what Samuel said of his choosing the father, "the Lord looketh on the heart," 1 Samuel xvi, 7.

XVII. You proceed in your enumeration of the good that sin does to the pleasant children. "How has many a poor soul, who has been faithless through fear of man, even blessed God for Peter's denial!" Surely, sir, you mistake: none but the fiend, who desired to have Peter "that he might sift him," could bless God for the apostle's crime; nor could any one, on such a horrible account, bless any other God but "the god of this world." David said, "My eyes run down with water, because men keep not thy law;" but the author of *Pietas Oxoniensis* tells us, that "many a poor soul has blessed God" for the most horrid breaches of his law! Weep no more, perfidious apostle! thou hast "cast the net on the right side of the ship;" thy three *curses* have procured God multitudes of *blessings!* Surely, sir, you cannot mean this! "Many a poor soul has blessed God" for *granting a pardon to Peter,* but never *for Peter's denial.* It is extremely dangerous thus to confound *a crime* with *the pardon* granted to a penitent criminal.

XVIII. Upon the same principle you add, "How have many others been raised out of the mire, by considering the tenderness shown to the incestuous Corinthian!" I am glad you do not say, "by considering *the incest* of the Corinthian." The good received by many did not then spring from this horrid crime, but from the tenderness of the apostle. This instance, therefore, by your own confession, does not prove that sin does any good to believers.

But as you tell us with what "tenderness the apostle restored that man, when he was swallowed up in godly sorrow, you will permit me to remind you of the severity which he showed him while he continued impenitent. "In the name of our Lord Jesus Christ," said he, "when ye are gathered together, deliver such a one unto Satan for the destruction of the flesh, that his spirit may be saved in the day of the Lord." Hence it appears, the apostle thought his case so desperate, that his body must be solemnly delivered to Satan, in order, if possible, to bring his soul to repentance. Now, if the incestuous man's sins "had been for ever and for ever cancelled;" if he had not forfeited the Divine favour, and cut himself off from "the general assembly of the first born" by his crime; what power could the apostle, who acted under the influence of the Spirit, have had to cut him off from the visible Church as a corrupt member? What right to deliver the body of one of God's pleasant children" to destruction? Was this "finished salvation?" For my part, as I do not believe in a *two-fold,* I had almost said *Jesuitical,* will in God, I am persuaded he would have us consider things as they are; an impenitent adulterer as a profligate heathen; and a penitent believer as his "pleasant child."

XIX. You add, (1.) A "grievous fall serves to make believers know their place." No, indeed, it serves only to make them *forget* their place; witness David, who, far from *knowing* his place, wickedly took that of Uriah; and Eve, who, by falling into the condemnation of the devil, took her Maker's place, in her imagination, and esteemed herself as wise as God. (2.) "It drives them nearer to Christ." Surely, you mistake, sir; you mean nearer the devil: for a fall into pride may drive me nearer Lucifer, a fall into adultery and murder may drive me nearer Belial and Moloch; but not nearer Jesus Christ. (3.) "It makes them more dependent on his strength." No such thing. The genuine effect of a fall into sin, is to stupify the conscience and harden the heart: witness the state of obduracy in which God found Adam, and the state of carnal security in which Nathan found David, after their crimes. (4.) "It keeps them more watchful for the future." Just the reverse: it prevents their watching for the future. If David had been made more watchful by falling into adultery, would he have fallen into treachery and murder? If Peter had been made more watchful by his *first* falling into perjury, would he have fallen *three times* successively? (5.) "It will cause them to sympathize with others in the like situation." By no means. A fall into sin will naturally make us desirous of drawing another into our guilty condition. Witness the devil and

Eve, Eve and Adam, David and Bathsheba. The royal adulterer was so far from sympathizing with the man who had unkindly taken his neighbour's favourite ewe lamb, that he directly swore, "As the Lord liveth, the man that has done this thing shall surely die."

6. "It will make them sing louder to the praise of restoring grace throughout all the ages of eternity." I demand proof of this. I greatly question whether Demas, Alexander the coppersmith, Hymeneus, Philetus, and many of the fallen believers mentioned in the Epistles of our Lord to the Churches of Asia, in the Epistle to the Hebrews, and in those of St. Peter, St. James, and St. Jude, shall sing restoring grace at all. The apostle, far from representing them all as singing louder, gives us to understand, that many of them shall be "thought worthy of a much sorer punishment" than the sinners consumed by fire from heaven; and that "there remaineth therefore no more sacrifice for their sins;" (a sure proof that Christ's sacrifice availed for them, till they "accounted the blood of the covenant an unholy thing;") for, adds the apostle, "The Lord will judge his people;" and, notwithstanding all that Dr. Crisp says to the contrary, "there remaineth [for apostates] a certain fearful looking for of judgment, and fiery indignation, which shall devour the adversaries. Weeping, wailing, and gnashing of teeth," and not "louder songs," await "the unprofitable servant."

But supposing some are "renewed to repentance, and escape out of the snare of the devil;" can you imagine they will be upon the footing of those who, standing "steadfast and immovable, always abounded in the work of the Lord?" Shall then "the labour of these be in vain in the Lord?" Are not our works to follow us? Shall the unprofitable servant, if restored, receive a crown of glory equal to his, who, from the time he listed, has always "fought the good fight, and kept the faith?" The doctrine you would inculcate, at once bears hard upon the equity of the Divine conduct, and strikes a fatal blow at the root of all diligence and faithfulness, so strongly recommended in the oracles of God.

You will be sensible of your error, if you observe, that all the fine things which you tell us of a fall into sin, belong not to *the fall*, but to *a happy recovery from it*: and my honoured correspondent is as much mistaken, when he ascribes to *sin* the effects of *repentance and faith*, as if he ascribed to a frost the effects of a thaw, or to sickness the consequence of a recovery.

And now that we have seen how you have done a *pious* man's strange work, permit me, sir, to tell you, that, through the prevalence of human corruption, a word spoken *for* sin generally goes farther than ten thousand spoken *against* it. This I know; that if a fall, in an hour of temptation, appears only half so profitable as you represent it, thousands will venture after David into the whirlpool of wickedness. But alas! *facilis descensus Averni, &c:* it is easier to follow him when he plunges in, than when he struggles out, with his eyes wasted, his flesh dried up, and his bones broken.

XX. I gladly do you the justice, honoured sir, to observe, that you exclaim against sin in the next page; but does not the antidote come too late? You say, "Whatever may be God's secret will, we are to keep close to the declaration of his own written word, which binds us to resist sin." But, alas, you make a bad matter worse, by representing God as having two wills, a secret, effectual will that we should sin, and a revealed will, or written word, commanding us to resist sin! If these insinuations are just, I ask, Why should we not regard God's *secret*, as much as his *revealed* will? Nay, why should we not regard it more, since it is the more efficacious, and consequently the stronger will?

You add, "He would be mad who should wilfully fall down, and break a leg or an arm, because he knew there was a skilful surgeon at hand to set it." But I beg leave to dissent from my honoured opponent. For, supposing I had a crooked leg, appointed to be broken for good, by God's secret will intimated to me; and supposing a dear friend strongly argued, not only that the surgeon is at hand, but that he would render my leg straighter, handsomer, and stronger than before; must I not be a fool, or a coward, if I hesitate throwing myself down?

O sir, if "the deceitfulness of sin" is so great that thousands greedily commit it, when the gallows on earth, and horrible torments in hell, are proposed for their just wages; how will they be able to escape in the hour of temptation, if they are encouraged to transgress the Divine law, by assurances that they shall reap eternal advantages from their sin? O! how highly necessary was it that Mr. Wesley should warn his assistants against talking of a state of justification and sanctification in so unguarded a manner as you and the other admirers of Dr. Crisp so frequently do!

You conclude this letter by some quotations from Mr. Wesley, whom you vainly try to press into the doctor's service, by representing him as saying of established Christians what he speaks of babes in Christ, and of the commission of adultery and murder, what he only means of evil desire resisted, and evil tempers restrained: but more of this in a "Treatise on Christian Perfection."

REMARKS ON THE FIFTH LETTER.

This letter begins by a civil reproof for "speaking rather in a sneering manner of that heart-cheering expression so often used by awakened divines, *the finished salvation of Christ;*" an expression which, by the by, you will not find once in all my letters. But why some divines, whom you look upon as unawakened, do not admire the unscriptural expression of finished salvation, you may see in the Second Check, p. 119*.

I am thankful for your second reproof, and hope it will make me more careful not to "speak as a man of the world." But the third I really cannot thank you for. "You are not very sparing of hard names against Dr. Crisp," says my honoured correspondent; and again' "The hard names and heavy censures thrown out against the doctor, are by far more unjustifiable than what has been delivered against Mr. Wesley." The hardest names I give to your favourite divine are, *the doctor, the good doctor,* and *the honest doctor,* whom, notwithstanding all his mistakes, I represent, (Second Check, p. 88†) as a good man shouting aloud, *Salvation to the Lamb of God!* Now, sir, I should be glad to know by what rule, either of criticism or charity, you can prove that these are hard names, more

---

* [117]

† [85]

unjustifiable than the names of "Papist unmasked, heretic, apostate, worse than Papists," &c, which have been of late so liberally bestowed upon Mr. Wesley?

I confess, that those branches of Dr. Crisp's doctrine which stand in direct opposition to the practical Gospel of Christ, I have taken the liberty to call *Crispianity;* for had I called them CHRISTIANITY, my conscience and one half of the Bible would have flown in my face; and had I called them *Calvinism,* Williams, Flavel, Alleine, Bishop Hopkins, and numbers of sound Calvinists, would have proved me mistaken; for they agree to represent the peculiarities of the doctor as *loose Antinomian tenets;* and if any man can prove them either legal or *evangelical,* I shall gladly recant those epithets, which I have sometimes given, not to the good doctor, but to his unscriptural notions.

In the meantime, permit me to observe, that if any one judges of my letters by the 36th page of your book, he will readily say of them what you say of the Rev. Mr. Sellon's Works: "I have never read them, and from the accounts I hear of the abusive, unchristian spirit with which they are written, I believe I shall never give myself that trouble." Now, sir, I have read Mr. Sellon's books, and have therefore more right than you, who never read them, to give them a public character. You tell us," you have heard of the imbecility of the performance," &c,[*] and I assure my readers, I have found it a masterly mixture of the skill belonging to the sensible scholar, the good logician, and the sound anti-Crispian divine.

He is blunt, I confess, and sometimes to an excess. "Really," says he in a private letter, "I cannot set my razor; there is a roughness about me I cannot get rid of. If honest truth will not excuse me, I must bear the blame of those whom nothing will please but smooth things." But sharp (you will say *abusive*) as he is, permit me to tell you, that my much admired countryman, Calvin, was much more so.

For my part, though I would no more plead for abuse than for adultery and murder, yet, like a true Suisse, I love *blunt honesty;* and to give you a proof of it, I shall take the liberty to observe, It is much easier to say, a book is full of *hard names, and heavy censures, written in an abusive, unchristian spirit;* and to insinuate it is "dangerous, or not worth reading;" than it is fairly to answer one single page of it. And how far a late publication proves the truth of this observation, I leave our candid readers to decide.

Page 38, you "assure me upon honour that Mr. Wesley's pieces against election and perseverance [Why did you forget *reprobation?*] have greatly tended to establish your belief in those most comfortable doctrines." Hence you conclude, that "Mr. Wesley's pen has done much service to the Calvinistic cause;" and add, that "some very experienced Christians hope he will write again upon that subject, or publish a new edition of his former Tracts."

You are too much acquainted with the world, dear sir, not to know that most Deists declare, they were established in their sentiments by reading the Old and New Testament. But would you argue conclusively, if you inferred from

---

[*] Some of the Rev. Mr. Sellon's Works are, *Arguments against the Doctrine of General Redemption considered; a Defence of God's Sovereignty;* and *the Church of England vindicated from the Charge of Calvinism.* All these are well worth the reading of every pious and sensible man.

thence, that the sacred writers have done infidelity much service? And if some confident infidels expressed their hopes that our bishops would reprint the Bible to propagate Deism, would you not see through their empty boast, and pity their deistical flourish? Permit me, honoured sir, to expose by a simile the similar wish of the persons you mention, who, if they were "very experienced Christians," will hardly pass for very modest logicians.

The gentleman of fortune you mention never read *all* Mr. Wesley's Tracts, nor one of Mr. Sellon's on the Crispian orthodoxy. And I am no more surprised to see you both dissent from those divines, than I should be to find you both mistaken upon the bench, if you passed a decisive sentence before you had so much as heard one witness out. The clergyman you refer to has probably been as precipitate as the two pious magistrates; therefore, you will permit me to doubt whether he, any more than my honoured opponent, "has had courage enough to see for himself."

CONCLUSION.

Having so long animadverted upon your letters, It is time to consider the present state of our controversy. Mr. Wesley privately advances, among his own friends, some propositions, designed to keep them from running into the fashionable errors of Dr. Crisp. These proposition are secretly procured, and publicly exposed through the three kingdoms, as dreadfully heretical, and subversive of the Protestant doctrine of justification by faith. In Mr. Wesley's absence, a friend writes in defence of his propositions. The Rev. Mr. Shirley, instead of trying to defend his mistakes by argument, publicly recants his Circular Letter and his volume of sermons by the lump. Some of the honest souls, who have been carried away by the stream of fashionable error, begin to look about them, and ask, whether narratives and recantations are to pass for scriptures and arguments? The author of *Pietas Oxoniensis,* to quiet them, enters the lists, and makes a stand against the anti-Crispian propositions: but what a stand!

1. *"Man's faithfulness,"* says he, "I have no objection to, in a *sober, Gospel sense* of the word." So Mr. Wesley's first proposition, by my opponent's confession, bears a sober Gospel sense.

2. He attacks the doctrine of *working for life,* by proposing some of the very objections answered in the Vindication, without taking the least notice of the answers; by producing scriptures quite foreign to the question, and keeping out of sight those which have been advanced; by passing over in silence a variety of rational arguments; jumbling all the degrees of spiritual life and death, acceptance and justification, mentioned in the sacred oracles; confounding all the dispensations of Divine grace toward man: and levelling at Mr. Wesley a witticism which wounds Jesus Christ himself.

3. He acknowledges the truth of the doctrine that we must *do some. Thing in order to attain justification;* and after this candid concession, fairly gives up the fundamental Protestant doctrine of *justification by faith:* the very doctrine which Luther called *Articulus stantis vel cadentis Ecclesiæ,* and which our Church so strongly maintains in her articles and homilies. The Rev. Mr. Shirley throws his sermon on justification by faith overboard. His second comes up to mend the matter, and

does it so unfortunately, as to throw the handle after the axe. He renounces the doctrine itself. "I maintain," says he, "that believing cannot be previous to justification, that is, to complete justification." As dangerous a proposition as was ever advanced by Crisp, and refuted by all the sober Calvinists of the last century!

4. He opposes St. Peter's, Mr. Henry's, and Mr. Wesley's doctrine, that "Cornelius was accepted of God in consequence of his *fearing God and working righteousness,*" and insinuates that Cornelius was completely accepted before he feared God and worked righteousness. Upon this scheme, the words of St. Peter, "He that feareth God and worketh righteousness is accepted of him," may mean, *He that dareth God and worketh unrighteousness is completely accepted of him!*

5. He represents Mr. Wesley as a Papist, for having privately observed among his friends that we have been too much afraid of the word *merit,* while he allows real Protestants, the countess of Huntingdon, and the Rev. Mr. Shirley, to publish and sing, *We* MERIT *heaven by the righteousness which Christ has supplied.* Nay, he sings the same bold words at the Lock chapel. The Rev. Mr. Madan's *"we merit"* passes for Gospel; his hymns are every where recommended as evangelical' but "Popery is about midway between Protestantism and Mr. Wesley!" What strange prejudice! And yet, surprising! my honoured correspondent accuses *me* of betraying "no small degree of chicanery" upon the article of merit!

6. He attempts to "'split the hair," which the Rev. Mr. Shirley is wise enough not to attempt. But how? Without ceremony he cuts off the middle term between being "rewarded according to our works," and "as our works deserve;" he throws out of the question this proposition, that *we are rewarded* BECAUSE *of our works,* though it is supported by the plainest scriptures.

7. Notwithstanding this unwarrantable liberty, when he confidently soars upon the wings of orthodoxy, to find his broad passage between "east and west," he directly falls into Mr. Wesley's sentiment about the *rewardableness* of works; and, before he is aware, shakes hands with thegood Papist Scotus, and the good Protestant Baxter.

8. The last proposition which he attacks, is, that "we are continually pleasing or displeasing to God, according to the whole of our inward and outward behaviour." And what does he advance against it? Assertions and distinctions contradicted by the general tenor of the Bible; scriptures detached from the context, and set at variance with the clearest declarations of God, and loudest dictates of conscience: and, what is worse than all, dangerous enumerations of the good that falling into adultery, murder, perjury, and incest does to them that love God!

And now, honoured sir, let the Christian world judge, whether you have been able to fix the mark of error upon one of the propositions so loudly decried as heretical; and whether the letters you have honoured me with, do not expose the cause which you have attempted to defend, and demonstrate the absolute necessity of erecting and defending such a seasonable rampart as the Minutes, to check the rapid progress of Dr. Crisp's Gospel.

Permit me, honoured and dear sir, to conclude by assuring you, that Although I have thought myself obliged publicly to show the mistakes in the five letters which you have publicly directed to me, I gladly do you the justice to acknowledge that your principles have not that effect upon your conduct which they naturally have upon the conversation of hundreds who are consistent Antinomians. See *Second Check,* page 114*.

If I have addressed my *Three Checks* to the Rev. Mr. Shirley and yourself, God is my witness, that it was not to reflect upon two of the most eminent characters in the circle of my religious acquaintance. Forcible circumstances have overruled my inclinations. *Decipimur specie recti.* Thinking to attack error, you have attacked the very truth which Providence calls me to defend; and the attack appears to me so much the more dangerous, as your laborious zeal and eminent piety are more worthy of public regard, than the boisterous rant and loose insinuations of twenty *practical* Antinomians. The tempter is not so great a novice in antichristian politics as to engage only such to plead for *doctrinal* Antinomianism. This would soon spoil the trade. It is his masterpiece of wisdom to get *good men* to do him that eminent service. He knows that their good lives will make way for their bad principles. Nor does he ever deceive with more decency and success, than under the respectable cloak of their genuine piety.

If a wicked man plead for sin, *foenum habet in cornu,* "he carries the mark upon his forehead:" we stand upon our guard. But when a good man gives us to understand that "there are no lengths God's people may not run, nor any depths they may not fall into, without losing the character of *men after God's own heart;* that many will praise God for our denial of Christ; that sin and corruption work for good; that a fall into adultery will drive us nearer to Christ, and make us sing louder to the praise of free grace:" when he quotes Scripture too in order to support these assertions, calling them *the pure Gospel,* and representing the opposite doctrine as *the Pelagian heresy,* worse than Popery itself; he casts the Antinomian net "on the right, side of the ship," and is likely to enclose a great multitude of unwary men; especially if some of the best hands in the kingdom drive the frighted shoal into the net, and help to drag it on shore.

This is, honoured sir, what I apprehend you have done, not designedly, but thinking to do God service. And this is what every good man, who does not look at the Gospel through Dr. Crisp's glass, must resolutely oppose. Hence the steadiness with which I have looked in the face of a man of God, whose feet I should be glad to wash at any time, under a lively sense of my great inferiority.

And now, as if I were admitted to show you that humble mark of brotherly love, I beg you would not consider the unceremonious plainness of a Suisse (mountaineer) as the sarcastic insolence of an incorrigible Arminian.

I beseech you to make some difference between the wisdom and poison of the serpent. If charity forbids to meddle with the latter, does not Christ recommend the former? Is every mild, well-meant irony a bitter and cruel sarcasm? Should we directly insinuate that it is the sign of "a bad spirit," the mark of murder in the heart; and that he who uses it to sharpen the truth,† "scatters firebrands, arrows, and death?" To say nothing of Elijah and the priests of Baal,

---

* [111]

† This assertion is the grand argument of an evangelical writer, in the Gospel Magazine, and of a charitable gentleman (a Baptist minister, I think) in a printed letter dated Bath. If this method of arguing is Calvinistically evangelical, my readers will easily perceive it is very far from being either legal or Scripturally logical.

did our Lord want either deep seriousness or ardent love, when, coming more than conqueror from his third conflict in Gethsemane, he roused his nodding disciples by this compassionate irony, "Sleep on now and take your rest!" Did not the usefulness of a loud call, a deserved reproof, a seasonable expostulation, and a solemn warning, meet in that well-timed figure of speech? And was it not more effectual than the two awful charges which he had given them before?

I entreat you to consider that when the meanest of God's ministers has truth and conscience on his side, without being either abusive or uncharitable, he may say, even to one whom the Lord has exalted to the royal dignity, "Thou art the man!" God has exalted you, not only among the gentlemen of fortune in this kingdom, but, what is an infinitely greater blessing, among the converted men who are "translated into the kingdom of his dear Son!" Yet, by a mistake, fashionable among the religious people, you have unhappily paid more regard to Dr. Crisp than to St. James. And as you have pleaded the dangerous cause of the impenitent monarch, I have addressed you with the honest boldness of the expostulating prophet. I have said to my honoured opponent, "Thou art the man!" With the commendable design of comforting "mourning backsliders," you have inadvertently "given occasion to the enemies of the Lord to blaspheme," and unscripturally assured believers, "that falls even into enormous sins shall work for their good, and accomplish God's purposes for his glory and their salvation." And as I have supported my expostulations about your *doctrinal* mistakes with plain Scripture, which amounts to a *Thus says the Lord;* I beseech you to take them in as good a part as King David did the prophet's reproofs about his *practical* miscarriages.

I owe much respect to you, but more to truth, to conscience, and to God. If, in trying to discharge my duty toward them, I have inadvertently betrayed any want of respect for you, I humbly ask your pardon; and I can assure you, in the face of the whole world, that, notwithstanding your strong attachment to the peculiarities of Dr. Crisp, as there is no family in the world to which I am under greater obligation than yours, so there are few gentlemen for whom I have so peculiar an esteem, as for the respectable author of *Pietas Oxoniensis.* And till we come where no mistake will raise prejudice, and no prejudice will foment opposition to any part of the truth; till we meet where all that "fear God and work righteousness," however jarring together now, will join in an eternal chorus, and with perfect harmony ascribe a common "salvation to the Lamb that was slain," I declare, in the fear of God and in the name of Jesus, that no opposite views of the same truths, no clashing diversity of contrary sentiments, no plausible insinuations of narrow-hearted bigotry, shall hinder me from remaining, with the greatest sincerity, honoured and dear sir, your most obedient and obliged servant, in the bonds of a peaceful Gospel,

J. FLETCHER.

MADELEY, *February* 3, 1772

POSTSCRIPT.

As I have cleared my conscience with respect to Antinomianism, a subject which at this time appears to me of the last importance, I should be glad to employ my leisure hours in writing on subjects more suitable to my taste and private edification. It is by no means my design to obtrude my sentiments upon my Calvinian, any more than upon my Arminian brethren. I sincerely wish peace to both, upon the terms of mutual forbearance, *Veniam petimusque, damusque vicissim.* Should, therefore, a fourth publication call for a *Fourth Check;* if I can help it, it shall be short. I shall just thank my antagonist for his deserved reproofs, or point out his capital mistakes, and quote the pages in the *Three Checks* where his objections are already answered. But if his performance is merely Calvinistical, I shall take the liberty of referring him to the Rev. Mr. Sellon's "imbecile performance," which, I apprehend, every unprejudiced person, who has courage to see and read for himself, will find strong enough to refute the strongest arguments of Elisha Coles and the Synod of Dort.

Before I lay by my pen, I beg leave to address, a moment, the true believers who espouse Calvin's sentiments. Think not, honoured brethren, that I have no eyes to see the eminent services which many of you render to the Church of Christ; no heart to bless God for the Christian graces which shine in your exemplary conduct; no pen to testify, that by "letting your light shine before men, you adorn the Gospel of God our Saviour," as many of your predecessors have done before you. I am not only persuaded that your opinions are consistent with a genuine conversion, but I take Heaven to witness, how much I prefer a Calvinist who loves God, to a remonstrant who does not. Yes, although I value Christ infinitely above Calvin, and St. James above that good, well-meaning man, Dr. Crisp, I had a thousand times rather be *doctrinally* mistaken with the latter, than *practically* deluded with those who speak well of St. James' "perfect law of liberty," and yet remain lukewarm Laodiceans in heart, and perhaps gross Antinomians in conduct.

This I observe, to do your piety justice, and prevent the men of this world, into whose hands these sheets may fall, from "falsely accusing your good conversation in Christ," and confounding you with practical Antinomians, some of whose dangerous notions you inadvertently countenance. If I have, therefore, taken the liberty of exposing your favourite mistakes, do me the justice to believe, that it was not to pour contempt upon your respectable persons; but to set your peculiarities in such a light, as might either engage you to renounce them, or check the forwardness with which some have lately recommended them as the only *doctrine of grace,* and the *pure Gospel* of Jesus Christ; unkindly representing their remonstrant brethren as enemies to free grace, and abettors of a dreadful heresy.

If you think I have exceeded, in my Checks, the bounds which brotherly love prescribes to a controversial writer, permit me to remind you and myself, that we are parties, and therefore peculiarly liable to think the worst of each other's intentions and performances. By our respective publications we have appealed to the serious world; let us not then take the matter out of their hands. And while we leave to our merciful God the judging of our spirits, let us leave our serious readers to judge of our arguments, and pass sentence upon the manner in which they are proposed.

And you, my remonstrant brethren, who attentively look at our controversial engagement; while a Geneva anti-Calvinist solicits an interest in your prayers for "meekness of wisdom," permit him to offer you some reasonable advices, which he wants to inculcate upon his own mind also.

1. More than ever let us confirm our love toward our Calvinist brethren. If our arguments gall them, let us not envenom the sore by maliciously triumphing over them. Nothing is more likely to provoke their displeasure, and drive them from what we believe to be the truth. If we, that immediately "bear the burden and heat of *this controversial* day," are obliged to cut; help us to act the part of friendly opponents by directly pouring into the wound the healing balsam of brotherly love: and if you see us carried beyond the bounds of moderation, instantly admonish us, and check our Checks. Your whispers will go farther than the clamours of our opponents. The former, we know, must proceed from truth: but we are apt to suspect that the latter spring from partiality or a mere stratagem not uncommon in controversial wars. Witness the clamours of the Jews, and those of the Ephesians, when the one saw that their idol temple, the other, that great Diana was in danger.

2. Do not rejoice in the mistakes of our opponents, but in the detection of error. Desire not that we, but that *truth,* may prevail. Let us not only be willing that our brethren should win the day, if they have truth on their side; but let us make it matter of solemn, earnest, and constant prayer. While we decry confined, shackled grace, obtruded upon us as free grace, let not bigotry confine our affections and shackle our hearts. Nothing would be more absurd than to fall into Calvinian narrowness of spirit, while we oppose Calvin's narrow system. If we admit the temper, we might as well be quite consistent, and at once embrace the doctrine. The best method of recommending God's universal love to mankind, is to love all men universally. If absolute reprobation has no place in our principles, let it have none in our affections. If we believe that all share in the Divine mercy, let all be interested in our brotherly kindness. Should such practical demonstrations of universal love second our Scriptural arguments for it, by God's blessing bigotry would soon return to Rome, and narrow grace fly back to Geneva.

3. Let us strictly observe the rules of decency and kindness, taking care not to treat, upon any provocation, any of our opponents in the same manner that they have treated Mr. Wesley. The men of the world hint sometimes that he is a Papist and a Jesuit: but good mistaken men have gone much farther in the present controversy. They have published to the world that they "do verily believe his principles are too rotten for even a Papist to rest upon; that it may be supposed Popery is about the midway between Protestantism and him; that he wades through the quagmires of Pelagianism, deals in inconsistencies, manifest contradictions, and strange prevarications; that if a contrast was drawn from his various assertions, upon the doctrine of sinless perfection, a little piece might extend into a folio volume; and that they are more than ever convinced of his prevaricating disposition." Not satisfied with going to a Benedictine monk, in Paris, for help against his dreadful heresy, they have wittily extracted an argument

ad hominem, from the comfortable dish of tea which he drinks with Mrs. Wesley: and, to complete the demonstration of their respect for that grey-headed laborious minister of Christ, they have brought him upon the stage of the controversy in a dress of their own contriving, and made him declare to the world, that "whenever he and fifty-three of his fellow labourers say one thing, they mean quite another." And what has he done to deserve this usage at their hands? Which of them has he treated unjustly or unkindly? Even in the course of this controversy, has he injured any man? May he not say to this hour, *Tu pugnas: Ego vapulo tantum?* Let us avoid this warmth, my brethren, remembering that personal reflections will never pass for convincing arguments with the judicious and humane.

I have endeavoured to follow this advice with regard to Dr. Crisp; nevertheless, lest you should rank him with practical Antinomians, I once more gladly profess my belief that he was a good man; and desire that none of you would condemn all his sermons, much less his character, on account of his unguarded Antinomian propositions, refuted by Williams and Baxter, some of which I have taken the liberty to produce in the preceding Checks. As there are a few things exceptionable in good Bishop Hopkins, so there are many things admirable in Dr. Crisp's works. And as the glorious truths advanced by the former should not make you receive his Calvinian mistakes as Gospel, so the illegal tenets of the latter should by no means make you reject his evangelical sayings as Antinomianism. "Prove, therefore, all things, and hold fast that which is good," though it should be advanced by the warmest of our opponents; but whatever unadvised step their zeal, for what they believe to be the truth, makes them take, "put ye on (as the elect of God, holy and beloved) bowels of mercies, kindness, humbleness of mind, long suffering, forgiving one another, if any man have a quarrel against any: even as Christ forgave you, so also do ye."

4. If you would help us to remove the prejudices of our brethren, not only grant with a good grace, but strongly insist upon the great truths for which they make so noble a stand. Steadily assert with them, that the scraps of morality and formality, by which Pharisees and Deists pretend to merit the Divine favour, are only "filthy rags" in the sight of a holy God; and that no righteousness is current in heaven but "the righteousness which is of God by faith." If they have set their heart upon calling it "the imputed righteousness of Christ," though the expression is not strictly Scriptural, let it pass; but give them to understand, that as *Divine* imputation of righteousness is a most glorious reality, so *human* imputation is a most delusive dream; and that of this sort is undoubtedly the Calvinian imputation of righteousness to a man, who actually defiles his neighbour's bed, and betrays innocent blood.[*] A dangerous contrivance this! not

---

[*] God's imputation of righteousness is always *according to truth.* As all sinful men actually partake of Adam's sinful nature, by the defiling seed of his corruption, before God accounts them *guilty* together with him; so all righteous men partake of Christ's holy nature by the seed of Divine grace, before God accounts them *righteous* together with Christ. This dictate of reason is confirmed by Scripture. "Abraham was fully persuaded that what God had promised he was able also to perform; and therefore it wall imputed to him for righteousness; and it shall be imputed to us, if we believe on him that raised up Jesus from the dead," Romans iv, 21, &c. From this passage it is evident that faith, which unites to Christ and "purifies the heart," is previous to God's imputation of righteousness,

less subversive of common heathenish morality, than of St. James' *"pure* and undefiled religion."

Again: our Calvinist brethren excel in setting forth a part of Christ's priestly office; I mean the immaculate purity of his most holy life, and the all-atoning, all-meritorious sacrifice of his bloody death. Here imitate, and if possible surpass them. Shout a finished atonement louder than they. Behold with raptures of joy, and bid all around you behold, with transports of gratitude, "the Lamb of God that taketh away the sin of the world." If they call this complete atonement *finished salvation,* or *the finished work of Christ,* indulge them still; for peace' sake, let those expressions pass. Nevertheless, at proper times give them to understand, that it is absolutely contrary to reason, Scripture, and Christian experience, to think that *all* Christ's mediatorial work is finished. Insinuate you should be very miserable if he had nothing more to do *for* you and *in* you. Tell them, as they can bear it, that he works daily as a Prophet to enlighten you, as a Priest to make intercession for you, as a King to subdue your enemies, as a Redeemer to deliver you out of all your troubles, and as a Saviour to help you to work out your own salvation; and hint, that, in all these respects, Christ's work is no more finished, than the working of our own salvation is completed.

The judicious will understand you: as for bigots on all sides, you know, they are proof against Scripture and good sense, Nevertheless, mild irony, sharply pointing a Scriptural argument, may yet pass between the joints of their impenetrable armour, and make them feel — either some shame, or some weariness of contention. But this is a dangerous method, which I would recommend to very few. None should dip his pen in the wine of irony till he has dipped it in the oil of love; and even then he should not use it without constant prayer, and as much caution as a surgeon lances an imposthume. If he goes too deep, he does mischief; if not deep enough, he loses his time; the virulent humour is not discharged, but irritated by the skin-deep operation. And "who is sufficient for these things?" Gracious God of wisdom and love! if thou callest us to this difficult and thankless office, let all "our sufficiency be of thee;" and should the operation succeed, thine and thine alone shall be all the glory.

5. And yet, brethren, "I show you a more excellent way" than that of mild irony sharpening a strong argument. If love is the fulfilling of the law, love,after all, must be the destruction of Antinomianism. We shall do but little good by exposing the doctrinal Antinomianism of Dr. Crisp's admirers, if our own tempers and conduct are inconsistent with our profession of evangelical legality. When our antagonists cannot shake our arguments, they will upbraid us with our practice. Let us then take care not to "hold the truth in unrighteousness:" let our moderation and evangelical legality appear even to our candid opponents: so shall "the righteousness of the law be fulfilled in us" that believe the anti-Crispian truth: so shall our faith "establish the law" of ardent love to God and man; and wherever that law is established, Antinomianism is no more. And if, when we truly love our antagonists, they still look upon our

---

although not to Crisp's imputation, which, by a little mistake of only five or six thousand years, he dates from "before the foundation of the world." One is sadly out, either the good doctor or the great apostle.

opposition to their errors as an abuse of their persons, and call our exposing their mistakes "sneering at the truth," let us wrap our souls in the mantle of that "love which is not provoked;" remembering, "the disciple is not above his Master, nor the servant above his Lord."

6. Above all, while we expostulate with our brethren for going to one extreme, let us not go to another. Many in the last century so preached what Christ did for us in the days of his flesh, as to overlook what he does in us in the days of his Spirit. The Quakers saw their error; but while they exposed it they ran into the opposite. They so extolled Christ *living in us,* as to say but little of Christ *dying for us.* At this time, many hearing *our salvation is so finished by Christ, that we need not "work it out with fear and trembling,"* are justly shocked; and thinking they cannot fly too far from so wild a notion, they run headlong into Pelagianism, Socinianism, or gross infidelity. Let us, my brethren, learn wisdom by their contrary mistakes. While some run full east, and others full west, keep we under the bright meridian line of evangelical truth, at an equal distance from their dangerous extremes. By cordial faith let us daily "receive the atonement;" and making our perpetual boast of Christ crucified, let us recommend his inestimable merits to all convinced sinners, cheerfully commending our souls to him "in well doing," and growing in his knowledge, till we experience that he "is all and in all." So shall we "adorn the Gospel of God our Saviour in all things;" nor will our opponents have any occasion to reprove us for Pharisaic unbelief, when we reprove them for Antinomian faith.

LOGICA GENEVENSIS:

OR,

A FOURTH CHECK TO ANTINOMIANISM

IN WHICH

ST. JAMES' PURE RELIGION

IS DEFENDED

AGAINST THE CHARGES,

AND

ESTABLISHED UPON THE CONCESSIONS,

OF MR. RICHARD AND MR. ROWLAND HILL.

IN A SERIES OF LETTERS TO THOSE GENTLEMEN,

BY JOHN FLETCHER, A.M.,

VICAR OF MADELEY.

Reprove, rebuke, exhort, with all long suffering and *(Scriptural)* doctrine; for the time will come when they will not endure sound doctrine, 2 Timothy iv, 2, 3.
Wherefore rebuke them sharply, that they may be sound in the faith. But let brotherly love continue, Titus i, 13; Hebrews xiii, 1.

TO ALL CANDID CALVINISTS

IN THE

CHURCH OF ENGLAND.

HONOURED AND DEAR BRETHREN, — A student from Geneva, who has had the honour of being, admitted a minister of your Church, takes the liberty of dedicating to you these strictures on GENEVA LOGIC, which were written both for the better information of your candid judgment, and to obtain tolerable terms of peace from his worthy opponents.

Some, who mistake blunt truth for sneering insolence, and mild ironies for bitter sarcasms, will probably dissuade you from looking into this FOURTH CHECK TO ANTINOMIANISM. They will tell you that *"Logica Genevensis* is a very bad book," full of "calumny, forgeries, vile slanders, acrimonious sneers, and horrid misrepresentations." But candour, which condemns no one before he is heard, which weighs both sides of the question in an impartial balance, will soon convince you, that, if every irony proceeds from spleen and acrimony of spirit, there is as much of both in these four words of my honoured opponent, *Pietas Oxoniensis* and *Goliah Slain,** as in all the four Checks; and that I have not exceeded the apostolic direction of my motto, "Rebuke them sharply," or rather, αποτομως, cuttingly, but "let brotherly love continue."

I do not deny, that some points of doctrine, which many hold in great veneration, excite pity or laughter in my Checks. But how can I help it? If a painter, who knows not how to flatter, draws to the life an object excessively ridiculous in itself, must it not appear excessively ridiculous in his picture? Is it right to exclaim against his pencil as *malicious,* and his colours as *unfair,* because he impartially uses them according to the rules of his art? And can any unprejudiced person expect that he should draw the picture of the night without using any black shades at all?

If the charge of "bitterness" do not entirely set you against this book, they will try to frighten you from reading it, by protesting that I throw down the foundation of Christianity, and help Mr. Wesley to place works and merit on the Redeemer's throne. To this dreadful charge I answer, (1.) That I had rather my right hand should lose its cunning to all eternity, than use it a moment to detract

---

* The ironical titles of two books written by my opponent, to expose the proceedings of the university of Oxford, respecting the expulsion of six students belonging to Edmund Hall.

from the Saviour's real glory, to whom I am more indebted than any other man in the world. (2.) That the strongest pleas I produce for holiness and good works, are quotations from the homilies of our own Church, as well as from the Puritan divines, whom I cite preferably to others, because they held what you are taught to call *the doctrines of grace*. (3.) That what I have said of those doctrines recommends itself to every unprejudiced person's reason and conscience. (4.) That my capital arguments in favour of practical Christianity are founded upon our second justification by the evidence of works in the great day; a doctrine which my opponent himself cannot help assenting to. (5.) That from first to last, when the *meritorious cause* of our justification is considered, we set works aside; praying God "not to enter into judgment with us," or "weigh our merits, but to pardon our offences" for Christ's sake; and gladly ascribing the whole of our salvation to his alone merits, as much as Calvin or Dr. Crisp does. (6.) That when the word *meriting, deserving*, or *worthy*, which our Lord himself uses again and again, is applied to good works, or good men, we mean absolutely nothing but *rewardable*, or qualified for the reception of a gracious reward. And, (7.) That even this *improper* merit or rewardableness of good works is entirely derived from Christ's *proper* merit, who works what is good in us, and from the gracious promise of God, who has freely engaged himself to recompense the fruits of righteousness, which his own grace enables them to produce.

I hope, honoured brethren, these hints will so far break the waves of prejudice which beat against your candour, as to prevail upon you not to reject this little means of information. If you condescend to peruse it, I trust it will minister to your edification, by enlarging your views of Christ's prophetic and kingly office; by heightening your ideas of that practical religion which the Scriptures perpetually enforce; by lessening your regard for some well-meant mistakes, on which good men have too hastily put the stamp of orthodoxy; and by giving you a more favourable opinion of the sentiments of your remonstrant brethren, who would rejoice to live at peace with you in the kingdom of grace, and walk in love with you to the kingdom of glory. But whether you consent to give them the right hand of fellowship or not, nobody, I think, can be more glad to offer it to you, than he who, with undissembled respect, remains, honoured and dear brethren, your affectionate brother, and obedient servant in Christ,

J. FLETCHER.

CONTENTS OF FOURTH CHECK.

Letter IX.
To Mr. Rowland Hill.

An answer to Mr. Rowland Hill's arguments against justification by works in the day of judgment, closed by some strictures upon the friendliness of his friendly remarks.

Letter X.
To the same, and to Richard Hill, Esq.

An answer to Mr. Richard and Mr. Rowland Hill's remarks upon the Third Check, in which the Scriptural doctrine of justification, in its several branches, is vindicated from their witticisms, and Mr. Hill cut off from some of his subterfuges.

Letter XI.
To both the same.

The doctrine of a believer's justification by works is reconciled with the doctrine of a sinner's justification by grace: and it is proved that Calvinism makes way for barefaced Antinomianism, absolutely destroys the law of Christ, and casts his royal crown to the ground.

Letter XII.
To Richard Hill, Esq.

In which the author shows how far the Calvinists and the remonstrants agree, wherein they disagree, and what makes the latter dissent from the former concerning the famous doctrine of imputed righteousness.

Letter XIII.
To the same.

Containing a view of the present state of the controversy, especially with regard to free will; and a conclusion, descriptive of the loving, apostolic method of carrying on controversy; — expressive of brotherly love and respect for all pious Calvinists; — and declarative of a desire to live with them upon peaceable and friendly terms.

Postscript.

Containing an account of the reasons which engage us to make at last a firm stand against our pious opponents; and of the hope we entertain, that in so doing, our labour will not be in vain in the Lord.

LOGICA GENEVENSIS;

OR,

A FOURTH CHECK TO ANTINOMIANISM

LETTER I.

To Richard Hill, Esq.

HON. AND DEAR SIR, — My entering the field of controversy to defend St. James' "pure religion," procured me your Five Letters, which I compare to a shower of rain, gently descending from the placid heaven. But the six which have followed resemble a storm of hail, pouring down from the lowering sky, ushered by some harmless flashes of lightning, and accompanied by the rumbling of distant thunder. If my comparison is just, it is no Wonder that when I read them first I was almost thunderstruck, and began to fear, lest, instead of adding light, I had only added heat, to the hasty zeal which I endeavoured to check.

But at the second perusal, my drooping hopes revive: the disburdened clouds begin to break: the air, discharged of the exhalations which rendered it sultry or hazy, seems, clearer or cooler than before; and the smiling plains of evangelical truth, viewed through that defecated medium, appear more gay after the unexpected storm. Methinks even *moderation*, the phoenix consumed by our polemic fires, is going to rise out of its ashes' and that, notwithstanding the din of a controversial war, "the voice of the turtle is *still* heard in our land."

May the gentle sound approach nearer and nearer, and tune our listening hearts to the melodious accents of Divine and brotherly love! And thou Prince of Peace, thou true Solomon, thou pacific Son of warlike David, should an evil spirit come upon me as it did upon Saul, to make me dip my pen in the envenomed gall of discord, or turn it into a javelin to strike my dear opponent through and through; mercifully bow the heavens, gently touch the strings of my heart, and play upon them the melting tune of forgiving love! Teach me to check the rapid growth of Antinomian errors, without hindering the slow progress of thy precious truth; and graciously instruct me how to defend an insulted, venerable father, without hurting an honoured, though, alas! prepossessed brother. If the latter has offended, suffer me not to fall upon him with the whip of merciless revenge; and if I must use the rod of reproof, teach me to weigh every stroke in the balance of the sanctuary with tender fear, and yet with honest impartiality.

Should I, in this encounter, gracious Lord, overcome by *thy wisdom* my worthy antagonist, help me by *thy meekness* to give him an example of Christian moderation; and while I tie him with the cords of a man and a believer, while I bind him with reason and Scripture to the left wheel of thy Gospel chariot, which, alas! he mistakes for a wheel of antichrist's carriage; let me rejoice to be tied by him with the same easy bonds to the *right* wheel, which he, without reason, fears I am determined to stop. And when we are thus mutually bound to thy triumphant car, draw us with double swiftness to the happy regions where the good, as well as "the wicked, cease from troubling," and those who are "weary *of contention* are at rest." So shall we leave for ever behind the deep and noisy "waters of strife," in which so many bigots miserably perish; and the barren mountains of Gilboa, where hurried Saul falls upon the point of his own controversial sword, and lovely Jonathan himself receives a mortal wound.

You remember, honoured sir, that I opened the Second Check to Antinomianism by demonstrating that in the day of judgment we shall be justified by works, that is, by the evidence of works. A person of your penetration could not but see, that if this legal proposition stood, your favourite doctrine of finished salvation, and *Calvinian* imputation of righteousness to an impenitent adulterer, would lose their exorbitant influence. You design, therefore, to bend yourself, with Samson's might, upon this adamantine pillar of our "heretical" doctrine. Let us see whether your redoubled efforts have shaken it, or only shown that it stands as firm as the pillars of heaven.

You enter upon the arduous labour of deciding, in your first paragraph, that I deal in "sneer, banter, sarcasm, notorious falsehood, calumny, and gross perversions;" and to confirm this charge, you produce three anonymous letters, one of which deposes, that what I have written upon finished salvation "is enough to make every child of God shudder;" while another pronounces, that my "book is full of groundless and false arguments;" and the third, that I am "infatuated," and have "advanced pernicious doctrines in bitter expressions." Your initial charge, supported by this three-fold authority, will probably pass for a demonstration with some of your readers; but as I consider it only as a faint imitation of Calvin's book, called *Responsio ad calumnias Nebulonis,* I hasten to what looks a little like an argument.

Page 4, you say, concerning justification by works, that is, by the evidence of works, in the last day, "I may *safely affirm,* that it has no existence in the word of God." So, honoured sir, the plainest and fullest passages of the sacred oracles are, it seems, to fly like chaff before your "safe affirmation;" for you have not supported it by one single text. Near twenty have I produced, which declare, with one consent, that we shall be judged, not according to our faith, but according to our works; and that *the doers* of the law, and they alone, shall be justified in the last day; but in your *"full* and particular answer to my book," you take a full and easy leap over most of these texts. Two, however, you touch upon; let us see if you have been able to press them into the service of your doctrine.

1. You find fault with our translation of Revelation xxii, 14: "Blessed are they that do his commandments, that they may have right to the tree of life." You

say, that the word which is rendered *right* properly signifies *privilege*. Granting it, for peace' sake, I ask, What do you get by this criticism? Absolutely nothing: for the word *privilege* proves my point as well as the word *right;* unless you can demonstrate that it makes a material difference in the sense of the following similar sentence: — "Blessed was the son of Aaron, whom Moses anointed high priest, that he might have the *right,* (or, that he might have the *privilege,*) of entering once a year into the holy of holies." If those different expressions convey the same idea, your objection is frivolous, and Revelation xxii, 14, even according to your own translation, still evidently confirms the words of our Lord and his favourite disciple,: "If thou wilt enter into life, keep the commandments. And this is his commandment, that we should believe on the name of his Son Jesus Christ, and love one another."

2. The other text you touch upon is Matthew xii, 36, 37, "In the day of judgment, by thy WORDS shalt thou be justified." Page 10, you thus comment upon it: "Our Lord points out the danger of vain and idle words; and affirms, that as every tree is known by its fruit, so may the true state of the heart be known by the evil or good things which proceed out of the mouth; and having laid down this rule of judgment, he adds the words which you have so often cited in defence of your doctrine, 'By thy words thou shalt be justified,' &c, that is, as Words and works are the streams which flow from the spring of the heart, so by these it will appear whether that spring *was ever* [I would say, with more propriety, *is now*] purified by grace; or whether it still remains in its natural corrupt state; the actions of a man being *the declarative evidences,* both here and at the great day, whether or no *he was* [I would say, *he is*] among the trees of righteousness which the Lord hath planted. This is the plain, easy sense of this passage."

Is it, indeed, honoured sir? Well then, I have the pleasure of informing you, that supposing you allow of my little alterations, we are exactly of the same sentiments; and I think that, upon second thoughts, you will not reject them; for it is evident, the actions of to-day show what a free agent is today, and not what he was yesterday, or he will be six months hence. By what argument will you prove, that because Lucifer was once a bright angel, and Adam a godlike creature, they continued such under all the horrors of their rebellion? Or that David's repentance after Nathan's expostulation, evidenced that he was a penitent before? In the last day the grand inquiry will not be, Whether Hymeneus, Philetus, and Demas, "were ever purified by grace;" but whether they were so at death. Because our last works will be admitted as the last, and consequently the most important and decisive evidences; for "as the tree falls, so it lies." Apostates, far from being justified for having been once "purified by grace," will be "counted worthy of a sorer punishment" for having "turned from the way of righteousness." Would not the world hiss a physician, who should publicly maintain, that by feeling people's pulse now, he can tell whether they were ever sick or well? Or that because one of his patients *was* alive ten years ago, he *is* alive now, though every symptom of death and corruption is actually upon him? And shall your hint, honoured sir, persuade your readers that what would be an imposition upon common sense in a gentleman of the faculty, is genuine orthodoxy in Mr. Hill?

The Works of John Fletcher

But I have too high an opinion of your good sense and piety, dear sir, to think that you will persist in your inaccuracy, merely for the pleasure of maintaining the ridiculous perseverance of Antinomian apostates, and contradicting the God of truth, who expressly mentions "the righteous turning from his righteousness, and dying in the sin that he has sinned." My hopes that you will give it up are the more sanguine, as it is rectified in the same page by two quotations which have the full stamp of your approbation.

"The judicious Dr. Guise," say you, "paraphrases thus on the place: "Your words, as well as actions, shall be produced in evidence for or against you, to prove [not whether you *ever were*, but] whether you *are* a saint or a sinner, a true believer or not; and, according to their evidence, you shall be either publicly acquitted or condemned in the great day."" And as it is absurd to suppose that Christ shall inquire whether men *are* believers in the day of judgment, because faith will then be lost in sight; Mr. Wesley, whom you quote next, as if he contradicted me, wisely corrects the little inaccuracy of the doctor, and says, "Your words, as well as actions, shall be produced in evidence for or against you, to prove [not whether you *are*, but] whether you *was* a true believer or not, and according to their evidence you will either be acquitted or condemned in the great day." The very doctrine this which I have advanced at large in the Second Check.

However, triumphing as if you had won the day, you conclude by saying, "In the mouth of these two witnesses may THE TRUTH be firmly established." To this pious wish, honoured sir, my soul breathes out a cordial *Amen!* I rejoice to see that God has given you candour to the acknowledgment of THE TRUTH; and as it is firmly established in the mouth of Dr. Guise and Mr. Wesley, may it be for ever confirmed by this spontaneous testimony of Mr. Hill! But, in the name of brotherly love, if you thus hold THE TRUTH which I contend for; that is, justification by the evidence of works in the last day; why do you oppose me? Why do you represent my sentiment "as full of rottenness and deadly poison?" Till you solve this problem, permit me to vent my surprise by a sigh, and to say, *Logica Genevensis!*

Having seen how *fully and particularly* you have granted the fundamental doctrine of the book, to which you was to give "a full and particular answer," namely, that our final justification will turn upon the evidence of works in the last day; I go back to page 4, where, to my utter astonishment, you affirm, "that as this doctrine has no existence in the word of God, so neither in any Protestant Church under heaven!" Thus, to unchurch Mr. Wesley and me, you unchurch Dr. Guise and yourself!

To support your assertion you quote Bishop Cowper, Dr. Fulke, and Mr. Hervey, who agree to maintain, that "justification is *one single act*, and must therefore be done or undone." As neither you nor they have supported this proposition by one single argument, I shall just observe, that a thousand bishops and doctors are lighter than vanity, when weighed in the balance against the authority of Christ and his apostles.

However, if you forget your proofs, I shall produce mine; and by the following syllogism I demonstrate that justification in the day of our conversion, and justification in the last day, are no more "one single act," than the day of the sinner's conversion and that of judgment are one single day.

Five Checks To Antinomianism

Two acts, which differ as to time, place, persons, witnesses, and circumstances, &c, cannot be "one single act;" (the one may be *done* when the other remains *undone*.) But our first justification at conversion thus differs from our second in the great day. Therefore our first and second* justification cannot be one single act, &c.

The second proposition, which alone is disputable, may be thus abundantly proved. Our first and second justification differ, (1.) With respect to *time:* the time of the one is the hour of conversion; and the time of the other the day of judgment. (2.) With respect to *place:* the place of the former is this earth; and the place of the latter the awful spot, in the new heaven or on the new earth, where the tribunal of Christ shall be erected. (3.) With respect to the *witnesses:* the witnesses of the former are the Spirit of God and our own conscience; or, to speak in Scripture language; "The Spirit beating witness with our spirits that we are the children of God:" but the witnesses of the latter will be the countless myriads of men and angels assembled before Christ. (4.) With respect to the *Justifier:* in the former justification "one God justifies the circumcision and the uncircumcision;" and in the latter, "one Mediator between God and man, even the man Christ Jesus," will pronounce the sentence: for, "the Father judgeth no man, but hath committed all judgment to the Son." (5.) With respect to the *justified:* in the day of conversion, *a penitent sinner* is justified; in the day of judgment, *a persevering saint.* (6.) With respect to *the article upon which justification will turn:* although the meritorious cause of both our justifications is the same, that is, the blood and righteousness of Christ, yet the instrumental cause is very different; by FAITH we obtain (not purchase) the first, and by WORKS the second. (7.) With respect *to the act of the Justifier:* at our conversion God covers and pardons our sins; but in the day of judgment Christ uncovers and approves our righteousness. And, (lastly,) with regard to *the consequences of both:* at the first justification we are enlisted by the Friend of sinners to "fight the good fight of faith" in the Church militant; and at the second we are admitted by the righteous Judge to "receive a crown of righteousness, and shine like the sun" in the Church triumphant.

Is it not strange that the enchanting power of Calvinian logic, should have detained us so long in Babel, where things so vastly different are perpetually confounded? Is it not deplorable that when Mr. Wesley has the courage to call us out of mystic Geneva, so many tongues and pens should be sharpened against him? Shall foreign logic for ever prevail over English good sense, and Christian brotherly kindness? Have we so "leaned toward Calvinism" as to be totally past recovery? And is the balance between St. Paul's and St. James' justification lost among pious Protestants for ever? O ye regenerate Britons, who have unhappily fallen in love with the Genevan Delilah, "awake! awake! put on strength," and leap out of the arms of that enchantress! If she rocks you asleep in her bosom, it is only to bind you fast with cords of Antinomian errors, and deliver you up to the horrors of Antinomian practices. Has she not already cut off the locks, and

---

* I still call them *first* and *second,* not only to accommodate myself to the Rev. Mr. Shirley's expression in his Narrative, but because they may with propriety be thus distinguished, when considered with respect to each other.

put out the eyes of thousands? And does not Samson publicly grind for the Philistine? Have we not seen Mr. Hill himself tell the world that "all sins work for good to the pleasant children," who go on frowardly from adultery to treachery, and from treachery to murder?

But you have an answer ready. Page 6, you insinuate that it is I who have erected a Babel, by denying that the two above-described justifications are one and the same. And, to prove it, you advance a dilemma which is already obviated in the Third Check, p. 161*. We readily grant you, honoured sir, that, if a man dies the moment he is justified by faith, the inward labour of his love, (for living faith always works by love,) will justify him in the day of judgment. But you must also grant us, that if he lives, and "turns from his righteousness;" or which is the same, if his faith, instead of working by love and obedience, works by lust and malice, by adultery and murder, it is no longer a living faith; it is a dead faith, of which St. James says, "What does it profit, though a man say he hath faith, and have not works? Can *that* faith save him? Faith, if it hath not works, is dead." You see, then, how that, in what you call "the intermediate state," as well as in the last day, "by works a man is justified, and not by faith only," James ii.

Page 6, you assert, that my "favourite scheme is rather overthrown than supported by the instance of the collier," on whose evidence I supposed myself acquitted in a court of judicature. "His testimony," say you, "proves indeed your innocence, but it does in no degree constitute that innocence." Are then, "to justify a man," and "to constitute him innocent," expressions of the same import? Nay, some believe that when God justifies returning prodigals at their conversion, he does not constitute them innocent, but for Christ's sake mercifully pardons their manifold sins, and graciously accepts their guilty persons; and that when Christ shall justify persevering saints in the last day, he will not constitute them innocent, but only declare, upon the evidence of their last works, that they are "pure in heart," and therefore qualified "to see God, and worthy to obtain that world, where the children of the resurrection are equal to angels."

To show that the instance of the grafted tree overthrows also the doctrine of a two-fold justification, you quote that great and good man, Mr. Hervey. But you forget that his bare assertion is no better than your own. I appeal from both your assertions to the common sense of any impartial man, whether there is not a material difference between declaring that a *crab stock* is properly grafted, and pronouncing that an *apple tree* is not cankered and barren, but sound and fruitful. Mr. Hervey's mistake appears to me so much the more surprising, as the distinction which he explodes is every where obvious.

Look into our orchards, and you will see some trees that were once properly grafted, but are now blasted, dead, rotten, and perhaps torn up by the roots. Consider our congregations, and you will cry out, as the pious divine† under whose ministry you sit at present, "O what sad instances does the present state of the Church afford us of persons, who set out with the most vehement

---

* [161]

† The Rev. Mr. De Courcy, in his "Delineation of true and false Zeal," a little edifying tract, which does justice to St. James' "pure religion," and shows, that some pious Calvinists clearly see the growth, and honestly check the progress of Antinomianism, so far as their principles will allow.

zeal at the beginning, seemed to promise great things, and to carry all before them, who are now like the snuff of an extinguished taper, devoid of any apparent life! We swarm with slumbering virgins on the right hand and on the left. The Delilah of this world has shorn their locks, their former strength is gone, their frame is totally enervated, and the Philistines are upon them."

But, above all, search the oracles of God, and there you will see various descriptions of apostates, that *is,* of men who, to the last, "tread under foot the Son of God, and account the blood of the covenant wherewith they were sanctified," and consequently justified, "a common, *despicable* thing." These, in a dying hour, have no right to say, "I have kept the faith;" for, alas! by "putting away a good conscience, concerning faith they have made shipwreck." These, like "withered branches" of the heavenly Vine, in which they once blossomed, shall be "taken away, cast forth, and burned," in the last day, together with the chaff, for not "bearing fruit, and ending in the flesh;" agreeable to that awful clause in the Gospel charter, "The works of the flesh are adultery, fornication, uncleanness, idolatry, hatred, variance, wrath, strife, envying, murder, drunkenness, revellings, and such like; of which I tell you, [justified believers,] as I have told you in time past, that they who Do such things SHALL NOT inherit the kingdom of heaven." Thus the numerous tribe of apostates, after having been "justified by FAITH" in the day of their conversion, shall be *condemned by* WORKS in the day of judgment. So real, so important is the. distinction, which Mr. Hervey looks upon as needless, and you, sir, as "full of deadly poison!"

However, says Bishop Cowper, "This distinction confounds two benefits, justification, and sanctification." To this assertion, which, according to a grand rule of your logic, is also to pass for proof, I answer, that our *sanctification* will no more be confounded with our *justification* in the last day, than our *faith* is confounded with our *acceptance* in the day of our conversion. When you shall demonstrate that the witnesses, upon whose testimony a criminal is absolved, are the same thing as the sentence of absolution pronounced by the judge, you will be able to make it appear, that sanctification is the same thing as justification in the last day; or, which is all one, that there is no difference between an instrumental cause and its proper effect. May both our hearts lie open to the bright beams of convincing truth! And may you believe that my pen expresses the feelings of my heart, when I subscribe myself, honoured and dear sir, your most obedient servant in Him who will justify us by our words,

JOHN FLETCHER.

LETTER II.

To Richard Hill, Esq.

HONOURED AND DEAR SIR, — An assertion of yours seems to me of greater moment than the quotation from Bishop Cowper, which I answered in my last. You maintain, (p. 11,) "that the doctrine of a two-fold justification is not to be found in any part of the liturgy of our Church."

1. Not to mention again the latter part of St. Athanasius' creed; permit me, sir, to ask you, if on the thirteenth and fourteenth Sundays after Trinity you never considered what is implied in these and the like petitions? "Grant that we may so *faithfully* serve thee in this life, that we *fail not finally* to attain thy heavenly promises, through the merits of Jesus Christ. Make us to *love* that which thou dost *command,* that we may *obtain* that which thou dost *promise.*" Again: on St. Peter's day, "Make all pastors *diligently* to preach thy holy word, and the people *obediently* to follow the same, *that they may receive the crown* of everlasting glory, through Jesus Christ." And on the third Sunday in Advent: "Grant that thy ministers may so prepare thy way, by *turning* the hearts of *the disobedient,* that at *thy second coming to judge the world,* we may be found *an acceptable people* in thy sight."

St. James' justification by works, consequent upon justification by faith, is described in the service for Ash Wednesday: "*If* we walk in his ways: *if* we follow him in lowliness, patience, and charity, and be ordered by the governance of his Holy Spirit, seeking always his glory, and serving him duly with thanksgiving:" — Then comes the description of our final justification, which is but a solemn and public confirmation of St. James' justification by works. — "This *if we do,* Christ will deliver us from the curse of the law, and from the extreme malediction which shall light upon them that shall be set on the left hand; and he will set us on his right hand, and give us the gracious benediction of his Father, commanding us to take possession of his glorious kingdom." — *Commination.*

I flatter myself, honoured sir, that you will not set these quotations aside, by just saying what you do on another occasion: "As to the quotation you have brought from Mr. Henry in defence of this doctrine, for any good it does your cause, it might as well have been urged in defence of extreme unction." I hope you will not object that the WORDS, *second justification by works,* are not in our liturgy; for if the THING be evidently there, what can a candid inquirer after truth require more? Should you have recourse to such an argument, you will permit me to ask you, what you would say to those who assert, that the DOCTRINE of the Trinity is not found in the Scripture, because the WORD *Trinity* is not read there? And the same answers which you would give to such opponents, I now beforehand return to yourself.

II. As final justification by the evidence of works is clearly asserted in our liturgy, so it is indirectly maintained in our articles. You know, honoured sir, that the eleventh treats of *justification by faith* at our conversion, and you yourself very justly observe, (p. 11,) "That our reformers seemed to have had an eye to the words of our Lord, 'The tree is known, [that is, is evidenced,] by its fruits,' when they drew up our twelfth article, which asserts, that a lively faith may be as evidently known by good works as a tree discerned by its fruit." This, honoured sir, is the very basis of Mr. Wesley's "rotten" doctrine; the very foundation on which St. James builds "his pure and undefiled religion." This being granted, it necessarily follows, to the overthrow of your favourite scheme, that a living, justifying faith may degenerate into a dead, condemning faith, as surely as David's faith, once productive of the fruits of righteousness, degenerated into a faith productive of adultery and murder.

You are aware of the advantage that the twelfth article gives us over you; therefore, to obviate it, you insinuate, in your Five Letters, that David's faith, when he committed adultery, was the same as when he danced before the ark. It was justifying faith still, only "in a winter season." This argument, which will pass for a demonstration in Geneva, will appear an evasion in England, if our readers consider that it is founded merely upon the Calvinian custom of forcing rational comparisons to go *upon all four* like brutes, and then driving far beyond the intention of those by whom they were first produced. We know that a tree on the banks of the Severn may be good in winter though it bear no good fruit; because no trees bear among us any fruit, good or bad, in January. But this cannot be the case either of believers or unbelievers — they bear fruit all the year round — unless you can prove that like men in an apoplectic fit they neither think, speak, nor act "in a winter season." Again:

Believers who commit adultery and murder are not good trees, even in a negative sense, for they *positively* bear fruit of the most poisonous nature, How then can either their faith or their persons be evidenced a *good* tree, by such bad fruit, such *detestable evidence?* While you put your logic to the rack for an answer, I shall take the liberty to encounter you a moment with your own weapons, and making the degraded comparison of our twelfth article walk upon all four against you, I promise you, that if you can show me an apple tree which bears poisonous crabs in summer, much more one that bears them "in a winter season," I will turn Antinomian, and believe that an impenitent murderer has justifying faith, and is complete in Christ's righteousness.

III. Having thus, I hope, rescued our twelfth article from the violence which your scheme offers to its holy meaning, I presume to ask, Why do you not mention *the homilies*, when you say that the doctrine of a two-fold justification is not found in any part of the offices and liturgy of our Church? Is it because you never consulted them upon the subject of our controversy? To save you the trouble of turning them over, and to undeceive those who are frighted from the pure doctrine of their own Church by the late cries of *Arminianism! Pelagianism!* and *Popery!* I shall present you with the following extract from our homilies, which will show you they are not less opposite to Antinomianism than our liturgy and articles: —

"The first coming unto God is through faith, whereby we are justified before God. And lest any man should be deceived, it is diligently to be noted, that there is one faith, which in Scripture is called *a dead faith,* which bringeth forth no good works, but is idle, barren, and unfruitful. And this faith, by the holy Apostle St. James, is compared to the faith of devils. And such faith have the wicked, naughty Christian people, who, as St. Paul saith, 'confess God with their mouth,' but deny him in their deeds. Forasmuch as 'faith without works is dead,' it is not *now* faith, as a dead man is not a man. The true, lively Christian faith liveth and stirreth inwardly in the heart. It is not without the love of God and our neighbour, nor without the desire to hear God's word and follow the same, in eschewing evil, and doing gladly all good works. Of this faith, this is first to be noted, that it does not lie dead in the heart, but is lively and fruitful in bringing forth good works. As the light cannot be hid, so a true faith cannot be kept secret, but shows itself by good works. And as the living body of a man ever exerciseth such things as belong to a living body, so the soul that has a lively faith in it will be doing always some good work which shall declare that it is living. For he is like a tree set by the water side, his leaf will be green, and he will not cease to bring forth his fruit." (*Hom. Of Faith, first part.*) Here is no Antinomian salvo; no "winter state" allowed of, to bring forth the dire fruits of adultery and murder.

"There is one WORK in which are all good works, that is, 'faith which WORKETH by charity.' If you have it, you have the ground of all good works; for wisdom, temperance, and justice, are all referred unto this faith: without it we have not virtues, but only their names and shadows. Many have no fruit of their works, because faith, *the chief work,* lacketh. Our faith in Christ must go before, and after be nourished by good works. The thief did believe only, and the most merciful God justified him. If he had lived and not regarded the WORKS *of faith,* [N. B.] he should *have lost his salvation* again." (*Hom. on Good Works, first part.*)

"The third thing to be declared unto you is, what manner of works they are which spring out of true faith, and lead faithful men to everlasting life. This cannot be known so well as by our Saviour himself, who, being asked of a certain great man this question, 'What works shall I do to come to everlasting life?' answered him, 'If thou wilt come to everlasting life, keep the commandments: Thou shalt not kill, thou shalt not commit adultery,' &c. By which words Christ declared, that the laws of God are the very way which leads to everlasting life. So that this is to be taken for *a most true* lesson, taught by Christ's *own mouth,* that the works of the moral commandments of God are the very true works of faith, which lead to the blessed life to come. But the blindness and malice of men hath ever been ready to fall from God and his *law,* and to invent a new way to salvation by works of *their own device.* Therefore Christ said, 'You leave the commandments of God to keep your own traditions.' You must have an assured faith in God, love him, and dread to offend him evermore. Then, for his sake, love ALL MEN, *friends and foes,* because they are his creation and image, and *redeemed by Christ as ye are.* Kill not; commit no manner of adultery in will nor deed, &c. Thus, in keeping the commandments of God (wherein standeth his pure honour, and which wrought in faith, he hath ordained to be the right trade and pathway to heaven) you *shall not fail* to come to everlasting life." (*Hom. on Good Works, third part.*)

"Whereas God hath showed, to all that *truly believe* his Gospel, his face of mercy in Jesus Christ, which does so enlighten their hearts, that if they behold it as they ought they are transformed to his image, and made partakers of the heavenly light and of his Holy Spirit; so, if they *after do neglect* the same, and order not their life according to his example and doctrine, he will take away from them his kingdom, because they bring not forth the fruit thereof. And if this will not serve, but still we remain disobedient, behaving ourselves uncharitably, by disdain, envy, malice, or by committing murder, adultery, or such detestable works; then he threateneth us by terrible comminations, swearing in great anger, that *whosoever* does these works shall *never* enter into his rest, which is the kingdom of heaven." *(Hom. of Falling from God, first part.)*

"We do call for mercy in vain, *if* we will not show mercy to our neighbour. For *if* we do not put wrath and displeasure forth out of our hearts to our brother, no more will God forgive the wrath that our sins have deserved before him. For under this *condition* doth God forgive us, *if* we forgive others. God commands us to forgive *if* we will have any part of the pardon which Christ purchased by shedding his precious blood. Let us then be favourable one to another, &c. By these means shall we move God to be merciful to our sins. He that hateth his brother* is *the child of damnation and of the devil,* cursed and hated of God *so long as he so remaineth.* For as peace and charity make us *the blessed children of God,* so do hatred and malice make us the cursed children of the devil." *(Hom. for Good Friday.)*

The Homily on DRESS brings to my mind what you say, p. 35, upon that head. If I am not mistaken, you quote Mr. Hervey in support† of finery, which surprises me so much the more, as the plainness of your dress is a practical answer to what can be advanced in support of that branch of Antinomianism. Permit me, however, to guard your ornamented quotation in the plain, nervous language of our Church. After mentioning "the round attires of the head," exposed by Isaiah, she says: "No less truly is the vanity used among us. For the proud and haughty stomachs of the daughters of England are so maintained with divers disguised sorts of costly apparel, that as Tertullian saith, *there is left no difference of apparel between an honest matron and a common strumpet!* Yea, many care not what they spend in disguising themselves, ever desiring new toys and inventing new fashions. Therefore we must needs look for God's fearful vengeance from heaven, to overthrow our pride, as he overthrew Herod, who, in his royal apparel, forgetting God, was smitten of an angel, and eaten up with worms.

"But some vain women will object, 'All which we do, in decking ourselves with gay apparel, is to please our husbands.' O most shameful answer to the reproach of thy husband! What couldest thou say more to set out his foolishness, than to charge him to be pleased with the devil's attire? Nay, nay, this is but a vain excuse of such as go about to please [themselves and] others, rather than their husbands. She does but deserve scorn to set out all her commendation in Jewish and heathenish apparel, and yet brag of her Christianity; and sometimes she is the cause of much deceit in her husband's dealings, that she may be the

---

* Did not David once hate Uriah as much as Jezebel did Naboth? Was not innocent blood shed in both cases by means of sanguinary letters? Is it to the honour of David that he outdid Jezebel in kindly desiring Uriah to carry his own death warrant to Joab?

† I blame, in the Second Check, only such professors of godliness as "wear gold, pearls, and precious stones, when no distinction of office or state obliges them to do it." As you find fault with this guarded doctrine, and insinuate that I "dwindle the noble ideas of St. Paul into a meanness of sense befitting the superstitious and contracted spirit of a hermit;" it necessarily follows that you plead for finery, or that you oppose me for opposition's sake, when you exactly mean the same thing with me.

more gorgeously set out to the sight of the vain world. O thou woman, not a Christian, but worse than a Pagan, thou settest out thy pride, and makest of thy indecent apparel the devil's net to catch souls. Howsoever thou perfumest thyself, yet cannot thy beastliness be hidden. The more thou garnishest thyself with these outward blazings, the less thou carest for the inward garnishing of thy mind. Hear, hear, what Christ's holy apostles do write." Then follow those passages of St. Peter and St. Paul, which you suppose "I do not rightly understand."

To convince you, however, that our Church has as much of "the superstitious and contracted spirit of a hermit" as myself, I shall plead a moment more against finery in her own words: "The wife of a heathen being asked *why she wore no gold?* she answered, That *she thought her husband's virtues sufficient ornaments.* How much more ought every Christian to think himself sufficiently garnished with our Saviour Christ's heavenly virtues! But perhaps some will answer *that they must do something to show their birth and blood:* as though these things, [jewels and finery] were not common to those who are most vile: as though thy husband's riches could not be better bestowed than in such superfluities: as though, when thou wast christened, thou didst not *renounce* the pride of this world and the pomp of the flesh. If thou sayest *that the custom is to be followed,* I ask of thee, Whose custom should be followed? Of the wise, or of fools? If thou sayest, *Of the wise;* then I say, Follow them; for fools' customs, who should follow but fools? If any lewd custom be used, be thou the first to break it; labour to diminish it, and lay it down, and thou shalt have more praise before God by it, than by all the glory of such superfluity. I speak not against convenient apparel, for every state agreeable; but against the superfluity whereby thou and thy husband are compelled to rob the poor, to maintain thy costliness. Hear how holy Queen Esther setteth out these goodly ornaments, as they are called, when, in order to save God's people, she put them on: 'Thou knowest, O Lord, the necessity which I am driven to, to put on this apparel, and that I abhor this sign of pride, and that I defy it as a filthy cloth.'" (*Hom. Against Excess of Apparel.*)

So far is our Church from siding with Antinomian Solifidianism, which perpetually decries good works, that she rather leans to the other extreme. "If Popery is about half way between Protestantism and the Minutes," you will hardly think that the mass itself is a quarter of the way between Dr. Crisp's scheme and the following propositions, extracted from the Homily on Alms Deeds.

"Most true is that saying of St. Augustine, *Via coeli pauper est,* 'relieving of the poor is the right way to heaven.' Christ promiseth a reward to those who give but a cup of cold water in his name to them that have need of it; and that reward is the kingdom of heaven. No doubt, therefore, God regardeth highly that which he rewardeth so liberally. He that hath been liberal to the poor, let him know that his godly, doings are accepted, and thankfully taken at God's hands, which he will requite with double and treble; for so says the wise man: 'He who showeth mercy to the poor doth lay his money in the bank to the Lord' for a large interest and gain; the gain being chiefly the possession of the life everlasting, through the merits of Christ."

When our Church has given us this strong dose of legality, that she may by a desperate remedy remove a desperate disease, and kill or cure the

Antinomian spirit in all her children; lest the violent medicine should hurt us, she, like a prudent mother, instantly administers the following balsamic corrective: —

"Some will say, *If charitable works are able to reconcile us to God, and deliver us from damnation, then are Christ's merits defaced; then are we justified by works, and by our deeds may we merit heaven.* But understand, dearly beloved, that no godly men, when they, in extolling the dignity, profit, and effect of virtuous and liberal alms, do say that it bringeth us to the favour of God, do mean that our work is the *original* cause of our acceptance before God, &c. For that were indeed to deface Christ, and to defraud him of his glory. But they mean, that the Spirit of God mightily working in them, who seemed before children of wrath, they *declare* by their outward deeds that they are the undoubted children of God. By their tender pity, (wherein they show themselves to be like unto God,) they declare openly and manifestly unto the sight of all men that they are the sons of God. For as the good fruit does argue the goodness of the tree, so doth the good deed of a man prove the goodness of him that doeth it."

In justice to our holy Church, whom some represent as a patroness of Antinomianism; in brotherly love to you, honoured sir, who seem to judge of her doctrines by a few expressions which custom made her use after St. Augustine; in tender compassion to many of her members, who are strangers to her true sentiments; and in common humanity to Mr. Wesley, who is perpetually accused of erecting Popery upon her ruins; I have presented you with this extract from our homilies. If you lay by the veil of prejudice, which keeps the light from your honest heart, I humbly hope it will convince you that our Church nobly contends for St. James' evangelical legality; that she pleads for the *rewardableness* (which is all we understand by the *merit*) of works, in far stronger terms than Mr. Wesley does in the Minutes; and that in perpetually making our justification, merited by Christ, turn upon the *instrumentality* of a lively faith, and the *evidence* of good works, as there is opportunity to do them, she tears up Calvinism and Antinomian delusions by the very roots.

Leaving you to consider how you shall bring about a reconciliation between your fourth letter and our *godly homilies,* I shall just take the liberty to remind you, that when you entered, or took your degrees at Oxford, you subscribed to the thirty-nine articles; the thirty-fifth of which declares, that "the homilies contain a godly and wholesome doctrine, necessary for these" Papistical and Antinomian "times."

That keeping clear from both extremes, we may evidence the godliness of that doctrine by the soundness of our publications, and the exemplariness of our conduct, is the cordial prayer of, honoured and dear sir, your obedient servant in the liturgy, articles, and homilies of the Church of England,

J. FLETCHER.

LETTER III.

To Richard Hill, Esq.

HONOURED AND DEAR SIR, — In my last I endeavoured to show you, that our Church, far from warping to CRISPIANITY, strongly enforces St. James' undefiled religion: let us now see what modern divines, especially the Puritan, thought about the important subject of our controversy.

Page 13, you oppose the doctrine which you have, (p. 11,) so heartily wished to be firmly *established* in the mouth of two witnesses: "If Mr. Whitefield had been now living," say you, "I doubt not but he would have told you, that if need should be, he was ready to offer himself among the foremost of those *true Protestants,* who, you tell us, could have burned against the doctrine of a second justification by works. And as to the Puritan divines, there is not one of the many hundreds of them but what *abhorred* the doctrine of a second justification by works, as full of rottenness and deadly poison. Surely then it is not without justice that I accuse you of the grossest perversions and misrepresentations, that perhaps ever proceeded from any author's pen. The ashes of that laborious man of God, Mr. Whitefield, you have raked up, in order to bring him as a coadjutor to support your tottering doctrine of a second justification by works." And again, (91, 92,) "I am not afraid to challenge Mr. Fletcher to fix upon one Protestant minister, either Puritan or of the Church of England, from the beginning of the reformation to the reign of Charles the Second, who held the doctrines he has been contending for." "Sure I am, that you have grieved many a pious heart among our dissenting brethren, by lathering upon their venerable ancestors such a spurious offspring, as can only trace its descent from the loins of 'the man of sin,' by which it was begotten out of the mother of abominations, the 'scarlet Babylonish whore, which sitteth upon many waters.'"

Your charges and challenge, honoured sir, deserve an answer, not because they fix the blot of the grossest perversions upon my insignificant character, but because they represent the holy Apostle James, whose doctrine I vindicate, as "the man of sin," begetting his *undefiled religion* "out of the Babylonish whore." I begin with what you say about Mr. Whitefield: —

I never thought he was clear in the doctrine of our Lord, "In the day of judgment by thy words shalt thou be justified;" for if he had seen it in its proper light, he would instantly have renounced Calvinism. All I have asserted is, that the most eminent ministers, Mr. Whitefield himself not excepted, perpetually allude to that doctrine, when their enlarged hearts, (under a full gale of God's free Spirit,) get clear of the shallows of bigotry, or the narrow channels of their favourite systems: for then, sailing in deep water, and regardless of the rocks of offence, they cut their easy way through the raging billows of opposition, and speak ALL the truth as it is in Jesus; or at least "allude" (this was my expression, see Second Check, p. 77*) to what, at another time, they would perhaps oppose with all their might.

And do you not, honoured sir, allow that Mr. Whitefield did this in the application of his sermons with regard to my doctrine, when you say, (p. 15,) "All that can be gathered from his expressions is, that he believed there would be a great and awful day, in which all who sit under the sound of the Gospel shall be called to give a solemn account of what they hear, and every minister as solemn an account of the doctrine delivered by him?" To convince you that you grant me all I contended for, permit me to ask, whether this solemn account will be in order to a mock trial, or to the solemn justification or condemnation mentioned by our Lord, Matthew xii, 37? If you affirm the former, you traduce heavenly Wisdom, you blaspheme Jesus Christ: if the latter, you give up the point; our hearing and speaking, that is, our works, will turn evidence for or against us in the day of judgment; and, according to their deposition, the scale of absolution and condemnation will turn for heaven or hell.

Let, therefore, the public judge who wrongs Mr. Whitefield; — I, who represent him as speaking agreeably to the plain words of his heavenly Master, Matthew xii, 37; — or you, dear sir, who make him advance as a zealot, at the head of a body of prejudiced men, to burn against as explicit and important a declaration as ever dropped from the Redeemer's lips. I say *important;* because the moment you strike at our justification by works in the last day, you strike at the doctrine of a day of judgment; and the moment that fundamental doctrine is overthrown, natural and revealed religion sink in a heap of common ruins.

Pass we on now to the other reason for which you "accuse me of the grossest misrepresentations and perversions that perhaps ever proceeded from any author's pen." I have affirmed, (Second Check, p. 78†) that "all the sober Puritan divines have directly or *indirectly‡* asserted a second justification by works;" and you tell us, (p. 13,) "There is *not one* of them but what abhorred it, as full of rottenness and deadly poison." One of us is undoubtedly mistaken; for our propositions are diametrically opposite. Let us see who is the man.

To dispute about words is unbecoming men of reason and religion; and that we may not be guilty of this common absurdity, and oppose one another, when perhaps we mean the same thing, permit me to state the question as clearly as I possibly can. Not considering the *meritorious,* but the *instrumental* cause of our justification, I ask, In the day of judgment, shall we be justified or condemned by the works which Christ did in the days of his flesh? Or, in other terms, Shall we be justified by the righteousness of Christ *imputed to us,* as Calvin supposes it was imputed to David in Uriah's bed? or by the righteousness of Christ *implanted in us,* as it was implanted in David when "his eyes ran down with water because men kept not God's law?" Or, if you please, Shall we be justified by Christ's loving God and man for us? or by our loving God and man ourselves? The former of these sentiments is that of Dr. Crisp and all his admirers. That the latter was the

---

* [73]

† [73]

‡ These were my limited expressions.

sentiment of Dr. Owen, and all the *sober* Puritan divines, when they regarded Christ more than Calvin, I prove thus: —

Dr. Owen, (the pious and learned champion of the Calvinists in the last century, whom you quote, p. 93,) speaking, in his *Treatise on Justification*, p. 222, of one justified at his conversion, says, "That God does indispensably require of him personal obedience, which may be called *his* evangelical righteousness. That *this* righteousness is pleadable* unto an acquitment against any charge from Satan, the world, or our own consciences. That upon *it* we shall be declared righteous in the last day; and, without *it*, none shall. And if any shall think meet from hence to conclude unto *an evangelical justification*, or call God's acceptance of *our* righteousness by that name, I shall by no means contend with them.† Whenever this inquiry is made, How a man that professeth evangelical faith in Christ shall be tried and judged; and whereon, as such, he shall be *justified?* we grant that it is, and must be, *by his own personal obedience.*"

This important quotation is produced by D. Williams, in his *Gospel Truth vindicated against Dr. Crisp's Opinions*, p. 149. It is introduced to confirm the following Gospel truth: "The Lord Jesus has of grace, for his own merits, promised to bring to heaven such as are partakers of true holiness, and do good works *perseveringly*. And he appoints these, as the way and means of a believer's obtaining salvation, requiring them as indispensable duties and qualifications, of all such whom he will save and bless; and excluding all that want and neglect them, or live under the power of what is contrary thereto." Here is evidently the pure doctrine of the Minutes, and the "undefiled religion" of St. James.

The same judicious author, in his preface, speaks thus upon the subject of our controversy: "The revival of these [Dr. Crisp's] errors must not only exclude that ministry as legal which is most apt to secure the practical power of religion, but also render unity among Christians impossible. Mutual censures are unavoidable; while one side [the sober Puritans] press *the terms* of the Gospel, under its promises and threats, for which they are accused as enemies to Christ and grace; and the other side [the followers of Dr. Crisp] ignorantly set up *the name* of Christ and free grace against *the government of Christ and the rule of judgment*.

"I believe many abettors of these mistakes are honestly zealous for the honour of free grace, but have not light to see how God has provided for this. By this pretence Antinomianism corrupted Germany: it bid fair to overthrow Church and state in New England; and by its stroke at the vitals of religion it alarmed most of the pulpits in England. Many of our ablest pens were engaged against these errors: — as Mr. Gataker, Mr. Rutherford, Anthony Burgess, the provincial Synod at London — with very many others, whose labours God was pleased to bless to the stopping the attempts of Dr. Crisp, by name opposed by the aforesaid divines, Saltmarsh, Eaton, &c.

---

* I have shown in the Vindication how David and Ezekiel pleaded this righteousness before God. Another instance of this plea I lately found in Nehemiah. That man of God, after describing his royal hospitality, and tender regard for the poor, says," Think upon me, my God, for good, according to all that I have done for this people," Nehemiah v, 19.

† Who indeed would contend with them, but such as are not afraid of flying in the face of St. Paul and Jesus Christ? See Romans ii,18, and Matthew vii, 37.

"To the grief of such as perceive the tendency of these principles, we are engaged in a new opposition, or must betray the truth as it is in Jesus. I believe many abettors of these notions have grace to preserve their minds and practices from their influence: but they ought to consider that the generality of mankind have no such antidote; and themselves need not fortify their own temptations, nor lose the defence which the wisdom of God has provided against remissness in duty, and sinful backslidings.

"In the present testimony of the *truth of the Gospel* I have studied plainness. To the best of my knowledge I have in nothing misrepresented Dr. Crisp's opinions, nor mistaken his sense: for most of them he oft studiously pleads: of each I could multiply proofs, and all of them are necessary for his scheme, although not consistent with all his other occasional expressions." I have carefully avoided any reflection on Dr. Crisp, whom I believe to be a holy man.

The whole work of D. Williams, and consequently the preceding quotations, have the remarkable sanction of the following certificate: "We, whose names are subscribed, do judge that our Rev. brother has, in all that is material, *fully* and *rightly* stated the truths and errors, mentioned as such, in the following treatise: and do account he has, in this work, done considerable service to the Church of Christ; adding our prayers, that these labours of his may be a mean for reclaiming those who have been misled into such dangerous opinions; and for establishing those that waver in any of these truths." Signed by near fifty Puritan ministers, the first of whom is William Bates; and the last Edmund Calamy, two of the greatest preachers in the last century.

The following Appendix closes the certificate. "I have by me near as many worthy names, such as Mr. Woodhouse, Mr. Hallet, Mr. Boys, &c, who have approved of this work. But I think this number sufficient to convince the world that the Presbyterian ministers, at least, espouse not the Antinomian dotages. Yea, I am credibly informed, that the most learned country ministers, of the Congregational persuasion, disallow the errors here opposed, and are amazed at such of their brethren in London as are displeased with this book."

Now, dear sir, you must either prove that what Dr. Owen, D. Williams, and such a cloud of Puritan divines consent to call *an evangelical justification in the last day, by our own personal obedience,* is not a justification; or, you must confess that you have given the world a true specimen of *Geneva logic,* when you have declared that "there is *not one* Puritan divine but what abhorred the doctrine of such a justification as full of rottenness and deadly poison." And you must do me the justice to acknowledge you did not give yourself time to weigh your words in the balance of brotherly kindness, when you accused me of "calumny and the grossest perversions, that perhaps ever proceeded from any author's pen," for asserting what I thought my quotations from Mr. Henry sufficiently proved, and what your groundless charge has obliged me fully to demonstrate. And now, permit me to apologize for the severity of your conduct toward me, by reminding my reader that your great Diana was in danger, and that on such a trying occasion, even a good man may be put into a hurry, and act, before he is aware, inconsistently with the Christian virtues which blazon his character.

D. Williams' *Gospel Truth Vindicated* might be confirmed by numberless quotations from Puritan authors, who directly or indirectly assert a second justification by works. Take one instance out of a thousand: — Anthony Burgess, fellow of Emmanuel college in Cambridge, (I think one of the ejected ministers,) speaking in his twelfth sermon of *obedience as a sign of grace*, concludes his discourse by this truly anti-Crispian paragraph: —

"Art thou *universal* in thy obedience? Then thou mayest take comfort. Otherwise, know if thou hast not respect to *all* the ways and duties required by God, thou wilt be confounded. Though with Ahab and Herod thou do *many things,* yet if not *all things,* confusion will be upon thee. O then how few are there who may claim a right to grace!* Many men have an external obedience only, and no internal; but most have a partial, and not entire, complete obedience; therefore it is that 'many are called, but few chosen.' Consider that terrible expression of St. James ii, 10, 11, where the apostle informs *believers* that if they are guilty but of that one sin, 'accepting of persons,' they are the transgressors of the law in general, which he farther urgeth by this assertion, 'He that keepeth all, and offendeth in one, is guilty of all;' not with the guilt of every particular sin, but in respect of the authority of the Lawgiver, according to that, 'Cursed is every one that continueth not in everything commanded by the law.' Seeing, therefore, God in regeneration does write his law in our hearts, which does seminally contain the exercise of all holy actions, so that there cannot be an instance of any godly duty of which God does not infuse a principle in us: and seeing glorification will be universal of soul and body, in all parts and faculties, how necessary is it that sanctification should be universal! Take heed therefore that the works of grace in thee be not abortive or monstrous, wanting essential and necessary parts. Let not thy ship be drowned by any one leak."

From this alarming quotation it appears holy Calvinist ministers saw, a hundred years ago, that if believers did not secure St. James' justification by universal obedience, the *works of grace* in them would prove *abortive,* their hopes would *perish,* their ship would *sink,* though by *one leak* only; and consequently they would be condemned as Hymeneus and Philetus in the day of judgment. And let nope complain of the legality of this doctrine; for our Lord himself fully preached it, when he said, *"Except* a man forsake all, he cannot be my disciple."

Take another instance of a later date. The Rev. Mr. Haweis, that has distinguished himself among the zealous ministers of our Church who have espoused Calvin's sentiments, speaks thus to the point, in his comment on Matthew xii, 37: "Not an idle word passes without the Divine notice, but we must answer for it at the day of judgment. With what circumspection then should we keep the door of our lips, when our eternal state is to be determined thereby, and our words must all be produced at the bar of God as evidences of our justification or condemnation, and sentence proceed accordingly!" If this is not maintaining, at least *indirectly,* justification by works in the day of judgment, my reason fails, and I can no more understand how two and two make four.

The Rev. Mr. Madan himself, if I am not mistaken, grants what I contend for, in the very title of the sermon quoted in my motto, *Justification by* WORKS *reconciled with Justification by* FAITH, &c, but much more in the following passages, which I extract from it: —

---

* Some of the Puritans understood by *grace* a state of justification and sanctification.

Five Checks To Antinomianism

"In every person that is justified, three particulars concur, (1.) The *meritorious cause* of our justification, which is Christ. (2.) The *instrumental cause*, which is faith. And then the justification in the text. [*Ye see how by works a man is justified, and not by faith only,*] which is to be understood in a *declarative* sense — no person being justified in Paul's sense, that is not also in the sense of our text," that is, in the sense of St. James.

The truth contained in this last sentence is the rampart of practical Christianity, and the ground of the Minutes. If Mr. Madan considers what his proposition necessarily implies, I am persuaded he will not only side with Mr. Wesley against the Benedictine monk, but also, give up Calvinism, with which his assertion is no more reconcilable, than it is with what you, sir, call "a *winter* (and I beg leave to name an *Antinomian)* state," in which we are supposed to be justified in Paul's sense, while we fly in the face of St. James by the commission of adultery and murder.

The same eminent minister asks, in the same discourse, "What does it profit though a man say he hath faith, and have not works? Can faith save him? [Can faith save David in Uriah's bed? Can it save Solomon worshipping Ashtaroth, perhaps with his seven hundred wives and three hundred concubines?] that is, such a faith as has not works, as is not productive of the fruit of the Spirit in the *heart* and *life?* Is this saving faith? *Certainly not;* for such a faith wants the evidence of its being true and real, and nothing but true faith can save. If my faith does not produce the proper fruits, it is no better than the devil's faith. We have no Scripture testimony of our being any other than *the devil's children,* unless we evidence the truth of our faith by showing forth the genuine fruits and works of faith. All this the apostle confirms, v, 20, 26; 'Faith without works is dead. As the body without the spirit is dead, so faith without works is dead also.'"

This excellent passage is the demolition of Calvinism, and the very doctrine of the Minutes, if you except the article about the word *merit*, which I do not read in our pious author's sermon. However, p. 12, I find the word *deserve* in the following important question: — "How can we, not only escape the penalty threatened, but *deserve* the *rewards* promised under the law?" And as I do not understand "splitting a hair," I think *that the two expressions,* MERITING *and* DESERVING, *when duly considered, are* NOT *as wide as east is from west:* and I fear, that if Mr. Wesley is a heretic for using the former at a conference among friends, the Rev. Mr. Madan is not quite orthodox, for using the latter in St. Vedast's church before friends and enemies. But as this question may turn upon some nicety of the English language, which, as a foreigner, I have not yet observed, I drop it, to obviate an objection.

You will perhaps say, honoured sir, that all the above-mentioned authors, being sound Calvinists, hold *your* election, and that you could produce passages out of their writings absolutely irreconcilable with the preceding quotations. To this I reply, that a volume of such passages, instead of invalidating the doctrine which I maintain, would only prove, that the peculiarities of Calvin are absolutely irreconcilable with St. James' undefiled religion; and that even the most judicious Calvinists cannot make their scheme hang tolerably together.

I hope, honoured sir, the preceding pages will convince my readers that you have spoken unwarily, when you have asserted, "that there is *not one* of the many hundred Puritan divines, but what abhorred my doctrine as full of rottenness;" and that the author of *Goliah slain* has been rather too forward in *challenging me "to* fix upon one Protestant minister, either Puritan, or of the Church of England, who, to the reign of Charles the Second, held the doctrine I have been contending for."

Your challenge, dear sir, provokes me to imitation; and I conclude this letter by challenging you, in my turn, to fix upon a man who will expose your mistakes more bluntly, and yet esteem and love you more cordially, than, honoured and dear sir, your most obedient servant, in St. James' pure religion.

J. FLETCHER.

LETTER IV.

To Richard Hill, Esq.

HONOURED AND DEAR SIR, — Before I take my leave of the Puritan writers, you will permit me to make some observations upon the fault you find with my quoting one of them. Page 94, you introduce a *judicious, worthy, reverend friend,* charging me with having "most notoriously perverted the quotation" which I produced out of Flavel, (*Vindication,* p. 41*) and you stamp with your approbation his exclamation on the subject, "Could you have expected such disingenuity from Madeley?"

Now, dear sir, full of *disingenuity* as you suppose me to be, I can yet act with *frankness.* And to convince you of it I publicly stand to my quotation, and charge your worthy friend with — what shall I call it? — a gross mistake. My quotation I had from that judicious Puritan divine, D. Williams, who, far from *notoriously perverting* the sense of the ministers that drew up Flavel's preface, has weakened it by leaving out some excellent anti-Crispian sentences. Permit me to punish your friend for his hasty charge, by laying the whole passage before my readers; reminding them, that only the sentences enclosed in crotchets, [   ] are quoted in the Vindication.

A body of seven eminent divines, all friends, it seems, to Dr. Crisp, but enemies to his *Antinomian dotages,* charitably endeavour to apologize for him, at the same time that they recommend Flavel's treatise on *Mental Errors* in general, and on *Antinomianism* in particular, where Dr. Crisp is opposed by name. Having mentioned two similar propositions of his, viz. "Salvation is not the end of any thing we do." and, "We are to act *from* life, and not *for* life," they bear this full testimony against the absurdity which they contain: —

---

* [33]

"[It were in effect to abandon human nature,] and to sin against a very fundamental law of our creation, not to intend our own felicity; it were to make our first and most deeply fundamental duty, in one great, essential branch of it, our sin; viz. To take the Lord for our God: for to take him for our God most essentially includes our taking him for our Supreme Good, which we all know is included in the notion of *the last end.* It were to make it unlawful to strive against all sin, and particularly against sinful aversion from God, wherein lies the very death of the soul, or the sum of its misery; or to strive after perfect conformity to God in holiness, and the full fruition of him, wherein the soul's final blessedness does principally consist.

"[It were to teach us to violate the great precepts of the Gospel:] "Repent, that your sins may be blotted out: strive to enter in at the strait gate: work out your own salvation with fear and trembling." To obliterate the patterns and precedents set before us in the Gospel: "We have believed in Jesus Christ, that we might be justified — I keep under my body lest I should be a castaway — that thou mayest save thyself, and them that hear thee."

"[It were to suppose us bound to do more for the salvation of others than our own] salvation. We are required to save others with fear, plucking them out of the fire. Nay, we were not (by this rule strictly understood) so much as to pray for our own salvation, which is a doing somewhat; when, no doubt, we are to pray for the success of the Gospel, to this purpose, on behalf of other men.

"[It were to make all the threatenings of eternal death, and promises of eternal life, we find in the Gospel of our blessed Lord, useless, as motives to shun the one and obtain the other:] for they can be motives no way, but as the escaping of the former, and the attainment of the other, have with us the place and consideration of an end.

"[It makes what is mentioned in the Scripture as the character and commendation of the most eminent saints, a fault,] as of Abraham., Isaac, and Jacob; that 'they sought the better and heavenly country;' and plainly declared that they did so, which necessarily implies their making it their end."

Now, honoured sir, it lies upon you to prove, that because Mr. Williams and I have not produced all that makes against you, we are guilty of a "most notorious perversion"* of the quotation. If you affirm that the *perversion* I am

---

* Want of argument in a bad cause, which people will defend "at all events," (if I may use the words which Mr. Hill too hastily lends me in his book, but justly claims as his own in the "errata,") obliges them to fly to personal charges. *Zelus arma ministrat.* Their Diana is in danger. They must raise dust, and make a noise, to divert the attention of the reader from the point. Who knows but she may escape in the hurry? At the end of the above-mentioned quotation I had added three lines, to throw some light upon the last clause, which D. Williams had cut off too short. As I did not enclose them in commas, it never entered into my mind that any body would charge me with presenting them as a quotation, nor do they in the least "misrepresent," much less "pervert" the sense of the author. Upon this, however, my opponent brings me to a trial. But if, at p. 97, he lets me escape, without condemning me point-blank for "forging quotations," he is not so mild, p. 27. I have observed in the Second Check, p. 100, [97], that Mr. Wesley in his Minutes guards the foundation of the Gospel by the two clauses, where he mentions the exclusion of the "merit of works" in point of salvation, and "believing in Christ." The two clauses I present in one point of view, in the very words of the Minutes, although not in the tense of the verb "believing," thus: "Not by the merit of works," but by "believing in Christ." My opponent is pleased here to overlook the commas, which show, that I produce two different places of the Minutes; and then he improves his own oversight thus: "Forgeries

charged with, consists in saying, that the divines who wrote Flavel's preface were *shocked* at Dr. Crisp's doctrine, when they nevertheless apologize for his person; I reply, that their apology confirms my assertion, even more than their arguments; for they say, "It is likely the doctor meant, [just what Mr. Wesley does,] that we shall not work FOR life ONLY, without aiming at working FROM life ALSO. For it is not tolerable charity to suppose that one would deliberately say, *that salvation is not the end of any good work we do, or that we are not to work for life in the rigid sense of the words."* And they profess their hopes, that, "upon consideration, he would presently unsay it, [namely, the absurd proposition, *We are not to work* FOR *life,*] being calmly reasoned with."

Thus hoped those pious divines concerning Dr. Crisp: and thus I once hoped also concerning his admirers. But, alas! experience has damped my hope; for, when they have been "calmly reasoned with," they have shown themselves much more ready to *unsay* what they had said right, than what the doctor had said wrong; and to this day they publicly defend those *Antinomian dotages,* which the authors of Flavel's preface could not believe Dr. Crisp could possibly mean, even when he preached and wrote them.

---

of this kind have long passed for no crime with Mr. Wesley. I did not think you would have followed him in these ungenerous artifices, which must unavoidably sink the writer in our esteem. But I am sorry to say, sir, that this is not the only stratagem of this sort which you have made use of. Instance your bringing in Mr. Whitefield as a maintainer of a second justification by works," &c, &c. The bare mention of such groundless accusations being a sufficient refutation of them, I shall close this note by observing, that the pure religion which I vindicate is too well grounded on Scripture to need the support, either of the pretended forgeries which my opponent contrives for me, or of the blackening charges which he is forced to produce for want of better arguments.

In almost any other but my pious opponent, I should think that this severity proceeded from palpable disingenuity; but my respect for him does not permit me to entertain such a thought. I urge for his excuse the inconceivable strength of prejudice, and the fatal tendency of his favourite system. Yes, O Calvinism, upon thee I charge the mistakes of my worthy antagonist! If at any time his benevolent temper is soured, thy leaven has done it. It is by thy powerful influence that he discovers "a forgery," where there is not so much as the printer's omission of a comma to countenance his discovery. It is through the mists which thou raisest that he sees in the works of one of our most correct authors, nothing but "a regular series of inconsistencies, a wheel of contradiction running round and round again." Thou lendest him thy deceitful glass, when he looks at my Second Check, and cries out, "Base and shocking slander! Acrimonious, bitter, and low sneers! Horrid misrepresentations, and notorious perversions! Abominable beyond all the rest! A wretched spirit of low sarcasm and slanderous banter runs through the whole book," which contains "more than a hundred close pages, as totally void of Scriptural argument as they are replete with calumny, gross perversions, equivocations," — and a "doctrine full of rottenness and deadly poison, the spurious offspring of the man of sin, begotten out of the scarlet whore."

I beg my readers would not think the worse of my opponent's candour, on account of these severe charges. In one sense they appear to me very moderate; for who can wonder, that a good, mistaken man, who finds Calvin's everlasting, absolute, and unconditional reprobation in the mild oracles of the God of love, should find "forgery, vile slander, calumny, horrid perversions, deadly poison," &c, in my sharp Checks, and perpetual contradictions in Mr. Wesley's works? Are we not treated with remarkable kindness, in comparison of the merciful God whom we serve? Undoubtedly; for neither of us is yet so much as indirectly charged with contriving in cool blood, the murder of "one" man; much less with forming, from all eternity, the evangelical plan to save unconditionally by "free grace" the little flock of the elect, and damn unconditionally by "free wrath" the immense herd of the reprobates! and with spending near six thousand years in bringing about an irresistible decree, that the one shall absolutely go to heaven, let them do what they please to be damned; and that the other shall absolutely go to hell, and burn there to all eternity, let them do what they can to be saved!

Five Checks To Antinomianism

You express, honoured sir, a most extraordinary wish, p. 94. Speaking of *Flavel's Discourse upon Mental Errors*, which is also called *A Blow at the Root*, you say, "I should have been glad could I have transcribed the whole discourse." But as you have not done it, I shall give *a blow at the root* of your system, by presenting you with an extract of the second Appendix, which is a pretty large treatise full against Antinomianism.

"The design of the following sheets," says that great Puritan divine, in the discourse you should be glad wholly to transcribe, "is to free the grace of God from the dangerous errors, which fight against it under its own colours; to prevent the seduction of some that stagger; and to vindicate my own doctrine. The Scripture, foreseeing there would arise such a sort of men in the Church as would wax wanton against Christ, and turn his grace into lasciviousness, has not only precautioned us in general to beware of such opinions as corrupt the doctrine of free grace: 'Shall we continue in sin that grace may abound? God forbid:' but has marked those very opinions by which it would be abused, and made abundant provision against them. As namely, (1.) All vilifying expressions of God's holy law, Romans vii. (2.) All opinions inclining men to the neglect of the duties of obedience, under pretence of free grace and liberty by Christ, James ii; Matthew xxv. (3.) All opinions neglecting sanctification as the evidence of justification, which is the principal scope of St. John's first epistle.

"Notwithstanding such is the *wickedness* of some, and *weakness* of others, that in all ages (especially in the last and present) men have notoriously corrupted the doctrine of free grace, to the great reproach of Christ, scandal of the world, and hardening of the enemies of the reformation. 'Behold, (says Contzen the Jesuit,) the fruit of Protestantism, and their Gospel preaching.'

"The Gospel makes sin more odious than the law did, and discovers the punishment of it in a more dreadful manner. 'For if the word spoken by angels was steadfast, and every disobedience received a just recompense of reward, how shall we escape if we neglect so great salvation? It shows us our encouragements to holiness greater than ever; and yet corrupt nature will still abuse it. The more luscious the food is, the more men are apt to surfeit upon it.

"This perversion of free grace is justly chargeable both upon *wicked* and *good* men. WICKED MEN corrupt it designedly, that, by entitling God to their sins, they might sin the more quietly. So the Nicolaitans, and school of Simon; the Gnostics, in the very dawning of Gospel light; and he that reads the preface of learned Mr. Gataker's book, will find that some Antinomians of our days are not much behind the vilest of them. One of them cries out, 'Away with the law! It cuts off a man's legs, and then bids him walk.' Another says, 'That if a man, by the Spirit, know himself to be in a state of grace, though he commit murder,* God sees no sin in him.'

"But others† there are, whose judgments are unhappily tainted with those loose doctrines; yet being, in the main GODLY PERSONS, they dare not take the liberty to sin, or live in the neglect of known duties, though their

---

* This is, I fear, the very doctrine of your fourth letter, where an impenitent murderer is represented as complete in Christ, &c.
† Here my worthy opponent is exactly described by Flavel.

- 229 -

principles too much incline that way. But though they dare not, others will, who imbibe *corrupt* notions from them; and *the renowned piety* of the authors will be no antidote against the danger; but make the poison operate the more powerfully, by receiving it in such a vehicle. Now it is highly probable these men were charmed into these opinions upon such accounts as these: —

"I. Some of them might have felt in themselves the anguish of a perplexed conscience under sin, and not being able to live under the terrors of the law, might too hastily snatch at such doctrines which promise them relief and ease. (2.) Others have been induced to espouse these opinions from the excess of their zeal against the errors of the Papists. (3.) Others have been sucked into those quicksands of Antinomian errors, by lathering their own fancies upon the Holy Spirit. (4.) And it is not unlike, but a comparative weakness of mind, meeting with a fervent zeal for Christ, may induce others to espouse such *taking* and *plausible*, though pernicious doctrines.

"Let all good men beware of such opinions and expressions as give a handle to wicked men to abuse the grace of God, which haply the author himself dares not do, and may strongly hope others may not do: but if the principle will yield it, it is in vain to think corrupt nature will not catch at it, and make a vile use, and dangerous improvement of it!

"For example: If such a principle as this be asserted before the world, 'That men need not fear that any or all the sins they commit shall do them any hurt:'* let the author warn and caution his readers, [as the Antinomian† author of that expression has done,] not to abuse this doctrine; it is to no purpose, the doctrine itself is full of dangerous consequences, and wicked men have the best skill to draw them forth to cherish their lusts. That which the author might design for the relief of the distressed, quickly turns into poison in the bowels of the wicked. Nor can we excuse it by saying any Gospel truth may be thus abused; for this is none of that number, but a principle that gives offence to the godly and encouragement to the ungodly. And so much as to the rise and occasion of Antinomian errors.

"II. Let us view next some of the chief errors of Antinomians. (1.) Some make justification to be an eternal act of God, and affirm that the elect were justified before the world had a being. Others, that they were justified at the time of Christ's death: with these Dr. Crisp harmonizes. (2.) That justification by faith is no more than a manifestation to us, of what was done before we had a being. (3.) That men ought not to question whether they believe or no. (*Saltmarsh on Free Grace*, p. 92, 95.) (4.) That believers are not bound to mourn for sin, because it was pardoned before it was committed; and pardoned sin is no sin. (*Eaton's Honeycomb of Justification*, p. 446.) (5.) That God sees no sin in believers, whatsoever sins they commit. (6.) That God is not angry with the elect, and that to say he smites them for their sins is an injurious reflection upon his justice. This is avouched generally in all their writings. (7.) That by God's laying our iniquities

---

* My worthy opponent has publicly advanced, not only that sin, even adultery and murder, does not hurt the pleasant children, but that it even *works for their good.*
† Dr. Crisp, who was publicly called *an Antinomian* by the Puritans, and his tenets *loose, corrupt, and pernicious doctrine; Antinomian dotages, &c.*

upon Christ, he became as completely sinful as we, and we as completely righteous as Christ. (*Dr. Crisp*, p. 270.) (8.) That no sin can do believers any hurt, nor must they do any duty for their own salvation. (9.) That the new covenant is not made properly with us, but with Christ for us; and that this covenant is all of it a promise, having no condition on our part. They do not absolutely deny that faith, repentance, and obedience are *conditions* in the new covenant; but say, they are no conditions on our side, but Christ's, and that he repented, believed, and obeyed for us. (*Saltmarsh on Free Grace*, p. 126.) (10.) They speak very slightingly of trying ourselves by marks and signs of grace. Saltmarsh calls it "a low, carnal way:" but the New-England Antinomians call it a fundamental error, to make sanctification an evidence of justification. They say, that the darker our sanctification is, the brighter is our justification.

"I look upon such doctrines to be of a very dangerous nature; and their malignity and contagion would certainly spread much farther than it does, had not God provided two powerful antidotes.

"1. The scope and current of the Scriptures. They speak of the elect as 'children of wrath' during their unregenerate state. They frequently discover God's anger, and tell us, his castigatory rods are laid upon them for their sins. They represent sin as the greatest evil; most opposite to the glory of God and good of his saints. They call the saints to mourn for their *sins*, &c. They put the people of God to the trial of their interest in Christ, by signs and marks from the divers branches of sanctification. They infer *duties* from privileges; and therefore the Antinomian dialect is a *wild note*, which the generality of serious Christians do easily distinguish from the Scripture language.

"2. The experience and practice of the saints greatly secure us from the spreading malignity of Antinomianism. They acknowledge that before their conversion they were equal in sin and misery with the vilest wretches in the world. They fear nothing more than sin. They are not only sensible that God sees sin in them, but they admire his patience, that they are not consumed for it. They urge his commands and threatenings, as well as promises, upon their own hearts to promote sanctification. They excite themselves to duty and watchfulness against sin. They encourage themselves by the rewards of obedience, knowing their 'labour is not in vain in the Lord.' And he that shall tell them, *their sins can do them no hurt, or their duties no good,* speaks to them not only as a barbarian, but in such a language as their souls abhor. The zeal and love of Christ being kindled in their souls, they have no patience to hear such doctrines as so greatly derogate from his glory, under a pretence of honouring and exalting him. It wounds and grieves their very hearts to see the world hardened in their prejudices against reformation, and a gap opened to all licentiousness. But notwithstanding this double antidote, we find, by daily experience, such doctrines too much obtaining in the professing world, *Tantum religio suadere malorum.*

"For my own part, He that searcheth my heart is witness: I would rather choose to have my right hand wither, and my tongue rot within my mouth, than to speak one word, or write one line, to cloud the free grace of God. Let it arise and shine in its meridian glory. None owes more to it, or expects more from it, than I do; and what I write in this controversy is to vindicate it from those opinions, which, under pretence of exalting it, do really militate against it."

Then follows a prolix refutation of the above-mentioned Antinomian errors, most of which necessarily flow from your second and fourth letters. When our pious author attacks them as a disciple of St. James, he carries all before him: but when he encounters them as an admirer of Calvin, his hands hang down, Amalek prevails, and a shrewd logician could, without any magical power, force him to confess, that most of the errors which he so justly opposes are the natural consequences of *unconditional* election, *particular* redemption, *irresistible* grace, Calvinian imputation of righteousness to impenitent murderers, the *infallible* perseverance of believers who defile their fathers' beds, and, in a word, salvation *finished* for all the "pleasant children," who go on frowardly in the way of their own heart. Thus it would appear that Calvinism is "the ωρωτον ψευδος," to use Mr. Flavel's words, *"The radical and prolific error from which most of the rest are spawned."*

He concludes his anti-Crispian treatise by the following truly Christian paragraph' "I call the Searcher of hearts to witness that I have not intermeddled with this controversy of Antinomianism, out of any delight I take in polemic studies, or an unpeaceable contradicting humour, but out of pure zeal for the glory and truths of God, for the vindication and defence whereof I have been necessarily engaged therein. And having discharged my duty thus far, I now resolve to return, if God permit me, to my much more agreeable studies: still maintaining my Christian charity for those whom I oppose, not doubting but I shall meet those in heaven from whom I am forced in lesser things to dissent upon earth."

While my heart is warmed by the love which breathes through the last words of Mr. Flavel's book, permit me to tell you, that I cordially adopt them with respect to dear Mr. Shirley and yourself, hoping that if you think yourself obliged "to cut off all intercourse and friendship with me" upon earth, on account of what you are pleased to call my "disingenuity and gross perversions," you will gladly ascribe to the Lamb of God a common salvation truly finished in heaven, together with, honoured and dear sir, your most obedient servant, in the pure Gospel of St. James,

J. FLETCHER.

LETTER V.

To Richard Hill, Esq.

HONOURED AND DEAR SIR, — I have hitherto endeavoured to show that the exploded doctrine of a second justification by works, (i.e. by the evidence or instrumentality of works,) in the day of judgment, is Scriptural, consonant to the doctrine of our Church, and directly or indirectly maintained, as by yourself, so by all anti-Crispian Puritan divines, whenever they regard St. James' holy doctrine more than Calvin's peculiar opinions. I shall now answer a most important question which you propose about it, p. 149. You introduce it by these words: —

"You cannot suppose that when Mr. Shirley said, *Blessed be God, neither Mr. Wesley nor any of his preachers,* (Mr. Olivers excepted,) *holds a second justification by works,* he intended to exclude good works in an evidential sense." Indeed, sir, I did suppose it; nor can I to this moment conceive how Mr. Shirley could lean toward Calvinism, if he were settled in St. James' doctrine of justification by the evidence of works. You proceed: —

"Neither Mr. Shirley, nor I, nor any Calvinist that I ever heard of, deny that a sinner is declaratively justified by works, both here and at the day of judgment." You astonish me, sir. Why then do you at the end of this very paragraph, find fault with me for saying, that it will be absurd in a man, set on the left hand as a rebellious subject of our heavenly King, to plead the works of Christ, when his own works are called for, as the only *evidences* according to which he must be justified or condemned? Why do you cry out in the fifth letter of your Review, "O shocking to tell! *Horresco referens,*" &c. Why do so many Calvinists shudder with horror because I have represented our Lord as condemning, by the evidence of works, (agreeably to his own express doctrine, Matthew xxv,) a practical Antinomian, a canting apostate, who had no good works to be *declaratively justified* by in the day of judgment? Why do you maintain, that when David committed adultery and murder he was "justified from all things; his sins past, present, and to come, were for ever and for ever cancelled?" And why do you (p. 70) call me a "snake that bites the Calvinist ministers," because I have exposed the Antinomianism of those preachers who, setting aside Christ's doctrine of justification by the evidence of works in the last day, give thousands to understand, that they shall then be abundantly justified by *righteousness imputed* in Calvin's way, and by nothing else? You go on: —

"Therefore, I say, if you utterly disclaim all human works, as the *procuring, meritorious* cause of justification, what need was there of addressing Mr. Shirley as you have done? Yea, what need was there of your making this point a matter of controversy at all? We are quite agreed both as to the expression and as to the meaning of it."

Are we indeed *quite agreed, both as to the expression* of a second justification by works in the day of judgment *and as to the meaning of it;* to which I once more set my seal, viz. that we shall be justified, *not by the merit, but by the evidence of works?* What a pity is it then, that you did not find this out till you came to the 149th page of your book! It would probably have saved you the trouble of writing it, and me the thankless office of exposing it.

However, it is but right I should requite your candid concession by answering your important question: "What need was there of making this point, [of justification by the evidence of works in the day of judgment,] a matter of controversy at all?" I will ingenuously tell you: I wanted an immovable point to fix my engine upon, in order to throw down your great Diana, and pull up by the roots the immense trees of Antinomian knowledge. And now you have so fully and repeatedly granted me the firm point which I desired, permit me, honoured sir, to throw myself at your feet, to return you thanks, and tell you that you are the happy prisoner of the truth which I vindicate.

"What do you mean?" What you little expect, dear sir, and what I think you cannot possibly avoid. Yes, whether you will or not, I must serve a friendly warrant, and "young ignorance" arrests you in the name of English logic, to make you publicly subscribe to the anti-Crispian propositions, which your Benedictine monk has rashly traduced. "I will never do it; I am ready to offer myself among the foremost of those true Protestants who could have burned against the doctrine of a second justification by works." Well then, sir, you shall go, not to the stake near Baliol college, but to "the ground and pillar of truth:" and that you may not make a needless resistance, I humbly presume to bind you before all the candid and judicious Calvinists in England, with the following *necessary consequences* of a capital doctrine, which, you tell us, "was never denied, either by Mr. Shirley, or yourself, or any Calvinist you ever heard of."

If we are *"justified* by works, i.e. by the evidence of works, both here and at the day of judgment," it follows, 1. That Mr. Wesley's doctrine, with respect to man's faithfulness in good works, is true; and that if a man (Judas for instance) is not "faithful in the unrighteous mammon, God will not give him the true riches" of glory. Though he should once have had faith enough to "leave all and follow Christ, his shipwrecked faith," sunk by bad works, "will profit him nothing." He shall as surely be condemned by the evidence of his unfaithfulness, as ever a highwayman was condemned upon the fullest evidence that he had robbed upon the highway.

2. The second proposition of the Minutes also stands now upon an immovable basis. "Every believer, till he comes to glory, works *for* as well as *from* life," since his works will appear as witnesses for or against him at the day of judgment, and life or death will be the certain consequence of their deposition.

3. The third proposition of the Minutes now shines like the meridian sun after an eclipse. Nothing is more false than the maxim, *That a man is to do nothing in order to justification,* either at conversion or in the last day. For the *work of faith* undoubtedly takes place in the day of conversion, agreeably to those words of St. Paul, "We have believed THAT we might be justified." And, if even Calvinists grant, that a sinner is "justified by the evidence of works, both here and at the day of judgment," it is indubitable that he must provide that evidence as there is opportunity; and that if even an apostle provides it not, he shall, notwithstanding his election, increase the number of those practical Antinomians, whose condemnation I have described in the Second Cheek. Hence appears also the error couched under the unguarded proposition which you advance, (p. 12.) "In the act of justification, we affirm good works have no place:" for the good work of faith has the important place of *an instrument,* when we are justified at our conversion; and the good work of love will have the place of *the chief witness,* by whose deposition we shall be justified in the great day.

You indeed produce the words of our Church: — "The thief did believe *only,* and the merciful God justified him;" but they make against you, for they intimate that the work of faith was previous to his justification. And that he was not saved *without works,* strictly speaking, although he was saved without *the merit* of works, I prove by your quotation from Bishop Cowper, *Justifying faith, whereby we are saved, cannot be without works;* and by these words of St. James and the Rev. Mr. Madan, adapted to the present case: Could "faith save him? i.e. such a faith as *hath not works;* as is not productive of the fruits of the Spirit in the heart and life? Is this saving faith? Certainly not." When our Church says, that he went to heaven without works, she means without the outward works which Pharisees trust to, such as receiving the sacraments, going to the temple, and giving alms; or she grossly contradicts St. James, Bishop Cowper, Mr. Madan, and herself. Therefore, notwithstanding all you have advanced, even the penitent thief's experience, who, as our Church says, *should have lost his salvation,* and consequently his justification and election, *if he had lived and not regarded the works of faith,* is "a formidable rampart" *for,* not *against,* St. James' undefiled religion. Again:

4. When, in the *review of the whole affair,* Mr. Wesley says, that "he who now believes in Christ with a loving, obedient heart, is now accepted of God," what does he say more than you, and your favourite bishop, who tells us, (p. 12,) "That justifying faith, whereby we are saved, *cannot* be without good works; for faith worketh by love?" Does it not evidently follow, from your own, as well as Mr. Wesley's position, that while the incestuous Corinthian defiled his father's bed, his living, justifying faith had degenerated into a dead, devilish faith? agreeably to that evangelically-legal proposition of Mr. Madan, "If my faith does not produce the proper fruits, it is no better than the devil's faith:" whence it necessarily follows, that the devil's faith is justifying, or that the Corinthian backslider was condemned; and consequently, that Calvinism and Antinomianism, the grand pillars of defiled religion, are two broken reeds.

5. It is now an indubitable truth, that a sincere heathen, who never heard the name of Christ, and nevertheless "feareth God and worketh righteousness, according to his light, is accepted of him:" for, if he perseveres, he will be justified in the last day by *the evidence* of his works of righteousness; and he is now justified by *the instrumentality* of his faith in the light of his dispensation; for this light, when we receive it by faith, if we may believe those excellent mystics,* St. John and St. Paul, is *"Christ* in us, the hope of glory," John i, 5, 9; Colossians i, 27; Ephesians iii, 27, and v, 14.

6. Nor can you now justly refuse to clear Mr. Wesley of the charge of heresy, because he says, *Salvation is not by the merit of works, but by works as a condition:*

---

* The word *mysticism,* like the word *enthusiasm,* may be used in a good or bad sense. I am no more ashamed of the true mystics, i.e. those who fathom the deep mysteries of inward religion, than of the true enthusiasts, those who are really inspired by the grace and love of God. When I said that Solomon was the great Jewish mystic, I took the word mystic in a good sense; if all are mystics who preach *Christ in us,* and *Christ the Light of the world,* (as you intimate in your Five Letters,) I affirm, that St. Paul and St. John are two of the greatest mystics in the world. And when I intimated, that Solomon's Song is a *mystical* book, and that the Rev. Mr. Romaine has given a *mystical,* and in general edifying explanation of the one hundred and seventh Psalm; I no more insulted those good men than our Church reflects upon our Lord, when she says, that "matrimony represents to us the *mystical* union between Christ and his Church." If Mr. Wesley has spoken against mysticism, it is undoubtedly against that which is wild and unscriptural; for he has shown us his approbation of rational and Scriptural mysticism, by publishing very edifying extracts from the works of the great German and English mystics, Kempis and Mr. Law. Permit me to recommend to you what Mr. Hartley, a clergyman whom you have quoted with honour, has written in defence of the mystics; and to remind you, that, abroad, those who go a little deeper into inward Christianity than the generality of their neighbours, are called pietists, or mystics, as commonly as they are called Methodists in England. On the preceding accounts I hope, that when Mr. Wesley, or Mr. Shirley, shall again condemn mysticism, they will particularly observe that it is only unscriptural and irrational mysticism which they explode.

for in the present case where is the difference between the word *evidence*, which you use, with Dr. Guise, Mr. Wesley, and me; and the word *condition*, which Mr. Wesley uses, and our Church, and most of the Puritan divines? An example will enforce my appeal to your candour: You sit upon the bench as a magistrate, and a prisoner stands at the bar: you say to him, "You are charged with calumny, forgery, and gross perversions; but you shall be acquitted, on *condition* that some of your reputable neighbours give you a good character." A lawyer checks you for using the treasonable word *condition*, insisting you must say, that the prisoner shall be acquitted or condemned, according to the *evidence* which his creditable neighbours will give of his good behaviour. You turn to the bar, and say, "Prisoner, did you understand me?" "Yes, sir," replies he, "as well as the gentleman who stops your honour." "That is enough," say you, "let us not *dispute about words;* I am persuaded the court understands we all mean that the acquittal or condemnation of the prisoner will entirely turn upon the deposition of proper witnesses."

7. With regard to the word *merit* I hope our controversy is at an end for Mr. Wesley and I, or to speak your own language, *old Mordecai and young Ignorance,* freely grant what Bishop Hopkins and you assert, (*Review*, p. 42,) namely, that "in all *proper merit* there must be an equivalence, or at least a proportion of worth between the work and the reward; and that the obedience we perform cannot be said, without *a grand impropriety*, to *merit* any reward from God." But you must also grant us, that if our Lord, speaking after the manner of men, by *a grand catechresis,*[*] a very condescending impropriety, frequently uses the word *meriting*, or *deserving*, we may without heresy use it after him.

Should you ask me how I can prove that our Lord ever used it, I reply, that if he used again and again words answering to it, as face answers to face in a glass, it is just as if he had used the English word *merit*, or Mr. Wesley's Latin word *meritum*: and to prove that he did so I appeal to the first Greek lexicon you will meet with. I suppose it is that of Schrevelius, because it is the most common all Europe over. Look for *mereor*, (to *merit* or *deserve*,) and you will find that the correspondent Greek is μισθον φερειν, literally *to carry a reward*, and αξιος ειναι, *to be worthy;* Αξια answers to *meritum, merit;* and αξιως to m*erito, deservedly*, or *according to one's merit.*

To prove, therefore, that our Lord did not scruple to use the word *merit* in an improper sense, I need only prove that he did not scruple applying the words Greek μισθος and αξιος to man. Take some instances of both: —

1. Matthew xx, 8, "Give them τον μισθον, *their hire*, or *reward.*" And again Matthew ver. 12, "Your *reward* (μισθος) is great in heaven," &c. Hence the apostle calls God (μισθαποδοτης) *the Rewarder;* and Moses is said "to look to (μισθαποδοσιαν) *the recompense of reward*," Hebrews xi, 6, 26. And the word μισθαποδοσια, *the bestowing of a reward*, as much answers to the word μισθοφορια, *the carrying of a reward*, or *merit*, as the relative words which necessarily suppose one another. He, therefore, that uses the former without

---

[*] A figure of speech, which consists in using a word in an improper sense, as when unfaithful ministers are called "dogs that cannot bark."

scruple, makes himself quite ridiculous before unprejudiced people if he scruples using the latter; much more if he thinks the doing it is *a dreadful heresy*.

2. As for the other word (αξιος) *meriting, deserving,* or *worthy,* it is as Scriptural as any word in the Bible. You find it used both in a proper and in an improper sense in the following scriptures: — (1.) In a PROPER sense: "The labourer is *worthy of,* or *merits,* his hire, Luke x, 7. *Worthy,* or *deserving,* stripes, Luke xii, 48. *Worthy of,* or *meriting* death, Acts xxi, 11. They have shed the blood of thy saints, and thou hast given them blood to drink, for they are *worthy:"* that is, they *merit,* they *deserve* it, Revelation xvi, 6. (2.) In an IMPROPER sense, which you represent as heretical: "They shall walk with me in white, for they *are worthy,* Revelation iii, 4. Inquire who *is worthy,* Matthew x, 11. *Worthy* of me, Matthew x, 37. They that were bidden *were not worthy,* Matthew xxii, 8. *Worthy* to escape these things, Luke xxi, 36. *Worthy* to obtain that world," Luke xx, 35, &c, &c.

In all these passages the original word is αξιος, *worthy, meriting,* or *deserving.* Bishop Cowper, therefore, whom you quote in your Five Letters, p. 26, spoke with uncommon rashness when he said, "No man led by the Spirit of Jesus, did ever use this word of *merit,* [i. e. αξιος ειναι] as applying to man. It is the proud speech of antichrist. Search the Scriptures, and ye shall see that none of all those who speak by Divine inspiration did ever use it: yea, the godly fathers always abhorred it." What! the sacred writers "never used the word αξιος ειναι!" "The godly fathers always abhorred" an expression which the Holy Ghost so frequently makes use of! Christ himself' spoke by the proud spirit of antichrist!" When I see such camels obtruded upon the Church, and swallowed down by thousands as glib truth, I am cut to the heart, and, in a pang of sorrow and shame, groan, "From such divinity, good Lord, deliver me, my worthy opponent, and all real Protestants!"

To this Mr. Rowland Hill answers beforehand, in his *Friendly Remarks,* p. 28. This is "a bad criticism upon the word αξιος, which more properly means *meet* or *fit."* Now, sir, to your bare assertion I oppose, (1.) All the Greek lexicons. (2.) The testimony of Beza, Calvin's successor, who speaking of the word αξιος, says, It is *properly* used of that which is of equal weight and importance. (3.) The testimony of Leigh, another learned Calvinist, who, in his *Critica Sacra,* says, "αξιος has its name from αγειν, *a trahendo: Quæ preponderant lancem attrahunt;* and is a metaphor taken from balances, when one scale doth counterpoise another." And speaking of αξιοω, a word derived from αξιος, he adds, "It signifieth when either *reward* or *punishment* is given according to the proportion of *merit."* And this he proves, by 1 Timothy v, 17, "Let the elders that rule well be counted *worthy* of double honour: for the Scripture says, The labourer is *worthy* of his reward."

When I see the learned Calvinists forced to grant all we contend for, I wish that no Protestant may any longer expose his prejudice, in denying what is absolutely undeniable, viz. That Christ and his apostles assert, some men *merit,* or *are worthy* of rewards. Taking care, therefore, never to fix to those Scriptural words the idea of *proper* worthiness, or *merit of condignity,* let us no longer fight against Christ, by saying, they are in no sense worthy, whom Christ himself *makes, accounts, and calls* WORTHY; yea, whom he gloriously *rewards* as such.

8. As for this modest proposition of the Minutes, "It is a doubt if God justifies any one that never did fear him, and work righteousness," it stands now

established by your concessions, not as matter of doubt, but as a matter of fact, if we speak of justification in the hour of conversion, or in the day of judgment. For, with respect to the former, you justly observe, (p. 12,) that "the faith whereby we are saved," and consequently justified, "cannot be without good works." And with regard to the latter, you say, (p. 149,) "What need is there of making our justification, by the evidence of works in the day of judgment, a matter of controversy at all? We are quite agreed that a sinner is declaratively justified by works." Now, honoured sir, if he is justified by *works*, it is undoubtedly by works of *righteousness;* unless it could be proved that he may be justified by works of *unrighteousness,* by adultery and murder.

9. It is likewise evident from your own concessions, that "talking of a justified, or a sanctified state," without paying a due regard to good works, *tends to mislead men,* and actually misleads thousands. If Judas, for instance, when he neglected good works, which are the *mark* of our first, and the *instrument* of our second justification, trusted to what was done in the moment, in which he was effectually called to leave all, and follow Jesus, he grossly deceived himself: or if he depended upon imputed righteousness, when he neglected personal holiness, he built upon the loosest sand.

The seasonableness of Mr. Wesley's caution in this respect will strike you, honoured sir, if you cast your eyes upon the numbers of fallen believers, who once, like obedient Judas, left all to follow Christ; but having resumed their besetting sin, like the apostolic traitor, now sell their Saviour and election, perhaps for a less valuable consideration than he did. However, they were once in a justified and sanctified state, and Mr. Hill tells them, that "in the act of justification good works have no place," and insinuates, that adulterers and murderers may be in the winter season of a sanctified state; therefore they reasonably conclude, that they are still justified and sanctified. Thus they live, and if God does not send them an honest Nathan, or if when he comes they stop their ears, and cry out, Heresy, thus like Judas they will die.

With respect to the last clause of the Minutes, you must acknowledge, "that we are every moment pleasing or displeasing to God, according to the whole of our inward tempers and outward behaviour:" or, to clothe Mr. Wesley's doctrine in words in which you agree with me, you must confess, that, "as we may die every hour, and every moment, we are liable to be every hour and every moment justified, or condemned, by the evidence of our works."* This is evident, if you consider St. Paul's words, "Without faith it is impossible to please God;" and if you do not recant what you say, (*Review,* p. 12,) "Justifying faith [the faith by which we please God] *cannot* be without good works." You must therefore prove that adultery, treachery, and murder, are *good works,* and by that means openly plead for Belial, Ball, and Beelzebub; or you must grant, that when David committed those crimes he had not justifying faith, and consequently did not please God. And the moment you grant this, you set your seal to the last proposition of the Minutes, which you esteem most contrary, and I entirely

---

* The reader is once more desired to remember, that by works we understand, not only the works of the tongue and hands, i.e. words and actions; but also, and chiefly, the works of the mind and heart, that is, thoughts, desires, and tempers.

agreeable, to *sound doctrine.* Having thus, by the help of *your* own concessions, once more removed the rock of offence, under which you try to crush the seasonable rampart of St. James' undefiled religion, which we call *the Minutes,* I leave you to consider how much Mr. Wesley has been misunderstood, and how much the truth of the Gospel has been set at naught. I am, honoured and dear sir, yours, &c,

J. FLETCHER.

LETTER VI.

To Richard Hill, Esq.

HON. AND DEAR SIR, — While my engine, common sense, stands yet firm upon the point of our *justification by the evidence of works,* which you have so fully granted me, permit me to level it a moment at the basis of the main pillars which support Antinomianism and Calvinism.

1. If righteous Lot had died when he repeated the crimes of drunkenness and incest, his justification would have been turned into condemnation, according to St. Paul's plain rule, *If thou be a breaker of the law, thy circumcision is made uncircumcision:* for neither the holy God, nor any virtuous man, can possibly justify a sinner upon the evidence of drunkenness and incest.

2. If old Solomon, doating upon heathenish young women, and led away by them into abominable idolatries, had died before he was brought again to repentance, he could never have seen the kingdom of God. He should have perished in his sin, unless Geneva logic can make it appear, in direct opposition to the word of God, that the *impenitent* shall not perish, and that *idolaters* shall inherit the kingdom of God, Luke xiii, 3; 1 Corinthians vi, 9.

3. If the incestuous Corinthian had been cut off while he defiled his father's bed, the justification granted him at his first conversion, far from saving him in the day of judgment, would have aggravated his condemnation, and caused him to be *counted worthy of a much severer punishment* than if he never had *known the way of righteousness,* — never been justified; unless you can prove that Christ would have acquitted him upon the horrid evidence of apostasy and incest, which appears to me as difficult a task as to prove that Christ and Belial are one and the same filthy god.

4. If David and Bathsheba had been run through by Uriah, as Zimri and Cosbi were by Phinehas; and if they had died in their flagrant wickedness, no previous justification, no Calvinian imputation of righteousness, would have secured their justification in the last day. For, upon the evidence of adultery and premeditated murder, they would infallibly have been condemned; according to those awful words of our Lord, *I come quickly to give* EVERY MAN, [here is no exception for the "pleasant children,"] *according as* HIS *work shall be,* not according as my work has been. *Blessed are they that do his commandments, that they may enter in*

through the gates into the city; for without are dogs, WHOREMONGERS, and MURDERERS, Revelation xxii, 12, &c.

Should you say, honoured sir, It is provided in the decree of absolute election that adulterers, who once walked with God, shall not die till they have repented: (1.) I demand proof that there ever was such a decree. In the second Psalm, indeed, I read about God's decree respecting Christ and mankind; but it is the very reverse of Calvin's decree, for it implies general redemption and conditional election. *I will declare the decree. Thou art my son. I will give thee the* HEATHEN *for thine inheritance, and the* UTTERMOST *parts of the earth for thy possession. Kiss the son, lest he be angry, and ye perish from the way.*

2. This evasion is founded upon a most absurd supposition, which sews pillows to the arms of backsliders and apostates, by promising them immortality if they persevere in sin. But setting aside the absurdity of supposing that old Solomon, for example, might have kept himself alive till now by assiduously worshipping Ashtaroth; or, which is the same, that he might have put off death by putting off repentance, because he could not die till he had repented: I ask, Where is this strange Gospel written? Certainly not in the Old Testament; for God asks there with indignation, "When the righteous turneth away from his righteousness, and committeth iniquity, SHALL HE LIVE?" No: "in his sin that he has sinned SHALL HE DIE," Ezekiel xviii, 24. Much less in the New, where Christ protests, that he will *spue lukewarm* believers *out of his mouth,* and that *every branch in him which bears not fruit, shall be taken away* or *cut off.* An awful threatening this, which was executed even upon one of the twelve apostles! For our Lord himself says, *Those that thou* GAVEST *me I have kept, and none of* THEM *is lost but Judas,* who fell finally, since he died in the very act of self murder, and is particularly called *the son of perdition.*

But granting you, that lest Lot, David, and Solomon should be condemned by works in the day of judgment, they were to be immortal till they repented and did their first works; this very supposition indicates, that till they repented they were *sons of perdition,* according to that solemn declaration of truth manifest in the flesh, *Except ye repent, ye shall all perish.*

As if you were aware of this difficulty, (p. 149,) you have recourse to a noted distinction in Geneva logic, by which you hope to secure your favourite doctrine, as well as fond Rachel once secured her favourite teraphim. You say, "that though a sinner [David, for instance, or Solomon] be justified *in the sight of God* by Christ alone, he is declaratively justified by works both here and at the day of judgment."

Now, honoured sir, this necessarily implies, that though David in Uriah's bed, and Solomon at the shrine of Ashtaroth, are justified in the sight of God by Christ's chastity and piety imputed to them; yet, before men, and before the Judge of quick and dead, they are justified by the evidence of their own chastity and piety. This distinction, one of the main supports of Calvinism, is big with absurdities; for if it be just, it follows,

1. That while God says of Solomon, worshipping the goddess of the Zidonians, he is still a true believer, "he is justified from all things;" Christ says, *By his fruit ye shall know him;* he is an impenitent, unjustified idolater; and St. James, siding with his Master, says roundly, that Solomon's *faith* being now *without works*

is a dead, unjustifying faith; by which, as well as by his bad works, he is condemned already. Now, sir, it remains that you should give up Antinomian Calvinism, or tell us who is grossly mistaken, God or Christ. For, upon your scheme, God says of an impenitent idolater, who once believed in him, "He is fully justified by the perfect law of liberty." And Christ says, "He is fully condemned by the same law!" And reason dictates, that both parts of a full contradiction cannot be true.

Do not say, honoured sir, that, upon the Calvinian plan, the Father and the Son never contradict one another in the matter of a sinner's justification; for if the Father justifies by the imputation of an external righteousness, which constitutes a sinner righteous while he commits all sorts of crimes; and if the Son, on the other hand, condemns a sinner for his *words,* much more for the commission of adultery, idolatry, and murder; their sentence must be as frequently different as a believer acts or speaks, contrary to the law of liberty. For Christ being *the same yesterday, to-day, and for ever,* cannot justify: he must condemn now, as well as in the day of judgment, every man who now acts or speaks wickedly.

Should you attempt to account for the Father's imaginary justification of an impenitent idolater, by bringing in Calvin's decrees, and saying that God reckoned Solomon a converted man at the shrine of Ashtaroth, because he had absolutely decreed to give him restoring grace; I reply, supposing such decrees are not imaginary, is it not absurd to say, God reckons that cold is heat, and confounds January with July, because he has decreed that summer shall follow winter Therefore, which way soever you turn, absurdities or impieties stare you in the face.

2. The unreasonableness of Calvinism will appear to you more glaringly still, if you suppose for a moment that David died in Uriah's bed. For then, according to Dr. Crisp's justification by the imputation of Christ's chastity, he must have gone straight to heaven; and, according to our Lord's condemnation, by the evidence of personal adultery, he must have gone straight to hell. Thus, by the help of Geneva logic, so sure as the royal adulterer might have died before Nathan stirred him up to repentance, I can demonstrate, that David might have been saved and damned, in heaven and in hell, at the same time!

3. Your distinction insinuates, that there will be two days of judgment; one to try us secretly *before God,* by imputed sin and imputed righteousness; and the other to try us publicly *before men and angels,* by personal sin and personal righteousness. A new doctrine this, which every Christian is bound to reject, not only because the Scripture is silent about it, but because it fixes a shocking duplicity of conduct upon God; for it represents him, first, as absolutely saving or damning the children of men, according to his own capricious imputation of Christ's righteousness, or of Adam's sin; and then as being desirous to make a show of justice before men and angels, by pretending to justify or condemn people "according to their works," when in fact he has already justified or condemned them without the least respect to their works; for, say Bishop Cowper and Mr. Hill, "In the act of justification, good works have no place;" and, indeed, how should they, if free grace and free wrath have unalterably cast the lot of all, before the foundation of the world? — or, in other terms, if finished

salvation and finished damnation have the stamp of God, as well as that of Calvin?

4. According to your imaginary distinction, Christ, as King of saints, frequently condemns for inherent wickedness, those whom he justifies, as a Priest, by imputed righteousness; and so, to the disgrace of his wisdom, he publicly recants, as a Judge, the sentence of complete justification, which he privately passes as a God. Permit me, honoured sir, to enforce this observation by the example of Judas, or any other apostate. I hope nobody will charge me with blasphemy, for saying that our Lord called Judas with the same sincerity with which he called his other disciples. Heaven forbid that any Christian should suppose the Lamb of God called Iscariot to get him into the pit of perdition, as the fowler does an unhappy bird which he wants to get into a decoy. Judas readily answered the call, and undoubtedly believed in Christ as well as the rest of the apostles; for St. John says, "This beginning of miracles did Jesus in Cana of Galilee, and manifested forth his glory, and his disciples [of whom Judas was one] believed in him." His faith was true so far as it went; for he was one of "the little flock to whom it was God's good pleasure to give the kingdom," Luke xii, 32. Our Lord pronounced him "blessed," with the rest of his disciples, Matthew xiii, 16, and conditionally promised him one of the twelve apostolic crowns in his glory, Matthew xix, 28.

If you say, that "he was always a traitor and a hypocrite," you run into endless difficulties; for, (1.) You make Christ countenance, by his example, all bishops, who knowingly ordain wicked men — all patrons, who give them livings — and all kings, who prefer ungodly men to high dignities in the Church. (2.) You suppose that Christ, who would not receive an occasional testimony from an evil spirit, not only sent a devil to preach and baptize in his name, but at his return encouraged him in his horrid dissimulation, by bidding him "rejoice that his name was written in heaven." (3.) You believe, "that the faithful and true Witness," in whose mouth no guile was ever found, gave this absurd, hypocritical charge to a goat, an arch hypocrite, a devil: "Behold, I send you forth as sheep in the midst of wolves; but fear not, the hairs of your head are all numbered. A sparrow shall not fall to the ground without your Father, and ye are of more value than many sparrows. Do not premeditate, it shall be given you what you shall speak: for it is not you that speak, but the Spirit of your Father which speaketh in you."

When our Lord spoke thus to Judas, he was a sheep, i.e. "he heard Christ's voice, and followed him." But, alas! he was afterward taken by the bright shining of silver and gold, as David was by the striking beauty of Uriah's wife. And when he had admitted the base temptation, our Lord, with the honesty of a Master, and tenderness of a Saviour, said, "Have not I chosen you twelve, and one of you is a devil?" He has let the tempter into his heart. This severe, though indirect reproof, reclaimed Judas for a time; as a similar rebuke checked Peter on another occasion. Nor was it, probably, till near the end of our Lord's ministry that he began to be "unfaithful in the mammon of unrighteousness:" and even then Christ kindly warned, without exposing him.

Some, indeed, think that our Lord was partial to Peter; but I do not see it: for with equal love and faithfulness he warned all his disciples of their approaching fall, and mentioned the peculiar circumstances of Judas and Peter's apostasy. "Aye, but he prayed for Peter that his faith might not fail." And is this a proof that he never prayed for Judas? That he always excepted him, when he prayed for his disciples, and that he would have excepted him, if he had been alive when he interceded for all his murderers? "However, he looked at Peter, to cover him with a penitential shame." Nay he did more than this for Judas; for he pointed at him, first indirectly, and then directly, to bring him to a sense of his crime. But, supposing our Lord had not at all endeavoured to stop him in his dreadful career, would this have been a proof of his reprobating partiality? Is it not said, that "the Lord weigheth the spirits?" As such, did he not see that Judas offended of malicious wickedness and calm deliberation; and that Peter would offend merely through fear and surprise? Supposing, therefore, he had made a difference between them, would it be right to account for it by Calvinian election and reprobation, when the difference might so naturally be accounted for from the different state of their hearts, and nature of their falls? Was it not highly agreeable to the notions we have of justice, and the declarations we read in the Scripture, that our Lord should reprobate, or give up Judas, when he saw him immovably fixed in his apostasy, and found that the last hour of his day of grace was now expired?

From all these circumstances, I hope I may conclude, that Judas was not always a hypocrite; that he may be properly ranked among apostates, that is, among those who truly fall from God, and therefore were once truly in him; and that our Lord spoke no untruth, when he called the Spirit of God the Spirit of Judas' Father, without making any difference between him and the other disciples.

If you ask, How he fell? I reply, That, overlooking an important part of our Lord's pastoral charge to him, "He that endureth unto the end the same shall be saved," he dallied with worldly temptations till the evil spirit, which was gone out of him, entered in again, with seven other spirits more wicked than himself, and took possession of his heart, which was once swept from reigning sin, and garnished with the graces which adorn the Christian in his infant state. Thus, like Hymeneus, Philetus, Demas, and other apostates, "by putting away a good conscience, concerning faith he made shipwreck," and evidenced the truth of God's declaration: "When the righteous turneth away from his righteousness, all his righteousness that he hath done shall not be mentioned: in his sin that he hath sinned he shall die."

"Nay, Judas kept his Master's money, and was a thief; therefore he was always a hypocrite, an absolute reprobate." To show the weakness of this objection, I need only retort it thus: David set his heart upon his neighbour's wife, as Judas did upon his Master's money, and like him betrayed innocent blood; therefore he was always a hypocrite, an absolute, reprobate. If the inference is just in one case, it is undoubtedly so in the other.

"But David repented, and did his first works."

I thank my objector for this important concession. Did Judas perish? It was then because he did not do his first works, though he repented. And is David saved? It is because he not only repented, but did also his first works; or, to use your own expressions, because he recovered "justifying faith, which cannot be without good works." Thus, when he had recovered justifying faith before God, he could again be justified by the evidence of works, both before his fellow mortals, and that God who "judges the world in righteousness," and who sentences every man according to *his own* works, and not merely according to works done by *another* near 6000 or 1800 years before they were born. Thus the royal adulterer, who died a justified, chaste penitent, can, through the merits of Christ, stand before the throne in a better and more substantial righteousness than the fantastic robe in which you imagine he was clothed, when his eyes were full of adultery, and his hands full of blood: an airy, loose, flimsy robe this, cut out at Geneva and Dort, not at Jerusalem or Antioch; a wretched contrivance, the chief use of which is to cover the iron-clay feet of the Calvinian Diana, and afford a safe asylum, a decent canopy to "the pleasant children," while they debauch their neighbours' wives, and hypocritically murder them out of the way.

O ye good men, how long will ye inadvertently represent our God, who is glorious in holiness, as the pander of vice? and Christ's immaculate righteousness as the unseemly cloak of such wickedness as is not so much as named among the Gentiles? "O that salvation, *from this evil*, were given unto Israel out of Sion!" O that the Lord would deliver his people from this preposterous error! O that the blast of Divine indignation, and the sighs of thousands of good men, lighting at once on the great image, might tear away the loose robe of righteousness which Calvin put upon her in a "winter season!" Then could all the world read the mark of the beast and the fiend, which she wears on her naked breast: "Free adultery, free murder, free incest, any length of sin for the pleasant children, the little flock of the elect: free wrath, free vengeance, free damnation for the immense herd of the reprobates!"

But to return to Judas, the first of all Christian apostates: waiving the consideration of his justification in his infancy, I observe, that as he had once true faith, he undoubtedly "believed to righteousness," and consequently "it was imputed to him for righteousness." Now, if this mean that God put upon him a loose robe of righteousness, which for ever screened him from condemnation, and under which he could conceal a bag of stolen money, as easily as you suppose David hid the ewe lamb which he conveyed away from Uriah's pasture, it follows, upon your scheme, that "justification being one single immutable act, in which works have no place," Judas is still completely justified before God by Calvinian imputation of righteousness; although Christians have hitherto believed works have so important a place in justification, that the apostate is no less condemned before God, than before men and angels, by his avarice and treason.

Let those who can split a hair as easily as an eagle can find her passage between east and west, take the chosen apostle, who did not make his election sure by the works of faith, and let them split him asunder: so shall happy Iscariot, the dear elected child of God, wrapped in imputed righteousness, and carried by everlasting love, infallibly go to heaven without works, in consequence of his Calvinian justification before God; while poor reprobated Judas, for accomplishing God's decree, shall infallibly go to his own place, in consequence of his condemnation by the evidence of wicked works.

Thus, honoured sir, by fixing my plain engine, common sense, upon the immovable point which you have granted me, i.e. St. James' justification by works, I hope I have not only removed the rock of offence from off Mr. Wesley's anti-Crispian propositions, but heaved also your great Diana, and her brother Apollo, (I mean unconditional election and absolute reprobation) from off the basis of orthodoxy, on which you suppose they stand firm as the pillars of heaven. May the God of pure, impartial love, whom they have so long indirectly traduced, as a God of blind dotage to hundreds, and implacable wrath to millions of his creatures, in the very same circumstances, — the God whom those unscriptural doctrines have represented as fond Eli, and grim Apollyon; may he, I say, arise for his name's sake, and touch the Geneva colossus with his own omnipotent finger; so shall it in a moment fall from the amazing height of reverence to which Calvin, the Synod of Dort, and Elisha Coles have raised it; and its undeceived votaries shall perceive, they had no more reason to call Geneva impositions "the doctrines of grace," than good Aaron and the mistaken Israelites to give the tremendous name of JEHOVAH to the ridiculous idol, which they had devoutly set up in the absence of legal Moses; so, giving glory to God, they shall confess that the robe of their image, with which some so officiously cover impenitent adulterers and murderers, is no more like the true wedding garment, than the imaginary appearances of armed men in the clouds are like the multitude of the heavenly host.

While you try to defend this robe, and I to tear it off the back of Antinomian Jezebel, let us not neglect "putting off the old man, putting on Christ Jesus, and walking in him" as St. Paul, or with him as Enoch, "arrayed in fine linen, clean and white, which is the righteousness *imparted* to the saints, when Christ is formed in their hearts by faith," and imputed to them so long as they walk, in their measure, "as he also walked." That, notwithstanding our warm controversy, we may "walk in love" with each other, and all the people of God, is the prayer of, honoured and dear sir, your obedient and devoted servant, in St. James' Gospel,

JOHN FLETCHER.

LETTER VII.

To Richard Hill, Esq.

HONOURED AND DEAR SIR, — The fourth letter of your Review you produce as "a full and particular answer" to what I have advanced against Dr. Crisp's scheme of finished salvation, and finished damnation. But to my great surprise, you pass in profound silence over my strongest arguments. Had I been in your place, I would have paid some regard to my word, printed in capitals in my title page: I would have tried to prove, that, upon the doctor's scheme, St. Paul might, consistently with wisdom, exhort the Philippians "to work out their [finished] salvation with fear and trembling." And if I could not have made it appear, that our Lord has finished his work, as an interposing Mediator, a teaching Prophet, and a ruling King; I would either have given up the point, or endeavoured to show, that he has finished it at least as a Priest.

But even this you could not do without setting aside two important parts of his priestly office: for the same Jesus, who offered up himself as the true paschal Lamb, is now exalted at the right hand of God, to bless us as our Melchisedec, and "make intercession for us" as our Aaron, saying daily concerning a multitude of barren fig trees in his vineyard, "Let them alone this year also, till I shall dig about them; and if they bear fruit, well: and if not, then after that thou shalt cut them down." Now if he daily carries on his own personal work of salvation, not only as a Prophet and a King, but also as a Mediator and a Priest, common sense dictates, that "his personal work" is no more finished than our own; and that the doctrine of finished salvation is founded upon a heap of palpable mistakes, if by that expression you mean any thing more than a finished atonement.

But, overlooking these insurmountable difficulties, you open your "full and particular answer" by saying, pp. 62, 63, "Finished salvation is a grand fortress, against which all your artillery is played, and at which your heavy bombs of bitter sneer and cutting sarcasm are thrown. Yet this very expression, in its full extent, I undertake to vindicate, and in so doing shall fly to the sword of the Spirit; and the Lord enabling me to wield it aright, I doubt not I shall put to flight the armies of the aliens." Let us now see how you manage your sword, put us to flight, and establish finished salvation.

I. Page 63, "When the Lord of glory gave up the ghost, he cried, 'It is finished.' And what was finished? Not merely his life, but 'the work which was given him to do.' And what was this work, but the salvation of his people? One would have imagined, that the Lord's own use of this expression might have silenced every cavil."

The Lord's own use of this contested expression, "finished salvation!" Pray, dear sir, where does he use it? Certainly not in the two passages you quote, "I have finished the work thou gavest me to do," previously to my entering on my passion; and "It is finished;" that is, all the prophecies relative to what I was to do, teach, and suffer *before* my death, are accomplished. These scriptures do not in the least refer to the work of salvation on our part; nor do they even take in the most important branches of salvation's work on Christ's part. To assert it, is to take a bold stride into Socinianism, and maintain, it was not needful to our salvation that Christ should die, and rise again. For when he said, "I have finished the work thou gavest me to do," he was not yet entered upon his passion: nor had he died for our *sins,* much less was he yet risen for our justification, when he said upon the cross, "It is finished." To suppose, then, that salvation's work on Christ's part was finished, not only before his resurrection, but also before his death, is to set aside some of his most important works, in direct opposition to the Scriptures, which testify, that "he died, the just for the unjust;" and affirm, that "if he is not raised, our faith is vain, we are yet in our sins." Thus, sir, you have so unhappily begun to "wield your sword," as to cut down, at the first stroke, the two grand articles of the Christian faith — the death and resurrection of Jesus Christ.

II. Page 33. To mend the matter, you have recourse to the mysterious doctrine of the decrees; and because "all events are present unto God, and were so from eternity to eternity," you affirm that "the glorification of the elect is as much finished as their predestination." By the same rule of Geneva logic, I may say, that because God has decreed the world shall melt with fervent heat, the general conflagration is as much finished as the deluge. Were ever more strange assertions obtruded upon mankind?

If this illustration does not convince you of your mistake, I turn the tables, and make your blood run cold with the dreadful counterpart of your own proposition. The damnation of the non-elect "born or unborn," is as much finished as their predestination. And are these "the good tidings of great joy which shall be to all people?" and is this the comfortable Gospel of free grace, which we are "to preach to every creature?" Alas, my dear sir, you wield your sword so unskilfully, as absolutely to cut down all hopes and possibility of mercy for millions of your fellow creatures; even for all the poor reprobates on the left side of the ship, who, "from eternity to eternity were irresistibly enclosed in the net of finished damnation!"

III. Page 63. To support your unscriptural assertion, you produce Romans viii, 29, "Whom he did predestinate, them he called: and whom he called, them he also justified; and whom he justified, them he also glorified." Indeed, sir, the apostle no more meant to insinuate by these words, that David was justified and glorified when he wallowed in the filth of adultery and murder, than that Judas was condemned and damned when he left all to follow Christ. He only lays before us an account of the method which God follows in the eternal salvation of obedient, persevering believers; who are the persons that, as such, he predestinated to life, "according to his foreknowledge, *and* the counsel of his *holy* will." These "he called," but not these alone. When they made their calling sure, by believing in the light of their dispensation, these "he also justified." And when they made their justification sure, by "adding to their faith virtue," &c, these "he also glorified;" for the souls of departed saints are actually glorified in Abraham's bosom; and living saints are not only called and justified, but also in part glorified; for, by "the Spirit of glory and of God, *which* rests upon them, *they are* changed into the Divine image from glory to glory;" yea, they are already "all glorious within."

How much more reasonable and Scriptural is this sense of the apostle's words than that which you fix upon them, by which you would make us believe, that, on the one hand, Solomon's salvation (including his justification and glorification) was finished, "in the full extent of the expression," when he worshipped the abomination of the Zidonians, and gloried in his shame: while, on the other hand, Demas' damnation was finished when he was St. Paul's zealous "companion in the kingdom and patience of Jesus Christ!" O sir, have you not here also inadvertently used the "sword of the Spirit," to oppose the "mind of the Spirit," and make way for barefaced Antinomianism? You proceed:

IV. Page 63. "The same apostle, in his Epistle to the Ephesians, speaking to believers, addresses them as already (virtually) 'seated in heavenly places in Christ Jesus.'" Hence you infer, that their salvation was finished, "in the full extent of the expression." But your conclusion is not just; for the apostle, instead of supposing their salvation finished, exhorts them "not to steal, not to be drunk with wine, and not to give place to the devil," by fornication, uncleanness, filthiness, or covetousness; "for this ye know," adds he, "that no unclean person, &c, hath any inheritance in the kingdom of Christ;" so far is he from being "already virtually seated in heavenly places in Christ.

What need is there of "darkening counsel by a word without knowledge?" By the dark word "virtually?" While the Ephesians kept the faith, did they not "set their affections on things above?" Were not their hearts in heaven with Christ agreeably to our Lord's doctrine, "Where your treasure is, there will your heart be also?" And by a lively faith, which is "the substance of things hoped for," did they not already share the glory of their exalted Head? Will you still endeavour to persuade the world, that when David defiled his neighbour's bed, he was "seated in heavenly places in Christ?" Is it not evident that these, and the like expressions of St. Paul, must not be understood of idle Antinomian speculations; but of such a real change as our Church mentions in her collect for Ascension day? "Grant, that as Christ ascended into the heavens, so we may also in heart and mind thither ascend, and continually dwell." Such powerful exertions of faith, hope, and love, as are described in the 77th hymn of the Rev. Mr. Madan's collection?

> By faith *we are come*
> *To our permanent home;*
> By hope *we the rapture improve:*
> By love *we still rise,*
> *And look down on the skies —*
> *For the heaven of heaven is* love!

But this is not all: if the elect, whether they be drunk or sober, chaste or unclean, "are already virtually seated in heavenly places in Christ," according to the doctrine of finished salvation; are not poor reprobates, whether they pray or curse, repent or sin, already virtually seated in hellish places in the devil, according to the doctrine of finished damnation? O sir, when you use the sword of the Spirit to storm the New Jerusalem, and cut the way through law and Gospel before an adulterer *in flagrante delicto,* that he may *virtually* [that is, I fear, *comfortably and securely*] "sit in heavenly places in Christ," do you not dreadfully prostitute God's holy word? Inadvertently fight the battle of the rankest Antinomians, and secure the foundation of Mr. Sandiman's, as well as Dr. Crisp's increasing errors? But you have an excuse ready: —

V. Page 63. "Christ has purchased the Spirit, to work mortification of sin, &c, in the hearts of his children: and in this respect their sanctification is really as much finished as their justification." I reply, (1.) If their justification by works is not finished before the day of judgment, as our Lord informs us, Matthew xii, 37, your observation proves just nothing. (2.) The Scriptures, in direct opposition to your scheme, declare, that the Spirit strives with, and consequently was purchased for all; those who "quench" it, and "sin against the Holy Ghost," not excepted. Therefore, neither the sanctification nor salvation of sinners is absolutely secured by the purchase you mention. If it were, all the world would be saved. But, alas! many "deny the Lord that bought them," and by "doing despite to the Spirit of grace" purchased for them, "bring upon themselves swift destruction," instead of finished salvation. Here, then, the sword which you wield flies again to pieces, by clashing with the real sword of the Spirit, brandished by St. Peter and St. Paul.

VI. Page 64. You bring in "the immutability of God's counsel confirmed by an oath," and add, "The will and testament is signed, sealed, and properly attested. The whole affair is finished. There remains nothing to do but to take possession." I thank you, dear sir, for this concession; something then "remains to do" we must, at least, "take possession;" and if we neglect doing it, farewell finished salvation. We shall as much fall short of the heavenly, as the Israelites, who perished in the wilderness, because they refused to take possession, fell short of the earthly Canaan.

Again: we grant that God's "will and testament is finished, and sealed by Christ's most precious blood:" and that "the everlasting covenant is ordered in all things, and sure." But if part of that will and covenant runs thus: "Ye are saved by grace through faith. You are kept by the power of God through faith. If ye continue in the faith. Faith without works is dead. Wherefore work out your own salvation with fear and trembling. For him that sinneth I will blot out of my book. If ye walk contrary to me, I will walk contrary to you. I will cut my staff, beauty, asunder, that I may break my covenant which I have made with all the people, Zechariah xi, 10. And ye shall know my breach of promise, Numbers xiv, 34. I will therefore put you in remembrance, though ye once knew this, how that the Lord, having saved the people out of the land of Egypt, afterward destroyed them that believed not; although through faith they kept the passover, and the sprinkling of blood, lest the destroyer should touch them. And did all drink the same spiritual drink, (for they drank of that spiritual rock that followed them; and that rock was Christ.) Now all these things happened to them for examples: and they are written for our admonition. Wherefore let him that thinketh he standeth take heed lest he fall." If part of God's will and covenant, I say, runs thus, is it not absurd to suppose, that any man's salvation is finished while he not only does not comply with the gracious terms of God's "sure covenant," but notoriously incurs the dreadful threatenings recorded in his unalterable "will and testament?" Here, then, instead of "turning to flight the armies of the aliens," you have given us weapons to beat you out of the field. But you soon come back again to say, —

VII. Page 64. "Certain it is, that the salvation of every soul given by the Father to the Son, in the eternal covenant of redemption, is as firmly secured as if those souls were already in glory." The certainty which you speak of, exists only in your own imagination. Judas was given by the Father to the Son; and yet Judas is lost. If the salvation of some people "was as firmly secured from the beginning as if they had already been in glory," all the Gospel ministers who have addressed them at any time as children of wrath, have been preachers of lies, and the Holy Spirit witnesses to an untruth, when he testifies to the unregenerate elect that they are in danger of hell. But this is not all: upon your dangerous scheme, the foundations are thrown down; man is no more in a state of trial; the day of judgment will be a mere farce; and the Scriptures are a farrago of the most absurd cautions, and the most scandalous lies: for they perpetually speak to believers as to persons in danger of "falling," and "being cut off," if they do not "walk circumspectly;" and they assert that some "perish for whom Christ died;" and that others, by "denying the Lord who bought them, bring upon themselves swift destruction."

But pray, sir, when you tell us, "The salvation of every soul given by the Father to the Son, in the eternal covenant of redemption, is as firmly secured as if those souls were already in glory," do you not see the cloven foot on which your doctrine stalks along? Permit me to uncover it a moment, and strike my readers with salutary dread, by holding forth the inseparable counterpart of your dangerous opinion, "Certain it is, that the damnation of every soul given by the Father to the devil, in the eternal covenant of reprobation, is as firmly secured as if those souls were already in hell." Shame on the man that first called such horrid tenets "the doctrines of grace, and the free Gospel of Jesus Christ!" Confusion on the lying spirit, who broke out of the bottomless pit, thus to blaspheme the Father of mercies, delude good men, and sow the tares of Antinomianism! O, sir, when you plead for such doctrines, instead of wielding aright "the sword of the Spirit," do you not plunge it in muddy, Stygian waters, till it is covered with sordid rust, and reeks with poisonous error? But you pursue: —

VIII. Page 64. "To scruple the use of that expression, finished salvation, argues the greatest mistrust of the Mediator's power, and casts the highest reflection upon his infinite wisdom, by supposing that he did not count the cost before he began to build, and therefore that either his own personal work, or that which he does in his members, (for they are only parts of the same salvation,) is left unfinished." If we do not admit your doctrine, honoured sir, it is not because we mistrust the Mediator's "power," and have low thoughts of his "wisdom;" but because we cannot believe that he will use his power in opposition to his wisdom and truth, in taking the elect by main force into heaven, as a strong man takes a sack of corn into his granary; much less can we think that he will use his omnipotence in opposition to his mercy and justice, by placing millions of his creatures in such forcible circumstances, as absolutely necessitate them to sin and be damned, according to the horrible doctrine of finished damnation.

Nor do we suppose that Christ unwisely forgot to "count the cost." No: from the beginning he knew that some would abuse their liberty, and bury their talent of good will, and gracious power to come unto him, "that they might have more abundant life." But far from being disappointed, as we are when things fall out contrary to our fond expectation, he declared beforehand, "I have laboured in vain, yet surely my work is with my God," Isaiah xlix, 4. As if he had said, "If I cannot rejoice over the obstinate neglecters of my great salvation; if my kindly dying for their sins, excepting that against the Holy Ghost, and my sincerely calling upon them to 'turn and live,' prove useless to them, through their 'doing despite to the Spirit of grace,' and committing 'the sin unto death;' yet my work will not be lost with respect to my God. For my impartial, redeeming love will effectually 'stop every mouth,' and abundantly secure the honour of all the Divine perfections, which would be dreadfully sullied, if, by an absolute decree that all should necessarily fall in Adam, and that millions should never have it in their power to rise by me, I had set my seal to the horrible doctrine of finished salvation."

Five Checks To Antinomianism

Here, then, in flourishing with your sword, you have "beaten the air," instead of "turning to flight the armies of" — those who are not clear in the doctrine of absolute predestination, whom you call — "aliens;" and in a quotation, p. 37, "absolutely place among the numerous hosts of the Diabolonians, who by the best of laws must die as election doubters."

IX. Page 64. "If any thing be left unfinished, Christ would never have said,'He that believeth hath everlasting life;' it is already begun in his soul." Well, if it is but begun, it is not yet finished. But you add, "It is so certain in reversion, that nothing shall deprive him of it." True, "if he continues in the faith *and* abides in Christ, hearing his voice *and* following him;" for who "shall pluck you out of *the Redeemer's* hand?" "Who shall harm you, if ye be followers of that which is good?" But if the believer "makes shipwreck of his faith," and "ends in the flesh," after having "begun in the Spirit," with all apostates he shall "of the flesh reap destruction." Again: —

"Everlasting life," in the passage you quote, undoubtedly signifies a title to eternal bliss, as it appears from these words of our Lord "He that has left brethren, &c, for my sake, shall receive in the world to come eternal life." And from these words of St. Paul, "Ye have your fruit unto holiness, and the end everlasting life." Now if we give over following after holiness, and do not continue to leave all for Christ's sake, may we not forfeit our title to glory, as the servant who had ten thousand talents forgiven him, forfeited his pardon and the privilege annexed to it, by "taking his fellow servant by the throat," and arresting him for a "hundred pence?" But supposing the expression "everlasting life," means, as you intimate, "the life of God, already begun in the soul," agreeably to these scriptures: "The life that I live, I live by faith in the Son of God; for the just shall live by faith;" how can you infer that the life of faith is inamissible? If you can believe that every child quickened in the womb grows up to be a man, because he has human life in embryo, I will grant that no soul, quickened by the seed of grace, can miscarry, and that the seed of the word brings forth fruit to maturity in every sort of ground.

Should you reply, "That the life of faith, or spiritual life, cannot be lost, because it is of an eternal nature," I deny the consequence. Suppose I have lost an everlasting jewel, do I not quibble myself out of my invaluable property, if I say "I have not lost it, for it is everlasting?" Did not Satan and Adam lose their spiritual life? Do not all apostates lose it also? Is there a damned soul but what has lost it twice? Once in Adam, and the second time by his own personal transgressions? Are not all men who burn" in fire unquenchable trees plucked up by the roots;" not because they "died in Adam," but because they "are twice dead;" because they personally "destroyed themselves," and, when Christ gave them a degree of life, "would not come to him that they might have it more abundantly?" Thus, by resisting to the last the quickening beams of the Spirit that "strove with them," they "quenched him" in themselves, and became apostates. If Christ is "the light and the life of men," and if he "enlightens every man that comes into the world," are not all the damned apostates? Have they not all fallen from some degree or other of quickening grace? Have they not all buried one or more talents? And is it not Satan's masterpiece of policy, to make good men assure quickened sinners that they cannot lose their life; no, not by plunging into the whirlpools of adultery, murder, and incest? The ancient serpent deceived our first parents by saying, "Ye shall not surely die," if ye eat of the forbidden fruit. But now, it seems, he may take his rest, for, O astonishing! Gospel ministers do his work; they inadvertently "deceive the very elect," and "overthrow the faith of some," by making them the very same false promise.

I have already observed, that he "who believeth" is said to "have everlasting life;" not only because, while he keeps the faith, he has a title to glory, but because living "faith *always* works by love," the grace that "never faileth," the grace that "lives and abides for ever;" not indeed in this or that individual, during his state of probation, but in the kingdom of heaven; "among the spirits of just men made perfect in love," and confirmed in glory. However, you still urge, "To say that everlasting life can be lost, is a contradiction in terms: if it is everlasting, how can it be forfeited or lost?" How? Just as the Jews forfeited the land which God gave to Abraham for an everlasting possession, Genesis xvii, 8. Just as the seed of Phinehas lost "the everlasting priesthood," Numbers xxv, 13. Just as the Israelites "broke the everlasting covenant," Isaiah xxiv, 5. Just as Hymeneus and Philetus forfeited the everlasting privileges of believers; that is, by "making shipwreck of faith and a good conscience." Here, then, the edge of your own sword is again blunted, and the stroke given to the "aliens" easily parried with the unbroken "sword of the Spirit:" I mean the word of God illustrated by itself, and taken in connection with itself. However, you proceed: —

X. Page 64. "The chosen vessel, Paul, tells his beloved Timothy, that God 'hath saved us, and called us with a holy calling,'" *&c.* Hence you conclude, that if we are elect, our salvation is finished. I grant, that God hath saved us from hell, placed us in a state of salvation begun, and "called us with a holy calling, to work out our salvation with fear and trembling;" under some dispensation of that" grace which was given us in Christ before the world began; according to God's own purpose, *that Christ should be* the Saviour of all men, especially of them that believe." But alas! Though "many are thus called, yet but few are chosen; because few walk worthy of their high vocation, few make their calling and election sure." Numbers, like David and Solomon, Demas and Sapphira, believe for awhile, and "in time of temptation fall away;" some of whom, instead of rising again, "draw back unto perdition."

Hence "the chosen vessel, Paul," himself cries to halting believers, "How shall we escape if we neglect so great salvation?" So far was he from imagining that the salvation of some, and the damnation of others "were as firmly secured" as if the one were already in heaven, and the other in hell! So little did he think that to preach the Gospel was to present the elect with nothing but the cup of finished salvation, even when they take away the wives and lives of their neighbours; and to drench the reprobates with the cup of finished damnation, even while they ask, seek, knock, and endeavour to make their mock calling sure!

Certain it is, that if the apostle spoke of your finished salvation, when he said, "God hath saved us, and called us with a holy calling," reprobated myriads may reasonably give over wrestling with almighty, ever, lasting wrath, and cry out, "He hath damned us, and called us with an unholy, hypocritical, and lying calling, according to his own purpose and wrath, which was given us in Adam before the world began." O sir, by this frightful doctrine you give a desperate thrust to the

Five Checks To Antinomianism

hopes which millions entertain, that God is not yet absolutely merciless toward them, and that they may yet repent and be saved; but happily for them, it is with the dagger of error, and not with "the sword of the Spirit."

XI. Page 65. "But farther. Believers are said to be 'saved by faith,' and tobe 'kept by the power of God through faith unto salvation.' Now true faith and salvation are here inseparably linked by the apostle." Inseparably linked! Pray, sir, where is the inseparable link? I see it not. Nay, when I consult the apostles, on whose strained words you raise your argument, they rise with one consent against your doctrine. The one says, Some branches in Christ "were broken off because of unbelief; thou standest by faith; [undoubtedly true faith;] nevertheless, fear, lest he also spare not thee. Behold his goodness toward thee, if thou continue in his goodness; otherwise thou also shalt be cut off." The other declares, "If after they [fallen believers, whom he does not call "pleasant," but cursed children] have escaped the pollutions of the world, through the knowledge of the Lord and Saviour Jesus Christ, (that is, through true faith,) they are again entangled therein, and overcome; the latter end is worse with them than the beginning, 2 Peter. ii, 20, compared with 2 Peter i, 2, 8, 9, 10. Thus, sir, St. Paul and St. Peter, whom you call to your assistance, agree to wrench your sword out of your own hand. But you soon take it up again.

XII. Page 64. "Christ being styled not only the author, but the finisher of our faith, he must be, consequently, the finisher of our salvation." So he undoubtedly is, when we are "workers together with him," that is, when using the gracious talent of will and power, which he freely gives us, we "work out our own salvation with fear and trembling." But if we bury that talent, "do despite to the Spirit of grace, forget that we were washed from our sins," and wallow again in the mire of iniquity; "Christ," the author of the faith which we destroy, "profiteth us nothing; we are fallen from grace."

Is it right to rock feeble believers in the cradle of carnal security, by telling them they can never lose the faith; when part of St. Paul's triumphant song, just before he received the crown of martyrdom, was, "I have kept the faith?" What wonder was it that he should have kept, what even the carnal, incestuous Corinthian could never lose! When the Scriptures mention, not only those who "have kept the faith," but those who "have made shipwreck of it, and of a good conscience; those who "believe for awhile, and in time of temptation fall away;" and those who one day believe, another day have little faith, and by and by have no faith; — are we not "wise above what is written," and sow we not Antinomian tares, when we give lukewarm Laodiceans to understand they can never lose what, alas! they have already lost?

If Christ was to believe in his own blood for us, I grant, that the work of faith and salvation could not miscarry. But what ground have we to imagine that this is the case? Did the apostles charge Christ or sinners to believe under pain of damnation? If believing is entirely the work of Christ, why did he marvel at the unbelief of the Jews? Did you ever marvel at the sessions that the constables in waiting did not act as magistrates? Did you ever send them to jail for not doing your work, as you suppose Christ sends unbelievers to hell for not believing, that is, upon your scheme, for not doing his work?

While we readily grant you, that the talent of faith, like that of industry, is the "free gift of God," together with the time, opportunity, and power to use it; should you not grant us, that God treats us as rational, accountable creatures? That he does not use the gift of faith for us: that we may bury our talent of faith, and perish; as some bury their talent of industry and starve? And that it is as absurd to say, the faith of every individual in the Church is inadmissible, because Christ is the author and finisher of our faith, as to affirm that no individual ear of corn can be blasted, because Christ (who upholds all things by the word of his power) is the unchangeable author and finisher of all our harvests?

Once more, permit me, honoured sir, to hang the mill stone of reprobation about the neck of your Diana, to cast her back with that cumbrous weight into the sea of error, from whose scum she, like another Venus, had her unnatural origin. If the salvation of the elect is finished, because "Christ is the author and finisher of their faith," it necessarily follows, that the damnation of the reprobates is also finished, because "Christ is the author and finisher of their unbelief." For he that absolutely withholds faith, causes unbelief as effectually, as he that absolutely withholds the light, causes darkness.

If, in direct opposition to the words of our Lord, John iii, 18, you say, with some Calvinists, that "Christ does not damn men for unbelief, but for their sins," I reply, This is mere trifling. If Christ absolutely refuses them power to believe in the light of their dispensation, how can they but sin? Does not Paul say, that "without faith it is impossible to please God?" Is not unbelief at the root of every sin? Did not even Adam eat the forbidden fruit through unbelief? And is not "this our only victory, even our faith?"

An illustration will, I hope, expose the emptiness of the pleas which some urge in favour of unconditional reprobation, or, if you please, non-election. A mother conceives an unaccountable antipathy to her sucking child. She goes to the brink of a precipice, bends herself over it with the passive infant in her bosom, and, withdrawing her arms from under him, drops him upon the craggy side of a rock, and thus he rolls down from rock to rock, till he lies at the bottom beaten to pieces, a bloody instance of finished destruction. The judge asks the murderer what she has to say in her own defence. The child was mine, replies she, and I have a right to do what I please with my own. Beside, I did neither throw him down nor murder him: I only withdrew my arms from under him, and he fell of his own accord. In mystic Geneva she is honourably acquitted; but in England the executioner is ordered to rid the earth of the cruel monster. So may God give us commission to rid the Church of your Diana, who teaches that he, the Father of mercies, does by millions of his passive children, what the barbarous mother did by one of hers; affirming, that he unconditionally withholds grace from them; and that, by absolutely refusing to be "the author and finisher of their faith," he is the absolute author and finisher of their unbelief, and consequently of their sin and damnation.

XIII. However, without being frightened at these dreadful consequences, you conclude as if you had won the day: p. 65, "Now I appeal to any candid judges, whether I have not brought sufficient authority from the best of authorities, God's unerring word, for the use of that phrase, finished salvation," which, p. 63, "in its full extent, I undertook to vindicate." I cordially join in your appeal, honoured sir, and desire our unprejudiced readers to say, if you have brought one solid proof from God's unerring word in support of your favourite scheme, which centres in the doctrine of finished salvation: and if that expression, when taken "in its full extent," is not the stalking horse of every wild Nicolaitan ranter; and the dangerous bait, by which Satan, transformed into an angel of light, prevails upon unstable souls to swallow the silver hook of speculative, that he may draw them into all the depths of practical, Antinomianism.

XIV. I do not think it worth while to dwell upon the lines you quote from Mr. Charles Wesley's hymns. He is yet alive to tell us what he meant by "It's finished; it's past," &c. And he informs me that he meant "the sufficient sacrifice, oblation, and satisfaction, which Christ made upon the cross for the sins of the whole world, except 'doing despite to the Spirit of grace,' or the sin against the Holy Ghost." The atonement, which is a considerable part of the Redeemer's work, is undoubtedly finished; and if by a figure of poetry, that puts a part for the whole, you choose to give the name of finished salvation to a finished atonement, I have already observed, in The Third Check, that we will not dispute about the expression. We only entreat you so to explain and guard it, as not to give sanction to "Antinomian dotages," and charge the God of love with the blasphemy of finished damnation.

XV. The Calvinistical passage which you produce from the Christian Library is unguarded, and escaped Mr. Wesley's or the printer's attention. One sentence of it is worthy of a place in the *Index Expurgatorius*, which he designs to annex to that valuable collection. Nevertheless, two clauses of that very passage are not at all to your purpose. "Christ is now thoroughly furnished for the carrying on of this work: he is actually at work." Now if Christ is actually at work, and carrying on his work, that work is not yet finished. Thus, even the exceptionable passage which you, or the friends who gave you their assistance, have picked out of a work of fifty volumes, shows the absurdity of taking the expression, "finished salvation," in its full extent.

Should you say, "Christ is thoroughly furnished for his work, (namely, the salvation of the elect,) therefore that work is as good as finished," I once more present you with the frightful head of Geneva Medusa, and reply, "Christ is thoroughly furnished for his work, (namely, the damnation of the reprobates,) therefore that work is as good as finished." Thus all terminates still in uncovering the two iron-clay feet of your great image, absolute election and absolute reprobation, or, which is all one, finished salvation and finished damnation.

O sir, the more you fight for Dr. Crisp's scheme of free grace, the more you expose his scheme of free wrath. I hope my judicious readers are shocked at it, as well as myself. Your "sword" really "puts us to flight." We start back, — we run away: but it is only from the depths of Satan, which you help us to discover in speculative Antinomianism, or barefaced Calvinism.

XVI. If you charge me with "calumny," for asserting that speculative Antinomianism and barefaced Calvinism are one and the same thing; to clear myself, I present you with the creed of an honest, consistent, plainspoken Calvinist. Read it without prejudice, and say if it will not suit an abettor of speculative Antinomianism, and, upon occasion, a wild Ranter, wading through all the depths of practical Antinomianism, as well as an admirer of "the doctrines of grace."

Five Letters, 1st edit. pp. 33, 34, 27. "I most firmly believe, that the grand cause of so much lifeless profession is owing to the sheep of Christ being fed in the barren pastures and muddled waters of a legalized Gospel. The doctrines of grace are not to be kept out of sight for fear men of corrupt minds should abuse them. I will no more be so fearful to trust God with his own truths, as to starve his children and my own soul: I will make an open confession of my faith."

"1. I believe in God the Father Almighty, who from all eternity unconditionally predestinated me to life, and absolutely chose me to eternal salvation. Whom he once loved he will love for ever; I am therefore persuaded, (pp. 28, 31,) that as he did not set his love on me at first for any thing in me, so that love, which is not at all dependent upon any thing in me, can never vary on account of my miscarriages: and for this reason; when I miscarry, suppose by adultery or murder, God ever considers me as one with his own Son, who has fulfilled all righteousness for me. And as he is 'always well pleased' with him, so with me, who am absolutely 'bone of his bone and flesh of his flesh.' (pp. 26, 31.) There are no lengths, then, I may not run, nor any depths I may not fall into, without displeasing him; as I see in David, who, notwithstanding his repeated backslidings, did not lose the character of the man after God's own heart. I may murder with him, worship Ashtaroth with Solomon, deny Christ with Peter, rob with Onesimus, and commit incest with the Corinthian, without forfeiting either the Divine favour or the kingdom of glory. 'Who shall lay any thing to the charge of God's elect?' to the charge of a believer? to my charge? For,

"2. (Pages 26, 27, 32.) I believe in Jesus Christ, that 'by one offering has for ever perfected' me, who am 'sanctified' in all my sins: in him I am complete in all my iniquities. What is all sin before his atoning blood? Either he has fulfilled the whole law, and borne the curse, or he has not. If he has not, no soul can be saved; if he has, then all debts and claims against his people and me, be they more (suppose a thousand adulteries, and so many murders) or be they less, (suppose only one robbery,) be they small or be they great, be they before or be they after my conversion, are for ever and for ever cancelled. I set up no more mountainous distinctions of sin, especially sins after conversion. Whether I am dejected with Elijah under the juniper tree, or worshipping Milcom with Solomon; whether I mistake the voice of the Lord for that of his priest, as Samuel, or defile my neighbour's bed, as David, I am equally accepted in the Beloved. For in Christ I am chosen, loved, called, and unconditionally preserved to the end. All trespasses are forgiven me. I am justified from all things. I already have everlasting life. Nay, I am now (virtually) set down in heavenly places with Christ; and as soon shall Satan pluck his crown from his head, as his purchase from his hand."

Pages 27, 28. "Yes, I avow it in the face of all the world; no falls or backslidings can ever bring me again under condemnation; for Christ hath made me free from the law of sin and death. Should I outsin Manasses himself, I should not be a less pleasant child; because God always views me in Christ, and in him I am without spot or wrinkle, or any such thing. Black in myself, I am still comely through the comeliness put upon me: and therefore He 'who is of purer eyes than to behold iniquity,' can, in the midst of all adulteries, murders, and incests, address me with, 'Thou art all fair, my love, my undefiled; there is no spot in thee!' And,

"3. I believe in the Holy Ghost, the Spirit of grace, against whom I can never sin, (p. 26,) whose light and love I can never quench, to whom I can never do despite, and who, in his good time, will irresistibly and infallibly (Review, p. 38) work in me to will and to do. In the meantime I am perfectly secure; for I can never perish, my salvation being already finished in the full extent of the expression." (Review, p. 63, &c.)

"Once, indeed, I supposed, that 'the wrath of God came,' at least for enormous crimes, 'upon the children of disobedience;' and I thought it would come upon me if I committed adultery and murder' but now I discover my mistake, and believe (p. 28 and 25) it is a capital error to confound me and my actions. While my murders, &c, certainly displease God, my person stands always absolved, always complete, always pleasant in the everlasting righteousness of the Redeemer. I repeat it, (2d edit. p. 37,) it is a most pernicious error of the school-men, to distinguish sins according to the fact, and not according to the person. He that believeth hath as great sin as the unbeliever: nay, his sins, (p. 32,) for the matter of them are perhaps more heinous and scandalous than those of the unbeliever; but although he daily sinneth, perhaps as David and the Corinthian, by adultery, murder, and incest, he continueth godly.

"Before I was acquainted with the truth, I imagined that sin would dishonour God and injure me: but since the preachers of finished salvation have opened my eyes, I see how greatly I was mistaken. And now I believe that God will overrule my sin, (whether it be adultery, murder, or incest,) for his glory and my good.

"(1.) For his glory. (Pages 36, 30, 31, 32.) God often permits his own dearest children to commit adultery, murder, and incest, to bring about his purposes. He has always the same thing in view, namely, his own glory and my salvation, together with that of the other elect. This Adam was accomplishing when he put the whole world under the curse; Onesimus when he robbed Philemon his master; Judah when he committed incest with Tamar; and David when he committed adultery with Bathsheba. How has many a poor, faithless soul even blessed God for Peter's denial! As for the incestuous Corinthian, the tenderness shown him after his crime, has raised many out of the mire, and caused them to recover their first love.

(2.) "For my good. (Page 32.) God has promised to make 'all things work for good to me;' and if all things, then my very sins and corruptions are included in the royal promise. Should I be asked, What particular good sin will do me in time and in eternity? I answer: A grievous fall [suppose into adultery, murder, or incest] shall serve to make me know my place, to drive me nearer to Christ, to make me more dependent upon his strength, to keep me more watchful, to cause me to sympathize with the fallen, and to make me sing louder to the praise of free, sovereign, restoring grace, throughout all the ages of eternity. Thus, although I highly blame (p. 33,) those who roundly say, 'Let us sin that grace may abound,' I do not legalize the Gospel, but openly declare, (p. 27,) that if I commit adultery, murder, or incest, before or after my conversion, grace shall irresistibly and infallibly abound over these, and all my other sins, be they small or be they great, be they more or be they less. My foulest falls will only drive me nearer to Christ, and make me sing (p. 32) his praises louder than if I had not fallen. Thus [to say nothing of the sweetness and profit which may now arise from sin] adultery, incest, and murder shall, upon the whole, make me holier upon earth, and merrier in heaven."

I need not tell you, honoured sir, that I am indebted to you for all the doctrines, and most of the expressions of this dangerous confession of faith. If any one doubt of it, let him compare this creed and your Letters together. Some clauses and sentences I have added, not to "misrepresent and blacken," but to introduce, connect, and illustrate your sentiments. You speak, indeed, in the third person, and I in the first, but this alters not the doctrine. Beside, if the privileges of a lean believer belong to me as well as to David, I do not see why I should be debarred from the fat pastures you recommend, (p. 34,) which, I fear, are so very rich, that if the leanest sheep of Christ do but range, and take their fill in them, they will in a few days wax wanton against him, butt at the sheep which do not bleat to their satisfaction, attack the under shepherds, and grow so excessively fat as to outkick Jeshurun himself.

XVII. Some half-hearted Calvinists, who are ashamed of their principles, and desirous to conceal their Diana's deformity, will probably blame you for having uncovered the less frightful of her feet, and shown it naked to the wondering world. But to the apology which you have already made about it, I hope I may, without impertinence, add one or two remarks.

1. Whoever believes either the doctrine of unconditional election, or that of righteousness absolutely imputed to apostatizing believers, or that of the infallible perseverance of all who were saints yesterday, and to-day commit adultery, murder, or incest; and, in a word, whoever believes the doctrine of finished salvation implicitly receives two-thirds of the Antinomian creed which you have helped me to. And those who have so strong a faith, and so large a conscience, as to swallow so much, (together with the doctrine of finished damnation, eternal wrath flaming against myriads of unborn creatures, and everlasting fire prepared for millions of passive, sensible machines, which have only fulfilled God's secret and irresistible will,) might, one would think, receive the whole creed without any difficulty: for why should those who can swallow five or six camels as a glib morsel, strain at three or four gnats, as if they were going to be quite choked. Again:

2. If Calvinism is true, you are certainly, honoured sir, the honest and consistent Calvinist, so far as consistency is compatible with the most inconsistent of all schemes. Permit me to produce one instance, which I hope will abate the prejudices which some unsettled Calvinists have conceived against you for speaking quite out with respect to the excellent effects of sin in believers.

If man is not a free agent, (and undoubtedly he is not, if from all eternity he has been bound by ten thousand chains of irresistible and absolute decrees,) it follows, that he is but a curious machine, superior to a brute, as a brute is superior to a watch, and a watch to a wheelbarrow. Upon Calvin's principles this wonderful machine is as much guided by God's invisible hand, or rather by his absolute decrees, as a puppet by the unseen wire which causes its seemingly spontaneous motions. This being the case, it is evident that God is as much the author of our actions, good or bad, as a show-man is the author of the motions of his puppets, whether they turn to the right or to the left. Now as God is infinitely wise, and supremely good, he will set his machines upon doing nothing but what, upon the whole, is wisest and best. Hence it appears, that if the doctrine of absolute decrees, which is the fundamental principle of Calvinism, is true, whatever sin we commit, we only fulfil the absolute will of God, and do that which, upon the whole, is wisest and best; and therefore that you have not unadvisedly pleaded for Baal, but rationally spoken for God, when you have told us what great advantages result from the commission of the greatest crimes. In doing this strange work, then, you have acted only as a consistent predestinarian; and though some thoughtless Calvinists may, yet none that are judicious will blame you, for having spoken agreeably to the leading principle of "the doctrines of grace."

I have observed, that speculative Antinomianism, or barefaced Calvinism, stalks along upon the doctrine of finished salvation, and finished damnation, which we may consider as the two feet of your great Diana; and the preceding creed, which is drawn up for an elect, uncovers only her handsome foot, finished salvation. To do my subject justice, I should now make an open show of her cloven foot, by giving the world the creed of a reprobate, according to the dreadful doctrine of finished damnation. But as I flatter myself that my readers are already as tired of Calvinism as myself, I think it needless to raise their detestation of it, by drawing before their eyes a long chain of blasphemous positions, capable of making the hair of their heads stand up with horror. I shall, therefore, with all wise Calvinists, draw a veil over the hideous sight, and conclude by assuring you, few people more heartily wish you delivered from speculative Antinomianism, and possessed of salvation truly finished in glory, than, honoured and dear sir, your affectionate and obedient servant, in the bonds of what you call the "legalized Gospel,"

JOHN FLETCHER.

LETTER VIII.

To Richard Hill, Esq.

HON. AND DEAR SIR, — Having endeavoured, in my last, to convince you out of your own mouth, that undisguised Calvinism and speculative Antinomianism exactly coincide, before I turn from you to face you brother, I beg leave to vindicate good works from an aspersion, which zealous Calvinists perpetually cast upon them. For as practical Antinomianism destroys the fruits of righteousness, as a wild boar does the fruit of the vine; so speculative

Antinomianism besprinkles them with filth, as an unclean bird does the produce of our orchards.

Hence it is, that you charge me (Review, p. 69,) with "vile slander," for insinuating that our free-grace preachers do not "raise the superstructure in good works." Page 41, as if you wanted to demonstrate the truth of my "vile slander," you say, "Though we render the words χαλα εργα, 'good works,' yet the exact translation is 'ornamental works;' and truly, when brought to the strictness of the law, they do not deserve the name of 'good.' But, however grating the expression may sound to those who hope to gain a second justification by their works, yet we have Scripture authority to call them dung, dross, and filthy rags."

Now, sir, if Scripture authorizes us to call them thus, they are undoubtedly very useless, loathsome, and abominable; and the Minutes, which highly recommend them, are certainly dreadfully heretical. I must then lose all my controversial labour, or once more take up the shield of truth, and quench this *fiery* (should I not say, this "filthy") dart, which you have thrown at St. James' *undefiled* religion: I begin with your criticism.

I. "Though we render the words χαλα εργα, good works, yet the exact translation is ornamental works." I apprehend, sir, you are mistaken. The Greek word χαλος exactly answers to the Hebrew (טוב,) which conveys the joint ideas of *goodness* and *beauty*. Before there was any "filthy rag" in the world, "God saw every thing that he had made; and behold it was (טוב מאד) very good," which the Septuagint very exactly renders χαλα λιαν. Fully to overthrow your criticism, I need only to observe, that good works are called *good*, with the very same word by which the *goodness* of the law, and the *excellence* of the lawgiver are expressed. For St. Paul, speaking of the law, Romans vii, 16, says that it is χαλος, "good;" and our Lord, speaking of himself, says "I am ο ωοιμην ο χαλος, the GOOD Shepherd." Now, sir, as you are too pious to infer from the word Greek χαλος, that neither the law nor Christ "deserved to be called *good*," I hope you will be candid enough to give up your similar inference concerning *good works*.

Inconsistency is the badge of error. You give us, if I mistake not, a proof of it, by telling us with one breath that "good works do not deserve the name of *good*," but that of "*ornamental*;" and, with the next, that Scripture authorizes us to call them "dung, dross, and filthy rags." Are then dung, dross, and filthy rags *ornamental* things? or did you try to render Geneva criticism as famous as Geneva logic? But,

II. You have recourse to divinity as well as to criticism: for you say, "When good works are brought to the strictness of the law, they do not deserve the name of *good.*" I answer: If our Lord himself called them *good*, it does not become us to insinuate that in so doing he passed a wrong judgment, and countenanced "proud justiciars" in their legal error. With respect to the "strictness of the law," which you so frequently urge, your frightful notions about it cannot drive us into Antinomianism; because we think that Christ and St. Paul were better acquainted with the law than Calvin and yourself. If "all the law and the prophets hang on the grand commandment of love," as our Lord informs us; and if "he that loveth another hath fulfilled the law," as the apostle declares, we see no reason to believe that the law condemns as "dung" the labour of that love by which it is fulfilled, and rejects as "filthy rags" works which Christ himself promises to crown with eternal rewards. You probably reply: —

III. "Many Pharisees go to church without devotion, and many fornicators give alms without charity, fancying that such good works make amends for their sins, and merit heaven." *Good works,* do you call them? The Scriptures never gave them that honourable name. They are the hypocritical righteousness of unbelief, and not "works meet for repentance," or "the fruits of the righteousness of faith." Treat *them* as you please, but spare *good works.* It is as unjust to asperse good works on their account, as to hang the honest men who duly carry on the king's coinage at the mint, because the villains who counterfeit his majesty's coin evidently deserve the gallows.

IV. Should you object that "the best works have flaws, blemishes, and imperfections; and therefore may properly be called dung, dross, and filthy rags," I deny the consequence. The best guineas may have their flaws: nay, some dust or dirt may accidentally cleave to them; but this does not turn them into dross. As therefore a good guinea is gold, and not dross, though it has some accidental blemishes; so, God himself being judge, a good work is *a good work,* and not a filthy rag, though it is not free from all imperfections.

V. Not so, do you say? "We have Scripture authority to call good works *filthy rags.*" You build, it seems, your mistakes upon Isaiah lxiv, 6, "All our righteousness are as filthy rags:" a passage which, upon mature consideration, I beg leave to rescue from the hands of the Calvinists. The Jews were extremely corrupted in the days of Isaiah: hence he opens his prophecy by calling the rich, "Ye rulers of Sodom," and the poor, *"Ye* people of Gomorrah." And what says he to them? "How is the faithful city become a harlot! Righteousness lodged in it, but now murderers!" Yet these murderers hypocritically went on keeping their Sabbaths and new moons. They "fasted," but it was "for strife," and "to smite with the fist of wickedness." They "made many prayers," and offered multitudes of sacrifices, but "their hands were full of blood." Nor did they consider that he who, under these circumstances, "sacrifices an ox, is as if he slew a man."

This corruption of the Jews, though general, was not universal: for the Lord of hosts had left to them a remnant, though very small. Now Isaiah, one of that very little flock, being humbled at the sight of the general wickedness of his people, confesses it in the first person (*we*) as ministers always do on such occasions; and he uses the word *all,* because the small remnant of the righteous was as lost in the multitude of the wicked. The verse, taken in connection with the context, runs thus' "Thou meetest him that rejoiceth, and worketh righteousness, those that remember thee in thy ways." But, alas! we are not the people. " Behold, thou art wroth, for we have sinned. We are all as an unclean thing, and all our righteousnesses are as filthy rags." Therefore, instead of meeting us, as thou dost the righteous, thou hast hid thy face from us, and hast consumed us because of our iniquities. "We all do fade as a leaf; and our iniquities, like the wind, have taken us away:" so far are we from resembling the righteous, who "are like a tree planted by the water side, whose leaf does not wither." Who does not see that the prophet here opposes the happiness of the righteous to the misery of the wicked? And that it is the hypocritical righteousness of the ungodly, and not the precious obedience of believers, which he compares to filthy rags?

VI. However, "We have Scripture authority to call good works *dross.*" Your mind, I suppose, runs upon Isaiah i, 22, 25, where God expostulates with the obstinate Jews, by saying, "Thy silver is become dross," thy righteousness is all hypocrisy: yet, if thou returnest, "I will purge away thy dross," I will make thee truly righteous. Is it not evident, that it is hypocrisy and *bad* works, not *good* works, which God here calls *dross?* Will he, think you, purge away *good* works from his people? Is it not enough that armies of Antinomians do the devil that service? Must we also suppose that God promises to be his drudge?

VII. But, "we have Scripture authority to call good works *dung.*" Not at all: for the two passages you probably think of, are against you. In the first, God speaks to the disobedient Jews, and says, "If ye will not hear, and give glory unto my name, I will send a curse upon you: yea, I have cursed your blessings already. Behold, I will spread upon your faces the dung of your solemn feasts," Malachi ii, 2, 3. Now, sir, who does not see by the context that festivals kept by cursed hypocrites are called dung, and not the solemn worship performed by penitent believers?

If you quote Philippians iii, 8, it will be to as little purpose. Do you tightly understand that passage? "I count all things but loss, for the excellency of the knowledge of Christ, for whom I have suffered the loss of all things, and do count them but dung, that I may win Christ, and be found in him, not having mine own righteousness, which is of the law, but that which is through the faith of Christ." You know, sir, that the apostle once made far too much of his privileges as a Jew, his morals as an honest man, and his observance of the law as a strict disciple of Moses. And you remember that when he wrapped himself up in that kind of external righteousness, his heart breathed nothing but contempt toward Christ, and slaughter against his people. What wonder is it that he should count such a righteousness, together with all earthly, perishing things, loss and dung, for Christ? Who does not see that it was not the precious righteousness of faith, which consists in pardon, acceptance, and power to do good works, but the paltry righteousness of an unbeliever, a blasphemer, a murderer?

Should you say that when the apostle declares, "he counts all things but dung, that he may be found in Christ," he certainly includes good works, and counts them dung: I reply, You have as good reason to say that he certainly includes repentance, faith, obedience, grace, and glory, and counts them dung also!

Some gentlemen invite you to go a hunting, or play at cards, to keep you from the sessions; and you answer, "I am determined to do my duty. Once your sports were gain to me, but now I count them but loss of time: yea, doubtless, I count all things, that stand in competition with my office, vile and contemptible as dung' they no more tempt me to pursue them, than yonder dung hill tempts me to take my rest; I am ready to trample upon them as filthy dust, rather than not to be found upon the bench doing my duty as a magistrate: not according to my own former mistaken notions of justice, but according to the equitable laws of my country."

Now, sir, should I not very much wrong you if I inferred from your very generous answer that you call doing justice dung? And do you not greatly wrong St. Paul, when, upon a pretence equally frivolous, you insinuate that he gave to good works such an injurious name? That he called the will of God, done in faith by the Spirit of Christ, dung?

Again: when the apostle prayed to "be found in Christ, not having his own *Pharisaic* righteousness, which was of the *letter of* the law, but the righteousness which is of God by faith;" is it not evident that (beside the desire of being pardoned and accepted through faith in Christ) he wished to be found to the last a branch grafted "in the true vine," by faith? A living branch, filled with the righteous sap of the root that bore him? A branch made fruitful by the principle of all acceptable righteousness, which is "Christ in us, the hope of glory?" And, to use his own words in this very epistle, a branch "filled with the fruits of righteousness, which are by Jesus Christ to the glory of God?" Philippians i, 11, compared with iii, 9.

Let men of reason and religion say if this sense is not more agreeable to the letter of Scripture in general, and the apostle's words in particular, than the fantastic imputation of righteousness, which Calvinists build upon them. An imputation this, which constitutes a man righteous, while he commits adultery, murder, or incest. Is it not deplorable that such an unscriptural and unnatural idea should ever have entered the minds of pious men? Especially when St. John says, "Little children, let no man deceive you: he that does righteousness" and not barely he for whom Christ hath done righteousness, "is righteous?" Is it not lamentable that good men, influenced by prejudice, should be able to persuade thousands that St. John meant, "Let not Mr. Wesley deceive you; he that actually liveth with another man's wife, worships abominable idols, and commits incest with his father's wife, may not only be righteous, but complete in imputed righteousness; in a righteousness which exceeds, not only the righteousness of the Pharisees, but the personal righteousness of converted Paul, and of the brightest angel in glory!"

O sir, if you have told it in Paris, tell it not in Constantinople, lest the daughters of the Mohammedans bless God, that, lewd and bloody as their prophet was, he never so far lost sight of morality and decency as to give Mussulmen a cloak, under the specious name of a "robe of righteousness," under which they can curse, swear, and get drunk, commit adultery, robbery, murder, and incest, without being less righteous than if they had kept all the commandments of God; less in favour with the Most High than if they had personally abounded in all the works of piety, mercy, and self denial, which adorned the life of Jesus Christ; and less interested in finished salvation than if they were already in glory. O sir, is not this doctrine more dangerous than that of transubstantiation? Is it not more dishonourable to Christ, more immoral, and consequently more pernicious to society? And would it not absolutely destroy the morals of all those who receive it, if our Lord, for his name's sake, did not in mercy deny to thousands of them sense or attention, to draw a dreadful conclusion from their dreadful premises; while he graciously gives to thousands more hearts infinitely better than their immoral principles!

Having thus endeavoured to rescue the passages on which you found your assertion concerning good works, and proved that there is not one scripture which gives you the least authority to call them either dung, dross, or filthy rags; to convince you that a heap of impious absurdities lies concealed under that doctrine, permit me to produce some of the scriptures where good works are mentioned: and to substitute to that phrase the hard names which, you tell us, the Scripture authorizes you to call them.

"Let your light so shine before men, that they may see your good works, [i.e. your dung,] and glorify your Father who is in heaven." "She has wrought a good work [i.e. a filthy rag] upon me, against my burial." "Dorcas was full of good works," [i.e. of dung and rags.] "God make you to abound in every good work," i.e. in every sort of dung and dross. "We are created in Christ Jesus to good works," i.e. to filthy rags, "which God had prepared for us to walk in." "Walk worthy of the Lord, being fruitful in every good work," i.e. in every filthy rag. "God establish you in every good work," i.e. in dung of every sort. "Provoke one another to love and good works," i.e. to dross and rags. "Be zealous of good works," i.e. of filthy rags. "Be rich in good works," i.e. in dross. "Be careful to maintain good works," i.e. dung. "Let the Gentiles by your good works," i.e. your dung, "which they shall behold, glorify God in the day of visitation." "Be thoroughly furnished to every good work: be perfect in every good work," i.e. in dung and dross of every kind. "Blessed are they that die in the Lord, for their works," i.e. their dung and rags, "follow them." "God is not unrighteous, to forget your work," i.e. your dung, "that proceedeth of love." "The Gentiles should do works," i.e. dung, "meet for repentance." "Esteem ministers highly in love for their work's [i.e. their dung's,] sake." "If he have not works," i.e. dung, "can faith save him?" "Faith without works," i.e. without filthy rags, "is dead." "By works," i.e. dung, "was Abraham's faith made perfect." "He and Rahab were justified by works," by filthy rags. "He that believeth in me, the works that I do shall he do also, and greater works than these," i.e. filthier rags, and more ornamental dung, "shall he do." "This is the work," i.e. the dung, "of God, that you believe," &c.

Indeed, sir, I am almost ashamed to take up the "filthy rag" of this bad divinity, though it is only with the point of my pen, to hold it out a moment to public view, that the world may be sick of barefaced Antinomianism. I drop it again into the sink of defiled religion, out of which Dr. Crisp raked it; and beg for the honour of Christ and your own, that you will no more recommend it as pure Gospel.

And now, dear sir, permit me to expostulate a moment with you. Against whom have you employed your pen, when you have taught the world to call good works dung, dross, and filthy rags; pretending to have authority from the Scripture thus to revile the best thing under heaven? Is it only against the "proud justiciars?" Is it not also indirectly, though I am persuaded undesignedly, against the adorable trinity? Has not the Father "created us to good works?" Did not the Son "redeem us, that we might be a people zealous of good works?" And does not the Holy Ghost sanctify us, that "all our works being begun, continued, and ended in him, we may glorify God's holy name," and cause it to be glorified by all around us?

What harm did good works ever do you, or any one, that you should decry them in so public a manner as you have done? Did you ever duly consider their nature and excellence? Or have you condemned them in a hurry, without so much as casting an attentive look upon them? Permit me to bring them to you, as God brought the beasts of the field to Adam, that he might give them names according to their nature; and tell me which of them you will call dung, which dross, and which filthy rags?

First, then, what objection have you against the *good works of the heart?* Against the awaking out of sin, returning to God, repenting, offering the sacrifice of a contrite spirit, and believing unto righteousness? What objection against trusting in the Lord Jehovah, in whom is everlasting strength? casting the anchor of our hope within the veil? loving God for himself, and all mankind for God's sake? Do you see any of these good works of the heart that look like a "filthy rag?"

No sooner is the "inward man of the heart" truly engaged in any one of the preceding works, than the outward man is all in motion. The candle of the Lord is not lighted in the soul to be "put under a bushel," and extinguished, but to be set as "on a candlestick" of the body, "that it may give light to all" around, and that men "seeing our light, may glorify our heavenly Father." Hence arise several classes of external good works.

Consider the man of God as he is clothed with a corruptible body, which must be nourished without being pampered. He "keeps it under," by moderate fasting or abstinence. He "daily denies himself, and takes up his cross." He works with cheerful diligence. He eats, drinks, or sleeps, "with gladness and singleness of heart;" and if he is sick, he bears his pain with joyful resignation, doing or suffering "all to the glory of God," in the spirit of sacrifice, and "in the name of the Lord Jesus."

View him in his family. Not satisfied with mental prayer, he bends the knee "to his Father who sees in secret;" and not contented with private devotions, he reads to his assembled household select portions of God's word, and solemnly worships him with them "in spirit and in truth." Nor does he think, that doing his duty toward God excuses him from fulfilling it toward his neighbour. Just the reverse. Because his soul is all reverence to his heavenly Father, it is all respect to his earthly parents. Because he ardently loves the Bridegroom of souls, he feels the warmest regard for his wife, he bears the tenderest, and yet the most rational affection to his children. Nor is he less desirous that his servants should serve God and "work out their salvation," than he is that they should serve him and do his work. Hence arise his familiar instructions, mild reproofs, earnest entreaties, encouraging exhortations. His strict honesty and meekness of wisdom, his moderation and love of peace are known to all around him; and even those who despise his piety are forced to speak well of his morals.

Behold his works as a member of society in general. In his little sphere of action he makes his star "to shine upon the just and the unjust," his charity is universal. To the utmost of his ability he opposes vice, countenances virtue, promotes industry, and patronizes despised piety. Humble faith kindles him into "a burning and shining light:" he is a minister of the God of all mercies, he is a flaming fire. He feeds Christ in the hungry, gives him drink in the thirsty, clothes him in the naked, entertains him in strangers, attends him on sick beds, visits him in prisons, and comforts him in the mournful apartments, where the guilty are stretched on the rack of despair, or where the godly, forsaken of their friends, pledge their dying Lord with the dregs of the cup of sorrow. How easily does he overlook the unkindness of his neighbours! How readily does he forgive injuries! How cordially heaps he coals of melting fire upon the heads of his enemies! How sincerely does he pray for all his slanderers and persecutors! And how ardently desire "to grow in grace," and endeavour "to adorn" more and more "the doctrine of God our Saviour in all things!"

Consider him as a member of a religious society. How excellent, how Divine are his works! He respectfully holds up the hands of his minister, and kindly bears the burdens of his brethren. He watches over them for good, "rejoices with those that rejoice, "and "mourns with those that mourn." He compassionately sympathizes with the tempted, impartially reproves sin, meekly restores the fallen, and cheerfully animates the dejected. Like undaunted Caleb, he spirits up the fearful; and, like valiant Joshua, he leads them to the conquest of Canaan; and goes on "from conquering to conquer."

And suppose he "went on *even* unto perfection," and "took the kingdom of heaven by violent" faith, and humble, patient, importunate prayer; would you call him a filthy rag man, and insinuate that he had only done a dung work? O, sir, if you can so publicly call good works, dross, dung, and filthy rags; and (what is worse still) assert, that the Holy Ghost in the Scriptures, authorizes you so to do; who will wonder to see you represent the doctrine of Christian perfection as a pernicious Popish heresy, which turns men "into temporary monsters?" Would you be consistent, if you did not rise against it with the collected might of credulous uncharitableness, and barefaced Antinomianism? For,

What is, after all, the perfection that Mr. Wesley contends for? Nothing but two good works, productive of ten thousand more; or, if you please, two large filthy rags, in which ten thousand other filthy rags are wrapped; that is, "loving God with all our hearts, and our neighbour as ourselves." it is nothing but "perfect love shed abroad in our hearts by the Holy Ghost given unto us," making us "steadfast, immovable, always abounding in the work of the Lord," always "zealous of good works," always the reverse of the easy elect, who, by means of Calvin's contrivance, are "all fair and undefiled," while they wallow in the adulterer's mire, and the murderer's gore. Or, in other terms, it is nothing but Christ, through the Holy Spirit, "dwelling in our hearts by faith," and making us always "zealous of good works." Now, if good works are dross, dung, and filthy rags; it is evident that perfection is a rich mine of dross; a heap of dung, as immense as that which Hercules got out of Augeas' stables; and a vast store house of filthy rags, spun by "proud justiciars," as cobwebs are by venomous spiders.

In this wrong view of Christian perfection, I no more wonder to see multitudes of careless professors agree, like Pilate and Herod, to destroy it out of the earth; nor am I surprised to hear even good, mistaken people cry out, "Down with it! down with it!" While I complain of their want of candour, I commend their well-meant zeal, and wish it may flame out against objects worthy of their detestation; against perfection itself, suppose it is what they imagine. Yes, if it is a mine of "dross," let them drown it: I give my consent; but let them do it with the floods of Scripture and argument. If it is a dung hill in the Church, let them carry it out, and permit even the swine, which come "from wallowing in the mire," to shake themselves upon it: I will not say it is improper. If it is a repository of filthy rags, more infectious than those which convey the jail distemper or the plague; let them agree to set fire to it, and burn it down to the ground: but let them do it with "fire from the altar," and not with "tongues set on fire" of prejudice or malice.

But if Christian perfection is (next to angelic perfection) the brightest and richest jewel which Christ purchased for us by his blood; if it is the internal kingdom of God ruling over all; if it is Christ *fully* formed in our hearts, the *full* hope of glory; if it is the fulfilment of the promise of the Father, that is, "the Holy Ghost given unto us," to make us abound in righteousness, peace, and joy, through believing; and in a word, if it is the Shekinah, filling the Lord's human temples with glory; is it right, sir, to despise it as some do, or to expose it as you have so frequently done?

Should you apologize for your conduct, by saying, "I have only treated YOUR perfection as you have treated OUR finished salvation, and OUR imputed righteousness:" I reply, The case is widely different. I hope I have made it appear, that you have not one single text in all the Bible to prove that a bloody adulterer (*in flagrante delicto*) stands complete in imputed righteousness; or that the salvation of idolatrous and incestuous apostates, who now work out their damnation with both hands, is actually finished, in the full extent of the expression. The whole stream of God's word runs counter to these "Antinomian dotages." Nor are they less repugnant to conscience and common sense, than to the law and the prophets. But you cannot find one word in all the Scriptures against the pure love of God and our neighbour, against perfect love, which is all the perfection we encourage believers to press after. The law and the Gospel, the Old and the New Testament, are equally for it. All who are "filled with the Spirit," sweetly experience it. A heathen, that fears God and regards man, cannot speak evil of it, but through misapprehension. And even while, through the amazing force of prejudice, you write against it with so much severity, it recommends itself to your own reason, and conscience. Are you not then, dear sir, under a mistake, when you think you may take the same liberty with God's undeniable truth, which I have taken with Dr. Crisp's indefensible error?

Permit me to state the case more fully still. Mr. Wesley cries to believers' "It is your privilege so to believe in Christ, and receive the Spirit, as to 'love God with all your hearts, and your neighbours as yourselves.'" And you say to them: "Mr. Wesley is blinder than a Papist, regard not his heretical words. Your salvation is finished. Whatever lengths you go in sin, you are as sure of heaven as if you were already there. It is your privilege to commit adultery, murder, and incest, not only without fearing that the Lord will be displeased with you; but conscious that, black as ye are in yourselves by the actual commission of these crimes, through Christ's comeliness put upon you, God can address each of you with, Thou art all fair, my love, my undefiled, there is no spot in thee!" (*Five Letters*, p. 28.) Now, sir, are you not a partial judge, when, by way of retaliation, you serve the holy doctrine maintained by Mr. Wesley, as I have served the unholy tenet propagated by Calvin and yourself?

Think you, really, that because a judge, after a fair trial, justly condemns a notorious robber to be hanged; another judge, to retaliate, has a right to quarter a good man, after a mock trial, or rather without any trial at all? And do you suppose, that because Jehu deservedly made "the house of Baal a draught house;" or because Josiah burned dead men's bones upon the unhallowed "altar in Bethel," to render it detestable to idolaters, Antiochus had a right to turn the temple of the Lord into a stye, and to pollute "the altar of incense," by burning "dung. and filthy rags" upon it, that true worshippers might abominate the offering of the Lord, and loathe the holy of holies? Thus, however, have you (inadvertently I hope) treated good works and Christian perfection, which are ten thousand times more sacred and precious in the sight of God than the holy, and the most holy place in the temple of Jerusalem.

And now, dear sir, please to look at the preceding list of the good works, which adorn the Christian's breast, or blazon his shining character; and tell us if there is one, which, upon second thoughts, you object against as a nuisance: one, which you would put away like "dross;" one, which you would have carried out of his apartment as "dung," or remove from his pious breast as a "filthy rag."

Methinks I hear you answer, "Not one. May they all abound more and more in my heart and life, and in the hearts and lives of all God's people!" Methinks that all the Church militant and triumphant cry out, "Amen!" A Divine power accompanies their general exclamation. The veil of prejudice begins to rend. Your honest heart relents. You acknowledge that Calvinism has deceived you. You retract your unguarded expressions. The Spirit of holiness, whom you have grieved, returns. The heavenly light shines. The Antinomian charm is broken. "Dross" is turned into fine gold; "dung" into savoury meat, which every believer loveth next to the bread of life; and "filthy rags," into the "linen, fine and white, which is the righteousness of the saints, and the robe made white in the blood of the Lamb." Far from pouring contempt, through voluntary humility, upon this precious garment, you give praise to God, and in humble triumph put it on, together with the Lord Jesus Christ.

In that glorious dress you "walk with Christ in white," and in love with Mr. Wesley. Paris, and the convent of Benedictine monks, disappear. The "New Jerusalem," and "the tabernacle of God, come down from heaven. Leaving the things that are behind, *you solemnly* hasten unto the day of the Lord. Following peace with all men, and holiness, without which no man shall see the Lord, *you daily* perfect it in the fear of God." You feel the amazing difference there is between a real and an imaginary imputation of righteousness. You tear away with honest indignation the pillow of finished salvation from under the head of Laodicean backsliders, who sleep in sin; and of bloody murderers, who defile their neighbour's bed. You set fire to the fatal canopy, under which you have inadvertently taught them to fancy that the holy and righteous God calls them "My love, my undefiled!" even while they wallow in the poisonous mire of the. most atrocious wickedness. And to undo the harm you have done, or remove the offence you have given by your letters, you show yourself reconciled to St. James' pure religion; you openly give Mr. Wesley the right hand of fellowship, and gladly help him "to provoke" believer's to uninterrupted "love and good works," that is, to Christian perfection.

Such is the delightful prospect which my imagination discovers through the clouds of our controversy; and such are the pleasing hopes that sometimes soothe my polemical toil, and even now make me subscribe myself, with an additional pleasure, honoured and dear sir, your affectionate brother and obedient servant, in the bonds of a pure Gospel,

JOHN FLETCHER.

LETTER IX.

To Mr. Rowland Hill.

DEAR SIR, — Your uncommon zeal for God, so far as it is guided by knowledge, entitling you to the peculiar love and reverence of all that fear the Lord; I should be wanting in respect to you, if I took no notice of the arguments with which you are come from Cambridge to the help of your pious brother. In the *Friendly Remarks* that you have directed to me, you say with great truth, (page 31,) "the principal cause of controversy among us is the doctrine of a second justification by works. Thus much you indicate throughout, that a man is justified before the bar of God a second time by his own good works."

So I do, dear sir; and I wonder how any Christian can deny it, when Christ himself declares, "In the day of judgment, by thy words shalt thou be justified," &c. Had he said "By my words imputed to thee thou shalt be justified," you might indeed complain. But now, what reason have you to assert, as you do, that I "have grossly misrepresented the Scriptures," and "made universal havoc of every truth of the Gospel?" The first of these charges is heavy, the second dreadful. Let us see by what arguments they are supported. After throwing away a good part of your book in passing a long, Calvinian, juvenile sentence upon my spirit as a writer, you come at last to the point, and attempt to explain some of the scriptures, which you suppose I have "misrepresented."

I. Page 32, "'Not every one that saith unto me, Lord, Lord, shall enter into the kingdom of heaven, but he that doeth the will of my Father,'" Matthew 7:21. "And what is this (say you) more than a description of those who are to be saved?"

What, sir, is it nothing but a description? Is it not a solemn declaration, that no practical Antinomian shall be saved by faith in the last day? And that Christ is really a Lord and a King, who has a law, which he will see obeyed? Had he not just before, (verse 12,) admitted the law and the prophets into his Gospel dispensation, saying, "All things which ye would that men should do unto you, do ye even so unto them, for this is the law and the prophets?" Are we not under this law to him? And will he not command his subjects, who obstinately violate it, to be brought and slain before him?

Again: when he declares that they who "hate a brother, and call him, Thou fool! are in danger of hell fire as murderers!" do we not expose his legislative wisdom, as well as his paternal goodness, by intimating, that, without having an eye to the murder of the heart or the tongue, he only describes certain wretches whom he unconditionally designs for everlasting burnings?

What I say of a punishment threatened is equally true of a reward promised, as you may see by the following illustration of our controverted text. A general says to his soldiers, as he leads them to the field of battle, "Not every one that calls me, Your honour, your honour, shall be made a captain; but he that fights manfully for his king and country." You say, "What is this more than a description of those that shall be promoted?" And I reply, If warlike exploits have absolutely nothing to do with their promotion; and if the general's declaration is only a description of some favourites, whom he is determined to raise at any rate; could he not as well have described them by the colour of their hair, or height of their stature? And does he not put a cheat upon all the soldiers, whom he is absolutely determined not to raise; when he excites them to quit themselves like men, by the fond hope of being raised? Apply this simile to the case in hand, and you will see, dear sir, how frivolous, and injurious to our Lord is your intimation, that one of his most awful royal proclamations is nothing but an empty description. O Calvinism! is this thy reverence for Jesus Christ? Hast thou no way of supporting thyself but by turning the Lord of glory into a Virgil? The supreme Lawgiver of men and angels into a maker of descriptions?

II. Much of the same nature is the observation which you make (p. 37) upon these words of our Lord. "They that have done good shall go into life everlasting; and they that have done evil into everlasting punishment." You say "What does this text prove more than has been granted before? What does it more than characterize those that shall be saved?" Nay, sir, it undoubtedly characterizes all those that shall be damned; and this too by as essential a character, as that according to which the king would appoint some of his servants for a gracious reward, and others for a capital punishment, if he said to them, "They that serve me faithfully shall be richly provided for; and they that rob me shall be hanged." If such characterizing as this passes at Geneva for a bare description of persons whom royal humour irrespectively singles out for reward, I hope the time is coming when at Cambridge it will pass for a clear declaration of the reason why some are rewarded, or punished, rather than others; and for a proof that the king is no more a capricious dispenser of rewards, than a tyrannical inflicter of punishments.

III. Page 33. After mentioning these words of St. Paul, "Without holiness no man shall see the Lord;" and those words which St. James wrote to believers, "Be ye doers of the word and not hearers only, deceiving your own selves;" you say, "What is this to the purpose respecting a second justification? Just about as much as, 'Now an omer is the tenth part of an ephah.'" Now, sir, although I do not immediately rest the cause upon such scriptures, I maintain, that they are much more to the purpose of our second justification by works than Moses' definition of an omer.

Five Checks To Antinomianism

Will you dare to say, dear sir, that impious Jezebel, and unconverted Manasses, were persons "just about as" properly qualified for justification in the great day, because they had an omer in their palace, as pious Deborah, and holy Samuel, who had holiness in their hearts, and were doers of the word in their lives? And when the apostle declares that "Christ is the author of eternal salvation to them that obey him," does he mean, that to obey is a thing just about as important to eternal salvation, as to know that a bushel holds four pecks, and an ephah ten omers? Were ever holiness and obedience inadvertently set in a more contemptible light? For my part, if "by our words we shall be justified in the day of judgment," I believe it shall be by our words springing from holiness of heart; and therefore I cannot but think that holiness will be more to the purpose of our justification by works in the great day, than all the omers and ephahs, with all the notions about imputed righteousness and finished salvation, in the world.

IV. Page 33. After quoting that capital passage, "Not the hearers of the law are just before God, but the doers shall be justified," Romans ii, 13, you say, "This certainly proves that the doers of the law shall be justified." Well, then, it directly proves a justification by works. But you immediately insinuate the "impossibility of salvation by the law." I readily grant, that in the day of conversion, we are "justified by faith," not only "without the deeds of the *ceremonial law*," but even without a previous observance of the law of love. But the case is widely different in the day of judgment; for then "by thy words shalt thou be justified." Now, sir, it remains for you to prove, that the apostle did not speak of the text under consideration, with an eye to our final justification by works.

In order to this, (p. 33,) you appeal to "the place which this text stands in, and the connection in which the words are found." I answer,

1. This text stands in the Epistle to the Romans, to whom the apostle says, "Love is the fulfilling of the law: he that loveth another hath fulfilled the law," Romans xiii, 8, 10. Now, if "he that loveth another hath fulfilled the law," you must show that it is impossible to "love another," or acknowledge that there are persons who "fulfil the law;" and consequently persons who can be justified as "doers of the law." Nay, in the very chapter such persons are thus mentioned, "If the uncircumcision keep the righteousness of the law, and fulfil the law, shall it not judge thee who dost transgress the law?" That is, shall not a Cornelius, an honest heathen, that "fears God and works righteousness," rise in judgment against thee who "committest adultery;" vainly supposing that Abraham's chastity is imputed to thee? Romans ii, 22, 27. But,

2. Going back to the beginning of the chapter where our controverted text stands, I affirm that "the connection in which it is found" establishes also justification by works in the great day: and to prove it I only lay the apostle's words before my judicious readers. "Thou art inexcusable, O Jew, whosoever thou art that judgest, or condemnest *the heathens,* who do such things, *and* doest them thyself. The judgment of God is according to truth," and not according to thy Antinomian notions, that thou wast unconditionally elected in Abraham; that thou standest complete in his righteousness; and that thy salvation was finished when he had offered up Isaac. Be not deceived, "God will render to every man according to his *deeds:* [and not according to his notions:'] to them who by patient continuance in well doing, seek for immortality, he will render eternal life:

anguish to every man that doeth evil; but glory to every man that worketh good: for not the hearers of the law are just before God, but the doers of the law shall be justified — in the day when he shall judge the secrets of men by Jesus Christ, according to my Gospel," Romans ii, 1-16.

Now, sir, is it not evident from "the connection" to which you appeal, that Mr. Henry did not pervert the text, when he had the courage to say upon it, "It is not hearing but doing that will save us" in the great day? Hearing, mixed with faith, saves us indeed instrumentally in the day of conversion; but in the day of judgment, neither hearing nor faith will do it; but "patient continuance in well doing," from the principle of a living faith in Christ, will have that honour.

V. Page 34. After criticising in the same frivolous manner as your brother on Revelation xxii, 14, "Blessed are they that keep his commandments," &c, you add, "This is his commandment, That we should believe on the name of his Son Jesus Christ," and omitting what follows, "and love one another, as he gave us commandment," you ask, "What then is the conclusion? To believe is the great New Testament command of God." No, sir; according to 1 John iii, 23, the text you have quoted by halves, that commandment is to believe and to love, or to believe with a "faith working by love." Our Lord informs us, that on the grand commandment of love "hang all the law and the prophets." St. Paul says, "Though I have all faith, yet if I have not love, I am nothing." "Devils believe," says St. James. To believe, then, without loving, is not "doing God's commandments," but doing the devil's work. Because the word commandments, being in the plural number, denotes more than one, and therefore is incompatible with Solifidianism.

To add, as you do, "They that believe will and must obey," as if they could not help it, is supporting one mistake by another. That they may, can, and should obey, we grant: but that they will and must, are two articles of Calvin's creed, to which we cannot subscribe; for, to say nothing of daily experience, we read in the Scripture dismal accounts of those fallen believers, who, instead of "adding to their faith virtue," &c, proceeded so far "in wilful disobedience," as to "worship the abomination of the Zidonians, shed innocent blood," forswear themselves, and defile their father's bed.

It follows then still from Revelation xxii, 14, that although "upon believing, not for obeying, we are initiated into all the new covenant blessings" in the day of conversion; yet in the great day, only upon persevering in faith and obedience, shall we have right, or, if you please, "privilege, power, and authority, through our Surety, to partake of the tree of life." For "he that endureth unto the end, the same shall be saved;" and "Christ is the author of eternal salvation to *none but* them that obey him."

VI. Page 36. You quote, against yourself, Revelation xiv, 13, "'Blessed are the dead that die in the Lord.' Their blessedness arises from their dying in the Lord." Granted. But how shall it be known they died in the Lord? The Spirit says, "Their works [not their faith] do follow them," namely, in order to their final justification. To this you reply, "Their works do not go before them — but follow after, to prove that they were in the Lord, whose prerogative alone is to 'justify the ungodly.'" I answer,

1. When you grant that works prove that we are in the Lord, if they are good, or in the wicked one if they are evil, you give up the point.

2. Do you not confound truth and error? Because in the day of conversion "God justifies the ungodly," who renounces his ungodliness to believe in Jesus, does it follow that Jesus will justify the ungodly in the day of judgment? Is not the insinuation as unscriptural as it is dangerous? Does not our Lord himself say, that, far from justifying them, he will bid them "depart from him into everlasting fire?"

3. Your observation, that works follow the righteous, and "do not go before them," is frivolous: for what matters it, whether the witnesses, by whose evidence a prisoner is to be acquitted, follow him to the bar, or are there before him? Is their following him a proof that he is not justified by their instrumentality? To support your cause by such arguments will do it no service.

VII. Page 37. You think to set aside these words of Solomon, "Keep God's commandments, for this is the whole [duty] of man; for God shall bring every work into judgment, whether it be good or bad," by just saying, "This passage asserts, that we are to be accountable for our actions." Then it asserts the very thing for which it was produced: for how can those be really accountable for their actions, who can never be justified or condemned by their words, never be rewarded or punished according to their works? Here, then, again you grant what we contend for.

VIII. Page 38. "Circumcision is nothing — but the keeping the commandments of God," 1 Corinthians vii, 19. "This passage (say you) would equally as well prove the supremacy of the pope, as your doctrine of a second justification by works."

I answer, (1.) If you compare this text with Ecclesiastes xii, 13, 14; Revelation xxii, 14, and Matthew xii, 37, you will see it is very much to the purpose. (2.) Love is keeping of the commandments. If I have not love, which is "the keeping of the commandments, I am only a tinkling cymbal." Now, sir, you must prove that God will justify tinkling cymbals by imputed righteousness in the great day; or acknowledge that the keeping of the commandments, or, which is the same, love, makes more toward our final justification than toward placing his holiness the pope in the pretended chair of St. Peter. (3.) If the doers of the law shall be finally justified, and none but they; and if keeping the commandments is the same thing as being a doer of the law, you boldly hoist the Geneva flag when you insinuate that the keeping of the commandments has no more to do with our final justification than with the supremacy of the pope. Lastly, If keeping the commandments will have nothing to do with our justification in the last day, by a parity of reason, breaking of them will have nothing to do with our condemnation. Thus we are insensibly come to the dreadful counterpart of your comfortable doctrine, that is, absolute reprobation, free wrath, and finished damnation. And when the apostle says, "God shall judge the world in righteousness," should he not rather, according to your plan, have said, in unrighteousness?

IX. Instead of answering such passages as these: "Behold; I come quickly, and my reward is with me, to give to every man as his work shall be." He that knoweth the heart, "shall render to every man according to his works. We shall all appear before the judgment seat of Christ, that every one may receive the things done in the body, according to that he hath done, whether it be good or bad. The Father, without respect of persons, judgeth according to every man's work. The dead were judged out of the things written in the books, according to their works." Instead, I say, of answering such passages, you leap over fifty pages of my book, to blame me (p. 35) for saying after St. Peter, Acts ii, 40, "SAVE YOURSELVES from this untoward generation!"

Granting you, sir, that the Greek word means literally, "Be ye saved;" yet you wrong our translation when you say that its language is "glaringly inconsistent." The words that immediately precede, "He exhorted them, saying, Save yourselves," &c, convinced our translators of the absurdity of exhorting people to be saved, that could absolutely do nothing in order to salvation. And you make Calvinism ridiculous before all Cambridge, when (p. 36) you make σωθητε, "Be ye saved;" or when spoken in a way of exhortation, "Save yourselves," to mean, "Know that ye cannot save yourselves."

Page 35, you say, "Let the context illustrate this: Thousands 'were pricked to the heart;' they ask 'what they shall do?' doubtless meaning 'to be saved.' The apostle directs them immediately to Jesus for salvation." What! without doing any thing toward it? No such thing. To the overthrow of your criticism, and of Calvinism, he sets them immediately upon doing. Their question was, "What shall we do to be saved?" and the immediate answer is, "Repent and be baptized." Just as if he had said, Be ye saved, or, Save yourselves by repenting and coming to Christ: or, to use the words of Christ to the people of Capernaum, and those of St. Paul to the jailer of Philippi, "Do the work of God," i.e. the work which God first calls for; "believe in the Lord Jesus, and you shall be saved."

You add, "This language ('Save yourselves') ill becomes the mouth of inspiration." I am sorry, sir, you should be so exceedingly positive. I rather think, that your "language ill becomes the mouth of" modesty. Does not St. Jude say, "Save some with fear?" Does not St. Paul mention his endeavours to "save some of his own flesh," Romans xi, 14, and his "becoming all things to all men, that he might save some?" 1 Corinthians ix, 22.

Does he not speak of a husband "saving his wife," and of a wife "saving her husband?" 1 Corinthians vii, 16. Does he not write to the Philippians, "Work out your own salvation;" and to Timothy, "In doing this, thou shalt save thyself and them that hear thee?" 1 Timothy iv, 16. You are too good a scholar, sir, to say, that Greek σωσεις σεαυτον "is passive:" and too modest a divine to insinuate, upon second thoughts, that St. Paul speaks like a heretic, and you like an apostle.

X. After opposing our doctrine of justification by the evidence of works in the last day, as warmly as your pious brother, you give yore public assent to it as well as he. Page 34, speaking of the day that shall declare every man's work, and the fire that shall try of what sort it is, you say, "Who that reads the Bible denies, that every man's works shall be examined as a proof of his faith, and that upon their evidence the Judge will pass sentence?" Undoubtedly you mean sentence of absolution or condemnation, according to our Lord's words, "By thy words shalt thou be justified or condemned," Matthew xii, 37.

Now, sir, this is the very doctrine which we maintain; as you may see, Second Check, pp. 86, 88*; the very doctrine for which you represent me to the world as a Papist, and fierce enemy to the Gospel. Gentle reader, take notice of my capital crime. I have dared to vindicate a truth, which, my opponent himself being judge, "no man that reads the Bible denies!" Is this a dreadful heresy? O sir, when this shall be known in our universities, will not Oxford cry to Cambridge, and Cambridge echo back to Oxford, the substance of your book, and the title of mine? *Logica Genevensis!*

XI. Now that you have granted the doctrine of justification by the evidence of works in the day of judgment, let us see how you endeavour to keep your system in countenance. Page 34, you say, contrary to your own concession, "Though works have not the least to do in justifying our persons, yet they will appear to the justifying of that faith, as sound, by which alone we are to be saved."

To cut you off from this last subterfuge, I observe, (1.) That works will have as much to do in justifying our persons in the last day, as faith in justifying them at our conversion. (2.) This doctrine of faith, being justified by works in the day of judgment, is irrational: for faith shall then be no more; and common sense dictates, that Christ, the wisdom of God, will not lose time in justifying or condemning a grace which shall not exist. (3.) It is quite unscriptural. Our Lord says, "By thy words shalt thou [not by faith] be justified." St. Paul says, "The doers of the law [not their faith] shall be justified." And St. James declares, that "Rahab [not her faith] and Abraham [not his faith] were justified by works," in the day of trial. (4.) Your scheme fathers nonsense upon that apostle: for if faith is justified by works, and not a man, it follows, that when St. James says "Ye see then how that by works a man is justified, and not by faith only," it is just as if he said, "Ye see then how that by works faith is justified, and not by faith only." (5.) If the believer's faith is justified in the last day, and not the believer himself; by a parity of reason, the unbeliever's unbelief will be condemned, and not the unbeliever himself. (6.) We have as good ground to assert, that the faith of believers shall be saved in the last day, and not their persons; as you to maintain, that the faith of believers shall be justified, and not their persons. Thus, according to your curious doctrine, faith, not believers, shall go to heaven; and unbelief, not unbelievers, shall depart into hell. Lastly: If " works have not the least to do in justifying our persons" in the great day; it follows, they will not have the least to do in condemning them. Thus are we come again to the doctrine of finished damnation; and thus you point blank contradict your own Scriptural concession, "Upon the evidence of works the Judge will pass sentence."

From the preceding pages it appears, if I am not mistaken, that justification by works, i.e. by the works of faith, in the last day, is a solid anvil, which the twelve strokes of your hammer have settled more than ever upon its firm basis, "The word of God, that abideth for ever." To this anvil I shall, by and by, bring Calvinian Antinomianism, and endeavour to work it, in meekness of wisdom, with a hammer, I hope, a little heavier than your own.

---

* [83, 85]

Having answered your objections to what you justly call "the principal cause of controversy among us," I may make one or two observations upon the *friendliness* of your *Friendly Remarks*.

Candid reader, if thou hast read my Checks without prejudice, and attentively compared them with the word of God, wouldst thou ever think that the following lines contain an extract from the *friendly* sentence, which my young opponent passes upon them? "Hard names, banter, sarcasm, sneer, abuse, bravado, low arts of slander, slanderous accusations, opprobrious names, ill-natured satire — odious, deformed, detestable colours — unfair and ungenerous treatment, terms void of truth, unmerciful condemnations, false humility, irritating spirit — provoking, uncharitable style — continual sneers, most odious appellations, abusive words, notorious scandalizing — lines too dreadful to be transcribed, unworthy of an answer, beneath contempt — most indecent ridicule — a wretched conclusion, as bitter as gall — and slanders, which ought even to make a Turk blush!"

If thou canst not yet see, gentle reader, into the nature of Mr. Rowland Hill's *Remarks,* peruse the following *friendly* sentences. "In regard to the fopperies of religion, you certainly differ from the Popish priest of Madeley. You have made universal havoc of every truth of the Gospel. You have invented dreadful slanders. You plentifully stigmatize many with the most unkind language. You have blackened our principles, and scandalized our practice. You place us in a manner among murderers. It shocks me to follow you. Our characters lie bleeding under the cruelty of your pen, and complain loudly against your great injustice. Blush for the characters you have injured by the rashness and bitterness of your pen. You have invented a set of monsters; and raised a hideous ghost by your own spells, and incantations of banter and contempt. Numberless sneers, taunts, and sarcasms dreadfully decorate the whole of your performance: they are nothing better than infernal terms of darkness, which it is hateful to transcribe. Your Second Check, I fear, must prove the concluding bar of separation," that is, of excommunication.

When I cast my eye upon this extract, I cannot help crying out, If this is my antagonist's friendliness, alas! what will be his displeasure? And what have I done to deserve these tokens of Calvinian benevolence? Why are these flowers of Geneva rhetoric so plentifully heaped upon my head? And why? But I must not complain; for my friendly opponent has patiently stayed till the publication of the Second Check, to talk of a "concluding bar of separation." But if I am a reprobate, upon his scheme of unconditional election and gratuitous reprobation, Calvin's God put "the concluding bar of separation" between me and himself, not only before I wrote the Second Check, but thousands of years before I drew my first breath. When I consider this, far from feeling the least resentment against Mr. Hill, I see it my duty to thank him for showing much greater patience toward me than the God whom he worships; and I wonder that his severe principles should not be productive of more *unfriendly Remarks,* than those which he is pleased to call *friendly*.

Five Checks To Antinomianism

Yes, sir, though I thought at first that the title of your book was ironical, I now believe it literal, and am persuaded you really meant to show me much friendliness. For a temporary excommunication, yea, a "concluding bar of separation," must appear an act of grace to one who truly relishes the doctrines of limited grace and unprovoked wrath.

I do not hereby intimate that I have done nothing displeasing to you. Far from insinuating it, I shall present my readers with a list of the manifold, but well-meant provocations, which have procured me your public correspondence. I say well-meant provocations; for all I want to provoke any one to is love and good works. And may not a minister use even the rod for that purpose? If you think not, please to inform me what the apostle meant, when he said "What will ye? Shall I come unto you with the rod, or in love, and in the spirit of meekness?"

1. I have written my Checks with the confidence with which the clear dictates of reason, and the full testimonies of Scripture, usually inspire those who love what they esteem truth more than they do their dearest friends.

2. After speaking most honourably of many Calvinists, even of all that are pious, I have taken the liberty to insinuate, that the schemes of finished salvation, and imputed righteousness, will no more save a Calvinist guilty of practical Antinomianism, than the doctrine of general redemption will save an ungodly Remonstrant. Thus I have made no difference between the backsliding elect of the Lock, and the apostates of the Foundery, when death overtakes them in their sins and in their blood.

3. I have maintained that our Lord did not speak an untruth, when he said, "In the day of judgment, by thy words shalt thou be justified;" and that St. Paul did not propagate heresy, when he wrote, "Work out your own salvation!"

4. I have sprinkled with the salt of irony* your favourite doctrine. (*Friendly Remarks*, page 39,) "Salvation wholly depends upon the purpose of God according to election, without any respect to what may be in them," that is, the elect. Now, sir, as by the doctrine of undeniable consequences, he who receives a guinea with the king's head on the one side, cannot but receive the lion's on the other side; so he that admits the preceding proposition, cannot but admit the inseparable counterpart, namely, the following position, which every attentive and unprejudiced person sees written in blood upon that side of Calvin's standard which is generally kept out of sight, "Damnation wholly depends upon the

---

* If I make use of irony in my Checks, I can assure thee, reader, it is not from "spleen," but reason. It appears to me that the subject requires it; and that ridiculous error is to be turned out of the temple of truth, not only with Scriptural argument, which is "the sword of the Spirit," but also with mild irony, which is a proper scourge for a glaring an obstinate mistake. I have already observed, that our Lord himself used it with his apostles, when he came out of his agony and bloody sweat. Some other remarkable instances of it we find in Scripture, 1 Kings xxii, 15. Micaiah, a prophet of the Lord, being requested by King Ahab and pious King Jehoshaphat to tell them, whether Israel should go against Ramoth Gilead to battle: he ironically answered," Go, and prosper; for the Lord shall deliver it into the hands of the king." Well known is that solemn, though ironical, or, as Mr. Hill would call it, sarcastic reproof of Solomon to a young prodigal, "Rejoice, O young man, in thy youth, let thine heart cheer thee, and walk in the way of thy heart, and in the sight of thy eyes," Eccles, xi, 9. From these examples I conclude, that an irony dictated by love not only is no sign of "a bad spirit," but is a useful figure of speech, especially where the rapid progress of a preposterous error calls for the sharp rebukes mentioned by St. Paul in my motto.

The Works of John Fletcher

purpose of God according to reprobation, without respect to what may be in the reprobates." Here is no "inventing a monstrous creed," but merely turning the leaf of your own, and reading what is written there, namely, Damnation finished, evidently answering to finished salvation.

5. You have done more, says my opponent, (p. 47,) "You scarce write a page without unjust reflections. To follow you through all your accusations would be endless. One passage, however, which seems to me to shine conspicuous among the rest for calumny and falsehood, as the moon does among the stars, shall be the last we will notice."

I say, in the Second Check, "How many intimate, that Christ has fulfilled all righteousness, that we might be the children of God with hearts full of unrighteousness!" And you reply," How many? There are a generation it seems of these black blasphemers. [I would say, of these mistaken Calvinists.] Produce but a few of them."

Well, sir, I produce first the author of Pietas Oxoniensis, next yourself, and then all the Calvinists who admire your brother's Fourth Letter, where he not only insinuates, but openly attempts to prove, that David was "a man after God's own heart," a "pleasant child" of God, and that he stood absolved and complete in the everlasting righteousness of Christ, while his eyes were full of adultery, and his hands full of blood: consequently, while his heart was full of all unrighteousness. Now if this was the case of David, it may not only be that of many, but of all the elect. They may all be the children of God, not only with hearts full of unrighteousness, but even while they cloak adultery with deliberate murder.

Now, pray sir, do you not show yourself completely master of Geneva logic, when you assert that what is so abundantly demonstrated by your brother's Letters, and the well-known principles of all sound Calvinists, is a calumny and a falsehood as conspicuous as the luminary that rules the night? This imaginary moon of calumny, which you discover through the telescope of Calvinian prejudice, will help my judicious readers to guess at the magnitude of the stars of falsehood, with which, you say, almost all the pages of my book are bespangled.

I conclude by entreating you not to put any longer a wrong construction upon the Helvetic bluntness with which I continue to expose barefaced Antinomianism. Do not account me an enemy, because I tell you the truth as it is in the Epistle of St. James: and deprive me not of an interest in your valuable friendship, merely because I follow the word of God, and the dictates of my conscience.

I can with truth assure you, dear sir, that your groundless charges of "calumny, falsehood, bitterness, injustice," &c, instead of putting "a concluding bar of separation" between us, only give me an opportunity of fulfilling delightfully that precept of the evangelical law, according to which we shall be justified in the great day, "Forgive one another, even as God for Christ's sake hath forgiven you." I confirm my love toward you, by rejoicing in all your pious labours, and sincerely wishing you the most unbounded success, whenever you do not give up the "right foundation," or substitute Dr. Crisp to St. James, and Calvin's narrow election to the free Gospel of Jesus Christ. And if I may trust the feelings of my own heart, which continues quite open toward you, I remain just as if you were not my opponent, dear sir, your affectionate friend, and obedient servant, in a pure Gospel,

J. FLETCHER.

LETTER X.

To Mr. Richard and Mr. Rowland Hill.

HONORED AND DEAR OPPONENTS, — Do you hate that foul monster, Antinomianism? I know you cordially hate practical, and would cheerfully oppose doctrinal Antinomianism, if it were not inseparably connected with the favourite doctrines you have embraced. Yes, your true regard for holiness would make you wish me success, if (while I attack sin, our common adversary,) Calvinism, which passes with you for Christianity, did not justly appear to you to be sapped in its very foundation. For, to my great astonishment, I find that Calvin's doctrine of unconditional election, and Dr. Crisp's doctrine of finished salvation, are now substituted to Jesus Christ, and openly made the foundation of the present Calvinists. "Finished salvation and electing love, (says Mr. Hill, *Friendly Remarks*, p. 19,) is their foundation."

Is it, indeed? Alas! I really thought that all the Calvinists still maintained, with Mr. Wesley, that other "foundation can no man lay than that is laid, which is Jesus Christ," 1 Corinthians iii, 11: but I now fear the breach between us is wider than I imagined; for it seems we disagree no less about the foundation than about the superstructure; and my younger opponent does me justice when be adds, "Surely you never mean to praise the Calvinists for guarding this foundation." No, indeed, sir, no more than I would praise them for placing two of Rachel's Teraphim upon the Mediator's throne.

You are both conscious that your two favourite doctrines will appear empty dreams, if the doctrine of the justification of all infants without faith is true; much more, if the doctrine of the justification of adult persons by works, both in the day of trial and in the day of judgment, is Scriptural. You agree, therefore, to bear your public testimony against the Third Check, where these doctrines are set in a clearer point of view, than in my preceding publications. Permit me to remind my readers of the reasonableness of the assertions which have so greatly excited your surprise.

In the Third Check, (pp. 161-163)* to make my readers sensible, that Calvinism has confusion, and not Scripture, for its foundation, I made a Scriptural distinction between the four degrees that constitute a saint's eternal justification, and each of these degrees I called a justification, because I thought I

---

* [161 and 162]

could speak as the oracles of God, without exposing the truth of the Gospel to the smiles of Christian wits.

I. From Romans v, 18, I proved the justification of infants: "As by the offence of Adam, (says the apostle,) judgment came upon all men to condemnation, even so by the righteousness of Christ, the free gift came upon all men to justification of life." In support of this justification, which comes upon all men in their infancy, I now advance the following arguments: —

1. The Scripture tells us, that "Christ in all things hath the preeminence." But if Adam is a more public person, a more general representative of mankind, than Jesus Christ, it is plain, that in this grand respect, Adam hath the pre-eminence over Christ. Now, as this cannot be, as Christ is at least equal to Adam, it follows, that as Adam brought a general condemnation, and a universal seed of death upon all infants, so Christ brings upon them a general justification, and a universal seed of life.

2. I never yet saw a Calvinist who denied that Christ died for Adam. Now, if the Redeemer died for our first parent, he undoubtedly expiated the original sin, the first transgression of Adam. And if Adam's original sin was atoned for, and forgiven to him, as the Calvinists, I think, generally grant, does it not follow, that although all infants are by nature children of wrath, yet through the redemption of Christ they are in a state of favour or justification? For how could God damn to all eternity any of Adam's children for a sin which Christ expiated? A sin which was forgiven almost six thousand years ago to Adam, who committed it in person?

3. The force of this observation would strike our Calvinist brethren, if they considered that we were not less in Adam's loins when God gave his Son to Adam in the grand, original Gospel promise, than when Eve prevailed upon him to eat of the forbidden fruit. As all in him were included in the covenant of perfect obedience before the fall, so all in him were likewise interested in the covenant of grace and mercy after the fall. And we have full as much reason to believe, that some of Adam's children never fell with him from a state of probation, according to the old covenant, as to suppose that some of them never rose with him to a state of probation, upon the terms of the new covenant, which stands upon better promises.

Thus, if we all received an unspeakable injury, by being seminally in Adam when he fell, according to the first covenant, we all received also an unspeakable blessing by being in his loins when God spiritually raised him up, and placed him upon Gospel ground. Nay, the blessing which we have in Christ is far superior to the curse which Adam entailed upon us' we stand our trial upon much more advantageous terms than Adam did in paradise. For according to the first covenant, "judgment was by one offence to condemnation." One sin sunk the transgressor. But according to the free gift, or second covenant, provision is made in Christ for repenting of, and rising from "many offences unto justification," Romans v, 16.

4. Calvinists are now ashamed of consigning infants to the torments of hell:they begin to extend their election to them all. Even the translator of Zanchius believes, that all children who die in their infancy are saved. Now, sir, if all children, or any of them, are saved, they are unconditionally justified according

to our plan; for they cannot be "justified by faith," according to St. Paul's doctrine, Romans v, 1, as it is granted, that those who are not capable of understanding, are not capable of believing. Nor can they be "justified by works," according to St. James' doctrine, James ii, 24, for they are not accountable for their works, who do not know good from evil, nor their right hand from their left. Nor can they be justified by words, according to our Lord's doctrine, Matthew xii, 37, because they cannot yet form one articulate sound. It follows, then, that all infants must be damned, or justified without faith, words, or works, according to our first distinction. But as you believe they are saved, the first degree of an adult saint's justification is not less founded upon your own sentiments than upon reason and Scripture.

II. When infants grow up, they are all called to believe in the light of their dispensation; and till they do, their personal sins condemn them. Here appears the absolute need of justification by the instrumentality of faith. This justification we preach to Jews and heathens, to Pharisees and publicans. Upon it we chiefly insist, when we address penitent prodigals and mourning backsliders. This the apostle chiefly defends in his Epistles to the Romans and Galatians. Our Church strongly maintains it in her eleventh article: and as we are all agreed about it, I shall only refer to some passages where it is evidently mentioned, Romans v, 1; Galatians ii, 16; Acts xiii, 39.

III. Whoever hath present access unto that grace wherein they who are justified by faith do stand, is also justified by works. True justification by faith is then inseparable from justification by works; for "faith works by love," so long as it is living; and love is productive of good works. In the apostolic age as well as in ours, "the love of many grew cold," and "concerning faith they made shipwreck, by not adding to it brotherly kindness, godliness, and charity." But as they still professed the saving faith of God's elect, which works by love, St. James was directed by the Holy Ghost to enforce the justification of a believer by works.

Now, dear sirs, before you can reasonably explode this justification, you must execute the Antinomian wish of Luther, and tear St. James' Epistle out of your Bible. But as we can never give you leave to take this liberty with ours, we shall still oppose the justification of evil workers, or practical Antinomians, in the day of trial, by such scriptures as these: "Know, O vain man, that faith without works is dead: Rahab was justified by works: Abraham was justified by works;" and so are all his legitimate children; "for by works a man is justified, and not by faith only."

IV. As for the last degree of an adult saint's justification, it is so fully established upon the words of our Lord, "In the day of judgment by thy words shalt thou be justified," that Dr. Owen and multitudes of the Puritan divines, as I have made it appear from their own writings, avowed it as the Gospel truth, in opposition to Dr. Crisp's Antinomian error. Nay, during our controversy, truth has prevailed; for, notwithstanding the strong resistance you have made against it, you have both granted all that we contend for: witness the two first letters of this Check.

Now, instead of attempting to prove, at least by one argument, that these distinctions are contrary either to Scripture or reason, Mr. Hill, sen., says, in his *Remarks*, (pp. 5, 6,) "What really surprises me beyond all the rest, is, your having brought out two new justifications since the Second Check: no apologies can excuse you for having concealed the matter so long." Mr. Hill, jun., adds in the postscript to his *Friendly Remarks*, (pp. 65, 66, 67,) "Your doctrine is a mysterious jumble. Your three publications contain a farrago. You are quite become unanswerable. In your first Check we hear but of one justification; in your Second you treat us with two: two more are lately invented, and shoved in among the rest. These four justifications may be doubled and doubled, till they amount to four-score. Your imagination is fertile, you can invent them by dozens."

1. Before I answer these witticisms, permit me to trouble you with a simile. I maintain that the age of man in general may properly, and at times necessarily must be considered, as made up of four different stages; infancy, youth, ripe years, and old age. Two masters of arts, who would make the world believe that youth and old age are the same, smile at the absurdity of this four-fold distinction. "How inconsistent are you," say they: "some time ago you spoke of the age of man in general, and told us it was three-score years and ten. Yesterday, you treated us with a dissertation upon youth and old age. To-day, two more ages, infancy and ripe years, are invented, and shoved in among the rest. Your fertile imagination may double and double these four ages till they amount to four-score; nay, you can invent them by dozens." This humorous answer highly delights thousands, and in mystic Geneva such wit passes for argument; but some in England begin to ask, "Shall we be for ever the dupes of Geneva logic?"

2. It is a very great mistake, that, "In the First Check we hear but of one justification;" for though I there treat principally of justification by faith, because Mr. Wesley principally meant it in the Minutes, yet, p. 34, the justification of infants is thus described: — It is "that general benevolence of our merciful God toward sinful mankind, whereby, through the Lamb slain from the foundation of the world, he casts a propitious look upon us, and freely makes us partakers of 'the light that enlightens every man who comes into the world.' This general loving kindness is certainly previous to any thing we can do to find it; for it always prevents us, saying to us in our very infancy, Live, and in consequence of it, our Lord says, 'Let little children come unto me, for of such is the kingdom of heaven.'" This is not all: pp. 34 and 35, I particularly describe "justification by faith" in the day of conversion, and expressly mention "justification by words (or works) in the day of judgment;" and common sense dictates that none can be justified by works in the day of judgment but those who, according to St. James' doctrine, have been justified by works in this life. How rash, then, is the assertion that I have invented any new Justification since the First Check! How weak is that cause, which a master of arts cannot support but by witticism, founded upon as palpable a mistake as that "one and three do not make more than one!"

And is the doctrine of a glorified saint's complete justification changed in the Second Check! No: for the author of *Pietas Oxoniensis*, in his answer to that book, (*Review*, p. 12,) upbraids me with saying therein, "By faith a man is justified at his conversion, but by works he is justified" on earth "in the hour of trial, as Abraham when he offered up Isaac," or "in a court of judicature, as St. Paul at the bar of Festus." And again: "By works he is justified before the judgment seat of Christ, as every one will be whose faith when he goes hence is found working by love." I grant, however, that I did not mention the justification of infants in the Second Check; but this does not prove that I "concealed a matter of such importance." For I had plainly mentioned it in the *Vindication,* and Mr. Shirley not having opposed it in his *Narrative,* as he had done justification by works in the great day, it would have been absurd to spend time in establishing it.

If you ask why I have distinguished between justification by works to-day, and justification by works in the day of judgment, I answer, For two reasons, (1.) St. James and Mr. Hill, jun., do so: "Rahab was justified by works, AT THE TIME WHEN she received the spies." (*Friendly Remarks,* p. 38.) (2.) The propriety and importance of this distinction appear from the following consideration: — Many may be justified by works to-day, who shall be condemned by works "in the day of judgment."

Take an instance: When St. Paul chose Demas to be his fellow labourer, Demas was undoubtedly justified by works, and not by faith only; for the apostle would not have been unequally yoked with an evil worker, any more than with an unbeliever. Nevertheless, in the day of judgment, if we may believe John Bunyan, Demas shall be condemned by his latter, instead of being justified by his former works.

But I have said, Second Check, that "a man is justified by faith when his backslidings are healed," as well as at his first conversion. And as he may fall from, and return to God ten times, a facetious opponent is ready to charge me with holding ten, perhaps "three-score justifications" by faith. Witty, but groundless is the charge; for supposing I lose and find the same guinea ten times, am I not mistaken if I fancy that I have found ten guineas? Or if you draw back sixty times from a bright sunshine into a dark cave, and sixty times come into the sunshine again, do I not offer violence to reason if I maintain that you have got into "three-score" sunshines? Here you say, "Illustrations are no proofs at all." I grant it: nevertheless, when the proofs are gone before, just illustrations wonderfully help many readers to detect the fallacy of a plausible argument.

But supposing I had not mentioned the different degrees of an adult saint's justification either in the First or Second Check, would you not, gentlemen, have exposed Geneva logic, as you have now done your inattention, if you had hoped to set plain Scripture aside by saying, "It comes too late. You placed it in the Third Check; it should have been produced in the First?" Does not such an argument hurt your cause more than a prudent silence would have done?

However, if you cannot put out the candle with which we search the streets of mystic Geneva, and examine the foundation of its towers, you both agree to amuse the Calvinists, by bringing Mr. Wesley* upon the stage of

---

* The prejudice of my opponents against Mr. Wesley makes them catch at every shadow of opportunity to place him in a contemptible light before the world. Witness their exclaiming against him for having suffered me to make an honourable mention of his labours in the Vindication, to counterbalance a little the loads of contempt poured upon him on all sides.

Those gentlemen do not consider that there are times when a greyheaded, useful, and yet slighted, insulted minister of Christ, may not only suffer another to speak honourably of his labours, but when he ought to magnify his own office in person.

controversy. He said, above twenty years ago in one of his journals, "I cannot but maintain, at least till I have clearer light, that the justification which is spoken of by St. Paul to the Romans, and in our articles, is not two-fold; it is one and no more." Here Mr. Hill, jun., particularly triumphs; "By your four degrees of a glorified saint's justification, you have thrown your own friend in the dirt," says he, "help him out if you can."

To this I answer, That if Mr. Wesley, by the justification spoken of by St. Paul to the Romans, meant that which the apostle purposely maintains in that epistle, and which our Church explicitly asserts in her eleventh article, my vindicated friend speaks a great truth when he says that this justification is one and no more; for it is evidently justification by faith. But supposing he had not properly considered either the justification of infants without faith and works, or the justification of believers by works in the day of trial, and in the day of judgment; what would you infer from thence? That the Scriptures which speak of such justifications are false? The conclusion would be worthy of Geneva logic! Weigh your argument in the balance of English logic, and you will find it is wanting. Twenty-three, or, if you please, three years ago, Mr. Wesley wanted clearer light, to distinguish between the justification of a sinner by faith, and the justification of a believer by works: but two years ago God gave him this clearer light, and he immediately called his friends to "review the whole affair," and help him to make a firm stand for St. James' pure religion, against Dr. Crisp's defiled Gospel. Therefore, say my opponents, St. James' and Jesus Christ's justification of a believer by works is a "dreadful heresy," and Mr. Wesley is "thrown in the dirt." Is the conclusion worthy of two masters of arts? May I not more reasonably draw just a contrary inference, and say, therefore, Mr. Wesley shakes the very dust, or, if you please, the very "dirt" of Geneva from off his feet, and exhorts his flocks to do the same through the three kingdoms?

II. As our controversy centres in the point of justification by works, both in the day of the trial of faith and in the day of judgment, whatever my opponents advance against this I shall endeavour to answer.

"The Scriptures, (says Mr. Hill, sen., Remarks, p. 5,) always speak of justification as perfect, full, and complete." For an answer to this bold, unscriptural assertion, I refer the reader to the preceding pages, where he will

---

St. Paul certainly did so, when he said, "In nothing am I behind the very chiefest apostles. I have laboured more abundantly than they all. Are they ministers of Christ, I am more; in labours more abundant," &c. After the apostle's example, might not Mr. Wesley himself say, (giving, like him, all the glory to Divine grace,) "I am nothing behind the chief of Gospel ministers. I have laboured more abundantly than they all?" Nay, might he not add, "I have broken the ice, and stood in the gap for them all?" Now if, instead of answering for himself, he has permitted me to vindicate his aspersed character, and despised ministry, where is the harm? If Timothy was to let no man despise his youth, is Mr. Wesley guilty of an unpardonable crime because he has permitted me to bear my testimony against the impropriety of despising his old age? And does not even young Mr. Hill say much more for himself than I have done for Mr. Wesley the aged? The whole of what I have advanced in his favour centres in this assertion, "He has done much for God." But my opponent addresses me thus before the public, "Friendly Remarks," (p. 69,) "You know my character, that I have suffered much, very much for God." And yet this very gentleman takes Mr. Wesley to task, and accuses him of self importance! O partiality, how long wilt thou blind and divide us? And how long wilt thou cause the astonished world to say, "See how these sheep bite and devour one another?"

easily see that although God's work is always perfect so far as it goes; yet as final justification depends upon perseverance in the faith, and as perseverance in the faith is inseparably connected with "patient continuance in well doing," it is unscriptural and absurd to assert that final justification is complete, before we can say, with St. Paul, "I am ready to be offered up; I have fought the good fight, I have finished my course, I have kept the faith;" or rather, before Christ himself says to us, "Well done, good and faithful servants, enter into the joy of your Lord."

III. Page 4. "You do us great injustice in supposing that we believe, or assert, any souls may strive, reform, and pray without any possibility of escaping hell. When you made the above assertion, did you not know, in your own conscience, that you charged us wrongfully?"

In the presence of God, I answer in the negative. If you maintain that Christ never died for a certain, fixed number of men, you must of consequence believe that those whom he never died for, can never flee from the wrath to come, though they should strive, reform, and pray ever so much.

If you are consistent, you must be persuaded that though Mr. Wesley, for example, has prayed, strove, and reformed for above forty years, yet if he is not one of what you call "the happy number," he shall inevitably bedamned.

IV. Page 8. You refer me to your "striking quotation of Luther, concerning the distinction between a believer and his actions." I answer, (1.) Luther's bare assertions go for nothing with us, when they stand in direct opposition to St. James' Epistle, which, in one of his Antinomian fits, he wanted to burn out of the way. (2.) This assertion contradicts common sense and daily experience, which agree to depose that, excepting the case of lunatics and delirious persons, men are like their actions, when those actions are taken together with their principle and design.

V. You add in the same page, "It was happy for David that, when he fell so grossly, he had a merciful, gracious, promise-keeping God to deal with; and that he fell not into the hands of Arminians and Perfectionists." I retort, "It was happy for Clodius that, if he turned from his wicked way, he had not an unmerciful, ungracious, and promise-breaking God to deal with, and fell not into the hands of an inexorable Moloch, before whom poor reprobated heathens can find no place for repentance, though they should seek it carefully with tears." As for your insinuation, that Arminians and Perfectionists (as such) are merciless to backsliders, it is groundless; we are taught to "restore the fallen in the spirit of meekness," as well as you. And (to the praise of Divine wisdom I write it) we are enabled to do it without encouraging them to return to their wallowing in the mire of sin, by dangerous insinuations that relapses into it will "work for their good."

VI. While we speak of David and Clodius, it may be proper to dwell a moment upon their ease. Clodius, a young heathen, forsakes his one wife, and David, an elderly Jew, forsakes his seven wives and ten concubines to commit the crime of adultery with women whose husbands they have just murdered. I maintain that David is more guilty than Clodius, and that his crime is so much the more atrocious than that of the noble heathen, as he commits it against greater light and knowledge, against greater mercies and more solemn vows, perhaps with more deliberation, and certainly with less temptation from the ferments of youthful blood, and the want of variety.

But you still dissent from me, and persist to say (p. 9,) that "David remained absolved from the curse of the law, while Clodius lay under it." And how can you prove it? "David," say you, "was a believer." I reply, No: he was an impenitent adulterer, and a treacherous murderer; and these characters are as incompatible with that of a believer, as heaven is irreconcilable with hell, and Christ with Belial. If a man can be a believer, i.e. a member of Christ, a child of God, and an inheritor of the kingdom of heaven, while he wallows in the filth of adultery, and imbrues his hands in innocent blood, farewell Christianity, farewell heathen morality, farewell common decency! We are come to the *non plus ultra* of Antinomianism. Truth and virtue, law and Gospel, natural and revealed religion, are buried in a common grave. Alas! my dear sir, what can the wildest Ranter, what can Satan himself desire more?

A Deistical gentleman lately observed, that all religion consisted in morality; and that nevertheless revelation was a useful contrivance of wise politicians to keep the vulgar in awe, and enforce the practice of moral duties among the populace. But, alas! the unhappy turn which you give to revelation does not even leave it the poor use which a Deist will allow it to have. Nay, your scheme, far from enforcing morality, sets it aside at a stroke. For, if a man that actually commits adultery, treachery, and murder is a pleasant child of God, why should not a drunkard, a swearer, a thief, or a traitor, be also accomplishing God's holy decrees? Why should he not prove his pleasant child, as well as a wanton adulterer and a perfidious murderer? Is not this stripping the woman, the Christian Church, of the glorious garment of holiness, in which she came down from heaven? Is it not exposing her to horrid derision, without so much as a scrap, I shall not say of exalted piety, but even of heathen morality, to keep herself decent before a world of mocking infidels? Hath not this doctrine driven Geneva headlong into Deism? And is it not likely to have the same effect upon all who can draw a just inference from your dangerous premises?

Hitherto Protestants in general have granted to the Papists, that, although good works are not meritorious, (if any higher idea than that of rewardable is fixed to that word,) yet they are necessary to salvation. But since the doctrine of finished salvation pours in upon us like a flood; since good men do not scruple to tell the world that the salvation of a bloody adulterer, *in flagrante delicto*, is finished, and that he is a pleasant child of God, fully accepted and completely justified, what have good works to do with salvation? We may not only dispense with them, but do the most horrid works. Yea, "the wheel of" adultery, treachery, and murder, may "run round and round again," for ten months, without interrupting the finished salvation of the elect; any more than praying, weeping, and reforming for ten years will prevent the finished damnation of the reprobates.

But, lest you should say I "blind the eyes of the readers with deceitful dust," I meet you on the solid ground where St. James stood, when he opposed the primitive Antinomians; and, taking that holy apostle's Gospel trump, I sound an alarm in Laodicea, and cry out to the drowsy world of Nicolaitan professors, whether they hear the word at the Lock chapel, or at the Foundery, "Awake, ye that sleep, and arise from the dead. Show your faith by your works. Know ye not, O vain men, that faith without works is dead," that it is a putrefying, ill-smelling corpse? Help, ye men of God, help us to bury it out of the way of good works. Let frighted morality dig a grave; let indignant piety cast the horrid nuisance into it. And, while we commit it to hell, whence it came, while the devils who believe feed upon the noisome carcass, let Bishop Cowper himself, attended by the author of *Pietas Oxoniensis,* say over the grave, "Justifying faith, whereby we are saved, cannot be without good works. Dead and damnable is the faith which is consistent with adultery and murder." And let all the Church say, "Amen," and contend for "the faith of God's elect," the faith maintained by St. Paul and St. James, the faith recommended in Mr. Wesley's Minutes, the living faith that works by obedient love.

VII. Page 10. In defence of your cause you produce those words of our Lord to the proud Pharisees, "Publicans and harlots go into the kingdom of heaven before you." Surely, sir, you would not insinuate that God takes extortioners and strumpets into heaven as such, and that adultery and whoredom are a ready way to glory! I know you start from the horrid insinuation: and, nevertheless, I fear this doctrine naturally flows from the manner in which the passage is quoted. I always thought those words of our Lord meant, that publicans and harlots could sooner be reclaimed from their execrable courses of life than self-hardened Pharisees from their diabolical pride; and that while Christ would admit a penitent Magdalene into heaven, he would thrust an impenitent Pharisee into hell. But what is this to the purpose? Does this make the case of David or any other sinner better while they remain in a state of impenitency?

VIII. Page 9. You have answered this question: "David in Uriah's bed," you say, "in a sense was not impenitent. The grace of repentance, &c, did lie like a spark covered with ashes." To this I reply: —

1. If by a spark or seed of repentance, you understand a ray of that quickening "light, which enlightens every man who comes into the world," and endues him with a gracious capacity of repenting during the day of salvation, we are agreed; supposing you grant us, that while Clodius defiled his neighbour's bed in Rome, he was such a penitent as David when he committed the same crime in Jerusalem.

2. We deny, that a capacity of repentance is in a sense repentance, any more than a capacity of obeying is in a sense obedience. According to your idea of that sort of repentance, which David had when he committed murder, the most abandoned profligates, who have not yet filled up the measure of their iniquities, are all in a sort penitent; and Adam when he ate the forbidden fruit was in a sort obedient.

3. Your assertion is unscriptural. You cannot produce one passage to prove that a murderer, or an adulterer, *in flagrante delicto,* is a penitent in any sense. If David was a penitent, because repentance lay in his heart as a spark buried under ashes; I may say, in direct opposition to the words of our Lord, that "the wicked and slothful servant" was, in some sense, good and diligent, because his master's talent lay buried in his napkin.

4. You insinuate that the ashes which covered the spark of David's repentance were "his sin." The comparison is not very fortunate; for ashes

frequently preserve the spark which they cover; but the commission of murder always tends to quench the Spirit. If you say, "that David repented" in some sort while he sinned, because he undoubtedly sinned with remorse of conscience, I reply, (1.) That he seems to have enjoyed his crimes at least with as much carnal security as Clodius could possibly do. (2.) If remorse is confounded with repentance, hell is filled with penitents; and most drunkards and murderers are in a sort penitent; for when they sin, they do it frequently with much reluctance.

5. This scheme of a sort of repentance, covered as a spark in the heart of those whose eyes are full of adultery, and hands full of blood, is attended with the most fatal consequences. It tends to breed negligence in the hearts of believers, and carnal security in the breasts of apostates; for how can the former be careful not to lose what is inamissible? And how can the latter endeavour to recover what they have not lost? Again: it supersedes the distinction there is between the righteous and the wicked, and opens the door to the most horrid confusion in the moral world. Has not a traitor as much right to plead the spark of loyalty, a drunkard the spark of sobriety, and a highwayman the spark of honesty, covered under the ashes of his sin, as you have to plead the spark of repentance, chastity, and brotherly love, that lay covered in the heart of David during his long apostasy?

6. But this is not all. If your doctrine is true, that of Christ and his apostles is evidently false. For St. Paul says to the Corinthians, "Examine yourselves whether you are in the faith." And he gives them this rule of examination, "Be not deceived; neither fornicators, nor adulterers, &c, have any inheritance in the kingdom of Christ." Now, if a man who commits adultery and murder may have a spark of grace and repentance, which actually constitutes him a pleasant child of God, how can he know by the apostle's rule whether he is in the faith or not? St. John says, with apostolic bluntness, "He that committeth sin is of the devil." Yes, in Rome, replies one who is versed in your divinity; but in Jerusalem, he that committeth adultery and murder may be in a sort penitent, consequently a man after God's own heart. Again: "By their fruits ye shall know them," says our Lord, when he speaks of wolves in sheep's clothing. Now, it is clear, that if your doctrine is true even when they commit adultery and murder, it cannot be known whether they are wolves, because the spark of chastity and charity that constituted David a pleasant child during his dreadful fall may be concealed under their debaucheries and barbarities.

IX. (Page 13.) To enforce your doctrine of a two-fold, and, as it appears to me, Jesuitical will in God, you again produce God's forbidding murder to free agents: and to this prohibition you oppose the murder which the Jews committed as free agents, when "by wicked hands they crucified Christ, who was delivered to them by the determinate counsel and foreknowledge of God." I hope, sir, you would not insinuate that God solemnly forbids murder by his revealed, and forcibly enjoins it by his secret will! To what I have already said on the point in the Third Check, (p, 186,) I now add, (1.) God never instigated the Jews to murder Christ. On the contrary, he frequently restrained them from the commission of their intended crime. "Ye seek to kill me," said Jesus to them many months before they actually did it. They even made open attempts to stone him, and cast him down a precipice, before the time foretold. (2.) When that time was come, God being about to give his Son a ransom for the many, "by his determinate counsel," that one should die for all; and seeing "by his foreknowledge," that the Jews, who thirsted for his blood, would put him to death, he no longer hindered them from taking him. Thus Jesus went to meet their malicious band in the garden of Gethsemane, and said, "I am he whom ye seek." (3.) This only shows that Divine Providence sometimes suffers moral agents to commit outwardly the sins which they have already committed in their own breasts; and he suffers it that they may come to condign punishment, or that other wicked men may be punished. Sometimes also that good men may be tried, hypocrites detected, and the godly made perfect by sufferings, like their Lord.

X. (Page 13.) In support of the same mistake you add, "You believe it to be God's revealed will that every man should love his brother as himself; yet it was certainly according to the secret will of God, that Joseph's brethren should sell [why do you not say, should hate] him, and that he should go into Egypt; otherwise Joseph must have told a gross untruth, when he said, 'God did send me to preserve life: — it was not you that sent me hither, but God.'"

To vindicate what I beg leave to call God's honesty, permit me to observe, (1.) That I had rather believe Joseph told once a gross untruth, than suppose that God perpetually equivocates. (2.) You must not raise a doctrine upon two sentences which Joseph spake as a fond brother, rather than as a judicious divine. When he saw his brethren confounded, and when, in a cordial embrace, he mixed his tears of joy with their tears of shame and repentance, how natural was it for him to draw a veil over their crime, and to comfort them, by observing with what providential wisdom God had overruled a circumstance which attended their sin? (3.) All that you can therefore infer from Joseph's case is, that God would have his brothers love him as free agents; and that when, as free agents, they chose to hate and murder him, the Lord, to save his life and bring about his deep designs, excited some compassion in their breasts: hence they thought it less cruel, while the providential appearance of the Ishmaelites made it appear more profitable, to sell him as a slave, than to starve him to death in a pit. Thus God, contrary to their intention, but not contrary to his own law, sent him into Egypt to preserve life. But what is this to the purpose? Was it God's secret, effectual will, that Joseph's brothers should hate him, while his revealed will commanded them to love him under pain of eternal damnation? Before you can establish this doctrine, you must prove that man is a mere machine, and God a mere Moloch.

XI. But to excuse yourself, you ask, (p. 12,) "By speaking of the secret and revealed will of God, do I suppose that God has two contrary wills?" Undoubtedly you do, honoured sir, if you are consistent. God's revealed will, for example, is, that "all the families of the earth should be blessed in Christ" with "the grace that bringeth salvation to all men;" but by his secret will, if we may believe Calvin, most families of the earth are absolutely cursed: a decree of preterition eternally excludes them from an interest in Christ, and from the least degree of saving grace.

Again: it is God's revealed will, that "all men every where should repent," under penalty of destruction: but upon your plan of doctrine, it is his secret, effectual will, that most men, even all the reprobates, shall never repent.

And, indeed, how should they, if he hardens them either from their mother's womb, or from the loins of their first parent Once more: it is God's revealed will, that all men should believe the Gospel, and be saved as free agents, if they submit to his gracious and easy terms: but, according to your scheme, it is his secret, indefectible will, either that there shall be no Gospel, or only a lying gospel for most men; and that there shall be no conditions or terms in the Gospel. Hence we are openly told, that God does not treat with the sons of men in a way of condition; his language being absolute, like himself, "I WILL and you SHALL:" that is, "Ye elect, I will that ye believe and be saved, and you shall believe and be saved' and ye reprobates, I will that you sin and be damned, and you shall sin and be damned." If you do not hold those propositions, you are with reason ashamed of Calvinism; if you hold them, you certainly maintain that there are two contrary wills in God, whether you suppose that you do so or not.

XII. One more observation and I have done. In your Five Letters you have opposed this proposition, "Believing is previous to justification," and said, "I deny that believing precedes justification" in the day of conversion. I have observed, in my reply, that this assertion sets aside justification by faith; because, if believing does not precede justification, there is no need of believing in order to be justified. "This is disingenuous: (say you, Remarks, p. 10:) where do I assert that justification precedes believing? I believe that true faith and justification are as inseparable as fire and heat."

To this I answer, (1.) Your comparison is not just. Fire is not the instrument by which heat is apprehended, but the very fountain of heat itself: whereas faith justifies, not as being the very fountain of justification, but merely as an instrument that apprehends the truth of Him "who justifies the ungodly" that believes in Jesus. Here, then, you indirectly give to justifying faith the honour due to none but the heavenly Justifier.

(2.) We grant you, that as, in the very instant in which we open our eyes, we receive the light, and see: so in the very moment in which we believe, we receive Christ the truth, and are justified. But still you must grant us, that believing is as much previous to justification, as opening the eyes is previous to seeing. We are justified by faith, and common sense dictates, that the instrument by which a thing is apprehended, must exist before it can be apprehended.

Having thus endeavoured to follow you in your retreat, to cut you off from your various subterfuges; and having exposed, with my usual bluntness, the hard shifts you have been obliged to make, in order to keep your doctrine the least in countenance, permit me to assure you that I still remain, with brotherly love and respect, gentlemen, your obedient servant in the whole Gospel of Christ,

JOHN FLETCHER.

LETTER XI.

To Mr. Richard and Mr. Rowland Hill.

HONOURED AND DEAR SIRS, — Having answered the arguments which each of you has advanced against the doctrine of justification by works in the great day, permit me to consider what may farther be advanced against it.

I. We cry to sinners, "By grace shall ye be saved through faith," in the day of your conversion; but to believers we say, By grace shall ye be saved, through works, in the day of judgment. Turn, therefore, ye sinners; and ye saints, "work out your own salvation with fear and trembling."

"Saved by grace, through works, in the day of judgment! What a farrago of Popery and Gospel! Faith and works; what a shocking mixture! *Geminantur tigribus agni.* You have undoubtedly the full consent of Bellarmine and the scarlet whore for such a match. But with what detestation would St. Paul enter his protest against it! Does he not declare, that faith and works reciprocally exclude each other? Says he not, 'If by grace, then it is no more of works, otherwise grace is no more grace; but if it be of works, then it is no more grace, otherwise work is no more work. If Abraham was justified by works he hath whereof to glory; for to him that worketh is the reward not reckoned of grace but of debt: but Abraham believed God, and it was accounted to him for righteousness: and David also describeth the blessedness of the man to whom God imputeth righteousness without works.' Hence the apostle concludes, 'By grace ye are saved, through faith: not of works, lest any man should boast.' And again: 'Not by works of righteousness which we have done, but of his mercy he saved us,' &c. Now, how does this doctrine of justification and salvation without works agree with your doctrine of justification or salvation by works in the last day; and how can you reconcile St. Paul with Bellarmine, Mr. Wesley, and yourself?"

ANSWER 1. Should you not rather ask, how we can reconcile St. Paul with Jesus Christ, St. James, and himself? Is not the second chapter to the Romans as strong for works as the Minutes, the Epistle of St. James, and our Lord's sermon on the mount? Have we not observed, that even in the epistles where the apostle purposely maintains the doctrine of justification by faith in the day of conversion, he writes of works in such a manner as flatly to contradict himself, if they have nothing to do with our final justification in the last day?

Says he not to the believers at Rome, "If ye live after the flesh," or, if ye do not "cast off the works of darkness, rioting and drunkenness, strife and envying, &c, ye shall die; but if ye through the Spirit mortify the deeds of the body, ye shall live?" And again: "Be subject to the higher powers: for they that resist them shall receive to themselves damnation?"

And says he not to the Galatians, "All the law is fulfilled in one word, even in this, Thou shalt love thy neighbour as thyself?" And let no Antinomian persuade you that the law of obedient love is only a rule of life. No, it is also a rule of punishment; for, "I tell you before," says he, "as I have also told you in time past, [see how plainly and constantly the apostle preached the law of Christ!]

that they who do such things, [they who are guilty of] adultery, fornication, hatred, wrath, strife, envying, murder, drunkenness, and such like, shall not inherit the kingdom of God. Fulfil, therefore, the law of Christ. Let every man prove his own work; for every man shall bear his own burden. Be not deceived; whatsoever a man soweth, that shall he also reap; for he that soweth to his flesh, shall of the flesh reap corruption, [or rather, φθοραν, perdition:] but he that soweth to the Spirit, shall of the Spirit reap life everlasting."

When St. Paul, even in his Epistles to the Romans and Galatians, preaches so evidently justification and condemnation by works in the great day, do we not suppose him deprived of common sense, when we represent him as perpetually saying and unsaying, as building up one hour what he pulls down the next?

But as this general answer, though it vindicates our doctrine, does not vindicate the apostle from the charge of contradiction, I beg leave once more to carry the candle of the Lord into the tower of Calvinian confusion; thus shall we see the farrago made at Geneva with the words "justification, salvation, works, righteousness of the law, and righteousness of faith."

It is evident that every degree of justification is attended with a degree of salvation. Hence, when St. Paul preached to the Jews justification by faith, he said, "To you is the word of this salvation sent," and when he wrote to those who were justified, he says, "By grace are ye saved through faith." This holds with regard to the justification of infants, for "of such is the kingdom of heaven:" and by the same rule, eternal salvation answers to final justification.

This being premised, we may observe, that when the apostle excludes works from having any hand in our justification or salvation, it is only when he speaks of the justification of sinners, whether we consider them as infants or adults. For if he excluded works from the justification of believers, either in the day of trial or in the day of judgment, he would grossly contradict himself! But now he is quite consistent. Mr. Wesley and I, through grace, gladly join him and Titus when their say, "Not by works of righteousness which we have done, [either in our infancy or before the day of our conversion,] but according to his mercy he saved us, by the washing of regeneration, — that being justified by his grace, we should be made heirs according to the hope of eternal life."

But what does the apostle mean here by "the hope of eternal life?" Is it the hope of a Laodicean believer, who makes his boast of "imputed righteousness, and finished salvation," while he goes on in strife and envying, perhaps in adultery and murder? Certainly no: this is the "hope of the hypocrite, which shall perish." The hope, according to which we "are made heirs of eternal life" in glory, is a hope which "if any man hath," he will "purify himself even as God is pure;" and this hope, far from being contrary to our doctrine of justification by works in the last day, is inseparably connected with "the labour of love," by which persevering believers shall then be justified.

Inquire we now what are those works which St. Paul opposes to faith and free grace; and I observe: —

1. That it is not absolutely every work, or else he would oppose faith to itself; for believing is as much a work of the heart, as walking to church is a work of the feet.

Five Checks To Antinomianism

2. Neither does the apostle oppose to faith "works meet for repentance;" for he strongly recommended them himself, Acts xxvi, 20. Nor the works of upright Gentiles, that "fear God, and believe he is a rewarder of those who diligently seek him." If St. Paul represented these works as "dung and filthy rags," he would contradict the angel who said to Cornelius, "Thy prayers and alms, [far from being rejected,] are come up for a memorial before God."

3. Much less did it ever come into the apostle's mind to oppose "the work of faith and the labour of love," to faith and free grace; for they are no more contrary to each other, than the stalk and the ear are contrary to the root that bears them. Far from despising these works, see how honourably he speaks of them: "We give thanks always for you, remembering without ceasing your work of faith and labour of love, in our Lord Jesus Christ. God is not unrighteous to forget your work and labour that proceedeth of love. Always abound in the work of the Lord. Charge the rich, that they be rich in good works, laying up for themselves a good foundation, that they may lay hold on eternal life."

For want of attending to this, some have preposterously opposed the righteousness of faith to personal holiness. The latter they look upon as the "righteousness which is of the law," and which the apostle explodes, Philippians iii, 9. Thus they suppose, that St. Paul formed the horrid wish of not being found clothed with holiness, "without which no man shall see the Lord;" not considering that the pardon of sins and true holiness, the two inseparable fruits of a living faith, constitute "the righteousness which is through the faith of Christ, the righteousness which is of God by faith." A righteousness this that far exceeds the outside "righteousness of the scribes and Pharisees," with which the apostle had too long been satisfied, and which he so justly despised after his conversion.

One mistake makes way for another. Those who imagine that the apostle would not be found in his own inherent righteousness, flowing from Christ formed in his heart by faith, insinuate, that he desired to be found clothed with the personal actions of our Lord, put upon his soul by as irrational and unscriptural an imputation as if God had fed Peter, when he was hungry, by imputing to his empty stomach the meals which Christ ate in the days of his flesh; or, as if he had clothed St. Paul, when he was naked, by laying to his account our Lord's being wrapped up in swaddling clothes in the stable at Bethlehem.

But to return: the works which St. Paul excludes, are, —

1. The works of the ceremonial law of Moses, generally called the "works of the law." On these works most Jewish converts still laid a very great stress, and some of them went so far in this error as to say to their Gentile brethren, "Except ye be circumcised after the manner of Moses, ye cannot be saved," Acts xv, 1. Hence the apostles wrote, verse 24, "Certain men, subverting your souls, have troubled you, saying, Ye must be circumcised, and keep the law." Hence also it is said, that when St. Paul shaved, and "was at charges to purify himself," in the temple, he "walked orderly and kept the law," Acts xxi, 24.

2. The apostle likewise opposed to faith those hypocritical deeds of the moral law, those external works of partial piety and ostentatious mercy, by which proud Pharisees think to atone for their sins, and purchase the kingdom of

heaven. Such works of unbelief and spiritual pride cannot be too much decried. They do infinite mischief; they draw a veil over our apostasy; they breed self complacence, generate self conceit and feed the opposition of Pharisees against the Gospel. Hence their contempt of Christ, their enmity against his people, their ridiculing the atonement, despising others, and boasting of their own goodness. St. Paul was the more zealous in bearing his testimony against these fruits of self righteousness, as he knew, by fatal experience, that they are the reverse of "fruits meet for repentance," and of "the righteousness which is of God by faith;" and that they stood yet in the way of the Jews, as much as they once did in his own.

3. The apostle excludes also all the works of impious moralists, who make no scruple of robbing God, because they are just to man; all the works of Antinomian believers, who, like the Galatians, pray to the Lord, and devour their neighbours; or, like the Jews, fast to-day, and to-morrow "strike with the fist of wickedness;" all the works which are not ultimately referred to the glory of God through Jesus Christ; and all the works whose gracious rewardableness is not acknowledged to flow from the original and proper merit of the Redeemer. These works the apostle justly discards, as contrary to the doctrine of grace, because they do not spring from the grace of God, but from the pride of man. He explodes them as opposite to "the righteousness of faith," because they are not the works of humble faith, but of conceited unbelief; the constant language of faith being, "Not unto us, O Lord, not unto us, but unto thy name give glory, for thy mercy and truth's sake."

Let the judicious reader say, if by thus distinguishing between the justification of a sinner in the day of conversion, and the justification of a saint in the great day; and by making a proper difference between the works of an humble believer, which the apostle justly extols; and the works of a proud Pharisee, which he justly decries, we do not perfectly reconcile him to himself, and sufficiently secure the honour of free grace?

Is it possible to make larger concessions without sacrificing St. James' Epistle to Geneva logic, and our Lord's invaluable sermon on the mount to Antinomian obstinacy? If we continue to assert that no sort of works have any thing to do with any sort of justification and salvation, shall we not justly shock the moral and rational part of mankind? Is it not of the Lord that the contempt which unconverted men show to religious people rises no higher than it does? And do we not deserve that our candour or good sense should be suspected, when we go about to persuade the world that half a dozen strained verses of St. Paul, put in the favourite scale of a Geneva balance, are sufficient to outweigh fifty plain texts of the apostle, and the best half of the Bible, which testifies, directly or indirectly, that though the final justification and eternal salvation of adult persons are not by the merit, yet they are by the evidence or instrumentality of good works?

II. OBJECTION. "There is some plausibility in your answer, but we are still afraid that this doctrine of justification, or salvation by works in the last day, robs the Lord Jesus Christ of his glory."

ANSWER. Just the reverse. It delivers him from the shame of saving men by unaccountable humour, or damning them with unparalleled cruelty. But how do you prove your assertion? Of what glory does our doctrine rob the

Five Checks To Antinomianism

Redeemer? Does it rob him of the glory of atoning for our sins, as our High Priest? Or of leading us into all the truth necessary to our salvation, as our great Prophet? Does it rob him of the glory of pardoning our sins, and esteeming us righteous when we believe, as the Lord our righteousness? Does it rob him of the glory of making us fruitful branches in him as the true Vine? Or of rendering to every one according to his works, as an impartial Judge? On the contrary, is it not the opposite doctrine which refuses him the glory of maintaining the honour of his crown, as the King of kings, and Lord of lords?

Yes, we affirm, that to reject the doctrine of justification by works in the great day, is to set Christ at nought in the most glorious of his offices. Is it not enough that, in the days of his flesh, he was chiefly derided and crucified as the King of the Jews? Must he also, in the days of his Spirit, be every where put to open shame in his regal office? How useless is his sceptre, and contemptible his government, if he gives his subjects only shadows of laws, which amount to no laws at all? And if, leaving his immense dominions in a lawless condition, he saves the happy number of his favourites, and damns the rest of mankind, merely according to Calvin's notions of free grace and free wrath? Or according to Dr. Crisp's scheme of salvation and damnation finished?

To this Mr. Rowland Hill answers beforehand, (*Friendly Remarks*, pp. 45, 46,) "You slander the Calvinists. We grant, that in the point of justification, [and of course of condemnation,] we have nothing to do ,with the law' [but] though we boldly say, we are not under the law as a covenant of works, yet we never were so ignorant and daring as to say, we are not under the law to Christ as a rule of life."

Pardon my freedom, dear sir, if I tell you, without ceremony, that, like thousands more, you have learned to say shibboleth, before you have properly considered the sense of the expression. If you mean any thing by "being under the law to Christ only as a rule of life," you probably mean, with Dr. Crisp, that Christ has indeed a law; but that with regard to believers, who are the subjects of his kingdom, this law has no more the Divine sanction of a blessing for those who observe it, and of a curse for its violators. And is not this saying, in ambiguous words, that Christ's subjects are absolutely lawless? Let little children pompously give the name of laws to rules of play, or rules of grammar; but let not men of sense imitate their mistake, by giving that name to directions of conduct or rules of life, which are no longer enforced by rewards and penalties.

You decry "illustrations," and I do not wonder at it; for they carry light into Babel, where it is not desired. The father of errors begets darkness and confusion. From darkness and confusion springs Calvinism, who, wrapping himself up in some garments which he has stolen from the truth, deceives the nations, and gets himself reverenced in a dark temple, as if he were the pure and free Gospel.

To bring him to a shameful end, we need not stab him with the dagger of "calumny," or put him upon the rack of persecution. Let him only be dragged out of his obscurity, and brought unmasked to open light, and the silent beams of truth will pierce him through! Light alone will torture him to death, as the meridian sun does a bird of night that cannot fly from the gentle operations of its beams.

May the following illustration dart at least one luminous beam into the profound darkness in which your venerable Diana delights to dwell! And may it show the Christian world that we do not "slander you," when we assert, you inadvertently destroy God's law, and cast the Redeemer's crown to the ground. And that when you say, "in point of justification, [and consequently of condemnation,] we have nothing to do with the law; we are under the law as a rule of life," but not as a rule of judgment; you might as well say, "We are under no law, and consequently no longer accountable for our actions."

"The king," who I suppose is in love with your doctrines of free grace and free wrath, by the advice of a predestinarian council and parliament, issues out a Gospel proclamation, directed "to all his dear subjects, and elect people, the English." By this evangelical manifesto they are informed, "that in consequence of the prince of Wales' meritorious intercession, and perfect obedience to the laws of England, all the penalties annexed to the breaking of those laws are now abolished with respect to Englishmen: that his majesty freely pardons all his subjects, who have been, are, or shall be guilty of adultery, murder, or treason: that all their crimes, 'past, present, and to come, are for ever and for ever cancelled:' that, nevertheless, his loving subjects, who remain strangers to their privileges, shall still be served with sham warrants according to law, and frightened out of their wits, till they have learned to plead 'they are Englishmen,' [i.e. elect:] and then, they shall also set at defiance all legalists; that is, all those who shall dare to deal with them according to law: and that, excepting the case of the above-mentioned false prosecution of his chosen people, none of them shall ever be molested for the breach of any law.

"By the same supreme authority it is likewise enacted that all the laws shall continue in force against foreigners, [i.e. reprobates,] whom the king and the prince hate with everlasting hatred, and to whom they have agreed never to show mercy: that, accordingly, they shall be prosecuted to the utmost rigour of every statute, till they are all hanged or burned out of the way: and that, supposing no personal offence can be proved against them, it shall be lawful to hang them in chains for the crime of one of their forefathers, to set forth the king's wonderful justice, display his glorious sovereignty, and make his chosen people relish the better their sweet distinguishing privileges as Englishmen.

"Moreover his majesty, who loves order and harmony, charges his loving subjects to consider still the statutes of England, which are in force against foreigners, as very good rules of life for the English, which they shall do well to follow, but better to break; because every breach of those rules will work for their good, and make them sing louder the faithfulness of the king, the goodness of the prince, and the sweetness of this Gospel proclamation.

"Again: as nothing is so displeasing to the king as legality, which he hates even more than extortion and whoredom, lest any of his dear people, who have acted the part of a strumpet, robber, murderer, or traitor, should, through the remains of their inbred corruption, and ridiculous legality, mourn too deeply for breaking some of their rules of life, our gracious monarch solemnly assures them, that though he highly disapproves of adultery and murder, yet these breaches of rules are not worse in his sight than a wandering thought in speaking to him, or a moment's dulness in his service: that robbers, therefore, and traitors, adulterers, and murderers, who are free-born Englishmen, need not at all be uneasy about losing his royal favour; this being utterly impossible, because they always stand complete in the honesty, loyalty, chastity, and charity of the prince.

"Moreover, because the king changes not, whatever lengths the English go on in immorality, he will always look upon them as his pleasant children, his dear people, and men 'after his own heart;' and that, on the other hand, whatsoever lengths foreigners go in pious morality, his gracious majesty is determined still to consider them as 'hypocrites, vessels of wrath,' and 'cursed children, for whom is reserved the blackness of darkness for ever;' because he always views them as completely guilty, and absolutely condemned in a certain robe of unrighteousness, woven thousands of years ago by one of their ancestors. This dreadful *sanbenetto*[*] his majesty hath thought fit to put upon them by imputation; and in it it is his good pleasure that they shall hang in adamantine chains, or burn in fire unquenchable.

"Finally, as foreigners are dangerous people, and may stir up his majesty's subjects to rebellion, the English are informed, that if any one of them, were he to come over from Geneva itself, shall dare to insinuate that his most gracious Gospel proclamation is not according to equity, morality, and godliness, the first Englishman that meets him shall have full leave to brand him as a Papist, without judge or jury, in the forehead or on the back, as he thinks best; and that, till he is farther proceeded with according to the utmost severity of the law, the chosen people shall be informed, in the Gospel Magazine, to beware of him, as a man 'who scatters firebrands, arrows, and deaths,' and makes universal havoc of every article of this sweet Gospel proclamation.

"*Given at Geneva, and signed by four of his majesty's principal secretaries of state for the predestinarian department.*

"JOHN CALVIN.   DR. CRISP.
"THE AUTHOR OF P.O.   ROWLAND HILL."

What would wise men think of such a manifesto? Who does not see, his majesty might as well have informed us at once that all the laws of the land are now repealed; that instead of being laws, they shall be only moral finger posts, directing men in the narrow way of righteousness, or in the broad way of iniquity, if the one pleases them better than the other?

Suppose a courtier asserted, That we are still under the laws of the land as rules of life; would not thinking men answer, No: we are now absolutely lawless: for statutes, according to which no Englishman can be prosecuted, much less executed, are no laws at all for Englishmen; they are only directions, which every one is at full liberty to follow or not, as he pleases. It is not less absurd to give the name of laws to rules, which are not enforced with the sanction of proper rewards or penalties, than to call Baxter's Directory a code of laws, because it contains excellent rules of life.

O ye abettors of Dr. Crisp's mistakes, how long will you regard vain words, and inadvertently pour contempt upon the King of kings? How long will you rashly charge us with robbing him of his glory, because we cannot join you,

[*] A frock, painted with flames and devils, in which heretics are burned by the inquisition.

when, under the plausible pretence of advancing the honour of his priesthood, you explain away the most awful protestations which he made as a prophet, and rob him of the royal glory of punishing his rebellious, and rewarding his faithful subjects, according to law, as a righteous King?

Alas! even while you seem zealous for God's sovereignty, do you not unawares represent Jesus as the weakest of princes, or fiercest of tyrants? Do you not inadvertently, (for I know you would not do it deliberately for the world,) do you not, I say, inadvertently crown him with the sharpest thorns that ever grew in the territory of mystic Geneva? Instead of the "sceptre of his kingdom," which is "a right sceptre," do you not at one time put in his hand a reed, which the Antinomian elect may insult with more impunity than the frogs in the fable did the royal log sent by Jupiter to reign over them? And, at another time, while you give him Nimrod's iron sceptre, do you not put upon him Nero's purple robe; and even slip into his loving bosom a black book of horrible decrees, more full of the names of unborn reprobates than the Emperor Domitian's fatal pocket book was full of the names of the poor wretches to whom, in a gloomy day, he took an unaccountable dislike, and whom, on this account, as well as to maintain his dreadful sovereignty, he tyrannically appointed for the slaughter? Never, no never, shall you be able to do justice to the Scripture, and our Lord's kingly office, till you allow that, agreeably to his evangelical law, he will one day "reward every man according to his works;" and the moment you allow this, you give up what you unhappily call your foundation, that is, unconditional election and finished salvation: in a word, you allow justification by works in the great day, and are as heretical (should I not say as orthodox?) as ourselves. I am, honoured and dear sirs, yours, &c,

J. FLETCHER.

LETTER XII.

To Richard Hill, Esq.

HON. AND DEAR SIR, — Although I reserve for two separate tracts my answer to your objections against "the monstrous doctrine of perfection," and my reply to the argument which you draw from our seventeenth article, in favour of the doctrine of unconditional election; the already exorbitant length of this Check calls for a speedy conclusion; and I hasten toward it, by laying before my readers the present state of our controversy, enlarging chiefly upon imputed righteousness and free will, two points which I have not yet particularly discussed in this piece.

Imputed righteousness, as it is held by the Calvinists, I have endeavoured to expose in the Second Check, by the most absurd, and yet (upon your plan) most reasonable plea of a bare-faced Antinomian, who expects to be justified in the great day by Christ's imputed righteousness without works. To this you have answered, (Review, p. 68, &c,) by exclaiming, "Shocking slander, slanderous banter," &c, and I might reply only by crying out, *Logica Genevensis!* But, as honest inquirers after the truth would not be benefited, for their sakes I shall in this letter show how far we agree, wherein we disagree, and what makes us dissent from you, about the doctrine of imputed righteousness.

We agree that all the righteousness which is in the spiritual world is as much Christ's righteousness, as all the light that shines in the natural world at noon is the light of the sun. And we equally assert that, when God justifies a sinner who believes in Christ, he freely pardons his past sins, graciously accounts him righteous, and, as such, admits him to his favour, only through faith in the Redeemer's meritorious blood and personal righteousness.

To see clearly wherein we disagree, let us consider both your doctrine and ours; touching, as we go along, upon the capital arguments by which they are supported.

Consistent Calvinists believe, that if a man is elected, God absolutely imputes to him Christ's personal righteousness, that is, the perfect obedience unto death which Christ performed upon earth. This is reckoned to him for obedience and righteousness, even while he is actually disobedient, and before he has a grain of inherent righteousness. They consider this imputation as an unconditional and eternal act of grace, by which, not only a sinner's past sins, but his crimes present and to come, be they more or be they less, be they small or be they great, are for ever and for ever covered. He is eternally "justified from all things." And therefore, under this imputation, he is perfectly righteous before God, even while he commits adultery and murder. Or, to use your own expressions, whatever lengths he runs, whatever depths he falls into, "he always stands absolved, always complete in the everlasting righteousness of the Redeemer." (*Five Letters*, pp. 26, 27, 29.) In point of justification, therefore, it matters not how unrighteous a believer actually is in himself; because the robe of Christ's personal righteousness, which, at his peril, he must not attempt to patch up with any personal righteousness of his own, is more than sufficient to adorn him from head to foot; and he must be sure to appear before God in no other. In this rich garment of finished salvation, the greatest apostates shine brighter than angels, though they are "in themselves black" as the old murderer, and filthy as the brute that actually wallows in the mire. This "best robe," as it is called, is full trimmed with such phylacteries as these, "Once in grace, always in grace: once justified, eternally justified: once washed, always fair, undefiled, and without spot." And so great are the privileges of those who have it on, that they can range through all the bogs of sin, wade through all the puddles of iniquity, and roll themselves in the thickest mire of wickedness without contracting the least spot of guilt, or speck of defilement.

This scheme of imputation is supported, 1. By Scriptural metaphors, understood in a forced, unscriptural sense. Thus when a sound Calvinist reads about "the breastplate of righteousness," and "the garment of salvation;" or about "putting on Christ, walking in him, being in him, being found in him, or being clothed with righteousness," his prepossessed mind directly runs upon his imputation. And if he reads in the Psalms, "I will make mention of thy righteousness, and thine only," he immediately concludes that the psalmist meant the personal righteousness of the man Christ: as if David really made mention of no other righteousness but that in all the Psalms! or God had had no righteousness, before the Virgin Mary "brought forth her first-born Son!"

2. By the parable of the man who "was bound hand and foot, and cast into outer darkness, because he had not on a wedding garment;" that is, upon your scheme, because Christ's personal righteousness was not imputed to him: as if the Prince of Peace, the mild Jesus, who says, "Learn of me, for I am meek," had kindly invited a man to the feast, and then commanded him to be thrust into hell, merely because he had not on a garment which he never could procure; a robe which none but God could clothe him with; and which God determined should never be for him, when he decreed that Christ should never work out an inch of righteousness for one single reprobate. Does not this exceed Ovid's description of the iron age? *Non hospes ab hospite tutus.* The bare mention of such a dreadful reflection cast upon God's goodness, and our Lord's hospitality, will amount to a strong argument against your imputation, with those who are yet concerned for God's adorable perfections, and our Lord's amiable character.

3. By the parable of the prodigal son, who, it is supposed, was clothed with the "best robe" of Christ's personal righteousness. But this notion is overturned by the context itself: for the father had met, forgiven, and embraced his returning son in his own ragged garment, before the "best robe" was called for, and put upon him. Whence it would follow, that a sinner may be forgiven without the garment of righteousness; and as completely accepted out of Christ, as the prodigal was without the "best robe."

4. By the goodly raiment of Esau, in which Jacob got his father's blessing. But Moses' account of the cheat put upon the short-sighted Isaac, entirely overthrows the scheme of the Calvinists. The robe which they recommend is made of Christ's complete and personal righteousness; it is long and wide enough perfectly to cover even a giant in sin; nor must it be patched with any thing else. But Jacob's dress, far from being all of a-piece, was a mongrel sort of human and beastly garment. For, when Rebekah had clothed his body with Esau's raiment, "she put goat skins upon his hands, and upon the smooth of his neck," to make them feel like Esau's hairy hands and shaggy neck. And the worst is, that the goat skins, and not Esau's borrowed dress, deceived the aged patriarch, and got the blessing. Hear the historian. "Jacob went near to his father, and he felt him, and said, The voice is Jacob's voice, but the hands are the hands of Esau; and he discerned him not because his hands were hairy; so he blessed him," Genesis xxxvii, 22. Thus the skin of a goat, the emblem of a reprobate, unfortunately comes in to patch up your best robe. And I doubt not but, as the typical garment was too scanty to cover Jacob's hands and neck; so the fancied antitype will prove too short to cover the hands of those, who, like "Onesimus, rob their masters;" and the neck and heels of those, who, like David, are "swift to shed blood," and climb up into their neighbour's bed; if they do not get a more substantial righteousness than that in which you suppose they stand complete, while they commit their enormous crimes.

5. Plain Scripture is also brought to support this imputation. David says, "Blessed is he whose sin is covered: blessed is the man unto whom the Lord

imputeth not iniquity," Psalm xxxii, 1, 2. But, alas for your scheme! it is thrown down by the very next words, "And in whose spirit there is no guile." Thus, although you would make us believe the contrary, David's own doctrine shows that he was not the "blessed man whose sins are covered by non-imputation of iniquity," when his spirit was full of guile, adultery, and murder. And, indeed, he tells us so himself in this very Psalm: "When I kept silence," says he, when I harboured guile and impenitency, "day and night thy hand was heavy upon me: but when I acknowledged my sin unto thee," when I parted with my guile, "thou forgavest the iniquity, of my sin."

6. However, if David's words are flatly against your imputation, it is supposed, that as prefaced by St. Paul, they make greatly for it: "David describeth the blessedness of the man to whom God imputeth righteousness without works," Romans iv, 6. I have already observed, that as the apostle cannot contradict David and himself, he only means without the works of the law, as opposed to faith and to the work of faith. That this is the true meaning of St. Paul's words, is evident by those which introduce them: "To him that worketh not, but believeth, his faith is counted for righteousness." Who does not see here, that believing, which is the good work that begets all others, is opposed to the faithless works, about which the Pharisees made so much ado to so little purpose? Who does not perceive, that a man must believe, that is, do the work of God before his faith can be "counted for righteousness?" and consequently, that righteousness is imputed to him who believes, not absolutely without any sort of works; but only without the works of the law, emphatically called by the apostle, works, or "deeds of the law," when he contradistinguishes them from faith, and "the work of faith."

7. To the preceding scriptures our Calvinist brethren add a plausible argument. "God," say they, "may as well impute to us Christ's perfect righteousness in all our sins, and account us completely righteous without one grain of inherent righteousness; as he imputed the horrid crimes of the elect to Christ in all his obedience, and accounted him completely guilty without one single grain of inherent sin. To deny, therefore, that God imputes righteousness to an elect, while he is full of unrighteousness; or to suppose that he imputes sin to an apostate, who 'is sold under sin,' is but a decent way of denying the imputation of our personal sins to Christ, and the vicarious satisfaction which he made on the cross."

To detect the fallacy of this argument, we need only observe, (1.) That God never accounted Christ "completely guilty." Such expressions as these, "He made him sin for us: he laid upon him the iniquities of us all," &c, are only Hebrew idioms, which signify that God appointed Christ a sacrifice for sin; and that "the chastisement of our forfeited peace was upon him;" which no more implies that God put on his back, by an absolute imputation, a robe of unrighteousness, woven with all the sins of the elect, to make him completely guilty, than St. Luke, when he informs us that the Virgin Mary offered two young pigeons for her purification, supposes her ceremonial uncleanness was, somehow, woven into a couple of little garments, and put upon the back of the two young pigeons, which, by that mean, were made completely unclean. I hope the following illustration will convince you, sir, that such refinements as these are as contrary to sober reason as to Scripture duly compared with itself. Gallio gets drunk, and as he reels home from his midnight revels, he breaks thirty-six lamps in the streets, and sends out volleys of curses to the number of two hundred. He is brought before you, and you insist on his going to the house of correction, or paying so much money to buy three dozen of lamps, beside the usual fine for his profane language. As he is not worth a groat, his sober brother Mitio kindly offers to lay down the sum for him. You accept of the "vicarious satisfaction," and binding the rake to his good behaviour, you release him at his brother's request. Now, sir, would you be reasonable if you reckoned Mitio completely guilty of getting drunk, swearing two hundred oaths, and breaking thirty-six lamps? Far from supposing him guilty of breaking one lamp, or swearing one oath, even while he makes satisfaction for his brother's wildness, do you not esteem him according to his own excellent character?

And will you defend a doctrine which charges God with a mistake ten thousand times more glaring than that you would be guilty of, if you really reckoned Mitio an abandoned rake, and Gallio a man of an exemplary conduct? Will you indeed recommend still as Gospel an opinion which supposes that the God of everlasting unchangeable love once loathed and abhorred his beloved Son? and that the God of invariable truth could once say to the holy Jesus, "Thou art all foul, O thou defiled object of my hatred, there is no purity in thee:" while he addresses a bloody adulterer with, "Thou art all fair, my love, my undefiled, there is no spot in thee?"

A variety of Scriptural and rational arguments I have, directly or indirectly, advanced in every Check against that capital doctrine of yours, "the absolute imputation of Christ's personal righteousness to believers;" whether they live chastely with their own wives, or entice away other men's wives: whether they charitably assist their neighbours, or get them treacherously murdered. All those arguments centre in this: If that doctrine is true, the Divine perfections suffer a general eclipse; one half of the Bible is erased; St. James' epistle is made void; defiled religion justly passes for "pure Gospel;" the Calvinian doctrine of perseverance is true; and barefaced Antinomianism is properly recommended as the "doctrine of grace."

Having thus considered your doctrine of imputed righteousness, permit me, honoured sir, to submit to your inspection the harmonizing views that we have of God's perfections; while we see him impute righteousness to a man (i.e. reckon a man righteous) so long as he actually believes with a faith working by obedient love; and impute iniquity to an apostate (i.e. reckon him unrighteous) as soon as he departs from the faith, to work iniquity, and walk in the ways of unrighteousness.

We firmly believe that God's imputation, whether of sin or righteousness, is not founded upon sovereign caprice, but upon indubitable truth. As we are partakers by generation of Adam's original pollution before God imputes it to us, that is, before he accounts us really polluted; so are we partakers by regeneration of Christ's original righteousness before God imputes righteousness to us, that is, before he accounts us really righteous. And therefore a positive and substantial communication of Christ's righteousness, apprehended by faith, no less precedes God's imputation of righteousness to a believer, than

Bartimeus' receiving his sight, and admitting the light, were previous to God's reckoning that he actually saw.

Although we grant the Almighty "calls the things that are not, as though they were," and that, according to his foreknowledge, he frequently speaks of them in the prophetic style, as if they were now, or had been already; yet when he reckons what is, in order to pass sentence of absolution or condemnation, he cannot deny his truth, and reckon a man actually chaste and charitable that actually commits adultery and murder. We dare not impute this flagrant unrighteousness to God. And as "no guile was found in the Lord's mouth" while he was upon earth, we cannot admit the most distant thought of his being full of guile in heaven; which we apprehend would be the case, if he reckoned that a man who actually falls from adultery into murder is actually undefiled, and completely righteous.

Again: as Christ bore no manner of vicarious punishment for us; or, which is the same, as our iniquities were not actually laid upon him till he partook of our frail nature, and was positively interested in our corruptible blood; so, by a parity of reason, we are not indulged with the pardon and acceptance which he merited for us till we partake of his light and righteousness. Hence appears the weakness of that argument, "righteousness may as well be imputed to us, without any participation of the Divine nature, as sin was imputed to Christ, without any participation of our fallen nature." We absolutely deny the fact on which this argument is founded; and assert, with St. Paul, that Christ "was made sin for us," (i.e. a proper sacrifice for our sins,) not by an imaginary robe of unrighteousness put upon him according to your imputation; but by being really "made of a *fallen, mortal* woman," and "sent in the likeness of sinful flesh," that he might suffer and die for us; which he could not have done, if he had not assumed our fallen nature — unfallen man being quite above the reach of pain and death. It is not less certain, therefore, that "he was made in the likeness of sinful flesh," than it is indubitable that "he was in all points tempted like as we are, yet without sin."

As sure then as Christ was not "made sin [i.e. a sin offering] for us," by a speculative imputation of our personal sins; but by being actually made flesh, clothed with our mortality, and "sent in the likeness of sinful flesh;" so sure are "we made the righteousness of God in him," not by a speculative imputation of his personal good works, but by being "made partakers of the Divine nature, begotten of God, and clothed with essential righteousness;" which is the case when we "put on the new man, who after God is created in righteousness and true holiness." Thus it appears to us that your imputation may be demolished, only by retorting 2 Corinthians v, 21, the scripture with which it is chiefly supported; and, if we are not mistaken, the venerable fabric raised upon that passage, like Mohammed's venerable tomb, hangs in the air without one single prop.

That the seed of righteousness, by which we are first interested in Christ, is universal in all infants, appears to us evident from St. Paul's words' "As by one man's [Adam's] disobedience the many [the multitudes of mankind] were made sinners," by a seed of sin; "so by the obedience of one [Christ] shall the many [the multitudes of mankind] be made righteous," by a seed of righteousness, to the end of the world, Romans v, 19. Hence it is that righteousness is imputed to all infants; and that, as I have proved, Letter X, they stand justified before God, according to the inferior dispensation they are under.

When they grow up, and "hold the truth in unrighteousness," by sinning against their light, personal iniquity is imputed to them; and till they believe again in the light, and renounce the evil deeds which it reproves, they are "condemned already." But the moment they truly repent, and unfeignedly believe the Gospel belonging to their dispensation, condemnation vanishes; God again imputes righteousness to them — that is, for Christ's sake he again pardons their sins, accepts their persons, and considers them as branches that admit the righteous sap of the true vine, and bear "the fruits of righteousness."

Once more: If these branches do not believingly abide in Christ, the vine, they become such branches in him as bear not fruit. Nay, they bear the poison of unrighteousness. Iniquity therefore is again imputed to them; and so long as they continue in their sin and unbelief, they are every moment liable to be "taken away, cast into the fire, and burned," John xv. Nevertheless, through the Redeemer's intercession, God "bears long with them;" and if they despise not to the last the "riches of his forbearance and long suffering," duly considering how "his goodness leadeth them to repentance," their backslidings are healed. They believe again "with the heart unto righteousness." The righteous sap of the true vine has again a free course in their hearts. They again receive Christ, who "is the end of the law," and the sum of the Gospel, "for righteousness to every one that believeth:" and their faith, which once more admits the beams of the Sun of righteousness, is once more "imputed to them for righteousness."

This, honoured sir, is the holy imputation of righteousness, which we read of in the oracles of God; and we prefer it to yours for three reasons. (1.) It hath truth for its foundation; but your imputation stands upon a preposterous supposition, that Christ the righteous was an execrable sinner, and that an elect is perfectly righteous, while he commits execrable iniquity. (2.) Because it perfectly agrees with St. James' undefiled religion, which your scheme entirely overthrows. And (3.) Because it is supported by the plainest scriptures.

The popes have at least the letter of one passage to countenance their monstrous doctrine of transubstantiation. They save appearances when they make their dupes believe that a bit of bread is really the body of Christ: for, say they, Christ took bread, and declared, This is my body. But, O tell it not in Paris, lest the subjects of the triple crown triumph over us in their turn! The personal righteousness of Christ is not so much as once mentioned in all the Bible with the doctrine of imputation; and yet some divines can make whole congregations of men, who protest against the impious absurdities of the Church of Rome, believe that the imputation of Christ's personal righteousness is a Scriptural doctrine, and the very marrow of the Gospel! This garment of their own weaving they cast over adulterers and murderers, and then represent the filthy, bloody wretches, as complete in Christ's obedience, perfect in righteousness, and "undefiled" before God!

If I had a thousand tongues, could I employ them more to the glory of Christ, and the good of souls, than by crying to the thousands who are still" sold under sin," and still take their carnal ease in that imaginary garment of righteousness, "Awake to *true* righteousness, and sin not?" Search the Scriptures. Where is it said, that Christ's personal righteousness was ever imputed to either man or angel? And where is it written that righteousness was ever imputed to any one, farther than he was possessed of, and actuated by, a living, powerful inherent principle of righteous faith?

"To the law and the testimony!" Can any thing be plainer than the two following positions, on which all our doctrine of imputation is founded? (1.) Faith is a powerful, quickening, justifying, sanctifying, working, victorious, saving grace. (2.) This faith, as it springs from and receives Christ, and his righteous power, "is imputed to us for righteousness."

Does not the first of these propositions stand unshaken upon such scriptures as these? "Faith is the evidence of things not seen, and the substance of things hoped for: all things are possible to him that believeth: whosoever believeth is born of God: all that believe are justified: purifying their hearts by faith: sanctified through faith that is in me: this is the victory that overcometh the world, even our faith: ye are saved through faith: faith worketh by love: remembering your work of faith: faith without works is dead: he that believeth hath everlasting life: holding the mystery of faith in a pure conscience, which some having put away concerning faith have made shipwreck," &c. Is it not evident from these scriptures, that all who have a living faith have not only a pardon, but works, especially love, which is "the fulfilling of the law;" — love, the most excellent "fruit of righteousness," in which all others are contained? And surely, if they have a pardon, and true inherent righteousness in their Christ accepting, loving, and obedient faith, that faith may well be "imputed to them for righteousness," or God may well account them righteous.

Nor is the second proposition, upon which our imputation stands, less clearly laid down in the Scriptures. "Abraham believed in the Lord, and he counted,* [or imputed] it to him for righteousness," Genesis xv, 6. What says the Scripture? "Abraham believed God, and it was imputed unto him for righteousness," i.e. for preceding righteousness, through the remission of his past sins; for present acceptance in the Beloved, whom he received; and for present righteousness through the righteous exertions of a "faith that worketh by love." Again: "To him that believeth, his faith is imputed for righteousness: we say that faith was imputed to Abraham for righteousness: that he might be the father of all them that believe, that righteousness might be imputed to them also. He was strong in faith, giving glory to God; and therefore it was imputed to him for righteousness. Now it was not written for his sake alone, that it was imputed to him; but for us also, to whom it shall be imputed, if we believe," Galatians iii, 6; Romans iv, 3, &c.

As Moses had led the van of these testimonies in favour of our Scriptural imputation, and St. Paul the main body, permit St. James to bring up the rear. "Seest thou," says he, "how faith wrought with Abraham's works, and by works was faith made perfect, and the scripture was fulfilled, which says, Abraham believed God, and it was imputed to him for righteousness?" James ii,

---

* There is but one word in the original, which our translators indifferently render impute, count, or reckon.

23. The whole is thus summed up by the great defender of free grace: — "The Gentiles which followed not after righteousness have attained to righteousness, even the righteousness which is of faith. But Israel, which followed after the law of righteousness, hath not attained to it. Wherefore? Because they sought it not by faith; but, as it were, by [the faithless] works," which they did in self-righteous obedience to the letter of the law; trampling under foot the righteousness of faith, which speaketh on this wise: "If thou shalt confess with thy mouth the Lord Jesus, and shalt believe in thy heart that God hath raised him from the dead, thou shalt be saved: for with the heart man believeth unto righteousness, and with the mouth confession is made unto salvation," Romans ix, and x.

Who does not see, in reading these words, that we must do something unto righteousness, as well as unto salvation? Is it not evident that we must now "believe with the heart," in order to the former, and "make confession with the mouth," as we have opportunity, in order to the latter; and, consequently, that righteousness imputed, as well as salvation finished, without any thing done on our part, is a doctrine that is not less contrary even to St. Paul's Epistle to the Romans, fairly taken together, than to that strong rampart of undefiled religion, the Epistle of St. James.

However, a cloud of objections arises, to keep the light from a prejudiced reader: and as he thinks that three of them are remarkably strong, I beg leave to consider them with some degree of attention.

I. OBJECTION. "Your doctrine of justifying, sanctifying, and working faith imputed to us for righteousness, I bear my loud testimony against; because it confounds righteousness with sanctification, two Gospel blessings, which are clearly distinguished, 1 Corinthians i, 30."

ANSWER. It would be much better to confound, than to destroy them both; as I fear you do, when you cast a robe of finished salvation, i.e. of complete righteousness and finished holiness, over impenitent adulterers and murderers. But be that as it will, your objection is groundless. I have already observed, and I once more declare, that when we speak of the righteousness of faith we understand three things (1.) The non-imputation, or "forgiveness of the sins that are PAST," Romans iii, 25. (2.) Present "acceptance in the Beloved!" Ephesians i, 6. And, (3.) A principle of universal righteousness, by which we are interested in Christ's righteousness; just as a branch is interested in the excellence of the vine, by receiving the generous sap which it actually derives from it; and not by an imaginary imputation of the fine grapes which the vine bore seventeen hundred years ago. "Let no man deceive you; he that DOES righteousness," is a righteous branch; even as Christ is a righteous vine! 1 John iii, 7; John xv, 5.

On the other hand, when we speak of sanctification we understand the wonderful change wrought in us by the working of the above-mentioned principle of righteousness; and the internal fruits which it produces, till, by "growing up into Christ in all things, we come in the unity of the faith, and of the knowledge of the Son of God, unto a perfect man, unto the measure of the stature of the fulness of Christ." It is evident therefore, that, considering righteousness and sanctification even in their most intimate union, we do not confound them at all; but maintain as clear a distinction between them as that which subsists between the derivation of sap by a wild branch from the good olive tree, and the change produced in that branch upon such a derivation.

II. OBJECTION. "Your doctrine is Popery refined. By paying saving honours to a Christian grace, and taking the crown from Christ to set it upon faith, you shake the very foundation of the Mediator's throne. If this is not high treason against him, what crime deserves that name?"

ANSWER. Your fears are laudable, though absolutely groundless. (1.) Faith, the humble grace that will know nothing but Christ, for "wisdom, righteousness, sanctification, and redemption," can never dishonour his person, claim his crown, or shake the foundation of his throne. Is it not ridiculous to make so much ado about faith robbing Christ of saving honours, when Christ himself says, "Thy FAITH hath SAVED thee;" and when the apostle cries out, "Believe, and thou shalt be saved!" Were then Christ and St. Paul two refined Papists, and guilty of high treason against the Redeemer?

(2.) If some will be "wise above what is written," we dare not. If they are ashamed of the oracles of God, we are not: therefore, whatever they think of us, we must say, with the evangelical apostle, "Faith was imputed to Abraham for righteousness: and to him that believeth, HIS FAITH is imputed for righteousness."

(3.) Should you say that Abraham's faith, or his believing God, signifies either Christ's person or his personal righteousness, we reply, *Credat Judæus Apella!* There was indeed a time when Calvinist divines could make simple Protestants believe it, as easily as the pope can make credulous Papists believe that a wafer of the size of half a crown is the identical body of our Lord: but as many Romanists begin to shake off the yoke of Popish absurdities, so many Protestants will cast away that of Calvinian impositions. And as our fathers taught us to protest that the hocus pocus of a Popish priest cannot turn bread into flesh, so will we teach our children to protest that the bare assertion of a Calvinist minister cannot turn Abraham's faith into Christ's person, or into his personal righteousness; which must however be the case if those words, "Abraham's faith," or his believing God, "was imputed for righteousness," do only mean, as we are confidently told, that "Christ, or, his personal righteousness, was imputed to Abraham for righteousness."

(4.) Does it reflect any dishonour upon Christ to say, with St. Paul, that "FAITH is imputed to us for righteousness;" when believing includes its object, (Christ the way, the truth, and the life,) as necessarily as eating supposes food, and drinking, liquor? Is it not as impossible to "believe in the light," without Christ the light; or to believe in the truth, without Christ the truth, as it is to breathe without air, and hear without sounds? Again: if you affirm "that we warm ourselves by going to the fire," do you sap the foundation of natural philosophy because you do not say ten times over that the warming power comes from the fire, and not from our motion toward it? And do we destroy the foundation of Christianity, when we assert that "faith working by love" instrumentally saves us because we do not spend so much time as you in saying over and over that the saving merit and the saving power flow from the Saviour, and not from our own act of believing? Is not this as clear as it is that the light flows in upon us from the sun, and not from (though it is through) the opening of our eyes?

Lastly: would not physicians make themselves appear very ridiculous if they distressed their patients when they were going to take a medicine, with the fear of ascribing their recovery to their taking the remedy, i.e. to "their own doing," rather than to the virtue of the remedy itself? And are those divines alone partakers of heavenly wisdom who puzzle sinners that are coming to Christ, and place a lion in their way, by perpetually injecting into their minds a fear lest they should ascribe their salvation to faith rather than to the Saviour whom faith receives? Where does the apostle, whose evangelical sentiments they do so deservedly extol, set them the example of such refinements? Is it Romans iv, where he says, directly or indirectly, seven times, that "FAITH is imputed for righteousness?" Is it not strange that at last "orthodoxy" should consist in fairly setting aside, or explaining away the doctrine of St. Paul, as well as that of St. James?

III. OBJECTION. "Your mind is full of carnal reasonings. You do not know either Christ or yourself. If you did you would never set up the inherent righteousness of faith, which is nothing but our own righteousness, in opposition to imputed righteousness. If you were not quite blind, or 'very dark,' you would see that all our righteousnesses are as filthy rags; and you would humbly acknowledge that the holy breastplate and robe of righteousness, which we may with safety and honour appear in before God, are the breastplate and robe of Christ's personal righteousness freely imputed to us, without any of our doings. This best robe, which you so horribly bespatter, we must defend against all the Arminians, Pelagians, and Papists in the world."

ANSWER. To do this grand objection justice, it will be proper to consider it in its various parts, and give each a full answer.

1. We acknowledge that we cannot think nonsense is any more compatible with the wisdom of God, and flat contradiction with his sacred oracles, than adultery is compatible with undefiled religion, and murder with common morality. If these sentiments are "carnal reasonings," we beg leave to continue carnal reasoners, till you can recommend your spiritual reasonings, either by common sense or plain Scripture.

2. You confound, without reason, the inherent righteousness of faith with Pharisaic self-righteousness. I have already proved that the latter, which is the partial, external, and hypocritical righteousness of unbelieving formalists, is the only righteousness which the prophet compares to filthy rags. With respect to the former, that is our own righteousness of faith, far from setting it up in opposition to imputed righteousness rightly understood, we assert that it is the righteousness of God, the very thing which "God imputes to us for righteousness;" the very righteousness which has now the stamp of his approbation, and will one day have the crown of his rewards.

3. You affirm that the breastplate of righteousness which St. Paul charges the Ephesians to have on, is Christ's personal righteousness imputed to us; and we prove the contrary by the following arguments. The apostle, who is the best illustrator of his own expressions, exhorts the Thessalonians to "put on the breastplate of faith and love." Now, as we never heard of soldiers having two breastplates on; the imaginary breastplate of their general, which they wear by imputation; and the solid plate of metal, which actually covers their breasts; we

conclude, that the "breastplate of righteousness," which St. Paul recommends to the Ephesians, together with the "shield of faith," is nothing but the "breastplate of faith and love," which he recommends to the Thessalonians.

To help my readers to see your doctrine in a proper light, I might say, If the breastplate of our Lord's personal obedience has no more to do with our breasts than the personal dinner which he took in the Pharisee's house has to do with our empty stomachs; and the personal garment in which he shone upon Mount Tabor has to do with our naked shoulders; the judicious apostle would probably have called it a brainplate rather than a breastplate, as having far less to do with the breast and heart than with the brain and imagination. But as this argument would rather turn upon our translation than upon the original, I drop it, and present you with one that has more solidity.

If the breastplate of a Christian Warrior is as far from him, in time and place, as the personal righteousness wrought by our Lord in Judea seventeen hundred and sixty years ago, his shield may be at the same distance; and so undoubtedly may his helmet and sandals, his belt and sword. Thus, by Calvin's contrivance, you have a soldier of Christ armed cap-a-pee, without one single piece of armour from head to foot. And will you say of these imaginary accoutrements, in which the elect can with all ease commit adultery and incest, that they are "the armour of righteousness on the right hand and on the left," in which St. Paul fought his battles, and subdued so many kindreds and nations to his Lord's triumphant cross? O! if that champion were yet alive, who said, in the midst of Corinth, "The kingdom of God is not in word, but in power," how would he cry, in the midst of mystic Geneva, "The armour of God is not a Calvinian notion, but a Divine reality!"

What we are persuaded he would thunder out through the world, we are at last determined to proclaim on the walls of our Jerusalem. "Soldiers of Christ, have on the true breastplate of righteousness! Put on the solid breastplate of inherent faith and love. If Satan's temptations are not idle imputations of his dreadful assaults upon Christ; if his darts are really fiery and terrible, throw away Calvinian imputation: 'cast off the works of darkness; and put on the real armour of righteousness, the armour of light, the whole armour of God:' so shall you be 'able to stand in the evil day; and having DONE ALL, to stand with safety in judgment, and with honour in the congregation of the righteous.'"

4. We apprehend that you are not less mistaken about the ROBE than about the breastplate of righteousness. And we think we can prove it by the testimony of the three most competent judges in the universe, an apostle, an elder before the throne, and the Lamb in the midst of it. Hear we the apostle first.

1. If all the saints were clothed with the robe of Christ's personal righteousness, they would all be clothed exactly like Christ. But when St. John had a vision of the Redeemer's glory, he "saw him clothed with a vesture DIPPED IN BLOOD: and the armies which were in heaven followed him, clothed in fine linen WHITE and clean," Revelation xix, 13, 14. Now, as the white robes worn by the soldiers that compose an army cannot be the red robe worn by the general at the head of the army, we so far give place to what you call "carnal reasonings," as to conclude, that so sure as white is not red, the robes of the saints are not the robes of our Lord's personal righteousness. Nay, we, who

throw off the veil of prejudice, would be guilty of the very crime you charge us with, were we to entertain that daring idea. Christ's personal righteousness is the obedience of the Son of God, who, by living and dying for us, became the "propitiation for the sins of the whole world;" now, if we pretended that this identical, allmeritorious "obedience of Christ unto death," this active and passive righteousness, which made all atonement for all mankind, is fairly made over to, and put upon us; would it not be pretending to merit with Christ, not only our own salvation, but the salvation of all mankind? O sir, it is you, we are afraid, who affect the Saviour; for by presuming to put on his robes, you claim his mediatorial honours. For, after all your fears lest we should make humble faith share the Saviour's glory, or his glorious apparel, you not only put it on yourself without ceremony, but throw it also over the shoulders of ten thousand elect, without excepting even those who add drunkenness to thirst, and cruelty to lust.

You will, I hope, see the great impropriety of this conduct, if you consider that the Redeemer's personal and peculiar righteousness is his personal and peculiar glory; and that those who fancy themselves clad with it, (if they do not sin ignorantly,) are as guilty of ridiculous, not to say treasonable presumption before God, as country clergymen would be before the archbishop of Canterbury and the king, if they seriously gave it out that the sleeves of their surplures are the very lawn sleeves of his grace; and their gowns and cassocks the identical coronation robes of his majesty.

The fanciful parsons would no doubt be pitied by all men of sense; and so are we by all our Calvinist brethren; but, alas! for a very different reason. They wonder at and kindly pity us, because we cannot fancy ourselves clothed with robes a thousand times more sacred than those which Aaron wore on the great day of atonement: with robes ten thousand times more incommunicable than the king's coronation robes: with a Divine garment, that, in the very nature of things, can absolutely suit none but Him, "on whose head are many crowns, and who hath on his vesture and on his thigh a name written, King of kings, and Lord of lords; — the child born unto us of a virgin, the only begotten Son of the Father, given to put away sin by the sacrifice of himself: — the wonderful Counsellor, the mighty God, the everlasting Father, the Prince of Peace."

O ye sons of men, how long will you become so "vain in your imagination," as to put on robes on which the very finger of God has embroidered such incommunicable names with adamant and gold! If you are "saviours of the world," and "mediators between God and man;" if you are "emmanuels" and "gods over all, blessed for ever," wear them; they fit you, and they are your right. But if "ye all shall die like men," who cannot atone for one sin; and if the flesh of every one of you "shall see corruption," touch them not, unless it be with the reverential faith of the Syro-Phenician woman. Like her you may indeed steal a cure through them: but O! do not steal them, as those who "come" in the Redeemer's dress, and say, "I am Christ," or those who tell you, "I am carnal, sold under sin," but no matter! I am safe. In the robes of Christ's righteousness, I am as righteous as Christ himself. If nevertheless you are bent upon putting them on by self imputation, at the peril of your souls throw them not over the shoulders of impenitent sinners, lest you "turn the truth of God into a *flagrant* lie;" lest professing yourselves wise to salvation, you "become fools, and change the glory [the glorious robe] of the incorruptible God"-man into the infamous cloak of an incestuous adulterer.

2. Suppose that still despising the white robes, that is, the evangelical righteousness of the saints, you aspire at being clothed with the Redeemer's vesture dipped in blood; permit me. to oppose to your error the testimony of one of the twenty-four elders who stand nearest the throne, and therefore know best in what robes the saints can stand before it with safety and honour.

"I beheld, (says the beloved disciple,) and lo, a great multitude which no man can number, of all nations, people, and tongues, stood before the throne, and before the Lamb, clothed with WHITE ROBES," Revelation vii, 9. By comparing this verse with Revelation xix, 7, 8, it is evident, that great multitude was the Church triumphant, the wife of the Lamb, who has made herself ready. She is composed of souls who have fulfilled those awful commands, "O Jerusalem, wash thy heart from iniquity, that thou mayest be saved. Wash you, make you clean, put away the evil of your doings from before my eyes. Come, and let us reason together; though your sins be as red as scarlet, they shall be as white as snow." They continued instant in prayer, that God would "wash them thoroughly from their iniquity, and cleanse them from their sins." Nor did they give over pleading his gracious promises, till the living water, the cleansing blood, the fuller's soap, and the refiner's fire, had had their full effect upon them. Therefore, "to them it was granted, that they should be arrayed in fine linen, clean and white; for the fine linen is the righteousness of the saints."

Now the question between us is, whether the "fine linen, clean and white," and the "white robes" mentioned by St. John, are the evangelical, personal righteousness of the saints, or the mediatorial, personal righteousness of their Lord: but who shall help us to decide it? One of the elders before the throne, who advances and says unto John, "These, who are arrayed in white robes, are they who came out of great tribulation, and have washed their robes, and made them white in the blood of the Lamb," Revelation vii, 14. Does not this information, given by one to whom the beloved disciple had just said, "Sir, thou knowest," make it indubitable that the righteousness which the saints appear in before God, is a righteousness which was once defiled, and therefore stood in need of washing? Now, what Christian will assert, that the personal righteousness of the immaculate Lamb of God had ever one spot of defilement?

Again: those robes were washed and made white by the saints: "THEY have washed their robes." It is evident, therefore, that if these robes were the personal righteousness of Christ, the saints had washed it. And who is the good man, that, upon second thoughts, will dare to countenance a preposterous doctrine, which supposes, that the saints have washed the defiled righteousness of the Lord, and made it white?

Once more: These robes are washed "in the blood of the Lamb," that is, "in the fountain opened for sin and for uncleanness." Now, if they were the robes of Christ's personal righteousness, does it not necessarily follow, that Christ opened a fountain to wash his own spotted and sinful righteousness? Is it not strange, that those who pretend to a peculiar regard for the Redeemer's glory, should be such great sticklers for an opinion which pours such contempt upon him and his glorious apparel?

3. If the testimony of St. John, and that of one of the twenty-four elders, be not regarded, let our Lord's repeated declaration, at least, be thought worthy of consideration. All our righteousness flows from him, as all the sap of the branch flows from the vine. Therefore, speaking of righteousness, he says, "Buy of me white raiment, that thou mayest be clothed, and that the shame of thy nakedness do not appear," Revelation iii, 18. But that this white raiment cannot be his personal righteousness, we prove, first, from his own words mentioned in the same chapter: "Thou hast a few names in Sardis, which have not defiled their garments," Revelation iii, 4. Now, if these garments were the robes of Christ's personal obedience, which neither man nor devil can defile, how came our Lord to make it matter of praise to a few names, that they had not defiled them? If David could not in the least bespatter them by all his crimes, was it a wonder that some persons should have kept them clean? Is it not rather surprising that any names in Sardis should have had defiled garments, which remain "undefiled, and without spot," even while those who wear them welter in the mire of adultery, murder, and incest?

Once more: Our Lord says, "Behold, I come as a thief. Blessed is he that watcheth and keepeth his garments, lest he walk naked and they see his shame," Revelation xvi, 5. Who does not see here that the garments, which we are to keep with watchfulness, are garments which may be spotted or stolen? Garments of which we may be so totally stripped, as to be seen walking naked? Two particulars that perfectly suit our personal righteousness by faith, but can never suit the personal righteousness of Christ; that "best robe," which neither man nor devil can steal, neither adultery nor murder defile.

Having spent so much time with my objector, I beg leave to turn to you, honoured sir, and to conclude this essay upon imputed righteousness, by summing up the difference which subsists between us on that important subject; and inviting men of candour to determine who of us have reason, conscience, and Scripture on their side.

You believe that the uninterrupted good works and the atoning sufferings of Christ, which made up his personal righteousness while he was upon earth, are imputed to the elect for complete and eternal righteousness, be their own personal righteousness what it will: insomuch that, as you express it, (*Five Letters*, pp. 27 and 29,) "All debts and claims against them, be they more or be they less, be they small or be they great, be they before or be they after conversion, are for ever and for ever cancelled: they always stand absolved, always complete in the everlasting righteousness of the Redeemer." And you think that this imputed righteousness composes the robes of righteousness, in which they stand before God, both in the day of conversion and in the day of judgment.

On the other hand, we believe, that, for the alone sake of Christ's atoning blood and personal righteousness, our personal faith, working by obedient love, is imputed to us for righteousness. And we assert, that this living faith, working by obedient love, together with the privileges annexed to it, (such as pardon through, and acceptance in the Beloved,) makes up the robe of righteousness "washed in the blood of the Lamb," in which true believers now walk humbly with their God, and will one day triumphantly enter into the glory of their Lord.

I hope, honoured sir, that when we speak of personal faith, love, and righteousness, you will do us the justice to believe, we do not mean that we can have either faith, love, or righteousness of ourselves, or from ourselves. No: they all as much flow to us from Christ, the true vine, and the Sun of righteousness, as the sap and fruit of a branch come from the tree that bears it, and from the sun that freely shines upon it. "without him" we have nothing but helplessness; "we can do nothing" but sin; but with him we "can do all things." If we call any graces personal or inherent, it is not then to take the honour of them to ourselves, but merely to distinguish them from "imputed righteousness," which is nothing but the imputed assemblage of all the graces that were in our Lord's breast seventeen hundred and fifty years ago.

As some of my readers may desire to know exactly wherein the difference between personal and imputed grace consists, I shall just help their conception by three or four Scriptural examples. Joseph, struggling out of the arms of his tempting mistress, has personal chastity, a considerable branch of personal righteousness: and David, sparing his own flock, and taking the ewe lamb that lay in Uriah's bosom, is complete in imputed chastity, which is a considerable part of imputed righteousness. Solomon choosing wisdom, and dedicating the temple, has inherent wisdom and piety: but when he chooses Pagan wives, and with them worships deformed idols, he has imputed wisdom and piety. Again: when Peter confesses that Jesus is the Christ, the Son of the living God, he personally wears the girdle of truth: but when he denies his Lord with oaths and curses, saying, "I know not the man," he wears it only by imputation. Once more: When David killed proud Goliah with his own sword, he stood complete in the personal righteousness we plead for: but when he killed brave Uriah with the sword of the children of Ammon, he stood complete in what our opponents extol as the "best robe."

And now, ye unprejudiced servants of the most high God, ye men of candour and piety, scattered through the three kingdoms, to you, under God, we submit our cause. Impartially weigh the arguments on both sides; and judge whether the robe recommended by our brethren deserves to be called "the best robe," because it is really better than the robes of "righteousness and true holiness" which we recommend; or only because it is best calculated to pervert the Gospel, dishonour Christ, disgrace undefiled religion, throw a decent cloak over the works of darkness, render Antinomianism respectable to injudicious Protestants, and frighten moral men from Christianity, as from the most immoral system of religion in the world.

By this time, honoured sir, you are perhaps ready to turn objector yourself, and say, "You slander our principles. 'The doctrines of grace' are doctrines according to godliness. Far from opposing inherent righteousness in its place, we follow after it ourselves, and frequently recommend it to others. Imputed righteousness is highly consistent with personal holiness."

To this I answer: I know a mistaken man, who believes that he has a right to all his neighbour's property, because St. Paul says, "All things are yours;" and nevertheless he is so honest that you may trust him with untold gold. Just so it is with you, dear sir. You not only believe, but publicly maintain, that an elect who seduces his neighbour's wife "stands complete in the everlasting personal chastity of Christ," and that a fall into adultery will "work for his good:" and yet, I am persuaded that, if you were married, you would be as true to your wife as Adam was to Eve before the fall. But can you in conscience apologize for your errors, and desire us to embrace them, merely because your conduct is better than your bad principles?

Again: "You frequently recommend holiness," and perhaps give it out that the shortest way to it is to believe your doctrines of imputed righteousness and finished salvation: but this, far from mending the matter, makes it worse. As fishes would hardly swallow the hook, if a tempting bait did not cover it and entice them; so the honest hearts of the simple would hardly jump at imputed righteousness, if they were not deceived by fair speeches about personal holiness. Thus good food makes way for poison, and the right robe decently wraps fig leaves and cobwebs.

Once more: Every body knows, that bad guineas are never so successfully put off, as when they are mixed with a great deal of good gold. But suppose I made it my business to pass them, either ignorantly or on purpose, would not the public be my dupes, if they suffered me to carry on that dangerous trade upon such a plea as this: "I am not against good gold. I pass a great deal of it myself. I have even some about me now. I frequently recommend it to others; neither did I ever decry his majesty's coin?" Would not every body see through such a poor defence as this? And yet, poor as it is, you could not, with any show of truth, urge the last plea: for, in order to pass your notions about imputed righteousness, you have publicly spoken against inherent righteousness, and all its fruits. In the face of the whole world you have decried the coin that bears the genuine stamp of the Lord's goodness. You have called good works, "dung, dross, and filthy rags;" and what is still worse, you have given it out that you had "Scripture authority" so to do.

Should you to the preceding objection add the following question: "If you were now dying, in which robe would you desire to appear before God; that of Christ's personal righteousness imputed to you, without any of your good works; or, that of your own self righteousness and good works, without the blood and righteousness of Christ?" My answer is ready.

I would be found in neither, because both would be equally fatal to me: for the robe of an Antinomian is not better than that of a Pharisee; and all are foolish virgins who stand only in the one or in the other. Were I then come to the awful moment you speak of, I would beg of God to keep me from all delusions, and to strengthen my heartfelt faith in Christ, that I might be found clothed, like a wise virgin, with "a robe washed and made white in the blood of the Lamb;" that is, with the righteousness of a living faith working by love: for such a faith is the blessed reality that stands at an equal distance from the Antinomian and Pharisaic delusion. And, I say it Again,* this righteousness of

---

* I have on purpose been guilty of several such repetitions, not only because the same answers solve frequently different objections; but because I should be glad to stop the mouths of some of my readers, if I may give that name to prejudiced persons, who cast a careless, and perhaps a malignant

faith includes, (1.) A pardon through the blood and righteousness of Christ. (2.) Acceptance in the Beloved. And (3.) A universal principle of inherent righteousness. For the kingdom of God is not meat and drink, much less whim and delusion; but "righteousness, peace, and joy in the Holy Ghost."

But perhaps you ask, "Which would you depend upon for pardon and acceptance in a dying hour, — your own inherent righteousness of faith, or the atoning blood and meritorious righteousness of Jesus Christ?" If this is your question, I reply, that it carries its own answer along with it. For if I have the inherent righteousness of a living faith, and if the very nature of such a faith is (as I have already observed) to depend upon nothing but Christ for "wisdom, righteousness, sanctification, and redemption," is it not absurd to ask, whether I would depend on any thing else? Suppose I have faith working by humble love, do not I know that the moment I rely upon myself, or my works, as the meritorious cause of my acceptance, I put off the robe "made white in the blood of the Lamb," and put on the spotted robe of a proud Pharisee?

However, it is by self-contradictory objections and false dilemmas that the hearts of the simple are daily deceived, as well as by fair speeches, which carry an appearance of great self abasement, and of a peculiar regard for the Redeemer's glory. Who can tell how many pious souls are driven by the tempter upon one rock, through an excessive fear of dashing against the other? Every judicious, moderate man,

Auream quisquis mediocritatem
Diligit,

sees their well-meant error, and can say to each of them,

Procellas
Cautus horrescis, nimium premendo
Littus iniquum.

Lest you should be found in the odious apparel of a Pharisee, you put on unawares the modish dress of an Antinomian.

But, O thou man of God, whosoever thou art, have nothing to do with the one or the other, except it be to decry and tear them both. In the meantime be thou really "found in Christ, not having thine own Pharisaic righteousness, which is of the *letter* of the law;" nor yet notions about righteousness imputed to thee in the Antinomian way; but the substantial, evangelical "righteousness, which is through the faith of Christ: the righteousness which is of God by faith: the true armour of righteousness," with which St. Paul cut in pieces the forces of Pharisaism "on the right hand," and St. James those of Antinomianism "on the left." Rejoicing, dear sir, that if our arguments should strip you of what appears to us an imaginary garment, you shall not be found naked; and thanking "the

---

look over here and there a page; and, without one grain of candour, condemn me for not saying in one letter what I have perhaps already said in half a dozen. In these perilous times we must run the risk of passing for fools with men of unbiassed judgment, that we may not pass for heretics with some of our brethren. And it is well, if, after all our repetitions, we are not still charged with not holding what we have so frequently asserted. For, alas! what repetitions, what scriptures, what expostulations can reach breasts, covered with a shield of prejudice, which bears such a common motto as this, "Non persuadebis etiamsi persuaseris?" I could wish, that such readers as will not do justice to the arguments of our opponents, as well as to our own, would never trouble themselves with our books.

God of all grace" for giving you, and thousands of pious Calvinists, a more substantial robe than that for which you so zealously plead; in the midst of chimerical imputations of "calumny," I remain, with personal and inherent truth, honoured and dear sir, your affectionate brother, and obedient servant in our common Lord,

JOHN FLETCHER.

LETTER XIII.

To Richard Hill, Esq.

HONOURED AND DEAR SIR, — Having so fully considered in my last the state of our controversy with respect to imputed righteousness, I proceed to the doctrine of free will, which I have not discussed in this Check, because you seem satisfied with what we grant you, and we are entirely so with what you grant us concerning it. Let us, however, just cast three looks, one upon our concessions, another upon yours, and a third upon the difference still remaining between us, with regard to that capital article of our controversy.

I. We never supposed that the natural will of fallen man is free to good, before it is more or less touched or rectified by grace. All we assert is, that whether a man chooses good or evil, his will is free, or it does not deserve the name of will. It is as far from us to think, that man, unassisted by Divine grace, is sufficient to will spiritual good, as to suppose, that when he wills it by grace he does not will it freely. And therefore, agreeable to our tenth article, which you quote against us without the least reason, we steadily assert, that "we have no power to do good without the grace of God preventing us," not that we may have a free will, for this we always had in the above-mentioned sense, but that we may have a good will: believing that, as confirmed saints and angels have a free will, though they have no evil will; so abandoned reprobates and devils have a free will, though they have no good will.

Again: We always maintained that the liberty of our will is highly consistent with the operations of Divine grace, by which it is put in a capacity of choosing life. We are therefore surprised to see you quote in triumph, (*Review*, p. 33,) the following paragraph out of the Second Check: "Nor is this freedom derogatory to free grace; for as it was free grace that gave an upright free will to Adam at his creation, so, whenever his fallen children think or act aright, it is because their free will is mercifully prevented, touched, and rectified by free grace."

At the sight of these concessions you cry out, "Amazing! Here is all that the most rigid Calvinist ever contended for granted in a moment. Your words, sir, are purely evangelical." Are they, indeed? Well, then, honoured sir, I have the pleasure to inform you, that, if this "is all you ever contended for," you need not

Five Checks To Antinomianism

contend any more with us; since Mr. Wesley, Mr. Sellon, J. Goodwin, and Arminius himself, never advanced any other doctrine concerning free will. For they all agree to ascribe to the free grace of God, through the Redeemer, all the freedom of man's will to good. Therefore, you yourself being judge, their sentiments, as well as my "words, are purely evangelical."

II. You cannot be more satisfied with our concessions than we are with yours: for you grant us as much freedom of will as constitutes us free willers, or moral agents; and in so doing, you expose the ignorance and injustice of those who think, that when they have called us free willers, they have put upon us one of the most odious badges of heresy.

We are particularly pleased with the following concessions, (*Review*, p. 38:) "Grace may not violate the liberty of the will: God forceth not a man's will to do good or ill. He useth no violence. The freedom of the regenerate is such, that they may draw back to perdition if they will."

We are yet better satisfied with what you say, (p. 35:) "Still it is your own opinion, that, to the end of the world, this plain, peremptory assertion of our Lord, 'I would, and ye would not,' will throw down and silence all the objections which can be raised against free will — it proves that those to whom it was addressed, might have come if they would. Granted." And (p. 43) you add: "I have granted Mr. Fletcher his own interpretation of that text, 'I would, and ye would not.'" Now, sir, if you stand to your concession, you have granted me, that Christ had eternal life for the Jews who rejected it: that he had a strong desire to bestow it upon them: that he had made them so far willing and able to come to him for it, as to leave them inexcusable if they did not: and that his saving grace, which they resisted, is by no means irresistible. Four propositions that sap the foundation of your system, and add new solidity to ours.

However, you try to make your readers believe, that "still we are but just where we were. The fault yet remains in the corruption of the will:" giving us to understand, that because the Jews would not be gathered by Christ, he had never touched and rectified their will. Thus you suppose, that their choosing death is a demonstration that they could not have chosen life: that is, you suppose just what you should have proved.

You imagine that a wrong choice always demonstrates the previous perverseness of the will that makes it; but we show the contrary by matter of fact. Satan and his legions, as well as our first parents, were created perfectly upright. Their will was once as free from corruption as the will of God himself. Nevertheless, with a will perfectly capable of making a right choice; with a will that a few moments before had chosen life, they all chose the ways of death. Hence appears the absurdity of concluding, that a wrong choice always proves the will was so corrupted, previously to that choice, that a better choice was morally impossible. Take us right, however. We do not suppose that the will of the obstinate Jews had not been totally corrupted in Adam. We only maintain, that they made as free and fatal a choice with their free will, which free grace had rectified, as Adam, Eve, and all the fallen angels once made with the upright free will with which free grace had created them.

But I return to your concessions. That which pleases us most of all, I find, (*Review*, p. 39:) "For my own part, (you say,) I have not the least objection to the expression *free will*, and find it used in a very sound sense by St. Augustine, Luther, and Calvin, the great patrons for the doctrine of man's natural inability to do that which is good since the fall. God does not force any man to will either good or evil; but man. through the corruption of his understanding, naturally and freely wills that which is evil; but by being wrought upon and enlightened by converting grace, he as freely wills that which is good, as before he freely willed the evil. In this sense the assembly of divines speak of the natural liberty of the will, and affirm that it is not forced."

These, honoured sir, are our very sentiments concerning free will. How strange is it, then, when you have so fully granted us the natural and necessary freedom of the will, to see you as flushed with an imaginary victory, as if you had just driven us out of the field! How astonishing to hear you cry out, (p. 34,) "Jesus Christ on the side of free will! What! The Gospel on the side of free will! What!" Yes, honoured sir, Jesus Christ and the Gospel on the side of free will! And if that is not enough, appeal to the thirty-fourth page of your Review, to show that the assembly of divines and yourself are on the side of free will also.

III. Consider we now the difference still remaining between us. From our mutual concessions, it is evident we agree, (1.) That the will is always free. (2.) That the will of man, considered as fallen in Adam, and unassisted by the grace of God, is only free to evil, — free to live in the element of sin, as a sea fish is only free to live in salt water. And, (3.) That when he is free to good, free to choose life, he has this freedom from redeeming grace.

But although we agree in these material points, the difference between us is still very considerable; for we assert, that, through the Mediator promised to all mankind in Adam, God, by his free grace, restores to all mankind a talent of free will to do good, by which they are put in a capacity of "choosing life or death," that is, of acquitting themselves well or ill, at their option, in their present state of trial.

This you utterly deny, maintaining that man is not in a state of probation; and that, as Christ died for none but the elect, none but they can ever have any degree of saving grace, i.e. any will free to good. Hence you conclude, that all the elect are in a state of finished salvation; and necessarily, infallibly, and irresistibly choose life: while all the reprobates are shut up in a state of finished damnation; and necessarily, infallibly, and irresistibly choose death. For, say your divines, God has not decreed the infallible end, either of the elect or the reprobates, without decreeing also the infallible means conducing to that end. Therefore, in the day of his irresistible power, the fortunate elect are absolutely made willing to believe and be waved; and the poor reprobates to disbelieve and be damned.

I shall conclude this article by just observing, that we are obliged to oppose this doctrine, because it appears to us a doctrine of wrath, rather than a doctrine of grace. If we are not mistaken, it is opposite to the general tenor of the Scriptures, injurious to all the Divine perfections, and subversive of this fundamental truth of natural and revealed religion, "God shall judge the world in righteousness." It is calculated to strengthen the carnal security of Laodicean professors, raise horrid anxieties in the minds of doubting Christians, and give damned spirits just ground to blaspheme to all eternity. Again: it withdraws from thinking sinners and judicious saints the helps which God has given them, by multitudes of conditional promises and threatenings, designed to work upon their hopes and fears. And, while it unnecessarily stumbles men of sense, and hardens infidels, it affords wicked men rational excuses to continue in their sins, and gives desperate offenders full room to charge, not only Adam, but God himself, with all their enormities.

I shall now be shorter in the review of the state of our controversy. Free will to good is founded upon general free grace, and general free grace upon the perfect oblation which Christ made upon the cross for the sins of the whole world. General redemption, therefore, I have endeavoured to establish upon a variety of arguments, which you decline answering.

Justification by (the evidence of) works in the last day is the doctrine which you and your brother have most vehemently attacked. You nave raised against it a great deal of dust, and some objections, which I hope you will find abundantly answered in the three first letters of this Check, and in the ninth. But suppose I had not answered them at all, you could not have won the day; because after all your joint opposition against our doctrine, both you and your brother bear your honest testimony to the indubitable truth of it, as our readers may see in our first, fifth, and ninth letters.

I need not remind you, sir, that upon this capital doctrine, the Minutes in general stand as upon a rock. If you doubt it, I refer you to the fifth and sixth letters.

The doctrine of a four-fold justification appears monstrous to your orthodoxy. Both you and your brother, therefore, have endeavoured to overturn it. But as you had neither Scripture nor argument to attack it with, you have done it by some witticisms, which are answered in the tenth letter.

Calvinian everlasting love, according to which the elect were never children of wrath, and apostates may go any length in sin without displeasing God, is a doctrine which I have attacked in all the Checks. You cannot defend it, and yet you will not give it up. You just intimate, that when the elect commit adultery and murder, they are in a sense penitent. This frivolous plea, this last shift, is exposed, letter tenth.

Finished salvation, which you call your" grand fortress," and which your brother styles, "the foundation of the Calvinists," you have endeavoured to support by a variety of arguments, answered, I trust, letter vii, in such a manner that our impartial readers will be convinced your foundation is sandy, and your grand fortress by no means impregnable.

The oneness of speculative Antinomianism and of barefaced Calvinism is the point in which our controversy insensibly terminates. I will not say that what we have advanced upon this subject is unanswerable; but I shall wonder to see it answered to the satisfaction of unprejudiced readers. In the meantime, I confess that I cannot cast my eyes upon the Calvinian creed in the seventh letter, and the Gospel proclamation in the eleventh, without being astonished at myself, for not seeing sooner that there is no more difference between Calvinism and speculative Antinomianism than there was between the disciple who betrayed our Lord, and Judas, surnamed Iscariot.

The Works of John Fletcher

Such, honoured sir, is, I think, the present state of our controversy; but what is that of our hearts? Do we love one another the better, and pray for each other the oftener, on account of our theological contest? Alas! if we sell love to buy the truth, we shall be no gainers in the end. Witness those awful words of St. Paul' "Though I have all knowledge, and all faith, if I have not charity, I am nothing but a tinkling cymbal." O sir, we stand in great danger of being carried away by our own spirits beyond the sacred lines of truth and love, which should bound the field of Christian controversy. Permit me, then, to propose to our common consideration, and future imitation, the most perfect patterns in the world.

Let us consider Him first, "who in all things has the pre-eminence." With what wisdom and fortitude, with what a happy mixture of rational and Scriptural arguments, does Christ carry on his important controversy with the Pharisees! He stands firm as a rock against all the frothy billows of their cavils and invectives. With astonishing impartiality he persists in telling them the most galling truths, and condemning them out of their own mouths, consciences, and sacred records. In so doing, he loses indeed their love and applause; but he maintains a good conscience, and secures the praise which comes from God. Nor does he give over bearing his testimony against them by day, and praying for them by night, till they shed his innocent blood: and when they have done it, he revenges himself by sending them the first news of his pardoning love. "Go," says he to the heralds of his grace, "preach forgiveness of sins among all nations, beginning at Jerusalem," the city of my murderers. O sir, if the Lord of glory was so ready to forgive those who, for want of better arguments, betook themselves first to pitiful sophisms, and groundless accusations, and then to the nails, the hammer, and the spear; how readily ought we to forgive each other the insignificant strokes of our pens!

Let St. Paul be our pattern next to Jesus Christ. Consider we with what undaunted courage, and unwearied patience, he encounters his brethren, the Jews, who engrossed the election to themselves, and threw dust into the air, when they heard that there was salvation for the Gentiles. In every city, he mightily convinces them out of the Scriptures. They revile him, and he entreats them; they cast him out of the temple, and he wishes himself "accursed from Christ for their sake." And yet, when they charge him with crimes of which he is perfectly innocent, he scruples not to appeal to the Gentiles, from whose candour he expected more justice than from their bigotry.

Fix we our eyes also upon the two greatest apostles, encountering each other in the field of controversy. Because St. Peter is to blame, St. Paul "withstands him to the face," with all the boldness that belongs to truth. He does not give him place for a moment, although Peter is his superior in many respects; and he sends to the Churches of Galatia, for their edification, a public account of his elder brother's mistakes. But does Peter resent it? Does he write disrespectfully of his opponent? Does he not, on the contrary, call him his "beloved brother Paul," and make honourable mention of his wisdom?

When I behold these great patterns of Christian moderation and brotherly love, I rejoice to have another opportunity of recommending, to the love and esteem of my readers, the two pious brothers, whom I now encounter, and all those who were more or less concerned in the Circular Letter; in particular, our Christian Deborah, the countess of Huntingdon, and my former opponent, the Rev. Mr. Shirley, who are far less honourable and right honourable by the noble blood that flows in their veins, than by the love of Christ which glows in their hearts, and the zeal for God's glory which burns in their breasts: being persuaded that their hasty step was intended to defend the first Gospel axiom, which, for want of proper attention to every part of the Gospel, they imagined Mr. Wesley had a mind to set aside, when he only wanted to secure the second Gospel axiom.

Once more: I profess also my sincere love and unfeigned respect for all pious Calvinists; protesting, I had a thousand times rather be an inconsistent Antinomian with them, than an inconsistent legalist with many, who hold the truth in practical unrighteousness. I abhor, therefore, the very idea of "dressing them up in devils' clothes, as the Papists did John Huss; and burning them for heretics in the flames of hell." (*Review*, p. 92.) If I have represented an Antinomian in practice, as standing on the left hand with wicked Arminians; it was not to condemn the mistaken persons who lead truly Christian lives, though their heads are full of Antinomian opinions; but to convince my readers that it is much better to be really a sheep, than to have barely a sheep's clothing; and that our Lord will not be deceived, either by a goat, who imputes to himself the clothing of a sheep, or by a wolf, who tries to make his escape, by insolently wrapping himself up in the shepherd's garment.

Should it be objected, that, after all the severe things which I have said against the sentiments of the Calvinists, my professions of love and respect for them cannot possibly be sincere: I answer, That although we cannot in conscience make a difference between a man and his actions, candour and brotherly kindness allow and command us to make a difference between a man and his opinions, especially when his exemplary conduct is a full refutation of his erroneous sentiments.

This, I apprehend, is the case with all pious Calvinists. They talk much, I grant, about finished salvation; but consider them with attention, and you will find a happy inconsistency between their words and their actions; for they still "work out their own salvation with fear and trembling." Again: they make much ado about a robe of imputed righteousness: but still they go on "washing their own robes, and making them white in the blood of the Lamb." Therefore, their errors, which they practically renounce, do not endanger their salvation: and it would be the highest degree of injustice to confound them with abandoned Nicolaitans.

Fantasticus tells you he is possessed of an immense estate in the territories of Geneva; where, by the by, he has not an inch of ground. But though he talks much about his fine estate abroad, he wisely considers that he stands in need of food and raiment; that he cannot live upon a chimera: and that he must work or starve at home. To work therefore he goes, though much against his will. In a little time, by the Divine blessing upon his labour and industry, he gets a good estate, and lives comfortably upon it. And though he frequently entertains you with descriptions of the rich robes which he has at Geneva, he takes care to have always a good, decent coat upon his back. Now, is it not plain, that though

Fantasticus would be a mere beggar, for all his great estate near Geneva; yet, as matters are at present, you cannot justly consider him as burthensome to his parish, unless you can make it appear, that his trusting to his imaginary property abroad has lately made him squander away his goods personal, and real estate, in England.

This simile needs very little explanation. A pious Calvinist does not so dream about his imaginary imputation of Christ's personal obedience and good works, as to forget that he must personally believe, or be damned; yea, and "believe *too* with the heart unto *personal* righteousness," and good works. Therefore, he cries to God for the living "faith which works by love." He receives it; "Christ dwells in his heart by faith," and "this faith is imputed to him for righteousness," because it really makes him righteous. Thus, while he talks about the false imputation of righteousness, he really enjoys the true: he has inherent righteousness, peace, and joy in the Holy Ghost. When he speaks against good works, he is so happily inconsistent as to do them. If he ignorantly builds up the Antinomian Babel with one hand, he sincerely tries to pull it down with the other: and while he decries the perfection of holiness, he goes on "perfecting holiness in the fear of God." Thus his doctrinal mistakes are happily refuted by his godly conversation.

Hence it is, that, although we severely expose the mistakes of godly Calvinists, we sincerely love their persons, truly reverence their piety, and cordially rejoice in the success which attends their evangelical labours. And although we cannot admit their logic, while they defend a bad cause with bad arguments; we should do them great injustice, if we did not acknowledge that there have been, and still are among them, men eminent for good sense and good learning; — men as remarkable for their skill in the art of logic as for their deep acquaintance with the oracles of God. How they came to embrace doctrines, which appear to us so unscriptural and irrational, will be the subject of a peculiar dissertation.

In the meantime, I observe, again, that as many, who have right opinions concerning faith, holiness, and good works, go great lengths in practical Antinomianism; so many Antinomians in principle distinguish themselves by the peculiar strictness and happy legality of their conduct. Both are to be wondered at: the one for doing "the works of darkness," in the clearest light; and the other for "walking as children of light," under the darkest cloud. The former we may compare to green wood, that is always upon the altar, and never takes the hallowed fire. The latter to the bush which Moses saw in the wilderness. The flames of Antinomianism surround them and ascend from them; and yet they are not consumed! Would to God I could say they are not singed!

Nay, what is a greater miracle still, the love of Christ burns in their breasts, and shines in their lives. They preach him, and they do it with success. "Some, indeed, preach him of envy and contention, and some of love and good will. What then? notwithstanding, every way, whether in pretence or in truth, Christ is preached; and we therein do rejoice; yea, and will rejoice." Add to this that some are prudent enough to keep their opinions to themselves. You may hear them preach most excellent sermons, without one word about their peculiarities; or, if they touch upon them, it is in so slight a manner as not to endanger either the foundation or superstructure of undefiled religion. Nay, what is a greater blessing still, sometimes their hearts are so enlarged, and their views of the Gospel so brightened, that they preach free grace as well as we: and in the name of God seriously "command ALL [men] EVERY WHERE to repent."

Far be it from us, therefore, to "cut off all intercourse and friendship" with such favoured servants of the Lord. On the contrary, we thank them for their pious labours; we ask the continuance or the renewal of their valuable love. Whereinsoever we have given them any just cause of offence, we entreat them to forgive us. Upon the reasonable terms of mutual forbearance, "we offer them the right hand of fellowship," together with our brotherly assistance. We invite them to our pulpits, and assure them, that if they admit us into theirs, we shall do by them as we would be done by; avoiding to touch there, or among their own people occasionally committed to our charge, upon the points of doctrine debated between us; and reserving to ourselves the liberty of bearing our full testimony, in our own pulpits, and from the press, against Antinomianism and Pharisaism in all their shapes.

With these pacific sentiments toward all pious Calvinists, and in particular toward your brother and yourself; and with my best thanks for the condescending manner in which you have closed your Remarks upon the Third Check, I conclude this, assuring you, that, (notwithstanding the repeated proofs, which I find in your *Review,* of your uncommon prejudice against the second Gospel axiom, and against Mr. Wesley, who is set for the defence of it,) I remain, with all my former love, and a considerable degree of my former esteem, honoured and dear sir, your affectionate companion in tribulation, and obedient servant in Christ,

J. FLETCHER.

MADELEY, *Nov.* 15, 1772.

POSTSCRIPT.

SOME persons think our controversy will offend the world; and, indeed, we were once afraid of it ourselves. Of this ill-judged fear, and of the voluntary humility which made us reverence the very errors of the good men from whom we dissent, the crafty, diligent tempter has so availed himself as to sow his Antinomian tares with the greatest success. Messrs. John and Charles Wesley, and Mr. Sellon have, indeed, made a noble stand against him: but an impetuous torrent of triumphant opposition still rolls and foams through the kingdom, bent upon drowning their works and reputation in floods of contempt and reproach. And some good, mistaken men, warmly carry on still the rash design of publicly turning the second Gospel axiom out of our Bibles, and out of the Church of England, under the frightful names of "Arminianism and Popery."

The question With us, then, is not so much whether Mr. Wesley shall be ranked with heretics, as whether the undefiled religion, particularly described in the Epistle of St. James, and in our Lord's sermon on the mount, shall pass for a dreadful heresy, while barefaced Antinomianism passes for pure Gospel.

Now, we apprehend, that, to debate such a question in a fair and friendly manner, will rather edify than offend either the religious or the moral world. Fair arguments, plain scriptures, honest appeals to conscience, and a close pursuit of ridiculous error, hunted down to its last recesses, will never displease inquirers after truth: and among the bystanders, few, beside these, will trouble themselves with our publications. If we offend our readers, it is only when we take our leave of Scripture and argument, to cry out, without rhyme and reason, "Disingenuity! Slander! Falsehood! Calumny! Forgery! Heresy! Popery!"

Bad as we are, the moral world regards yet a good argument, and the religious world still shows some respect for Scripture quoted consistently with the context. Fight we then lovingly with such weapons, for what we esteem to be the truth; and be the edge of our controversial swords ever so keen, we shall be sure to wound nobody but the bigots of the opposite party, and such as are so great a disgrace to Christianity, that we shall do the cause of religion service by stumbling them out of their profession of it, if they are above learning the lessons of moderation.

Undoubtedly we are severely condemned by some good people who forget that Moses was once obliged to oppose not only Korah, Dathan, and Abiram, who styled themselves the Lord's people, but his own dear elect brother Aaron himself: and that St. Paul was forced by peculiar circumstances, at all hazards, to withstand St. Peter himself. Well-meaning Elis also, who do not consider consequences, and love to enjoy their own ease rather than to make a vigorous resistance against error and sin, will be very apt to conclude that our opposition springs from mere obstinacy and party spirit. But should such hasty judges read attentively the Epistle of St. Jude, that of St. James, the first of St. John, and the second of St. Peter, which are all levelled at Antinomianism, they will think more favourably of the stand we make against our pious brethren who inadvertently countenance the Antinomian delusion.

However, it is objected, "This controversy will hurt the men of the world, and set them against all religion." Just the contrary. There are, indeed, Galios, men that care for no religion at all, who, upon hearing of our controversy, will triumph, and cry out, "If these men do not agree among themselves, how can they desire that we should agree with them?" As if we had ever desired them to agree with us any farther than the plain letter of Scripture, and the loud dictates of conscience invite them so to do! But such prepossessed judges will not be hurt by our controversy though they should pretend they are: for they have their stumbling block in their own breast. They would not have wanted pretences to ridicule religion, if our controversy had never been set on foot; nor would they entertain more favourable thoughts of it, if we dropped it without coming to a proper *eclaircissement*.

But these, however numerous, are not all the world. There are, in our universities, and throughout the kingdom, hundreds, and we hope thousands, of judicious and candid men who truly fear God, and sincerely desire to love him.

These, we apprehend, are offended at the first Gospel axiom, and driven farther and farther from it by the mixture of "Antinomian dotages," which renders it ridiculous. They are tempted to throw away the marrow of the Gospel, on account of the luscious, fulsome additions made to it, to make it richer. And to these, we flatter ourselves, that our controversy will prove useful, as well as to our candid brethren.

We hope it will open to the view of these Gamaliels and Obadiahs the confused heap of truth and error at which they so justly stumble, and help them precisely to separate the precious from the vile, that while they "abhor that which is evil, they may cleave to that which is good." This is not all: when they shall see that some of those men, whom they accounted wild enthusiasts, candidly take their part, where they are in the right, and fight their battles in a rational and Scriptural manner, their prejudices will be softened, the light will imperceptibly steal in upon them, and, by Divine grace, convince them, that they go as far out of the way to the left hand, as our opponents do to the right.

The truth, which we maintain, lies between all extremes, or rather, it embraces and connects them all. The *Calvinists* fairly receive only the *first* Gospel axiom, and the *moralists,* the *second.* If I may compare the Gospel truth to the child contended for in the days of Solomon, both parties, while they divide, inadvertently destroy it. We, like the true mother, are for no division. Standing upon the middle Scriptural line, we embrace and hold fast both Gospel axioms. With the Calvinists, we give God in Christ all the glory of our salvation; and, with the moralists, we take care not to give him in Adam any of the shame of our damnation: we have need of patience with both, for they both highly blame us because we follow the poet's direction,

Inter utrumque tene, medio tutissimus ibis:

Both think hardly of us, because we do not so maintain the particular Gospel axiom which they have justly espoused as to exclude that which they rashly explode. But if we can use, with meekness of wisdom, the "armour of righteousness on the right hand and on the left," and give our opposite adversaries, on every side, a Scriptural and rational "account of the hope that is in us," moderate Calvinists and evangelical moralists will at last kindly "give us the right hand of fellowship." Discovering that the advantages of both their doctrines join in ours, they will acknowledge, that the "faith working by love," which we preach, includes all the privileges of solifidianism and morality; that we do justice to the Gospel, without making "void the law through faith; that we establish the law," without superseding free grace; and that we extol our High Priest's cross, without pouring contempt upon his throne. In a word, they will perceive, that we perfectly reconcile St. Paul with St. James, and both with reason, conscience, and all the oracles of God.

Thus shall all good men of all denominations agree at last among themselves, and bend all their collected force against Pharisaic unbelief, which continually attacks the first Gospel axiom; and against Antinomian contempt of good works, which perpetually militates against the second. The Father of lights grant that this may be the happy effect of our controversy! So shall we bless the hour when a variety of singular circumstances obliged us to come to a full *eclaircissement,* and to lay, by that mean, the foundation of a solid union, not only with each other, but also with all good and judicious men, both in the religious and in the moral world.

LOGICA GENEVENSIS

CONTINUED:

OR,

THE FIRST PART

OF THE

FIFTH CHECK TO ANTINOMANISM:

CONTAINING

AN ANSWER TO "THE FINISHING STROKE"

OF RICHARD HILL, ESQ.

IN WHICH SOME REMARKS UPON MR. FULSOME'S ANTINOMIAN CREED, PUBLISHED
BY THE REV. MR. BERRIDGE, ARE OCCASIONALLY INTRODUCED.

WITH AN APPENDIX,

UPON THE REMAINING DIFFERENCE BETWEEN THE
CALVINISTS AND THE ANTICALVINISTS, WITH RESPECT TO OUR LORD'S DOCTRINE
OF JUSTIFICATION BY WORDS, AND ST. JAMES' DOCTRINE OF JUSTIFICATION
BY WORKS, AND NOT BY FAITH ONLY.

**"As deceivers and yet true."— "In meekness instructing them that oppose
themselves," 2 Corinthians 6:18; 2 Timothy 2:25.**

CONTENTS OF FIFTH CHECK.

Section XI.
An answer to two capital charges of gross misrepresentation,

Section XII.
Some queries concerning Mr. Hill's forwardness to accuse his opponents of disingenuity, gross perversion, calumny, forgery, &c, and concerning his abrupt manner of quitting the field of controversy.

Section XIII.
A perpetual noise about gross perversions, and base forgeries, becomes Mr. Hill as little as any writer, considering his own inaccuracy with regard to quotations, some flagrant instances of which are produced out of his Finishing Stroke.

Section XIV.
The author, after professing his brotherly love and respect for all pious Calvinists, apologizes for his antagonist before the Anti- Calvinists; and,

Section XV.
Takes his friendly leave of Mr. Hill, after promising him to publish a sermon on Romans 11:5, 6, to recommend and guard the doctrine of free grace in a Scriptural manner.

In the Appendix, the author proves, by ten more arguments, the absurdity of supposing, with the Solifidians, that believers are justified by works before men and angels, but not before God.

AN ANSWER

TO

THE FINISHING STROKE

OF RICHARD HILL, ESQ.

HON. AND DEAR SIR, — I have received your *Finishing Stroke*, and return the following answer to you; or, if you have quitted the field, to your pious second, the Rev. Mr. Berridge, who, by a public attack upon *sincere obedience*, and upon the doctrine of a believer's *justification by works, and not by faith only*, has already entered the lists in your place.

Sec. i, p. 6. You complain that I represent you as fighting the battles of the rankest Antinomians, "because (say you) we firmly believe and unanimously assert, that 'the blood of Christ cleanseth from all sin,' and that, 'if any man sin, we have an Advocate with the Father,' &c, and that this advocacy prevails." Not so, dear sir: I apprehend you give your readers totally wrong ideas of the question. You know I never opposed you for saying that "the blood of Christ cleanseth *penitent believers* from all sin." On the contrary, this I insist upon in a fuller sense than you do, who, if I mistake not, suppose that death, and not the blood of Christ, applied by the sanctifying Spirit, is to be our cleanser from all sin. The point which we debate is not then whether Christ's blood cleanses from all sin, but whether it actually cleanses from all guilt an impenitent backslider, a filthy apostate; and whether God says to the fallen believer, that commits adultery and murder, "Thou art all fair, my love, my undefiled, there is no spot in thee." This you affirm in your fourth letter; and this I expose as the very quintessence of Ranterism, Antinomianism, and Calvinistic perseverance.

The second part of your mistake is yet more glaring than the first. The question is not, (as you inform your readers,) whether, if "any man sin, we have an Advocate with the Father," &c. You know, sir, that far from denying this comfortable truth, I maintain it in full opposition to your narrow system, which declares that if any man, who is passed by or nonelected, sinneth, there is no advocate with the Father for him: and that there are thousands of absolutely reprobated wretches, born to have the devil for a tempter and an accuser, without any help from our Redeemer and Advocate.

Nor yet do we debate whether Christ's advocacy prevails in the full extent of the word, for all that know the day of their visitation; this is a point of doctrine in which I am as clear as yourself. But the question about which we divide is, (1.) Whether Christ's advocacy never prevails when he asks that barren fig trees, which are at last cut down for persisting in their unfruitfulness, may be "spared this year also?" (2.) Whether it prevails in such a manner for all those, who once made ever so weak an act of true faith, that they shall never "make shipwreck of the faith," never "deny the Lord that bought them," and "bring upon themselves swift destruction?" (3.) Whether Aaron and Korah, David and Demas, Solomon and Hymeneus, Peter and Judas, Philetus and Francis Spira, with all that fall from God, shall infallibly sing louder in heaven for their grievous falls on earth? In a word, whether the salvation of some, and the damnation of others, are so finished, that, during "the day of their visitation," it is absolutely impossible for one of the former to draw back to perdition from a state of salvation; and for one of the latter to draw back to salvation from a state of perdition?

These important questions you should have laid before your readers as the very ground of our controversy. But instead of this you amuse them with two precious scriptures, which I hold in a fuller sense than yourself. This is a stroke of your logic, but it is not the finishing one, for you say: —

Sec. ii, p. 6. "We cannot admit the contrary doctrine [that of the Checks] without at once undermining both law and Gospel. For the law is certainly undermined by supposing that any breach of it whatever is not attended with the curse of God." What law do I undermine? Is it the law of innocence? No: for I insist upon it as well as you, to convince unhumbled sinners that there can be no salvation but in and through a Mediator. Is it the Mediator's law, "the law of liberty?" Certainly not: for I defend it against the bold attacks you make upon it; and shall now ward off the dreadful blow you give it in this argument.

O sir, is it right to confound, as you do, the law of paradisiacal innocence with the evangelical law of liberty, that in point of personal, sincere obedience, you may set both aside at one stroke? Is not this Calvinistic stroke as dangerous as it is unscriptural? "There is no law but one which damns for want of absolute innocence: all those that are under any law, must be under this law, which curses for a wandering thought as well as for incest. But believers are not cursed for a wandering thought. Therefore they are under no law: they are not cursed even for incest; they may break their 'rule of life' by adultery, as David, or by incest, as the unchaste Corinthian, without falling under the curse of any Divine law in force against them: in a word, without ceasing to be men 'after God's own heart.'"

Now whence arises the fallacy of this argument? Is it not from overlooking the Mediator's law, the law of Christ? Can you see no medium between being under "a rule of life," the breaking of which shall "work for our good," and being under a law that curses to the pit of hell for the least want of absolute innocence? Between those two extremes is there not the evangelical "law of liberty?"

O sir, be not mistaken: the Gospel has its law. Hear St. Paul: "God shall JUDGE, the secrets of men by Jesus Christ, according to my *Gospel,*" Romans ii, 16. Hear St. James: "So speak ye [believers] and so do, as they that shall be judged by the LAW OF LIBERTY; for he [the believer] shall have judgment without mercy, that hath showed no mercy," James ii, 12, 13, illustrated by Matthew xviii, 23-35.

Christ is neither an Eli nor a Nero, neither a dolt nor a tyrant; but a priestly king, a "Melchisedec." If he is a king, he has a law; his subjects may, and the disobedient shall, be condemned by it. If he is a priestly king, he has a gracious law; and if he has a gracious law, he requires no absolute impossibilities. Thus the covenant of grace keeps a just medium between the relentless severity of the first covenant, and the Antinomian softness of the covenant trumpeted by some Calvinists.

Be not then frightened, O Sion, from meditating in Christ's law day and night; for it is the law of thy gracious "King, who cometh unto the meek, and sitting upon the foal" of a mild, pacific animal: and not that of thy fierce and fond monarch, O Geneva, who comes riding upon the wings of storms and tempests, to damn the reprobates for the preordained, unavoidable consequences of Adam's preordained, unavoidable sin; and to encourage fallen believers, that climb up into their neighbours' beds, by saying to each of them, "Thou art all fair, my love, my undefiled, there is no spot in thee." But more of this to Mr. Berridge. When you have given us a wrong idea of the Mediator's law, you proceed to do the same by the Gospel, with which that law is so closely connected. For you say: —

Page 6. "The Gospel is certainly undermined, by supposing that there is provision made in it for some sins, and not for others." Well then, sir, Christ and the four evangelists have "certainly undermined the Gospel;" for they all mention the blasphemy against the Holy Ghost, "the sin unto death," or the sin of final impenitency and unbelief; and they not only suppose, but expressly declare, that it is a sin for which "no provision is made," and the punishment of which obstinate unbelievers and apostates must personally bear. Is it not strange that the capital doctrine by which our Lord guards his own Gospel, should be represented as a capital error, by which "the Gospel is certainly undermined?"

See. iii, p. 6. To show that your scheme is different from speculative Antinomianism, you ask, "Is the experience of David, Lot, and Solomon, that of all those who abide by those doctrines?" I answer, It may be that of thousands for aught you know, and if it is not that of myriads, no thanks to you, sir, for you have given them encouragement enough: (though I still do you the justice to say, you have done it undesignedly:) and lest they should forget your former innuendo, in this very page you say, that "the covenant of grace [including, no doubt, finished salvation] standeth sure in behalf of the elect, under every trial, state, and circumstance they can possibly be in," which, if I mistake not, implies, that they may be in the impenitent "state" of drunken Lot, and adulterous David, or in the dangerous "circumstance" of idolatrous Solomon, and the incestuous Corinthian, without being less interested in finished salvation than if they served God with Noah, Job, and Daniel. To this answer I add Flavel's judicious observation: "If the principle will yield it, it is in vain to think corrupt nature will not catch at it, and make a vile use and dangerous improvement of it." But you say, (p. 7,) "You know in your conscience that we detest and abhor that damnable doctrine and position of real Antinomians: 'Let us sin, that grace may abound.'" I believe, dear sir, that all pious Calvinists, and consequently you, abhor that horrible tenet practically, so far as you are saved from sin. And yet, to the great encouragement of practical Antinomianism, you have made an enumeration of the good that sin, yea, any length in sin, unto adultery, robbery, murder, and incest, does to the pleasant children. You have assured them that sin shall work for their good; and you have closed the strange plea by saying, that "a grievous fall will make them sing louder the praises of free, restoring grace, to all eternity in heaven." Now, honoured sir, pardon me if I tell you my whole mind. Really, to this day, I think, that if I wanted to make Christ publicly the minister of sin, and to poison the minds of my hearers by preaching an Antinomian sermon from these words, *Let us sin, that grace may abound*, I could not do it more effectually than by showing, according to the doctrine of your fourth letter: (1.) That, upon the whole, sin can do us no harm. (2.) That, far from hurting us, it will Work for our good. And, (3.) That even a grievous fall into adultery and murder will make us "sing louder in heaven; all debts and claims against believers, be they more or be they less, be they small or be they great, be they before or be they after conversion, being for ever and for ever cancelled by Christ's fulfilling the law for them." In the name of reason, I ask, Where is the difference between publishing these unguarded tenets and saying roundly, *Let us sin, that grace may abound?*

Do not reply, sir, that this objection was brought against St. Paul as well as against you, and therefore the apostle's doctrine and yours exactly coincide; for this would be impeaching the innocent to screen the guilty. The charge of indirectly saying, "Let us sin, that grace may abound," is absolutely false, when it is brought against St. Paul; but alas, it is too true when produced against the author of *Pietas Oxoniensis*. Where did that holy apostle ever say that sin works for our good? When did he declare that the Lord overrules sin, even adultery and murder, for the good of his backsliding people; and that grievous falls in this world will make us more joyful in the next? But you know, sir, who has published those maxims, and who stands to them, even in a *Finishing Stroke:* intimating still, that it is God's "secret will" to do good to his people by "the abominable thing which his soul hateth," (p. 55, 1. 36, &c.) O sir, hell is not farther from heaven than this doctrine from that of the apostle: for while you absolutely promise fallen believers louder songs in heaven, he conditionally threatens them with "much sorer punishment" in hell, Hebrews x, 29, and Christ says, "Go and sin no more, lest a worse thing happen unto thee." But your scheme says, "Go any length in sin, and a more excellent thing shall happen unto thee: *a grievous fall will drive thee nearer to Christ."*

Leaving you to reconcile yourself with holy Paul and our blessed Lord, I beg leave to account for the warmth with which you sometimes plead for and sometimes against sin. As a good man, you undoubtedly "detest and abhor" this dangerous maxim of the great Diana of the Antinomians; "sin works for good to believers;" but, as a sound Calvinist, you plead for it, yea, and you father it upon the apostle too. (See Third Check, p. 185*) This contrariety, in your sentiments, may be illustrated by Judah's inconsistent behaviour to Tamar.

As Tamar was an agreeable woman, Judah took an Antinomian fancy to her, gave her his "signet, bracelets, and staff," for a pledge; and faithfully "sent her a kid from the flock." But as she was his disgraced daughter-inlaw, big with a bastard child, though he himself was the father of it, he rose against her with uncommon indignation, and said, in a fit of legality, "Bring her forth that she may

---

* [186]

be burnt!" O! that instead of calling me "a spiritual calumniator," and accusing me of "vile falsehood and gross perversion," for bearing testimony against a similar inconsistency, you would imitate the undeceived patriarch, take your signet and bracelets again; I mean, call in your fourth letter, that fatal pledge sent me from the press of your great Diana, and from this time "know her again no more!" Genesis xxxviii, 26.

Sec. iv. But you are not put out of countenance by your former mistakes, for, (pp. 8, 9,) speaking, it seems, of those mistaken good men, "who say more at times for sin than against it," or of those who traduce obedience, and make void the law through faith, representing it as a bare rule of life, the breaking of which will in the end work for the believer's good, you say, "Though I have begged you so earnestly in my Review to point out by name who these wretches [you should say these *persons*] are: though I have told you that without this the charge of slander must be for ever at your door; still neither they nor their converts are produced; no, nor one quotation from their writings, in order to prove these black charges upon them." Here is a heap of gross mistakes. I have not only produced one quotation, but many, both from Dr. Crisp's writings and your own. See Second Check, from p. 117 to 120 [115 to 118], and Third Check, from p. 175 to p. 190 [176 to p. 191]. Again: that "neither they nor their converts are produced," is a capital oversight. Turn to Fourth Check, p. 278 [282]: "Produce a few of them," says your brother; to which I answer, "Well, sir, I produce, first, the author of *Pietas Oxoniensis,* next yourself, and then all the Calvinists who admire your brother's fourth letter, where he not only insinuates, but openly attempts to prove, that David, &c, stood absolved and complete in the everlasting righteousness of Christ, while his eyes were full of adultery and his hands of blood. Now, sir, if this was the case of David, it may not only be the case of many, but of all the elect:" for the imaginary covenant of finished salvation stands as sure for fallen believers, who cheat, swear, and get drunk, as for those who commit adultery, murder, and incest.

But since you press me still to produce witnesses, I promise you to produce by and by the Rev. Mr. Berridge, your second, together with his Antinomian pleas against sincere obedience. In the meantime I produce "Mr. Fulsome," together with a quotation from "The Christian World Unmasked." It contains a ludicrous description of a consistent Antinomian, brought over to the doctrines of grace by, I know not which of our Gospel ministers.

His name, says Mr. Berridge, was Mr. Fulsome, and his mother's maiden name was Miss Wanton. "When the cloth was removed, and some few tankards had gone round, Mr. Fulsome's face looked like the red lion painted on my landlord's sign, and his mouth began to open. He talked swimmingly about religion, and vapoured much in praise of [Calvinistic] perseverance. Each fresh tankard threw a fresh light upon his subject, &c. No sin; he said, can hurt me. I have had a call, and my election is safe. Satan may pound me, if he please: but Jesus must replevy me. What care I for drunkenness or whoredom, for cheating, or a little lying? These sins may hurt another, but they cannot hurt me. Let me wander where I will from God, Jesus Christ must fetch me back again. I may fall a thousand times, but I shall rise again: yes, I may fall exceeding foully. And so he did, for instantly he pitched with his head upon the floor, and the tankard in his hand." (*Christian World Unmasked.* 2d ed. p. 191.)

Thus fell the Antinomian champion of Calvinistic perseverance. "The tankard (adds Mr. Berridge) was recovered, but no one thought it worth his while to lift up Mr. Fulsome." And what does Mr. Fulsome care for it, if Jesus Christ himself is absolutely engaged to raise him up, though he had spilt not only some of my landlord's ale, but all my landlord's blood? Let Mr. Fulsome take a peaceful nap upon the floor, till he can call for another tankard; it will never hurt him, for Mr. Hill declares that "the covenant of grace standeth sure in behalf of the elect under every trial, state, and circumstance they can possibly be in: and that God overrules sin for their good." (*Finishing Stroke,* pp. 6, and 55.)

Upon the principles of Calvinism, no logician in the world can, I think, find a flaw in the following arguments of Mr. Fulsome: — If I am unconditionally elected, irresistible grace will certainly save me at last; nay, my salvation is already finished: and for this tankard and twenty more, I shall only sing "louder" in heaven the praises of free, distinguishing, restoring grace, which, passing by thousands, viewed me with unchangeable love, and determined to save me with an everlasting salvation, without any regard to that "Jack o'lantern, sincere obedience." If, on the other hand, I am unconditionally reprobated, I shall absolutely be damned. Again: supposing Christ never died for me, not only all my faith, but also all my endeavours and works, (were they as many as those of Mr. J. W.) like a "Jack o'lantern," will only dance before me to the pit of hell. Once more: if I am absolutely justified, it is not all the tankards and harlots in the world that can blot my name out of the book of life. And if I am in the black book, my damnation is as good as finished. My sincere obedience will never reverse a personal, absolute decree, older and firmer than the pillars of heaven. Nay, it maybe the readiest way to hell: for our vicar, who is one of the first Gospel ministers in the kingdom, tells us, that "the devil was surely the author of the condition of sincere obedience," and that "thousands have been lost by following after it." Landlord, bring in another tankard. Here is the health of all who do not legalize the Gospel!

Mr. Berridge is too good a logician to attempt proving that Mr. Fulsome's creed is not quite rational, upon the principles of Calvinism. He only says, (p. 192,) "Such scandalous professors are found at all times, in our day, and in St. Paul's day, yet St. Paul will not renounce the doctrine of perseverance. True; he will not renounce his own doctrine of conditional perseverance, because it is the very reverse of the doctrine of absolute, or Calvinistic perseverance, from which Mr. Fulsome draws his horrible, and yet just inferences.

But, says Mr. B., (p. 178,) "A believer's new nature makes him hunger for implanted righteousness;" insinuating that a believer's holy nature puts him upon such spontaneous obedience to his "rules of life," that he needs not the help of a law, as a rule of rewards and punishments, to encourage him in the path of duty, and to keep him from the broad way of disobedience. As this is one of the grand arguments by which pious Calvinists defend the Antinomian Babel, I shall answer it first as an anti-Calvinist, and Mr. Fulsome next as a Calvinist.

1. Experience shows, that to secure the creature's obedience, or the Creator's honour, the curb of a law is necessary for all free agents who are yet in a

state of probation; and that so long as we are surrounded with so many temptations to faint in duty, and to leave the thorny way of the cross for the flowery paths of sin, the spur and bridle of a promising and threatening law are needful, even with respect to those duties which natural or supernatural inclination renders in general delightful; such as for mothers to take care of their own children, and believers to do good to their own neighbour. Now as the civil law, that condemns murderers to death, does not except mothers who destroy the fruit of their womb, because natural affection makes them in general glad to preserve it; so the penal law of Christ makes no exception in favour of believers who fall into adultery and murder, under the Calvinistic pretence that their new nature makes them in general hunger after purity and love. See 1 Corinthians vi, 8, 9. Again: all sophisms flee before matter of fact. Fallen angels and our first parents once naturally hungered after righteousness, more than most believers do; and yet they grossly apostatized. And if you object to these instances, I produce David and the incestuous Corinthian: both had a "new nature" as believers; and yet as fallen believers, the one could thirst after Uriah's blood, and the other hunger after his father's wife, far more than after "implanted righteousness." But,

2. Mr. Fulsome may answer Mr. Berridge as a Calvinist thus: — My new nature will make me hunger for implanted righteousness "in the day of God's power:" God will do his own work: in the meantime I am "in a winter season:" "I am carnal and sold under sin," as well as St. Paul, and I thirst after my tankard as David did after Bathsheba's beauty, and Uriah's blood: thus the Antinomian gap remains as wide as ever.

It is true also that Mr. Berridge says, (p. 173,) "Cheats will arise: and how must we deal with them? Deal with them, sir! why, hang them, when detected; as Jesus hanged Judas." I thought that Judas, and not Jesus, was the hangman. But I let that pass, to observe, that Mr. Fulsome may justly ask, Why will you hang me? Does not our Lord, speaking of his elect, say, "He that touches you, touches the apple of mine eye?" If Mr. Berridge answers, You are no elect; you are a hypocrite; you never had grace: Mr. Fulsome may justly reply, upon the plan of the Calvinistic doctrines of grace, "I have had a call, and my election is safe. Who shall lay any thing to the charge of God's elect? Whom he called, them he also justified: yea, they are justified from all things. You have no more right to condemn me as a hypocrite, because you see me with a tankard in my hand, than to pass a sentence of hypocrisy upon all backsliders. How will you prove that I have not as much right to toss my tankard, as David to write a sanguinary letter; Solomon to worship devils; and the incestuous Corinthian to invade the rights of his father's bed? I will maintain the privileges of God's children against all the legalists and the Wesleys in the world: I will fight for free grace to the last drop in my tankard' my service to you!"

If Mr. Fulsome's arguments are conclusive, as well as Calvinistical, how can he be brought to give up his Antinomian creed? Undoubtedly, by being brought to give up Calvinism. Till then it is evident that he will still hold his doctrines of grace in theory, or in practice: indirectly and with mental reserves, as all pious Calvinists do; or openly and without shuffling, as he does in his confession of faith. Thus has Mr. Berridge presented the world with an Antinomian creed as horrid as that which I have composed with the unguarded principles of your fourth letter. And by acknowledging that "such scandalous professors as Mr. Fulsome are found at all times," he has confirmed the necessity of my Checks, shown they are really Checks to Antinomianism, and not "Checks to the Gospel," silenced those who have accused me of misrepresentation, and helped me to give the world a just idea of Calvinistic principles. I say principles, because many, very many Calvinists, like Mr. Berridge, are too moral not to reject in their practice, and not to explode as detestable in their discourse, the immoral inferences consistent Antinomians justly draw from their doctrines of grace.

Sec. v. Having thus complied with your request, sir, by producing "a quotation" from an eminent Calvinist divine, to show that I do not fight against a shadow when I oppose Mr. Fulsome; and having described a rational "convert" to your doctrines of grace, I return to the *Finishing Stroke,* where, to ward off the blow given to your system by the orthodoxy and bad conduct of the Fulsomes,

Page 9. You offer to show me "a long black list of deluded creatures, (some of whom have been principal leaders in Mr. Wesley's classes, &c,) who have been carrying on abominations, and wicked practices under the mask of religion." And you tell us they are "some of the fruits which the doctrines" of Mr. Wesley "have produced." But you have forgot the proof, unless you think that your bare assertion is quite sufficient. Suppose that one out of twelve of Mr. Wesley's class leaders had actually turned out a "temporary monster," what could you infer from it against Mr. Wesley's doctrine, but what the Pharisees could, with equal truth, or rather with equal justice, have inferred against the doctrine of our Lord?

By what plain and easy consequence, or by what Scriptural argument will you make it appear that even the most abhorred of all Mr. Wesley's doctrines, that of Christian perfection, (or, which is all one, that of believing in Christ with a penitential faith, till we love God with all our heart, and our neighbour as ourselves,) has any more tendency to turn his hearers into "temporary monsters," than our Lord's sermon upon the mount had to turn his apostles into covetous traitors? But how can you free your doctrine from the dangerous consequences which flow from it as naturally as a river does from its source? Have I not just proved, I hope to the satisfaction of judicious readers, that Mr. Fulsome's practice perfectly agrees with your Calvinistic principles? O sir, that vapourer, in favour of your perseverance, fairly and consistently builds upon what your brother calls "the foundation of the Calvinists," that is, unconditional election and finished salvation: he is a wise master builder. Apply the most exact plummet of reason to the walls of his Antinomian Babel, and you will find them straight. They do not project a hair's breadth from your doctrines of grace, which are the foundations laid in some our celebrated pulpits for him and all the clan of the Fulsomes to build upon. He is a judicious monster; he has reason and your orthodoxy on his side. But the monsters of your long black list (supposing it to be a true one) are barefaced hypocrites, equally condemned by their reason and profession: for, so far as they adhere to Mr. Wesley's doctrine, their principles are diametrically opposed to their practice, and therefore he is no more accountable for their "abominations" than our Lord was for Judas' treason.

Sec. vi, pp. 12, 13. You leave me in full possession of the scriptures, arguments, and quotations from our homilies and liturgy which I have advanced

Five Checks To Antinomianism

in the Fourth Check, supposing that when you have called them "the novel chimeras of the Fourth Check," or a "mingle mangle;" and that when you have referred your readers to "the faith of Mr. Ignorance," you have given my sentiments a *Finishing Stroke.* To such forcible arguments I can make no better and shorter reply than that of my title page, *Logica Genevensis!* However,

Page 11. You decide that my illustration of the woman dropping her child down the precipice "is totally foreign to the purpose," i.e. does not at all prove that Calvinism fathers "unprovoked wrath" upon the God of love. But how do you make it appear? Why, you insinuate that "man has forfeited all right and title to the favour of God by his fall in Adam;" and therefore God has been justly provoked to drop the reprobates down the precipice of sin into hell, by an eternal, unconditional, absolute decree of non-election.

The argument is specious, and has deceived thousands of simple souls into Calvinism: but can it bear examination? Who, or what provoked God to make, from all eternity, a decree of absolutely dropping Adam down the precipice of sin, and the reprobated part of his posterity down the precipice of damnation? Was it the sin of reprobates? No: for millions of them are as yet unconceived, and therefore sinless; for what has not yet a substance cannot yet have a mode; what does not yet exist cannot yet be sinful. Was it a foresight of their sin? No: for, upon the Calvinistic plan, God certainly foresees what will happen, only because he has absolutely decreed what shall happen. Was it Adam's sin, as you insinuate? No: for Adam's sin was committed in time, and therefore could not influence an absolute decree of personal reprobation made before time, yea, from all eternity. But you add: —

Pages 11, 12, "If you believe that the transgression of our first parent entailed no condemnation upon his posterity, why did you subscribe to the ninth article of our Church, which says, that *in every man born into the world it deserves God's wrath and damnation?*" I apprehend you mistake, sir: that article says no such thing. What it affirms of a derivation of Adam's corruption, or of "the fault and corruption of the nature of every man," you represent as spoken of Adam's personal transgression; which is absolutely confounding the cause and the effect. Every anti-Calvinist may, and I, for one, do believe, that *in every man born into the world,* and considered according to the first covenant, original corruption (not Adam's transgression) deserves God's wrath and damnation at the hands of a holy and righteous God, without dreaming that any man shall be ever damned for it: seeing that according to God's mercy and goodness displayed in the second covenant, Christ, "the second Adam," is come "to taste death for every man;" and to be "the Saviour of all men;" so that for his sake "the free gift is come upon all men to justification of life." (See the *Fourth Check,* p. 279*, &c.) Thus, by looking at our Divine compass, the word of God, we sail through the straits of error, keeping at an equal distance from the rocks against which Calvinists run on the right hand, and the Pelagians on the left.

I have warded off the *Stroke* which you have attempted to give my sentiments with our ninth article; and now it is but just you should suffer me to

* [283]

- 339 -

return it. If I am not mistaken, that article is repugnant to Calvinism in two respects. (1.) It says not one word about the imputation of the demerits of Adam's first transgression; but makes original sin to consist only in the "infection of our nature;" which saps the foundation of your imaginary imputation of Adam's personal sin, and consequently ruins its counterpart, namely, your imaginary imputation of Christ's personal good works distinct from some actual participation of his holiness. (2.) It affirms that this infection, in every person born into the world, deserves God's wrath: a strong intimation this that it did not actually deserve that wrath before we were actually defiled by a sinful birth or conception, Now this, if I mistake not, implies, that of all the men now living upon the earth, not one actually deserved God's wrath and damnation two hundred years ago. So that if God absolutely reprobated one man now living, three hundred, much more six thousand years ago, much more from all eternity, he did it according to Calvin's doctrine of rich, free, unprovoked, gratuitous, undeserved wrath. O ye considerate Englishmen, stand to your articles, and you will soon shake off Geneva impositions!

Sec. vii, p. 12. You say in your moral creed about faith and works: "Faith when genuine will always manifest its reality by bringing forth good works, and all the fruits of a holy life." Now, sir, if you stand to this, without secret reserves about "a winter state," in which a genuine believer (so called) may commit adultery, murder, and incest, for many months, without losing the character of' a man after God's own heart," and his title to heaven; you make up the Antinomian gap, you set your seal to St. James' Epistle, you ratify the Checks; and consequently you give up your fourth letter, which contains the very marrow of Calvinism: unless, by some salvo of Geneva logic, you can reconcile these two propositions, which, upon the rational and moral plan of the Gospel, appear to me utterly irreconcilable. (1.) Faith, when genuine, always brings forth all the fruits of a holy life. (2.) A man s faith may be genuine while he goes any length in sin, and brings forth all the fruits of an unholy life — adultery and murder not excepted.

Sec. viii. My quotation from Dr. Owen, which sets Calvinistic contradiction in a most glaring light, seems to embarrass you much, (p. 14, &c.) You produce passage upon passage out of his writings to show that he explodes "the distinction of a double justification." But you know, sir, the doctor had as much right to contradict himself in his writings as you to militate against yourself in your Review. (See *Fourth Check*, letter I.) Beside, I have already observed, (*Fourth Check*, letter X,) that" a volume of such passages, instead of invalidating the doctrine I maintain, (or the quotation I produce,) would only prove that the most judicious Calvinists cannot make their scheme hang tolerably together." However, you say,

Pages 13, 14. "He [Dr. Owen] drops not the least intimation of any fresh act of justification which is then to pass upon a believer's person." What, sir, has not the doctor said, in his Treatise upon Justification, (p. 222,) "Whenever this inquiry is made, not how a sinner, &c, shall be justified, which is [as we are all agreed, by faith, or to use the doctor's unscriptural phrase] by the righteousness of Christ alone imputed to him; but how a man that professes evangelical faith in Christ shall be tried and judged; and whereon, as such, [that is, as a believer,] he shall be justified: we grant that it is, and must be by his own personal obedience." Now, sir, if the doctor has said this, and you dare not deny it, has he not said the very thing which I contend for?

When you affirm that he makes no mention of a fresh act of justification, do you not betray your inattention? Does he not declare that a sinner is justified by imputed righteousness, and that a believer as such shall be tried and justified by his own personal obedience? Now, if justification is the act of justifying, are you not greatly mistaken, when you represent the justification of a sinner by Christ's imputed righteousness, and the justification of a believer, or a saint, by his own personal obedience, as one and the same act? Permit me, sir, to refer you to the argument contained in the *Fourth Check*, p. 211*; on which, next to the words of our Lord, Matthew xii, 37, I chiefly rest our controversy about justification. An argument, the answering of which (if it can be answered) Would have done your cause more honour and service than what you are pleased to insinuate next concerning Mr. Wesley's honesty and mine.

D. Williams, out of whose book I copied my quotation from Dr. Owen, being a Calvinist, and as clear about a sinner's justification by faith as Dr. Owen himself, for brevity's sake, left out what the doctor says about it under the Calvinistic phrase of *Christ's imputed righteousness*. Here, as if D. Williams' wisdom were duplicity in me, (p. 14,) you triumph not only over me, but over Mr. Wesley, thus: "I never dare trust to Mr. Wesley or Mr. Fletcher in any quotations, &c. More words expunged by Mr. Fletcher out of the short quotation he has taken from Dr. Owen." But suppose I had *knavishly expunged* the words which D. Williams *wisely left out* as useless to his point, what need was there of reflecting upon Mr. Wesley on the occasion? O ye doctrines of free grace and free wrath, how long will ye mislead good men? How long will ye hurry them into that part of practical Antinomianism which consists in rash accusations of their opponents, in a lordly contempt of their gracious attainments, and in repeated insinuations that they pay no regard to common honesty?

When a combatant is too warm, he frequently gives an unexpected advantage to his antagonist. You are an instance of it, sir; your eagerness to reflect upon Mr. Wesley and me, has engaged you to present the world with a clause, which, though it was useless to the question debated by D. Williams, is of singular use to me in the present controversy, and in a manner decides the point. For in the passage left out by D. Williams, Dr. Owen speaks of the justification of a sinner, and says, as I have observed, that he is "justified by the righteousness of Christ alone, imputed to him: and this justification he evidently opposes to that of a believer, which" says he, "is and must be by his own personal obedience." So that the world (thanks be to your controversial heat!†) sees now that even your champion, in one of those happy moments when the great Diana did not stand in his light, saw, and held forth the important distinction between St. Paul's and St. James' justification, that is, between the justification of a sinner by Christ's proper merits, according to the first Gospel axiom; and the

---

* [213]

† The second instance of this heat, so favourable to my cause, may be seen in the appendix, (No. 10.)

justification of a saint by his own personal obedience of faith, or by Christ's derived merits, according to the second Gospel axiom.

Nor is this a new distinction, you would say, a "novel chimera," among Protestants: for, looking lately in a treatise upon good works, written by La Placette, that famous Protestant champion and confessor abroad, who, after he had left his native country for righteousness' sake, was minister of the French Church at Copenhagen, p. 272, Amst. edition, 1700, I fell upon this passage: — *"Les Protestants de leur cote distinguent une double justification, celle du pecheur, et celle du juste,"* &c. That is, "Protestants on their part distinguish a two-fold justification, that of the sinner and that of the righteous," &c. Then speaking of the latter, he adds, "The justification of the righteous, considered as an act of God, implies three things: (1.) That God acknowledges for righteous him that is actually so. (2.) That he declares him such. And, (3.) That he treats him as such." How different is this threefold act of God from that which constitutes a sinner's justification? For this justification, being also considered as the act of God, implies: (1.) That he pardons the sinner. (2.) That he admits him to his favour. And, (3.) That, under the Christian dispensation, he witnesses this double mercy to the believing sinner's heart, by giving him a sense of "the peace which passes all understanding," and a taste of the "glory which shall be revealed." However, as if all this was a mere "chimera," you say, —

Page 17. "Having fully vindicated Dr. Owen from the charge you have brought against him of holding two justifications," &c. Nay, sir, you have not vindicated him at all in this respect. All that you have proved, is, that he was no stranger to your logic, and that his love for the great Diana of the Calvinists made him inconsistently deny at one time what at another time his hatred of sin forced him to confess. Nor is this a new thing in mystic Geneva: you know, sir, a pious gentleman, who, after militating in a book called the Review against the declarative justification by works, which I contend for, drops these words, which deserve to be graven in brass, as an eternal monument of Calvinistic contradiction: — 'Neither Mr. Shirley, nor I, nor any Calvinist, that I ever heard of, denies that a sinner [should you not have said a believer?] is declaratively justified by works, both here and at the day of judgment." (*Review*, p. 149.) Now, if no Calvinist you ever heard of denies, in his luminous intervals, the very justification which I contend for in the Checks, do you not give a *Finishing Stroke* to Calvinistic consistency, when you say, (p. 18,) "I am determined to prove my former assertion against you, viz. that you cannot find one Protestant divine among the Puritans, &c, till the reign of Charles II., who held your doctrines!" You mean those of a sinner's justification by faith, and of a saint's justification by works, according to Galatians ii, 16, and Matthew xii, 37. Is it not granted on all sides that they all held the former justification? And do you not tell the world, No Calvinist that you ever heard of denied the latter? However, while you thus candidly confess that all Protestant divines held those capital doctrines of the Checks, I should not do you justice if I did not acknowledge that few, if any of them, held them uniformly and consistently, in England, till Baxter began to make a firm stand against "Antinomian dotages."

Sec. ix, p. 20. You produce these words of mine, taken from the Fourth Check, "Your imputation stands upon a preposterous supposition that Christ the righteous was an execrable sinner." To this you reply with the warmth of a gentleman, who has learned politeness in mystic Geneva' "I tell you, Rev. sir, with the bluntness and honesty of an Englishman, that this is execrable Swiss slander." Now, sir, that what you call "execrable Swiss slander," is *sterling English truth*, I prove by these quotations from your favourite divine, Dr. Crisp, who, as quoted by D. Williams, says, (p. 328:) "God makes Christ as very a sinner as the creature himself *was.*" Again, (p. 270:) "Nor are we so completely sinful, but Christ, being made sin, was as completely sinful as we." And it is well known that Luther, in one of his unguarded moments, called Christ the greatest, and consequently the most execrable sinner in the world. Now, sir, if "Christ was as completely sinful as we," (to use the words of your oracle,) does it not follow that he was a sinner as completely execrable as we are? And that you deviate a little from brotherly kindness when you call Dr. Crisp's Calvinistic mistake an execrable slander of mine?

Sec. x, pp. 21, 22. You find fault with my saying, "Is this (Christ's praying for Peter) a proof that he never prayed for Judas?" And you declare that this "assertion" (you should have said *query*) "does little honour to the advocacy of Christ." Permit me, sir, to explain myself. Though I believe, with Bishop Latimer, that *Christ shed as much blood for Judas as for Peter,* I never said nor believed, as you insinuate, "that Christ took more pains for the salvation of Judas than for that of Peter." You cannot justly infer it from my mentioning a matter of fact recorded in Scripture, viz. that once our Lord spoke to Judas, when he only looked at Peter; for he had explicitly warned Peter before. Therefore, in either Case, Christ showed himself void (not of a peculiar regard for Peter's peculiar sincerity, but) of Calvinistic partiality. Again: I am persuaded that during the day of Judas' visitation, Christ prayed for him, and sincerely too; for if Christ had borne him a grudge, and, in consequence of it, had always made mental reserves, and excepted him when he prayed for his apostles; would he not have broken the second table of the law? And might he not be proposed as a pattern of inveterate malice, rather than of perfect charity?

You reply, (p. 22,) "If this were the case, [i.e. if our Lord prayed for Judas,] those words of his, 'I know thou hearest me always,' must be untrue; for when he prayed for Judas his prayer was rejected." But is your inference just? Christ always prayed with Divine wisdom, and according to his Father's will. Therefore he prayed consistently with the eternal decree, that moral agents shall be invited, drawn, and gently moved, but not forced, to obey the Gospel. Now, if our Lord prayed conditionally for Judas, (as he certainly did for all his murderers, since they were not all forgiven,) he might say, "I know thou hearest me always;" and yet Judas might, by his perverseness, as a free agent, "reject against himself" the gracious counsel of God, till he was absolutely given up. Thus our scheme of doctrine, instead of dishonouring Christ's advocacy, represents it in a rational and Scriptural light; while yours, I fear, wounds his character in the tenderest part, and fixes upon him the blot of cunning uncharitableness, and profound dissimulation.

Sec. xi, p. 25. You say, "Time would fail me to pretend to enumerate the many gross misrepresentations," &c. However, as you have actually represented me as saying, that the more a believer sins upon earth, the merrier he will be in heaven, I beg you will point out to me where, in the plain, easy sense of my words, I have spoken any such thing; or where I have ever used so ludicrous an expression as mirth, &c, when speaking of those "pleasures which are at God's right hand for evermore."

I conclude my Antinomian creed thus, (*Fourth Check*, p. 257*) "Adultery, incest, and murder, shall, upon the whole, make me holier upon earth and merrier in heaven." Two lines below, I observe that "I am indebted to you for all the doctrines, and most of the expressions of this creed." You have therefore no right to say, "Where have I used the expression merry?" For I never said you have used it, though our Lord has, Luke xv, 32. But as you have a right to say, Where is the doctrine? I reply, In your fourth letter, sir, where you tell us, that "a grievous fall will make believers sing louder in heaven to all eternity." Now as louder songs are a certain indication of greater joy, where nothing is done in hypocrisy, I desire even Calvinists to say if I have wrested "the plain, easy sense of your words," in observing that, according to your scheme, apostates shall be merrier, or, if you please, more joyful in heaven for their grievous falls on earth.

Page 27. "Now, sir, give me leave to pluck a feather out of your high soaring wings, &c, by asking you simply, Whence have you taken it? [this quotation so called.] Did I ever assert any thing like this? &c. Prove your point, and then I will confess that you are no calumniator of God's people." I answer, —

(1.) I did not produce as a quotation the words which you allude to: I put them in commas, as expressive of the sentiments of "many good men." How then could you think that you alone are many good men? (2.) But you say that you, for one, understand the words of St. John, "He that does righteousness is righteous," of personal holiness. Now, sir, to prove me a "calumniator," you have only to prove that David did righteousness when he defiled Uriah's wife; for you teach us directly, or indirectly, that when he committed that crime he was "undefiled," and continued to be "a man after God's own heart," i.e. a righteous man, for "the Lord alloweth the righteous, but the ungodly does his soul abhor." (3.) However, if I have mistaken one of the scriptures, on which you found your doctrine, I have not mistaken the doctrine itself. What are the words for which you call me a "calumniator," and charge me with "horrid perversion, falsehood, and base disingenuity?" Why, I have represented "many good men" as saying, (by the general tenor of one of their doctrines of grace, the absolute perseverance of fallen, adulterous, idolatrous, incestuous believers,) "Let not Mr. Wesley deceive you: he that actually liveth with another man's wife, worships abominable idols, and commits incest with his father's wife, may not only be righteous, but complete in imputed righteousness," &c. This is the doctrine I charge upon many good men. and if you, for one, say, "Did I ever assert any thing like this?" I reply, Yes, sir, in your fourth letter, which is a professed attempt to prove that believers may, like adulterous David, idolatrous Solomon, and the incestuous Corinthian, go any length in sin without ceasing to stand complete in, what I beg leave to call,

* [261]

Calvinistic righteousness. Thus, instead of "plucking a feather out of my wings," you wing the arrow which I let fly at your great Diana.

Sec. xii. For brevity's sake I shall reduce my answer to the rest of your capital charges into plain queries, not doubting but my judicious readers will see their unreasonableness without the help of arguments.

1. Is it right in Mr. Hill to call (pp. 34, 35) my extract from Flavel "a citation," and "a quotation;" and then to charge me with "disingenuity, gross perversion, expunging," &c, because I have not swelled my extract by transcribing all Flavel's book, or because I have taken only what suits the present times, and what is altogether consistent? Especially when I have observed, (*Fourth Check*, p. 232*) "that, when Flavel encounters Antinomian errors as a disciple of Calvin, his hands hang down, Amalek prevails; and a shrewd logician could, without any magical power, force him to confess, that most of the errors which he so justly opposes are the natural consequences of Calvinism?"

2. Is it right in Mr. Hill to charge me (p. 57) with "base forgeries;" and to represent me (p. 56) as "descending to the poor, illiberal arts of forgery, and defamation," because I have presented the public with a parable in the dress of a royal proclamation, which I produce as a mere "illustration;" because I charge him with indirectly propagating tenets which as necessarily flow from his doctrines of grace, as light does from the sun; and because I have distinguished by commas a creed framed with his avowed principles? Although I have added these words, to show that I took the composition of it upon myself: "You speak indeed in the third person, and I in the first; but this alters not the doctrine. Some clauses and sentences I have added, not to misrepresent and blacken, (for what need is there of blackening the sable mantle of midnight?) but to introduce, connect, and illustrate your sentiments."

3. Angry as the Pharisees were at our Lord when he exposed their errors by parables, did they ever charge him with base forgery, because his "illustrations" were not true stories? Is it not strange that this admirable way of defending "the truth" should have been found out by the grand defender of "the doctrines of grace?" Again: if marking with commas a paragraph of our composing, to distinguish it from our own real sentiments, is a crime; is not Mr. Hill as criminal as myself? Does he not (p. 31,) present the public with a card of his own composing, in which he holds forth the supposed sentiments of many clergymen, and which he distinguishes with commas thus: "The Feather's Tavern fraternity present compliments to Messrs J. Wesley and Fletcher," &c. Shall what passes for wit in the author of *Pietas Oxoniensis*, be gross disingenuity, and base forgery, in the author of the Vindication? O ye candid Calvinists, partial as your system is, can you possibly approve of such glaring partiality?

4. Is it right in Mr. Hill to take his leave of me in this abrupt manner, (pp. 39, 40:) "The unfair, quotations you have made, and the shocking misrepresentations and calumnies you have been guilty of, will for the future prevent me from looking into any of your books, if you should write a thousand volumes:" and this especially under pretence, that I have "shamefully perverted

---

* [234]

and misrepresented the doctrines of Anthony Burgess," when I have simply produced a quotation from him, in which there is not a shadow of misrepresentation, as the reader will see by comparing Fourth Check, (p. 226,) with the last paragraph of the twelfth Sermon of Mr. Burgess on *Grace and Assurance?*

Sec. 13. This perpetual noise about "gross misrepresentations, shameful perversions, interpolations, base forgeries," &c, becomes Mr. Hill as little as any man; his own inaccuracy in quotation equalling that of the most inattentive writer I am acquainted with. Our readers have seen on what a slender basis he rests his charge of "base forgeries." I beg leave to show them now on what solid ground I rest my charge of uncommon inaccuracy; and not to intrude too long upon their patience, I shall just produce a few instances only out of his *Finishing Stroke.**

---

* To produce such instances out of the "Review," would be almost endless. One, however, Mr. Hill forces me to touch upon a second time. This is the case. The sword of the Spirit, which Mr. Wesley uses, is two edged. When he defends the first Gospel axiom against the Pharisees, he preaches "salvation, not by the merit of works, but by believing in Christ:" and when he defends the second Gospel axiom against the Antinomians, he preaches "salvation, not by the merit of works, but by works as a condition." No sooner did the Calvinists see this last proposition at full length in the Minutes than they took the alarm, fondly imagining that Mr. Wesley wanted to overthrow the Protestant doctrine of salvation by faith. To convince them of their mistake, I appealed to Mr, Wesley's works in general, and to the Minutes in particular; two sentences of which evidently show that he had not the least intention of setting aside faith in Christ, in order to make way for the antichristian merit of works. Accordingly, I laid those sentences before my readers, taking special care to show by commas that I produced two different parts of the Minutes, thus: "Not by the merit of works," but by "believing in Christ." Here is not a shadow of disingenuity, either as to the quotations, for they are fairly taken from the Minutes; or as to the sense of the whole sentences, for fifty volumes, and myriads of hearers can testify, that it perfectly agrees with Mr. Wesley's well-known doctrine. But what does Mr. Hill? Biassed by his system, he tampers with my quotations; he takes off the two commas after the word works; he overlooks the two commas before the word believing! He (inadvertently, I hope) throws my two distinct quotations into one; and by that means adds to them the words "but by," which I had particularly excluded. When he has thus turned my two just quotations into one that is false, he is pleased to put me into the Geneva pillory for his own mistake; and as his doctrines of grace teach him to kill two birds with one stone, he involves Mr. Wesley in my gratuitous disgrace, thus: "Forgeries of this kind have long passed for no crime with Mr. Wesley: I did not think you would have followed him in these ungenerous artifices." ("Review," p. 27.)

Upon the remonstrance I made about this strange way of proceeding, (see note, Fourth Check, p. 229,) I hoped that Mr. Hill would have hanged down his head a moment, and dropped the point for ever. But no: he must give a Finishing Stroke, and drive home the nail of his rash accusation, by calling my remarks upon his mistakes "attempts to vindicate that most shameful, false quotation he [Mr. Fletcher] has twice made from the Minutes." (Log. Wesl. p. 35.) And to prove that my attempts have been unsuccessful, he produces passages out of a newspaper, which represent "his majesty," — "stealing bread," — "her majesty," — "committed to the house of correction." To this I answer, that if such unconnected quotations (of which I only give here the substance) were properly distinguished by commas; if they were separated by intervening words; and if they did not in the least misrepresent the author's sense, it would be great injustice to call them either "a most shameful false quotation," or a "forgery." Now these three particulars meet in my two quotations from the Minutes. (1.) They are both properly distinguished with commas. (2.) They are parted by intervening words. And (3.) They do not in the least misrepresent Mr. Wesley's meaning: whereas, (to say nothing more of my commas expunged in the Review,) no word intervenes between Mr. Hill's supposed quotations out of the papers; and they form a shameful misrepresentation of the publisher's meaning.

O! but as the quotations from the Minutes are linked, they "speak a language directly opposite to the Minutes themselves." So says Mr. Hill, without producing the shadow of a proof. But, upon the arguments of the five Checks, I affirm that the two Gospel axioms, or my linked quotations and the

Five Checks To Antinomianism

1. That performance does not do my sermon justice; for, (p. 51,) Mr. Hill quotes me so: "They [good works] are declarative of our free justification;" whereas my manuscript runs thus: "They are the declarative cause of our free justification," viz. in the day of trial and of judgment. The word "cause" here is of the utmost importance to my doctrine, powerfully guarding the Minutes and undefiled religion. Whether it is left out, because it shows at once the absurdity of pretending that my old sermon "is the best confutation of Mr. Wesley's Minutes," or because Mr. Hill's copier omitted it first, is best known to Mr. Hill himself.

2. I say in the Fourth Check, (p. 289*) "To vindicate what I beg leave to call God's honesty, permit me to observe, first, that I had rather believe Joseph told once 'a gross untruth,' than to suppose that God perpetually equivocates." For undoubtedly of two evils I would choose the least, if a cogent dilemma obliged me to choose either. But this is not the case here: the dilemma is not forcible; for in the next lines I show that Joseph, instead of "telling a gross untruth," only spake the language of brotherly kindness. However, without paying any regard to my vindication of Joseph's Speech, Mr. Hill catches at the conditional words, "I had rather believe:" just as if I had said, I do actually believe, he turns them into a peremptory declaration of my faith, and three times represents me as asserting what I never said nor believed. Thus, (p. 38,) "your wonderful assertion, that Joseph told his brethren a gross untruth." Once more, (p. 39,) "The repeated words of inspiration you venture to call gross untruth." Solomon says, "Who can stand before envy?" And I ask, "Who can stand before Mr. Hill's inattention?" I am sure, neither I, nor Mr. Wesley. At this rate he can undoubtedly find a blasphemy in every page, and a farrago in every book.

3. Take another instance of the same want of exactness. I say in the Fourth Check, (p. 220†) "I never thought Mr. Whitefield was clear in the doctrine of our Lord: 'In the day of judgment by thy words shalt thou be justified;' for if he had seen it in a proper light, he would instantly have renounced Calvinism." This passage Mr. Hill quotes thus, in italics and commas, (p. 23:) *"You never thought him clear in our Lord's doctrine; for if he had, he would have renounced his Calvinism."* The inaccuracy of this quotation consists in omitting those important words of our Lord: "In the day of judgment," &c. By this omission that sense of the preceding clause is indefinite; and I am represented as saying, that Mr. Whitefield was not clear in any doctrine of our Lord, no not in that of the fall, repentance, salvation

---

Minutes, agree as perfectly with each other as those positions of St. Paul to which they answer: "By grace ye are saved through faith." Therefore "work out your salvation with fear."

From this redoubled stroke of Mr. Hill, I am tempted to think, that, like Justice, "Logica Genevensis" has a covering over her eyes; but, alas! for a very different reason. Like her also she has a balance in her left hand; but it is to weigh out and vend her own assertions as proofs. And, like her, she holds a sword in her right hand; but, alas! it is often to wound brotherly love, and stab evangelical truth. Bring her into the field of controversy, and she will at once cut down Christ's doctrine as dreadful heresy. Set her in the judgment seat to pass sentence over good works, and over honest men, that do not bow at her shrine; and without demur she will pronounce, that the former are dung, and that the latter are knaves.

* [293]

† [222]

by faith, the new birth, &c. This one mistake of Mr. Hill is sufficient to make me pass for a mere coxcomb in all the Calvinistic world.

 4. It is by the like inattention that Mr. Hill prejudices also against me the friends of Mr. Wesley. In the Fourth Check, after having answered an objection of the Rev. Mr. Hill against Mr. Wesley, I produce that objection again for a fuller answer, and say: "But, supposing that Mr. Wesley had not properly considered, &c, what would you infer from thence? &c. Weigh your argument, &c, and you will find it is wanting." Then I immediately produce Mr. Hill's objection in the form of an argument, thus: "Twentythree, or, if you please, three years ago, Mr. Wesley wanted clearer light," &c. Now what I evidently produce as a supposition, and as the Rev. Mr. Hill's own argument unfolded in order to answer it, my opponent fathers upon me thus: — "The following are your own words, '*Three years ago Mr. Wesley wanted clearer light,*'" &c. True, they are my own words: but, to do me justice, Mr. Hill should have produced them as I do, namely, as a supposition, and as the drift of his brother's objection, in order to show its frivolousness. This is partly such a mistake as if Mr. Hill said: "The following are David's own words,' *Tush! there is no God.*'"

 However, he is determined to improve his own oversight, and he does it by asking, (p. 17,) "What then is become of thousands of Mr. Wesley's followers who died before this clearer light came?" An argument this by which the most ignorant Papists in my parish perpetually defend their idolatrous superstitions' "What is become of all our forefathers," say they, "before Luther and Calvin? Were they all damned?" Is it not surprising that Mr. Hill, not contented to produce a Popish friar's conversation, should have thus recourse to the argument of every Popish cobbler who attacks the doctrine of the reformation? O *Logica Genevensis!* how dost thou show thyself the genuine sister of *Logica Romana!*

 5. I return to the mistakes by which Mr. Hill has supported, before the world, his charge of "calumny." I say, in the Second Cheek, (p. 112*) "How few of our celebrated pulpits are there where more has not been said *at times* for sin than against it?" Mr. Hill (p. 7) says, "The ministers, who preach in these (our most celebrated pulpits,) are condemned *without exception,* as such *pleaders for sin, that they say more for it than against it.*" Here are two capital mistakes, (1.) The question, How few? &c, evidently leaves room for some exceptions; but Mr. Hill represents me as condemning our most celebrated pulpits "without exception." (2.) This is not all. To mitigate the question, I add, "at times," words by which I give my readers to understand that sin is in general attacked in our celebrated pulpits, and that it is only at times, that is, on some particular occasion, or in some part of a sermon, that the ministers alluded to say more for sin than against it. Now, Mr. Hill leaves out of his quotation the words, at times, and by that means effectually represents me as "a calumniator of God's people:" for what is true with the limitation that I use, becomes a falsehood when it is produced without. This omission of Mr. Hill is the more singular, as my putting the words, *at times,* in italics, indicates that I want my readers to lay a peculiar stress upon it on account of its importance. One more instance of Mr. Hill's inaccuracy, and I have done.

<hr />

* [109]

6. Pages 7, 8. He presents his readers with a long paragraph produced as a quotation from the Second Check. It is made up of some detached sentences picked here and there from that piece, and put together with as much wisdom as the patches which make up a fool's coat. And among these sentences he has introduced this, which is not mine in sense any more than in expression: "They [celebrated ministers] handle no texts of Scripture without distorting them," for I insinuate just the contrary, in the Second Check.

7. But the greatest fault I find with that paragraph of Mr. Hill's book is the conclusion, which runs thus: "They [celebrated ministers] do the devil's work till they and their congregations all go to hell together. Second Check, pp. 100, 106 [97, 103]." Now, in neither of the pages quoted by Mr. Hill, nor indeed any where else, did I ever say so wild and wicked a thing. Nothing could engage my pious opponent to father such a horrid assertion upon me, but the great and severe Diana, that engages him to father absolute reprobation upon God.

It is true, however, that, alluding to the words of our Lord, Matthew xxv, I say, in the Second Check, p. 131 [129], "If these shall go into everlasting punishment," &c. But who are these? *All celebrated ministers, with all their congregations!* So says Mr. Hill; but, happily for me, my heart starts from the thought with the greatest detestation, and my pen has testified that these condemned wretches are in general "obstinate workers of iniquity," and, in particular, "unrenewed anti-Calvinists, and impenitent Nicolaitans." Page 128 [126], (the very page which Mr. Hill quotes,) I describe the unrenewed anti-Calvinists thus: "Stubborn sons of Belial, saying, Lord, thy Father is merciful; and if thou didst die for all, why not for us? Obstinate Pharisees, who plead the good they did in their own name to supersede the Redeemer's merits." Impenitent Nicolaitans or Antinomians, I describe thus, (pp. 131, 137, 138 [129, 136, 137]: "Obstinate violators of God's law, who scorned personal holiness; rejected Christ's word of command; have gone on still in their wickedness; have continued in doing evil; have been unfaithful unto death; and have defiled their garments to the last." Is it possible that Mr. Hill should take this for a description of *all* celebrated ministers, and of all their congregations, and that, upon so glaring a mistake, he should represent me as making them "*all* go to hell together?"

Sec. xiv. O ye pious Calvinists, whether ye fill our celebrated pulpits, or attend upon them that do, far from sending "you all to hell together," as you are told I do, I exult in the hope of meeting you *all together in heaven.* I lie not. I speak the truth in Him that shall justify us by our words; even now I enjoy a foretaste of heaven in lying at your feet in spirit; and my conscience bears me witness, that, though I try to detect and oppose your mistakes, I sincerely love and honour your persons. My regard for you, as zealous, defenders of the first Gospel axiom, is unalterable. Though your mistaken zeal should prompt you to think or say all manner of evil against me, because I help Mr. Wesley to defend the second; I am determined to offer you still the right hand of fellowship. And if any of you should honour me so far as to accept it, I shall think myself peculiarly happy; for, next to Jesus and truth, the esteem and love of good men is what I consider as the most invaluable blessing. A desire to recover the interest I once had in the brotherly kindness of some of you, has in part engaged me to clear myself from the mistaken charges of calumny and forgery, by which my hasty opponent has prejudiced you against me and my Checks. If you find that he has defended your cause with carnal weapons, hope with me that precipitation, and too warm a zeal for your doctrines have misled him, and not malice or disingenuity.

Hope it also, ye anti-Calvinists, considering that if St. James and St. John, through mere bigotry and impatience of opposition, were once ready to command fire from heaven to come down upon the Samaritans, it is no wonder that Mr. Hill, in an unguarded moment, should have commanded the fire of his Calvinistic zeal to kindle against Mr. Wesley and me. As you do not unchristian now the two rash apostles for a sin, of which they immediately repented, let me beseech you to confirm your love toward Mr. Hill, who has probably repented already of the mistakes into which his peculiar sentiments have betrayed his good nature and good breeding.

Sec. xv. I return to you, honoured sir, and beg you would forgive me the liberty I have taken to lay before the public what I should have been glad to have buried in eternal oblivion. But your *Finishing Stroke* has been so heavy and desperate, as to make this addition to *Logica Genevensis* necessary to clear up my doctrine, to vindicate my honesty, to point out the mistaken author of the Farrago, and give the world a new specimen of the arguments by which your system must be defended, when reason, conscience, and Scripture, (the three most formidable batteries in the world,) begin to play upon its ramparts.

You "earnestly entreat" me, in your *postscript,* to publish a manuscript sermon on Romans xi, 5, 6, that I preached about eleven years ago in my Church, in defence of the first Gospel axiom. You are pleased to call it three times "excellent," and you present the public with an extract from it, made up of some unguarded passages; detached from those that in a great degree guard them, explain my meaning, confirm the doctrine of the Checks, and sap the foundation of your mistakes. As I am not less willing to defend free grace, than to plead for faithful obedience, I shall gladly grant your request, so far at least as to send my old sermon into the world with additions in brackets, just as I preached it again last spring; assuring you that the greatest addition is in favour of free grace. By thus complying with your "earnest entreaty," I shall show my respect, meet you half way, gratify the curiosity of our readers, and yet give them a specimen of what appears to me a free guarded Gospel.

That discourse will be the principal piece of *An Equal Check to Pharisaism and Antinomianism* which I have prepared for the press. Upon the plan of the doctrines it contains, I do not despair to see moderate Calvinists, and unprejudiced anti-Calvinists acknowledge their mutual orthodoxy, and embrace one another with mutual forbearance. May you and I, dear sir, set them the example! In the meantime, may the brotherly love, with which we forgive each other the real or apparent unkindness of our publications, continue and increase! May the charity that is "not easily provoked," and "hopeth all things," uniformly influence our hearts! So shall the words that drop from our lips, or distil from our pens, evidence that we are, or desire to be, the close followers of the meek, gentle, and yet impartial, plainspoken Lamb of God. For his sake, to whom we are both so greatly indebted, restore me to your former benevolence, and be persuaded, that notwithstanding the severity of your *Finishing Stroke,* and the plainness of my answer, I really think it an honour, and feel it a pleasure to subscribe myself, honoured and dear sir, your affectionate and obedient servant, in the Gospel of our common Lord,

J. FLETCHER.

MADELEY, *Sept.* 13, 1773.

APPENDIX.

Upon the remaining difference between the Calvinists and the anti-Calvinists with respect to our Lord's doctrine of justification by words, and St. James' doctrine of justification by works.

To force my dear opponents out of the last entrenchment in which they defend their mistakes, and from behind which they attack the justification by words and works peculiarly insisted on by our Lord and St. James, I only need to show how far we agree with respect to that justification; to state the difference that remains between us; and to prove the unreasonableness of considering us as Papists, because we oppose an unscriptural and irrational distinction, that leaves Mr. Fulsome in full possession of all his Antinomian dotages.

On both sides we agree to maintain, in opposition to Socinians and Deists, that the grand, the primary, and properly meritorious cause of our justification, from first to last, both in the day of conversion and in the day of judgment, is only the precious atonement, and the infinite merits of our Lord Jesus Christ. We all agree, likewise, that, in the day of conversion, faith is the instrumental cause of our justification before God. Nay, if I mistake not, we come one step nearer each other, for we equally hold that after conversion the works of faith are in this world, and will be in the day of judgment, the evidencing cause of our justification; that is, the works of faith (under the above-mentioned primary cause of our salvation, and in subordination to the faith that gives them birth) are now, and will be in the great day, the evidence that shall instrumentally cause our justification as believers. Thus Mr. Hill says, (*Review*, p. 149:) "Neither Mr. Shirley, nor I, nor any Calvinist that I ever heard of, denies, that though a sinner be justified in the sight of God by Christ alone, he is declaratively justified by works, both here and at the day of judgment." And the Rev. Mr. Madan, in his sermon on *justification by works, &c, stated, explained, and reconciled with justification by faith, &c,* says, (p. 29,) "By Christ only are we meritoriously justified, and by faith only are we instrumentally justified in the sight of God; but by works, and not by faith only, are we declaratively justified before men and angels." From these two quotations, which could easily be multiplied to twenty, it is evident, that pious Calvinists hold the doctrine of a justification by the works of faith; or, as Mr. Madan expresses it, after St, James, "by works, and not by faith only."

It remains now to show wherein we disagree. At first sight the difference seems trifling, but upon close examination it appears that the whole Antinomian gulf still remains fixed between us. Read over the preceding quotations; weigh the clauses which I have put in italics; compare them with what the Rev. Mr. Berridge says in his "Christian World Unmasked," (p. 26,) of "an absolute impossibility of being justified in any manner by our works," namely, before God; and you will see that although pious Calvinists allow we are justified by works before men and angels, yet they deny our being ever justified by works before God, in whose sight they suppose we are for ever "justified by Christ alone," i.e. only by Christ's good works and sufferings absolutely imputed to us, from the very first moment in which we make a single act of true faith, if not from all eternity. Thus works are still entirely excluded from having any hand either in our intermediate or final justification before God, and thus they are still represented as totally needless to our eternal salvation. Now, in direct opposition to the above-mentioned distinction, we anti-Calvinists believe that adult persons cannot be saved without being justified by faith as sinners, according to the light of their dispensation; and by works as believers, according to the time and opportunities they have of working. We assert that the works of faith are not less necessary to our justification before God as believers, than faith itself is necessary to our justification before him as sinners: and we maintain, that when faith does not produce good works, (much more when it produces the worst works, such as adultery, hypocrisy, treachery, murder, &c,) it dies, and justifies no more, seeing it is a living and not a dead faith that justifies us as sinners; even as they are living, and not dead works that justify us as believers. I have already exposed the absurdity of the doctrine, that works are necessary to our final justification before men and angels, but not before God. However, as this distinction is one of the grand subterfuges of the decent Antinomians, and one of the pleas by which the hearts of the simple are most easily deceived into Solifidianism, to the many arguments that I have already produced upon this head in the sixth letter of the Fourth Check, I beg leave to add those which follow: —

1. The way of making up the Antinomian gap, by saying, that works are necessary to our intermediate and final justification before men and angels, but not before God, is as bad as the gap itself. "If God is for me (says judicious Mr. Fulsome) who can be against me? If God has for ever justified me only by Christ, and if works have absolutely no place in my justification before him, what care I for men and angels? Should they justify when God condemns, what would their absolution avail? And if they condemn when God justifies, what signifies their condemnation? All creatures are fallible. The myriads of men and angels are as nothing before God. He is all in all." Thus, Mr. Fulsome, by a most judicious way of arguing, keeps the field of licentiousness where the Solifidian ministers have inadvertently brought him, and whence he is too wise to depart upon their brandishing before him the broken reed of an absurd distinction.

2. Our justification by works will principally, and in some cases entirely, turn upon the works of the heart, which are unknown to all but God. Again: were men and angels in all cases to pass a decisive sentence upon us according to our works, they might judge us severely, as Mr. Hill judges Mr. Wesley: they might brand us for forgery upon the most frivolous appearances; at least they might condemn us as rashly as Job's friends condemned him. Once more: were our fellow creatures to condemn us decisively by our works, they would often do it as

unjustly as the disciples condemned the blessed woman, who poured a box of very precious ointment on our Lord's head. They had indignation, and blamed as uncharitable waste what our Lord was pleased to call "a good work wrought upon him," — a good work, which shall be told for a memorial of her as long as the Christian Gospel is preached. To this may be added the mistake of the apostles, who, even after they had received the Holy Ghost, condemned Saul of Tarsus by his former, when they should have absolved him by his latter works. And even now, how few believers would justify Phinehas for running Zimri and Cosbi through the body, or Peter for striking Ananias and Sapphira dead, without giving them time to say once, "Lord, have mercy upon us!" Nay, how many would condemn them as rash men, if not as cruel murderers! In some cases, therefore, none can possibly justify or condemn believers by their works, but He who is perfectly acquainted with all the outward circumstances of their actions, and with all the secret springs whence they flow.

3. The Scriptures know nothing of the distinction which I explode. When St. Paul denies that Abraham was justified by works, it is only when he treats of the justification of a sinner, and speaks of the "works of unbelief." When Christ says, "By thy words thou shalt be justified," he makes no mention of angels. To suppose that they shall be able to justify a world of men by their words, is to suppose that they have heard, and do remember, all the words of all mankind, which is supposing them to be gods. Nay, far from being judged by angels, St. Paul says, that "we shall judge them;" not indeed as proper judges, but as Christ's assessors and mystical members: for our Lord, in his description of the great day, informs us that he, and not men or angels, will justify the sheep, and condemn the goats, by their works.

4. St. Paul discountenances the evasive distinction which I oppose when he says, "Thinkest thou, O man, who doest such things, that thou shalt escape the righteous judgment of God, who will render eternal life to them that by patient continuance in well doing seek for glory, &c, when he shall judge the secrets of men by Jesus Christ?" For reason dictates, that neither men nor angels, but the Searcher of hearts alone will be able to justify or condemn us by secrets, unknown possibly to all but himself.

5. If you say, Most men shall have been condemned or justified long before the day of judgment; therefore the solemn pomp of that day will be appointed merely for the sake of justification by men and angels: I exclaim against the unreasonableness of supposing that "the great and terrible day of God," with an eye to which the world of rationals was created, is to be only the day of men and angels. And I reply: Although I grant, that judgment certainly finds us where death leaves us; final justification and condemnation being chiefly a solemn seal set, if I may so speak, upon the forehead of those whose consciences are already justified or condemned, according to the last turn of their trial on earth: yet it appears, both from Scripture and reason, that mankind cannot properly be judged before the great day. Departed spirits are not men; and dead men cannot be tried till the resurrection of the dead takes place, when departed spirits and raised bodies will form men again by their re-union. Therefore, in the very nature of things, God cannot judge mankind before the great day; and to suppose that the Father has appointed such a day, that we may be finally justified by our works

before men and angels, and not before him, is to suppose that he has committed the chief judgment to the parties to be judged, i.e. to men and angels, and not to Jesus Christ.

6. But, if I mistake not, St. James puts the matter out of all dispute, where he says: "You see, then, that by works a man is justified, and not by faith only," James ii, 24. This shows that a man is justified by works before the same judge, by whom he is justified by faith; and here is the proof. Nobody was ever justified by faith before men and angels, because faith is an inward act of the soul, which none but the Trier of the reins can be a judge of. Therefore, as the Justifier by faith alluded to in the latter part of the verse is undoubtedly God alone, it is contrary to all the rules of criticism to suppose that the Justifier by works, alluded to in the very same sentence, is men and angels. Nay, in the preceding verse, God is expressly mentioned, and not men or angels: "Abraham believed God, and it was imputed to him for righteousness," i.e. he was justified before God. So that the same Lord, who justified him *as a sinner by faith* in the day of his conversion, justified him also *as a believer by works* in the day of his trial.

7. But this is not all. Turning to Genesis xxii, the chapter which St. James had undoubtedly in view when he insisted upon Abraham's justification by works, I find the best of arguments, matter of fact. "And it came to pass, that God did tempt [i.e. try] Abraham." The patriarch acquitted himself like a sound believer in the hard trial; he obediently offered up his favourite son. Here St. James addresses a Solifidian, and bluntly says, "Wilt thou know, O vain man, that faith without works is dead," i.e. that when faith gives over working by obedient love, it sickens, dies, and commences adead faith? Was not Abraham our father justified by works when he offered up Isaac upon the altar? If Mr. Hill answer, Yes, he was justified by works before men and angels, but not before God; I reply, Impossible! For neither men nor angels put him to the trial to bring out what was in his heart. God tried him that he might justly punish, or wisely reward him; therefore God justified him. If a judge, after trying a man on a particular occasion, acquits him upon his good behaviour, in order to proceed to the reward of him, is it not absurd to say, that the man is acquitted before the court, but not before the judge; especially if there is neither court nor jury present, but only the judge? Was not this the case at Abraham's trial? Do we hear of any angel being present but יהוה מלאך, the Angel Jehovah? And had not Abraham left his two servants with the ass at the foot of the mount? Is it reasonable then to suppose that Abraham was justified before them by a work, which as yet they had not heard of; for, says St. James, "When [which implies as soon as] he had offered Isaac, he was justified by works?" If you say that he was justified before Isaac, I urge the absurdity of supposing that God made so much ado about the trial of Abraham before the lad; and I demand proof that God had appointed the youth to be the justifier of his aged parent.

8. But let the sacred historian decide the question. "And the Lord called to Abraham out of heaven, and said, Lay not thy hand upon the lad, for now I know [declaratively] that thou fearest God," (i.e. believest in God.) Now I can praise and reward thee with wisdom and equity: "Seeing thou hast not withheld thy son, thy only son from me." Upon Calvinistic principles, did not God speak improperly? Should not he have said, Now angels and men, before whom thou

hast offered Isaac, do know that thou fearest me? But if God had spoken thus, would he have spoken consistently with either his veracity or his wisdom? Is it not far more reasonable to suppose, that although God as omniscient, with a glance of his eyes, "tries the hearts, searches the reins," and foresees all future contingencies; yet, as a judge, and a wise dispenser of punishments and rewards, he condemns no unbelievers, and justifies no believers, in St. James' sense, but by the evidence of tempers, words, and actions, which actually spring from their unbelief, or their faith?

9. Was it not from the same motive that God tried Job in the land of Uz, chap. i, 12, Israel in the wilderness, Deuteronomy viii, 1, compared with Joshua xxii, 2, and King Hezekiah in Jerusalem, 2 Chronicles xxxii, 31. "God (says the historian) left him [to the temptation] that he [God] might know [declaratively] all that was in his heart." It is true, Mr. Hill supposes, in the second edition of his Five Letters, that the words, *he might know,* refer to Hezekiah; but Canne more judiciously refers to Genesis xxii, 1, where God tried Abraham — not that Abraham might know, but that he himself might declaratively know what was in Abraham's heart. If the word *that* HE *might know,* did refer to Hezekiah, should not the affix (ו) *he,* or *him,* have been added to רצד, thus, לדצתו, as it is put to the two preceding verbs, צזב, *he left* HIM, לנמותו, *to try* HIM?

10. Our Lord himself decides the question, where he says to his believing disciples, "Whosoever shall confess me before men, him will I also confess before my Father who is in heaven. But whosoever shall deny me before men, him will I also deny before my Father who is in heaven." It was undoubtedly an attention to this scripture that made Dr. Owen say: "Hereby [by personal obedience] that faith whereby we are justified [as sinners] is evidenced, proved, manifested in the sight of God and man." And yet, astonishing! this passage, which indirectly gives up the only real difference there is between Mr. Hill's justification by works and ours; this passage, which cuts him off from the only way he has of making his escape, (except that by which his brother tried to make his own, see *Fourth Check,* p. 275*) this very passage which makes so much for my sentiment, is one of those concerning which he says, *(Finishing Stroke,* p. 14:) "Words *prudently* expunged by Mr. Fletcher," when they are only words, which for brevity's sake I very *imprudently* left out, since they cut down Solifidianism, even with Dr. Owen's sword.

To conclude. Attentive reader, peruse James ii, where the justification of believers by works before God is so strongly insisted upon. Observe what is said there of the law of liberty; of believers being judged by that law; of the "judgment without mercy," that shall be shown to fallen, merciless believers according to that law. Consider that this doctrine exactly coincides with the sermon upon the mount, and the Epistle to the Hebrews; that it perfectly tallies with Ezekiel xviii, xxxiii; Matthew xii, xxv; Romans ii; Galatians vi, &c; and that it is delivered to brethren, yea, to the beloved brethren of St. James, to whom he could say, "Out of his own will the Father of lights begat us with the word of truth." Take notice that the charge indirectly brought against them is that they "had the faith of the

---

* [279]

Lord Jesus Christ with respect of persons;" and that they "deceived their own selves," by not being as careful doers as they were diligent "hearers of the word." Then look round upon some of our most famous believers: see how foaming, how roaring, how terrible are the billows of their partiality. Read *"An Address from candid Protestants to the Rev. Mr. Fletcher;"* read "The *Finishing Stroke;"* read "More *Work for Mr. Wesley;"* read the *Checks to Antinomianism;* and say if there is not as great need to insist upon a believer's justification by words and works as there was in the days of our Lord and St. James: and if it is not high time to say to modern believers, "My brethren, have not the faith of our Lord Jesus Christ with respect of persons. So speak ye, and so do, as they that shall be judged by the law of liberty. For he shall have judgment without mercy, that hath showed no mercy: for with what judgment ye judge, ye shall be judged; and with what measure ye mete, it shall be measured to you again, [by Him that] shall render to every one according to what he has done in the body, whether it be good or bad." But "candid Protestants" have an answer ready in their "Address." This is "the Popish doctrine of justification by works," and "Arminian Methodism turned out rank Popery at last." This is a mingle mangle of "the most high and mighty, self-righteous, self-potent, selfimportant, self-sanctifying, self-justifying, and self-exalting medley minister."[*] The misfortune is, that amidst these witticisms of "the Protestants," (for it seems the Calvinists engross that name to themselves,) we, "rank Papists," still look out for arguments; and when we find none, or only such as are worse than none, we still say *Logica Genevensis!* And remain confirmed in our "dreadful heresy," or rather in our Lord's anti-Calvinistic doctrine, "By thy words thou shalt be justified, and by thy words thou shalt be condemned."

END OF THE FIRST PART.

---

[*] See the above-mentioned "Address from Candid Protestants."

LOGICA GENEVENSIS CONTINUED:

OR,

THE SECOND PART

OF THE

FIFTH CHECK TO ANTINOMIANISM:

CONTAINING

DEFENCE OF "JACK O'LANTERN," AND "'THE PAPER KITE," I.E. SINCERE
OBEDIENCE; — OF THE "COBWEB," I.E. THE EVANGELICAL LAW OF LIBERTY; —
AND OF THE "VALIANT SERGEANT IF," I.E. THE CONDITIONALITY OF
PERSEVERANCE, ATTACKED BY THE REV. MR. BERRIDGE, M. A., VICAR OF
EVERTON, AND LATE FELLOW OF CLARE HALL, CAMBRIDGE, IN HIS BOOK CALLED
"THE CHRISTIAN WORLD UNMASKED."

Quandoque bonus dormitat Homeius. — HOR.

CONTENTS

The Works of John Fletcher

Section V.

Mr. Berridge candidly grants the conditionality of perseverance, and consequently of election, by showing much respect to "Sergeant IF," who "guards the camp of Jesus:" but soon picking a quarrel with the valiant sergeant, oddly discharges him as a Jew, opens the camp to the Antinomians, by opposing to them only a sham sentinel, and shows the foundation of Calvinism in a most striking light.

Conclusion.

In which the author expresses again his brotherly love for Mr. Berridge, makes an apology for the mistakes of his pious antagonist, and accounts for the oddity of his own style in answering him.

INTRODUCTION.

HAVING animadverted on Mr. Hill's *Finishing Stroke,* I proceed to ward off the first blow which the Rev. Mr. Berridge has given to practical religion. But before I mention his mistakes, I must do justice to his person. It is by no means my design to represent him as a divine who either leads a loose life, or intends to hurt the Redeemer's interest. His conduct as a Christian is exemplary; his labours as a minister are great; and I am persuaded that the wrong touches which he gives to the ark of godliness are not only undesigned, but intended to do God service.

There are so many things commendable in the pious vicar of Everton, and so much truth in his *Christian World Unmasked,* that I find it a hardship to expose the unguarded parts of that performance. But the cause of this hardship is the ground of my apology. Mr. Berridge is a good, an excellent man, therefore the Antinomian errors, which go abroad into the world with his letters of recommendation, which speak in his evangelical strain, and are armed with the poignancy of his wit, cannot be too soon pointed out, and too carefully guarded against. I flatter myself that this consideration will procure me his pardon for taking the liberty of despatching his valiant "sergeant," with some doses of rational and Scriptural antidotes for those who have drunk into the pleasing mistakes of his book, and want his piety to hinder them from carrying speculative into practical Antinomianism.

SECTION I.

ONE of my opponents has justly observed, that "the principal cause of controversy among us "is the doctrine of our justification by the works of faith in the day of judgment. At this rampart of practical godliness Mr. Berridge levels such propositions as these, in his *Christian World Unmasked:* (second edition, pp. 170, 171:) "*Final* justification by faith is the *capital* doctrine of the Gospel. Faith being the term of salvation, &c, must *utterly* exclude *all* justification by works." And, (p. 26,) we read of "an *absolute* impossibility of being justified in any *manner* by our works."

If these positions are true, say, reader, if St. James, St. Paul, and Jesus Christ, did not advance great untruths when they said: "By works a man is justified, and not by faith only," James ii, 24. "For not the hearers of the law [of

Christ] are just before God, but the doers shall be justified, &c, in the day when God shall judge the secrets of men by Jesus Christ," Romans ii, 13, 16. "For (adds our Lord, when speaking of the day of judgment) by thy words thou shalt be justified," &c, Matthew xii, 37. Christian reader, say, who is mistaken, Christ and his apostles, or the late fellow of Clare Hall?

Mr. Berridge goes farther still. Without ceremony he shuts the gate of heaven against every man who seeks to be justified by works, according to our Lord's and St. James' doctrine. For when he has assured us, (p. 171,) that faith must utterly exclude all justification by works, he immediately adds, "And the man who seeks to be justified by his passport of obedience, will find no passage through the city gates." Might not our author have unmasked Calvinism a little more, and told the Christian world that the man who minds what Christ says shall be turned into hell.

See the boldness of Solifidianism!* In our Lord's days believers were to keep their mouths as with a bridle, and to abstain from every idle word, lest in the day of judgment they should not be justified. In St. John's time they were to do Christ's commandments, that they might enter through the gates into the city, Revelation xxii, 14. But in our days, a Gospel minister assures us, (p. 171,) that the believer, who, according to our Lord's doctrine, seeks to be "justified by his passport of obedience, will find *no* passage through the city gates. He may talk of the tree of life, and soar up with his *paper kite* to the gates of paradise, but will find no entrance." I grant it, if an Antinomian pope has St. Peter's key; but so long as Christ has the key of David, so long as he opens, and no Solifidian shuts, the dutiful servant, instead of being sent flying to hell after the "paper kite" of obedience, will, through his Lord's merits, be honourably admitted into heaven by the passport of good works which he has about him. For though the remembrance of his sins, and the sight of his Saviour, will make him ashamed to produce it; yet he had rather die ten thousand deaths than be found without it. The celestial Porter, after having kindly opened it for him, will read it before an innumerable company of angels, and say, "Enter into the joy of thy Lord, for I was hungry and thou gavest me meat," &c, Matthew xxv, 35, &c.

If the vicar of Everton throws in an Antinomian caveat against this "passport of obedience,"† and ridicules it still as a "paper kite," Isaiah and St. Paul will soon silence him. "Open ye the gates," says the evangelical prophet, "that the righteous nation which keepeth the truth [of the Gospel doctrines] may enter in:" for, adds the evangelical apostle, "Circumcision [including all professions of faith] is nothing, but the keeping of the commandments of God. Yea, though I have all faith and no charity, I am nothing," Isaiah xxvi, 2; 1 Corinthians vii, 19; xiii, 2.

---

* *Solifidianism* is the doctrine of the Solifidians; and the Solifidians are men who, because sinners are justified (*sola fide*) by "sole faith" in the day of conversion, infer, as Mr. Berridge, that "believing is the total term of all salvation," and conclude, as Mr. Hill, that the doctrine of final justification by the works of faith in the great day is "full of rottenness and deadly poison." It is a softer word for *Antinomianism.*

† I speak only of the obedience of faith. It is only for that obedience, and for the works of faith, that St. James pleads in his epistle, Mr. Wesley in the Minutes: and I in the Checks. All other obedience is insincere; all other works Pharisaical.

Five Checks To Antinomianism

If I am at the city gates when Mr. Berridge will exclaim against the "passport of obedience," I think I shall venture to check his imprudence by the following questions: — Can there be a medium between not having a passport of obedience, and having one of disobedience? Must a man, to the honour of free grace, take a passport of refractoriness along with him? Must he bring a certificate of adultery and murder to be welcome into the New Jerusalem? I am persuaded that, with the utmost abhorrence, Mr. Berridge answers, "No!" But his great Diana speaks louder than he, and says, before all the world: "There is no need that he should have a testimonium of adultery and murder, but he may if he pleases. Nay, if he is so, inclined, he may get a diploma of treachery and incest; it will never invalidate his title to glory; for, if David and the incestuous Corinthian had saving faith, inamissible, eternal life, and finished salvation, when they committed their crimes; and if faith or believing (as Mr. Berridge affirms, p. 168,) be the total term of all salvation," why might not every Christian, if he is so minded, murder his neighbour, worship idols, and gratify even incestuous lusts, as well as primitive backsliders, without risking his finished salvation! Upon this Antinomian axiom, advanced by Mr. Berridge, "believing is the total term of all salvation," I lay my engine, a grain of reason, and ask every unprejudiced person who is able to conclude that two and two make four, whether we may not, without any magical power, heave morality out of the world, or Calvinism out of the Church?

If Mr. Berridge pleads, that, when he says, (p. 168,) "Believing is the total term of all salvation," he means a faith "including and producing all obedience," I reply, Then he gives up Solifidianism; he means the very faith which I contend for in the Checks; and pressing him with his own definition of faith, I ask, How can a "faith including all obedience," include murder, as in the case of David; idolatry, as in the case of Solomon; lying, cursing, and denying Christ, as in the case of Peter; and even incest, as in the case of the apostate Corinthian? Are murder, idolatry, cursing, and incest, "all obedience?" If Mr. Berridge replies," No:" then David, Solomon, &c, lost the justifying faith of St. Paul when they lost the justifying works of St. James; and so Mr. Berridge gives up the point together with Calvinism. If he says, "Yes:" he not only gives up St. James' justification, but quite unmasks Antinomianism: and the rational world, who "come and peep," may see that his doctrine of grace is not a *chaste virgin*, but a *great Diana*, who pays as little regard to decency as she does to Scripture.

If this is a sophism, I humbly entreat the learned fellow of Clare Hall to convince the world of it, by showing where the fallacy lies. He can do it, if it can be done, "having consumed a deal of candle at a noted hall at Cambridge in lighting up a good understanding," even after he was declared *master of* the *art* of logic. But if the dilemma is forcible, and grinds Calvinism as between an upper and nether mill stone, I hope that he will no longer oppose the dictates of reason, merely to pour contempt upon our Lord's doctrine of a believer's justification by the works of faith; and to sport himself with obedience, rendered as ridiculous as Samson was when the Philistines treated him as a blind mill horse.

SECTION II.

WE have already seen how Mr. Berridge gives "the passport of obedience" to the winds, as a boyish trumpery. To render the "paper kite" more contemptible, (p. 145,) he ties to it, instead of a tail, "a spruce new set of duties half a yard long, called legally evangelical and evangelically legal, unknown to Christ and his apostles, but discovered lately by some ingenious gentlemen." Just as if I, who have ventured upon those expressions, to indicate the harmony that subsists between the promises of the Gospel and the duties of the law of liberty, and Mr. Wesley, who has let those compounded words pass in the Second Check, were the first men who have taught that believers "are not without law to God, but under a law to Christ," 1 Corinthians ix, 21. Just as if nobody had said before us, "Do we make void the law through faith," or through the Gospel? "God forbid! Yea, we establish the law," Romans iii, 31: that is, by preaching "a faith that worketh by love," we establish the moral law; for" love is the fulfilling of it, and he that loveth another has fulfilled the law," Romans xiii, 8, 10. Not indeed the ceremonial law of Moses, for ceremonies and love are not the same thing; nor yet the Adamic law of innocence, for if the apostle had spoken of that law, he would have said, "He that has always loved another with perfect love has fulfilled the law." Therefore he evidently speaks of the evangelical law preached thus by St. James to believers: "So speak ye, and so do, as they that shall be judged by the law of liberty," James ii, 12. A law which is so called, not because it gives us the least liberty to sin; but because, during the day of salvation, it indulges us with the precious liberty to repent Of our former sins, and come to Christ for pardon, and for stronger supplies of sanctifying grace.

However, 'Mr. Berridge, as if the Antinomians had already burned St. James' Epistle, says, (p. 144,) after speaking of the law of innocence given to Adam before the fall, "All other laws [and consequently the law of liberty] are cobwebs of a human brain." What, sir, do you think that Moses was a spiritual spider, when he wove the ceremonial law? Can you possibly imagine that David's "blessed man, whose delight is in the law of the Lord, meditates day and night in a law" Which bids him "stand upon his own legs," and absolutely despair of mercy upon "a single trip?" Would you, on second thoughts, say that St. Paul and St. James weave "cobwebs" in the brains of mankind, when they declare that "the end of the commandment [or of Christ's law] is charity, from a pure heart, a good conscience, and faith unfeigned:" when they speak of fulfilling the royal law, according to the Scripture: "Thou shalt love thy neighbour as thyself:" or when they assure us, "that he who loveth another hath fulfilled it:" and exhort us to "bear one another's burdens, and so fulfil the law of Christ?" See 1 Timothy i, 5; James ii, 8; Galatians v, 13, and vi, 2.

I shall not borrow here the rash expression which Mr. Berridge uses when he confounds original worthiness and derived merit, and reflects upon Christ, who evidently attributes the latter to believers: I shall not say that my new opponent's mistake "is enough to make* a devil blush:" but I may venture to affirm, that before he can prove the law of liberty is "a cobweb," he must not only burn St. James' Epistle, but sweep away the Epistles of St. Paul to the Romans and to the Galatians; together with the law, the prophets, and the Psalms. While he considers whether the tree of Antinomianism will yield a besom strong enough for that purpose, I beg leave to dwell a moment upon another of his mistakes. It respects obedience and good works, against which Solifidians indirectly wage an eternal war. It runs through several pages, but centres in the following unguarded propositions: —

Page 35, 50. 18. "Sincere obedience is no where mentioned in the Gospel as a condition of salvation,'" and, (p. 36, 50. 4,) "Works have no share in the covenant of grace as a condition of life." I grant it, if by *salvation,* in the first proposition, and by *life* in the second, Mr. Berridge means *initial salvation,* and *life begun* in the world of grace. For undoubtedly the "free gift is come upon all men to justification," or salvation from the damning guilt of original sin, and consequently to some interest in the Divine favour previous to all obedience and works. Again and again have I observed, that as "by one man's disobedience many [οι ωολλοι, 'the multitudes of men,'] were made sinners; so by the obedience of one, many [οι ωολλοι, 'the multitudes of men,'] shall, [to the end

---

* How strangely may prejudice influence a good man! Mr. Berridge (page 164, &c,) raises a masked battery against the article of the Minutes, where Mr. Wesley hints that the word merit might be used in a Scriptural sense to express what Dr. Owen, by an uncouth circulocution, calls "the rewardable condecency, that our whole obedience, through God's gracious appointment, has unto eternal life." "O sir," says Mr. Berridge, "God must abominate the pride, the insolence of human pride, which could dream of merit: it is enough to make a devil blush." There is great truth in these words, if Mr. Berridge speaks only of proper merit, or merit of condignness and equivalence; but if he extends them to the evangelical worthiness so frequently mentioned by our Lord — if he applies them to improper merit, generally called merit of congruity — he indirectly charges Christ with teaching a doctrine so excessively diabolical, that the devil himself would be ashamed of it: and what is more surprising still, if I mistake not, he indirectly enforces the dreadful heresy himself by an illustration, which, in some degree, shows how God rewards us "for" our works, and "according to" our works. "A tender-hearted gentleman," says he, "employs two labourers out of charity to weed a little spot of four square yards: both are old and much decrepit, but one is stronger than the other. The stronger weeds three yards, and receives three crowns; the weaker weedeth one, and receives one crown. Now both are rewarded for their labour, and according to their labour, but not for the merit of their labour." Granted, if merit is taken in the sense of proper merit, or merit of condignness and equivalence; but absolutely denied if it is taken in the sense of improper worthiness, or merit of congruity. Let Thomas Aquinas, the most famous of all the Papist divines, bring his standard of merit, and measure Mr. Berridge; and if the vicar of Everton (how loud soever he may exclaim against the word) is not found holding the doctrine of merit of congruity as much as Mr. Baxter, let me for ever forfeit all pretensions to a grain of common sense. "The angelic doctor" defines merit thus: *Dicitur aliquis mereri ex condigno, quando invenitur equalitas inter præmium et meritum secundum estimationem; ex congruo autem, tantum quando talis æqualitas non invenitur: sed solum secundum liberalitatem dantis munus tribuitur quod dantem decet:* that is, "A man is said to merit with a merit of condignness, [i.e. to merit properly,] when, upon an average, there appears an equality between the reward and the merit. But he is said to merit only with a merit of congruity [i.e. to merit improperly] when there is no such equality; and when a benefactor, out of mere liberality, makes a present which it becomes him to make." Now, let candid men compare Mr. Berridge's *illustration* with the definition that the most renowned Papist doctor has given *us* of merit; and let them say if Mr. Berridge, instead of splitting the hair, does not maintain and illustrate the doctrine of merit of congruity: and if one of the blushes which he supposes our Lord's doctrine Of worthiness, or merit, would bring upon the face of some modest devil, does not become the author of the "Christian World Unmasked," more than the author of the Minutes.

of the world,] be made righteous," i.e, partakers of the above-mentioned justification, inconsequence of Christ's atonement, and the talent of free grace, and supernatural light, which "enlightens every man that comes into the world;" compare Romans v, 18, 19, with John i, 4, 5, 9. Far from opposing this initial life of free grace, this salvation unconditionally begun, I assert its necessity against the Pelagians, and its reality against the Papists and Calvinists, who agree to maintain that God has* absolutely reprobated a considerable part of mankind. But Mr. Berridge's propositions are Antinomianism unmasked, if he extends their meaning (as his scheme does) to finished salvation, and to a life of glory, unconditionally bestowed upon adulterous backsliders: for sincere obedience, or the good works of faith, are a condition, (or, to use Mr. Berridge's word, "a term,") indispensably required of all that stay long enough upon the stage of life to act as moral agents. "Every branch in me that beareth not fruit he taketh away," John xv, 2. "Be not deceived: neither fornicators, &c, shall inherit the kingdom of God," 1 Corinthians vi, 9: see Ezekiel xviii, and xxxiii. "If the

---

* Some of my readers will wonder at my coupling the Calvinists and the Romanists, when I speak of those who hold absolute reprobation; but my observation is founded upon matter of fact. We are too well acquainted with the opinion of the Calvinists concerning the vessels of wrath. The sentiments of the papists not being so public, may be brought to light by the following anecdote: — Being some years ago at Ganges, in the south of France, I went with Mr. Pomaret, the Protestant minister of that town, to recommend to Divine mercy the soul of a woman dying in child bed. When he came out of the house, he said: "Did you take notice of the person who was by the bed side? He is a man-midwife, and a strenuous Papist. You see by the consequences that this poor woman had a very hard labour. As it was doubtful whether the child would be born alive, he insisted upon baptizing it in the womb, *avec une seringue,* according to custom. The Protestant women in the room exclaimed against his intention of tormenting a woman in that extremity, by so ridiculous and needless an operation. 'Needless!' replied he, 'how can you call that needless, which will save a soul? Do you not know that if the child dies unbaptized it will certainly be lost?'" The doctrine of the Romish Church is, then, free wrath, or free reprobation, for the myriads of infants who die without baptism all the world over.

I beg leave to confirm this anecdote by a public testimony. My opponents have frequently mentioned the agreement of my sentiments with those of the Popish champion Bellarmine. This gave me a desire of looking into his works. Accordingly I procured them last winter; and, to my great surprise, before I had read a page, I found him a peculiar admirer of the great Predestinarian St. Augustine, whom he perpetually quotes. Nay, he is so strenuous an assertor of Calvinistic election, that, to prove "we can give no account of God's election on our part," among the reasons advanced by Calvin, Coles, Zanchius, &c, in support of unconditional election and reprobation, he proposes the following argument: — *Tertia ratio, &c, ducitur a parvulorum diversitate, quorum aliqui rapiuntur statim a baptismo, alii paulo ante baptismum, quorum priores ad gloriam prædestinatorum, posteriors ad pænam reproborum pertinere non est dubium; nec possunt hic ulla merita previsa, ullusve bonus usus liberi arbitrii, aut gratis fingi."* (Bell. Opera de gratia et libero arbitrio. Cap. v, Antverpiæ, 1611, p. 766.) That is, "The third reason is taken from the different lot of little children; some being snatched immediately after baptism, and others a little before baptism: the former of whom undoubtedly go to the glory of the elect; and the latter to the punishment of the reprobates. Nor can any desert foreseen, or any good use of free will, or of grace, be here pretended." This argument is truly worthy of the cause which it supports. The very essence of Calvinism is an irreconcilable opposition to the second Gospel axiom. And as Bellarmine's argument demolishes that axiom, (it being impossible that the damnation of reprobated infants should be from themselves,) he necessarily builds up Calvinism, with all its gracious doctrines. I might here return my last opponent these words of his "Finishing Stroke," (p.!5,) which he writes in capitals, "So BELLARMINE." "See, sir, what company you are again found in!" But I do not admire such arguments. Were father Walsh and Cardinal Bellarmine in the right, it would be no more disgrace to Mr. Hill to stand between them both, than it is to me to believe, with the cardinal, that Christ has said, "In the day of judgment, by thy words thou shalt be justified:" for, as a diamond does not become a pebble upon the finger of a Papist, so truth does not become a lie under his pen.

penitent thief had lived, (says our Church,) and not regarded the works of faith, he should have lost his salvation again." As for the argument taken from these words' "He that believeth *now* with the heart unto righteousness, hath everlasting life," (i.e. has a title to it, and a taste of a life of glory, and shall have the enjoyment of it, "if he continues in the faith rooted and grounded,") it is answered at large in the *Fourth Check,* p. 251*.

Page 38, Mr. Berridge unmasks Antinomianism in the following proposition: — "I have gathered up my ends, respecting this matter; and I trust you see, at length, that sincere obedience is nothing but a Jack o'lantern, dancing here and there and every where: no man could ever catch him, but thousands have been lost by following him."

If I mistake not, Mr. Berridge here exceeds Mr. Hill. The author of *Pietas Oxoniensis* only supposes that works have nothing to do before the Judge of all the earth in the matter of our eternal salvation, and that all believers shall "sing louder" in heaven for all their crimes upon earth: but the vicar of Everton represents *sincere obedience* (which is a collection of all the good works of upright heathens, Jews, and Christians,) as "a *Jack o'lantern;* and thousands," says he, "have been lost by following him." Here is a blow at the root! What! thousands lost by following after sincere obedience to God's commands! Impossible! Our pious author, I hope, means insincere obedience; but if he stands to what he has written, he must not be surprised, if, with the "good folks cast in a Gospel foundry, I ring a fire bell," and warn the Protestant world against so capital a mistake. That thousands have been lost by resting in faithless, superficial, hypocritical, insincere obedience, I grant: but thousands! lost! by following after sincere obedience, i.e. after the obedience we uprightly perform according to the light we have! This is as impossible as that the Holy Spirit should lie when he testifies, "In every nation, he that feareth God and worketh righteousness, is accepted of him:" according to one or another of the Divine dispensations: he is accepted as a converted heathen, Jew, or Christian.

Had I the voice of a trumpet, I would shout upon the walls of our Jerusalem: "Let no man deceive you'" nobody was ever lost, but for not following after, or for starting from sincere obedience; Christian faith itself being nothing but sincere obedience to this grand Gospel precept: "Believe in the Lord Jesus Christ, and thou shalt be saved." "We have received apostleship," says St. Paul, "for obedience to the faith among all nations," Romans i, 5. No adult children of Adam were ever eternally saved, but such as followed after sincere obedience, at least from the time of their last conversion, if they once drew back toward perdition. For "Christ," says the apostle, "is the author of eternal salvation to them that obey him:" and he undoubtedly means, that obey him sincerely. "He will render eternal life to them who by patient continuance in well doing," or by persevering in sincere obedience, "seek for glory." "Has the Lord as great delight in burnt offerings," says Samuel, "as in obeying [and I dare say he meant sincerely obeying] the voice of the Lord? Behold! [whatever Solifidians may say] to obey is better than sacrifice, and to hearken than the fat of rams: for rebellion [or disobedience] is as the sin of witchcraft, and stubbornness as idolatry," Hebrews v, 9; Romans ii, 7; 1 Samuel xv, 22.

God, to show the high value he puts upon sincere obedience, sent Jeremiah to the Rechabites with this message: "Thus saith the Lord of hosts, Because ye have obeyed the commandment of Jonadab your father, and kept all his precepts; therefore Jonadab the son of Rechab shall not want a man to stand before me for ever." His capital charge against Israel is that of disobedience. St. Peter, who observes that the believing Jews had purified their souls by obeying the truth, asks, "What shall the end be of them that obey not the Gospel?" And St. Paul answers, that "Christ will come in flaming fire, taking vengeance on them," — and that "God will render tribulation and wrath to them that do not obey the truth, but obey unrighteousness:" and even that famous passage, "He that believeth on the Son, hath everlasting life, and he that believeth not the Son, shall not see life," John iii, 36, is in the original a rampart against Solifidianism; for in the last sentence of it, the word rendered "believeth not," is not Greek ου ωισευων, in opposition to the first clause; but απειθων, an expression which, by signifying equally "he who disobeyeth," and "he who believeth not," guards the doctrine of obedience as strongly as that of faith.

SECTION III.

An answer to Mr. Berridge's capital arguments against sincere obedience.

THE serious reader probably wonders at the pious vicar of Everton and asks, if he supports his assertions against sincere obedience by arguments? Yes, he does, and some of them are so plausible that the simple can hardly avoid being deceived by them; nay, and some of the judicious too: for asking, last summer, a sensible clergyman what part of Mr. Berridge's book he admired most, he convinced me of the seasonableness of this publication, by replying, "I think him most excellent upon sincere obedience." A glaring proof this, that the impossibility of deceiving the very elect is not absolute, and that our Lord did not give them an impertinent caution, when he said, "Take heed that no man deceive you." But let us hear Mr. Berridge: —

Page 24. "Perhaps you think that Christ came to shorten man's duty, and make it more feasible by shoving a commandment out of Moses' tables, as the Papists have done; or by clipping and paring all the commandments, as the moralists do. Thus sincere obedience, instead of perfect, is now considered as the law of works. But if Jesus Christ came to shorten man's duty, he came to give us a license to sin. For duty cannot be shortened without breaking commandments. And thus Christ becomes a minister of sin with a witness, and must be ranked at the head of Antinomian preachers." To this specious argument I reply: —

(1.) After the fall, Christ was given in the promise to mankind as a Mediator; and "help was laid upon him" to make man's duty (as a redeemed sinner) feasible. To deny it, is to deny man's redemption. At that first promulgation of the Gospel, what St. Paul calls "the law of faith," and St. James,

Five Checks To Antinomianism

"the law of liberty," took place. This gracious law has been in force under all the dispensations of the everlasting Gospel ever since. And according to its tenor, in the day of judgment, we shall "be justified or condemned," Matthew xii, 37. (2.) To assert that "the law of liberty," or "the law of faith," requires of us paradisiacal innocence, and such a perfection of bodily and rational powers as Adam had before the fall, is to set Christ's mediation aside: and to suppose that it leaves us just where it found us, that is, under the old Adamic covenant. (3.) "The law of liberty" "neither shoves out, pares, nor clips" any moral commandment; for it condemns a man for the adultery of the eye, as well as for gross fornication; and for the murder of the. tongue or heart, as well as for manual assassination; and it requires us to "love God with all our heart, and our neighbour as ourselves," according to the light of our dispensation, and the talent of power we have received from above. He that "keeps this whole law, and breaks it in one point," (as Saul did in the matter of Agag, David in the matter of Uriah, Judas in the matter of Mammon, some Corinthians and Galatians in biting one another, and some of the Christians, to whom St. James wrote, in despising the poor, and showing a mean partiality to the rich,) he, I say, that knowingly and wilfully "breaks this law in one point, is guilty of all:" and he remains under the curse of it, till he has repented, and resumed the obedience of faith. Therefore, when our Lord substituted the law of liberty for the law of innocence, he neither "gave us a license to sin," nor "became a minister of sin with a witness," as Mr. Berridge rashly affirms. (4.) The fourth Mosaic commandment allows "no manner of work," but the last edition of the law of liberty allows all manner of works of necessity and mercy to be done on the Sabbath. Our Lord, therefore, dispenses with the uncommon rigour with which the Jews observed the sacred day: and if Mr. Berridge will call that indulgence "clipping, paring," or altering the fourth commandment, he is at liberty; but if we break a commandment in availing ourselves of our Lord's gracious dispensation, why does Mr. Berridge allow his man servant, his maid servant, or his horse to work on the Saturday? Why does he not keep the seventh day holy, "like the circumcised race?"

(5.) Innocent man, with unimpaired powers, could yield perfect obedience to the law of innocence; therefore that law made no allowance, no provision, for any deficiency in duty. Not so "the law of liberty:" for although it allows no wilful sin, yet it does not reject sprinkled, though as yet imperfect, obedience. Nor does it, as some divines would persuade the world, curse the bud because it is not yet the blossom, nor the blossom because it is not yet the fruit, nor the fruit because it is not yet ripe; provided it tends to maturity, and harbours not insincerity, the worm that destroys evangelical obedience. It declares that our works of faith are accepted according to what we have, and not according to what we have not. It graciously receives from a heathen the obedience of a heathen, and from a babe in Christ the obedience of a babe: and instead of sentencing to hell the man, whose pound has only gained five pounds, and in whom the seed of the word has only produced thirty fold, it kindly allows him half the reward of him whose pound has gained ten pounds, or in whom the seed has brought forth sixty fold. But it shows no mercy to the unprofitable servant, who buries his talent; and it threatens with sorer punishment the wicked servant who "turns the grace of God into lasciviousness."

(6.) "Thus sincere obedience is now considered as the law of works." Not so: but it is considered, even by judicious Calvinists, as that obedience which the law of liberty accepts of, by which it is fulfilled, and through which believers shall be justified in the great day. I might fill a volume with quotations from their writings; but three or four will sufficiently prove my assertion. Joseph Alleine; that zealous and successful preacher, says, in his *Sure Guide to Heaven,* or *Alarm to the Unconverted,* Lond. 1705, (pp. 153, 154,) "The terms of mercy," (he should have said,) "The terms of eternal salvation are brought as low as possible to you. God has stooped as low to sinners as with honour he can. He will not be thought a fautor of sin, nor stain the glory of his holiness; and whither could he come lower than he hath, unless he should do this? He has abated the impossible terms of the first covenant, Acts xvi, 31; Proverbs xxviii, 13. He does not impose any thing unreasonable or impossible, as a condition of life." Alleine should have said, *as a condition of eternal life in glory;* for God in Christ most freely gives us *an initial life of grace* before he puts us upon performing any terms, in order to an *eternal life of glory.* "Two things were necessary to be done by you according to the first covenant, &c. And for future obedience, here he is content to yield to your weakness and remit the rigour. He does not stand upon [legal] perfection, &c, but is content to accept of sincerity," Genesis xvii, 11.

Matthew Mead, in his treatise on *The Good of Early Obedience,* London, 1683, (p. 402,) says: "It must be an upright and sincere obedience. 'Walk before me, and be thou perfect,' Genesis xvii, 1. In the margin it is *sincere* or *upright.* So that sincerity and uprightness is new covenant perfection. The perfection of grace in heaven is glory; but the perfection of grace on earth is sincerity," Mr. Henry perfectly agrees with Mr. Mead when he thus comments upon Genesis vi, 9: "'Noah was a just man and perfect" he was perfect, not with a sinless perfection, (according to the first covenant,) but a perfection of sincerity. And it is well for us, that, by virtue of the covenant of grace, upon the score of Christ's righteousness, sincerity is accepted as our Gospel perfection!" Hence it is that Dr. Owen says, a believer as such shall be tried, judged, and justified "by his own personal sincere obedience." (*Of Justification,* p. 111.) By comparing these fair quotations with Mr. Berridge's argument, my reader, without having the sagacity of "an old fox," will see that Antinomianism has lost all decency in our days, and is not ashamed to call "Jack o'lantern," &c, what the sober Calvinists of the last century called Gospel perfection.

Lastly: to insinuate, as Mr. Berridge does, that "Christ becomes a minister of sin with a witness, and must be ranked at the head of the Antinomian preachers," because he has substituted the law of liberty for the old Adamic covenant, is something so ungrateful in a believer, so astonishing in a Gospel minister, that — but I spare the pious vicar of Everton, and rise against thee, O Crispianity! Thou hast seduced that man of God, and upon thee I charge his dreadful mistake. However, he will permit me to conclude this answer to his shrewd argument by the following query: — If "Christ becomes a minister of sin, and must be ranked at the head of Antinomian preachers," for placing us under the law of liberty, which curses a fallen believer that breaks it in one point, (though it should be only by secretly harbouring malice or lust in his heart,) what must we say of the divines, who give us to understand that believers are not under the law preached by St. James, but under directions, or "rules of life," which they may break unto adultery and murder, without ceasing to be God's pleasant children, and men after his own heart? Must these popular men be ranked at the head, or at the tail of the Antinomian preachers?

Page 24. Mr. Berridge advances another argument' "If sincere obedience means any thing, it must signify either doing what you can, or doing what you will." I apprehend it means neither the one nor the other, but doing with uprightness what we know God requires of us, according to the dispensation of grace which we are under; meekly lamenting our deficiencies, and aspiring at doing all better and better every day. "So we are [not] got upon the old swampy ground again," but stand upon the Rock of Ages, and there defend the law of liberty against mistaken Solifidians.

Page 27. Mr. Berridge, instead of showing that our obedience is insincere, if we live in sin, and despise Christ's salvation, goes on mowing down all sincere obedience without distinction. "I perceive," says he, "you are not yet disposed to renounce sincere obedience." And, to engage us to it, he advances another argument, which, if it were sound, would demolish, not only "sincere obedience," but true repentance, faith unfeigned, and all Christianity. To answer it, therefore, I only need to produce it; substituting the words true repentance, or faith unfeigned, for "sincere obedience," which Mr. Berridge ridicules, thus: —

"You might have reason to complain, if God had made sincere obedience, [I say, true repentance, or faith unfeigned,] a condition of salvation. Much talk of it there is, like the good man in the moon, yet none could ever ken it. I dare defy the scribes to tell me truly what sincere [repentance] is: whether it means [leaving] half my or one fiftieth, or one hundredth part; [shedding] half [a score of tears,] 'or fifty, or one hundred. I dare defy all the lawyers in the world to tell me, whether [faith unfeigned,] means [believing] half [the Bible,] or three quarters, or one quarter, or one fiftieth, or one hundredth part: or whether it means [believing with*] half [a grain of the faith which removes a mountain load of guilt,] or one fiftieth, or one hundredth part [of a grain: or whether it implies believing with all our hearts, or with] half, or three quarters, or one quarter, &c. Where must we draw the line? It surely needs a magic wand to draw it.'" (See p. 27, &c.)

Mr. Berridge turns his flaming argument against sincere obedience, like the cherub's sword, "every way." Take two more instances of his skill: still giving me leave to level at faith unfeigned "the total term of all salvation," what he says against sincere obedience. Page 28: "If God has made sincere obedience [I retort, faith unfeigned] the condition [or term] of salvation, he would certainly have drawn the line, and marked out the boundary precisely, because our life depended on it." Page 28: "Sincere obedience [I continue to say, faith unfeigned] is called a condition, [or a term,] and no one knows what it is, &c. O fine condition! Surely Satan was the author of it."

---

* Mr. Berridge invites me thus to retort his bad argument against sincere obedience, (p. 94, 50. 18:) "I have been praying fifteen years for faith with some earnestness, and am not yet possessed of more than half a grain. Jesus assures you that a single grain, &c, would remove a mountain load of guilt from the conscience," &c.

The Works of John Fletcher

Page 24. "It is Satan's catch word for the Gospel." Page 38. It is "nothing but a Jack o'lantern, dancing here and there and every where," &c. For, (p. 29,) "If God has drawn no boundary, man must draw it, and will draw it where he pleaseth. Sincere obedience [I still retort, *sincere* repentance, or true faith] thus becomes a nose of wax, and is so fingered as to fit exactly every human face. I look upon this doctrine as the devil's masterpiece," &c.

And I look upon these assertions as the masterpiece of Antinomian rashness, and Geneva logic in the mouth of the pious vicar of Everton. Is it not surprising, that he who *unmasks the Christian World* should be so hood-winked by Calvinism, as not to see that there are as many false professors of *sincere repentance* and *true faith,* as there are of *sincere obedience;* that even the Turks call themselves Mussulmen, or true believers; and that he has full as much reason to call sincere repentance, or true faith, "a rotten buttress, a nose of wax, a paper kite, a Jack o'lantern," &c, as sincere obedience?

What a touch has this learned divine given here to the ark of God, in order to prop up that of Calvin? And how happy is it for religion, that this grand argument against obedience, repentance, and faith, is founded upon a hypothetical proposition, (p. 29, 50. 8,) "If God has drawn no boundary!" This supposition Mr. B. takes for granted, though it is evidently false; the boundaries of sincere obedience being full as clearly drawn in the Scriptures, as those of true repentance, and faith unfeigned.

God himself, without "a magic wand," has "drawn the line," both in every man's conscience, and in his written word. The line of Jewish obedience is drawn all over the Old Testament, especially Exodus xx; Psalm xv; Ezekiel xviii, and Micah vi, 8. The line of Christian obedience is exactly drawn all over the New Testament, and most particularly in our Lord's sermon on the mount. And the line of heathen faith and obedience is, without the Scripture, drawn in every breast by the gracious "light that enlightens every man who comes into the world." Through this light even Mohammedans and heathens may "believe that God is, and that he is a rewarder of those who diligently seek him:" and by this faith they may "work righteousness," do to others as they would be done by, and so "fulfil the law of liberty," according to their dispensation. And that some do is evident from these words of the apostle: "When the Gentiles, who have not the [written] law, do by nature [in its present state of initial restoration, without, any other assistance than that which Divine grace vouchsafes to all men universally] the things contained in the law: these having no [written] law are a law unto themselves, and show the work [or precepts] of the law written in their hearts; their conscience also bearing witness, and their thoughts accusing or excusing one another," Romans ii, 14, 15. Therefore the dreadful blow inadvertently struck at all religion, through the side of sincere obedience, is happily given with a broken reed. Christianity stands. The important term of sincere obedience, with respect to adult persons, has not Satan, but God for its author; and Antinomianism is more and more "unmasked."

But these are not all Mr. Berridge's objections against sincere obedience: for (p. 30) he says, "If works are a condition in the Gospel covenant, then works must make the whole of it." Why so? May not faith and repentance, so long as they continue true and lively, produce good works, their proper fruit? Why must the fruit "make the whole" of the tree? Beside, works being the evidencing cause of our salvation according to the Gospel, you have no warrant from Scripture to say, they must make the whole cause of it. They agree extremely well with faith, the instrumental cause; with Christ's blood, the properly meritorious cause; and with God's mercy, the first moving cause. May I not affirm, that the motion of the fourth wheel of a clock is absolutely necessary to its pointing the hour, without supposing that such a wheel must make the whole of the wheel work? O how have the lean kine, ascending out of the lake of Geneva, eaten those that fed so long near the river Cam!

But you add, (p. 30,) "Sincere obedience, as a condition, will lead you unavoidably up to perfect obedience." And suppose it should, pray, where would be the misfortune? Is it right to frighten the Christian world from sincere obedience, by holding out to their view Christian perfection, as if it were Medusa's fearful head? Are we not commanded to "go on to perfection?" Was not this one of our Lord's complaints against the Church of Sardis: "I have not found thy works perfect before God?" Does not St. Paul sum up all the law, or all obedience, in love? And does not St. John make honourable mention of perfect love, and excite those who are "not made perfect in love to have fellowship with him:" and With those who could say, "Our love is made perfect?" 1 John iv, 17. Why then should the world be driven from sincere, by the fear of perfect, obedience? Especially as our Lord never required absolute perfection from archangels, much less from fallen man. The perfection which he kindly calls us to being nothing but a faithful improvement of our talents, according to the proportion of the grace given us, and the standard of the dispensation we are under. So that, upon this footing, he whose one talent gains another, obeys as perfectly in his degree as he whose five talents gain five more. Notwithstanding all the insinuations of those "fishers of men," who beat the streams of truth to drive the fishes from Christian perfection into the Antinomian net, God is not an austere master, much less a foolish one. He does not expect to reap where he has not sown; or to reap wheat where he sows only barley. Those gracious words of our Lord, repeated four times in the Gospel, might alone silence them that discourage believers from going on to the perfection of obedience peculiar to their dispensation: "To every one that hath *to purpose* shall be given, and he shall have abundance," he shall attain the perfection of his dispensation: "but from him that hath not," because he buries his talent under pretence that his Lord requires unattainable obedience, "shall be taken away even that which he hath." Compare Matthew xiii, 12, with Matthew xxv, 29; Mark iv, 24, and Luke viii, 18.

The two last arguments of Mr. Berridge against sincere obedience may be retorted thus: — (1.) If faith is a condition (or term) in the Gospel covenant, then faith must make the whole of it. But if this be true, what becomes of Christ's obedience unto death? You reply, Faith necessarily supposes it. But you cannot escape. I follow you step by step, and say, The works I plead for necessarily suppose not only our Lord's obedience unto death, but faith, which you call "the only term of all salvation." (2.) You say, "Sincere obedience, as a condition, will lead you unavoidably up to perfect obedience." And I retort' faith unfeigned, as a term or condition, will lead you unavoidably up to perfect faith: for if "the law of liberty" commands us to love God "with all our soul," it charges us also to believe in Christ "with all our heart," Acts viii, 37. Should you reply, I am not afraid of being led up to perfect faith: I return the same answer with regard to perfect obedience.

This argument against sincere obedience, taken from the danger of going on to the perfection of it, is so much the more extraordinary, when dropping from Mr. Berridge's pen, as it is demolished by the words of his mouth, when he sings: —

> *Thee we would be always blessing,*
> *Serve thee as thine hosts above,*
> *Pray and praise thee without ceasing,*
> *Glory in thy perfect love.*

> *Finish then thy new creation;*
> *Pure and spotless may we be!*
> *Triumph in thy full salvation,*
> *Perfectly restor'd by thee!*

See A *Collection of Divine Songs, by J. Berridge*, M. A., &c, p. 178.

To conclude. Another argument is often urged by this pious author to render the doctrine of a believer's final justification by the evidence of works odious to humble souls. He takes it for granted that it encourages boasting; still confounding the works of faith, which he at times recommends as well as I, with the Pharisaical works of unbelief, which I perpetually decry as well as he. But even this argument, about which the Calvinists make so much noise, may be retorted thus: There is as much danger of being proud of one's faith, as of one's works of faith. And if Mr. Berridge presses me with Romans iii, 27, "Boasting is excluded by the law of faith:" I reply, that the works I plead for being the works of faith, his argument makes as much for me as for him: and I press him in my turn with Romans xi, 18, 20, "Boast not thyself against the branches. Thou standest by faith. Be not high minded, but fear:" which shows it is as possible to be proud of faith, as of the works of faith. Nor can a believer boast of the latter, unless his humble faith begins to degenerate into vain fancy.

Such are the capital objections that Mr. Berridge, in his unguarded zeal for the first Gospel axiom, has advanced against the second. Should he attempt to exculpate himself by saying, that all his arguments against sincere obedience are levelled at the hypocritical obedience which Pharisaic boasters sometimes call sincere: I reply, (1.) It is a pity he never once told his readers so. (2.) It is surprising that he who *unmasks the Christian World*, should so mask himself, as to say just the reverse of what he means. (3.) If he really designs to attack insincere obedience, why does he not attack it as insincere? And why does he advance no arguments against it, but such as would give the deepest wound to truly sincere obedience, if they were conclusive? (4.) What would Mr. Berridge say of me, if I published an impious essay against Divine worship in general, and, to vindicate my own conduct, gave it out, some months after, that I only meant to attack "the worship of the host," which makes a part of what the Papists call "Divine worship?" Would so lame an excuse clear me before the unprejudiced world? But, (5.) The worst is, that if Calvinism is true, all Mr. Berridge's arguments are as conclusive against evangelical, sincere obedience, as against the hypocritical works of Pharisees: for, if Christians (who have time to add the works chiefly recommended by St. James to the faith chiefly preached by St. Paul,) have a full, inamissible title to final justification without those works, nay, with the most horrid works, such as adultery and murder; is it not evident that the passport of good works and sincere obedience is as needless to their eternal salvation as "a rotten buttress, a paper kite, or a Jack o'lantern?"

SECTION IV.

When Mr. Berridge grants "that our damnation is wholly from ourselves," he grants that our salvation is suspended upon some term, which through grace we have power to fulfil; and in this case, unconditional reprobation, absolute election, and finished salvation, are false doctrines: and Calvin's whole system stands upon a sandy foundation.

WHEN a man grants me *two and two*, he grants me *four;* he cannot help it. If he exclaims against me for drawing the necessary inference, he only exposes himself before men of sense. Mr. Berridge, (p. 190,) fully grants the second Gospel axiom: "Our damnation," says he, "is wholly from ourselves." Nevertheless, he declares, (p. 26,) that there is "an absolute impossibility of being justified [or saved] in any manner by our works:" and part of his book seems levelled at this proposition of the Minutes, "Salvation, not by the merit of works, but by works as a condition." Now, if I am not mistaken, by granting the above-mentioned Gospel axiom, as all moderate Calvinists do, he grants me Mr. Wesley's proposition, together with the demolition of Calvinism. For,

1. If my damnation is wholly from myself,* it is not the necessary consequence of an absolute, efficacious decree of non-election, for then my damnation would be wholly from God. Nor is it the necessary consequence of the devil's temptation, for then it would be from the devil. Nor is it (upon the Gospel plan) the necessary consequence of Adam's fall: because, although I fell seminally into a state of damnation in the loins of Adam, yet the free gift came seminally upon me as well as upon all men unto initial justification; for I was no less in Adam when God raised him up by the true promise of a Mediator, than when he fell by the lying promise of the tempter.

Now, if my damnation is neither from any unconditional decree of reprobation, nor from the fall of Adam, what becomes of Apollo and his sister,

---

* By the word wholly, Mr. Berridge cannot mean that our damnation may not have secondary causes — such as a tempting devil, an alluring world, wicked company, a bad book, &c. He is too wise to deny it. All I suppose he means, as well as myself, is, that every reprobate is the primary, meritorious cause of his damnation. Just as Divine grace in Christ is the primary, meritorious cause of our salvation; although under that original, principal leading cause, there are inferior, instrumental, evidencing causes — such as Bibles, ministers, religious conversation, faith, good works. &c.

the great Diana? What becomes of absolute reprobation, and its inseparable companion, unconditional election? What becomes of all the horrors that St. Paul is supposed to father upon the God of love, Romans ix? In a word, what becomes of Calvinism?

Again: If "my damnation is wholly from myself," the just Judge of all. The earth must damn me personally for something which he had put it in my power personally to do or to leave undone. My damnation, then, and consequently my salvation, is necessarily suspended on some term or condition, the performance or non-performance of which is at my option. Nor is light more contrary to darkness than these two propositions of Mr. Berridge are to each other, "Our damnation is wholly from ourselves:" and, "St. Paul plainly shuts out all works of sincere obedience as a condition" of eternal salvation. On the first stand the Minutes and the Cheeks: on the second, Calvinism and Antinomianism. And as some of Mr. Berridge's readers cannot receive two incompatible propositions, they desire to know which of them we must give to the winds, with the paper kite of sincere obedience.

I hope that gentleman will not endeavour to screen Calvinism by saying, that the reprobates are damned merely for their personal sins, and therefore "their damnation is wholly from themselves." An illustration will easily show the fallacy of this argument, by which Calvinism is frequently kept in countenance.

A monarch, in whose dominions all children are naturally born *lame*, makes a law, that all who shall not walk *straight* before a certain day shall be cast into a fiery furnace. The terrible day comes, and myriads of lame culprits stand before him. His anger smokes against them; and with a stretched-out arm he thunders, Depart from me, ye cursed, into that place of torment prepared for obstinate offenders; for when I bid you walk upright, ye persisted to go lame. Go, burn to all eternity, and, as ye burn, clear my justice; and remember, that "your misery is wholly from yourselves."

"Wholly from ourselves!" they reply with one voice: "Was it ever in our power not to be born lame; or to walk upright in our crippled condition? Wast not thou acquainted with our natural misfortune? When a wonderful man came into thy kingdom to heal the lame, didst thou not order that he should pass us by? If he and his servants have tantalized us with general offers of a free cure, dost thou not know they were complimental, lying offers? Hast thou forgotten, how thou orderedst the loving physician, who wept over us, never to prepare one drop of his purple tincture for us? And how thy 'secret will' bound us with the invisible chains of an efficacious decree of preterition, that we might never come at that precious remedy? In a word, was it not from the beginning thy fixed determination, that, as we were born lame and helpless subjects to thy crown, so we should remain the lame and remediless victims of thy wrath? If therefore thou wilt show the boundless extent of thy grim sovereignty, by casting us into that flaming abyss, do it; for we cannot resist thee! But do not pretend that we have pulled down thy wrath upon us. Rob, O rob us not of the only alleviation that our deplorable case can admit of, viz. the comfort of thinking that our destruction is not from ourselves. If thou wilt be fierce as a lion, at least be not hypocritical as a crocodile."

"Hear, ye heavens," replies the absolute monarch, "give ear, O earth, and judge of the justice of my proceedings against these lame culprits. In consequence of a permissive, efficacious decree of mine, five or six thousand years ago, one of their ancestors brought lameness upon himself and upon them' therefore their necessary lameness, and the fearful destruction with which I am going to punish their lame steps, are wholly from themselves. Are not my ways equal, and theirs unequal? And far from being a crocodile toward them, am I not a lamb in whose mouth is no guile? or at least a lion who, like that of the tribe of Judah, use my sovereign power only according to the dearest dictates of justice and equity?" "Out of thine own mouth," reply the wretched culprits, "the world of rational beings will condemn thee, thou true king of terrors! Thou acknowledgest that thousands of years before we were born, one of our ancestors brought upon us the necessary lameness, in consequence of which we must be cast into that fiery furnace, without having ever had it in our power to take one straight step; and yet thou sayest that our destruction is wholly from ourselves! If thou wert not lost to all sense of equity and regard for truth, thou wouldst say that our condemnation is not from ourselves. but wholly from a man whom most of us never heard of; unless thou wast the grand contriver of the fall, which brought on his lameness and ours; and in that case our destruction is far less from him than from thyself. Beside, thou hast published a decree, in which thou declarest, 'They shall say no more, The fathers have eaten sour grapes, and the children's teeth are set on edge; but every one shall die for his own iniquity. Behold, all souls are mine, as the soul of the father, so also the soul of the son is mine. The soul that sinneth it shall die' the death thou designest us. Now iniquity that we could never personally help, an iniquity caused by one of our ancestors can never be our own iniquity, contradistinguished from that of our fathers. If thou didst cast all the asses of thy kingdom into thy fiery furnace, because they do not bray as melodiously as the nightingale sings; or all the ravens, because they are not as white as swans; couldst thou with any truth say, 'Their torments *are wholly from themselves?'* And hast thou any more reason to say that our perdition is from ourselves, when thou burnest us merely for our natural, necessary lameness, and for the lame steps that it has naturally and necessarily occasioned?"

The judicious reader will enter into this illustration without being presented with a key of my own making; and, trusting his candour and good sense with that business, I draw the following inferences from the second Gospel axiom, which Mr. Berridge has explicitly granted. (1.) God does not prevaricate, but speaks a melancholy truth, when he says, "O Israel, thou hast destroyed thyself." (2.) Every reprobate is his own destroyer, not only because he has willfully sinned away the justification mentioned Romans v, 18, by which all infants are entitled to the kingdom of heaven, but also because he willfully rejects the salvation really prepared for, and sincerely offered to him in Christ. (3.) According to the second covenant, we are never in a state of personal damnation till we have personally buried the talent of that "grace which bringeth salvation, and hath appeared to all men." (4.) Calvinism, which teaches the reprobates fully to exculpate themselves, and justly to charge God with shuffling, lying, injustice, cruelty, and hypocrisy, is a system that does the reprobates infinite honour, and the Divine perfections unspeakable injury. And, (5.) When Mr. Berridge maintains that "our damnation is wholly from ourselves," he maintains indirectly that the Minutes and Checks, which necessarily stand or fall with that Gospel axiom, are truly Scriptural. Thus, like other pious Calvinists,* he gives us an excellent dose of antidote to expel Antinomian poison. But who shall recommend it to the Calvinistic world? Mr. Wesley they will not hear. My Checks they will not read. Go, then, "valiant

---

* The warm author of a pamphlet, entitled, "Dr. Crisp's Ghost, or a Check upon Checks, being a Bridle for Antinomian, and a Whip for Pelagian and Arminian Methodists," with this motto, "Without are dogs, and whosoever loveth and maketh a lie:" designed, it seems, to whip the Arminian dogs, and to prove that Flavel, Baxter, Williams, and I, make a lie, when we represent Dr. Crisp as an abettor of "Antinomian dotages." This warm author, I say, informs us, that even Dr. Crisp, overcome by the glaring evidence of truth, once said, "I must read the fearful doom of all who have not learned this lesson [denying ungodliness,] and are not yet taught it of God, &c. They are yet in the gall of bitterness, and in the bond of iniquity, and have not their part in this matter. I say, as yet, this is their fearful doom; and if they continue thus untaught their lesson, there can be no salvation by grace for them. ' Not every one that says, Lord, Lord, shall enter the kingdom of heaven, but he that doeth the will of my Father, which is in heaven,' &c. Some licentious, ungodly wretches I know reply, though to their own ruin, &c, that Christ justifies the ungodly, and we are saved by faith without works. But, alas! they observe not how cunningly the devil equivocates to lull them asleep in their ungodly practices. It is true indeed that Christ justifies the ungodly; that is, he finds them ungodly when he imputes his righteousness to them: but he does not leave them ungodly after he has inspired them: he teacheth them to deny ungodliness. He affords no cloak to perseverance in ungodliness; but will come in flaming fire, with his mighty angels, to render vengeance unto such. He that denies not ungodliness, him will Christ deny before his Father which is in heaven. Why, then, wilt thou be deluded with gross sophistry in so clear a sunshine of the Gospel? Is not the light so bright that thine own heart checks thee? And if thine heart condemns thee, God is greater, and searches all things."
Hail: Crisp. Far from checking my Checks, and whipping the Arminian dog, in a happy moment thou manfully tightest St. James' battle. Thou callest the doctrine of the Checks "sunshine:" and whippest thine own speculative error out of the Church as "gross sophistry."
Dr. Crisp (as quoted by his opponent,) almost discovered once the important difference between the salvation of a sinner previous to works; and the salvation of a believer consequent upon works.
His excellent words run thus: "It is true, also, we are saved by faith without works; but here also Satan equivocates as grossly as in the other case: for though faith only saves without works efficiently, yet not consequentially, as I said before; that is, though faith only saves, yet that faith must not be alone that saves, but must be attended with its fruits, to wit, denying ungodliness; else it is so far from saving, that it is but a dead faith; and he is but a vain man that has no better, as St. James well affirms. The person believing must deny ungodliness, though this denial works not his salvation." This is very true, if it is understood either of initial salvation, or of the primary cause of eternal salvation. "Our Saviour speaks to the same purpose: 'A good tree bringeth forth good fruit.' He does not say, the fruit makes it a good tree; yet the good fruit is inseparable. I speak not of quantities or degrees, &c, but of the truth; to wit, a real and sincere denial of ungodliness." Excellent! To whip the dogs, the Rev. Mr. P — I need only prove, that when David robbed Uriah of the ewe lamb that lay in his bosom, tried to kill his soul with drunkenness, and treacherously killed his body with the sword of the Ammonites, he "really and sincerely denied ungodliness." And that his faith produced the good fruit, which is INSEPARABLE from saving faith. The moment this is done I promise the public to clear the pious Calvinists in general from the charge of speculative Antinomianism, Dr. Crisp in particular from that of glaring contradiction, and his zealous second, who accuses me with "gross falsities," from Calvinistic rashness.
We can no more exculpate warm Calvinists, when they betray holiness into the hands of practical Antinomians, because they now and then speak honourably of good works, than we can clear Pontius Pilate from the guilt of delivering the Messiah to the Jews, because he once solemnly "took water, and washed his hands before the multitude, saying, I find no fault in this just person: I am innocent of his blood: see ye to it." If the author of the "Whip for the Arminians" considers this, or if he turns to Fourth Check, p. 222 [224], where I produce D. Williams' observation concerning Dr. Crisp's inconsistency, he will be probably less forward in checking Checks that he has not candidly considered; and in making whips for the backs of his honest neighbours, lest some of them should take them from him to lash his mistakes, and chastise his precipitation.

Sergeant IF." Thou comest from Everton, therefore thou shalt be welcome. Thou knowest the way to the closets of Solifidians: nay, thou art there already with" The *Christian World Unmasked.*"

SECTION V.

Mr. Berridge candidly grants the conditionality of perseverance, and consequently of election, by showing much respect to "Sergeant IF," who "guards the camp of Jesus." But soon picking a quarrel with the valiant sergeant, he discharges him as a Jew, opens the camp to the Antinomians, by opposing to them only a sham centinel, and shows the foundations of Calvinism in a most striking light.

THE pious author of *"The Christian World Unmasked,"* speaking of the Calvinistic doctrine of unconditional perseverance, which he confounds with the evangelical doctrine of *conditional* perseverance, (p. 194,) says with great truth, provided he had spoken of the latter: It "affords a stable prop to upright minds, yet lends no wanton cloak to corrupt hearts. It brings a cordial to revive the faint, and keeps a guard to check the forward. The guard attending on this doctrine is Sergeant IF; low in stature, but lofty in significance; a very valiant guard, though a monosyllable. Kind notice has been taken of the sergeant by Jesus Christ and his apostles; and much respect is due unto him, from all the Lord's recruiting officers, and every soldier in his army. Pray listen to the sergeant's speech: 'IF ye continue in my word, then are ye my disciples indeed,' John viii, 31. 'IF ye do these things, ye shall never fall,' 2 Peter i, 10. 'IF what ye have heard shall abide in you, ye shall continue in the Son and in the Father,' 1 John ii, 24. 'We are made partakers of Christ, IF we hold steadfast unto the end,' Hebrews iii, 14. 'Whoso looketh and continueth [that is, IF he that looketh doth continue] in the perfect law of liberty, that man shall be blessed in his deed,'" James i, 25. And again, (p. 194,) "IF back-sliders fancy they must all be restored by repentance, because David was restored, and Peter was; they might as well suppose they must all be translated into heaven without dying,* because Enoch and Elijah were." (Page 199, l. 17.)

Upon this plan of doctrine, we are ready to lay by our controversial pens, and shake hands with our Calvinist brethren. All that we desire of them, in order to a lasting agreement, is, (1.) To consider what is implied in the preceding concessions; and not to gag Sergeant IF, when he honestly speaks the very words of "the Captain of our salvation," or those of the apostles, his lieutenant generals. (2) Not to call him a *Galatian* or a *Papist*, when he is found in company with St. James. (3.) Not to enter an action against him, for disturbing the peace of those backsliders, who, having denied the faith, and lost their first love now quietly hug

---

* Here Mr. Berridge, in a fit of legality, far exceeds the limits of the truth which I maintain in the Checks; for he insinuates that the recovery of backsliders is as improbable as their bodily translation into heaven. For my part, severe as I am represented to backsliders, I believe their return is ten thousand times more probable, than their going to heaven as Enoch and Elijah did.

a bosom sin, or take their Laodicean rest on the pillow of self election. (4.) Not to put him under arrest, for heading a platoon of those whom some of the elect call *diabolonians,* because they *doubt* the truth of *unconditional* election, or election without IF; and choose to fire at *sin,* rather than at their *captain.* And, (5.) Not to say to him, Hail! sergeant, kissing him as if he were a good Christian, in order to betray him with some decency into the hands of the Antinomians, as "a circumcised caitiff."

Whether my pious opponent has not treated the honest sergeant in that manner, I leave the candid reader to determine. "Yet take notice," says he, (p. 194,) "that Sergeant IF is not of Jewish, but Christian parentage: not sprung from Levi, though a son of Abraham: no centinel of Moses, but a watchman for the camp of Jesus. He wears no dripping beard, like the circumcised race; and is no legal blustering condition to purchase man's salvation, but a modest Gospel evidence to prove the truth of grace. He tells no idle tales." Enough, Rev. sir: if "he tells no idle tales," he does not cavil and quibble, much less does he deny his proper name, and well known meaning. Although he no more dreams of "purchasing man's salvation" than you do, yet he is conditional IF, — Sergeant IF, — a very valiant guard to the Scriptural doctrine of perseverance, and an irreconcilable enemy to Calvinian election, and "Antinomian dotages."

O ye opposers of the second Gospel axiom, "Pray come and peep!" See Calvinism *"unmasked"* by one of your principal leaders, who shows to the world the futile foundation of your doctrine of grace! Thanks be to his humourous honesty, we see now that those famous doctrines stand upon the super-metaphysical difference there is between IF and IF; between Jewish IF, and Christian IF; legal IF, and evangelical IF; IF at Madeley, and IF at Everton. When IF, the culprit, appears in the Foundry pulpit, he tells idle tales, it seems! He slily disguises himself! But when IF the orthodox shows himself in the desk at Everton, (for it is to be feared that he seldom appears in the pulpit valiantly to guard Bible perseverance,) he never equivocates! When he says to people that never stood, or to people that can never fall, "IF ye do these things ye shall never fall," he, he is not a condition, and yet he never shuffles! These are strange hints indeed!

Patient reader, permit me to try, by the following questions, the solidity of the Calvinistic distinction between IF and IF, which supports the amazing weight of the great Diana. (1.) When the Gospel said to David, "IF thou dost these things thou shalt never fall," and he fell into adultery; was "Sergeant IF a *modest* Gospel evidence to prove the truth of his grace?" And supposing he was such a modest evidence, did he "lend no wanton cloak to a corrupt heart?" (2.) When our Lord said to the young ruler, "IF thou wilt be perfect, sell all:" was Sergeant IF of Jewish or Christian parentage? (3.) How shall I know when the sergeant is "a centinel of Moses," or when he is "a watchman for the camp of Jesus?" Should you answer, "A Jewish IF wears a dripping beard," you may indeed, by such an argument, convince and entertain some Calvinists; but you leave me quite in the dark; and with "some very honest folks, who are cast in a Gospel foundery," instead of "ringing a fire bell," I smile at your wit and orthodoxy, but can no more understand what you mean by an IF, "with a dripping beard," than you could conceive what I would be at, if I spoke of a *yes,* with a long tail, or a *perhaps,* with dreadful horns! (4.) How shall I distinguish a "legal" From an evangelical IF? Should you say, that the "legal, blustering" sergeant wears a halberd, but the evangelical, mild IF has no weapon at all? I ask, What business has an unarmed IF in "the camp of Jesus?" Why do you call him sergeant? Is he not a sham centinel, a ridiculous scarecrow, to deceive the simple, rather than "a very valiant guard to check the forward?" (5.) How shall I make a difference between an Everton IF, and a Madeley IF? When I have read my Bible in both places, I have always found the sergeant exactly of the same stature; he always appeared in the same black regimentals: and to this day a Madeley IF exactly answers to the description that the pious vicar of Everton gives of him. He is "a monosyllable, low in stature, but of lofty significance." Whereas the Everton IF is yet lower in significance than in stature, since you make him signify just nothing. Should you reply, that a Madeley IF is "like one of the circumcised race:" I answer that, although about eleven years ago, I circumcised him with an Antinomian knife, yet I did not mutilate him. But I could name a Gospel minister, who has "served more than three apprenticeships at a noted hall of physic," by whom the unhappy sergeant has not only been "circumcised," but quite emasculated; yea, deprived of his very vitals. For when IF, in the above-quoted scriptures, is absolutely divested of conditionality, and turned into an unnecessary evidence of grace, which the elect can do without, as well as David and Solomon; may it not be compared to a dead sergeant, whose lungs and heart are pulled out: and whose ill-smelling remains, far from being a "valiant guard" against the forward, prove an enticing lure to unclean birds, who fly about in search of a carcass!

Excuse, reader, this prolix and ludicrous defence of the sergeant. The subject, though treated in so queer a manner, is of the utmost importance; for the Minutes, the Checks, and the second Gospel axiom, stand or fall with Sergeant IF. If he is a coward, a knave, or a cipher, Antinomianism will still prevail; but if he recovers his true and lofty significance, he will soon rid the Church of Antinomian dotages. As "much respect is due unto him," and to St. James' undefiled religion, which the ingenious book I quote indirectly undermines, I thought it my duty to "open my bag" also, and let out a ferret; or to speak exactly the language of Everton, "a fox," to chase "a straggling goose hard at hand." Take notice, however, that by the "goose," I do not mean the reverend author of *The World Unmasked*, for he has wit enough, and to spare; but the "*waddling dame*," Calvinistic contradiction, alias *Logica Genevensis*. And now, reader, I lay her before thee, not to make thee "sup" upon her, "amidst a deal of cackling music," but that thou wouldst help me to nail her up to the everlasting doors of the temple of truth, as sportsmen do cranes and foxes to the doors of their rural buildings.

CONCLUSION.

WERE I to conclude these strictures upon the dangerous tenets, inadvertently advanced, and happily contradicted, in *The Christian World Unmasked*, without professing my brotherly love and sincere respect for the ingenious and pious author; I should wrong him, myself, and the cause which I defend. I only do him justice, when I say, that few, very few of our elders, equal him in devotedness to Christ, zeal, diligence, and ministerial success. His indefatigable labours in the word and doctrine, entitle him to a double share of honour; and I invite all my readers with me to "esteem him highly in love for" his Master's and "his work's sake:" entreating them not to undervalue his vital piety, on account of his Antinomian opinion; and beseeching them to consider, that his errors are so much the more excusable, as they do not influence his moral conduct, and he refutes them himself, far more than his favourite scheme of doctrine allows him to do. Add to this, that those very errors spring, in a great degree, from the idea, that he honours Christ by receiving, and does God service by propagating them.

The desire of catching the attention of his readers has made him choose a witty, facetious manner of writing, for which he has a peculiar turn; and the necessity I am under of standing his indirect attack, obliges me to meet him upon his own ground, and to encounter him with his own weapons. I beg that what passes for evangelical humour in him may not be called indecent levity in me. A sharp pen may be guided by a kind heart; and such, I am persuaded, is that of my much esteemed antagonist, whom I publicly invite to my pulpit; protesting that I should be edified, and overjoyed, to hear him enforce there the guarded substance of his book, which, notwithstanding the vein of Solifidianism I have taken the liberty to open, contains many great and glorious truths.

END OF THE SECOND PART

For additional copies of this book and a list of other titles available from Apprehending Truth please visit our website:

http://www.publishers.apprehendingtruth.net

Apprehending Truth Publishers

Proclaiming Truth in the Age of Deceit

AD LEGEM MAGIS ET AD TESTIMONIUM

Published by

Apprehending Truth

Brookfield, Missouri

2011

Apprehending Truth Publishers is a division of Apprehending Truth Ministry.

http://www.ApprehendingTruth.net

Also Published By Apprehending Truth:

DEFINING BIBLICAL HOLINESS

John Wesley, Asa Mahan

ed. Jeffrey L. Wallace

The Biblical doctrine of "Christian Perfection" has been denied even by those who call themselves by the name of Christ. "Defining Biblical Holiness" takes a look at this all important doctrine by casting our gaze into the past, and attempting to clearly define the truth presented in this doctrine. John Wesley and Asa Mahan both had a firm grasp upon a Biblical understanding of the teaching of holiness and Christian Perfection. Their two works on the subject, along with a new introduction, are here presented in juxtaposition in order to shed light on the current antinomian trend which continues unabated in the modern professing "Church".

- ISBN: 0615444040
- EAN13: 9780615444048
- Page Count: 296
- Binding Type: US Trade Paper
- Trim Size: 6" x 9"
- Language: English
- Color: Black and White
- Related Categories: Religion / Christian Theology / Ethics

Available at:

Apprehending Truth

Apprehending Truth Publishers
Proclaiming Truth in the Age of Deceit
AD LEGEM MAGIS ET AD TESTIMONIUM

http://www.publishers.apprehendingtruth.net

www.ingramcontent.com/pod-product-compliance
Lightning Source LLC
Chambersburg PA
CBHW031231090426
42742CB00007B/151

9 780615 533414